THE *unofficial* GUIDE®
ᵀᴼ Walt Disney World® with Kids

2014

D0167785

Other Unofficial Guides:

THE *unofficial* GUIDE®

TO Walt Disney World® with Kids

2014

BOB SEHLINGER *and* LILIANE J. OPSOMER
with LEN TESTA

(Walt Disney World® is officially known as Walt Disney World® Resort.)

keen
communications

Please note that prices fluctuate in the course of time and that travel information changes under the impact of many factors that influence the travel industry. We therefore suggest that you write or call ahead for confirmation when making your travel plans. Every effort has been made to ensure the accuracy of information throughout this book, and the contents of this publication are believed to be correct at the time of printing. Nevertheless, the publishers cannot accept responsibility for errors or omissions, for changes in details given in this guide, or for the consequences of any reliance on the information provided by the same. Assessments of attractions and so forth are based upon the authors' own experiences; therefore, descriptions given in this guide necessarily contain an element of subjective opinion, which may not reflect the publisher's opinion or dictate a reader's own experience on another occasion. Readers are invited to write the publisher with ideas, comments, and suggestions for future editions.

Published by:
Keen Communications, LLC
P.O. Box 43673
Birmingham. AL 35243

Cover design by Scott McGrew

Text design by Vertigo Design and Annie Long

For information on our other products and services or to obtain technical support, please contact us from within the United States at 888-604-4537 or by fax at 205-326-1012.

Keen Communications, LLC, also publishes its books in a variety of electronic formats. Some content that appears in print may not be available in electronic formats.

ISBN: 978-1-62809-006-2; eISBN: 978-162809-007-9

Distributed by Publishers Group West

Manufactured in the United States of America

5 4 3 2

CONTENTS

◼◼ LIST *of* MAPS

ACKNOWLEDGMENTS

THANKS TO OUR TEAM OF YOUNG PUNDITS, Ian Geiger, Hannah Testa, and Shelton Siegel for their unique wisdom and fun-loving attitude (gotta have attitude, right?). Also thanks to Idan Menin and Katie Sutton. Disney-trivia guru Lou Mongello created the theme-park trivia quizzes, and entertainment reporter Jim Hill provided insightful and funny glimpses of the World behind the scenes. The cartoons were drawn by Tami Knight, possibly the nuttiest artist in Canada, and Chris Eliopoulos, a talented illustrator–Disney fanatic based in New Jersey. Much appreciation to Eve Zibart for her characteristically droll comments concerning Walt Disney World attractions, hotels, and dining. For research and contributions concerning family dynamics and child behavior, thanks to psychologists Karen Turnbow, Susan Corbin, Gayle Janzen, and Joan Burns. Kudos also to *Unofficial Guide* Research Director Len Testa and his team for the data collection and programming behind the touring plans in this guide.

To the Ortiz-Valle gang: We love your reports from the parks and the insights from your annual takeover of the Disney fleet. The next expedition will include a wedding on Castaway Cay; we can't wait to get your insider tips on tying the knot with the Mouse.

Many thanks also to Amber Kaye Henderson and Ritchey Halphen for their editorial and production work on this book. Annie Long contributed the fine design work. Scott McGrew and Steve Jones created the maps, and Ann Cassar prepared the index.

INTRODUCTION

■ HOW COME "UNOFFICIAL"?

DECLARATION OF INDEPENDENCE

THE AUTHORS AND RESEARCHERS OF THIS GUIDE specifically and categorically declare that they are and always have been totally independent of the Walt Disney Company, Inc.; of Disneyland, Inc.; of Walt Disney World, Inc.; and of any and all other members of the Disney corporate family not listed.

The authors believe in the wondrous variety, joy, and excitement of the Walt Disney World attractions. At the same time, we recognize that Walt Disney World is a business. In this guide, we represent and serve you, the consumer. If a restaurant serves bad food, or a gift item is overpriced, or a certain ride isn't worth the wait, we can say so, and in the process we hope to make your visit more fun, efficient, and economical.

YOUR *UNOFFICIAL* WALT DISNEY WORLD TOOLBOX

WHEN IT COMES TO WALT DISNEY WORLD, a couple with kids needs different advice than does a party of seniors going to the Epcot International Flower & Garden Festival. Likewise, adults touring without children, honeymooners, and folks with only a day or two to visit all require their own special guidance.

To meet the varying needs of our readers, we've created *The Unofficial Guide to Walt Disney World,* or what we call the "Big Book." At about 850 pages, it contains all the comprehensive information that anyone traveling to Walt Disney World needs to have a super vacation. More than 25 years in the making, it's our cornerstone.

As thorough as we try to make the main guide, there still isn't sufficient space for all the tips and resources that may be useful to certain readers. Therefore, we've developed four additional guides that provide information tailored to specific visitors. Although some advice from the Big Book, such as arriving early at the theme parks, is echoed in these guides, most of the information is unique.

Here's what's in the toolbox:

The guide you're reading now presents detailed planning and touring tips for a family vacation, along with more than 20 special touring plans for families that you won't find anywhere else. *The Unofficial Guide to Walt Disney World with Kids* is the only Unofficial Guide created with the guidance of a panel of kids, all of varying ages and backgrounds.

The Unofficial Guide Color Companion to Walt Disney World, by Bob Sehlinger and Len Testa, is a visual feast that proves a picture is worth a thousand words. In the Big Book, for instance, you can learn about the best guest rooms to request at the Wilderness Lodge, but in the *Color Companion* you can *see* the rooms, along with the pool and the magnificent lobby. Full-color photos illustrate how long the lines get at different times of day, how wet riders get on Splash Mountain, and how the parks are decked out for various holidays. The *Color Companion* whets your appetite for Disney fun, pictures all the attractions, serves as a keepsake, and, as always, helps make your vacation more enjoyable. Most of all, the *Color Companion* is for fun. For the first time, we're able to use photography to express our zany *Unofficial* sense of humor. Think of it as Monty Python meets Walt Disney . . . in Technicolor.

Mini-Mickey: The Pocket-Sized Unofficial Guide to Walt Disney World, by Bob Sehlinger, Len Testa, and Ritchey Halphen, is a portable CliffsNotes-style version of the Big Book. It distills information to help short-stay or last-minute visitors decide quickly how to plan their limited hours at Disney World.

Beyond Disney: The Unofficial Guide to Universal, SeaWorld, and the Best of Central Florida, by Bob Sehlinger and Robert N. Jenkins with Len Testa, is a guide to non-Disney theme parks, attractions, restaurants, outdoor recreation, and nightlife in Orlando and Central Florida.

THE MUSIC OF LIFE

ALTHOUGH IT'S COMMON in our culture to see life as a journey from cradle to grave, Alan Watts, a noted late-20th-century philosopher, saw it differently. He viewed life not as a journey but as a dance. In a journey, he said, you are trying to get somewhere, and are consequently always looking ahead, anticipating the way stations, and thinking about the end. Though the journey metaphor is popular, particularly in the West, it is generally characterized by a driven, goal-oriented mentality: a way of living and being that often inhibits those who subscribe to the journey metaphor from savoring each moment of life.

When you dance, by contrast, you hear the music and move in harmony with the rhythm. Like life, a dance has a beginning and an end. But unlike a journey, your objective is not to get to the end but to enjoy the dance while the music plays. You are totally in the moment and care nothing about where on the floor you stop when the dance is done.

As you begin to contemplate your Walt Disney World vacation, you may not have much patience for a philosophical discussion about journeys and dancing. But you see, it is relevant. If you are like most travel guide readers, you are apt to plan and organize, to anticipate and control, and you like things to go smoothly. And truth be told, this leads us to suspect that you are a person who looks ahead and is outcome-oriented. You may even feel a bit of pressure concerning your vacation. Vacations, after all, are special events and expensive ones as well. So you work hard to make the most of your vacation.

We also believe that work, planning, and organization are important, and at Walt Disney World they are essential. But if they become your focus, you won't be able to hear the music and enjoy the dance. Though a lot of dancing these days resembles highly individualized seizures, there was a time when each dance involved specific steps, which you committed to memory. At first you were tentative and awkward, but eventually the steps became second nature and you didn't think about them anymore.

Metaphorically, this is what we want for you and your children or grandchildren as you embark on your Walt Disney World vacation. We want you to learn the steps ahead of time, so that when you're on your vacation and the music plays, you will be able to hear it, and you and your children will dance with grace and ease.

YOUR PERSONAL TRAINERS

WE'RE HERE TO WHIP YOU INTO SHAPE by helping you plan and enjoy your Walt Disney World vacation. Together we'll make sure that it really *is* a vacation, as opposed to, say, an ordeal or an expensive way to experience heatstroke. Our objective, simply put, is to ensure that you and your children have fun.

Because this book is specifically for adults traveling with children, we'll concentrate on your special needs and challenges. We'll share our most useful tips as well as the travel secrets of more than 42,000 families interviewed over the years we've covered Walt Disney World.

So who *are* we? There's a bunch of us, actually. Your primary personal trainers are Liliane and Bob. Helping out big-time are Ian, Hannah, and Shelton. Ian is a 18-year-old from Tampa, Florida. His mop of surfer-boy hair nearly covers his hazy-blue peepers. He gets a kick out of playing soccer and just started a whole new life at college. Hannah, age 14, lives near Winston-Salem, North Carolina, really knows Disney, and will read you the riot act if you mess up. The rest of us work for her. Our most recent team member is Shelton, from Arlington, Virginia. He sings, plays keyboard, and loves to

IAN   HANNAH   SHELTON

BOB   LILIANE

chow down on ethnic food. Ian, Shelton, and Hannah, needless to say, have a lot of opinions when it comes to Disney. So many, in fact, that they think Liliane's and Bob's are largely irrelevant.

Faithful readers will notice that one is missing in the bunch. After contributing for some years to the guide, Idan skipped ship during a cruise. He was last seen at Castaway Cay, and rumor has it that he's searching for the *Flying Dutchman*. We'll miss his witty observations.

Help wanted: Are you age 16 or younger? Consider joining our *Unofficial Guide* Kids' Panel. All you need are opinions you'd like to share. About what? Most anything: Disney and Universal, rides you love, rides you hate, favorite restaurants and treats, things that work and things that don't. E-mail us at **unofficialguides @menasharidge.com** (put "Kids' Panel" in the subject line) and tell us about youself.

Liliane comes from Belgium and works in New York City. She's funny and very charming in the best European tradition, and she puts more energy into being a mom than you'd think possible without performance-enhancing drugs. Optimistic and happy, she loves the sweet and sentimental side of Disney World. You might find her whooping it up at the *Hoop-Dee-Doo Musical Revue*, but you'll never see her on a roller coaster with Bob.

Speak of the devil, Bob is not exactly a curmudgeon, but he likes to unearth Disney's secrets and show readers how to beat the system. His idea of a warm fuzzy might be the Rock 'n' Roller Coaster, but he'll help you save lots of money, find the best hotels and restaurants, and return home less than terminally exhausted. The caricatures above pretty much sum up the essence of Bob and Liliane.

If you're thinking that the cartoons paint a somewhat conflicted picture of your personal trainers, you're right. Admittedly, Bob and Liliane have been known to disagree on a thing or two. Together, however, they make a good team. You can count on them to give you both sides of every story. Let's put it this way: Liliane will encourage you to bask in the universal-brotherhood theme of "It's a Small World." Bob will show up later to help you get the infernal song out of your head.

Hannah's dad, occasionally known as "Len," is our research dude. His really complicated scientific wizardry will help you save a bundle of time—would you believe 4 hours in a single day?—by staying out of those pesky lines.

 Oops, almost forgot: There's another team member you need to meet. Called a Wuffo, she's our very own character. She'll warn you when rides are too scary, too dark, or too wet. You'll bump into her throughout the book doing, well, what characters do.

Why did we create our own character when Disney has dozens just sitting around? Simple—Disney characters toe the company line. We needed a tough (but lovable) independent character who would give you the straight skinny on what Disney rides do to your stomach and central nervous system.

▍ABOUT *this* GUIDE

WALT DISNEY WORLD HAS BEEN OUR BEAT for more than two decades, and we know it inside out. During those years, we've observed many thousands of parents and grandparents trying—some successfully, others less so—to have a good time at Walt Disney World. Some of these, owing to unfortunate dynamics within the family, were handicapped right from the start. Others were simply overwhelmed by the size and complexity of Walt Disney World; whereas still others fell victim to a lack of foresight, planning, and organization.

Walt Disney World is a better destination for some families than for others. Likewise, some families are more compatible on vacation than others. The likelihood of experiencing a truly wonderful Walt Disney World vacation transcends the theme parks and attractions offered. In fact, the theme parks and attractions are the only constants in the equation. The variables that will define the experience and determine its success are intrinsic to your family: things like attitude, sense of humor, cohesiveness, stamina, flexibility, and conflict resolution.

The simple truth is that Walt Disney World can test you as a family. It will overwhelm you with choices and force you to make decisions about how to spend your time and money. It will challenge you physically as you cover miles on foot and wait in lines touring the theme parks. You will have to respond to surprises (both good and bad) and deal with hyperstimulation.

This guide will forewarn and forearm you. It will help you decide whether a Walt Disney World vacation is a good idea for you and your family at this particular time. It will help you sort out and address the attitudes and family dynamics that can affect your experience. Most important, it will provide the confidence that comes with good planning and realistic expectations.

THE SUM OF ALL FEARS

EVERY WRITER WHO EXPRESSES an opinion is accustomed to readers who strongly agree or disagree: it comes with the territory. Extremely troubling, however, is the possibility that our efforts to be objective have frightened some readers away from Walt Disney World or made others apprehensive. For the record, if you enjoy theme parks, Disney World is as good as it gets, absolute nirvana. It's upbeat, safe, fun, eye-popping, happy, and exciting. If you arrive without knowing a thing about the place and make every possible mistake, chances are about 90% that you'll have a wonderful vacation anyway. In the end, guidebooks don't make or break great destinations. Rather, they are simply tools to help you enhance your experience and get the most for your money.

Bob: Be prepared to read experienced Disney World visitors' opinions of the parks in this book and to apply them to your own travel circumstances.

As wonderful as Walt Disney World is, however, it's a complex destination. Even so, it isn't nearly as challenging or difficult as New York, San Francisco, Paris, Acapulco, or any other large city or destination. And, happily, there are numerous ways to save money, minimize hassle, and make the most of your time. That's what this guide is about: giving you a heads-up regarding potential problems or opportunities. Unfortunately, some *Unofficial Guide* readers add up the warnings and critical advice and conclude that Walt Disney World is too intimidating, too expensive, or too much work. They lose track of the wonder of Disney World and focus instead on what might go wrong.

Our philosophy is that knowledge is power (and time and money too). You're free to follow our advice—or not—at your discretion. But you can't exercise that discretion if we fail to present the issues.

With or without a guidebook, you'll have a great time at Walt Disney World. If you let us, we'll help you smooth the potential bumps. We're certain that we can help you turn a great vacation into an absolutely superb one. Either way, once there, you'll get the feel of the place and quickly reach a comfort level that will allay your apprehensions and allow you to have a great experience.

LETTERS AND COMMENTS FROM READERS

MANY WHO USE *The Unofficial Guide to Walt Disney World with Kids* write us to comment or share their own touring strategies. We appreciate all such input, both positive and critical, and encourage our readers to continue writing. Their comments and observations are frequently incorporated into revised editions of the guide and have contributed immeasurably to its improvement.

Privacy Policy

If you write us or complete our reader survey, rest assured that we won't release your name and address to any mailing-list companies, direct-mail advertisers, or other third parties. Unless you instruct us otherwise, we'll assume that you don't object to being quoted in the guide.

How to Contact the Authors
  Bob, Liliane, and Len
  The Unofficial Guide to Walt Disney World with Kids
  P.O. Box 43673
  Birmingham, AL 35243
  unofficialguides@menasharidge.com

When e-mailing us, please tell us where you're from. If you snail-mail us, put your address on both your letter and envelope; the two sometimes get separated. It's also a good idea to include your phone number. Because we're travel writers, we're often out of the office for long periods of time, so forgive us if our response is slow. *Unofficial Guide* e-mail isn't forwarded to us when we're traveling, but we'll respond as soon as possible after we return.

Online Reader Survey

Express your opinions about your Walt Disney World visit at **touring plans.com/walt-disney-world/survey.** This online questionnaire lets every member of your party, regardless of age, tell us what he or she thinks about attractions, hotels, restaurants, and more.

If you'd rather print out and mail us the survey, send it to **Reader Survey, *The Unofficial Guides*, P.O. Box 43673, Birmingham, AL 35243.** In any case, let us know what you think!

A **QUICK TOUR** *of* *a* **BIG WORLD**

WALT DISNEY WORLD ENCOMPASSES 43 SQUARE MILES, an area twice as large as Manhattan. Situated strategically in this vast expanse are the **Magic Kingdom, Epcot, Disney's Hollywood Studios,** and **Disney's Animal Kingdom** theme parks; 2 swimming theme parks; a sports complex; 5 golf courses; 36 hotels and a campground; more than 100 restaurants; 4 interconnected lakes; a shopping complex; 8 convention venues; a nature preserve; and a transportation system consisting of four-lane highways, elevated monorails, and a network of canals.

THE MAJOR THEME PARKS

The Magic Kingdom

When people think of Walt Disney World, most think of the Magic Kingdom, opened in 1971. It consists of the adventures, rides, and shows featuring the Disney cartoon characters, and Cinderella Castle. It's only one element of Disney World, but it remains the heart.

The Magic Kingdom is divided into six "lands," with five arranged around a central hub. First you come to **Main Street, U.S.A.,** which

Continued on page 12

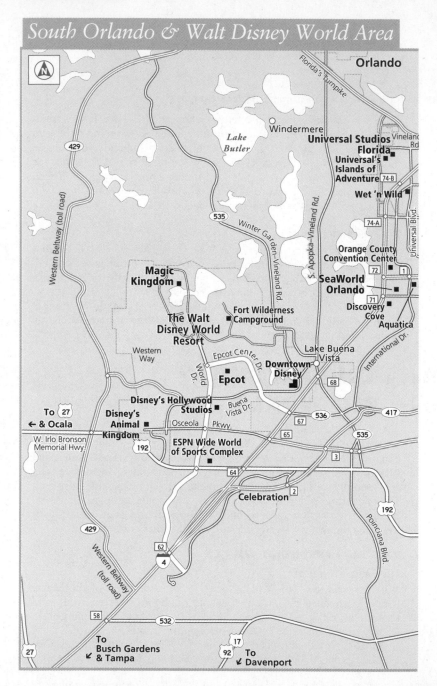

South Orlando & Walt Disney World Area

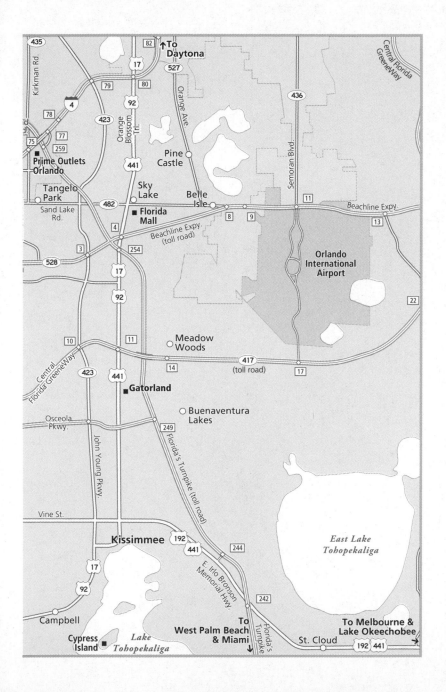

Walt Disney World

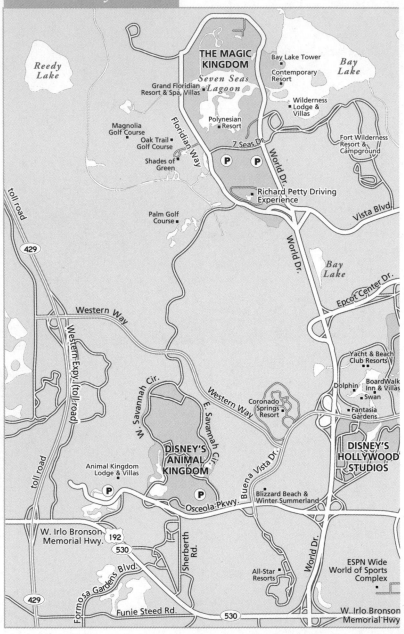

Reedy Lake

THE MAGIC KINGDOM

Bay Lake Tower

Contemporary Resort

Bay Lake

Seven Seas Lagoon

Grand Floridian Resort & Spa, Villas

Wilderness Lodge & Villas

Magnolia Golf Course

Polynesian Resort

Oak Trail Golf Course

Fort Wilderness Resort & Campground

Floridian Way

7 Seas Dr.

Shades of Green

World Dr.

toll road

Richard Petty Driving Experience

Vista Blvd.

Palm Golf Course

World Dr.

429

Bay Lake

Epcot Center Dr.

Western Way

Western Expy. (toll road)

Yacht & Beach Club Resorts

BoardWalk Inn & Villas

Dolphin

Swan

W. Savannah Cir.

Western Way

Coronado Springs Resort

Fantasia Gardens

E. Savannah Cir.

DISNEY'S ANIMAL KINGDOM

DISNEY'S HOLLYWOOD STUDIOS

Animal Kingdom Lodge & Villas

Buena Vista Dr.

toll road

Blizzard Beach & Winter Summerland

Osceola Pkwy.

W. Irlo Bronson Memorial Hwy.

192

Sherberth Rd.

530

World Dr.

ESPN Wide World of Sports Complex

Formosa Gardens Blvd.

All-Star Resorts

429

Funie Steed Rd.

530

W. Irlo Bronson Memorial Hwy

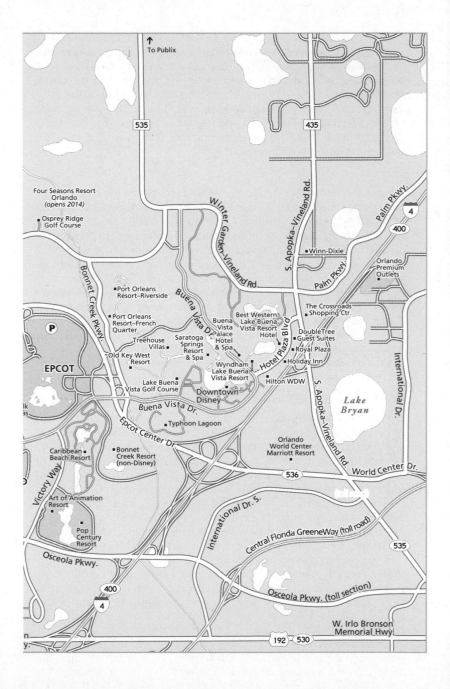

↑
To Publix

535

435

Four Seasons Resort
Orlando
(opens 2014)

Osprey Ridge
Golf Course

Winter Garden-Vineland Rd.

S. Apopka-Vineland Rd.

Palm Pkwy.

4

400

Winn-Dixie

Palm Pkwy.

Orlando
Premium
Outlets

Bonnet Creek Pkwy.

Buena Vista Dr.

Port Orleans
Resort–Riverside

Port Orleans
Resort–French
Quarter

Treehouse
Villas

P

Saratoga
Springs
Resort
& Spa

Buena
Vista
Palace
Hotel
& Spa

Best Western
Lake Buena
Vista Resort
Hotel

The Crossroads
Shopping Ctr.

DoubleTree
Guest Suites

Royal Plaza

Hotel Plaza Blvd.

International Dr.

Old Key West
Resort

EPCOT

Lake Buena
Vista Golf Course

Wyndham
Lake Buena
Vista Resort

Holiday Inn

Hilton WDW

Lake
Bryan

lk
as

Downtown
Disney

Buena Vista Dr.

Typhoon Lagoon

Epcot Center Dr.

S. Apopka-Vineland Rd.

Orlando
World Center
Marriott Resort

World Center Dr.

536

Caribbean
Beach Resort

Bonnet
Creek Resort
(non-Disney)

Victory Way

Art of Animation
Resort

Pop
Century
Resort

International Dr. S.

Central Florida GreeneWay (toll road)

535

Osceola Pkwy.

400

4

Osceola Pkwy. (toll section)

W. Irlo Bronson
Memorial Hwy.

n.
y.

192   530

Continued from page 7

connects the Magic Kingdom entrance with the hub. Clockwise around the hub are **Adventureland, Frontierland, Liberty Square, Fantasyland,** and **Tomorrowland.** Five hotels (**Bay Lake Tower;** the **Contemporary, Polynesian,** and **Grand Floridian** resorts; and **The Villas at the Grand Floridian**) are connected to the Magic Kingdom by monorail and boat. Two other hotels, **Shades of Green** (operated by the U.S. Department of Defense) and **Wilderness Lodge & Villas,** are nearby but aren't served by the monorail. Also nearby and served by boat and bus is **Fort Wilderness Resort & Campground.**

Epcot

Opened in October 1982, Epcot is twice as big as the Magic Kingdom and comparable in scope. It has two major areas: **Future World** consists of pavilions concerning human creativity and technological advancement; **World Showcase,** arranged around a 40-acre lagoon, presents the architectural, social, and cultural heritages of almost a dozen nations, each country represented by replicas of famous landmarks and settings familiar to world travelers.

The Epcot resort hotels—the **BoardWalk Inn & Villas, Caribbean Beach Resort, Dolphin, Swan,** and **Yacht & Beach Club Resorts and Beach Club Villas**—are within a 5- to 15-minute walk of the International Gateway, the World Showcase entrance to the theme park. The hotels are also linked to Epcot and Disney's Hollywood Studios by canal and walkway. Epcot is connected to the Magic Kingdom and its hotels by monorail.

Disney's Hollywood Studios

Opened in 1989 as Disney-MGM Studios and a little larger than the Magic Kingdom, Disney's Hollywood Studios consists of two areas. One, occupying about 75% of the Studios, is a theme park focused on movies, music, and television. Park highlights include a re-creation of Hollywood and Sunset Boulevards from Hollywood's Golden Age, four high-tech rides, several musical shows, and a movie stunt show.

The second area encompasses soundstages, a back lot of streets and sets, and an outdoor theater for an automobile stunt show. Public access to the soundstages is limited to a tour which takes visitors behind the scenes of Disney animation and moviemaking.

Disney's Hollywood Studios is connected to other Walt Disney World areas by highway and canal but not by monorail. Guests can park in the Studios' pay parking lot or commute by bus. Guests at Epcot resort hotels can reach the Studios by boat or on foot.

Disney's Animal Kingdom

About five times the size of the Magic Kingdom, Disney's Animal Kingdom combines zoological exhibits with rides, shows, and live entertainment. The park is arranged in a hub-and-spoke configuration somewhat like the Magic Kingdom. A lush tropical rainforest serves as Main Street, funneling visitors to **Discovery Island,** the park's hub. Dominated by the park's central icon, the 14-story-tall, hand-carved **Tree of Life,** Discovery Island offers services, shopping, and dining. From there, guests can access the themed areas: **Africa, Asia, DinoLand U.S.A.,** and **Camp Minnie-Mickey.** Discovery Island, Africa, Camp Minnie-Mickey, and DinoLand U.S.A. opened in 1998, followed by Asia in 1999. Africa, the largest themed area, at 100 acres, features free-roaming herds in a recreation of the Serengeti Plain. Camp Minnie-Mickey is likely to be the site of the park's next expansion phase, with construction taking place from late 2013 to around 2017.

Disney's Animal Kingdom has its own parking lot and is connected to other Walt Disney World destinations by the Disney bus system. Although no hotels lie within Animal Kingdom proper, the **All-Star Resorts, Animal Kingdom Lodge & Villas,** and **Coronado Springs Resort** are all nearby.

THE WATER PARKS

DISNEY WORLD HAS TWO MAJOR water parks: **Typhoon Lagoon** and **Blizzard Beach.** Opened in 1989, Typhoon Lagoon is distinguished by a wave pool capable of making 6-foot waves. Blizzard Beach is newer, having opened in 1995, and it features more slides. Both parks are beautifully landscaped, and great attention is paid to atmosphere and aesthetics. Typhoon Lagoon and Blizzard Beach have their own adjacent parking lots and can be reached by Disney bus.

OTHER WALT DISNEY WORLD VENUES

Downtown Disney, a.k.a. Disney Springs

Downtown Disney is a large shopping, dining, and entertainment complex that encompasses **Downtown Disney Marketplace** on the east, **Downtown Disney West Side** on the west, and what used to be **Pleasure Island** in the middle. Downtown Disney Marketplace contains the world's largest Disney-character-merchandise store, upscale resort-wear and specialty shops, and several restaurants, including **Rainforest Cafe** and **T-REX.** Downtown Disney West Side combines nightlife, shopping, dining, and entertainment. The **House of Blues** serves Cajun-Creole dishes in its restaurant and electric blues in its music hall. **Bongos Cuban Cafe,** a nightclub and café created by Gloria Estefan and her husband, Emilio, offers Cuban rhythms and flavors. **Wolfgang Puck Grand Cafe,** sandwiched among pricey boutiques, is the West Side's prestige eatery. For entertainment, you'll find a 24-screen **AMC Theater; Splitsville,** an upscale bowling alley and restaurant; a permanent showplace for the extraordinary 70-person cast of **Cirque du Soleil** *La Nouba;* and **DisneyQuest,** an interactive virtual reality and electronic-games venue. Access Downtown Disney via Disney buses from Disney resorts.

Since the nighttime-entertainment venues at the former Pleasure Island were shuttered in 2008, The Big Mouse has suffered great angst in trying to arrive at an overall vision for Downtown Disney. After several false starts, Disney has embarked on an expansion with a Florida-waterfront-town theme. Called **Disney Springs,** it will encompass the current three areas and add a fourth. Pleasure Island will become **Town Center** and be built out toward the parking lot. Adjacent to the waterfront will be **The Landing,** with shops, restaurants, docks, and a promenade. Construction began in April 2013 and will be completed in 2016.

Disney's BoardWalk

Near Epcot, the BoardWalk is an idealized replication of an East Coast 1930s waterfront resort. Open all day, the BoardWalk features upscale restaurants, shops and galleries, a brewpub, and an ESPN sports bar. In the evening, a nightclub with dueling pianos and a DJ dance club join the lineup. Both are for guests age 21 and up only. There's no admission fee for the BoardWalk, but the piano bar levies a cover charge at night. This area is anchored by the BoardWalk Inn and Villas, along with its adjacent convention center. The BoardWalk is within walking distance of the Epcot resorts, Epcot's International Gateway, and Disney's Hollywood Studios. Boat transportation is available to and from Epcot and Disney's Hollywood Studios; buses serve other Disney World locations.

ESPN Wide World of Sports Complex

The 220-acre Wide World of Sports is a state-of-the-art competition and training facility consisting of a 9,500-seat ballpark, two field houses, and venues for baseball, softball, tennis, track and field, beach volleyball, and 27 other sports. The spring-training home of the Atlanta Braves, the complex also hosts a mind-boggling calendar of professional and amateur competitions. Walt Disney World guests not participating in events may pay admission to use the PlayStation Pavilion or watch any of the scheduled competitions.

Disney Cruise Line: The Mouse at Sea

In 1998, the Walt Disney Company launched (literally) its own cruise line with the 2,400-passenger *Disney Magic.* Its sister ship, the *Disney Wonder,* first sailed in 1999. Most cruises depart

Liliane: If you go for a cruise and Disney World package, visit the parks first, then sail away for more fun, as well as some much-deserved rest. *La dolce vita, here I come!*

from Port Canaveral, Florida (about a 90-minute drive from Walt Disney World) or Miami, on three-, four-, and seven-night itineraries. Caribbean and Bahamian cruises include a day at **Castaway Cay,** Disney's private island. Cruises can be packaged with a stay at Disney World. In 2011 and 2012, respectively, two new ships, the *Disney Dream* and the *Disney Fantasy,* joined the fleet, enabling Disney Cruise Line to expand sailings to the Caribbean, Alaska, the Mexican Riviera, and the Mediterranean.

Disney cruises are perfect for families and for kids of all ages. Although the cruises are family-oriented, extensive children's programs and elaborate child-care facilities allow grown-ups plenty of opportunities to relax and do adult stuff. The ships are modern ocean liners with classic steamship lines. Cabins are among the most spacious in the cruise industry, and the staff is very attentive and accommodating. From the waitstaff at breakfast, lunch, and dinner to the cabin stewards, yours truly has not experienced any better.

Cabin design reveals Disney's finely tuned sense of the needs of families and children and offers a cruise-industry first: a split bathroom with a bathtub and shower combo and sink in one room, and toilet, sink, and vanity in another. This configuration, found in all but standard inside cabins, allows any family member to use the bathroom without monopolizing it. All bathrooms have a tub and shower, except rooms for persons with disabilities (shower only). Decor includes unusual features such as bureaus designed to look like steamer trunks. Cabins also have a telephone, TV, hair dryer, and a cooling box. In some cabins, pull-down Murphy beds or drop-down bunk beds allow for additional daytime floor space. Storage is generous, with deep drawers and large closets.

Liliane: Board the ship as early as possible. Check on your dining rotation, and reserve Palo or Remy, spa treatments, and kids' programs. Relax and get ready for the departure party.

A big party with appearances by Mickey and Minnie marks departures, when the ship's horn toots "When You Wish upon a Star." Halfway through your voyage Disney throws a deck party, where Mickey saves all passengers from Captain Hook and his evil plans.

Dining is a true pleasure. Each night, passengers move to a different family restaurant—each with its own unique theme and menu—and take their table companions and waitstaff with them. In addition to the family restaurants, the ships have a range of cafés offering pizza, burgers, sandwiches, and ice-cream bars. Room service is available 24/7.

For a night out without kids, Palo, which offers tables with a view, is a must. Reservations are also a must, and a surcharge of $20 is added for this service to your onboard bill. The food is excellent, the ambience sophisticated. Disney enforces a strict policy for diners at Palo to be 18 years of age or older.

In addition to Palo, the *Dream* and the *Fantasy* crank it up a notch with Remy. Chefs Scott Hunnel of Victoria & Albert's and Arnaud Lallement from L'Assiette Champenoise—a Michelin two-star restaurant outside Reims, France—created the French-inspired menu, served in an Art Nouveau–style dining room. This upscale dining experience on the high seas costs $75; an additional $99 is needed for wine pairing. If you think this is a little over-the-top, we completely agree. It remains to be seen if the wine list presented at the table by a sommelier is worth the hefty surcharge. Whatever happened to the no-frills, great-food philosophy we learned from Remy in *Ratatouille*?

Liliane: Disney strictly enforces a minimum age limit (18) for dining at Palo or Remy's, and a jacket (no ties) is a must.

The Disney ships offer 15,000-plus square feet of playrooms and other kids' facilities. Programs include interactive activities, play areas supervised by trained counselors, and a children's drop-off service in the evening. Passengers can register their children for the nursery, and group babysitting is available for select hours every day. Cost is $6 per child, per hour. **Oceaneer's Club,** with its Never Land theme, is perfect for kids ages 3–7, though children up to age 10 can participate. (Programs on the *Wonder* allow children up to age 12.) **Oceaneer's Lab** offers high-tech play. Kids wear ID bracelets, and parents receive pagers. There are also special clubs for tweens and teens.

Big with kids of all ages are the pools and the nightly entertainment on board, which show Disney at its best. The **Walt Disney Theatre** stages several musical productions each cruise, and the **Buena Vista Theatre,** with its full-screen cinema, shows first-run and digital 3-D movies as well as classic Disney films. Movies are also played poolside on a state-of-the-art 24 x 14–foot LED screen affixed to the forward funnel in the **Goofy's Pool** area.

The *Dream* and the *Fantasy* feature the first-ever on-board water coaster. At 765 feet long and the height of four decks, **AquaDuck** is a major attraction for kids and grown-ups alike. Following an initial drop, guests glide through a translucent tube in a loop that extends 12 feet over the side of the vessel, allowing them to look down on the ocean 150 feet below. The ride lasts about 90 seconds and comes with climbs and drops, twists and turns. If you can keep your eyes open while riding, the AquaDuck will provide you with a spectacular view of the ship.

Vista Spa & Salon (known as **Senses** on the *Dream* and the *Fantasy*) is an area reserved exclusively for adults and a great place to relax. The treatments are pricey, and there's a surcharge of $15 per day for the use of the saunas and steam rooms, as well as two aromatic showers. (The fitness center's showers and lockers are free of charge.)

Sessions, the piano bar on the *Magic*, and **Cadillac Lounge,** on the *Wonder*, are the most relaxing and beautiful lounges on the Seven Seas. Make a before-or-after dinner drink there part of your routine.

Shore excursions depend on the itinerary, but all Cape Canaveral, New York, and Bahamian sailings make at least one call at **Castaway Cay,** Disney's 1,000-acre private island. The natural environment and miles of white-sand beaches have been nicely preserved. The best way to enjoy the island is to disembark first thing in the morning and secure a prime spot at the beach complete with hammock and shade. **Castaway Family Beach** is served by a tram running every 5 minutes. We walked the quarter-mile to the beach but realize that it could be tiresome to walk in the blistering summer heat. **Cookie's BBQ** and **Cookie's Too** serve an array of food that is included in the price of your cruise. Programs for kids on Castaway Cay give parents a chance to enjoy **Serenity Bay,** the adults-only beach. Another great family experience is a wedding or vows renewal, offered both at sea and on Castaway Cay. For more information, visit **disneyweddings.com**.

Disney Cruise Line fared better than most during the recession, but throughout the industry, demand has declined and capacity, with the introduction of a number of new ships, has gone up. Disney Cruise Line offers a distinctive product and has a loyal client base. However, when other cruise lines heavily discount their cruises, the deals are often so good that Disney Cruise Line is forced to struggle to hang onto its market share. When you can buy a seven-night Alaska cruise on another line for less than a four-night Disney cruise to Nassau and Castaway Cay, it strains the loyalty of even the most ardent Mouseketeer. Disney, therefore, has been discounting and offering "Kids Sail Free" specials for children who share a cabin with their parents.

Cruises are unequivocally the best deal in travel right now and for the immediate future. Deals abound. Check websites such as **cruise critic.com, cruisemates.com, vacationstogo.com,** and **lastminutetravel .com** for the latest discounts. Search engine **kayak.com** is another great resource for uncovering cruise bargains. If you prefer to buy directly from Disney, here's how to get in touch:

Disney Cruise Line
☎ 800-951-6499 or 800-951-3532
disneycruise.com

Disney Cruise Line offers a free planning DVD that tells you all you need to know about Disney cruises and then some. To obtain a copy, call ☎ 888-DCL-2500, or order online at **disneycruise.com.**

DISNEY-SPEAK POCKET TRANSLATOR

ALTHOUGH IT MAY COME AS A SURPRISE to many, Walt Disney World has its own somewhat peculiar language. Here are some terms you're likely to bump into.

DISNEY-SPEAK	ENGLISH DEFINITION
ADVENTURE	Ride
ATTRACTION	Ride or theater show
ATTRACTION HOST	Ride operator
AUDIENCE	Crowd
BACKSTAGE	Behind the scenes, out of view of customers
CAST MEMBER	Employee
CHARACTER	Disney character impersonated by an employee
COSTUME	Work attire or uniform
DARK RIDE	Indoor ride
DAY GUEST	Any customer not staying at a Disney resort
FACE CHARACTER	A character who does not wear a head-covering costume (Snow White, Cinderella, Jasmine, and the like)
GENERAL PUBLIC	Same as day guest

DISNEY-SPEAK	ENGLISH DEFINITION
GREETER	Employee positioned at an attraction entrance
GUEST	Customer
HIDDEN MICKEYS	Frontal silhouette of Mickey's head worked subtly into the design of buildings, railings, vehicles, golf greens, attractions, and just about anything else
ON STAGE	In full view of customers
PRESHOW	Entertainment at an attraction prior to the feature presentation
RESORT GUEST	A customer staying at a Disney resort
SECURITY HOST	Security guard
SOFT OPENING	Opening a park or attraction before its stated opening date
TRANSITIONAL EXPERIENCE	An element of the queuing area and/or preshow that provides a story line or information essential to understanding the attraction

PART ONE

BASIC CONSIDERATIONS

IS WALT DISNEY WORLD *for* YOU?

ALMOST ALL VISITORS ENJOY WALT DISNEY WORLD on some level and find things to see and do that they like. In fact, for many, the theme park attractions are just the tip of the iceberg. The more salient question, then (because this is a family vacation), is whether the members of your family basically like the same things. If you do, fine. If not, how will you handle the differing agendas?

A mother from Toronto wrote a couple of years ago describing her husband's aversion to Disney's (in his terms) "phony, plastic, and idealized version of life." Touring the theme parks, he was a real cynic and managed to diminish the experience for the rest of the family. As it happened, however, dad's pejorative point of view didn't extend to the Disney golf courses. So mom packed him up and sent him golfing while the family enjoyed the theme parks.

If you have someone in your family who doesn't like theme parks or, for whatever reason, doesn't care for Disney's brand of entertainment, it helps to get that attitude out in the open. Our recommendation is to deal with the person up front. Glossing over or ignoring the contrary opinion and hoping that "Tom will like it once he gets there" is naive and unrealistic. Either leave Tom at home or help him discover and plan activities that he will enjoy, resigning yourself in the process to the fact that the family won't be together at all times.

DIFFERENT FOLKS, DIFFERENT STROKES

IT'S NO SECRET THAT WE AT THE *Unofficial Guides* believe thorough planning is an essential key to a successful Walt Disney World vacation. It's also no secret that our emphasis on planning rubs some folks the wrong way. Bob's sister and her husband, for example, are spontaneous people and do not appreciate the concept of detailed planning or, more particularly, following one of our touring plans when they visit the theme parks. To them the most important thing is to relax, take things as they come, and enjoy the moment. Sometimes they arrive at Epcot at 10:30 in the morning (impossibly late for us *Unofficial Guide* types), walk around enjoying the landscaping and architecture, and then sit with a cup of espresso, watching other guests race around the park like maniacs. They would be the first to admit that they don't see many attractions, but experiencing attractions is not what lights their sparklers.

Not coincidentally, most of our readers are big on planning. When they go to the theme park, they want to experience the attractions, and the shorter the lines, the better. They are willing to sacrifice some spontaneity for touring efficiency.

We want you to have the best possible time, whatever that means to you, so plan (or not) according to your preference. The point here is that most families (unlike Bob's sister and her husband) are not entirely in agreement on this planning versus spontaneity issue. If you are a serious planner and your oldest daughter and husband are free spirits, you've got the makings of a problem. In practice, the way this and similar scenarios shake out is that the planner (usually the more assertive or type-A person) just takes over. Sometimes daughter and husband go along and everything works out, but just as often they feel resentful. There are as many ways of developing a win-win compromise as there are well-intentioned people on different sides of this situation. How you settle it is up to you. We're simply suggesting that you examine the problem and work out the solution *before* you go on vacation.

THE NATURE OF THE BEAST

THOUGH MANY PARENTS DON'T REALIZE IT, there is no law that says you must take your kids to Walt Disney World. Likewise,

Bob: Sehlinger's Law postulates that the number of adults required to take care of an active toddler is equal to the number of adults present, plus one.

there's no law that says you will enjoy Walt Disney World. And although we will help you make the most of any visit, we can't change the basic nature of the beast . . . er, mouse. A Walt Disney World vacation is an active and physically demanding undertaking. Regimentation, getting up early, lots of walking, waiting in lines, fighting crowds, and (often) enduring heat and humidity are as intrinsic to a Walt Disney World vacation as stripes are to a zebra. Especially if you're traveling with children, you'll need a sense of humor, more than a modicum of patience, and the ability to roll with the punches.

KNOW THYSELF AND NOTHING TO EXCESS

THIS GOOD ADVICE WAS MADE AVAILABLE to ancient Greeks courtesy of the oracle of Apollo at Delphi, who gave us permission to pass it along to you. First, concerning the "know thyself" part, we want you to do some serious thinking concerning what you want in a vacation. We also want you to entertain the notion that having fun and deriving pleasure from your vacation may be very different indeed from doing and seeing as much as possible.

Because Walt Disney World is expensive, many families confuse "seeing everything" in order to "get our money's worth" with having a great time. Sometimes the two are compatible, but more often they are not. So, if sleep-
ing in, relaxing with the paper over coffee, sunbathing by the pool, or taking a nap ranks high on your vacation hit parade, you need to accord them due emphasis on your Disney visit (are you listening?), even if it means you see less of the theme parks.

Liliane: You can enjoy a perfectly wonderful time in the World if you're realistic, organized, and prepared.

Which brings us to the "nothing to excess" part. At Walt Disney World, especially if you are touring with children, less is definitely more. Trust us, you cannot go full tilt dawn to dark in the theme parks day after day. First you'll get tired, then you'll get cranky, and then you'll adopt a production mentality ("we've got three more rides and then we can go back to the hotel"). Finally, you'll hit the wall because you just can't maintain the pace.

Plan on seeing Walt Disney World in bite-size chunks with plenty of sleeping, swimming, napping, and relaxing in between. Ask yourself over and over in both the planning stage and while you are at Walt Disney World: What will contribute the greatest contentedness, satisfaction, and harmony? Trust your instincts. If stopping for ice cream or returning to the hotel for a dip feels like more fun than seeing another attraction, do it—even if it means wasting the remaining hours of an expensive admissions pass.

Bob: Get a grip on your needs and preferences before you leave home, and develop an itinerary that incorporates all the things that make you happiest.

The AGE THING

THERE IS A LOT OF SERIOUS COGITATION among parents and grandparents in regard to how old a child should be before embarking on a trip to Walt Disney World. The answer, not always obvious, stems from the personalities and maturity of the children, as well as the personalities and parenting style of the adults.

Walt Disney World for Infants and Toddlers

We believe that traveling with infants and toddlers is a great idea. Devel-
opmentally, travel is a stimulating learning experience for even the youngest of children. Infants, of course, will not know Mickey Mouse from a draft horse but will respond to sun and shade, music, bright colors, and the extra attention they receive from you. From first steps to full mobility, toddlers respond to the excitement and spectacle of Walt Disney World, though of course in a much different way than you do. Your toddler will prefer splashing in fountains and clambering over

curbs and benches to experiencing most attractions, but no matter: He or she will still have a great time.

Somewhere between 4 and 6 years of age, your child will experience the first vacation that he or she will remember as an adult. Though more likely to remember the comfortable coziness of the hotel room than the theme parks, the child will be able to experience and comprehend many attractions and will be a much fuller participant in your vacation. Even so, his or her favorite activity is likely to be swimming in the hotel pool.

As concerns infants and toddlers, there are good reasons and bad reasons for vacationing at Walt Disney World. A good reason for taking your little one to Walt Disney World is that you want to go and there's no one available to care for your child during your absence. Philosophically, we are very much against putting your life (including your vacation) on hold until your children are older.

Liliane: Traveling with infants and toddlers sharpens parenting skills and makes the entire family more mobile and flexible, resulting in a richer, fuller life for all.

Especially if you have children of varying ages (or plan to, for that matter), it's better to take the show on the road than to wait until the youngest reaches the perceived ideal age. If your family includes a toddler or infant, you will find everything from private facilities for breast-feeding to changing tables in both men's and women's restrooms to facilitate baby's care. Your whole family will be able to tour together with fewer hassles than on a picnic outing at home.

An illogical reason, however, for taking an infant or toddler to Walt Disney World is that you think Walt Disney World is the perfect vacation destination for babies. It's not, so think again if you are contemplating Walt Disney World primarily for your child's enjoyment. For starters, attractions are geared more toward older children and adults. Even designer play areas like Tom Sawyer Island in the Magic Kingdom are developed with older children in mind.

By way of example, Bob has a friend who bought a camcorder when his first child was born. He delighted in documenting his son's reaction to various new experiences on video. One memorable night when the baby was about 18 months old, he recorded the baby eating a variety of foods (from whipped cream to dill pickles) that he had never tried before. While some of the taste sensations elicited wild expressions and animated responses from the baby, the exercise was clearly intended for the amusement of Dad, not Junior.

That said, let us stress that for the well prepared, taking a toddler to Walt Disney World can be a totally glorious experience. There's truly nothing like watching your child respond to the color, the sound, the festivity, and, most of all, the characters. You'll return home with scrapbooks of photos that you will treasure forever. Your little one won't remember much, but never mind. Your memories will be unforgettable.

Along similar lines, remember when you were little and you got that nifty electric train for Christmas, the one Dad wouldn't let you play with? Did you ever wonder who that train was really for? Ask yourself the same question about your vacation to Walt Disney World. Whose dream are you trying to make come true: yours or your child's?

If you elect to take your infant or toddler to Walt Disney World, rest assured that their needs have been anticipated. The major theme parks have centralized facilities for infant and toddler care. Everything necessary for changing diapers, preparing formula, and warming bottles and food is available. Dads in charge of little ones are welcome at the centers and can use most services offered. In addition, men's rooms in the major theme parks have changing tables.

 Liliane: Baby supplies—including disposable diapers, formula, and baby food—are for sale, and there are rockers and special chairs for nursing mothers.

Infants and toddlers are allowed to experience any attraction that doesn't have minimum height or age restrictions. A Minneapolis mom suggests using a baby sling:

> We used a baby sling on our trip and thought it was great when standing in the lines—much better than a stroller, which you have to park before getting in line (and navigate through crowds). My baby was still nursing when we went to Walt Disney World. The only really great place I found to nurse in the Magic Kingdom was a hidden bench in the shade in Adventureland in between the snack stand (next to the Enchanted Tiki Room) and the small shops. It is impractical to go to the baby station every time, so a nursing mom better be comfortable about nursing in very public situations.

Two points in our reader's comment warrant elaboration. First, the rental strollers at all of the major theme parks are designed for toddlers and children up to 3 and 4 years old but are definitely not for infants. If you bring pillows and padding, the rental strollers can be made to work. You can bring your own stroller, but unless it's collapsible, you will not be able to take it on Disney trams, buses, or boats.

Even if you opt for a stroller (your own or a rental), we nevertheless recommend that you also bring a baby sling or baby/child backpack. Simply put, there will be many times in the theme parks when you will have to park the stroller and carry your child. As an aside, if you haven't checked out baby slings and packs lately, you'll be amazed by some of the technological advances made in these products.

The second point that needs addressing is our reader's perception that there are not many good places in the theme parks for breast-feeding unless you are accustomed to nursing in public. Many nursing moms recommend breast-feeding during a dark Disney theater presentation. This only works, however, if the presentation is long enough for the baby to finish nursing. *The Hall of Presidents* at the Magic Kingdom and *The American Adventure* at Epcot will afford you about 23 and 29 minutes, respectively.

Many Disney shows run back to back with only 1 or 2 minutes in between to change the audience. If you want to breast-feed and require more time than the length of the show, tell the cast member on entering that you want to breast-feed and ask if you can remain in the theater and watch a second showing while your baby finishes. Also keep in mind that many shows may have special effects or loud sound tracks that may make children even as old as 7 uncomfortable.

Liliane: In addition to providing an alternative to carrying your child, a stroller serves as a handy cart for diaper bags, water bottles, and other items you deem necessary.

If you can adjust to nursing in more public places with your breast and the baby's head covered with a shawl or some such, nursing will not be a problem at all. Even on the most crowded days, you can always find a back corner of a restaurant or a comparatively secluded park bench or garden spot to nurse. Finally, the Baby Care Centers, with their private nursing rooms, are centrally located in all of the parks except the Studios.

Walt Disney World for 4-, 5-, and 6-Year-Olds

Children ages 4–6 vary immensely in their capacity to comprehend and enjoy Walt Disney World. With this age group, the go–no-go decision is a judgment call. If your child is sturdy, easygoing, fairly adventuresome, and demonstrates a high degree of independence, the trip will probably work. On the other hand, if your child tires easily, is temperamental, or is a bit timid or reticent in embracing new experiences, you're much better off waiting a few years. Whereas the travel and sensory-overload problems of infants and toddlers can be addressed and (usually) remedied on the go, discontented 4- to 6-year-olds have the ability to stop a family dead in its tracks, as this mother of three from Cape May, New Jersey, attests:

> My 5-year-old was scared pretty bad on [a dark ride] our first day at Disney World. From then on, for the rest of the trip, we had to coax and reassure her before each and every ride before she would go. It was like pulling teeth.

If you have a tiring, clinging, and/or difficult 4- to 6-year-old who, for whatever circumstances, will be part of your group, you can sidestep or diminish potential problems with a bit of pretrip preparation. Even if your preschooler is plucky and game, the same prep measures (described later in this section) will enhance his or her experience and make life easier for the rest of the family.

Parents who understand that a visit with 3- to 6-year-old children is going to be more about the cumulative experience than it is about seeing it all will have a blast, as well as wonderful memories of their children's amazement.

The Ideal Age

Although our readers report both successful trips as well as disasters with children of all ages, the consensus ideal children's ages for family compatibility and togetherness at Walt Disney World are 8–12 years. This age group is old enough, tall enough, and sufficiently stalwart to experience, understand, and appreciate practically all Disney attractions. Moreover, they are developed to the extent that they can get around the parks on their own steam without being carried or collapsing. Best of all, they are still young enough to enjoy being with mom and dad. From our experience, ages 10–12 are better than 8 and 9, though what you gain in maturity is at the cost of that irrepressible, wide-eyed wonder so prevalent in the 8- and 9-year-olds.

Walt Disney World for Teens

Teens love Walt Disney World, and for parents of teens the World is a nearly perfect, albeit expensive, vacation choice. Although your teens might not be as wide-eyed and impressionable as their younger sibs, they are at an age where they can sample, understand, and enjoy practically everything Walt Disney World has to offer.

For parents, Walt Disney World is a vacation destination where you can permit your teens an extraordinary amount of freedom. The entertainment is wholesome, the venues are safe, and the entire complex of hotels, theme parks, restaurants, and shopping centers is accessible via the Walt Disney World transportation system. The transportation system allows you, for example, to enjoy a romantic dinner and an early bedtime while your teens take in the late-night fireworks at the theme parks. After the fireworks, a Disney bus, boat, or monorail will deposit them safely back at the hotel.

Because most adolescents relish freedom, you may have difficulty keeping your teens with the rest of the family. Thus, if one of your objectives is to spend time with your teenage children during your Disney World vacation, you will need to establish some clear-cut guidelines regarding togetherness and separateness before you leave home. Make your teens part of the discussion and try to meet them halfway in crafting a decision everyone can live with. For your teens, touring on their own at Walt Disney World is tantamount to being independent in a large city. It's intoxicating, to say the least, and can be an excellent learning experience, if not a rite of passage. In any event, we're not suggesting that you just turn them loose. Rather, we are just attempting to sensitize you to the fact that for your teens, there are some transcendent issues involved.

Most teens crave the company of other teens. If you have a solitary teen in your family, do not be surprised if he or she wants to invite a friend on your vacation. If you are invested in sharing intimate, quality time with your solitary teen, the presence of a friend will make this difficult, if not impossible. However, if you turn down the request to bring a friend, be prepared to go the extra mile to be a companion to your teen at Walt Disney World. Expressed differently, if you're a teen, it's not much fun to ride Space Mountain by yourself.

One specific issue that absolutely should be addressed before you leave home is what assistance (if any) you expect from your teen in regard to helping with younger children in the family. Once again, try to carve out a win-win compromise. Consider the case of the mother from Indiana who had a teenage daughter from an earlier marriage and two children under age 10 from a second marriage. After a couple of vacations where she thrust the unwilling teen into the position of being a surrogate parent to her stepsisters, the teen declined henceforth to participate in family vacations.

Many parents have written the *Unofficial Guide* asking if there are unsafe places at Walt Disney World or places where teens simply should not be allowed to go. Although the answer depends more on your family values and the relative maturity of your teens than on Walt Disney World, the basic answer is no. Though it's true that teens (or adults, for that matter) who are looking for trouble can find it anywhere, there is absolutely nothing at Walt Disney World that could be construed as a precipitant or a catalyst.

As a final aside, if you allow your teens some independence and they are getting around on the Walt Disney World transportation system, expect some schedule slippage. There are no posted transportation schedules other than when service begins in the morning and when service terminates at night. Thus, to catch a bus, for example, you just go to a bus station and wait for the next bus to your Disney World destination. If you happen to just miss the bus, you might have to wait 15–45 minutes (more often 15–20 minutes) for the next one. If punctuality is essential, advise your independent teens to arrive at a transportation station an hour before they are expected somewhere in order to allow sufficient time for the commute.

About **INVITING** *Your* **CHILDREN'S FRIENDS**

IF YOUR CHILDREN WANT TO INVITE FRIENDS on your Walt Disney World vacation, give your decision careful thought. There's more involved here than might be apparent. First, consider the logistics of numbers. Is there room in the car? Will you have to leave something at home that you had planned on taking to make room in the trunk for the friend's luggage? Will additional hotel rooms or a larger condo be required? Will the increased number of people in your group make it hard to get a table at a restaurant?

If you determine that you can logistically accommodate one or more friends, the next step is to consider how the inclusion of the friend will affect your group's dynamics. Generally speaking, the presence of a friend will make it harder to really connect with your own children. So if one of your vacation goals is an intimate bonding experience with your children, the addition of friends will probably frustrate your attempts to realize that objective.

If family relationship building is not necessarily a primary objective of your vacation, it's quite possible that the inclusion of a friend will make life easier for you. This is especially true in the case of only children, who may otherwise depend exclusively on you to keep them happy and occupied. Having a friend along can take the pressure off and give you some much-needed breathing room.

If you decide to allow a friend to accompany you, limit the selection to children you know really well and whose parents you also know. Your Walt Disney World vacation is not the time to include "my friend Eddie from school" whom you've never met. Your children's friends who have spent time in your home will have a sense of your parenting style, and you will have a sense of their personality, behavior, and compatibility with your family. Assess the prospective child's potential to fit in well on a long trip. Is he or she polite, personable, fun to be with, and reasonably mature? Does he or she relate well to you and to the other members of your family?

Because a Walt Disney World vacation is not, for most of us, a spur-of-the-moment thing, you should have adequate time to evaluate potential candidate friends. A trip to the mall including a meal in a sit-down restaurant will tell you volumes about the friend. Likewise, inviting the friend to share dinner with the family and then spend the night will provide a lot of relevant information. Ideally this type of evaluation should take place early on in the normal course of family events, before you discuss the possibility of a friend joining you on your vacation. This will allow you to size things up without your child (or the friend) realizing that an evaluation is taking place.

By seizing the initiative, you can guide the outcome. Ann, a Springfield, Ohio, mom, for example, anticipated that her 12-year-old son would ask to take a friend on their vacation. As she pondered the various friends her son might propose, she came up with four names. One, an otherwise sweet child, had a medical condition that Ann felt unqualified to monitor or treat. A second friend was overly aggressive with younger children and was often socially inappropriate for his age. Two other friends, Chuck and Marty, with whom she had had a generally positive experience, were good candidates for the trip. After orchestrating some opportunities to spend time with each of the boys, she made her decision and asked her son, "Would you like to take Marty with us to Disney World?" Her son was delighted, and Ann had diplomatically preempted having to turn down friends her son might have proposed.

We recommend that you do the inviting, instead of your child, and that you extend the invitation to the parent (to avoid disappointment, you might want to sound out the friend's parent before broaching the issue with your child). Observing this recommendation will allow you to query the friend's parents concerning food preferences, any medical conditions, how discipline is administered in the friend's family, how the friend's parents feel about the way you administer discipline, and the parents' expectation regarding religious observations while their child is in your care.

Before you extend the invitation, give some serious thought to who pays for what. Make a specific proposal for financing the trip a part of your invitation, for example: "There's room for Marty in the hotel room, and transportation's no problem because we're driving. So we'll just need you to pick up Marty's meals, theme park admissions, and spending money."

A **FEW WORDS** *for* **SINGLE PARENTS**

BECAUSE SINGLE PARENTS GENERALLY are also working parents, planning a special getaway with your children can be the best way to spend some quality time together. But remember, the vacation is not just for your child—it's for you too. You might invite a grandparent or a favorite aunt or uncle along; the other adult provides nice company for you, and your child will benefit from the time with family members. You might likewise consider inviting an adult friend.

Though bringing along an adult friend or family member is the best option, the reality is that many single parents don't have friends, grandparents, or favorite aunts or uncles who can make the trip. And while spending time with your child is wonderful, it is very difficult to match the energy level of your child if you are the sole focus of his or her world.

One alternative: Try to meet other single parents at Walt Disney World. It may seem odd, but most of them are in the same boat as you; besides, all you have to do is ask. Another option, albeit expensive, is to take along a trustworthy babysitter (18 or up) to travel with you.

The easiest way to meet other single parents at the World is to hang out at the hotel pool. Make your way there on the day you arrive, after traveling by car or plane and without enough time to blow a full admission ticket at a theme park. In any event, a couple of hours spent poolside is a relaxing way to start your vacation.

If you visit Walt Disney World with another single parent, get adjoining rooms; take turns watching all the kids; and, on at least one night, get a sitter and enjoy an evening out.

Throughout this book we mention the importance of good planning and touring. For a single parent, this is an absolute must. In addition, make sure that you set aside some downtime back at the hotel every day.

Finally, don't try to spend every moment with your children on vacation. Instead, plan some activities for your children with other children. Disney educational programs for children, for example, are worth considering. Then take advantage of your free time to do what you want to do: Read a book, have a massage, take a long walk, or enjoy a catnap.

While pricey, one of the best ways for single parents to relax is to add a three- or four-night cruise to their Disney stay. Onboard activities will keep your child occupied and give you time to relax.

"HE WHO HESITATES IS LAUNCHED!" *Tips and Warnings for Grandparents*

SENIORS OFTEN GET INTO PREDICAMENTS caused by touring with grandchildren. Run ragged and pressured to endure a blistering pace, many seniors just concentrate on surviving Walt Disney World rather than enjoying it. The theme parks have as much to offer older visitors as they do children, and seniors must either set the pace or dispatch the young folks to tour on their own.

An older reader from Alabaster, Alabama, writes:

> *The main thing I want to say is that being a senior is not for wusses. At Disney World particularly, it requires courage and pluck. Things that used to be easy take a lot of effort, and sometimes your brain has to wait for your body to catch up. Half the time, your grandchildren treat you like a crumbling ruin and then turn around and trick you into getting on a roller coaster in the dark. What you need to tell seniors is that they have to be alert and not trust anyone. Not their children or even the Disney people, and especially not their grandchildren. When your grandchildren want you to go on a ride, don't follow along blindly like a lamb to the slaughter. Make sure you know what the ride is all about. Stand your ground and do not waffle. He who hesitates is launched!*

If you don't get to see much of your grandchildren, you might think that Walt Disney World is the perfect place for a little bonding and togetherness. Wrong! Walt Disney World can potentially send children into system overload and can precipitate behaviors that pose a challenge even to adoring parents, never mind grandparents. You don't take your grandchildren straight to Disney World for the same reason you don't buy your 16-year-old son a Ferrari: Handling it safely and well requires some experience.

Begin by spending time with your grandchildren in an environment that you can control. Have them over one at a time for dinner and to spend the night. Check out how they respond to your oversight and discipline. Most of all, zero in on whether you are compatible, enjoy each other's company, and have fun together. Determine that you can set limits and that they will accept those limits. When you reach this stage, you can contemplate some outings to the zoo, the movies, the mall, or the state fair. Gauge how demanding your grandchildren are when you are out of the house. Eat a meal or two in a full-service restaurant to get a sense of their social skills and their ability to behave appropriately. Don't expect perfection, and be prepared to modify your behavior a little too. As a senior friend of mine told her husband (none too decorously), "You can't see Walt Disney World sitting on a stick."

If you have a good relationship with your grandchildren and have had a positive one-on-one experience taking care of them, you might consider a trip to Walt Disney World. If you do, we have two recommendations. First, visit Walt Disney World without them to get an idea of what you're getting into. A scouting trip will also provide you with an opportunity to enjoy some of the attractions that won't be on the itinerary when you return with the grandkids. Second, if you are considering a trip of a week's duration, you might think about buying a Disney package that combines four days at Walt Disney World with a three-day cruise. In addition to being a memorable experience for your grandchildren, the cruise provides plenty of structure for children of almost every age, thus allowing you to be with them but also to have some time off. Call the Disney Cruise Line at ☎ 800-951-3532 or visit **disneycruise.com**.

Tips for Grandparents

1. It's best to take one grandchild at a time, two at the most. Cousins can be better than siblings because they don't fight as much. To preclude sibling jealousy, try connecting the trip to a child's milestone, such as finishing the sixth grade.

2. Let your grandchildren help plan the vacation, and keep the first one short. Be flexible and don't overplan.

3. Discuss mealtimes and bedtime. Fortunately, many grandparents are on an early dinner schedule, which works nicely with younger children. Also, if you want to plan a special evening out, be sure to make the reservation ahead of time.

4. Gear plans to your grandchildren's age levels, because if they're not happy, you won't be happy.

5. Create an itinerary that offers some supervised activities for children in case you need a rest.

6. If you're traveling by car, this is the one time we highly recommend headphones. Kids' musical tastes are vastly different from most grandparents'. It's simply more enjoyable when everyone can listen to his or her own preferred style of music, at least for some portion of the trip.

7. Take along a night-light.

8. Carry a notarized statement from parents for permission for medical care in case of an emergency. Also be sure you have insurance information and copies of any prescriptions for medicines the kids may be on. Ditto for eyeglass prescriptions.

9. Tell your grandchildren about any medical problems you may have so they can be prepared if there's an emergency.

10. Many attractions and hotels offer discounts for seniors, so be sure you check ahead of time for bargains.

11. Plan your evening meal early to avoid long waits. And make advance reservations if you're dining in a popular spot, even if it's early. Take some crayons and paper to keep younger kids occupied.

ORDER *and* DISCIPLINE *on the* ROAD

OK, OK, WIPE THAT SMIRK OFF YOUR FACE. Order and discipline on the road may seem like an oxymoron to you, but you won't be hooting when your 5-year-old launches a screaming stem-winder in the middle of Fantasyland. Your willingness to give this subject serious consideration before you leave home may well be the most important element of your pretrip preparation.

Discipline and maintaining order are more difficult when traveling because everyone is, as a Boston mom put it, "in and out" (in strange surroundings and out of the normal routine). For children, it's hard to contain excitement and anticipation that pop to the surface in the form of fidgety hyperactivity, nervous energy, and sometimes, acting out. Confinement in a car, plane, or hotel room only exacerbates the situation, and kids are often louder than normal, more aggressive with siblings, and much more inclined to push the envelope of parental patience and control. Once in the theme parks, it doesn't get much better. There's more elbow room, but there's also overstimulation, crowds, heat, and miles of walking. All this coupled with marginal or inadequate rest can lead to meltdown in the most harmonious of families.

The following discussion was developed by leading child psychologist Dr. Karen Turnbow, who has contributed to the *Unofficial Guides* for years and who has spent many days at Walt Disney World conducting research and observing families.

 Liliane: Discuss your vacation needs with your children and explore their wants and expectations well before you depart on your trip.

Sound parenting and standards of discipline practiced at home, applied consistently, will suffice to handle most situations on vacation. Still, it's instructive to study the hand you are dealt when traveling. For starters, aside from being jazzed and ablaze with adrenaline, your kids may believe that rules followed at home are somehow suspended when traveling. Parents reinforce this misguided intuition by being inordinately lenient in the interest of maintaining peace in the family. While some of your home protocols (cleaning your plate, going to bed at a set time, and such) might be relaxed to good effect on vacation, differing from your normal approach to discipline can precipitate major misunderstanding and possibly disaster.

Children, not unexpectedly, are likely to believe that a vacation (especially a vacation to Walt Disney World) is expressly for them. This reinforces their focus on their own needs and largely erases any consideration of yours. Such a mind-set dramatically increases their sense of hurt and disappointment when you correct them or deny them something they want. An incident that would hardly elicit a pouty lip at home could well escalate to tears or defiance when traveling.

The stakes are high for everyone on a vacation; for you because of the cost in time and dollars, but also because your vacation represents a rare opportunity for rejuvenation and renewal. The stakes are high for your children too. Children tend to romanticize travel, building anticipation to an almost unbearable level. Discussing the trip in advance can ground expectations to a certain extent, but a child's imagination will, in the end, trump reality every time. The good news is that you can take advantage of your children's emotional state to establish pre-agreed rules and conditions for their conduct while on vacation. Because your children want what's being offered sooooo badly, they will be unusually accepting and conscientious regarding whatever rules are agreed upon.

According to Dr. Turnbow, successful response to (or avoidance of) behavioral problems on the road begins with a clear-cut disciplinary policy at home. Both at home and on vacation, the approach should be the same and should be based on the following key concepts:

1. LET EXPECTATIONS BE KNOWN. Discuss what you expect from your children but don't try to cover every imaginable situation. Cover expectations in regard to compliance with parental directives, treatment of siblings, resolution of disputes, schedule (including wake-up and bedtimes), courtesy and manners, staying together, and who pays for what.

2. EXPLAIN THE CONSEQUENCES OF NONCOMPLIANCE. Detail very clearly and firmly the consequences of unmet expectations. This should be very straightforward and unambiguous. If you do X (or don't do X), this is what will happen.

3. WARN YOUR KIDS. You're dealing with excited, expectant children, not machines, so it's important to issue a warning before meting out discipline. It's critical to understand that we're talking about one unequivocal warning rather than multiple warnings or nagging. These undermine your credibility and make your expectations appear relative or less than serious. Multiple warnings or nagging also effectively pass control of the situation from you to your child (who may continue to act out as an attention-getting strategy).

4. FOLLOW THROUGH. If you say that you're going to do something, do it. Period. Children must understand that you are absolutely serious and committed.

5. BE CONSISTENT. Inconsistency makes discipline a random event in the eyes of your children. Random discipline encourages random behavior, which translates to a nearly total loss of parental control. Long-term, both at home and on the road, your response to a given situation or transgression must be perfectly predictable. Structure and repetition, essential for a child to learn, cannot be achieved in the absence of consistency.

Although the previous five are the biggies, several other corollary concepts and techniques that are worthy of consideration.

First, understand that whining, tantrums, defiance, sibling friction, and even holding the group up are ways in which children communicate with parents. Frequently the object or precipitant of a situation has little or no relation to the unacceptable behavior. A fit may on the surface appear to be about the ice cream you refused to buy little Robby, but there's almost always something deeper, a subtext that is closer to the truth (this is the reason why ill behavior often persists after you give in to a child's demands). As often as not the real cause is a need for attention. This need is so powerful in some children that they will subject themselves to certain punishment and parental displeasure to garner the attention they crave.

To get at the root cause of the behavior in question requires both active listening and empowering your child with a "feeling vocabulary." Active listening is a concept that's been around a long time. It involves being alert not only to what a child says, but also to the context in which it is said, to the language used and possible subtext, to the child's emotional state and body language, and even to what's not said. Sounds complicated, but it's basically being attentive to the larger picture, and more to the point, being aware that there is a larger picture.

Helping your child to develop a feeling vocabulary consists of teaching your child to use words to describe what's going on. The idea is to teach the child to articulate what's really troubling him, to be able to identify and express emotions and mood states in language. Of course learning to express feelings is a lifelong experience, but it's much less dependent on innate sensitivity than being provided the tools for expression and being encouraged to use them.

It all begins with convincing your child that you're willing to listen attentively and take what he's saying seriously. Listening to your child, you help him transcend the topical by reframing the conversation to address the underlying emotional state(s). That his brother hit him may have precipitated the mood, but the act is topical and of secondary importance. What you want is for your child to be able to communicate how that makes him feel and to get in touch with those emotions. When you reduce an incident (hitting) to the emotions triggered (anger, hurt, rejection, and so on), you have the foundation for helping him to develop constructive coping strategies. Not only are being in touch with one's feelings and developing constructive coping strategies essential to emotional well-being, but they also beneficially affect behavior. A child who can tell his mother why he is distressed is a child who has discovered a coping strategy far more effective (not to mention easier for all concerned) than a tantrum.

Children are almost never too young to begin learning a feeling vocabulary. And helping your child to be in touch with, and try to communicate, his emotions will stimulate you to focus on your feelings and mood states in a similar way.

SIX MORE TIPS

UNTIL YOU GET THE ACTIVE LISTENING and feeling vocabulary going, be careful not to become part of the problem. There's a whole laundry list of adult responses to bad behavior that only make things worse. Hitting, swatting, yelling, name calling, insulting, belittling, using sarcasm, pleading, nagging, and inducing guilt (as in: "We've spent thousands of dollars to bring you to Disney World and now you're spoiling the trip for everyone") figure prominently on the list.

Responding to a child appropriately in a disciplinary situation requires thought and preparation. Following are key things to keep in mind and techniques to try when your world blows up while waiting in line for Dumbo.

1. BE THE ADULT. It's well understood that children can punch their parents' buttons faster and more lethally than just about anyone or anything else. They've got your number, know precisely how to elicit a response, and are not reluctant to go for the jugular. Fortunately (or unfortunately) you're the adult, and to deal with a situation effectively, you must act like one. If your kids get you ranting and caterwauling, you effectively abdicate your adult status. Worse, you suggest by way of example that being out of control is an acceptable expression of hurt or anger. No matter what happens, repeat the mantra, "I am the adult in this relationship."

2. FREEZE THE ACTION. Being the adult and maintaining control almost always translates to freezing the action, to borrow a sports term. Instead of a knee-jerk response (at a maturity level closer to your child's than yours), freeze the action by disengaging. Wherever you are or whatever the family is doing, stop in place and concentrate on one thing and one thing only: getting all involved to calm down. Practically speaking, this usually means initiating a time-out. It's essential that you take this action immediately. Grabbing your child by the arm or collar and dragging him toward the car or hotel room only escalates the turmoil by prolonging the confrontation and by adding a coercive physical dimension to an already volatile emotional event. If, for the sake of people around you (as when a toddler throws a tantrum in church), it's essential to retreat to a more private place, choose the first place available. Firmly sit the child down and refrain from talking to him until you've both cooled off. This might take a little time, but the investment is worthwhile. Truncating the process is like trying to get on your feet too soon after surgery.

3. ISOLATE THE CHILD. You'll be able to deal with the situation more effectively and expeditiously if the child is isolated with one parent. Dispatch the uninvolved members of your party for a Coke break or have them go on with the activity or itinerary without you (if possible) and arrange to rendezvous later at an agreed time and place. In addition to letting the others get on with their day, isolating the offending child with one parent relieves him of the pressure of being the group's focus of attention and object of anger. Equally important, isolation frees you from the scrutiny and expectations of the others in regard to how to handle the situation.

4. REVIEW THE SITUATION WITH THE CHILD. If, as discussed previously, you've made your expectations clear, stated the consequences of failing those expectations, and administered a warning, review the situation with the child and follow through with the discipline warranted. If, as often occurs, things are not so black and white, encourage the child to communicate his feelings. Try to uncover what occasioned the acting out. Lecturing and accusatory language don't work well here, nor do threats. Dr. Turnbow suggests that a better approach (after the child is calm) is to ask, "What can we do to make this a better day for you?"

5. FREQUENT TANTRUMS OR ACTING OUT. The preceding four points relate to dealing with an incident as opposed to a chronic condition. If a child frequently acts out or throws tantrums, you'll need to employ a somewhat different strategy.

Tantrums are cyclical events evolved from learned behavior. A child learns that he can get your undivided attention by acting out. When you respond, whether by scolding, admonishing, threatening, or negotiating, your response further draws you into the cycle and prolongs the behavior. When you accede to the child's demands, you reinforce the effectiveness of the tantrum and raise the cost of capitulation next time around. When a child thus succeeds in monopolizing your attention, he effectively becomes the person in charge.

To break this cycle, you must disengage from the child. The object is to demonstrate that the cause and effect relationship (that is, tantrum elicits parental attention) is no longer operative. This can be accomplished by refusing to interact with the child as long as the untoward behavior continues. Tell the child that you're unwilling to discuss his problem until he calms down. You can ignore the behavior, remove yourself from the child's presence (or visa versa), or isolate the child with a time-out. The important thing is to disengage quickly and decisively with no discussion or negotiation.

Most children don't pick the family vacation as the time to start throwing tantrums. The behavior will be evident before you leave home, and home is the best place to deal with it. Be forewarned, however, that bad habits die hard, and a child accustomed to getting attention by throwing tantrums will not simply give up after a single instance of disengagement. More likely, the child will at first escalate the intensity and length of his tantrums. By your consistent refusal over several weeks (or even months) to respond to his behavior, however, he will finally adjust to the new paradigm.

Liliane: Tantrums are about getting attention. Giving your child attention when things are on an even keel often preempts acting out.

Children are cunning as well as observant. Many understand that a tantrum in public is embarrassing to you and that you're more likely to cave in than you would at home. Once again, consistency is the key, along with a bit of anticipation. When traveling, it's not necessary to retreat to the privacy of a hotel room to isolate your child. You can carve out space for time-out almost anywhere: on a theme park bench, in a park, in your car, in a restroom, even on a sidewalk. You can often spot the warning signs of an impending tantrum and head it off by talking to the child before he reaches an explosive emotional pitch.

6. SALVAGE OPERATIONS. Children are full of surprises, and sometimes the surprises are not good. If your sweet child manages to make a mistake of mammoth proportions, what do you do? This happened to an Ohio couple, resulting in the offending kid pretty much being grounded for life. Fortunately there were no injuries or lives lost, but the parents had to determine what to do for the remainder of the vacation. For starters, they split the group. One parent escorted the offending child back to the hotel where he was effectively confined to his guest room for the duration. That evening, the parents arranged for in-room sitters for the rest of the stay. Expensive? You bet, but better than watching your whole vacation go down the tubes.

A family at Walt Disney World's Magic Kingdom theme park had a similar experience, although the offense was of a more modest order of magnitude. Because it was their last day of vacation, they elected to place the child in time-out, in the theme park, for the rest of the day. One parent monitored the culprit while the other parent and the siblings enjoyed the attractions. At agreed times the parents would switch places. Once again, not ideal, but preferable to stopping the vacation.

PART TWO

GETTING *Your* ACT TOGETHER

Visiting Walt Disney World is a bit like childbirth—you never really believe what people tell you, but once you have been through it yourself, you know exactly what they were saying!

—Hilary Wolfe, a mother and *Unofficial Guide* reader from Swansea, United Kingdom

GATHERING INFORMATION

IN ADDITION TO USING THIS GUIDE, we recommend that you visit our website, **touringplans.com,** which offers essential tools for planning your trip and saving you time and money, and its companion blog, **blog.touringplans.com,** which lists breaking news for Walt Disney World, Universal Orlando, the Disney Cruise Line, and Disneyland.

We sent our photography team door-to-door at Disney's resorts for the site's newest feature—**hotel-room views,** which show the scenery you'll get at all 30,000-plus hotel rooms in Walt Disney World. Spend some time looking at these photos and videos, and you'll be surprised at how much the views can vary even within the same resort. (Case in point: Some standard-view rooms at All-Star Music look out over a quiet little pond in the woods. Other rooms face a giant green electrical box.) We show you which rooms have the best views and the exact wording to use when requesting a specific room from Disney. The photos and videos can also show you whether upgrading to a more expensive category, like a water-view room, is worth the cost.

Though the guide you're reading now contains our best and most effective touring plans, the site offers **computer-optimized touring plans** for Disney World and Universal. With these, you choose the attractions you want to experience, including character greetings, parades, fireworks, meals, and midday breaks, and we'll give you a step-by-step itinerary for your specific dates of travel showing you how to see everything with minimal waits in line. The touring plans can incorporate your existing Fastpass+ reservations (see page 234) and suggest where to use any remaining Fastpass+ opportunities.

You can update the touring plans when you're in the parks, too. Let's say your touring plan calls for riding The Haunted Mansion next but your family really needs an ice-cream break and 30 minutes out of the sun. Get the ice cream and take the break; then, when you're done, click the "Optimize" button for your plan and you'll get an update on what to do next. The ability to redo your plan lets you recover from any situation while still minimizing your waits for the rest of the day.

Another really popular part of touringplans.com is our **Crowd Calendar,** which shows crowd projections for each Disney and Universal theme park for every day of the year. Look up the dates of your visit, and the calendar will not only show the projected wait times for each day but will also indicate for each day which theme park will be the least crowded. Historical wait times are also available, so you can see how crowded the parks were last year for your upcoming trip dates.

We've also got complete **dining menus** for every food cart, stand, kiosk, counter-service restaurant, and sit-down restaurant in Walt Disney World, including wine lists—more than 20,000 items. The whole thing is searchable, too, so you can find every restaurant in Epcot that serves prime rib (and its prices) or see which snacks at Starring Rolls Cafe are eligible for the Disney Dining Plan. Updated regularly, these menus represent the most accurate collection of Disney dining information available anywhere.

The touring plans, menus, Crowd Calendar, and more are available within **Lines,** our mobile app, which provides continuous real-time updates on wait times at Walt Disney World, Universal, and Disneyland. Using in-park research and updates sent in by readers, Lines shows you the current wait and Fastpass+ distribution times at every attraction in every park, as well as our estimated actual waits for these attractions for the rest of the day. For example, Lines will tell you that the posted wait time for Space Mountain is 60 minutes, and that based on what we know about how Disney manages Space Mountain's queue, the actual time you'll probably wait in line is 48 minutes. Lines is the only Disney-parks app that shows you both posted and actual wait times.

Lines' chat feature, through which you can ask questions and give travel tips, has grown into a thriving virtual community. Hundreds of "Liners" interact every day in discussions that stay remarkably on-topic for an Internet forum, and the group organizes regular in-park meets. We're thrilled with it.

Lines is available free to touringplans.com subscribers for the Apple iPhone and iPad at the iTunes Store (search for "TouringPlans"; requires iOS 4.3 or later) and for Android devices at the Google Play Store (requires Android 2.1 Eclair or later). Owners of BlackBerries, Windows Phones, and other Internet-capable phones can use the Web-based version at **m.touringplans.com.**

As long as you've got that smartphone handy while visiting the World, we and your fellow *Unofficial Guide* readers would love it if you'd pitch in and report on the actual wait times you get while you're there. Simply open Lines, log in to your user account, and click "+Time" in the upper right corner. Because Walt Disney World has free Wi-Fi now, you international users can help, too. We'll use your findings to update the wait times for everyone in the park.

Lines has been extremely well received—it's rated higher than Disney's official park apps—and we get lots of comments on it. A family from New York used Lines and got neighborhood bragging rights:

> We used your iPhone mobile app for our trip to WDW and barely waited for anything! We have neighbors whose vacation overlapped ours by a couple of days. They didn't have your app, and they complained about long lines (they waited 60 minutes for Soarin', we waited 10!) and crowds. Lines made our visit so much smoother, and your Crowd Calendar even made us change park strategy one evening and it benefitted us greatly!

A father from Brazil appreciated Lines' touring plans and wait-time estimates:

> The plans worked perfectly! At a certain point around halfway, I checked the plan and we were running within minutes of the schedule. I did not even have to use Fastpass.

From a Zionsville, Indiana, mom:

> Take the nap, use the app. By using a touring plan every day as our basic guide, updating the plan with real-time park information on my phone, and leaving the park each afternoon for a nap, we managed seven days in the parks—and only one toddler meltdown!

Much of our online content, including new research, menus, the Least Expensive Ticket Calculator, and updates and changes to this book, is completely free. Access to parts of the site, including the Crowd Calendar, hotel room views, and more touring plans, requires a small subscription fee (current-book owners get a substantial discount). This nominal charge—less than a meal at Flame Tree Barbecue in Disney's Animal Kingdom—pays the salaries of the staff who keep the site running day and night. And if you're not satisfied, we offer a 45-day money-back guarantee.

Bob: Request information as far in advance as possible and allow 6 weeks for delivery. Make a checklist of information you request, and follow up if you haven't received your materials within 6 weeks.

Next, we recommend that you obtain the following:

1. THE WALT DISNEY TRAVEL COMPANY FLORIDA VACATIONS BROCHURE AND DVD These cover Walt Disney World in its entirety, list rates for all Disney resort hotels and campgrounds, and describe Disney World package vacations. They're available from most travel agents, by calling the Walt Disney Travel Company at ☎ 407-828-8101 or 407-934-7639, or by visiting **disneyworld.com.** Be prepared to hold. When you get a representative, ask for the DVD vacation planner.

2. **THE DISNEY CRUISE LINE BROCHURE AND DVD** This brochure provides details on vacation packages that combine a cruise on the Disney Cruise Line with a stay at Disney World. Disney Cruise Line also offers a free DVD that tells you all you need to know about Disney cruises and then some. To obtain a copy, call ☎ 800-951-3532 or order at **disneycruise.com.**

3. **ORLANDO MAGICARD** If you're considering lodging outside Disney World or if you think you might patronize out-of-the-World attractions and restaurants, obtain an Orlando Magicard, a Vacation Planner, and the Orlando Official Vacation Guide (all free) from the Orlando Official Visitor Center. The Magicard entitles you to discounts for hotels, restaurants, ground transportation, shopping malls, dinner theaters, and non-Disney theme parks and attractions. The Orlando Magicard can be conveniently downloaded for printing at **orlandoinfo.com/magicard.** To order the accommodations guide, call ☎ 800-643-9492. For more information and materials, call ☎ 407-363-5872 weekdays during business hours and 9 a.m.–3 p.m. Eastern time weekends, or go to **visitorlando.com.**

4. *HOTELCOUPONS.COM FLORIDA GUIDE* Another good source of discounts on lodging, restaurants, and attractions statewide is the *HotelCoupons .com Florida Guide*. You can sign up at **hotelcoupons.com** to have a free monthly guide sent to you by e-mail, or you can view the guide online. If you prefer a hard copy over a digital version, you can request one by calling ☎ 800-222-3948 Monday–Friday, 8 a.m.–5 p.m. Eastern time. The guide is free, but you pay $3 for handling ($5 if it's shipped to Canada).

5. *KISSIMMEE VISITOR'S GUIDE* This full-color guide is one of the most complete resources available and is of particular interest to those who intend to lodge outside of Disney World, featuring ads for hotels, rental houses, time-shares, and condominiums, as well as a directory of attractions, restaurants, special events, and other useful info. For a copy, call the Kissimmee Convention and Visitors Bureau at ☎ 800-327-9159 or 407-944-2400, or view it online at **floridakiss.com.**

6. *GUIDEBOOK FOR GUESTS WITH DISABILITIES* Available at Guest Relations when entering the theme/water parks, at resort front desks, and wheelchair-rental areas (listed in each theme park chapter). More-limited information is available at **disneyworld.disney.go.com/plain-text.**

DISNEY ONLINE: OFFICIAL AND OTHERWISE

THE WALT DISNEY COMPANY is rolling out a set of high-tech enhancements to its theme parks and hotels. This collection of initiatives, officially known as **MyMagic+,** includes issuing rubber wristbands (**MagicBands**) with embedded computer chips that function as admission tickets and hotel keys; it also involves major changes to Disney's Fastpass ride-reservation system, restaurants, and attractions.

The Fastpass changes require that you make reservations months in advance to ride Disney's headliner attractions, if you want any chance of avoiding long waits in line. Other features, such as MagicBands and restaurant reservations, require you to enter detailed information about your traveling party.

Disney has revamped its website (**disneyworld.com**) and mobile app to be the "glue" binding all of this together. Because you've got to plan so much more before you leave home, we're covering the basics of Disney's website and app in this section. While we provide navigational instructions here, Disney's Web designers change direction faster than hypercaffeinated squirrels in traffic, so you may have to hunt around to find some features. Full coverage of MagicBands starts on page 72; details on the new Fastpass, dubbed Fastpass+, starts on page 234.

My Disney Experience at DisneyWorld.com

A lot of work has gone into the new Disney website. You can make hotel, dining, and recreation reservations; buy admission; and get park hours, attraction information, and much more.

The most important of the site's features support the new My Disney Experience campaign. To make use of some of these, you'll need to register by providing your e-mail address and choosing a password. You'll also need to have reserved a room at a Disney-owned hotel or have in your possession a valid theme park ticket.

GETTING STARTED First, click "My Disney Experience" in the upper-right corner of the home page. The site will then display a list of your existing hotel and dining reservations. The first thing to do on that page is click the "My Family" link; then enter the names and ages of everyone traveling with you. You'll need this information when you make your dining and Fastpass+ reservations.

From the "My Disney Experience" page, click "My Itinerary" in the lower-right corner of the page (use your browser's "find" feature to locate it, if needed). If you haven't already created an account, you'll be asked to do that now; otherwise, a calendar will appear. If you've got a Disney-hotel reservation, the calendar should display those dates of travel. If not, you'll need to select your travel dates using the calendar.

For each day of your trip, the website will display operating hours for the theme and water parks. Select the theme park you'll be visiting on a particular day; if you're visiting more than one, select the one at which you want to make reservations now.

MAKING FASTPASS+ RESERVATIONS A list of the park's attractions will appear as a series of rows going down the page. One attraction per row is listed. In each row is a description of the attraction, including operating hours, height requirements, and whether it supports Fastpass+. You can adjust the list of attractions shown by using the filtering criteria at the top of the page.

Clicking an attraction's name will bring up another page dedicated to that attraction, including available Fastpass+ ride times for a given day. If all the attraction's Fastpass+ opportunities have been exhausted, you'll get a message informing you so. If Fastpass+ times are still available, select one and indicate which members of your group will be riding. You'll need to repeat these steps for every attraction for which you want Fastpass reservations, for every day you're in the theme parks.

Depending on when you arrive and what you want to see, you may not need Fastpasses for most attractions. If you're unsure of the attractions or times of day for which you should use Fastpass+, our touring plan software can make recommendations that will minimize your overall time in line. See page 234 for details.

MAKING DINING RESERVATIONS From the "My Itinerary" page, click the "Book Dining" link. (You may have to reenter your travel dates.) A list of every Disney World eatery will be displayed. Use the filtering criteria at the top of the page to narrow the list.

Once you've settled on a restaurant, click the restaurant's name to check availability for your dining time and number of people. If space is available, you'll need to indicate which members of your party will be joining you. If you want to make other dining reservations, you'll need to repeat this process for every reservation.

Once you've made your initial set of Fastpass+ and dining reservations, you'll be able to view and edit them (along with your hotel reservation) in the "My Reservation" section of My Disney Experience.

OTHER WEBSITE CHANGES Besides these new features, some existing functions were made much easier to use. In particular, Disney's site now displays prices for every room category available at a specific hotel in a clean, easy-to-read vertical format, and it longer defaults you to the most expensive options for room views or tickets.

My Disney Experience Mobile App

Along with the website changes, Disney has released a companion app for iOS and Android devices. It includes park hours, attraction operating hours and descriptions, restaurant hours and descriptions, the ability to make dining reservations online, GPS-based directions, and more. Upcoming releases will include the ability to make Fastpass+ and counter-service-dining reservations online. My Disney Experience is optimized for the latest phones and tablets, so some features may not be available on all devices.

Users report many issues with the app, including frequent crashes, slow response time, battery drain, and difficulty using it in the parks. But Disney's a big company with lots of money, so we expect MDE to improve. Search for "My Disney Experience" on iTunes, Google Play, or the Amazon Appstore for Android if you'd like to try the latest version.

Our Recommended Websites

Searching online for Disney information is like navigating an immense maze for a very small piece of cheese: There's a lot of information available, but you may find a lot of dead-ends before getting what you want. Our picks follow.

BEST Q&A SITE Who knew? Walt Disney World has a **Mom's Panel** all chosen from among 10,000-plus applicants. The panelists have a website, **disneyworldmoms.com,** where they offer tips and discuss how to plan a Disney World vacation. Several moms have specialized experience in areas such as the Disney Cruise Line, runDisney, and traveling with sports groups; some speak Spanish, too. The parents are unpaid and are free to speak their minds.

BEST GENERAL UNOFFICIAL WALT DISNEY WORLD WEBSITE Besides touringplans.com, Deb Wills's **allears.net** is the first website we recommend to friends who want to make a trip to Disney World. Updated several times a week, the site includes breaking news, tons of photos, Disney restaurant menus, resort and ticket information, tips for guests with special needs, and more. We also check **wdwmagic.com** for news and happenings around Walt Disney World.

BEST MONEY-SAVING SITE Mary Waring's **MouseSavers (mousesavers .com)** keeps an updated list of discounts and reservation codes for use at Disney resorts. Codes are separated into categories such as "For the general public" and "For residents of certain states." Anyone who calls or books online can use a current code and get the discounted rate. Savings can be considerable—up to 40% in many cases. MouseSavers also has discount codes for rental cars and non-Disney hotels in the area, along with a calendar showing when Disney sales typically launch.

BEST WALT DISNEY WORLD PREVIEW SITE If you want to see what a particular attraction is like, visit **YouTube (youtube.com)**. Enter the name of the desired attraction in the search bar at the top of the page, and multiple videos should come up. Videos of indoor ("dark") rides are usually inferior to those of outdoor rides due to poor lighting, but even the videos of indoor rides generally provide a good sense of what the attraction is about.

SOCIAL MEDIA Facebook, Twitter, and **Instagram** are popular places for Disney fans to gather online and share comments, tips, and photos. Following fellow Disneyphiles as they share their in-park experiences can make you feel like you're there, even as you're stuck in a cubicle at work. Join more than 4,000 fans for daily news and insights on our very own Facebook page: **tinyurl.com/wdwkidsfb.**

BEST INTERNET RADIO STATION MouseWorld Radio (mouseworld radio.com) plays everything from attraction themes and hotel background music to sound clips from old TV ads for Disney resorts. What makes MouseWorld Radio special is that the tracks match what the Disney parks are playing at the time of day you're listening.

BEST THEME-PARK-INSIDER SITE It's been said that people who eat sausage should never watch it being made. If you have the stomach to learn how theme parks get built, take a look around **jimhillmedia.com.** Jim's got insider accounts of the politics, frantic project management, and pipe dreams that somehow combine into the attractions that Disney and Universal build.

BEST DISNEY DISCUSSION BOARDS There are tons of these; among the most active are **disboards.com, forums.wdfwmagic.com, micechat .com,** and for Brits, **thedibb.co.uk** (*DIBB* stands for "Disney Information Bulletin Board").

Important WDW Telephone Numbers

General Information	☎ 407-824-4321 or 407-824-2222
General Information for the Hearing-Impaired (TTY)	☎ 407-827-5141
General Information for Guests with Disabilities	☎ 407-939-7807
Accommodations/Reservations	☎ 407-W-DISNEY (934-7639)
Blizzard Beach Information	☎ 407-560-3400
Centra Care	☎ 407-200-2273
Formosa Gardens	☎ 407-397-7032
Kissimmee	☎ 407-390-1888
Lake Buena Vista	☎ 407-934-2273
Universal–Dr. Phillips	☎ 407-291-9960
Dining Advance Reservations	☎ 407-WDW-DINE (939-3463)
Disabled Guests Special Requests	☎ 407-939-7807
DisneyQuest	☎ 407-828-4600
ESPN Wide World of Sports Complex	☎ 407-939-GAME (4263)
Golf Reservations and Information	☎ 407-WDW-GOLF (939-4653)
Guided-Tour Information	☎ 407-WDW-TOUR (939-8687)

BEST SITE FOR GUESTS WITH FOOD ALLERGIES At **allergyeats.com /disney,** you put in your allergies and your park, and it shows you where and what you can eat.

BEST SITES FOR TRAFFIC, ROADWORK, CONSTRUCTION, AND SAFETY INFORMATION Visit **expresswayauthority.com** for the latest information on roadwork in the Orlando and Orange County areas. The site also contains detailed maps, directions, and toll-rate information for the most popular tourist destinations. Check **flhsmv.gov/fhp/cps** to learn about state child-restraint requirements. Finally, we like **mapquest.com** for driving directions.

Liliane's Favorite Podcasts

If you just can't make it through the year without the Mouse, don't despair. Sounds, images, and news from the World are available in abundance online. Here are some of our favorites.

WDW TODAY *Unofficial Guide* Research Director Len Testa cohosts three podcasts a week (Monday, Wednesday, and Friday) on all things Disney. Subscriptions are available free through iTunes. These programs consistently rank among the top 10 iTunes travel podcasts, drawing almost 40,000 listeners per show. Visit **wdwtoday.com.**

Lost and Found	
Yesterday or before *(all Disney parks)*	☎ 407-824-4245
Yesterday or before *(Downtown Disney)*	☎ 407-828-3150
Today at Disney's Animal Kingdom	☎ 407-938-2785
Today at Disney's Hollywood Studios	☎ 407-560-7500
Today at Epcot	☎ 407-560-7500
Today at the Magic Kingdom	☎ 407-824-4521
Today at Universal Orlando	☎ 407-224-4233
Outdoor Recreation Reservations and Information	☎ 407-WDW-PLAY (939-7529)
Resort Dining and Recreational Information	☎ 407-WDW-DINE (939-3463)
Security	☎ 407-560-7959 *(routine)* or 407-560-1990 *(urgent)*
Tennis Reservations/Lessons	☎ 407-621-1991
Ticket Inquiries	☎ 407-566-4985
Typhoon Lagoon Information	☎ 407-560-6296
Walt Disney Travel Company	☎ 407-939-6244
Weather Information	☎ 407-827-4545
Wrecker Service *(or call Security after hours; see above)*	☎ 407-824-0976

WINDOW TO THE MAGIC Paul Barrie, your smooth-voiced host, brings you all the magic with his weekly podcast. The show includes a game called "Where in the Park?" and delivers sounds, pictures, prizes, and more. Check it out at **windowtothemagic.com/podcast.html**.

SOUNDS OF DISNEY Every other Sunday you can join Jeff Davis, also known as The Sorcerer, as he delights his audience with music, news, and Disney songs right from the parks. In addition to the podcast, Davis's website, **srsounds.com**, provides music, videos, pictures, and a message board.

THE MINNIE MINXES Recorded in the U.K., this all-female podcast promotes "Disney Girl Power." Visit **theminnieminxes.blogspot.com**.

IMPORTANT WALT DISNEY WORLD TELEPHONE NUMBERS

WHEN YOU CALL THE MAIN INFORMATION NUMBER, you'll be offered a menu of options for recorded information on operating hours, recreation areas, shopping, entertainment, tickets, reservations, and driving directions. If you have a question not covered by recorded information, press 8 at any time to speak to a representative. See the table above for a list of phone numbers.

ALLOCATING TIME

YOU SHOULD ALLOCATE 6 DAYS for a whirlwind tour (7–10 days if you're old-fashioned and insist on some relaxation during your vacation). If you don't have 6-plus days, be prepared to make some hard choices.

Bob: If you must visit during the busy summer season, cut your visit short by one or two days so that you will have the weekend or a couple of vacation days remaining to recuperate when you get home.

A seemingly obvious point lost on many families is that Walt Disney World is not going anywhere. There's no danger that it will be packed up and shipped to Iceland anytime soon. This means that you can come back if you don't see everything this year. Disney has planned it this way, of course, but that doesn't matter. It's infinitely more sane to resign yourself to the reality that seeing everything during one visit is impossible. We recommend, therefore, that you approach Walt Disney World the same way you would an eight-course Italian dinner: leisurely, with plenty of time between courses. The best way not to have fun is to cram too much into too little time.

WHEN TO GO TO WALT DISNEY WORLD

LET'S CUT TO THE ESSENCE: Walt Disney World between mid-June and mid-August 18 is rough. You can count on large summer crowds as well as Florida's trademark heat and humidity. Avoid these dates if you can. Ditto for Memorial Day weekend at the beginning of the summer and Labor Day weekend at the end. Other holiday periods (Thanksgiving, Christmas, Easter, Halloween, spring break, and so on) are extremely crowded, but the heat is not as bad.

Bob: Though crowds have grown in September and October as a result of promotions aimed at families without school-age children and the international market, these months continue to be good for touring.

The least busy time is from Labor Day in September through the beginning of October. Next slowest are the weeks in mid-January after the Martin Luther King Jr. holiday weekend up to Presidents Day in February (except when the Walk Disney World Marathon runs after MLK Day). The weeks after Thanksgiving and before Christmas are less crowded than average, as is mid-April–mid-May, after spring break and before Memorial Day.

Late February, March, and early April are dicey. Crowds ebb and flow according to spring-break schedules and the timing of Presidents Day weekend. Besides being asphalt-melting hot, July brings throngs of South American tourists on their winter holiday.

So, parents, what to do? If your children are of preschool age, definitely go during a cooler, less-crowded time. If you have school-age children, look first for an anomaly in your school-year schedule: in other words, a time when your kids will be out of school when most schools elsewhere are in session. Anomalies are most often found at the beginning or end of the school year (for example, school starts late or lets out early), at Christmas, or at spring break. In the event that no such anomalies exist, and providing that your kids are good students, our recommendation is to ask permission to take your children out of school either just before or after the Thanksgiving holiday. Teachers can assign lessons that can be made up at home over the Thanksgiving holiday, either before or after your Walt Disney World vacation.

If none of these options are workable for your family, consider visiting Walt Disney World the week immediately before school starts (excluding Labor Day weekend) or the week immediately after school lets out (excluding Memorial Day weekend). This strategy should remove you from the really big mob scenes by about a week or more.

The time that works best for kids is the week before school ends. Because grades must be finalized earlier, there is often little going on at school during that week. Check far in advance with your child's teacher to determine if any special exams or projects will occur in that last week. If no major assignments are on the child's schedule, then go for it.

Incidentally, taking your kids out of school for more than a few days is problematic. We have received well-considered letters from parents and teachers who don't think taking kids out of school is such a hot idea. A Fairfax, Virginia, dad put it thus:

> My wife and I do not encourage families to take their children out of school in order to avoid the crowds at Walt Disney World during the summer months. My wife is an eighth-grade science teacher of chemistry and physics. She has parents pull their children, some honor-roll students, out of school for vacations, only to discover when they return that the students are unable to comprehend the material. Several students have been so thoroughly lost in their assignments that they ask if they can be excused from the tests. Parental suspicions [about] the quality of their children's education should be raised when children go to school for 6 hours a day yet supposedly can complete this same instruction with "less than an hour of homework" each night.

A Martinez, California, teacher offers this compelling analogy:

> There are a precious 180 days for us as teachers to instruct our students, and there are 185 days during the year for Disney World. I have seen countless students during my 14 years of teaching struggle to catch up the rest of the year due to a week of vacation during critical instructional periods. The analogy I use with my students' parents is that it's like walking out of a movie after watching the first 5 minutes, then returning for the last 5 minutes and trying to figure out what happened.

But a schoolteacher from Penn Yan, New York, expresses a different opinion:

> I've read the comments by teachers saying that they all think it's horrible for a parent to take a child out for a vacation. As a teacher and

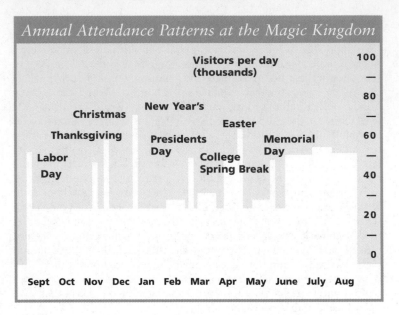

Annual Attendance Patterns at the Magic Kingdom

Visitors per day
(thousands)

New Year's

Christmas

Easter

Thanksgiving   Presidents   Memorial
                 Day   Day
Labor   College
Day   Spring Break

100
—
80
—
—
60
—
40
—
20
—
0

Sept Oct Nov Dec Jan Feb Mar Apr May June July Aug

*a parent, I disagree. If a parent takes the time to let us know that a
child is going to be out, we help them get ready for upcoming home-
work the best we can. If the child is a good student, why shouldn't
they go have a wonderful experience with their family? I also don't
understand when teachers say they can't get something together for
the time the student will be out. We all have to plan ahead, and we
know what we are teaching days, if not weeks, in advance. Take 20
minutes out of your day and set something up.* Learn to be flexible!

Though we strongly recommend going to Disney World in the fall,
winter, or spring, there are a few trade-offs. The parks often close early
during the off-season, either because of low crowds or special events
such as the Halloween and Christmas parties at the Magic Kingdom.
This drastically reduces touring hours. Even when crowds are small,
it's difficult to see big parks such as the Magic Kingdom between
9 a.m. and 7 p.m. Early closing also usually means no evening parades
or fireworks. And because these are slow times, some rides and attractions may be closed. Finally, Central Florida temperatures fluctuate
wildly during late fall, winter, and early spring; daytime highs in the
40s and 50s aren't uncommon.

On the other hand, Disney generally has the best lodging offers
during these times of the year, including free dining plans. If you plan
to stay on-property, this could represent some serious savings.

BE UNCONVENTIONAL The Orange County Convention Center in
Orlando hosts some of the largest conventions and trade shows in the
world. Rooms anywhere near Walt Disney World are hard to find when

Walt Disney World Climate

	JAN	FEB	MAR	APR	MAY	JUN	JUL	AUG	SEP	OCT	NOV	DEC
AVERAGE DAILY LOW (°F)												
	47	50	54	59	65	71	73	73	72	66	58	51
AVERAGE DAILY HIGH (°F)												
	71	73	78	83	89	91	92	92	90	84	78	72
AVERAGE DAILY TEMPERATURE (°F)												
	60	61	67	71	77	81	82	83	81	75	68	62
AVERAGE DAILY HUMIDITY PERCENTAGES												
	62	73	71	70	68	70	74	76	76	75	74	73
AVERAGE RAINFALL PER MONTH (INCHES)												
	2.9	2.7	4.0	2.3	3.1	8.3	7.0	7.7	5.1	2.5	2.1	2.9
NUMBER OF DAYS OF RAIN PER MONTH												
	6	7	8	6	8	14	17	16	14	9	6	6

there's a big convention, and as this Toronto, Ontario, reader points out, are also expensive:

> If saving money on accommodations is an important part of your trip, be sure to check rates on the Net before you settle on a date. Trade shows at the Orange County Convention Center can host over 100,000 attendees, with most of them staying one to a room. This drives rates on even average properties to two or three times normal rates. Since all large conventions are scheduled over one year out, these spikes in room rates should be visible up to 12 months prior.

Check the convention schedule for the next seven months at **occc .net/global/calendar.**

DON'T FORGET AUGUST Kids go back to school pretty early in Florida (and in a lot of other places too). This makes mid- to late August a good time to visit Walt Disney World for families who can't vacation during the off-season. A New Jersey mother of two school-age children spells it out:

> The end of August is the PERFECT time to go. There were virtually no wait times, 20 minutes at the most.

JUNE AND THE EARLY BIRD It's not an easy turnaround, but heading for Walt Disney World in late May or early June as soon as school is out will net big rewards. Late May through about June 12 is still considered shoulder season, so the crowds will not have spiked to summer levels. Also the weather is usually cooler than in late August. An exception to the above is Memorial Day weekend, though the week following the holiday is one of the best of the whole summer crowd-wise.

HOLIDAYS AND SPECIAL EVENTS AT WALT DISNEY WORLD

YOU CAN'T BEAT THE HOLIDAYS FOR live entertainment, special events, parades, fireworks, and elaborate decorations at the theme parks and resort hotels. Unfortunately, you also can't beat holiday periods for crowds. A mom from Ogden, Utah, puts it this way:

> We know the lines will be outrageous, but the special shows, parades, and decorations more than make up for it. For first-timers who want to see the rides, Christmas is not ideal, but for us it's the most colorful and exciting time to go.

Here's a look at the larger special events and major holidays at Walt Disney World.

JANUARY Usually held the second weekend after New Year's, the **Walt Disney World Marathon** pulls in more runners every year. In 2013, some 65,000 runners participated in the event—enough people to affect crowd conditions throughout Disney World. *Unofficial Guide* coauthor Len Testa usually runs one of the 5K, 10K, half, or full marathons. Following the marathon by a week is the **Tinker Bell Half Marathon** weekend, featuring shorter races for families and kids. Information on all Disney running events can be found at **rundisney.com**. Also check **wdw today.com** podcast archives for in-depth coverage and tips.

Each year the China Pavilion in Epcot has a Chinese New Year celebration (which is usually in late January or early February). There are typically Chinese acrobats and special activities for kids.

FEBRUARY **Black History Month** is celebrated throughout Walt Disney World with displays, artisans, storytellers, and entertainers. The Kinsey Collection at Epcot's United States Pavilion is a highlight.

Presidents Day February 17 in 2014, will increase attendance starting the weekend before the holiday, At the end of that week is the **Princess Half-Marathon** event, running February 20–23. The schedule for that weekend includes a health expo, kids' races, a family 5K, a 10K on Saturday, and the big race on Sunday. The 2013 event—in which *Unofficial Guide* coauthor Liliane Opsomer ran her first 5K—drew more than 21,000 runners, enough to affect vehicular and pedestrian traffic.

MARCH March 4, 2014, is **Mardi Gras** and will draw crowds from Louisiana that week. The **Epcot International Flower & Garden Festival** runs annually from mid-March to mid-May or June. Expert horticulturists showcase exotic floral displays and share gardening tips. The 30 million blooms from some 1,200 species will make your eyes pop, and best of all, the event doesn't seem to affect crowd levels at Epcot. In 2013 Disney added food and beverage kiosks to the festival, making it more like September's Food & Wine event (see page 52), only with flowers. Check out **johnnyjet.com/2013/03/epcot-international-flower-garden-festival** for a review with lots of pictures.

The **Atlanta Braves** hold spring training and play exhibition games at Disney's Wide World of Sports mid-February–March. You can get the exhibition schedule and purchase tickets by calling TicketMaster at ☎ 800-745-3000 or visiting **ticketmaster.com**. You can watch the training sessions at no charge when you buy general admission to ESPN Wide World of Sports ($15.50 for adults, $10.50 for ages 3–9). In Downtown Disney, the **Mighty St. Patrick's Day Festival,** a weeklong celebration culminating on St. Patrick's Day (March 17), pays tribute to Irish music, dance, and food.

APRIL Disney doesn't need much to boost attendance, what with **Easter** (April 20 in 2014) and some spring-break vacations happening. By far the most interesting event of the month is the **Easter Parade** at the Magic Kingdom. Outstanding floats carry Mickey, Minnie, and the gang, all dressed in their Sunday best, in a special parade. Of course, the appearance of the Easter Bunny is guaranteed. Ask at the front desk about special activities (such as egg hunts) at your hotel and other Disney resorts.

MAY Disney's Hollywood Studios hosts *Star Wars* **Weekends** annually beginning this month, with appearances from that franchise's actors and technicians. These events draw mainly local sci-fi fans, but some come from all over the country. While the impact on regular Disney World crowds is low, you'll find long lines if you want to meet the celebrities.

Also this month: the **Expedition Everest Challenge,** a 5K race at Disney's Animal Kingdom. Impact on crowds is low, but traffic is affected by the runners getting to and from the park.

JUNE Events this month include both *Star Wars* Weekends and **Gay Days,** June 3–9. June 3–9. Since 1991, gay, lesbian, bisexual, and transgender (GLBT) people from around the world have been converging on and around the World in early June for a week of events centered around the theme parks. Today, Gay Days attracts more than 160,000 GLBT visitors and their families and friends. Universal Studios and Wet 'n Wild also participate. For additional information, visit **gaydays.com.**

All summer long, you can dance to classic rock-and-roll hits under the skies of the open-air America Gardens Theatre at Epcot. The **Sounds Like Summer Concert Series** features a lineup of cover bands performing timeless tunes. Included in park admission are three nightly shows, at 5:30 p.m., 6:45 p.m., and 8 p.m.

JULY Independence Day at Disney World basically means crowds and more crowds. All parks are in a festive and patriotic mood, and the fireworks are incredible. A very special place to visit is *The Hall of Presidents* at the Magic Kingdom. We recommend leaving the parks prior to the evening fireworks and watching them from the Polynesian Resort. Most parks will reach full capacity by 10 a.m., and no advance reservations will get you into a park once it is closed. So pick your park and be prepared to stay there all day. If partying is your thing, consider Downtown Disney, which throws a DJ dance party and a fireworks show of its own.

SEPTEMBER Radio personality Tom Joyner hosts an extremely popular party at Walt Disney World. Held Labor Day weekend (around September 4–8 in 2014), the **Allstate Tom Joyner Family Reunion** typically features live musical performances, comedy acts, and family-oriented discussions. For more information, visit **familyreunion.blackamericaweb.com.**

Night of Joy, a Christian-music festival, is staged at the Magic Kingdom the first or second weekend of the month (September 6 and 7 in 2013). About 16 nationally known acts perform concerts on Friday and Saturday evenings after the park has closed. For information or to purchase tickets, call ☎ 407-W-DISNEY (934-7639) or visit **tinyurl.com/wdwnightofjoy.** Advance tickets for the 2013 event went on sale in early May and were $55 for one night or $99 for both nights; same-day tickets cost $65.

Those who say Christmas is the most wonderful time of year have never been to the **Epcot International Food & Wine Festival.** Held in the World Showcase late September–mid-November, the celebration represents 25 nations and cuisines, including demonstrations, wine seminars, tastings, and opportunities to see some of the world's top chefs. Although many activities are included in Epcot admission, some workshops and tastings are by reservation only and cost over $100. Call ☎ 407-WDW-DINE starting around the beginning of August for more information. We think the culinary demos (around $11–$14) and wine-and-beverage seminars ($11–$14) are the best values at the festival. Because most food kiosks are set up around World Showcase, it can be difficult to walk through the crowds at some of the popular spots. Wait times at Epcot's attractions, however, are affected only slightly.

Held two dozen or so nights each year mid-September–October 31 (and occasionally into November), **Mickey's Not-So-Scary Halloween Party** runs 7 p.m.–midnight at the Magic Kingdom. The event includes trick-or-treating in costume, parades, live music, storytelling, and a fireworks show. See **tinyurl.com/mickeysnotsoscary** for more information. Several times that evening, Disney villains will put on a great show followed by a Villains' Mix and Mingle in front of Cinderella Castle. Aimed primarily at younger children, the party is happy and upbeat rather than spooky and frightening.

The park will be crowded, so arrive early (we recommend arriving an hour before the beginning of the party, as Disney starts letting guests with party tickets inside the park around 6:30 p.m., sometimes much earlier). Proceed directly to the table where the wristbands identifying you as a party guest are obtained. Also, get the special map for the event with details and hours of all the happenings. Go straight to the rides that are on your must-do list, and after that just enjoy the party. If trick-or-treating is a priority, do that first thing after you arrive or toward the end of the night, when crowds thin out and there are no long lines in front of the trick-or-treating stations.

An absolute must-ride is **The Haunted Mansion,** which is especially spooky but only in the sweetest way. Look for the ghost in the garden of the mansion when queuing up. His hilarious tales and interaction with the guests will make you forget you are standing in line. Characters are out in force all over the park, and the Boo to You Parade is pretty amazing. Our two favorite parts of the parade are the Headless

Horseman riding at full speed through the park and The Haunted Mansion's groundskeeper, with his dim lantern in one hand and his bloodhound, followed by a large group of ghosts and gravediggers. Don't be shy: Wear a costume—about 50% of all the adults will be wearing a getup of some kind.

Advance tickets for the 2013 events went on sale in early May and cost $59–$73 for adults, $54–$68 for kids; same-day tickets cost $65–$73 for adults, $60–$68 for kids. Discounts are available for members of the U.S. military, Disney Annual Pass holders, and Disney Vacation Club members. The least-crowded events are typically in September and on Tuesdays. Tickets for the late-October dates usually sell out one to four days in advance.

In addition to activities in the theme parks, Disney's **Fort Wilderness Resort & Campground** offers haunted carriage rides. The carriage rides include a performer who tells the story of Ichabod Crane and the Headless Horseman from Washington Irving's story "The Legend of Sleepy Hollow." The rides leave from Pioneer Hall and cost $60 per carriage. A carriage can accommodate four adults, or two adults with three small children. This excursion can be booked up to 180 days in advance by calling ☎ 407-WDW-PLAY.

Also check out the different Halloween activities organized at the Disney properties. Activities range from pet costume parades, Halloween movies under the stars, and trick-or-treating to costume parades and contests. Check at the reception for a detailed schedule of events happening during your stay.

Teens and young adults looking for a non-Disney Halloween happening should check out the party at **Universal CityWalk.** And if you'd rather have a monster with a chain saw running after you, consider attending Universal theme parks' **Halloween Horror Nights.** (*Note:* No costumes are allowed at the parks on these special nights.) For more information, visit **halloweenhorrornights.com.**

OCTOBER Disney's Hollywood Studios hosts the **Twilight Zone Tower of Terror 10-Miler** road race in October. Registration usually opens in February and sells out quickly. See **rundisney.com** for details.

NOVEMBER The **Wine and Dine Half-Marathon** early this month revolves around a 13.1-mile race that ends with a party amid Epcot's International Food & Wine Festival. The number of runners and their "cheer squads"—combined with the guests who descend upon Epcot for the food festival alone—blows up the crowd levels like an agitated pufferfish. Again, vehicular and pedestrian traffic is disturbed by the running courses throughout Disney property.

There are no special Thanksgiving events or decorations in the parks, so if you're looking for the equivalent of the Macy's Thanksgiving Parade, you're out of luck, although many of the Christmas decorations are normally in place the day after Thanksgiving. But the kids are out of school, and this is the busiest travel weekend of the year. Your best bet for the least-crowded park will be Epcot.

Remember to make your dining arrangements long before your visit, especially if you want a traditional Thanksgiving meal. While there is plenty of food at the World, note that not all restaurants offer turkey with all the trimmings. Some that do include **Liberty Tree Tavern** at the Magic Kingdom; **50's Prime Time Cafe** at Disney's Hollywood Studios; **Cítricos** at the Grand Floridian; **Artist Point** at the Wilderness Lodge; and **'Ohana** (which means "family" in Hawaiian) at the Polynesian Resort, which is perfect for families with small children. For information and reservations, call ☎ 407-WDW-DINE.

The annual **Disney Parks Christmas Day Parade**, televised on December 25, is usually taped at the Magic Kingdom on the weekend that falls nine days after Thanksgiving, roughly the last weekend in November or first week of December. The parade ties up pedestrian traffic on Main Street, U.S.A. all day.

DECEMBER If you're visiting during Christmas week, don't expect to see all the attractions in a single day of touring at any park. All parks, especially the Magic Kingdom, will be filled to capacity, and Disney will stop admitting visitors as early as 10 a.m. (Not to mention that women will have to wait up to 20 minutes to use the restrooms in the Magic Kingdom during Christmas week.) As you might have guessed by now, your only way in is getting there early. Be at the gates with admission passes in hand at least 1 hour before scheduled opening time. Most of all, bring along a humongous dose of patience and humor. The daily tree-lighting ceremonies and the parades are wonderful. Again, most parks will reach full capacity by 10 a.m., and no advance reservations will get you into the park once it is closed. So *pick your park* and be prepared to stay there all day.

Liliane: Did I mention that it's going to be packed? This is not a good time for first-time visitors, but fun can be had by all at the parks even at peak times. (I actually stayed at Walt Disney World on Christmas Eve and Christmas Day and loved it.)

Also, be sure to make dinner reservations long before your visit, especially if you are spending Christmas Eve and Christmas Day at the parks. Christmas festivities at Walt Disney World usually run November 24–December 30. From the Monday following Thanksgiving weekend until December 20 or so, you can enjoy the decorations and holiday events without the crowds. This between-holidays period is one of our favorite times of year at Walt Disney World.

The **Magic Kingdom** is home to a stunning display of holiday decorations, a **tree-lighting ceremony** on Main Street, and **Mickey's Once Upon a Christmastime Parade** on select days. Check the *Times Guide* for days and hours. The Magic Kingdom is also the scene of **Mickey's Very Merry Christmas Party,** held from mid-November to mid-December, 7 p.m.–midnight. Advance tickets for the 2013 events went on sale in early May and cost $62–$71 for adults, $57–$66 for kids; same-day tickets cost $67–$71 for adults, $62–$66 for kids. Tickets for busier dates usually sell out one to four days in advance. Admission includes the use of all attractions during party hours, holiday-themed stage shows, cookies and hot chocolate, carolers, "a magical snowfall on Main Street," white lights on Cinderella Castle, and fireworks. The least crowded dates are usually the weeks before Thanksgiving week, and the week after. Tuesday (and the rare Wednesday) parties are the slowest, too. See **tinyurl.com/mickeysverymerryxmas** for more details. We don't recommend the party for first-time visitors.

With about twice the land of the Magic Kingdom, **Epcot** is a good option on Christmas Day, but this doesn't mean it's a ghost town, just somewhat less crowded than the Magic Kingdom. Again, if your heart is set on touring a park on Christmas Day, you'll have to get up early.

At Epcot don't miss the **Candlelight Processional,** featuring a celebrity narrator accompanied by a huge live choir and a full orchestra. The show takes place daily at the America Gardens Theatre and is included with regular Epcot admission. Special lunch and dinner packages are available for an additional charge and include preferred seating for the processional (call ☎ 407-WDW-DINE for reservations). If you don't want to spring for one of the packages, we recommend lining up at least 60 minutes prior to the show of your choice. Guests with preferred seating are well advised not to come at the last minute, either—instead, arrive at the reserved-seating entrance 30 minutes before the beginning of the show. Seats within this section are available on a first-come, first-served basis and are opened to general admission 15 minutes before the beginning of the show. Check the *Times Guide* for performance hours and information on the day's narrator.

The nightly fireworks, water, and laser show *IllumiNations: Reflections of Earth* is always worth watching and has an extra-special holiday finale.

Liliane: A word of advice for families with small children: Reassure the kids that Santa knows where the family is on Christmas Day. You don't want your little ones to suddenly worry that Santa won't find them on Christmas because they're not at home. Consider shipping a small tree and holiday decorations to your hotel. Kids can decorate the window of your hotel room with their drawings.

Our favorite Epcot holiday event, however, is **Holidays from Around the World** (check out Liliane's online review at **tinyurl.com/holidaysaroundtheworld**). While strolling from land to land, visitors can enjoy storytellers in each country. In **Canada,** Santa Claus explains how Christmas is celebrated by our neighbor to the north. At the **United Kingdom Pavilion,** Father Christmas tells of his country's holiday customs. **France** is the home of Père Noël, and in **Morocco,** Taariji explains the Feast of Ashoora. In **Japan,** the Daruma Seller talks about how Japanese celebrate the New Year. (*Daruma* dolls are symbols of the New Year and are said to bring good luck.)

At the **American Adventure Rotunda,** you can visit Santa's Bake-shop, a life-size gingerbread house made with real gingerbread, candies, and icing. Santa himself is also on hand to tell Christmas stories. Special programs are held for Kwanzaa and Hanukkah as well. (To learn more about Kwanzaa, an African American celebration of family, community, and culture, visit **kwanzaaguide.com**. The History Channel offers a nice description of Hanukkah, the Jewish Festival of Lights, at **history.com/topics/hanukkah.**)

In **Italy,** meet La Befana, the good witch who brings gifts to children on Epiphany. (For more information on La Befana, check out **en .wikipedia.org/wiki/befana.**) **Germany** honors St. Nicholas on December 6, and he welcomes visitors throughout the afternoon. Visitors can also hear the story of the nutcracker's origin. (To find out more about the legend of St. Nicholas, visit **tinyurl.com/729xnot.**)

Visit **China** and listen to the funny stories of the Monkey King. In **Norway,** meet the Christmas elf Julenissen, who represents simplicity and peace (to learn more, visit **tinyurl.com/norwaysanta**). In **Mexico,** the Three Sage Kings (Los Tres Reyes Magos) make appearances throughout the afternoon telling the story of Epiphany. (Discover the story at **mexonline.com/history-lostresreyes.htm.**)

At **Disney's Hollywood Studios,** the park is also dressed for the season, but the big attraction is the **Osborne Family Spectacle of Lights.** Millions—yes, millions—of lights decorate the buildings on the Streets of America, and snow machines provide the perfect atmosphere. There is no additional fee to see the display, but be prepared for huge crowds. A little background: Jennings Osborne of Little Rock, Arkansas, began putting up Christmas lights on his house about 10 years ago and expanded his display by buying the two houses next to his home. As his collection grew, so did the displeasure of his neighbors. Eventually the matter was brought to court, and in 1994 the Arkansas Supreme Court ruled that his houses, with their 3 million lights, were a public nuisance. The Walt Disney Company brought Osborne's Christmas lights to Disney's Hollywood Studios in 1995 and has a special agreement with him to keep the display.

At **Disney's Animal Kingdom,** don't miss **Mickey's Jingle Jungle Parade.** The park has festive holiday decorations and a gigantic Christmas tree with carolers performing throughout the day. At Camp Minnie-Mickey, kids can meet Santa Goofy and other favorite Disney characters all dressed in their holiday finest. If you don't mind the lines, this is the perfect place for taking holiday photographs.

Downtown Disney features holiday decor and offers photo ops with Santa but is mainly about shopping. The atmosphere is festive, and shops and restaurants have special window dressings.

You thought we were done? No way—there's much more to see outside of the parks.

The holiday decorations at the Walt Disney resorts are attractions in their own right. Generally speaking, each resort incorporates its theme into its holiday finery. At **Port Orleans Resort,** for example, expect Mardi Gras colors in the trees, while the **Yacht Club** has trees adorned with miniature sailboats. At the **Polynesian Resort,** kids will love the gingerbread workshop complete with Santa sleeping in a hammock and elves taking it easy under the sun. For the mother of all Christmas trees, make sure to visit the **Grand Floridian,** where a five-story tree dominates the lobby, flanked by a gingerbread dollhouse and a miniature railroad. Don't miss the free daily classes in decorating gingerbread houses, led by a Grand Floridian pastry chef; guests get a free recipe brochure and a taste of freshly made gingerbread. At the **Beach Club,** poinsettias, artificial snow, and a gingerbread carousel are the big draw. For a more natural approach, visit the **Wilderness Lodge** and **Animal Kingdom Lodge.**

If you're staying at a Walt Disney resort over Christmas, check with the concierge to see what holiday event your particular resort might be offering. Happenings can range from carolers, brass bands, and country singers to Christmas-cookie decorating, visits with Santa, and readings of *The Night Before Christmas*. Many hotels also offer free cookies and punch in their lobbies.

During December, Disney offers 25-minute "sleigh" rides through the woods from the Fort Wilderness Campground. (The horse-drawn vehicle is wheeled but made to look like a red sleigh, complete with sleigh bells!) Rides are offered every 30 minutes 5:30–9:30 p.m., departing from Crockett's Tavern at Fort Wilderness. The cost is $60 per sleigh. (Each sleigh can accommodate up to four adults or two adults plus up to three children age 9 and under.) You can book up to 180 days in advance by calling ☎ 407-WDW-PLAY (939-7529).

If you are looking for a perfect Christmas card, visit Downtown Disney. Santa appears in his chalet at Downtown Disney Marketplace, and you can take pictures with your own camera or use PhotoPass. For a less classical picture, Santa Goofy appears in the chalet December 25–January 3. Ask Guest Relations for the daily schedule.

Ring in the New Year with Mickey and friends. If you're in the mood for a night of partying and live entertainment, there's no better place than **Downtown Disney** or **Universal CityWalk.** Both offer a choice of parties and midnight fireworks. The Magic Kingdom shows the New Year's Eve fireworks on both December 30 and 31 for those who either wish to see fireworks in multiple parks or who don't wish to be caught in the largest crowds of the year on New Year's Eve.

Though all parks, with the exception of Animal Kingdom, have spectacular fireworks at midnight, here are a few different options for the last night of the year:

- Cirque du Soleil offers a special New Year's production of *La Nouba*. For more information, visit **cirquedusoleil.com.**

- Forget the rides—the lines will be long. Relax at your hotel pool and go out for a great dinner that night. If you have little children, get a babysitter. The trick is to arrive a day before New Year's, settle in, go to a water park, and start the touring after January 2, when crowds thin out.

• At Epcot, welcome the New Year several times. Have a drink before 6 p.m. at the Biergarten in Germany. (When the clock strikes 6, it will be midnight in Germany.) Then go over to the Rose & Crown Pub in the United Kingdom and repeat the celebration at 7 p.m., as guests and staff alike will be welcoming the New Year in the United Kingdom. Best of all, you get to start all over again a few hours later when the clock finally strikes midnight at Epcot.

HIGH-LOW, HIGH-LOW, IT'S OFF TO DISNEY WE GO

THOUGH WE RECOMMEND OFF-SEASON TOURING, we realize that's not possible for many families. We want to make it clear, therefore, that you can have a wonderful experience regardless of when you go. Our advice, irrespective of season, is to arrive early at the parks and avoid the crowds by using one of our touring plans. If attendance is light, kick back and forget the touring plans.

Selecting the Day of the Week for Your Visit

We receive thousands of e-mails and letters from readers each year asking which park is the best bet on a particular day. To make things easier for you (and us!), we provide at **touringplans.com** a calendar covering the next year (click "Crowd Calendar" on the home page). For each date, we offer a crowd-level index based on a scale of 1–10, with 1 being least crowded and 10 being most crowded. The calendar also lists the best and worst park(s) to visit in terms of crowd conditions on any given day.

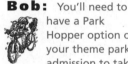

Bob: You'll need to have a Park Hopper option on your theme park admission to take advantage of Extra Magic Hours at more than one park on the same day.

Extra Magic Hours (EMHs)

This program is a perk for families staying at a Walt Disney World resort, including the Swan, Dolphin, and Shades of Green, and the Hilton in the Downtown Disney Resort Area. On selected days of the week, Disney resort guests will be able to enter a Disney theme park 1 hour earlier or stay in a selected theme park about 2 hours later than the official park-operating hours. Theme park visitors not staying at a Disney resort may stay in the park for Extra Magic Hour evenings, but they can't experience any rides, attractions, or shows. In other words, they can shop and eat. The swimming theme parks, Typhoon Lagoon and Blizzard Beach, rarely offer EMHs. If they do, it's usually during the summer.

Bob: Extra Magic Hours draw more Disney resort guests to the host park, which results in longer lines than you would otherwise experience.

WHAT'S REQUIRED? A valid admission ticket or MagicBand wristband is required to enter the park, and you must show your Disney resort ID or have your MagicBand scanned when entering. For evening EMHs, you may be asked to show your Disney resort ID or MagicBand to experience rides or attractions.

WHEN ARE EMHS OFFERED? You can check the Crowd Calendar at **touringplans.com** for the dates of your visit, check the parks calendar at **disneyworld.com,** or call Walt Disney World Information at ☎ 407-824-4321 or 407-939-6244 (press *0* for a live representative).

TYPICAL EXTRA MAGIC HOURS SCHEDULE *(frequently varies)*						
MORNING						
MON	TUES	WED	THUR	FRI	SAT	SUN
Animal Kingdom	Epcot	Animal Kingdom	Magic Kingdom	–	DHS	—
EVENING						
MON	TUES	WED	THUR	FRI	SAT	SUN
DHS	—	—	—	Epcot	—	Magic Kingdom

In addition to these, it's common for Epcot to have EMHs on Friday mornings and Tuesday evenings.

WHAT DO EXTRA MAGIC HOURS MEAN TO YOU? Disney seems to use EMHs in two ways: to provide Disney resort guests some extra park time on days when those parks are traditionally crowded, and as an incentive to visit one park on days when another park is typically more crowded.

Crowds typically range from slightly below average to average at Disney's Animal Kingdom and the Magic Kingdom on days when those parks host Extra Magic Hours. Crowds are higher than average at Disney's Hollywood Studios, and slightly higher at Epcot, on days when they have EMHs.

Not many families have the stamina to take advantage of morning and evening EMHs on consecutive days. If you have to choose between morning or evening Extra Magic Hour sessions, consider first whether your family functions better getting up early or staying up late. Also, consider the time at which the parks close to day guests. Evening EMHs are most useful when the crowds are low and the parks close relatively early to the general public, so your family doesn't have to stay up past midnight to take advantage of the perk.

MORNING EXTRA MAGIC HOURS (A.K.A. EARLY ENTRY) These are offered at all four theme parks throughout the year, and rarely (during summer) at Blizzard Beach and Typhoon Lagoon water parks. Several days of the week, Disney resort guests are invited to enter a designated theme park 1 hour before the general public. During this hour, guests can enjoy selected attractions opened early just for them.

Morning Extra Magic Hours strongly affect attendance at Disney's Hollywood Studios and Epcot, especially during busier times of year. Crowds at those parks are usually larger than average, as a Winston-Salem, North Carolina, mom discovered:

Disney Hollywood Studios was a MADHOUSE. Do NOT go on Extra Magic Hours days. After spending about 3 hours to ride three rides, I just wanted to trample the people stampeding to the exit.

Magic Kingdom crowds are about average when it has morning EMHs (usually Thursday). Because Disney's Animal Kingdom typically has two morning EMHs but no evening EMHs, crowds are spread out, resulting in lower-than-average waits on both days. Disney's decision to drop Animal Kingdom's single evening session in favor of two morning sessions seems like it was the correct thing to do.

If you're staying at a Disney resort, remember these three things about Extra Magic Hours:

1. The Magic Kingdom has more attractions open for morning EMHs than any other park. Coupled with a good touring plan, we think the Magic Kingdom's morning session is the most worthwhile of any EMHs at any park.

2. Morning EMHs are least useful at Disney's Animal Kingdom because it has fewer rides overall. There's simply not as much benefit for the lost sleep.

3. If you think it unlikely that you'll be at the park offering morning Extra Magic Hours 30 minutes before it opens, visit another park instead.

During holiday periods and summer, when Disney hotels are full, getting in early makes a tremendous difference in crowds at the designated park. The program funnels so many people into the EMH park that it fills by about 10 a.m. and is practically gridlocked by noon. A mother of three from Lee's Summit, Missouri, writes:

Our first full day at WDW, we went to the Magic Kingdom on an early-entry day for resort guests. We were there at 7:30 a.m. and were able to walk onto all the rides in Fantasyland with no wait. At 8:45 a.m. we positioned ourselves at the Adventureland rope and ran toward Splash Mountain when the rope dropped. We were able to ride Splash Mountain with no wait and then Big Thunder with about a 15-minute wait. We then went straight to the Jungle Cruise and the wait was already 30 minutes, so we skipped it. The park became incredibly crowded as the day progressed, and we were all exhausted from getting up so early. We left the park around noon. After that day, I resolved to avoid early-entry days and instead be at a non-early-entry park about a half-hour before official opening time.

Note that during holidays, the Magic Kingdom opens to regular guests at 8 a.m. Morning Extra Magic Hours begin at 7 a.m., so you'll need to be at the Magic Kingdom entrance at around 6:30 a.m. You won't be alone, but relatively few people are willing to get up that early for a theme park, and your first hour in the parks will be (please pardon us) magical.

This note from a North Bend, Washington, dad emphasizes the importance of arriving at the beginning of the early-entry period.

We only used early entry once—to Disney's Hollywood Studios. We got there 20 minutes after early entry opened, and the wait for Tower of Terror was 1½ hours long without Fastpass. We skipped it.

An alternative strategy for Disney resort guests is to take advantage of morning Extra Magic Hours, but only until the designated park gets crowded. At that time, move to another park.

A Dillsburg, Pennsylvania, mom has another tip:

If you have Fastpass+ opportunities [see page 234], schedule them for the park you're visiting second.

This works particularly well at the Magic Kingdom for families with young children who love the attractions in Fantasyland. However, it will take you about an hour to commute to the second park of the day. If, for example, you depart the Magic Kingdom for Disney's Hollywood Studios at 11 a.m., you'll find the Studios pretty crowded when you arrive at about noon, as this Texas mom found:

We made the mistake of doing a morning at the Magic Kingdom and an afternoon at the Studios. Worst idea ever. By the time we got to the Studios, all the Fastpasses were gone for Toy Story Mania!, the Tower of Terror, and Rock 'n' Roller Coaster. And all three rides had at least 90-minute waits.

Keeping these and other considerations in mind, here are some guidelines:

1. Use the morning-EMH–park-hopping strategy during the less busy times of year when the parks close early. You'll get a jump on the general public and add an hour to what, in the off-season, is an already short touring day.

2. Use the morning-EMH–park-hopping strategy to complete touring a second park that you've already visited on a previous day, or specifically to see live entertainment in the second park.

Don't hop to Disney's Animal Kingdom if it closes before 7 p.m. Crowds generally start leaving between 3 and 4 p.m. If the park closes at 5 or 6, you'll have only 1–3 hours of touring with lower crowds.

On any day except its EMH days, hopping to Epcot is usually good. Epcot is equipped to handle large crowds better than any other Disney park, minimizing the effects of a midday arrival. Also, World Showcase has a large selection of interesting dining options, making it a good choice for evening touring.

Don't hop to the park with morning EMHs. The idea is to avoid crowds, not join them. Finally, limit your hopping to two parks per day. Hopping to a third park in one day would result in more time spent commuting than saved by avoiding crowds.

EVENING EXTRA MAGIC HOURS These let Disney resort guests enjoy a different theme park on specified nights for about 2 hours after it closes to the general public. Guests pay no additional charge to participate but must show their resort IDs at each ride or attraction they wish to experience. You can also show up at the turnstiles at any point after evening Extra Magic Hours have started. Note that if you've been in another park that day, you'll need the Park Hopper feature on your admission ticket to enter. Evening Extra Magic Hours are offered at the Magic Kingdom, Epcot, and Disney's Hollywood Studios, but not at Disney's Animal Kingdom.

Evening sessions are usually more crowded at the Magic Kingdom and the Studios than at Epcot. Those evening EMH crowds can be just as large as those throughout the day. During summer, when the Magic Kingdom's evening EMH session runs until 1 a.m., lines at headliner attractions can still be long at midnight. A mom from Fairhaven, Massachusetts, doesn't mince words:

> *I say steer clear of a park that is open late. There are only a few attractions open and tons of people trying to get on them.*

More attractions operate during evening EMHs than during morning EMHs. Certain fast-food and full-service restaurants remain open as well.

PLANNING *Your* WALT DISNEY WORLD VACATION BUDGET

HOW MUCH YOU SPEND DEPENDS on how long you stay at Walt Disney World. But even if you only stop by for an afternoon, be prepared to drop a bundle. Later we'll show you how to save money on lodging. This section will give you some sense of what you can expect to pay for admissions and food. And we'll help you decide which admission option will best meet your needs.

WALT DISNEY WORLD ADMISSION OPTIONS

DISNEY OFFERS A NUMBER OF different admission options in order to accommodate various vacation needs. These range from the humble **1-Day Base Ticket,** good for a single day's entry into one Disney theme park, to the blinged-out **Premium Annual Pass,** good for 365 days of admission into every Disney theme or water park, plus DisneyQuest.

The number of ticket options available makes it difficult to sort out which option represents the least expensive way to see and do everything you want. The average family staying for a week at an off-World hotel and planning a couple of activities outside the theme parks has about a dozen different ticket options to consider.

Adding to the complexity, Disney's reservation agents are trained to avoid answering subjective questions about which ticket option is "best." Many families, we suspect, become overwhelmed trying to sort out the different options and simply purchase an expensive ticket with more features than they'll use.

As an example, a family of two adults and two children who want to visit the theme parks for five days and a water park for one day could buy everyone a 5-Day Base Ticket plus the Water Park Fun and More option, for $1,442 total. Or they could buy separate admissions to the theme and water parks from a third-party vendor for $1,321, a saving of $121. The problem is that comparing options requires detailed knowledge of the myriad perks included with specific admissions.

THIS IS A JOB FOR . . . A COMPUTER!

IT'S COMPLICATED ENOUGH that we wrote a computer program to solve it. Visit **touringplans.com** and try our **Park Ticket Calculator,** on the home page. It aggregates ticket prices from Disney and a number of online ticket vendors. Just answer a few simple questions relating to the size of your party and the theme parks you intend to visit, and the calculator will identify your four least expensive ticket options. It'll also show you how much you'll save.

The program will also make recommendations for considerations other than price. For example, Annual Passes might cost more, but they make sense in certain circumstances because Disney often offers substantial resort discounts and other deals to Annual Pass holders. Those resort discounts, especially during the off-season, can more than offset a small incremental charge for the Annual Pass.

The Park Ticket Calculator has saved readers millions of dollars over the past few years, as this husband discovered:

You just saved me from making a $408 mistake and needless expense!

MAGIC YOUR WAY

WALT DISNEY WORLD OFFERS AN ARRAY of ticket options, grouped into a program called Magic Your Way. The simplest option, visiting one theme park for one day, is called a **1-Day Base Ticket.** Other features, such as the ability to visit more than one park per day ("park-hopping"), or the inclusion of admission to Disney's minor venues (Typhoon Lagoon, Blizzard Beach, DisneyQuest, mini-golf, and the like), are available as individual add-ons to the Base Ticket.

In 2013 Disney introduced separate pricing for a single day's admission to the Magic Kingdom versus the World's other theme parks. An adult 1-Day Base Ticket for the Magic Kingdom costs $101.18, while one day's admission to any other theme park is $95.85 (including tax).

Multiday pricing is still uniform across the parks. The more days of admission you buy, the lower the cost per day. For example, if you buy an adult 5-Day Base Ticket for $307.79 (taxes included), each day will cost $61.56, compared with $95.85 a day for a one-day pass to Epcot, the Studios, or Animal Kingdom and $101.18 for the Magic Kingdom. Tickets can be purchased from 1 up to 10 days and admit you to exactly one theme park per day; you can reenter your chosen park as many times as you like on that day.

Disney says its tickets expire within 14 days of the first day of use. In practice, they really mean 13 days after the first day of use. If, say, you purchase a 4-Day Base Ticket on June 1 and use it that day for admission to the Magic Kingdom, you'll be able to visit a single Disney theme park on any of your three remaining days from June 2 through June 14. After that, the ticket expires and any unused days will be lost.

WDW Theme Park Ticket Options

	1-day	2-day	3-day	4-day	5-day
BASE TICKET AGES 3–9					
MK: $94.79 EP/AK/DHS: $89.46 –	$183.18 ($91.59/day)	$259.86 ($86.62/day)	$276.90 ($69.23/day)	$287.55 ($57.51/day)
BASE TICKET AGE 10 AND UP					
MK: $101.18 EP/AK/DHS: $95.85 –	$195.96 ($97.98/day)	$279.03 ($93.01/day)	$297.14 ($74.28/day)	$307.79 ($61.56/day)

Base Ticket admits guest to one theme park each day of use.

	1-day	2-day	3-day	4-day	5-day
FOR PARK HOPPER, ADD:					
Ages 3–9: $131.00 Age 10+: $137.39 –	$62.84 ($31.42/day)	$62.84 ($20.95/day)	$62.84 ($15.71/day)	$62.84 ($12.57/day)

Park Hopper option entitles guest to visit more than one theme park on each day of use.

	1-day	2-day	3-day	4-day	5-day
FOR WATER PARK FUN AND MORE, ADD:					
Ages 3–9: $152.30 Age 10+: $158.69 2 visits	$62.84 2 visits	$62.84 3 visits	$62.84 4 visits	$62.84 5 visits

Water Park Fun and More option entitles guest to a specified number of visits (between 2 and 10) to a choice of entertainment and recreation venues.

	1-day	2-day	3-day	4-day	5-day
FOR PARK HOPPER *PLUS* WATER PARK FUN AND MORE, ADD:					
Ages 3–9: $178.92 Age 10+: $185.31 –	$89.46 ($44.73/day)	$89.46 ($29.82/day)	$89.46 ($22.37/day)	$89.46 ($17.89/day)
FOR NO EXPIRATION, ADD:					
–	$37.28 ($18.64/day)	$47.93 ($15.98/day)	$101.18 ($25.29/day)	$154.43 ($30.89/day)

No Expiration means unused admissions on a ticket have no expiration date.

Through another add-on, however, you can avoid the 14-day expiration and make your ticket valid forever. More on that later.

BASE-TICKET ADD-ONS

NAVIGATING THE MAGIC YOUR WAY PROGRAM is like ordering dinner à la carte at an upscale restaurant: many choices, mostly expensive, virtually all of which require some thought.

Three add-on options are offered with the Magic Your Way Ticket, each at an additional cost:

Note: All ticket prices include 6.5% sales tax.

	6-day	7-day	8-day	9-day	10-day
BASE TICKET AGES 3–9					
	$298.20 ($49.70/day)	$308.85 ($44.12/day)	$319.50 ($39.94/day)	$330.15 ($36.68/day)	$340.80 ($34.08/day)
BASE TICKET AGE 10 AND UP					
	$318.44 ($53.07/day)	$329.09 ($47.01/day)	$339.74 ($42.47/day)	$350.39 ($38.93/day)	$361.04 ($36.10/day)

Park choices are Magic Kingdom, Epcot, Disney's Hollywood Studios, or Disney's Animal Kingdom.

$62.84 ($10.47/day)	$62.84 ($8.98/day)	$62.84 ($7.85/day)	$62.84 ($6.98/day)	$62.84 ($6.28/day)

Park choices are any combination of Magic Kingdom, Epcot, Disney's Hollywood Studios, or Disney's Animal Kingdom on each day of use.

$62.84 6 visits	$62.84 7 visits	$62.84 8 visits	$62.84 9 visits	$62.84 10 visits

Choices are Disney's Blizzard Beach water park, Disney's Typhoon Lagoon water park, DisneyQuest, Oak Trail Golf Course, ESPN Wide World of Sports Complex, or Winter Summerland or Fantasia mini-golf.

$89.46 ($14.91/day)	$89.46 ($12.78/day)	$89.46 ($11.18/day)	$89.46 ($9.94/day)	$89.46 ($8.95/day)

$202.35 ($33.73/day)	$234.30 ($33.47/day)	$260.93 ($32.62/day)	$298.20 ($33.13/day)	$346.13 ($34.61/day)

Note: Check **touringplans.com** for the latest ticket prices, which are subject to change. All tickets expire 14 days after first use unless **No Expiration** is purchased.

PARK HOPPER Adding this feature to your ticket allows you to visit more than one theme park per day. The cost is about $42–$46 (including tax) on top of the price of an adult 1-Day Base Ticket and $62.84 added to the price of adult and child multiday tickets—exorbitant for one or two days, but more affordable the longer your stay. As an add-on to a 7-Day Base Ticket, the flat fee would work out to $8.98 per day for park-hopping privileges. If you want to visit the Magic Kingdom in the morning and eat at Epcot in the evening, this is the feature to request.

NO EXPIRATION Adding this option to your ticket means that unused admissions to the major theme parks and the swimming parks, as well as other minor venues, never expire. If you added this option to a 10-Day Ticket and used only 4 days this year, the remaining 6 days could be used for admission at any date in the future. No Expiration ranges from $37.28 with tax for a 2-Day Base Ticket to $346.13 for a 10-Day Base Ticket. This option is unavailable for single-day tickets and must be added in person before the ticket expires. (*Note:* No Expiration is no longer available for purchase at the Disney website.)

WATER PARK FUN AND MORE (WPFAM) This option gives you a single admission to one of Disney's water parks (Blizzard Beach and Typhoon Lagoon), DisneyQuest, Oak Trail Golf Course, Fantasia Gardens or Winter Summerland mini-golf, or the ESPN Wide World of Sports Complex. The cost is a flat $62.84 (including tax). Except for the single-day WPFAM ticket, which gives you two admissions, the number of admissions equals the number of days on your ticket. If you buy an 8-Day Base Ticket, for example, and add the WPFAM option, you get eight WPFAM admissions. What you *can't* do is, say, buy a 10-Day Base Ticket with only three WPFAM admissions or a 3-Day Base Ticket with four WPFAM admissions. You can, however, skip WPFAM entirely and buy an individual admission to any of these minor parks—that's almost always the best deal if you want to visit only one of the venues above.

Liliane: Research indicates that less than 1 in 10 admission passes with unused days are ever used. I can report, however, that I have successfully kept track of all the partially used tickets I've taken home over the years. The secret? I keep them in the same place all the time with my passport, insurance papers, and other travel documents. And one more thing: I always keep a copy of my credit card receipt documenting the purchase. I even make a digital copy because receipts fade as time goes by.

Disney also offers a **Park Hopper–WPFAM combo** for $89.46 including tax. If you plan to spend a lot of time at the water parks and other WPFAM venues, the combo will save you $36 over buying the two options separately.

The foregoing add-ons are available for purchase in any combination (except for No Expiration, which can't be added to 1-Day Base Tickets). If you buy a ticket and then decide later on that you want one or more of the options, you can upgrade the ticket to add the feature(s) you desire. Disney doesn't prorate the cost, so you'll pay the same price regardless of when you buy the option. If you add the Park Hopper option on the last day of your trip, you'll pay the same $62.84 as if you'd bought it before you left home.

Annual Passes

An **Annual Pass** provides unlimited use of the major theme parks for one year; a **Premium Annual Pass** also provides unlimited use of the minor parks. Annual Pass holders also get perks, including free parking and seasonal offers such as room-rate discounts at Disney resorts. The

Annual Pass is not valid for special events, such as admission to Mickey's Very Merry Christmas Party. Tax included, Annual Passes run $648.59 for both adults and kids age 3 and up. A Premium Annual Pass, at $776.39 for adults and kids age 3 and up, provides unlimited admission to Blizzard Beach, Typhoon Lagoon, DisneyQuest, and Oak Trail Golf Course, in addition to the four major theme parks, plus mini-golf discounts and 30 minutes of game access at ESPN Wide World of Sports' PlayStation Pavilion (when the pavilion is open).

Florida Resident Passes

Disney offers several special admission options to Florida residents. The **Florida Resident Annual Pass** ($494.16 for adults and kids age 3 and up) and the **Florida Resident Premium Annual Pass** ($621.96 for adults and kids age 3 and up) both offer unlimited admission and park-hopping privileges to the four major theme parks. The Florida Resident Premium Annual Pass also provides unlimited admission to Blizzard Beach, Typhoon Lagoon, DisneyQuest, and Oak Trail Golf Course, in addition to the four major theme parks, plus mini-golf discounts and 30 minutes of game access at ESPN Wide World of Sports' PlayStation Pavilion (when the pavilion is open). AAA offers some nice discounts on these passes. And the **Florida Resident Seasonal Pass** ($329.09 for adults and kids age 3 and up) provides unlimited admission to the four major theme parks except on select blackout dates. In addition to Annual Passes, Florida residents are eligible for discounts on one-day theme park Base Tickets (about 10%) as well as on various add-on options.

ANOTHER ONE BITES THE DUST

DISNEY CLOSES MONEY-SAVING LOOPHOLES each time it updates admission prices and options. Considering that most guests need only four or five days' admission, the most cost-effective strategy would seem to be to buy a 10-Day Base Ticket plus the No Expiration option so you could roll over any unused admission days to a subsequent trip. When Disney first rolled out Magic Your Way, the No Expiration option made this investment a reasonable choice.

Well, they couldn't let *that* continue, could they?

If you buy an adult 10-Day Base Ticket for $361.04 plus No Expiration for $346.13, you'll pay $707.17 including tax, or $70.72 a day— $9 more a day compared with simply buying a 5-Day Base Ticket each time you visit Walt Disney World. While it's true that admission prices might go up before you visit again, in which case No Expiration would be to your benefit, it's equally true that you might misplace the tickets you bought in the previous scenario, or that you might have some better use for the $346.13 you shelled out on top of your ticket purchase.

HOW TO GET THE MOST FROM MAGIC YOUR WAY

FIRST, HAVE A REALISTIC IDEA of what you want out of your vacation. As with anything, it doesn't make sense to pay for options you won't use. A seven-day theme park ticket with seven WPFAM admissions might seem like a wonderful idea when you're snowbound and planning your trip in February. But actually trying to visit all those parks in a week in July might end up feeling more like Navy SEAL training. If you're going to make only one visit to a water park, DisneyQuest, or ESPN Wide World of Sports, you're almost always better off purchasing that admission separately rather than in the WPFAM option. If you plan to visit two or more WPFAM venues, you're better off buying the add-on.

Next, think carefully about paying for No Expiration. An inside source reports that fewer than 1 in 10 admission tickets with unused days are ever used at a Disney theme park. The rest are misplaced, discarded, or forgotten. Unless you're absolutely certain you'll be returning to the World within the next year or two and you've identified a safe place to keep those unused tickets, we don't think the additional cost is worth the risk. (We've lost a few of these passes ourselves.)

ANTICIPATING PRICE INCREASES

DISNEY USUALLY RAISES PRICES ONCE A YEAR, typically in late summer. (The last three hikes came in June, the five before that in August.) Price increases have generally run about 5% a year, but specific ticket categories are frequently bumped much more. In 2013, the average increase across all admissions was 7%; in 2012, it was a greedy 14%. If you're putting a budget together, assume at least a 5% increase, but know that it could be *much* higher.

A Georgia dad puts Disney's price hikes in perspective:

> *In the spring of 1983 as a working student, I purchased a [pre–Magic Your Way] 3-Day Park Hopper for $35 (including tax). Minimum wage was $3.35/hour, meaning it took less than 11 hours of work to pay for that ticket. With the latest increase, a 3-Day Base Ticket plus Park Hopper costs $341.87, or about **47 hours** of work at today's minimum wage of $7.25/hour. WDW simply is no longer the affordable vacation it once was.*

TICKETS, BIOMETRICS, WRISTBANDS, AND RFID

IF YOU'RE STAYING AT A DISNEY RESORT, your Magic Your Way ticket will have your name printed on it, a first line of defense against you selling your unused days to someone else. In addition, Disney's computer systems store biometric information about you—the dimensions of one finger from your right hand. A reference to this data is stored on the ticket, too. Contrary to popular myth, the turnstile finger-scanners don't record your fingerprints.

Recording this biometric information requires a quick and painless measurement, taken the first time the ticket is used. When the ticket is used again, you'll be asked to scan the same finger to validate your identity. If the scans don't match—if you use a different finger, for example—you may be asked for photo ID.

If you're buying admission for your entire family and you're worried about keeping everyone's tickets straight, Disney's computer system should link every family member's data to every ticket, allowing anyone to enter with anyone else's ticket. We've confirmed this by having a platoon of *Unofficial Guide* researchers (including men, women, and children) swap passes with each other; all were admitted.

We've been using the word *ticket* to describe the thing you carry around to indicate you've purchased entry into the park. In fact, Disney admission media comes in two types, neither of which is a ticket. Here's what you'll be handed when you plunk down your money:

For Disney resort guests, your admission media is a piece of credit card–size plastic. Called a **Key to the World (KTTW) Card,** it's printed with your name and travel dates. Each KTTW Card also displays a unique ID number internal to Disney, used to access your hotel reservation and other trip and ticket info.

If you're staying off-property or you bought your admission from a third-party vendor, your admission media is a flexible, credit card–sized piece of plastic-coated paper.

The other form of Disney admission media is a rubber wristband about the size and shape of a small wristwatch. Called a **MagicBand** and introduced in 2013, it contains no visible printing at all. What it does have is a tiny radio-frequency-identication (RFID) chip, on which is stored a link to your biometric info on Disney's computers.

If you're staying at a Disney resort, you can choose either a KTTW Card or a MagicBand as your "ticket." KTTW Cards already come with RFID chips, and we expect third-party tickets to incorporate them eventually; in the meantime, off-site guests and those with third-party tickets can switch to a MagicBand for a small fee. The inner workings of RFID chips and MagicBands are discussed in more detail starting on page 72.

WHERE TO PURCHASE MAGIC YOUR WAY TICKETS

YOU CAN BUY YOUR ADMISSION PASSES on arrival at Walt Disney World or purchase them in advance. Admission passes are available at Walt Disney World resorts and theme parks. Passes are also available at some non-Disney hotels and shopping centers, as well as through independent ticket brokers. Because Disney admission prices are only marginally discounted in the Walt Disney World–Orlando area, the chief reason for you to purchase from an independent broker is convenience. Offers of free or heavily discounted tickets abound, but they generally require you to attend a time-share sales presentation.

Magic Your Way tickets are available at Disney Stores and at **disney world.com** for the same prices listed in the chart on pages 64–65.

If you're trying to keep costs to an absolute minimum, consider using an online ticket wholesaler, such as **Undercover Tourist, Kissim-mee Guest Services, Maple Leaf Tickets,** or the **Official Ticket Center,** especially for trips with five or more days in the theme parks. All tickets sold are brand-new, and the savings can range from $2 to more than $65, depending on the ticket and options chosen. We've spoken with representatives from each company, and they're well versed in the pros and cons of the various tickets and options. If the new options don't make sense for your specific vacation plans, the reps will tell you so.

All four companies offer discounts on tickets for almost all Central Florida attractions, including Disney, Universal, SeaWorld, and Cirque du Soleil. Discounts for the major theme parks range from about 6% to 8.5%. Tickets for other attractions are more deeply discounted. **Undercover Tourist** (U.S.: ☎ 800-846-1302; Monday–Friday, 9 a.m.– 4 p.m. Eastern time; U.K.: ☎ 0800 081 1702; Monday–Friday, 2 p.m.– 9 p.m. Greenwich mean time; worldwide: ☎ +1 386-239-8624; fax +1 386-252-3469; **undercovertourist.com**) offers free delivery and has a sweetheart relationship with **MouseSavers** (**mousesavers.com**). If you subscribe to the MouseSavers e-newsletter, you can access Undercover Tourist by way of a special "secret" link that provides additional savings on top of the normal discount. **Kissimmee Guest Services** (950 Celebration Blvd., Suite H, Celebration; ☎ 321-939- 2057; Monday–Saturday, 8 a.m.–5 p.m., Sunday, 8 a.m.–noon, all Eastern time; U.K.: ☎ 0208 432 4024; **kgstickets.com**) offers free ticket delivery to Orlando-area hotels for tickets ordered over the phone, but tickets ordered online are cheaper. The **Official Ticket Center** (3148 Vineland Rd., Kissimmee; daily, 8 a.m.–8:30 p.m. Eastern time; ☎ 407-396-9020 or 877-406-4836; fax 407-396-9323; **official ticketcenter.com**) offers USPS certified mail for free or U.S. Priority Mail for $8. For $10 they'll also deliver to Orlando-area hotels; it's of course free if you pick up at their office. **Maple Leaf Tickets** (4647 W. Irlo Bronson Memorial Hwy. [US 192], Kissimmee; daily, 8 a.m.– 6 p.m. Eastern time; ☎ 407-396-0300 or 800-841-2837; fax 407-396-4127; **mapleleaftickets.com**) offers the same deal on pickup at their store and for $6.95 delivery to Orlando-area hotels; U.S. Priority Mail service is a flat $6.95 per order.

Where Not to Buy Passes

In addition to the many authorized sellers of Disney admissions, a number of bricks-and-mortar sellers exist. They buy unused days on legitimately purchased passes, then resell them as if they were newly issued. These resellers are easy to identify: They insist that you specify exactly which dates you plan to use the ticket. They know, of course, how many days are left on the pass and when it expires. If you tell them you plan to use it tomorrow and the next two days, they'll sell you a ticket that has three days remaining and expires in three days. Naturally, because they don't tell you this, you assume the usual 14-day expiration period from the date of first use. In the case of your tickets, however, the original purchaser triggered the 14-day expiration period. If you decide to skip a day instead of using the pass on the next three consecutive days, you'll discover to your chagrin that it has expired.

Liliane: Also steer clear of passes offered on eBay, Craigslist, and the like.

FOR ADDITIONAL INFORMATION ON PASSES

IF YOU HAVE A QUESTION OR CONCERN regarding admissions that can be addressed only through a person-to-person conversation, contact **Disney Ticket Inquiries** at ☎ 407-566-4985 or **ticket.inquiries @disneyworld.com.** If you call, be aware that you may spend a considerable time on hold; if you e-mail, be aware that it can take up to three days to get a response. In contrast, the ticket section of the Disney World website—**disneyworld.disney.go.com/tickets**—is surprisingly straightforward in showing how ticket prices breaks down.

HOW MUCH DOES IT COST PER DAY?

A TYPICAL DAY WOULD COST $683.19, excluding lodging and transportation, for a family of four—Mom, Dad, 12-year-old Abner, and 8-year-old Agnes—driving their own car and staying outside the World. They plan to stay a week, so they buy 5-Day Base Tickets with the Park Hopper option.

Breakfast for four at Denny's with tax and tip	$33.32
Epcot parking fee (free for pass holders and resort guests)	$15.00
Four day admission on a 5-Day Ticket with Park Hopper Option	$292.47
Dad: *Adult 5-Day with tax is $370.63 divided by five days = $74.13*	
Mom: *Adult 5-Day with tax is $370.63 divided by five days = $74.13*	
Abner: *Adult 5-Day with tax is $370.63 divided by five days = $74.13*	
Agnes: *Child 5-Day with tax is $350.39 divided by five days = $74.13*	
Morning break (soda or coffee)	$11.89
Fast-food lunch (sandwich or burger, fries, soda), no tip	$51.03
Afternoon break (soda and popcorn)	$26.63
Dinner at Italy (3 appetizers, 4 entrees, 3 desserts), with tax and tip	$206.10
Souvenirs (Mickey T-shirts for Abner and Agnes) with tax*	$46.75
One-day total (without lodging or transportation)	**$683.19**

* *Cheer up—you won't have to buy souvenirs every day.*

A Birmingham, Alabama, mom of two begs to differ with our budget recommendation above for souvenirs:

> *Sorry, but Uncle Bob is totally out of touch when he says "you won't have to buy souvenirs every day." In my experience, you'll head home with several sets of character ears; enough dress-up costumes to outfit the neighborhood; and countless pins, toys, and knickknacks.*

BACK TO THE SALT MINES! Our math could be off, but it appears that the cost of a Disney vacation has increased roughly three times faster than U.S. worker's median wages (3.1% vs. 0.9%) since 1995. To put that in perspective, it took the average worker about 3.1 hours to earn enough money for a 1-Day Base Ticket in 1995. Today it's 4.5 hours. If current trends continue, it'll be 7.7 hours in a decade.

RFID: IT'S ALL IN THE WRIST

WITH ITS MYMAGIC+ CAMPAIGN (see page 40), Disney is introducing **MagicBands**—reusable rubber wristbands—as a sort of wearable theme park ticket. Because they're small and reusable across trips, Disney doesn't print your name or hotel information on the wristband. Rather, a tiny radio-frequency-identification (RFID) chip embedded in the wristband holds your ticket and travel information.

Each RFID chip—not much larger than the end of a pencil—sends a unique serial number over short distances via radio waves. When you purchase theme park admission, Disney's computers will store that serial number, along with your ticket information. To enter a theme park, you'll touch your MagicBand to an RFID reader instead of going through a turnstile. The RFID reader will collect your MagicBand's serial number, compare your biometric information, and verify with Disney's computer systems that you've got the correct admission to enter the park.

RFID technology has been used for many years in the retail and transportation industries to track everything from the location of cargo containers to the receipt, stocking, and purchase of T-shirts. Many bus and subway systems have switched to RFID-enabled cards from paper tickets. The U.S. government also puts RFID chips in all new passports to prevent forgery; the chip transmits the same information printed on your passport.

Disney hotel guests may use either a MagicBand or a **Key to the World (KTTW) Card** (see page 69) as their admission media. If you're staying off-site, you can upgrade to a MagicBand for a small fee (the default is a credit card–sized plastic-coated ticket).

Each member of your family gets his or her own MagicBand, each with a unique serial number. Along with the wristband, each family member will be asked to select a four-digit personal-identification number (PIN) for purchases—more on that below. The wristbands are resizable and waterproof, and they have ventilation holes for cooling. Eight colors are available: red, black, blue, green, pink, orange, yellow, and gray (the default). You can choose your colors and personalize your bands when you book your resort stay at the Disney World website.

According to Disney, using RFID at each park entrance will speed up admittance, because RFID readers are more reliable than the magnetic-stripe card readers currently in use. The old turnstiles should be replaced completely with RFID readers by early 2014.

Disney hasn't said how it's going to deal with old non-RFID tickets. Our guess, based on reading the legalese on the website, is that you'll need to convert old tickets to RFID media in order to use Fastpass+.

RFID for Payment, Hotel-Room Access, and Photos

Disney resort guests will find other uses for MagicBands and KTTW Cards beyond park admission. Disney's hotel-room doors now have

RFID readers, allowing you to enter your room simply by tapping your wristband or card against the reader. The same technology has been in use for years at upscale hotels around the world.

RFID readers are also installed at virtually every Disney cash register on property, allowing you to pay for food, drinks, and souvenirs by tapping your MagicBand/KTTW Card against the reader. You'll be asked to verify your identity by entering your PIN on a small keypad to complete your purchase. This technology, known as "contactless payment," has been in use worldwide for many years, too.

If you're using Disney's PhotoPass service, your MagicBand/KTTW Card will be the link between your photos and your family. Each photographer will have a small RFID reader, against which you'll tap your MagicBand before having your photo taken. The computers running the PhotoPass system will link your photos to you, and you'll be able to view them on the Disney World website.

Disney's onboard ride-photo computers will eventually incorporate RFID technology, too. As you begin to go down the big drop near the finale of Splash Mountain, for example, RFID sensors will read the serial number on your MagicBand and pass it to Splash Mountain's cameras. When those cameras snap your family plunging into the briar patch, they'll attach your MagicBands' serial number to the photo, allowing you to see your ride photos together after you've returned home. Because rides sensors may not pick up the signal from an RFID card sitting in a wallet or purse, we expect on-board ride photos to require MagicBands.

The Future of RFID

Knowing your family was on Splash Mountain is one example of Disney using RFID technology, and others are rumored. In one scenario we've heard, you provide Disney with some benign information about your child before your visit, such as his or her favorite color and pet's name. Later, when your child visits Cinderella, an RFID reader next to Cinderella will recognize your child's wristband and display the previously gathered information on a hidden prompter for Cinderella to work into conversation. And because Disney's computer systems will know from your MagicBand which rides you've been on and where you've eaten, Cinderella may mention those details, too.

Many people, however, are understandably concerned when multinational corporations start collecting information on their locations and behavior. Disney has addressed this by making MagicBands optional; guests who prefer not to wear them can obtain RFID cards instead, and these are somewhat more difficult to track. (Google "RFID blocking wallet" if you're looking for an inexpensive way to block virtually all RFID readers from tracking your RFID-enabled cards.) Disney, however, says that guests who opt out of using a MagicBand won't get the full range of ride experiences, so there's a trade-off to be made.

▌ BABYSITTING

CHILD-CARE CENTERS Child care isn't available inside the theme parks, but two Magic Kingdom resorts connected by monorail or boat (Polynesian and Wilderness Lodge & Villas), four Epcot resorts (the Yacht & Beach Club Resorts, the Swan, and the Dolphin), and Animal Kingdom Lodge, along with the Hilton at Walt Disney World, have child-care centers for potty-trained children age 3 and older (see table below). Services vary, but children generally can be left between 4:30 p.m. and midnight. Milk and cookies and blankets and pillows are provided at all centers, and dinner is provided at most. Play is supervised but not organized, and toys, videos, and games are plentiful. Guests at any Disney resort or campground may use the services.

CHILD-CARE CLUBS*		
HOTEL NAME OF PROGRAM	AGES	PHONE
ANIMAL KINGDOM LODGE		
Simba's Cubhouse	3–12	☎ 407-938-4785
DOLPHIN AND SWAN		
Camp Dolphin	4–12	☎ 407-934-4241
POLYNESIAN RESORT		
Never Land Club	3–12	☎ 407-824-1639
YACHT & BEACH CLUB RESORTS		
Sandcastle Club	3–12	☎ 407-934-3750
WILDERNESS LODGE & VILLAS		
Cub's Den	3–12	☎ 407-824-1083

*Child-care clubs operate afternoons and evenings. Before 4 p.m., call the hotels rather than the numbers listed above. All programs require reservations; call ☎ 407-WDW-DINE (939-3463).

The most elaborate of the child-care centers (variously called "clubs" or "camps") is **Never Land Club** at the Polynesian Resort. The rate for ages 3–12 is $12 per hour, per child (2-hour minimum).

All the clubs accept reservations (some six months in advance!) with a credit card guarantee. Call the club directly, or reserve through Disney at ☎ 407-WDW-DINE. Most clubs require a 24-hour cancellation notice and levy a hefty penalty of 2 hours' time or $22.50 per call for no-shows. A limited number of walk-ins are usually accepted on a first-come, first-served basis.

If you're staying in a Disney resort that doesn't offer a child-care club and you *don't* have a car, then you're better off using in-room babysitting. Trying to take your child to a club in another hotel by Disney bus requires a 50- to 90-minute trip each way. By the time you've deposited your little one, it will almost be time to pick him or her up again.

Babysitting Services

ALL ABOUT KIDS	KID'S NITE OUT	FAIRY GODMOTHERS
☎ 407-812-9300 or 800-728-6506 all-about-kids.com	☎ 407-828-0920 or 800-696-8105 kidsniteout.com	☎ 407-277-3724
HOTELS SERVED All WDW hotels and many outside the WDW area	**HOTELS SERVED** All WDW and Orlando-area hotels	**HOTELS SERVED** All WDW hotels and those in the general WDW area
SITTERS Men and women	**SITTERS** Men and women	**SITTERS** Mothers and grandmothers, female college students
MINIMUM CHARGES 4 hours	**MINIMUM CHARGES** 4 hours	**MINIMUM CHARGES** 4 hours
BASE HOURLY RATES 1 child, $14 2 children, $16 3 children, $18 4 children, $20	**BASE HOURLY RATES** 1 child, $16 2 children, $18.50 3 children, $21 4 children, $23.50	**BASE HOURLY RATES** 1 child, $16 2 children, $16 3 children, $16 4 children, $18
EXTRA CHARGES Transportation fee, $12; starting before 7 a.m. or after 9 p.m., +$2 per hour	**EXTRA CHARGES** Transportation fee, $10; starting before 6:30 a.m. or after 9 p.m., +$2 per hour; additional fee for holidays	**EXTRA CHARGES** Transportation fee, $14; starting after 10 p.m., +$2 per hour
CANCELLATION DEADLINE More than 24 hours before service to avoid cancellation charge	**CANCELLATION DEADLINE** 24 hours before service when reservation is made	**CANCELLATION DEADLINE** 3 hours before service
FORM OF PAYMENT Cash or traveler's checks for actual payment; gratuity in cash; credit card to hold reservation	**FORM OF PAYMENT** AE, D, MC, V; gratuity in cash	**FORM OF PAYMENT** Cash or traveler's checks for actual payment; gratuity in cash
THINGS SITTERS WON'T DO Transport children	**THINGS SITTERS WON'T DO** Transport children in private vehicle, take children swimming, give baths	**THINGS SITTERS WON'T DO** Transport children, give baths. Swimming is at sitter's discretion

IN-ROOM BABYSITTING Three companies provide in-room sitting in Walt Disney World and surrounding areas. They're **Kid's Nite Out, All About Kids,** and **Fairy Godmothers** (no kidding). Kid's Nite Out also serves hotels in the greater Orlando area, including downtown. All three provide sitters older than age 18 who are insured, bonded, screened, reference-checked, police-checked, and trained in CPR. In addition to caring for your kids in your room, the sitters will, if you direct (and pay), take your children to the theme parks or other venues. All three services offer bilingual sitters. (See table above for details.)

SPECIAL PROGRAMS
for CHILDREN

SEVERAL CHILDREN'S PROGRAMS ARE AVAILABLE at Walt Disney World parks and resorts. While all are undoubtedly fun, we find them somewhat lacking in educational focus.

BEHIND THE SEEDS AT EPCOT This 1-hour walking tour of the Land greenhouses and labs at Epcot has plenty of interaction for the kids, including guessing games and feeding fish at the fish farm. The greenhouses are home to more than 60 crops from around the world. Did you know that the food grown in the Land is used at the restaurants throughout Epcot? The price is $19 per adult and $15 per child (ages 3–9). Call ☎ 407-WDW-TOUR for additional information and reservations.

DISNEY'S FAMILY MAGIC TOUR This is a 1½- to 2-hour guided tour of the Magic Kingdom for the entire family. Even children in strollers (no younger than age 3) are welcome. The tour combines information about the Magic Kingdom with the gathering of clues that ultimately solve "diabolical" problems. There's usually a marginal plot such as saving Wendy from Captain Hook, in which case the character at the end of the tour is Wendy. The tour departs daily at 10 a.m. The cost is about $36 per person with tax, plus a valid Magic Kingdom admission. Maximum group size is 20 persons. Reservations can be made up to a year in advance by calling ☎ 407-WDW-TOUR (939-8687).

Liliane: Be aware that Disney is tinkering with prices and availability of packages now more than ever. Check ahead of time before promising your kids any activity. . .

DISNEY'S THE MAGIC BEHIND OUR STEAM TRAINS Kids must be age 10 or older for this 3-hour tour, presented Monday–Saturday. At the 7:30 a.m. start time, join the crew of the Walt Disney World Railroad as they prepare their steam locomotives for the day. Cost is about $52 per person with tax, plus a valid Magic Kingdom admission. Call ☎ 407-WDW-TOUR for information and reservations.

DISNEY'S PIRATE ADVENTURE Children ages 4–12 get to don bandannas, hoist the Jolly Roger, and set out on a boat trip to search for buried treasure by following a map. At the final port of call, the kids find the hidden treasure (doubloons, beads, and rubber bugs!) and wolf down PB&J sandwiches. The treasure is split among the kids. The adventure costs about $36 per child with tax and is offered at Port Orleans Riverside (Bayou Pirate Adventure), the Grand Floridian (Pirate Adventure), the Yacht Club (Albatross Cruise), and the Caribbean Beach Resort (Caribbean Pirate Adventure). The Grand Floridian runs the excursion every day except Sunday; the other resorts offer the program three days a week. Call ☎ 407-WDW-PLAY (939-7529) for days offered and other information. Boys and girls alike really love this outing—many report it as the highlight of their vacation. *Note:* No parents allowed.

If you want to go whole-hog, check out **The Pirates League** in Adventureland at the Magic Kingdom, where scoundrels and rogues of all ages can acquire special pirate costumes and accessories, as well as an official pirate name. Two different packages are available:

First Mate Package: Includes bandanna; choice of facial effects (scars, tattoos, fake teeth, earring, and eye patch); sword and sheath;

pirate-coin necklace; one 5-by-7-inch photo; and personalized pirate oath for $49.95, plus tax.

Empress Package: Comes with bandanna; shimmering makeup (face gem, tattoos, nail polish, earring, and eye patch); sword and sheath; pirate-coin necklace; one 5-by-7-inch photo; and personalized pirate oath for $49.95 plus tax.

These packages are available for boys, girls, and adults. Call ☎ 407-WDW-CREW to make an appointment.

WONDERLAND TEA PARTY Although the name of this enchanting event is enough to make most boys break out in hives, it is nevertheless available at the Grand Floridian on Monday–Friday afternoons, 2–3 p.m. The price tag is $43. Held at 1900 Park Fare restaurant in the Grand Floridian Monday–Friday afternoons at 1:30 p.m. for $43 per child (ages 4–12, with tax), the program consists of decorating (and eating) cupcakes and having lunch and tea with characters from Alice in Wonderland. Reservations can be made by calling ☎ 407-WDW-DINE 180 days in advance.

MY DISNEY GIRL'S PERFECTLY PRINCESS TEA PARTY It certainly takes a princely sum to cover the tab on this Grand Floridian shindig, hosted by Rose Petal, an enchanted storytelling rose. Your little princess gets dressed up in her favorite regal attire and sips tea with Princess Aurora. Girls receive an 18-inch My Disney Girl doll dressed in a matching Princess Aurora gown plus accessories. Other loot includes a ribbon tiara, silver link bracelet, fresh rose, scrapbook set, and "Best Friend" certificate. A luncheon is served as well. The cost is about $314 with tax and gratuity for one adult and one child ages 3–11; add an additional adult for $107 or an additional child for $208 (adults-only bookings not available). Princes who attend the tea party will receive a plush Duffy (the Disney bear) and a Mickey pirate cap. *Note:* **This event is not covered by the Disney Dining Plan.** Your credit card will be charged beforehand, and you can book up to 180 days in advance. The tea party is held every Sunday, Monday, and Wednesday–Friday, 10:30 a.m.–noon. Call ☎ 407-939-6397 for reservations and information. Check in 15 minutes prior to reservation time.

An Illinois mom ponied up for two of the programs:

We splurged and went to the Perfectly Princess Tea Party. It was nice but a bit too long with all the singing and stories. Not easy for a 4-year-old to sit that long. I'm not sure it was worth the cost, and I would not do it again. We also booked the Wonderland Tea Party. That was a much better cost, and I thought my daughter would love decorating a cupcake. She was so freaked out by the Mad Hatter that the nice workers there called me and asked me to come get her. They said many kids are scared of him, so I'm not sure why they don't have Alice and another character. I was pleased that they gave me a full refund (she was in there maybe 10 minutes).

BIRTHDAYS AND SPECIAL OCCASIONS

ALL GUESTS WHO CELEBRATE A BIRTHDAY or are visiting Walt Disney World for the first time can pick up a button corresponding to the celebration at Guest Relations when entering any of the parks. Often upon check-in the hotel clerks will ask if any member of your party is celebrating a special event. It is especially fun for birthday kids, as cast members will congratulate your child throughout the day in the hotel, on the bus, in the park, and at restaurants throughout the World. A Lombard, Illinois, mom put the word out and was glad she did:

> My daughter was turning 5 while we were there, and I asked about special things that could be done. Our hotel asked me who her favorite character was and did the rest. We came back to our room on her birthday and there were helium balloons, a card, and a Cinderella 5x7 photo autographed in ink! When we entered the Magic Kingdom, we received an It's My Birthday Today pin (FREE!), and at the restaurant she got a huge cupcake with whipped cream, sprinkles, and a candle. IT PAYS TO ASK!!

Another great and reasonably priced treat is to have your child's hair cut at the **Harmony Barber Shop** on Main Street, U.S.A. at the Magic Kingdom. Rest assured that your kid will walk away with a good haircut, and you may even be treated to a song by the Dapper Dans, Disney's famous barber-shop quartet. The best time to go is during a parade. You get a good view, and the staff sings along with the parade music. It's a great photo op. An Ohio mom celebrated her child's first haircut at the barber shop:

> The barber shop at the entrance of MK makes a big deal with baby's first haircut—pixie dust, photos, a certificate, and "free" mouse ears hat! ($14 total).

Lest you think the Harmony Barber Shop is strictly a boys' domain, a fashion- and dollar-conscious Kalamazoo, Michigan, mom writes that it's a great alternative to the Bibbidi Bobbidi Boutique (see page 427) for little girls who want to get gussied up Disney princess–style:

> I think I spent about $12, including tip. You don't need reservations, and in my opinion they do a better job than Bibbidi Bobbidi Boutique. They put my daughter's hair into a teased bun and use brightly colored paints and colorful confetti to match whatever princess dress she had on. I understand that Disney doesn't want the barber shop to compete with the BBB, so I don't know if I want you telling anyone this great secret or not!

Outside the theme parks, **Goofy's Candy Co.**, in Downtown Disney, offers a fun and special way to celebrate a kid's birthday. The 1½-hour party includes two hosts to entertain the children, themed balloons, a present for the birthday kid, invitations, and thank-you notes. All guests receive a Goofy Glacier beverage with keepsake cup and get to decorate one of Goofy's goodies, such as deluxe candy apples, crisped-rice treats, or marshmallows on a stick. The **Disney Perfectly Princess Party** for girls includes autographed photos of Cinderella and a light-up necklace for everyone, while the birthday girl receives a tiara and a boxed glass slipper. The **Goofy's Scien-terrific Birthday Bash!** for boys offers Goody's autograph and light-up glasses for all, while the birthday boy gets a Goofy Gumball machine filled with a pound of candy. The price for all the fun is $344.95 for up to 12 guests. Parties are held seven days a week, subject to availability. For more information, call ☎ 407-WDW-BDAY (939-2329).

PART THREE

WHERE *to* STAY

WHEN TRAVELING WITH CHILDREN, your hotel is your home away from home, your safe harbor, and your sanctuary. Staying in a hotel, an activity usually reserved for adults, is in itself a great adventure for children. They take in every detail and delight in such things as having a pool at their disposal and obtaining ice from a noisy machine. Of course, it is critical that your children feel safe and secure, but it adds immeasurably to the success of the vacation if they really like the hotel.

In truth, because of their youth and limited experience, kids are far less particular about hotels than adults tend to be. A Spartan room and a small pool at a budget motel will make most kids happier than a beagle with a lamb chop. But kids' memories are like little steel traps, so once you establish a lodging standard, that's pretty much what they'll expect every time. A couple from Gary, Indiana, stayed at the pricey Yacht Club Resort at Walt Disney World because they heard that it offered a knockout swimming area (which is true). When they returned two years later and stayed at Disney's All-Star Resorts for about a third of the price, their 10-year-old carped all week. If you're on a budget, it's better to begin with modest accommodations and move up to better digs on subsequent trips as finances permit.

 Bob: In our opinion, if you're traveling with a child age 12 or younger, one of your top priorities should be to book a hotel within easy striking distance of the parks.

"You Can't Roller-Skate in a Buffalo Herd"

THIS WAS A SONG TITLE FROM THE 1960s. If we wrote that song today, we'd call it "You Can't Have Fun at Disney World if You're Drop-Dead Tired." Believe us, Walt Disney World is an easy place to be penny-wise and pound-foolish. Many families who cut lodging expenses by booking a budget hotel end up so far away from Walt Disney World that it is a major hassle to return to the hotel in the middle of the day for swimming and a nap. By trying to spend the whole day at the theme parks, however, they wear themselves out quickly, and the dream vacation suddenly disintegrates into short tempers and exhaustion. And don't confuse this advice with a sales pitch for Disney hotels. There are, you will find, dozens of hotels outside Walt Disney World that are as close or closer to certain Disney theme parks than some of the resorts inside the World. Our main point—in fact, our only point—is to make it easy on yourself to return to your hotel when the need arises.

SOME BASIC CONSIDERATIONS

COST

AT DISNEY WORLD STANDARD HOTEL-ROOM RATES range from about $90 to more than $1,000 per night during high season. Outside, rooms are as low as $35 a night. Clearly, if you are willing to sacrifice some luxury and don't mind a 10- to 25-minute commute, you can really cut your lodging costs by staying outside Walt Disney World. Hotels in Walt Disney World tend to be the most expensive, but they also offer some of the highest quality, as well as a number of perks not enjoyed by guests who stay outside of the World.

Animal Kingdom Villas, Bay Lake Tower, Beach Club Villas, BoardWalk Villas, Grand Floridian Villas, Old Key West Resort, Saratoga Springs Resort & Spa, and **Wilderness Lodge Villas** offer condo-type accommodations with one-, two-, and (at Saratoga Springs, BoardWalk Villas, Old Key West, Animal Kingdom Villas, Grand Floridian Villas, and Bay Lake Tower) three-bedroom units with kitchens, living rooms, DVD players, and washers and dryers. Studios have a kitchenette (with microwave, mini-fridge, and sink) but no washer or dryer. Prices range from $313 per night for a studio suite at Animal Kingdom Villas to more than $3,300 per night for a three-bedroom villa at Grand Floridian Villas, the newest Disney Vacation Club property. Fully equipped cabins (minus a washer and dryer) at **Fort Wilderness Resort & Campground** cost $289–$481 per night. Family Suites at All-Star Music and Art of Animation have kitchenettes, separate bedrooms, and two bathrooms. A few suites without kitchens are available at the more expensive Disney resorts.

For any extra adults in a room (more than two), the nightly surcharge for each extra adult is $26.63 per night with tax at all resorts but DDV resorts, which levy no surcharge.

Also at Disney World are the seven hotels of the **Downtown Disney Resort Area (DDRA).** Accommodations range from fairly luxurious to motel-like. While the DDRA is technically part of Disney World, staying there is like visiting a colony rather than the motherland. Free parking at theme parks isn't offered—nor is early entry, with one exception, the Hilton—and hotels operate their own buses rather than use Disney transportation. For more information on DDRA properties, see the chart on page 108 and the discussion starting on page 107.

COSTS PER NIGHT OF DISNEY RESORT HOTEL ROOMS (rack rate)	
All-Star Resorts	$85–$192
All-Star Music Resort Family Suites	$202–$392
Animal Kingdom Lodge	$279–$3,088
Animal Kingdom Villas (Jambo House, Kidani Village)	$313–$2,380
Art of Animation Family Suites	$252–$433
Art of Animation Resort	$100–$191
Bay Lake Tower	$431–$2,640
Beach Club Resort	$350–$2,826
Beach Club Villas	$360–$1,284
BoardWalk Inn	$392–$2,949
BoardWalk Villas	$360–$2,380
Caribbean Beach Resort	$162–$322
Contemporary Resort	$330–$3,178
Coronado Springs Resort	$167–$1,364
Dolphin (Sheraton)	$189–$359
Fort Wilderness Resort & Campground (cabins)	$289–$481
Grand Floridian Resort & Spa	$480–$3,306
Grand Floridian Villas	$480–$3,345
Old Key West Resort	$327–$1,822
Polynesian Resort	$422–$3,187
Pop Century Resort	$95–$206
Port Orleans Resort (French Quarter, Riverside)	$162–$328
Saratoga Springs Resort & Spa	$327–$1,822
Swan (Westin)	$189–$359
Treehouse Villas	$709–$1,144
Wilderness Lodge	$284–$1,563
Wilderness Lodge Villas	$368–$1,279
Yacht Club Resort	$350–$3,002

LOCATION AND TRANSPORTATION OPTIONS

ONCE YOU'VE DETERMINED YOUR BUDGET, think about what you want to do at Walt Disney World. Will you go to all four theme parks or will you concentrate on one or two? If you intend to use your own car, the location of your Disney hotel isn't especially important unless you plan to spend most of your time at the Magic Kingdom. (Disney transportation is always more efficient than your car in this case because it bypasses the Transportation and Ticket Center and deposits you at the theme park entrance.)

WHAT IT COSTS TO STAY IN THE DOWNTOWN DISNEY RESORT AREA	
Best Western Lake Buena Vista Resort Hotel	$76–$149
Buena Vista Palace Hotel & Spa	$119–$214
DoubleTree Guest Suites	$189–$239
Hilton in the WDW Resort	$89–$169
Holiday Inn in the WDW Resort	$108–$181
Royal Plaza	$129–$305
Wyndham Lake Buena Vista Resort	$76–$168

Most convenient to the Magic Kingdom are the three resorts linked by monorail: the **Grand Floridian** and its **Villas, Contemporary, Bay Lake Tower,** and **Polynesian. Wilderness Lodge & Villas,** along with **Fort Wilderness Resort & Campground,** are linked to the Magic Kingdom by boat.

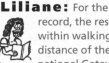

The most centrally located resorts in Walt Disney World are the Epcot hotels— **BoardWalk Inn, BoardWalk Villas, Yacht & Beach Club Resorts, Beach Club Villas, Swan,** and **Dolphin**—and **Coronado Springs,** an Animal Kingdom hotel. The Epcot hotels are within easy walking distance of Disney's Hollywood Studios and Epcot's International Gateway. Except at Coronado Springs, boat service is also available at these resorts, with vessels connecting to DHS.

Liliane: For the record, the resorts within walking distance of the International Gateway (the back door, so to speak, of Epcot) are expensive and are a long, long walk from Future World, the section of Epcot where families tend to spend most of their time.

Caribbean Beach Resort, Pop Century Resort, and **Art of Animation Resort** are just south and east of Epcot and DHS. Along Bonnet Creek, **Disney's Old Key West** and **Port Orleans Resorts** also offer quick access to those parks.

Though they're not centrally located, the **All-Star Resorts, Coronado Springs Resort,** and **Animal Kingdom Lodge & Villas** have very good bus service to all Disney World destinations and are closest to Animal Kingdom. Independent hotels on US 192 near the entrance to Walt Disney World are also just a few minutes from Animal Kingdom.

Bob: If you plan to use Disney transportation to visit all four major parks and one or both of the water parks, book a centrally located resort that has good transportation connections. The Epcot resorts and the Polynesian, Caribbean Beach, Art of Animation, Pop Century, and Port Orleans Resorts fill the bill.

Wilderness Lodge & Villas and Fort Wilderness Resort & Campground have the most convoluted and inconvenient transportation service of the Disney hotels. Old Key West Resort is also transportationally challenged in the sense that buses run less frequently there than they do at other Disney resorts. Spotty bus service is also a drawback shared by Saratoga Springs Resort and Treehouse Villas.

DRIVING TIME TO THE THEME PARKS				
MINUTES TO:	**MAGIC KINGDOM PARKING LOT**	**EPCOT PARKING LOT**	**DISNEY'S HOLLYWOOD STUDIOS PARKING LOT**	**DISNEY'S ANIMAL KINGDOM PARKING LOT**
FROM				
DOWNTOWN ORLANDO	35	31	33	37
NORTH INTERNATIONAL DRIVE AND UNIVERSAL STUDIOS	24	21	22	26
CENTRAL INTERNATIONAL DRIVE AND LAKE ROAD	26	23	24	27
SOUTH INTERNATIONAL DRIVE AND SEAWORLD	18	15	16	20
FL 535	12	9	10	13
US 192, NORTH OF I-4	10–15	7–12	5–10	5–10
US 192, SOUTH OF I-4	10–18	7–15	5–13	5–12

COMMUTING TO AND FROM THE THEME PARKS

FOR VISITORS LODGING INSIDE WALT DISNEY WORLD With three important exceptions, the fastest way to commute from your hotel to the theme parks and back is in your own car. And although many Walt Disney World guests use the Disney Transportation System and appreciate not having to drive, based on timed comparisons, it is almost always less time-consuming to drive. The exceptions are these: (1) commuting to the Magic Kingdom from the hotels on the monorail (Grand Floridian, Polynesian, Bay Lake Tower, and Contemporary Resorts); (2) commuting to the Magic Kingdom from any Disney hotel by bus or boat; and (3) commuting to Epcot on the monorail from the Polynesian Resort via the Transportation and Ticket Center.

If you stay at the Polynesian Resort, you can catch a direct monorail to the Magic Kingdom, and by walking 100 yards or so to the Transportation and Ticket Center, you can catch a direct monorail to Epcot. At the nexus of the monorail system, the Polynesian is certainly the most convenient of all hotels. From either the Magic Kingdom or Epcot, you can return to your hotel quickly and easily whenever you desire. Sound good? It is, but it costs $422–$1,060 per night.

Second to the Polynesian in terms of convenience are the Grand Floridian and Contemporary Resorts, also on the Magic Kingdom monorail, but they cost as much as or more than the Polynesian. Less expensive Disney hotels transport you to the Magic Kingdom by bus or boat. For reasons described below, this is more efficient than driving a car.

DRIVING TIME TO THE THEME PARKS FOR VISITORS LODGING OUTSIDE WALT DISNEY WORLD For vacationers staying outside Walt Disney World, we've calculated the approximate commuting time to the major theme parks' parking lots from several off-World lodging areas. Add a few minutes to our times to pay your parking fee and to park. Once parked at the Transportation and Ticket Center (Magic Kingdom parking lot), it takes an average of 20–30 more minutes to reach the Magic Kingdom. To reach Epcot from its parking lot, add 7–10 minutes. At Disney's Hollywood Studios and the Animal Kingdom, the lot-to-gate transit time is 5–10 minutes. If you haven't purchased your theme park admission in advance, tack on another 10–20 minutes.

Our WDW Resorts Chart on pages 109–111 shows the commuting time, with no consideration of getting to and from the parking lot to the turnstiles, to the Disney theme parks from each hotel listed. Those commuting times represent an average of several test runs. Your actual time may be shorter or longer depending on many variables.

SHUTTLE SERVICE FROM HOTELS OUTSIDE WALT DISNEY WORLD Many hotels in the Walt Disney World area provide shuttle service to the theme parks. They represent a fairly carefree alternative for getting to and from the parks, letting you off near the entrance (except for the Magic Kingdom) and saving you the cost of parking. The rub is that they might not get you there as early as you desire (a critical point if you take our touring advice) or be available at the time you wish to return to your lodging. Also, be forewarned that most shuttle services do not add vehicles at park opening or closing times. In the morning, your biggest problem is that you might not get a seat. At closing time, however, and sometimes following a hard rain, you can expect a lot of competition for standing space on the bus. If there's not room for everyone, you might have to wait 30 minutes to an hour for the next shuttle.

CONVENIENCE, CONVENIENTLY DEFINED Conceptually, it's easy to grasp that a hotel that is closer is more convenient than one that is far away. But nothing is that simple at Walt Disney World, so we'd better tell you exactly what you're in for. If you stay at a Walt Disney World resort and use the Disney transportation system, you'll have a 5- to 10-minute walk to the bus stop, monorail station, or dock (whichever applies). Once there, buses, trains, or boats generally run about every 15–25 minutes, so you might have to wait a short time for your transportation to arrive. Once you're on board, most conveyances make additional stops en route to your destination, and many take a less-than-direct route. Upon arrival, however, they deposit you fairly close to the entrance of the theme park. Returning to your hotel is the same process in reverse and takes about the same amount of time.

Regardless of whether or not you stay in Walt Disney World, if you use your own car, here's how your commute shakes out. After a 1- to 5-minute walk from your room to your car, you drive to the theme park, stopping to pay a parking fee or showing your Disney ID for free parking (if you are a Disney resort guest). Disney cast members then direct you to a parking space. If you arrive early, your space may be close enough to the park entrance (Magic Kingdom excepted) to walk. If you park farther afield, a Disney tram will come along every 5 minutes to collect you and transport you to the entrance.

At the Magic Kingdom, the entrance to the park is separated from the parking lot by the Transportation and Ticket Center (TTC) and the

Seven Seas Lagoon. After parking at the Magic Kingdom lot, you take a tram to the TTC and then board a ferry or monorail (your choice) for the trip across the lagoon to the park. All this is fairly time-consuming and is to be avoided if possible. The only way to avoid it, however, is to lodge in a Disney hotel and commute directly to the Magic Kingdom entrance via Disney bus, boat, or monorail. Happily, all of the other theme parks are situated adjacent to their parking lots.

Because families with children tend to spend more time on average at the Magic Kingdom than at the other parks, and because it's so important to return to your hotel for rest, the business of getting around the lagoon can be a major consideration when choosing a place to stay; the extra hassle of crossing the lagoon (to get back to your car) makes coming and going much more difficult. The half hour it takes to commute to your hotel via car from the Animal Kingdom, Disney's Hollywood Studios, or Epcot takes an hour or longer from the Magic Kingdom. If you stay in a Disney hotel and use the Disney transportation system, you may have to wait 5–25 minutes for your bus, boat, or monorail, but it will take you directly from the Magic Kingdom entrance to your hotel, bypassing the lagoon and the TTC.

DINING

DINING FIGURES INTO THE DISCUSSION of where to stay only if you don't plan to have a car at your disposal. If you plan on using the Disney Transportation System (for Disney hotel guests) or the courtesy shuttle of your non-Disney hotel, you will either have to dine at the theme parks or at or near your hotel. If your hotel offers a lot of choices or if other restaurants are within walking distance, then there's no problem. If your hotel is somewhat isolated and offers limited selections, you'll feel like Bob did on a canoe trip once when he ate northern pike at every meal for a week because that's all he could catch.

At Walt Disney World, although it's relatively quick and efficient to commute from your Disney hotel or campground to the theme parks, it's a long, arduous process requiring transfers to travel from hotel to hotel. Disney hotels that are somewhat isolated and that offer limited dining choices include the Old Key West, Caribbean Beach, All-Star, Pop Century, Art of Animation, Animal Kingdom Lodge, Coronado Springs, and Wilderness Lodge Resorts, as well as the Fort Wilderness Campground and most of the Saratoga Springs Resort.

If you want a condo-type accommodation so that you have more flexibility for meal preparation than eating out of a cooler, the best deals in Walt Disney World are the prefab log cabins at Fort Wilderness Resort & Campground. Other Disney lodgings with kitchens are available at the BoardWalk Villas, Old Key West, Saratoga Springs, Wilderness Lodge Villas, Animal Kingdom Villas, Bay Lake Tower, and the Beach Club Villas, but all are much more expensive than the cabins at the campground. Outside Walt Disney World, an ever-increasing number of condos are available, and some are very good deals. See our discussion of lodging outside of Walt Disney World later in this chapter.

THE SIZE OF YOUR GROUP

LARGER FAMILIES AND GROUPS MAY BE interested in how many people can stay in a Disney resort room, but only Lilliputians would be comfortable in a room filled to capacity. Groups requiring two or more rooms should consider condo, suite, or villa accommodations, either in or out of Walt Disney World. If there are more than six in your party, you will need either two hotel rooms, a suite (see Wilderness Lodge), or a condo.

STAYING IN OR OUT OF THE WORLD: WEIGHING THE PROS AND CONS

1. COST If cost is your primary consideration, you'll lodge much less expensively outside Walt Disney World.

2. EASE OF ACCESS Even if you stay in Disney World, you're dependent on some mode of transportation. It may be less stressful to use the Disney transportation system, but with the exception of commuting to the Magic Kingdom, the fastest, most efficient, and most flexible way to get around is usually a car. If you're at Epcot, for example, and want to take the kids back to Disney's Contemporary Resort for a nap, forget the monorail. You'll get back much faster by car.

 Liliane: If you share a room with your children, you all need to hit the sack at the same time. Establish a single compromise bedtime, probably a little early for you and a bit later than the children's usual weekend bedtime. Observe any nightly rituals you practice at home, such as reading a book before lights-out.

A reader from Raynham, Massachusetts, who stayed at the Caribbean Beach Resort writes:

Even though the resort is on the Disney bus line, I recommend renting a car if it fits one's budget. The buses don't go directly to many destinations, and often you have to switch buses. Getting a bus back to the hotel after a hard day can mean a long wait in line.

A Havertown, Pennsylvania, dad concurs regarding bus service:

WDW bus transportation is quite inefficient. When traveling from the BoardWalk to anywhere else, we had to pick up other passengers at the Swan, Dolphin, and Yacht and Beach Clubs before heading off to the parks. Same story upon return.

Although it's only for the use and benefit of Disney guests, the Disney transportation system is nonetheless public, and users must expect inconveniences: conveyances that arrive and depart on their schedule, not yours; the occasional need to transfer; multiple stops; time lost loading and unloading passengers; and, generally, the challenge of understanding and using a large, complex transportation network.

3. YOUNG CHILDREN Although the hassle of commuting to most non-Disney hotels is only slightly (if at all) greater than that of commuting to Disney hotels, a definite peace of mind results from staying in the World. Regardless of where you stay, make sure you get your young children back to the hotel for a nap each day.

HOTEL	MAXIMUM OCCUPANCY PER ROOM

All-Star Resorts | Standard room: 4 people plus child under age 3 in crib; **Family Suite:** 6 people plus child in crib

Animal Kingdom Lodge | 2–5 people plus child under age 3 in crib

Animal Kingdom Villas: Jambo House | Studio: 4 people; **1-bedroom:** 4 or 5 people; **2-bedroom:** 8 or 9 people; **Grand Villa:** 12 people; all plus child in crib

Animal Kingdom Villas: Kidani Village | Studio: 4 people; **1-bedroom:** 5 people; **2-bedroom:** 9 people; **Grand Villa:** 12 people; all plus child in crib

Art of Animation | Little Mermaid buildings: 4 people; **Cars, Finding Nemo, and Lion King buildings:** 6 people; all plus child in crib

Bay Lake Tower at the Contemporary Resort | Studio: 4 people; **1-bedroom:** 5 people; **2-bedroom:** 9 people; **Grand Villa:** 12 people; all plus child in crib

Beach Club Resort | 5 people plus child in crib

Beach Club Villas | Studio and 1-bedroom: 4 people; **2-bedroom:** 8 people; **Grand Villa:** 12 people; all plus child in crib

BoardWalk Inn | 4 people plus child in crib

BoardWalk Villas | Studio and 1-bedroom: 4 people; **2-bedroom:** 8 people; **Grand Villa:** 12 people; all plus child in crib

Caribbean Beach Resort | 4 people plus child in crib

Contemporary Resort | 5 people plus child in crib

Coronado Springs Resort | 4 people plus child in crib

Dolphin (Sheraton) | 4 people

Fort Wilderness Cabins | 6 people plus child in crib

Grand Floridian Resort | 5 people plus child in crib

Grand Floridian Villas | Studio and 1-bedroom: 5 people; **2-bedroom:** 9 or 10 people; **Grand Villa:** 12 people; all plus child in crib

Old Key West Resort | Studio: 4 people; **1-bedroom:** 5 people; **2-bedroom:** 9 people; **Grand Villa:** 12 people; all plus child in crib

Polynesian Resort | 5 people plus child in crib

Pop Century Resort | 4 people plus child in crib

Port Orleans French Quarter | 4 people plus child in crib

Port Orleans Riverside | 4 people plus child in crib or trundle bed

Saratoga Springs | Studio and 1-bedroom: 4 people; **2-bedroom:** 8 people; **Grand Villa:** 12 people; all plus child in crib

Swan (Westin) | 4 people

Treehouse Villas | 9 people plus child in crib

Wilderness Lodge | 4 people plus child in crib; junior suites with bunk beds accommodate 6 people

Wilderness Lodge Villas | Studio and 1-bedroom: 4 people; **2-bedroom:** 8 people

Yacht Club Resort | 5 people plus child in crib

4. SPLITTING UP If your party will likely split up to tour (as frequently happens in families with children of widely varying ages), staying in the World offers more transportation options, thus more independence. Mom and Dad can take the car and return to the hotel for a relaxed dinner and early bedtime, while the teens can remain in the park for evening parades and fireworks.

5. SLOPPIN' THE HOGS If you have a large crew that chows down like pigs at the trough, you may do better staying outside the World, where food is far less expensive.

6. VISITING OTHER ORLANDO-AREA ATTRACTIONS If you plan to visit SeaWorld, Kennedy Space Center, the Universal theme parks, or other area attractions, it may be more convenient to stay outside the World. Don't, however, book a hotel halfway to Orlando because you think you might run over to Universal or SeaWorld for a day. Remember the number-one rule: "Stay close enough to Walt Disney World to return to your hotel for rest in the middle of the day."

WALT DISNEY WORLD LODGING

BENEFITS OF STAYING IN WALT DISNEY WORLD

IN ADDITION TO PROXIMITY—especially easy access to the Magic Kingdom—Walt Disney World resort hotel and campground guests are accorded other privileges and amenities unavailable to those staying outside the World. Though some of these perks are only advertising gimmicks, others are potentially quite valuable. Here are the benefits and what they mean:

1. EXTRA MAGIC HOURS AT THE THEME PARKS 2. EXTRA MAGIC HOURS AT THE THEME PARKS Disney World lodging guests (excluding guests at the independent hotels of the Downtown Disney Resort Area, except the Hilton) are invited to enter a designated park 1 hour earlier than the general public each day or to enjoy a designated theme park for up to 2 hours after it closes to the general public in the evening. Early entry can be quite valuable if you know how to use it. It can also land you in gridlock.

2. THEME All of the Disney hotels are themed, in pointed contrast to non-Disney hotels, which are, well, mostly just hotels. Each Disney hotel is designed to make you feel that you're in a special place or period of history. See the chart on page 91 depicting the various hotels and their respective themes.

Themed rooms are a huge attraction for children, firing their imaginations and really making the hotel an adventure and a memorable place. Some resorts carry off their themes better than others, and some themes are more exciting. **Wilderness Lodge & Villas,** for example, is extraordinary. The lobby opens eight stories to a timbered ceiling supported by giant columns of bundled logs. One look eases you into the Northwest wilderness theme. The isolated lodge is heaven for kids.

Animal Kingdom Lodge & Villas replicates the grand safari lodges of Kenya and Tanzania and overlook their own private African-inspired game preserve. By far the most exotic of the Disney resorts, it's made to order for families with children.

Another kids' favorite is **Treehouse Villas at Saratoga Springs Resort.** Originally introduced in 1975, the tree house accommodations were closed and demolished in 2002. The new tree houses, designed in the adventurous image of their predecessors, are nestled in the woods alongside the Lake Buena Vista Golf Course.

The **Polynesian Resort,** also dramatic, conveys the feeling of the Pacific islands. It's great for families. Many waterfront rooms offer a perfect view of Cinderella Castle and the Magic Kingdom fireworks across Seven Seas Lagoon. Kids don't know Polynesia from amnesia, but they like those cool "lodge" buildings and all the torches at night.

Grandeur, nostalgia, and privilege are central to the **Grand Floridian,** the **Yacht & Beach Club Resorts,** the **Beach Club Villas, Saratoga Springs Resort,** and **BoardWalk Inn & Villas.** Although they're modeled after Eastern-seaboard hotels of different eras, the resorts are amazingly similar. Kids appreciate the creative swimming facilities of these resorts but are relatively neutral toward the themes.

The **Port Orleans Resort** lacks the real mystery and sultriness of the New Orleans French Quarter, but it's hard to replicate the Big Easy in a sanitized Disney version. The Riverside section of Port Orleans, however, hits the mark with its antebellum Mississippi River theme, as does **Old Key West Resort** with its Florida Keys theme. Children like each of these resorts, even though the themes are a bit removed from their frame of reference. The **Caribbean Beach Resort**'s theme is much more effective at night, thanks to creative lighting. By day, the resort looks like a Miami condo development. In 2009 the hotel created pirate-themed suites, which are a big hit with little buccaneers. The

Liliane: Coronado Springs and Port Orleans Riverside are among my favorite resorts.

playground and swimming pool fit in nicely with the pirate theme, and the shop has a large collection of toys from the *Pirates of the Caribbean* movies. All three resorts are more spread out and the buildings built to a more human (two- or three-story) scale.

Coronado Springs Resort offers several styles of Mexican and southwestern American architecture. Though the lake setting is lovely and the resort is attractive and inviting, the theme (with the exception of the main swimming area) isn't especially stimulating— more like a Scottsdale, Arizona, country club than a Disney resort.

The **All-Star Resorts** comprise 30 three-story, T-shaped hotels with almost 6,000 guest rooms. There are 15 themed areas: 5 celebrate sports (surfing, basketball, tennis, football, and baseball), 5 recall Hollywood movies, and 5 have musical motifs. The resort's design, with entrances shaped like giant Dalmatians, Coke cups, footballs, and the like, is pretty adolescent, sacrificing grace and beauty for energy and novelty. Guest rooms are small, with decor reminiscent of a teenage boy's bedroom. Despite the theme, there are no movies, sports, or music at All-Star Resorts. **Pop Century Resort** is pretty much a clone of All-Star Resorts, only this time the giant icons symbolize decades of the 20th century (Big Wheels, 45-rpm records, silhouettes of people doing

WALT DISNEY WORLD RESORT HOTEL THEMES	
HOTEL THEME	
ALL-STAR RESORTS Sports, movies, and music	
ANIMAL KINGDOM LODGE & VILLAS East African game-preserve lodge	
ART OF ANIMATION Disney's animated films	
BAY LAKE TOWER AT THE CONTEMPORARY Ultramodern high-rise	
BEACH CLUB RESORT & VILLAS New England beach club of the 1870s	
BOARDWALK INN East Coast boardwalk hotel of the early 1900s	
BOARDWALK VILLAS East Coast beach cottages of the early 1900s	
CARIBBEAN BEACH RESORT Caribbean islands	
CONTEMPORARY RESORT The future as envisioned by past and present generations	
CORONADO SPRINGS RESORT Northern Mexico and the American Southwest	
DOLPHIN (SHERATON) Modern Florida resort	
GRAND FLORIDIAN RESORT & VILLAS Turn-of-the-20th-century luxury hotel	
OLD KEY WEST RESORT Florida Keys	
POLYNESIAN RESORT Hawaii and South Seas islands	
POP CENTURY Popular-culture icons from various decades of the 20th century	
PORT ORLEANS FRENCH QUARTER Turn-of-the-19th-century New Orleans and Mardi Gras	
PORT ORLEANS RIVERSIDE Antebellum Louisiana plantation and bayou	
SARATOGA SPRINGS 1880s Victorian lakeside resort	
SWAN (WESTIN) Modern Florida resort	
TREEHOUSE VILLAS Rustic vacation homes with modern amenities	
WILDERNESS LODGE Grand national-park lodge of the early 1900s in the American Northwest	
YACHT CLUB RESORT New England seashore hotel of the 1880s	

period dances, and such), and period memorabilia decorate the rooms. Across the lake from Pop Century Resort is the **Art of Animation Resort,** with icons and decor based on four animated features: *Cars, Finding Nemo, The Lion King,* and *The Little Mermaid.*

Pretense aside, the **Contemporary, Bay Lake Tower, Swan,** and **Dolphin** are essentially themeless but architecturally interesting. The Contemporary is a 15-story, A-frame building with monorails running through the middle. Views from guest rooms in the Contemporary are among the best at Walt Disney World. Bay Lake Tower at the Contemporary Resort is a sleek, curvilinear high-rise offering bird's-eye views of Bay Lake. The Swan and Dolphin resorts are massive yet whimsical. Designed by Michael Graves, they're excellent examples of "entertainment architecture." Children are blown away by the giant sea creature and swans atop the Dolphin and Swan and love the idea of the monorail running through the middle of the Contemporary.

3. GREAT SWIMMING AREAS Walt Disney World resorts offer some of the most imaginative swimming facilities that you are likely to encounter anywhere. Exotically themed, beautifully landscaped, and equipped with slides, fountains, and smaller pools for toddlers, Disney resort swimming complexes are a quantum leap removed from the typical rectangular hotel pool. Some resorts, such as the Grand Floridian and the Polynesian, even offer a sand beach on the Seven Seas Lagoon in addition to swimming pools. Others, such as the Caribbean Beach and Port Orleans Resorts, have elaborately themed playgrounds near their swimming areas. Incidentally, lest there be any confusion, we are talking about Disney-hotel swimming areas and not the Disney paid-admission water theme parks (Typhoon Lagoon and Blizzard Beach).

Liliane: Just in case your luggage is delayed or your room isn't ready, always pack a change of clothes and bathing suits for all family members in your carry-on luggage.

4. DISNEY'S MAGICAL EXPRESS Checked baggage for those arriving in Orlando by commercial airliner are collected by Disney and sent via bus directly to your Walt Disney World resort, allowing you to bypass baggage claim. There's also a bus waiting to transport you to your hotel. If your flight arrives in Orlando close to or after 10 p.m., you must collect your own bags and bring them with you on the bus. Disney's Magical Express runs 24 hours a day.

If you are flying within the United States or Puerto Rico, when it's time to go home, you can check your baggage and receive your boarding pass at the front desk of your Disney resort. This service is available to all guests at Disney-owned resorts—but not the Swan, Dolphin, Shades of Green, or Downtown Disney resorts—even those who don't use the Magical Express service (folks who have rental cars, for example). Resort check-in counters are open 5 a.m.– 1 p.m., and you must check in no later than 3 hours before your flight. Participating airlines are **AirTran, Alaska, American, Delta, JetBlue, Southwest, United,** and **US Airways.** All of the preceding airlines have restrictions on the number of bags, checking procedures, and related items; consult your carrier before leaving home for specifics.

If your flight departs from Orlando before 8 a.m., Magical Express will pick you up before the Magical Express desk at your resort is open. In this case, because the desk isn't manned until 5 a.m., you cannot use the resort check-in for your bags or get your boarding pass. You'll need to handle your own luggage and get your boarding pass at the airport.

Travel agents report very few complaints about Magical Express. Still, the service is not without its faults. Luggage is transported by truck to Walt Disney World instead of accompanying you on the bus. Readers complain of luggage delivered to their hotel rooms hours late, sometimes in the middle of the night. If you want, you can collect your own luggage at the baggage claim and bring it along with you on the Magical Express bus. It isn't much extra trouble, and you will be at peace knowing where your luggage is at all times. If you arrive at your hotel with luggage in hand and your room isn't ready, the hotel will

WALT DISNEY WORLD RESORT SWIMMING POOLS:
Rated and Ranked

HOTEL	POOL RATING
1. YACHT & BEACH CLUB RESORTS & BEACH CLUB VILLAS *(shared complex)*	★★★★★
2. ANIMAL KINGDOM VILLAS *(Kidani Village)*	★★★★½
3. GRAND FLORIDIAN RESORT & VILLAS	★★★★½
4. PORT ORLEANS RESORT	★★★★½
5. SARATOGA SPRINGS RESORT & SPA, TREEHOUSE VILLAS	★★★★½
6. WILDERNESS LODGE & VILLAS	★★★★½
7. ANIMAL KINGDOM LODGE & VILLAS *(Jambo House)*	★★★★
8. BAY LAKE TOWER	★★★★
9. CORONADO SPRINGS RESORT	★★★★
10. DOLPHIN	★★★★
11. POLYNESIAN RESORT	★★★★
12. SWAN	★★★★
13. BOARDWALK INN & VILLAS	★★★½
14. CONTEMPORARY RESORT	★★★½
15. ALL-STAR RESORTS	★★★
16. ART OF ANIMATION RESORT	★★★
17. CARIBBEAN BEACH RESORT	★★★
18. OLD KEY WEST RESORT	★★★
19. FORT WILDERNESS RESORT & CAMPGROUND	★★★
20. POP CENTURY RESORT	★★★
21. SHADES OF GREEN	★★★

store your luggage and provide a phone number you can call to check the status of your room. Be forewarned that some buses go directly to your resort while others make multiple stops at other resorts. Regarding the return trip to the airport, we've received reports both of readers barely getting to the airport in time for their flight and of others made to depart from their hotel very early. One reader, for example, was picked up at 4:35 a.m. for a 7:40 a.m. flight.

3. BABYSITTING AND CHILD-CARE OPTIONS Disney hotel and campground guests have several options for babysitting, child care, and children's programs. The **Polynesian Resort** and **Animal Kingdom Lodge,** along with several other Disney hotels, offer "clubs"—themed childcare centers where potty-trained children ages 3–12 can stay while the adults go out.

Though somewhat expensive, the clubs do a great job and are highly regarded by children and parents. On the negative side, they're open only in the evening, and not all Disney hotels have them. If you're staying at a Disney hotel that doesn't have a child-care club, you're better off using a private in-room babysitting service (see page 75). In-room babysitting is also available at hotels outside Disney World.

5. PRIORITY THEME PARK ADMISSIONS On days of unusually heavy attendance, Disney may restrict admission into the theme parks for all customers. When deciding whom to admit into the parks, priority is given to guests staying at Disney resorts. In practice, no guest is turned away until a park's parking lot is full. When this happens, that park will be packed to gridlock.

7. CHILDREN SHARING A ROOM WITH THEIR PARENTS There is no extra charge per night for children younger than age 18 sharing a room with their parents. Many hotels outside Walt Disney World also observe this practice.

7. FREE PARKING Disney resort guests with cars pay nothing to park in theme park lots. This saves $15 per day.

WALT DISNEY WORLD HOTELS: *Strengths and Weaknesses for Families*

FOR THE SAKE OF ORIENTATION, we've grouped the Disney resorts, as well as the Swan and Dolphin resorts, by location. Closest to the Magic Kingdom are the **Grand Floridian, Polynesian, Bay Lake Tower,** and Contemporary Resorts, all on the monorail; the **Wilderness Lodge & Villas** and **Fort Wilderness Resort & Campground,** which are connected to the Magic Kingdom by boat; and the U.S. military resort, **Shades of Green,** served exclusively by bus.

Close to Epcot are the Yacht & Beach Club Resorts, the Beach Club Villas, the BoardWalk Inn & Villas, and the non-Disney-owned Swan and Dolphin Resorts. These are the closest hotels to Disney's Hollywood Studios.

Closer to Downtown Disney and Bonnet Creek are the Old Key West, Saratoga Springs, Port Orleans, Caribbean Beach, Pop Century, and Art of Animation Resorts. Also nearby are the seven independent hotels of the Downtown Disney Resort Area.

The All-Star and the Coronado Springs Resorts are located near both Disney's Hollywood Studios and the Animal Kingdom. Closest to the Animal Kingdom is The Animal Kingdom Lodge & Villas.

MAGIC KINGDOM RESORTS

Disney's Grand Floridian Resort & Spa

THE GRAND FLORIDIAN HAS A LOT TO OFFER: a white-sand beach, a spa and fitness center, tennis courts, elaborate theatrical dining from high tea to personal butler service, and so on. But the tone strikes some people as rather hoity-toity, the music in the lobby can be disconcertingly loud, the rooms are not as expansive or good-looking as the public spaces, and the complex is frequently crowded with sightseers and

STRENGTHS	WEAKNESSES
• On Magic Kingdom monorail	• Cavernous, impersonal lobby
• Ferry service to Magic Kingdom	• Overly large physical layout
• Excellent guest rooms	• Children don't get the theme
• Children's programs, character meals	• Only one on-site restaurant suitable for younger children
• Excellent children's pool	• Imposing, rather formal public areas
• Beach	• Distant guest self-parking
• Diverse recreational options	
• Good restaurant selection via monorail	
• On-site child care	

plantation nostalgics waving fat cigars. Also, because a wedding chapel is on the grounds, there are frequently receptions, photo sessions, and tizzies—which, depending on your outlook, add charm or are inconveniences. The Villas at the Grand Floridian, a Disney Vacation Club property, is scheduled to open in the fall of 2013. This new T-shaped building, situated between the main building and the Polynesian Resort, along Seven Seas Lagoon, will have 200 rooms in studio, one-, two-, and three-bedroom configurations, along with a 0.25-acre kids' pool.

Disney's Polynesian Resort

STRENGTHS	
• Relaxed and casual ambience	• Excellent swimming complex
• Ferry service to Magic Kingdom	• Recreational options
• Exotic theme that children love	• Good restaurant selection via monorail
• On Magic Kingdom monorail	• WDW's best child-care facility on-site
• Epcot monorail within walking distance	• Easily accessible self-parking
• Transportation and Ticket Center adjoins resort	**WEAKNESSES**
• Rooms among the nicest at WDW	• Overly large and confusing layout
• Children's programs, character meals	• Walkways exposed to rain
• Beach and marina	• Noise from nearby motor speedway and ferry
	• Front-desk inefficiency

THE POLYNESIAN IS ARRAYED along the Seven Seas Lagoon facing the Magic Kingdom. It's a huge complex, but the hotel buildings, laid out like a South Seas–island village around a ceremonial house, are of a decidedly human scale compared with the hulking Grand Floridian and Contemporary Resorts. From the tiki torches at night to the bleached-sand beach, kids love the Polynesian. The resort's location at WDW's transportation nexus makes it the most convenient resort for those without a car. Though the Polynesian is one of Disney's oldest resorts, periodic refurbishments keep it well maintained.

Disney's Contemporary Resort and Bay Lake Tower

THE CONTEMPORARY RESORT has a sleek, almost Asian look, although the pyramid structure itself is a period piece, of course. And it

DISNEY'S CONTEMPORARY RESORT AND BAY LAKE TOWER

STRENGTHS

- On Magic Kingdom monorail
- 10-minute walk to Magic Kingdom
- Interesting architecture
- Nicest guest rooms at WDW
- Super views of the Magic Kingdom or Bay Lake
- Character meals
- Excellent children's pool
- Marina
- Recreational options, including super games arcade
- Good restaurant selection via monorail
- On-site child care
- Good restaurant on-site

WEAKNESS

- Monorail aside, the theme leaves children cold

has lots to offer the active family: six lighted tennis courts, three swimming pools, a health club, volleyball courts, a beach, and a marina that rents sailboats of various sizes—you must be at least 18 years old, which helps limit the traffic a little—and offers parasailing and waterskiing. Guest rooms are quite stunning and, in our opinion, the nicest to be found at Walt Disney World. There's no compelling theme, but then show me a child who isn't wowed by monorails tearing though the inside of a hotel. The Bay Lake Tower is a high-rise Disney Vacation Club property situated on Bay Lake between the Contemporary Resort and the Magic Kingdom. Like other DVC developments, it offers one-, two-, and three-bedroom suites. Features include a fireworks-viewing deck, a rooftop lounge, a lakeside pool, and a sky bridge linking the tower to the Contemporary Resort's monorail station.

Wilderness Lodge & Villas

STRENGTHS

- Magnificently rendered theme that children can't get enough of
- Good on-site dining
- Great views from guest rooms
- Extensive recreational options
- Romantic setting and interesting architecture
- Elaborate swimming complex
- Health and fitness center
- On-site child care
- Convenient self-parking

WEAKNESSES

- Boat service only to Magic Kingdom
- No direct bus to many destinations
- No character meals
- Rooms sleep only four people (plus child in crib)
- Must take boat or bus to access off-site dining options

THIS DELUXE RESORT IS INSPIRED by national-park lodges of the early 20th century. Wilderness Lodge & Villas ranks with Animal Kingdom Lodge & Villas as one of the most impressively themed and meticulously detailed Disney resorts. It's also by far the hands-down favorite hotel of children. You won't have any trouble convincing the kids to abandon the theme parks for rest and a swim if you stay at the Wilderness Lodge.

On the shore of Bay Lake, the lodge consists of an eight-story central building flanked by two seven-story guest wings and a wing of studio and one- and two-bedroom condominiums. The hotel features exposed timber columns, log cabin–style facades, and dormer windows. The grounds are landscaped with evergreen pines and pampas grass. The lobby boasts an 82-foot-tall stone fireplace and two 55-foot Pacific Northwest totem poles. Timber pillars, giant tepee chandeliers, and stone- and wood-inlaid floors accentuate the lobby's rustic luxury. Although the resort isn't on vast acreage, it does have a beach and a delightful pool modeled on a mountain stream complete with waterfall and geyser. Adjoining the Wilderness Lodge are the Wilderness Lodge Villas, a Disney Vacation Club property.

Shades of Green

STRENGTHS	• Video arcade
• Large guest rooms	• Game room with pool tables
• Informality	• Ice-cream shop
• Quiet setting	**WEAKNESSES**
• Views of golf course from guest rooms	• No interesting theme
• Convenient self-parking	• Limited on-site dining
• Swimming complex, fitness center	• Limited bus service

THIS DELUXE RESORT IS OWNED and operated by the U.S. Armed Forces and is open only to U.S. military personnel (including members of the National Guard and reserves, retired military, and employees of the U.S. Public Health Service and the Department of Defense; others may be eligible; call for additional information). Shades of Green consists of one three-story building nestled among three golf courses. Tastefully nondescript, Shades of Green is at the same time pure peace and quiet. There's no beach or lake, but there are several pools, including one shaped like Mickey's head. Surrounding golf courses are open to all Disney guests. If you qualify to stay here, don't even think about staying anywhere else.

Disney's Fort Wilderness Resort & Campground

IF CAMPING IS ONE OF YOUR HOBBIES, you can rough it in beautiful territory at Fort Wilderness for as little as $48 per campsite. Either set up a tent and use the restrooms, showers, and Laundromat down the lane, or borrow your parents' RV. With the accessibility of two markets on-site, most visitors here choose to do their own cooking; do so and this becomes the absolute rock-bottom-priced Disney World vacation.

784 CAMPSITES $48–$132 per night; boat and bus service

408 WILDERNESS HOMES AND CABINS $289–$481 per night (sleep 4–6); boat and bus service

Fort Wilderness is ideal for nature lovers. For the less active, electric carts are for rent. Also available are pools, a marina, a beach, and outdoor games such as basketball, volleyball, shuffleboard, fishing, canoeing, biking, and even tennis and horseback riding. If you really get into the mood, you can sit around the evening campfire and watch a movie with the other happy campers. The campgrounds are the only accommodations that allow you to have pets (not running loose, of course).

FORT WILDERNESS RESORT & CAMPGROUND

STRENGTHS	WEAKNESSES
• Informality	• Isolated location
• Children's play areas	• Complicated bus service
• Best selection of recreational options at WDW	• Confusing campground layout
	• Lack of privacy
• Special day and evening programs	• Very limited on-site dining options
• Campsite amenities	• Extreme distance to store and restaurant facilities from many campsites
• Number of showers and toilets	
• *Hoop-Dee-Doo Musical Revue* dinner show	• Crowding at beaches and pools
	• Small baths in cabins
• Convenient self-parking	• Extreme distance to store and restaurant facilities from many campsites
• Off-site dining options via boat at Magic Kingdom resorts	

Here's what you *can't* do: drive anywhere within the campground, not even from your campsite back to the trading post. You must take the bus, bike, or golf cart (both are for rent), or walk (it's not far). And bus or boat transportation to the theme parks can be laborious.

Obviously, Fort Wilderness draws a lot of families (did we mention the petting farm and the hay rides?), and in hot weather, a lot of bugs and thunderstorms. If you want things a little more comfortable, ask for a full-service hookup and get water, electricity, an outdoor grill, sanitary disposal, and even a cable-TV connection. If you want super privacy and even more amenities, rent one of the prefab log cabins, which get you a full kitchen, housekeeping services, air-conditioning, a daily newspaper, voice mail, and, yes, cable TV.

Bob: All loops have a comfort station with showers, toilets, phones, an ice machine, and a coin laundry.

For tent and RV campers, there's a fairly stark trade-off between sites convenient to pools, restaurant, trading posts, and other amenities, and those that are most scenic, shady, and quiet. RVers who prefer to be near guest services, the marina, the beach, and the restaurant and tavern should go for Loops 100, 200, 700, and 400 (in that order). Loops near the campground's secondary facility area with pool, trading post, bike and golf-cart rentals, and campfire program are 1400, 1300, 600, 1000, and 1500, in order of preference. If you're looking for a tranquil, scenic setting among mature trees, we recommend Loops 1800, 1900, 1700, and 1600, in that order, and the backside sites on the 700 loop. The best loop of all, and the only one to offer both a lovely setting and proximity to key amenities, is Loop 300. The best loops for tents and pop-up campers are 1500 and 2000, with 1500 being nearest a pool, a convenience store, and the campfire program.

EPCOT RESORTS

Disney's Yacht & Beach Club Resorts and Beach Club Villas

SITUATED ON CRESCENT LAKE across from Disney's BoardWalk, the Yacht & Beach Club Resorts are connected and share a boardwalk,

STRENGTHS	
• Fun and nautical New England theme	• Best resort swimming complex at WDW
• Attractive guest rooms	• Health and fitness center
• Good on-site dining	• Convenient self-parking
• Children's programs, character meals	• View from waterside guest rooms
• Excellent selection of nearby off-site dining	• On-site child care
• Boat service to DHS and Epcot	**WEAKNESSES**
• 10-minute walk to rear entrance of Epcot	• No transportation to Epcot main entrance except by taxi
• 10-minute walk to BoardWalk	• No convenient counter-service food
• 15-minute walk to DHS	• Poor room-to-hall soundproofing

marina, and swimming complex. The Yacht Club Resort has a breezy Nantucket and Cape Cod atmosphere with its own lighthouse and boardwalks, lots of polished wood, and burnished brass (and boxes of chess or checkers pieces available for your room on request). Its sibling resort, the Beach Club, shares most of the facilities but is a little sportier and more casual in atmosphere. The Disney Vacation Club Villas at the Beach Club are available for rental, have their own small pool, and may offer more privacy. The resorts offer a shared mini–water park, Storm-along Bay, with a white-sand beach and marina, and an unusual number of sports facilities, such as croquet, tennis, and volleyball, plus fitness rooms, and so on. Many of the rooms have balconies with views looking out across the lagoon toward the BoardWalk.

Disney's BoardWalk Inn & Villas

STRENGTHS	
• Lively seaside and amusement-pier theme	• Health and fitness center
• Newly refurbished guest rooms	• View from waterside guest rooms
• 10-minute walk to Epcot rear entrance	• On-site child care
• 15-minute walk to DHS	**WEAKNESSES**
• Boat service to DHS and Epcot	• No restaurants in hotel
• Modest but well-themed swimming complex	• Limited children's activities and no character meals
• 3-minute walk to BoardWalk midway and nightlife	• No restaurants within easy walking distance suitable for children
• Selection of off-site dining within walking distance	• No transportation to Epcot main entrance
	• Distant guest self-parking

ALSO ON CRESCENT LAKE, the BoardWalk Inn is another of the Walt Disney World Deluxe resorts. The complex is a detailed replica of an early-20th-century Atlantic-coast boardwalk. Facades of hotels, diners, and shops create an inviting and exciting waterfront skyline. In reality, behind the facades, the BoardWalk Inn & Villas are a single integrated structure. Restaurants and shops occupy the boardwalk level, while accommodations rise up to six stories above. Painted bright red and yellow along with weathered pastel greens and blues, the BoardWalk resorts are the only Disney hotels that use neon signs as architectural detail. The inn and villas share one pool with an old-fashioned amusement-park theme and also have two quiet pools.

The BoardWalk Inn & Villas have a lot to offer in terms of entertainment, in that the ESPN Club, the carnival midway, street performers, and for adults, BoardWalk nightspots, are all literally at your feet. The downside: When you're ready to call it quits, the sound can come right up through the building, and odd lights are glaring at all hours.

The Walt Disney World Swan and Walt Disney World Dolphin

STRENGTHS	• Participates in Extra Magic Hours program
• Exotic architecture	• View from guest rooms
• Extremely nice guest rooms	**WEAKNESSES**
• Good on-site and nearby dining	• Primarily adult convention and business clientele
• Excellent beach and swimming complex	• No transportation to Epcot main entrance
• Health and fitness center	• Distant guest self-parking, requires daily fee
• Child-care facilities on-site	• Do not qualify for Disney's Magical Express service
• Children's programs, character meals	• Confusing layout
• Varied recreational offerings	
• 10-minute walk to BoardWalk nightlife	
• Boat service to DHS and Epcot	

THE SWAN AND DOLPHIN RESORTS were not designed by Disney Imagineers, though you might certainly think they were. They were the playgrounds of postmodern architect Michael Graves; in fact, they are not Disney-owned properties at all, though guests have most of the perks. The Swan and Dolphin are patronized by business types and adult travelers rather than families, and their theme runs more to the surrealistic rather than to the whimsical. That being said, a quick glance at the Swan and Dolphin's strengths will verify that they have as much or more to offer families than the Disney resorts.

BONNET CREEK/ DOWNTOWN DISNEY AREA RESORTS

Disney's Caribbean Beach Resort

THE CARIBBEAN BEACH RESORT OCCUPIES 200 acres surrounding a 45-acre lake called Barefoot Bay. This midpriced resort, modeled after resorts in the Caribbean, consists of the registration area (Custom House) and six two-story "villages" named after Caribbean islands. Each village has its own pool, laundry room, and beach. The Caribbean motif is maintained with red-metal roofs, widow's walks, and wooden-railed porches. The atmosphere is cheerful, with buildings painted blue, lime green, and sherbet orange. Rooms in the Trinidad South village have been refurbished and rethemed to include characters from *Finding Nemo* and *Pirates of the Caribbean*. In addition to the five village pools,

STRENGTHS	• No easily accessible off-site dining
• Attractive Caribbean theme	• No character meals
• Children's play areas	• Extreme distance of many guest
• Convenient self-parking	rooms from dining and services
• Walking, jogging, biking	• Occasionally poor bus service
• Lakefront setting	• Large, confusing layout
WEAKNESSES	• Long lines to check in
• Lackluster on-site dining	

the resort's main swimming pool is themed as an old Spanish fort, complete with slides and water cannons.

Disney's Port Orleans Resort: French Quarter and Riverside

STRENGTHS	WEAKNESSES
• Extremely creative swimming areas	• No character meals
• Nice guest rooms, especially in the French Quarter	• Insufficient on-site dining
• Pleasant setting along Bonnet Creek	• No easily accessible off-site dining
• Food courts	• Extreme distance of many guest rooms from dining and services
• Convenient self-parking	• Large, confusing layout
• Children's play areas	• Congested bus-loading areas
• Varied recreational offerings	
• Boat service to Downtown Disney	

PORT ORLEANS RIVERSIDE AND FRENCH QUARTER RESORTS are good-looking, lower-cost hotel alternatives that combine steamboat-era Southern decor and fairly easy access to Downtown Disney, and they're pretty popular among families too.

The 1,008-room French Quarter section is a sanitized Disney version of the New Orleans French Quarter. Consisting of seven three-story buildings next to Bonnet Creek, the resort suggests what New Orleans would look like if its buildings were painted every year and garbage collectors never went on strike. There are prim pink-and-blue guest buildings with wrought-iron filigree, shuttered windows, and old-fashioned iron lampposts. In keeping with the Crescent City theme, the French Quarter is landscaped with magnolia trees and overgrown vines. The centrally located Mint contains the registration area and food court and is a reproduction of a turn-of-the-19th-century building where Mississippi Delta farmers sold their harvests. The registration desk features a vibrant Mardi Gras mural and old-fashioned bank-teller windows. The section's Doubloon Lagoon swimming complex surrounds a colorful fiberglass creation depicting Neptune riding a sea serpent. We think that the French Quarter has the most attractive and tasteful rooms of any of the Disney Moderate resorts.

Port Orleans's Riverside Resort draws on the lifestyle and architecture of Mississippi River communities in antebellum Louisiana. Spread along Bonnet Creek, which encircles Ol' Man Island (the section's main swimming area), Riverside is subdivided into two more themed areas: the "mansion" area, featuring plantation-style architecture, and the "bayou" area, with tin-roofed imitation-rustic wooden buildings. Mansions are three stories tall, while bayou guesthouses are a story shorter. The river-life theme is augmented by groves of azalea and juniper. Riverside's food court houses a working cotton press powered by a 35-foot waterwheel. New at Riverside is a set of 512 rooms themed after Disney's *The Princess and the Frog.*

Disney's Old Key West Resort

STRENGTHS	WEAKNESSES
• Extremely nice studios and villas	• Old Key West theme meaningless to children
• Full kitchens in villas	• Large, confusing layout
• Quiet, lushly landscaped setting	• Substandard bus service
• Convenient self-parking	• Limited on-site dining
• Small, more private swimming pools in each accommodations cluster	• No easily accessible off-site dining
• Recreation options	• Extreme distance of many guest rooms from dining and services
• Boat service to Downtown Disney	• No character meals

THIS WAS THE FIRST DISNEY VACATION CLUB PROPERTY. Although the resort is a time-share property, units not being used by owners are rented on a nightly basis. Old Key West is a large aggregation of two- to three-story buildings modeled after Caribbean-style residences and guesthouses of the Florida Keys. Arranged subdivision-style around a golf course and along Bonnet Creek, the buildings are in small neighborhood-like clusters. They feature pastel facades, white trim, and shuttered windows. The registration area is in Conch Flats Community Hall, along with a full-service restaurant, modest fitness center, marina, and sundries shop. Each cluster of accommodations has a quiet pool; a larger pool is at the community hall. A waterslide in the shape of a giant sand castle is the primary kid pleaser at the main pool.

Disney's Saratoga Springs Resort & Spa

THE MAIN POOL IS THIS RESORT'S FOCAL POINT. Called High Rock Spring, it tumbles over boulders into a clear, free-form heated pool. The area offers a waterslide that winds among the rocks, two whirlpool spas, and an interactive wet-play area for children. The Saratoga Springs complex will eventually be the largest Vacation Club resort, with well over 800 units. It's expanding toward the Downtown Disney shopping area (across the lake) via a path and a pedestrian bridge. There is boat as well as bus service at the facility, although the boats are prohibited from running if lightning threatens. The resort's decor plays on the history and retro-Victorian style of the upstate New York racing resort, with traditional horse-country prints and drawings, stable boy uniforms for the bellhops, and so on. The spa, probably Disney's best, has a fitness center

STRENGTHS	WEAKNESSES
• Extremely nice studio rooms and villas	• Traffic congestion at resort's southeast exit
• Lushly landscaped setting	
• Best fitness center at Walt Disney World	• Small living areas in villas
	• Distance of some accommodations from dining and services
• Convenient self-parking	
• Close to Downtown Disney	• Limited dining options
• Best spa at Walt Disney World	• No character meals
• Excellent themed swimming complex	• Most distant of all Disney resorts from the theme parks
• Hiking, jogging, and water recreation	
	• Theme and atmosphere not very kid-friendly

attached. The Downtown Disney fireworks are visible from some areas. Favorites for children are the Treehouse Villas, nestled in a pine wood bordering the golf course. With the entire living and sleeping area about 12 feet off the ground, you really do feel like you're living in a tree house. Opened in 2009, the rustic Treehouse Villas are among Walt Disney World's most inventive accommodations. There are only 60 three-bedroom units, so if you want to reserve one of those, book well in advance.

Disney's Pop Century Resort

STRENGTHS	WEAKNESSES
• Kid-friendly theme	• Small guest rooms
• Low (for Disney) rates	• No full-service dining
• Large swimming pools	• Large, confusing layout
• Food court	• No character meals
• Convenient self-parking	• Limited recreation options
• Fast check-in	

ON VICTORY WAY near the ESPN Wide World of Sports Complex is Pop Century Resort. Originally designed to be completed in phases, the first section opened in 2004. The long-planned second phase of Pop Century was canceled in favor of a new Value resort, Art of Animation (see profile on the next page).

Pop Century is an economy resort. In terms of layout, architecture, and facilities, Pop Century is almost a clone of the All-Star Resorts (that is, four-story, motel-style buildings built around a central pool, food court, and registration area). Decorative touches make the difference. Where the All-Star Resorts display larger-than-life icons from sports, music, and movies, Pop Century draws its icons from decades of the 20th century. Look for such oddities as building-size Big Wheels, hula hoops, and the like, punctuated by silhouettes of people dancing the decade's fad dance.

The public areas at Pop Century are marginally more sophisticated than the ones at the All-Star Resorts, with 20th-century period furniture and decor rolled up in a saccharine, those-were-the-days theme. A food court, bar, playground, pools, and so on emulate the All-Star Resorts model in size and location. A Pop Century departure from the All-Star precedent has merchandise retailers thrown in with the fast-food concessions in a combination dining and shopping area. This apparently is what happens when a giant corporation tries to combine selling pizza with hawking Goofy hats. (You just know the word *synergy* was used like cheap cologne in those design meetings.) The resort is connected to the rest of Walt Disney World by bus, but because of the limited dining options, we recommend having a car.

If you're considering one of the Disney Value resorts, this reader from Dublin, Georgia, thinks Pop Century beats the All-Star Resorts hands-down.

Pop Century is far superior to the All-Stars. (1) There's a lake at a Value resort and a view of fireworks. (2) The courtyards have Twister games, neat pools, and a Goofy "surprise fountain" for little children. (3) The memorabilia is interesting to us over 18 years old. (4) I love the gift shop, food court, and bar combo. The shrimp lo mein is the best bargain and among the best food anywhere. (5) There are frozen Cokes in the refillable-mug section. (6) Bus transportation is better than anywhere else, including Grand Floridian! (7) The layout is more convenient to the food court. (8) I never hear construction noise, and the noise from neighbors is not worse than anywhere else. (9) Where else do the cast members do the shag to oldies?

Disney's Art of Animation Resort

OPENED IN MAY 2012, Art of Animation Resort draws its inspiration from four classic Disney animated films: *The Lion King, The Little Mermaid,* and Disney-Pixar's *Finding Nemo* and *Cars.*

The new Value resort, located across Hour Glass Lake from Pop Century, has 864 rooms and 1,120 family suites. These suites have two separate bathrooms, a master bedroom, three separate sleeping areas within the living space, and a kitchenette. The resort consists of four-story buildings and exterior-facing rooms and a series of themed swimming pools, including a large feature pool at the *Finding Nemo* courtyard. A water play area, as well as a 68,800-square-foot commercial building with shopping and dining space, completes the picture. Expect to see large, colorful icons of the film's characters throughout the grounds. The wall behind the front check-in desk is a dazzling rainbow of colors from floor to ceiling. In sharp contrast to the faded paints and photos at, say, the All-Star Resorts, Animation's backlight displays and wall art are bright and vibrant and should stand up better to Florida's weather.

Liliane: Anything that makes a food court feel less like a school cafeteria is very welcome.

Disney also tested new approaches with some of the hotel's fundamental features. For example, the massive counter-service-dining area is sectioned off into four separate themed seating areas featuring some new-for-Disney quick-service food concepts, including fresh-fruit smoothies, a Mongolian grill, and a customized hamburger station.

STRENGTHS	WEAKNESSES
• Kid-friendly theme	• Small standard guest rooms
• Low (for Disney) rates	• No full-service dining
• Large swimming pools	• Large, confusing layout
• Food court	• No character meals
• Convenient self-parking	• Limited recreation options

Reader reports on Art of Animation have mostly been positive. This comment from a Red Oak, Texas, mom is representative:

The Art of Animation Resort is fabulous. The rooms were very neat. Because we have a family of six, we stayed in a suite. There was plenty of room for our entire family. We had a queen bed in a separate room. Our kids slept in the living-room area. Two children shared the sofa bed while the other two shared the Murphy bed. We all slept very comfortably. I don't recall hearing any outside noises even though we faced the middle courtyard. We were in the Cars-*themed rooms, and the decorations were fantastic. Our family loved all of the life-size* Cars *characters outside on the grounds. The pool was beautiful with the* Finding Nemo *decorations. The kids were excited that they could hear real music when they were swimming under water.*

ANIMAL KINGDOM RESORTS

Disney's Animal Kingdom Lodge & Villas

STRENGTHS	
• Exotic theme	• On-site nature programs and storytelling
• Uniquely appointed guest rooms	• Health and fitness center
• Most rooms have private balconies	• Child-care center on-site
• View of savanna and animals from guest rooms	• Proximity to non-Disney restaurants on US 192
• Themed swimming areas	**WEAKNESS**
• Excellent on-site dining, including a buffet	• Remote location

ANIMAL KINGDOM LODGE is a snazzy take on safari chic, with balcony views of wildlife that alone may be worth the tabs, but its distance from the other parks may be a drawback for those planning to explore all of Disney World. On the other hand, if you have a car, it's the closest resort to all of the affordable family restaurants lining US 192 (Irlo Bronson Memorial Highway). By far the most exotic Disney resort, it's tailor-made for families.

Designed by Peter Dominick of Wilderness Lodge fame, Animal Kingdom Lodge fuses African tribal architecture with the rugged style of grand East African national-park lodges. Five-story thatched-roof wings fan out from a vast central rotunda housing the lobby and featuring a huge mud fireplace. Public areas and many rooms offer panoramic views of a private 33-acre wildlife preserve punctuated with streams and elevated kopje (rock outcrops) and populated with 100 types of free-roaming animals and 130 birds. Most guest rooms boast hand-carved furnishings and richly colored upholstery. Almost all rooms have full balconies.

Studio and one-, two-, and three-bedroom villa accommodations are available in Jambo House (the main building) and at adjacent Kidani Village, a Disney Vacation Club property. Having stayed at Kidani Village, we think it's a quieter, more relaxed resort. The lobby and rooms have a smaller, more personal feel than Jambo House. The building's exterior isn't anything special—essentially a set of green rectangles with oversize African-themed decorations attached. Kidani's distance from Jambo House makes it feel remote. The bus stops are a fair distance from the main building too, and it's easy to head in the wrong direction when you're coming back from the parks at night.

Disney's Coronado Springs Resort

STRENGTHS	• Nightclub on property
• Nice guest rooms	• Convenient self-parking
• View from waterside guest rooms	**WEAKNESSES**
• Food court	• Insufficient on-site dining
• Mayan-themed swimming area with waterslides	• *Extreme* distance of many guest rooms from dining and services
• Fitness center	• No character meals

TO SAVE A LITTLE MONEY without giving up services, consider the Coronado Springs Resort, a rich, Old Mexico–style complex with courtyards, fountains, stucco and terra-cotta buildings, a few Mayan ruins here and there, several swimming pools, a mini water park, a white-sand beach, a fitness center, a walking path circling a 22-acre lake, and a nightclub. Because it's also a convention hotel, expect a high percentage of guests to be business travelers. Coronado Springs has particularly good access to Animal Kingdom and Blizzard Beach.

Disney's All-Star Resorts: Movies, Music, and Sports

DISNEY'S VERSION OF A BUDGET RESORT features three distinct themes executed in the same hyperbolic style. Spread over a vast expanse, the resorts comprise almost 35 three-story motel-style guest-room buildings. Although the three resorts are neighbors, each has its own lobby, food court, and registration area. All-Star Sports Resort features huge sports icons: bright football helmets, tennis rackets, and baseball bats—all taller than the buildings they adorn. Similarly, All-Star Music Resort features 40-foot guitars, maracas, and saxophones, while All-Star Movies Resort showcases giant popcorn boxes and icons from Disney films. Lobbies of all are loud (in both decibels and brightness) and cartoonish, with checkerboard walls and photographs of famous athletes, musicians, and film stars. At 260 square feet, guest rooms at the All-Star Resorts are very small. They're so small that a family of four attempting to stay in one room might redefine family values by week's

STRENGTHS	• Small guest rooms (except family suites)
• Super kid-friendly theme	• No full-service dining
• Low (for Disney) rates	• Large, confusing layout
• Large swimming pools	• Congested bus-loading areas
• Food courts	• No character meals
• Convenient self-parking	• Limited recreation options
WEAKNESSES	• Close to McDonald's (no kidding!)
• Remote location	

end. Definitely a family resort, young children exercising their lungs make the All-Stars the noisiest Disney resorts, though guest rooms are well soundproofed and quiet.

All-Star Music has 192 Family Suites in the Jazz and Calypso Buildings. Suites measure roughly 520 square feet, slightly larger than the cabins at Fort Wilderness. Each suite, formed from the combination of two formerly separate rooms, includes a kitchenette with mini-refrigerator, microwave, and coffeemaker. Sleeping accommodations include a queen bed in the bedroom, plus a pullout sleeper sofa, a chair bed, and an ottoman bed. We're not sure we'd let adult friends (or friends we wanted to keep, anyway) sleep on the sofa bed or the chair or ottoman beds, but they're fine for children. A hefty door separates the two rooms.

We receive a lot of letters commenting on the All-Star Resorts. From a Massachusetts family of four:

> *I would never recommend the All-Star for a family. It was like dormitory living. Our room was about 1 mile from the bus stop, and the room was tiny—you needed to step into the bathroom, shut the door, then step around the toilet that blocked half the tub.*

But a Baltimore family had a very positive experience:

> *We were pleasantly surprised by All-Star Movies. Yes, the rooms are small, but the overall magic there is amazing. The lobby played Disney movies, which is perfect if you get up early and the buses aren't running yet. There are great photo ops everywhere (Donald and Daisy were awesome). Customer service was impeccable.*

Finally, a dad from Rogers, Arkansas, had this to say:

> *Make sure that people understand how inconvenient the shuttle service becomes when you have to share one bus for all three All-Star Resorts. This one issue ruined what was an otherwise very pleasant experience.*

INDEPENDENT HOTELS OF THE DOWNTOWN DISNEY RESORT AREA

THE SEVEN HOTELS OF THE DOWNTOWN DISNEY RESORT AREA (DDRA) were created in the days when Disney had far fewer of its own resorts. The hotels—the **Best Western Lake Buena Vista Resort**

Hotel, the **Buena Vista Palace Hotel & Spa, DoubleTree Guest Suites,** the **Hilton in the Walt Disney World Resort,** the **Holiday Inn in the Walt Disney World Resort, Royal Plaza,** and **Wyndham Lake Buena Vista Resort**—are chain properties with minimal or nonexistent theming, though the Buena Vista Palace, especially, is pretty upscale. All were hit hard by the recession, and several of the larger properties shifted their focus to convention and business travelers.

AMENITIES AT DOWNTOWN DISNEY RESORT AREA HOTELS

HOTEL	CHILDREN'S PROGRAMS	DINING	KID-FRIENDLY	POOL(S)	RECREATION
Best Western LBV Resort	None	★★½	★★★	★★½	★★
Buena Vista Palace	★★★★	★★★★	★★★½	★★★½	★★★★
DoubleTree Guest Suites	None	★★	★★★	★★½	★★½
Hilton WDW Resort	None	★★½	★★½	★★★	★★½
Holiday Inn WDW Resort	None	★★	★★	★★★	★★
Royal Plaza	★★½	★★	★★½	★★½	★★★
Wyndham LBV Resort	★★½	★★½	★★★	★★★	★★★

The main advantage to staying in the DDRA is being in Disney World and proximal to Downtown Disney. Guests at the Hilton, Wyndham Lake Buena Vista Resort, Buena Vista Palace, and Holiday Inn are an easy 5- to 15-minute walk from the Marketplace on the east side of Downtown Disney. Guests at the Royal Plaza, Best Western Lake Buena Vista, and DoubleTree Guest Suites are about 10 minutes farther by foot. Disney transportation can be accessed at Downtown Disney, though the Disney buses take a notoriously long time to leave due to the number of stops throughout the shopping and entertainment complex. Although all DDRA hotels offer shuttle buses to the theme parks, the service is provided by private contractors and is somewhat inferior to Disney transportation in frequency of service, number of buses, and hours of operation. All these hotels are easily accessible by car and are only marginally farther from the Disney parks than several of the Disney resorts (and DDRA hotels are quite close to Typhoon Lagoon water park).

All DDRA hotels try to appeal to families, even the business and meeting hotels. Some have pool complexes that rival those at any Disney resort, whereas others offer a food court or all-suite rooms. A few sponsor Disney-character meals and organized children's activities; all have counters for buying Disney tickets, and most have Disney gift shops. Take a peek at the combined website for the DDRA hotels at **downtowndisneyhotels.com.** Finally, check the cost chart on page 83 and the comparative chart above.

Continued on page 112

WDW Resorts Chart

All-Star Resorts ★★★
1701–1901 W. Buena Vista Dr.
Lake Buena Vista, FL 32830
☎ 407-934-7639
tinyurl.com/wdwvalueresorts

ROOM RATING	73
COST ($ = $50)	$$$–

commuting times to parks (*in minutes*)
MAGIC KINGDOM	6:15
EPCOT	5:45
ANIMAL KINGDOM	4:15
DHS	5:15

Animal Kingdom Lodge
★★★★
2901 Osceola Pkwy.
Lake Buena Vista, FL 32830
☎ 407-938-3000
tinyurl.com/aklodge

ROOM RATING	89
COST ($ = $50)	$ X 8–

commuting times to parks (*in minutes*)
MAGIC KINGDOM	8:15
EPCOT	6:15
ANIMAL KINGDOM	2:15
DHS	6:00

Animal Kingdom Villas (Jambo House)   ★★★★½
2901 Osceola Pkwy.
Lake Buena Vista, FL 32830
☎ 407-938-3000
tinyurl.com/akjambo

ROOM RATING	91
COST ($ = $50)	$ X 8+

commuting times to parks (*in minutes*)
MAGIC KINGDOM	8:15
EPCOT	6:15
ANIMAL KINGDOM	2:15
DHS	6:00

Animal Kingdom Villas (Kidani Village)   ★★★★½
2901 Osceola Pkwy.
Lake Buena Vista, FL 32830
☎ 407-938-7400
tinyurl.com/akkidani

ROOM RATING	95
COST ($ = $50)	$ X 10–

commuting times to parks (*in minutes*)
MAGIC KINGDOM	8:15
EPCOT	6:15
ANIMAL KINGDOM	2:15
DHS	6:00

Art of Animation Resort
★★★½
1850 Animation Way
Lake Buena Vista, FL 32830
☎ 407-938-7000
tinyurl.com/wdwartofanimation

ROOM RATING	80
COST ($ = $50)	$$$

commuting times to parks (*in minutes*)
MAGIC KINGDOM	12:00
EPCOT	10:00
ANIMAL KINGDOM	12:00
DHS	3:00

Beach Club Resort   ★★★★½
1800 Epcot Resorts Blvd.
Lake Buena Vista, FL 32830
☎ 407-934-8000
tinyurl.com/beachclubresort

ROOM RATING	90
COST ($ = $50)	$ X 9+

commuting times to parks (*in minutes*)
MAGIC KINGDOM	7:15
EPCOT	5:15
ANIMAL KINGDOM	6:45
DHS	4:00

Beach Club Villas   ★★★★½
1900 Epcot Resorts Blvd.
Lake Buena Vista, FL 32830
☎ 407-934-2175
tinyurl.com/beachclubvillas

ROOM RATING	90
COST ($ = $50)	$ X 10–

commuting times to parks (*in minutes*)
MAGIC KINGDOM	7:15
EPCOT	5:15
ANIMAL KINGDOM	6:45
DHS	4:00

BoardWalk Inn   ★★★★
2101 Epcot Resorts Blvd.
Lake Buena Vista, FL 32830
☎ 407-939-6200
tinyurl.com/boardwalkinn

ROOM RATING	89
COST ($ = $50)	$ X 10–

commuting times to parks (*in minutes*)
MAGIC KINGDOM	7:15
EPCOT	5:30
ANIMAL KINGDOM	7:00
DHS	3:00

BoardWalk Villas   ★★★★½
2101 Epcot Resorts Blvd.
Lake Buena Vista, FL 32830
☎ 407-939-6200
tinyurl.com/boardwalkvillas

ROOM RATING	90
COST ($ = $50)	$ X 10–

commuting times to parks (*in minutes*)
MAGIC KINGDOM	7:15
EPCOT	5:30
ANIMAL KINGDOM	7:00
DHS	3:00

WDW Resorts Chart (continued)

Caribbean Beach Resort
★★★½
900 Cayman Way
Lake Buena Vista, FL 32830
☎ 407-934-3400
tinyurl.com/caribbeanbeachresort

| ROOM RATING | 80 |
| COST ($ = $50) | $$$$+ |

commuting times to parks (in minutes)
MAGIC KINGDOM	8:00
EPCOT	6:00
ANIMAL KINGDOM	7:15
DHS	4:15

Contemporary Resort
★★★★½
4600 N. World Dr.
Lake Buena Vista, FL 32830
☎ 407-934-7639
tinyurl.com/contemporarywdw

| ROOM RATING | 94 |
| COST ($ = $50) | $ X 9– |

commuting times to parks (in minutes)
MAGIC KINGDOM	ON MONORAIL
EPCOT	11:00
ANIMAL KINGDOM	17:15
DHS	14:15

Coronado Springs Resort
★★★★
1000 W. Buena Vista Dr.
Orlando, FL 32830
☎ 407-939-1000
tinyurl.com/coronadosprings

| ROOM RATING | 83 |
| COST ($ = $50) | $$$$+ |

commuting times to parks (in minutes)
MAGIC KINGDOM	5:30
EPCOT	4:00
ANIMAL KINGDOM	4:45
DHS	4:45

Old Key West Resort
★★★★½
1510 North Cove Rd.
Lake Buena Vista, FL 32830
☎ 407-827-7700
tinyurl.com/oldkeywest

| ROOM RATING | 90 |
| COST ($ = $50) | $ X 8 |

commuting times to parks (in minutes)
MAGIC KINGDOM	10:45
EPCOT	6:00
ANIMAL KINGDOM	14:30
DHS	10:30

Polynesian Resort ★★★★½
1600 Seven Seas Dr.
Lake Buena Vista, FL 32830
☎ 407-824-2000
tinyurl.com/polynesianresort

| ROOM RATING | 92 |
| COST ($ = $50) | $ X 11 |

commuting times to parks (in minutes)
MAGIC KINGDOM	12:00
EPCOT	8:00
ANIMAL KINGDOM	16:15
DHS	12:30

Pop Century Resort ★★★
1050 Century Dr.
Lake Buena Vista, FL 32830
☎ 407-938-4000
tinyurl.com/wdwpopcentury

| ROOM RATING | 71 |
| COST ($ = $50) | $$$– |

commuting times to parks (in minutes)
MAGIC KINGDOM	8:30
EPCOT	6:30
ANIMAL KINGDOM	6:15
DHS	5:00

Shades of Green ★★★★½
1950 W. Magnolia Palm Dr.
Lake Buena Vista, FL 32830
☎ 407-824-3400
shadesofgreen.org

| ROOM RATING | 91 |
| COST ($ = $50) | $$$– |

commuting times to parks (in minutes)
MAGIC KINGDOM	3:30
EPCOT	4:45
ANIMAL KINGDOM	9:30
DHS	6:15

Swan ★★★★½
1200 Epcot Resorts Blvd.
Lake Buena Vista, FL 32830
☎ 407-934-4000
swandolphin.com

| ROOM RATING | 90 |
| COST ($ = $50) | $ X 5– |

commuting times to parks (in minutes)
MAGIC KINGDOM	6:30
EPCOT	4:45
ANIMAL KINGDOM	6:15
DHS	4:00

Treehouse Villas at Saratoga Springs Resort & Spa
★★★★½
1960 Broadway
Lake Buena Vista, FL 32830
☎ 407-827-1100
tinyurl.com/saratogawdw

| ROOM RATING | 90 |
| COST ($ = $50) | $ X 19– |

commuting times to parks (in minutes)
MAGIC KINGDOM	12:45
EPCOT	7:15
ANIMAL KINGDOM	16:45
DHS	12:30

Dolphin ★★★★½
1500 Epcot Resorts Blvd.
Lake Buena Vista, FL 32830
☎ 407-934-4000
swandolphin.com

| ROOM RATING | 90 |
| COST ($ = $50) | $$$$+ |

commuting times to parks (*in minutes*)
MAGIC KINGDOM	6:45
EPCOT	5:00
ANIMAL KINGDOM	6:15
DHS	4:00

Fort Wilderness Resort & Campground (cabins)
★★★★
4510 N. Fort Wilderness Trail
Lake Buena Vista, FL 32830
☎ 407-824-2639
tinyurl.com/ftwilderness

| ROOM RATING | 86 |
| COST ($ = $50) | $ X 8– |

commuting times to parks (*in minutes*)
MAGIC KINGDOM	13:15
EPCOT	8:30
ANIMAL KINGDOM	20:00
DHS	14:00

Grand Floridian Resort & Spa/ Grand Floridian Villas
★★★★½
4401 Floridian Way
Lake Buena Vista, FL 32830
☎ 407-824-3000
tinyurl.com/grandflresort

| ROOM RATING | 93 (hotel), 95 (villas) |
| COST ($ = $50) | $ X 17– (hotel), $ X 13 (villas) |

commuting times to parks (*in minutes*)
MAGIC KINGDOM	ON MONORAIL
EPCOT	4:45
ANIMAL KINGDOM	11:45
DHS	6:45

Port Orleans Resort (French Quarter) ★★★★
2201 Orleans Dr.
Lake Buena Vista, FL 32830
☎ 407-934-5000
tinyurl.com/portorleansfq

| ROOM RATING | 85 |
| COST ($ = $50) | $$$$+ |

commuting times to parks (*in minutes*)
MAGIC KINGDOM	12:00
EPCOT	8:00
ANIMAL KINGDOM	16:15
DHS	12:30

Port Orleans Resort (Riverside)
★★★★
1251 Riverside Dr.
Lake Buena Vista, FL 32830
☎ 407-934-6000
tinyurl.com/portorleansriverside

| ROOM RATING | 85 |
| COST ($ = $50) | $$$$+ |

commuting times to parks (*in minutes*)
MAGIC KINGDOM	12:00
EPCOT	8:00
ANIMAL KINGDOM	16:15
DHS	12:30

Saratoga Springs Resort & Spa
★★★★½
1960 Broadway
Lake Buena Vista, FL 32830
☎ 407-827-1100
tinyurl.com/saratogawdw

| ROOM RATING | 90 |
| COST ($ = $50) | $ X 8 |

commuting times to parks (*in minutes*)
MAGIC KINGDOM	14:45
EPCOT	8:45
ANIMAL KINGDOM	18:15
DHS	14:30

Wilderness Lodge ★★★★
901 Timberline Dr.
Lake Buena Vista, FL 32830
☎ 407-824-3200
tinyurl.com/wildernesslodge

| ROOM RATING | 86 |
| COST ($ = $50) | $ X 11 |

commuting times to parks (*in minutes*)
MAGIC KINGDOM	N/A **
EPCOT	10:00
ANIMAL KINGDOM	15:15
DHS	13:30

Wilderness Lodge Villas
★★★★½
901 Timberline Dr.
Lake Buena Vista, FL 32830
☎ 407-824-3200
tinyurl.com/wlvillas

| ROOM RATING | 90 |
| COST ($ = $50) | $ X 9 |

commuting times to parks (*in minutes*)
MAGIC KINGDOM	N/A*
EPCOT	10:00
ANIMAL KINGDOM	15:15
DHS	13:30

Yacht Club Resort ★★★★
1700 Epcot Resorts Blvd.
Lake Buena Vista, FL 32830
☎ 407-934-7000
tinyurl.com/yachtclubwdw

| ROOM RATING | 88 |
| COST ($ = $50) | $ X 9+ |

commuting times to parks (*in minutes*)
MAGIC KINGDOM	7:15
EPCOT	5:15
ANIMAL KINGDOM	6:45
DHS	4:00

*Primary transportation is by ferry boat rather than car.

Continued from page 108

HOW *to* GET DISCOUNTS *on* LODGING *at* WALT DISNEY WORLD

THERE ARE SO MANY GUEST ROOMS in and around Disney World that competition is brisk, and everyone, including Disney, wheels and deals to fill them. Disney, however, has its own atypical way of managing its room inventory. To uphold the brand integrity of its hotels, Disney prefers to use inducements rather than discounts per se. For example, Disney might include free dining if you reserve a certain number of nights at rack rate, or offer special deals only by e-mail to returning guests. Consequently, many of the strategies for obtaining discounted rates in most cities and destinations don't work well for Disney hotels. We'll explore these strategies in-depth when we discuss booking non-Disney hotels near Walt Disney World; for the moment, though, here are some tips for getting price breaks at Disney properties:

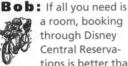 **Bob:** If all you need is a room, booking through Disney Central Reservations is better than booking online or through the Walt Disney Travel Company, because Central Reservations offers better terms for cancellation and payment dates.

1. SEASONAL SAVINGS You can save 15–35% or more per night on a Walt Disney World hotel room by scheduling your visit during the slower times of the year.

2. ASK ABOUT SPECIALS When you talk to Disney reservationists, ask specifically about specials. For example, "What special rates or discounts are available at Disney hotels during the time of our visit?" Being specific and assertive paid off for a Warren Township, New Jersey, dad:

> *Your tip on asking Disney employees about discounts was invaluable. They will not volunteer this information, but by asking we saved almost $500 on our hotel room using a AAA discount.*

3. KNOW THE SECRET CODE The folks at **MouseSavers** (**mousesavers .com**) maintain an updated list of discounts and reservation codes for Disney resorts. The codes are separated into categories such as "for anyone," "for residents of certain states," and "for Annual Pass holders." For example, the site recently listed code DGA, published in an ad in some Spanish-language newspapers and magazines, offering a rate of $72 per night for Disney's All-Star Resorts from August 15 through September 28. Anyone calling the Disney Reservation Center at ☎ 407-W-DISNEY can use a current code and get the discounted rate.

Be aware that Disney targets people with PIN codes in e-mails and direct mailings. PIN-code discounts are offered to specific individuals and are correlated with a given person's name and address. When you try to make a reservation using the PIN, Disney will verify that the street or e-mail address to which the code was sent is yours.

MouseSavers has a great historical list of when discounts were released and what they encompassed at **mousesavers.com/historical wdwdiscounts.html.** You can also sign up for the MouseSavers newsletter, with discount announcements, Disney news, and exclusive offers not available to the general public.

To get your name in the Disney system, call the Disney Reservation Center at ☎ 407-W-DISNEY and request that written info or the free trip-planning DVD be sent to you. If you've been to Walt Disney World before, your name and address will of course already be on record, but you won't be as likely to receive a PIN-code offer as you would by calling and requesting to be sent information. On the Web, go to **disneyworld.com** and sign up (via the trip-planning DVD) to automatically be sent offers and news at your e-mail address. You might also consider getting a **Disney Rewards Visa Card,** which entitles you to around two days' advance notice when a discount is released (visit **disney.go.com/visa** for details).

4. INTERNET SELLERS Online travel sellers **Expedia (expedia.com), Travelocity (travelocity.com),** and **One Travel (onetravel.com)** sell Disney hotels, but usually at a price approximating the going rate obtainable from the Walt Disney Travel Company or Walt Disney World Central Reservations. Most breaks are in the 7–25% range, but they can go as deep as 40%. Disney also places its hotel rooms on **Priceline (priceline .com).** While still abstaining from the "Name Your Own Price" aspect of the site, Disney's hotel rooms are now in Priceline's inventory and available through its conventional booking engine at a discounted rate.

5. WALT DISNEY WORLD WEBSITE Disney still offers deals when it sees lower-than-usual future demand. Go to **disneyworld.com** and look for "Explore Our Special Offers" on the home page. In the same place, also look for seasonal discounts, usually listed as "Summertime Savings" or "Fall Savings" or something similar. You can also go to "Places to Stay" at the top at the top right of the home page, where you'll find a link to Special Offers. You must click on the particular special to get the discounts: If you fill out the information on "Price Your Vacation," you'll be charged the full rack rate.

6. RENTING DISNEY VACATION CLUB POINTS The Disney Vacation Club (DVC) is Disney's time-share-condominium program. DVC resorts (a.k.a. Disney Deluxe Villa resorts) at Walt Disney World are **Animal Kingdom Villas, Bay Lake Tower** at the Contemporary Resort, the **Beach Club Villas, BoardWalk Villas, Old Key West Resort, Saratoga Springs Resort & Spa, Treehouse Villas at Saratoga Springs, Grand Floridian Villas,** and **Wilderness Lodge Villas.** Each resort offers studios and one- and two-bedroom villas (some resorts also offer three-bedroom villas). All accommodations are roomy and luxurious. The studios are equipped with kitchenettes, wet bars, and fridges; the villas come with full kitchens. Most accommodations have patios or balconies.

DVC members receive a number of "points" annually that they use to pay for their Disney accommodations. Sometimes members elect to "rent" (sell) their points instead of using them in a given year. Though Disney is not involved in the transaction, it allows DVC members to make these points available to the general public. The going rental rate is usually in the range of $13–$14 per point. Renting a studio for a week at Animal Kingdom Lodge & Villas would run you $3,424 with tax for Regular season if you booked through the Disney Reservation Center. The same studio costs the DVC member 76 points for a week. If you rented his points at $14 per point, the same studio would cost you $1,040 with tax—almost $2,400 less.

You have two options when renting points: go through a company that specializes in DVC points rental, or locate and deal directly with a selling DVC member. For a fixed rate of around $14 per point, the folks at **David's Disney Vacation Club Rentals** (**dvcrequest.com**) will act on your behalf as a points broker, matching your request for a specific resort and dates to their available supply. They'll also take requests months in advance and notify you as soon as something becomes available. We've used these folks for huge New Year's Eve events and last-minute trips, and they're tops. Plus they accept major credit cards.

The DVC discussion site **MouseOwners** (**mouseowners.com**) has a specific forum for matching DVC sellers and renters. When you deal directly with the selling DVC member, you pay him or her directly, such as by certified check (few members accept credit cards). The DVC member makes a reservation in your name and pays Disney the requisite number of points. Arrangements vary, but the going rate seems to be around $12 per point. Trust is required from both parties. Usually your reservation is documented by a confirmation sent from Disney to the owner and then passed along to you. Though the deal you cut is strictly up to you and the owner, you should always insist on receiving the aforementioned confirmation before making more than a one-night deposit.

We suggest using the discussion boards if you're going during the off-season, if you could stay at any of several resorts, and if you have the time and skills to invest in finding a seller at a low rate. If you're trying to book a certain resort, especially during a busy time of year, there's something to be said for the low-hassle approach of a points broker.

7. **TRAVEL AGENTS** are active players and particularly good sources of information on limited-time programs and discounts. We believe a good travel agent is the best friend a traveler can have. And though we at the *Unofficial Guide* know a thing or two about the travel industry, we always give our agent a chance to beat any deal we find. If she can't beat it, we let her book it anyway if she can get commission from it. We nurture a relationship that gives her plenty of incentive to roll up her sleeves and work on our behalf.

As you might expect, there are travel agents and agencies that specialize, sometimes exclusively, in selling Walt Disney World. These Disney specialists are so good we use them ourselves. The needs of our research team are many, and our schedules are complicated. When we work with an Authorized Disney Vacation Planner, we know we're dealing with someone who knows Disney inside and out, including where to find the deals and how to use all tricks of the trade that keep our research budget under control. Simply stated, they save us time and money, sometimes lots of both.

Each year we ask our readers to rate the travel agent who helped plan their Disney trip. The best of the best include **Sue Pisaturo** of **Small World Vacations,** whom we've used many times and who contributes to this guide (**sue@smallworldvacations.com**); **Kathy Atchue (kathy@ smallworldvacations.com**); **Jodie Ball (jodie@smallworldvacations .com**); **Coleen Bolton (coleen@mei-travel.com**); **Deanna Carrigan (deanna@smallworldvacations.com**); **Michelle Cunningham (michelle @mei-travel.com**); **Stephanie Hudson (stephanie@mousefantravel .com**); and **Leigh McCarty (leigh@smallworldvacations.com**).

Our reader-survey results indicate that for Walt Disney World, you'll be much more satisfied using a travel agent who specializes in Disney and much more likely to recommend those agents to a friend. While the agents above are the ones most consistently recommended in our surveys, you'll find good Disney specialists throughout the country if you prefer to work with someone close to home.

WALT DISNEY TRAVEL COMPANY MAGIC YOUR WAY PACKAGES

DISNEY'S MAGIC YOUR WAY travel-package program mirrors the admission-ticket program of the same name. Here's how it works: You begin with a base room-and-ticket package. Tickets can be customized to match the number of days you intend to tour the theme parks, and range in length from 1 to 10 days. As with theme park admissions, the package program offers strong financial incentives to book a longer stay. An adult 1-Day Base Ticket for the Magic Kingdom (with tax) costs $94.79, whereas if you buy a seven-day ticket, the average cost per day drops to $44.12. You can purchase options to add on to your Base Tickets, such as hopping between theme parks; playing miniature golf; visiting water parks, DisneyQuest, or ESPN Wide World of Sports; and buying your way out of an expiration date for any unused ticket features.

With Magic Your Way packages, you can avoid paying for features you don't intend to use. On a one-week vacation, for example, you might want to spend only five days in the Disney parks, saving a day each for Universal Studios and SeaWorld. With Magic Your Way, you can buy only five days of admission on a seven-day package. Likewise, if you don't normally park-hop, you can purchase multiday admissions that don't include the Park Hopper feature. If you don't use all your admissions, you can opt for the No Expiration add-on, and the unused days will be good forever. Best of all, you can buy the various add-ons at any time during your vacation.

The basic components of a Magic Your Way package are as follows:

- One or more nights of accommodations at your choice of any Disney resort
- Base Ticket for the number of days you tour the theme parks
- Unlimited use of the Disney transportation system
- Free theme park parking.
- Official Walt Disney Travel Company luggage tag (one per person)

The various **Magic Your Way Dining Plans,** an optional but very popular component, are covered in detail in the next chapter.

Number-Crunching

COMPARING A MAGIC YOUR WAY PACKAGE with purchasing the package components separately is a breeze.

1. Pick a Disney resort and decide how many nights you want to stay.

2. Next, work out a rough plan of what you want to do and see so you can determine the admission passes you'll require.

3. When you're ready, call the Disney Reservation Center (DRC) at ☎ 407-W-DISNEY and price a Magic Your Way package with tax for your selected resort and dates. The package will include both admissions and lodging. It's also a good idea to get a quote from a Disney-savvy travel agent (see page 114).

4. Now, to calculate the costs of buying your accommodations and admission passes separately, call the DRC a second time. This time, price a room-only rate for the same resort and dates. Be sure to ask about the availability of any special deals. While you're still on the line, obtain the prices, with tax, for the admissions you require. If you're not sure which of the various admission options will best serve you, consult our free Ticket Calculator at **touringplans.com.**

5. Add the room-only rates and the admission prices. Compare this sum to the DRC quote for the Magic Your Way package.

6. Check for deals and discounts for packages, room-only rates, and admission.

Throw Me a Line!

IF YOU BUY A PACKAGE FROM DISNEY, don't expect reservation-ists to offer suggestions or help you sort out your options. Generally, they respond only to your specific questions, ducking queries that require an opinion. A reader from North Riverside, Illinois, complains:

The representatives from WDW were very courteous, but they only answered the questions posed and were not eager to give advice on what might be most cost-effective. I feel a person could spend 8 hours on the phone with WDW reps and not have any more input than you get from reading the literature.

If you can't get the information you need from Disney, contact a good travel agent (see page 115 for our recommendations).

LODGING *outside*
WALT DISNEY WORLD

AT THIS POINT YOU'RE PROBABLY WONDERING HOW a hotel outside Walt Disney World could be as convenient as one inside Walt Disney World. Well, Mabel, Disney World is a *muy largo* place, but like any city or state, it has borders. By way of analogy, let's say you want to stay in a hotel in Cincinnati but can't find one you can afford. Would you rather book a hotel in Toledo or Cleveland, which are both still in Ohio but pretty darn far away, or would you be willing to leave Ohio and stay just across the river from Cincy in Covington, Kentucky?

Just south of Walt Disney World on US 192 are a bunch of hotels and condos, some great bargains, that are closer to Animal Kingdom and Disney's Hollywood Studios than are many hotels in Walt Disney World. Similarly, there are hotels along Disney's east border, FL 535, that are exceptionally convenient if you plan to use your own car.

Lodging costs outside Walt Disney World vary incredibly. If you shop around, you can find a clean motel with a pool within a few minutes of the World for as low as $40 a night. You also can find luxurious, expensive hotels. Because of hot competition, discounts abound.

GOOD NEIGHBOR HOTELS

SOME HOTELS PAY DISNEY a marketing fee to display a "Good Neighbor" designation. Usually a ticket shop in the lobby sells full-price Disney tickets. Other than that, the designation means nothing for the consumer. It doesn't guarantee quality—some Good Neighbor hotels are very nice, others not so much. Some are close to Walt Disney World, while others are quite far away. Disney requires Good Neighbor hotels to provide free shuttle service to Walt Disney World but prohibits them from offering shuttle service to Universal or SeaWorld.

SELECTING AND BOOKING A HOTEL
OUTSIDE WALT DISNEY WORLD

THERE ARE FOUR PRIMARY out-of-the-World areas to consider:

1. INTERNATIONAL DRIVE AREA This area, about 15–25 minutes northeast of Walt Disney World, parallels I-4 on its eastern side and offers a wide selection of both hotels and restaurants. Accommodations range from about $56 to $400 per night. The chief drawbacks of the International Drive area are its terribly congested roads, countless traffic signals, and inadequate access to westbound I-4. While the biggest bottleneck is the intersection with Sand Lake Road, the mile of International Drive between Kirkman Road and Sand Lake Road stays in near-continuous gridlock. It's common to lose 25–35 minutes trying to navigate this 1-mile stretch.

Hotels in the International Drive area are listed in the *Orlando Official Vacation Guide,* published by the Orlando–Orange County

Convention and Visitors Bureau. For a copy, call ☎ 800-972-3304 or 407-363-5872, or go to **visitorlando.com/vacation-planning-kit.**

2. LAKE BUENA VISTA AND THE I-4 CORRIDOR A number of hotels are situated along FL 535 and west of I-4 between Walt Disney World and I-4's intersection with the Florida Turnpike. These properties are easily reached from the interstate and are near a large number of restaurants, including those on International Drive. Most hotels in this area are listed in the *Orlando Official Vacation Guide.*

3. US 192 (IRLO BRONSON MEMORIAL HIGHWAY) This is the highway to Kissimmee, south of Walt Disney World. In addition to a number of large, full-service hotels, there are many small, privately owned motels that are often a good value. Several dozen properties on US 192 are closer to the Disney theme parks than are the more expensive hotels in the Downtown Disney Resort Area. The number and variety of restaurants on US 192 has increased markedly in the past several years, easing the area's primary shortcoming. Hotels on US 192 and in Kissimmee can be found in the *Kissimmee Visitor's Guide;* call ☎ 800-327-9159 or check **floridakiss.com.**

4. UNIVERSAL ORLANDO AREA In the triangular area bordered by I-4 on the southeast, Vineland Road on the north, and Turkey Lake Road on the west are Universal Orlando and the hotels most convenient to it. Running north–south through the middle of the triangle is Kirkman Road, which connects to I-4. On the east side of Kirkman are a number of independent hotels and restaurants. Universal hotels, theme parks, and CityWalk are west of Kirkman. Traffic in this area is not nearly as congested as on nearby International Drive, and there are good interstate connections in both directions.

THE BEST HOTELS FOR FAMILIES OUTSIDE WALT DISNEY WORLD

WHAT MAKES A SUPER FAMILY HOTEL? Roomy accommodations, in-room fridge, great pool, complimentary breakfast, child-care options, and programs for kids are a few of the things the *Unofficial Guide* hotel team researched in selecting the top hotels for families from among hundreds of properties in the Disney World area. Some of our picks are expensive, others are more reasonable, and some are a bargain. Regardless of price, be assured that these hotels understand a family's needs.

Though all the following hotels offer some type of shuttle to the theme parks, some offer very limited service. Call the hotel before you book and ask what the shuttle schedule will be when you visit. Because families, like individuals, have different wants and needs, we haven't ranked the following properties here. They're listed geographically and then alphabetically.

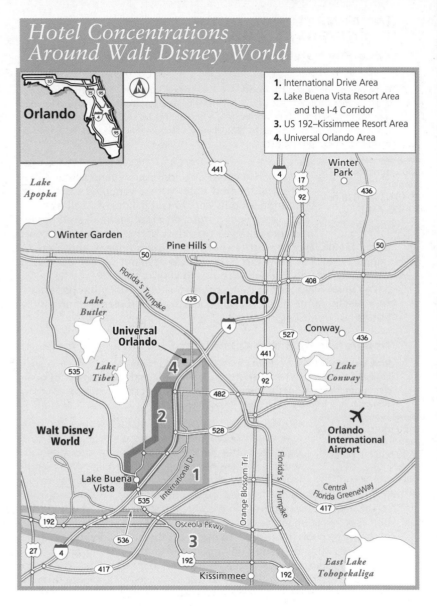

Hotel Concentrations Around Walt Disney World

1. International Drive Area
2. Lake Buena Vista Resort Area and the I-4 Corridor
3. US 192–Kissimmee Resort Area
4. Universal Orlando Area

INTERNATIONAL DRIVE & UNIVERSAL AREAS

CoCo Key Hotel and Water Resort–Orlando
★ ★ ★ ½

Rate per night $109–$279. **Pools** ★★★★. **Fridge in room** Yes. **Shuttle to parks** Yes (Aquatica, SeaWorld, Universal, Wet 'n Wild). **Maximum number of occupants per room** 4. **Special comments** Daily $19 room fee for use of the water park; day guests may use the water park for $22.95/person Monday–Friday ($24.95 on weekends and $17.95 for Florida residents).

7400 International Dr.
Orlando
☎ 407-351-2626 or
877-875-4681
cocokeyorlando.com

COCO KEY IS ON INTERNATIONAL DRIVE, not far from the Universal Orlando theme parks. It combines a tropical-themed hotel with a canopied water park featuring 3 pools and 14 waterslides, as well as poolside food and arcade entertainment. A full-service restaurant serves breakfast and dinner; a food court offers family favorites such as burgers, chicken fingers, and pizza. A unique feature of the resort is its cashless payment system: Bar-coded wristbands let you charge purchases to your room.

The unusually spacious guest rooms include 37-inch flat-panel TVs, free Wi-Fi, granite showers and countertops, and plenty of accessible outlets for guests' electronics.

DoubleTree by Hilton Orlando at SeaWorld   ★ ★ ★ ½

Rate per night $80–$700. **Pools** ★★★½. **Fridge in room** Standard in some rooms; available in others for $10/day. **Shuttle to parks** Yes. **Maximum number of occupants per room** 4. **Special comments** Good option if you're visiting SeaWorld or Aquatica. Pets welcome (1 per room, 25-pound limit, $75).

10100 International Dr.
Orlando
☎ 407-352-1100 or
800-327-0363
doubletreeorlando
idrive.com

ON 28 LUSH, TROPICAL ACRES with a Balinese feel, the DoubleTree is adjacent to SeaWorld and Aquatica water park. The 1,094 rooms and suites are suitable for business travelers or families. We recommend the tower rooms for good views and the resort rooms for maximum convenience. The Bamboo Grille serves steak and seafood, along with breakfast; you can also get a quick bite at Bangli Lounge, the deli, or the pool bar. Relax and cool off at one of the three pools (there are two more just for kids), or indulge in a spa treatment. A fitness center, mini-golf course and putting green, children's day camp, and game area afford even more diversions. The resort is about a 15-minute drive to Walt Disney World, a 12-minute drive to Universal, or a short walk to SeaWorld.

Hard Rock Hotel   ★ ★ ★ ★

Rate per night $200–$500. **Pool** ★★★★. **Fridge in room** $15/day. **Shuttle to parks** Yes (Universal, SeaWorld, Discovery Cove, Aquatica, and Wet 'n Wild). **Maximum number of occupants per room** 5 (double-queen) or 3 (king). **Special comments** Microwaves available for $15/day. Pets welcome ($50).

OPENED IN 2001, the Hard Rock Hotel is both Universal Orlando's least expensive on-site resort and the closest resort to Universal's theme parks. The exterior has a California Mission theme, with white stucco walls, arched entryways, and rust-colored roof tiles. Inside, the lobby is a tribute to rock-and-roll style, all marble, chrome, and stage lighting.

5800 Universal Blvd.
Orlando
☎ 407-503-2000 or
888-464-3617
hardrockhotel
orlando.com

The eight floors hold 650 rooms and 29 suites. Standard rooms are 375 square feet, slightly larger than rooms at Disney's Moderate resorts and a bit smaller than most Disney Deluxe rooms. They're furnished with two queen beds, with plush, comfortable linens and more pillows than you'll know what to do with. Rooms also include a flat-panel LCD television, refrigerator, coffeemaker, and an alarm clock with a 30-pin iPhone docking port. An optional rollaway bed, available at an extra charge, allows standard rooms to sleep up to five people.

Situated in the middle of the resort's C-shaped main building, the 12,000-square-foot pool includes a 250-foot waterslide, a sand beach, and underwater speakers so you can hear the music while you swim. Adjacent to the pool are a fountain play area for small children, a sand-volleyball court, hot tubs and a poolside bar. The Hard Rock also has a small, functional fitness center and a full-service Mandara Spa.

On-site dining includes The Kitchen, a casual full-service restaurant open for breakfast, lunch, and dinner, featuring American food such as burgers, steaks, and salads. The Palm Restaurant is an upscale steak house available for dinner only. And, of course, the Hard Rock Café is just a short distance away at Universal CityWalk.

In 2013, rack rates for standard rooms at the Hard Rock ranged from a low of $200 per night in mid-January to $500 per night during the last week of December, plus tax. What you're paying for isn't quality—the rooms are in need of new paint, carpet, and lighting—but a short walk to the theme parks and unlimited Universal Express.

Holiday Inn Resort Orlando–The Castle ★★★½

Rate per night $85–$250. **Pool** ★★★. **Fridge in room** Yes ($15/day). **Shuttle to parks** Yes (Universal, SeaWorld, and Wet 'n Wild). **Maximum number of occupants per room** 4. **Special comments** For an additional fee ($11.95 for adults, children age 12 and under free with paying adult), up to 4 people receive a full breakfast. Dogs up to 50 pounds welcome ($75).

YOU CAN'T MISS THIS ONE; it's the only castle on I-Drive. Inside you'll find royal colors (purple predominates), opulent fixtures, European art, Renaissance music, and a mystic Castle Creature at the door. The 216 guest rooms also receive the royal treatment in decor, though some guests may find them gaudy.

8629 International Dr.
Orlando
☎ 407-345-1511 or
877-317-5753
thecastleorlando.com

All, however, are fairly large and well equipped with TV, minibar (fridge is available at an extra charge), free Wi-Fi, coffeemaker, iron and board, hair dryer, and safe. The Castle Café off the lobby serves full or Continental breakfast. For lunch or dinner, you might walk next door to Vito's Chop House (dinner only) or Café Tu Tu Tango (an *Unofficial* favorite). The heated circular pool is 5 feet deep and features a fountain in the center, a poolside bar, and a whirlpool. There's no separate kiddie pool. Other amenities include fitness center, gift shop, lounge, valet laundry service and facilities, and guest-services desk with park passes for sale and babysitting recommendations. Security feature: Elevators require an electronic key card.

Loews Portofino Bay Hotel ★★★★½

Rate per night $209–$559. **Pools** ★★★★. **Fridge in room** Minibar; fridge available for $15/day. **Shuttle to parks** Yes (Universal, SeaWorld, Discovery Cove, Aquatica, and Wet 'n Wild). **Maximum number of occupants per room** 4. **Special comments** Character dinner on Friday.

5601 Universal Blvd.
Orlando
☎ 407-503-1000 or
888-464-3617
tinyurl.com/
 portofinobay

UNIVERSAL'S TOP-OF-THE-LINE HOTEL, intended to evoke the Italian seaside city of Portofino, was refurbished in 2013. Most guest rooms are 450 square feet, larger than most at Disney's Deluxe resorts, and have either one king bed or two queen beds. King rooms sleep up to three people with an optional rollaway bed; the same option allows queen rooms to sleep up to five. Two room-view options are available: "Garden" rooms look out over the landscaping and trees—many of these are the east-facing rooms in the resort's east wing, others face one of the three pools; "bay view" rooms face either west or south and overlook Portofino Bay, with a view of the piazza behind the lobby, too.

Rooms come furnished with a 32-inch LCD flat-panel TV, a refrigerator, a coffeemaker, and an alarm clock with a 30-pin iPhone docking port. Other amenities include a small desk with two chairs, a comfortable reading chair with lamp, a chest of drawers, and a standing closet. Wi-Fi is $10 per day in guest rooms, free in the lobby. Beds are large, plush, and comfortable.

Portofino Bay has three pools, the largest of which is the Beach Pool, on the west side of the resort. Two smaller quiet pools sit at the far end of the east wing and to the west of the main lobby. The Beach Pool has a zero-entry design and a waterslide themed after a Roman aqueduct, plus a children's play area, hot tubs, and a poolside bar and grill. The Villa Pool has private cabana rentals for that Italian Riviera feeling. Rounding out the luxuries are a full-service Mandara Spa and a complete fitness center with weight machines, treadmills, and more.

On-site dining includes three sit-down restaurants serving Italian cuisine; a deli; a pizzeria; and a café serving coffee and gelato. Perhaps because Universal figures that most guests have an expense account, some of the food prices go well beyond what we'd consider reasonable, even for a theme park hotel.

In 2013, rack rates ranged from $209 per night in January to $559 per night during the December holidays. The prices put Portofino Bay on par with the Ritz-Carlton, something its good points can't quite justify. On the other hand, the Ritz isn't a short walk from Harry Potter.

Loews Royal Pacific Resort ★★★★

Rate per night $224–$369. **Pools** ★★★★. **Fridge in room** Minibar; fridge available for $15/day. **Shuttle to parks** Yes (Universal, SeaWorld, Discovery Cove, Aquatica, and Wet 'n Wild). **Maximum number of occupants per room** 5 (double queen) or 3 (king). **Special comments** Microwaves available for $15/day.

YOU MAY BE TEMPTED, as we were initially, to write off the Royal Pacific, which opened in 2002, as a knockoff of Disney's Polynesian Resort. There are indeed similarities, but the Royal Pacific is attractive enough, and has enough strengths of its own, for us to recommend that you try a stay there to compare for yourself.

6300 Hollywood Way
Orlando
☎ 407-503-1000 or
888-464-3617
tinyurl.com/
    royalpacific

The South Seas–inspired theming is both relaxing and structured. Guests enter the lobby from a walkway two stories above an artificial stream that surrounds the resort. Once you're inside, the lobby's dark teak-wood accents contrast nicely with the enormous amount of light coming in from the windows and three-story A-frame roof. Palms line the walkway through the lobby, and through these you see that the whole lobby surrounds an enormous outdoor fountain.

The Royal Pacific's 1,000 guest rooms are spread among three Y-shaped wings attached to the resort's main building. Standard rooms are 335 square feet—about the size of a room at Disney's Moderate resorts—and feature one king or two queen beds. King rooms sleep up to three people with an optional rollaway bed; queen rooms sleep five with that rollaway bed.

Rooms are decorated in neutral beige tones, with dark wood and paint accents and forest-colored carpet, and include a 32-inch flat-panel LCD TV, a refrigerator, a coffeemaker, and an alarm clock with a 30-pin iPhone docking port. Other amenities include a small desk with two chairs, a comfortable reading chair, a chest of drawers, and a large closet. Wi-Fi is $10 per day in guest rooms, free in the lobby.

As at the Hard Rock, the Royal Pacific's zero-entry pool includes a sand beach, volleyball court, play area for kids, hot tub, and cabanas for rent, plus a poolside bar and grill.

The Royal Pacific includes a 5,000-square-foot fitness facility ($10 per day, free with club-level rooms), two full-service restaurants, three bars, and a luau. Of the table-service restaurants, only the Islands Dining Room is open for breakfast. Emeril Lagasse's Tchoup Chop, the other table-service option, serves Asian-inspired food, too; it's open for lunch and dinner (reservations recommended).

Nickelodeon Suites Resort ★★★½

Rate per night $129–$649. **Pools** ★★★★. **Fridge in room** Yes. **Shuttle to parks** Yes. **Maximum number of occupants per room** 8. **Special comments** Daily character breakfast; resort fee of $30/night.

SPONGEBOB SQUAREPANTS, eat your heart out. This resort is as kid-friendly as they come. Decked out in all themes Nickelodeon, the hotel is sure to please any fan of TV shows the likes of *SpongeBob, Dora the Explorer,* and *Avatar: The Last Airbender,* to name a few. Nickelodeon characters from the channel's many shows hang out in the resort's lobby and mall area, greeting kids while parents check in. Guests can choose from among 777 suites—one-bedroom Family Suites and two- and three-bedroom KidSuites—executed in a number of different themes—all very brightly and creatively decorated. All suites include kitchenettes or full kitchens; also standard are microwave, fridge, coffeemaker, TV, iron and board, hair dryer, and safe. KidSuites feature a semiprivate kids' bedroom with bunk or twin beds, pull-out sleeper bed, 32-inch TV, CD player, and activity table. The master bedroom offers ample storage space that the kids' bedroom lacks. Additional amenities include a high-tech video arcade, Studio Nick—a game-show studio that hosts several game shows a night for the entertainment of a live studio audience, a buffet (kids age 3 and younger eat free with a paying adult), a food court offering Subway and other choices, the full-service Nicktoons Cafe (offers character breakfasts), a convenience store, a lounge, a gift shop, a fitness center, a washer and dryer in each courtyard, and a guest-activities desk (buy Disney tickets and get recommendations on babysitting). Not to be missed—don't worry, your kids won't let you—are the resort's two pools, Oasis and Lagoon. Oasis features a water park complete with water cannons, rope ladders, geysers, and dump buckets, as well as a hot tub for adults (with a view of the rest of the pool so you can keep an eye on little ones) and a smaller play area for younger kids. Kids will love the huge, zero-entry Lagoon Pool with 400-gallon dump bucket, plus a nearby basketball court and nine-hole mini-golf course. Pool activities for kids are scheduled several times a day, seasonally; some games feature the infamous green slime. Whatever you do, avoid letting your kids catch you saying the phrase "I don't know" while you're here—trust us.

14500 Continental Gateway
Orlando
☎ 407-387-5437 or 877-NICK-111
nickhotel.com

Rosen Shingle Creek ★★★★

Rate per night $104–$294. **Pools** ★★★★. **Fridge in room** Yes. **Shuttle to parks** Yes (Universal, Wet 'n Wild, Discovery Cove, Aquatica, and SeaWorld only). **Maximum number of occupants per room** 4.

BEAUTIFUL ROOMS (east-facing ones have great views) and excellent restaurants distinguish this mostly meeting- and convention-oriented resort. The pools are large and lovely and include a lap pool, a family pool, and a kiddie wading pool. There's an 18-hole golf course on-site as well as a superior spa and an adequate fitness center. Child care is provided as well. Though a state-of-the-art video arcade will gobble up your kids' pocket

9939 Universal Blvd.
Orlando
☎ 407-996-9939
or 866-996-6338
rosenshinglecreek.com

change, the real kicker, especially for the 8-years-and-up crowd, is a natural area encompassing lily ponds, grassy wetlands, Shingle Creek, and an adjacent cypress swamp. Running through the area is a nature trail complete with signs to help you identify wildlife. Great blue herons, wood storks, coots, egrets, mallard ducks, anhingas, and ospreys are common, as are sliders (turtles), chameleons, and skinks (lizards). Oh yeah, there are alligators and snakes, too—real ones, but that's part of the fun. If you stay at Shingle Creek and plan to visit the theme parks, you'll want a car. Shuttle service is limited, departing and picking up at rather inconvenient times and stopping at three other hotels before delivering you to your destination.

LAKE BUENA VISTA & I-4 CORRIDOR

Buena Vista Palace Hotel & Spa   ★★★½

Rate per night $120–$500. **Pools** ★★★½. **Fridge in room** Yes. **Shuttle to parks** Yes (Disney only). **Maximum number of occupants per room** 4. **Special comments** Sunday character brunch available; resort fee of $22/night.

IN THE DOWNTOWN DISNEY RESORT AREA, the Buena Vista Palace is upscale and convenient. Surrounded by an artificial lake and plenty of palms, the spacious pool area contains three heated pools, the largest of which is partially covered (nice for when you need a little shade); a whirlpool and

1900 E. Buena Vista Dr.
Lake Buena Vista
☎ 407-827-2727 or
866-397-6516
buenavistapalace.com

sauna; a basketball court; and a sand volleyball court. Plus, a pool concierge will fetch your favorite magazine or fruity drink. On Sunday, the Watercress Café hosts a character brunch ($22 for adults and $10 for children). The 897 guest rooms are posh and spacious; each comes with desk, coffeemaker, hair dryer, satellite TV with pay-per-view movies, iron and board, and mini-fridge. There are also 117 suites. In-room babysitting is available through All About Kids (see page 75). One lighted tennis court, a European-style spa offering 60 services, a fitness center, an arcade, a playground, and a beauty salon round out amenities. Two restaurants and a mini-market are on-site. And if you aren't wiped out after time in the parks, consider dropping by the Lobby Lounge or the full-menu sports bar for a nightcap.

Hilton in the Walt Disney World Resort   ★★★★

Rate per night $100–$409. **Pools** ★★★½. **Fridge in room** Minibar; mini-fridge available free on request. **Shuttle to parks** Yes (Disney theme and water parks only). **Maximum number of occupants per room** 4. **Special comments** Sunday character breakfast and Disney Extra Magic Hours program; resort fee of $22/night.

THE HILTON IS THE ONLY DDRA HOTEL offering Disney's Extra Magic Hours program to its guests. Although Hilton's resort fees are outrageous and the decor is dated, the rooms are comfortable and nicer than some in the DDRA. On-site dining includes Covington Mill

1751 Hotel Plaza Blvd.
☎ 407-827-4000
hilton-wdwv.com

Restaurant, offering American sandwiches and pasta; Andiamo, an Italian bistro; and Benihana, a Japanese steak house and sushi bar (the last two are reviewed in Part Ten, Dining in and around Walt Disney World). Covington Mill hosts a Disney-character breakfast on Sundays. The two pools are matched with a children's "spray pool" and a 24-hour fitness center. An exercise room and a game room are available, as is a 24-hour market. Babysitting is available, but there are no organized children's programs.

Holiday Inn Resort Lake Buena Vista ★★★½

Rate per night $71–$200. **Pool** ★★★. **Fridge in room** Yes. **Shuttle to parks** Yes (Disney only). **Maximum number of occupants per room** 4–6. **Special comments** The first hotel in the world to offer KidSuites; resort fee of $11.95/night entitles guests to numerous perks, including use of fitness center and daily fountain drinks for kids.

13351 FL 535
Orlando
☎ 407-239-4500 or
866-808-8833
hiresortlbv.com

THE BIG LURE HERE IS KIDSUITES—405-square-foot rooms, each with a separate children's area. Themes include a tree house, jail, space capsule, and fort, among others. The kids' area sleeps two to four children in one or two sets of bunk beds. The separate adult area has its own TV, safe, hair dryer, and mini-kitchenette with fridge, microwave, sink, and coffeemaker. Standard guest rooms offer these adult amenities. Other kid-friendly amenities include the tiny Castle Movie Theater, which shows movies all day, every day; a playground; an arcade with video games and air hockey, among its many games; and a basketball court. Other amenities include a fitness center for the grown-ups and a large free-form pool complete with kiddie pool and two whirlpools. Applebee's serves breakfast and dinner and offers an à la carte menu for dinner. There's also a minimart. More perks: Kids age 12 and younger eat free from a special menu when dining with one paying adult (maximum four kids per adult), and "Dive-Inn" poolside movies are shown on Saturday nights. Finally, pets weighing 30 pounds or less are welcome for an additional $40 nonrefundable fee.

Hyatt Regency Grand Cypress ★★★★½

Rate per night $144–$399. **Pool** ★★★★★. **Fridge in room** Yes, plus minibar. **Shuttle to parks** Yes (Disney, Universal, SeaWorld). **Maximum number of occupants per room** 4. **Special comments** Wow, what a pool! Resort fee of $22/night.

1 Grand Cypress Blvd.
Orlando
☎ 407-239-1234
grandcypress.hyatt.com

THERE ARE MYRIAD REASONS to stay at this 1,500-acre resort, but the pool ranks as number one. The 800,000-gallon tropical paradise has two 45-foot waterslides, waterfalls, caves and grottoes, and a suspension bridge. New in 2013 were a waterslide tower, splash zone, pool bar, and children's rock-climbing facilities. The Hyatt also is a golfer's paradise. With 45 holes of Jack Nicklaus–designed championship golf, a nine-hole pitch-and-putt course, and a golf academy, there's something for golfers of all abilities. Other recreational perks include a racquet facility with hard and clay courts, a private lake with beach, a refurbished fitness center, and miles of trails for biking, walking, and jogging. The 769 standard guest rooms are 360 square feet and have a Florida ambience, with green and reddish hues, touches of rattan, and private balconies. Amenities include minibar, iron and board, safe, hair dryer, ceiling fan, and cable/satellite TV with pay-per-view movies and video games. The one- and two-bedroom Villas of Grand Cypress have a living room, dining room, fully equipped kitchen, and private patio; they can also double up through connecting doors for larger families. Camp Hyatt provides supervised programs for kids ages 3–12; in-room babysitting is available. Six restaurants offer dining options. If outdoor recreation is high on your family's list, Hyatt is an excellent high-end choice.

Marriott Village at Lake Buena Vista ★★★

Rate per night $79–$189. **Pools** ★★★. **Fridge in room** Yes. **Shuttle to parks** Disney only, $7. **Maximum number of occupants per room** 4 (Courtyard and Fairfield) or 5 (SpringHill). **Special comments** Free Continental breakfast at Fairfield and SpringHill.

THIS GATED HOTEL COMMUNITY INCLUDES a 388-room Fairfield Inn (★★★½), a 400-suite SpringHill Suites (★★★), and a 312-room Courtyard (★★★½). Whatever your budget, you'll find a room here to fit it. If you need a bit more space, book SpringHill Suites; if you're looking for value, try the Fairfield Inn; if you need limited business amenities, reserve at the Courtyard. Amenities at all three properties include fridge, cable TV, iron and board, hair dryer, and microwave. Cribs and roll-away beds are available at no extra charge at all locations. Swimming pools at all three hotels are attractive and medium-sized, featuring children's interactive splash zones and whirlpools; in addition, each property has its own fitness center. The incredibly convenient Village Marketplace food court includes Pizza Hut, Village Grill, Village Coffee House, and a 24-hour convenience store. Bahama Breeze and Golden Corral full-service restaurants are within walking distance. Other services and amenities include a Disney planning station and ticket sales, an arcade, and a Hertz car-rental desk. Shoppers will find the Orlando Premium Outlets adjacent. You'll get plenty of bang for your buck at Marriott Village.

8623 Vineland Ave.
Orlando
☎ 407-938-9001 or
800-761-7829
marriottvillage.com

Sheraton Lake Buena Vista Resort ★★★★

Rate per night $90–$351. **Pool** ★★★★. **Fridge in room** Yes. **Shuttle to parks** Yes (Disney only). **Maximum number of occupants per room** 4–6. **Special comments** Dogs 80 pounds and under allowed; $9.95/day resort fee.

12205 S. Apopka–
Vineland Rd.
Orlando
☎ 407-239-0444 or
800-325-3535
sheratonlakebuena
vistaresort.com

THE SHERATON'S 400 GUEST ROOMS and 90 family junior suites have a sleek, modern feel. Amenities in each room include Sheraton Sweet Sleeper beds, free Wi-Fi, 42-inch HDTV, refrigerator, coffeemaker, hair dryer, safe, clock-radio, and iron and board; micro-waves are available at an extra charge. The family junior suites provide bunk beds for children. The relaxing pool area features cabanas with food service (for a fee), and youngsters can enjoy the cascading water-fall and waterslide. The Top of the Palms Spa offers massages, facials, manicures, and pedicures. Also on-site are two restaurants, a business center, a fitness center, an arcade, and a gift shop.

Sheraton Vistana Resort Villas   ★ ★ ★ ★ ½

Rate per night $129–$209. **Pools** ★★★½. **Fridge in room** Yes. **Shuttle to parks** Yes (Disney free; other parks for a fee). **Maximum number of occupants per room** 4–8. **Special comments** Though time-shares, the villas are rented nightly as well.

8800 Vistana Centre Dr.
Orlando
☎ 407-239-3100 or
866-208-0003
tinyurl.com/vistanaresort

THE SHERATON VISTANA IS DECEPTIVELY LARGE, stretching across both sides of Vistana Cen-tre Drive. Because Sheraton's emphasis is on selling the time-shares, the rental angle is little known. But families should consider it; the Vistana is one of Orlando's best off-Disney properties. If you want a serene retreat from your days in the theme parks, this is an excellent base. The spacious villas come in one-bedroom, two-bedroom, and two-bedroom-with-lock-off models (which can be reconfigured as one studio room and a one-bedroom suite). All are decorated in beachy pastels, but the emphasis is on the profusion of amenities. Each villa has a full kitchen (including fridge/freezer, microwave, oven/range, dishwasher, toaster, and coffeemaker, with an option to prestock with groceries and laundry products), clothes washer and dryer, TVs in the living room and each bedroom (one with DVD player), stereo with CD player in some villas, separate dining area, and private patio or bal-cony in most. Grounds offer seven swimming pools (three with bars), four playgrounds, two restaurants, game rooms, fitness centers, a mini-golf course, sports equipment rental (including bikes), and courts for basketball, volleyball, tennis, and shuffleboard. A mind-boggling array of activities for kids (and adults) ranges from crafts to games and sports tournaments. Of special note: Vistana is highly secure, with locked gates bordering all guest areas, so children can have the run of the place without parents worrying about them wandering off.

Waldorf Astoria Orlando   ★ ★ ★ ★ ½

Rate per night $309–$4,000+. **Pool** ★★★★. **Fridge in room** Yes. **Shuttle to parks** Yes (Disney only) **Maximum number of occupants per room** 4, plus child in crib. **Spe-cial comments** Good alternative to Disney's Deluxe properties.

14200 Bonnet Creek
Resort Lane
Orlando
☎ 407-597-5500
waldorfastoria
orlando.com

OPENED IN 2009, the Waldorf Astoria is between I-4 and Disney's Pop Century Resort, near the Hilton Orlando at the back of the Bonnet Creek Resort property. Get-ting here requires a GPS or good directions, so be pre-pared with those before you travel. Once you arrive, however, you'll know the trip was worth it. Beautifully decorated and well manicured, the Waldorf is more elegant than any Disney resort. Service is excellent, and the staff-to-guest ratio is far lower than at Disney properties. At just under 450 square feet, standard rooms feature either two queen beds or one king. A full-size desk allows you to get work done if it's absolutely necessary, and rooms also have flat-panel televisions, high-speed Internet, and Wi-Fi. Amenities include a fitness center, a spa, a golf course, six restaurants, and two pools (including one zero-entry pool for kids). Poolside cabanas are available for rent. The resort offers shuttle service to the Disney parks about every half-hour, but check with the front desk for the exact schedule when you arrive.

Wyndham Bonnet Creek Resort ★★★★½

Rate per night $179–$329. **Pool** ★★★★. **Fridge in room** Yes. **Shuttle to parks** Yes (Disney only). **Maximum number of occupants per room** 4–12 depending on room/suite. **Special comments** A non-Disney suite hotel within Walt Disney World.

THIS CONDO HOTEL lies on the south side of Buena Vista Drive, about a quarter-mile east of Disney's Caribbean Beach Resort. The Wyndham is part of the Bonnet Creek resort, a hotel, golf, and convention complex on the same site that includes the Waldorf Astoria (see opposite) along with a Hilton. The development is surrounded on three sides by Disney property and on one side by I-4.

9560 Via Encinas
Lake Buena Vista
☎ 407-238-3500 or
888-743-2687
wyndham
bonnetcreek.com

One- and two-bedroom condos have fully equipped kitchens, washers and dryers, jetted tubs, and balconies. Activities and amenities include two outdoor swimming pools, a "lazy river" float stream, a children's activities program, a game room, a playground, and miniature golf. Free scheduled transportation serves all the Disney parks. One-bedroom units are furnished with a king bed in the bedroom and a sleeper sofa in the living area; two-bedroom condos have two double beds in the second bedroom, a sleeper sofa in the living area, and an additional bath.

US 192 AREA

Clarion Suites Maingate ★★★½

Rate per night $49–$149. **Pool** ★★★. **Fridge in room** Yes. **Shuttle to parks** Yes (Disney, Universal, and SeaWorld). **Maximum number of occupants per room** 6 for most suites. **Special comments** Free Continental breakfast is served daily.

THIS PROPERTY HAS 150 SPACIOUS one-room suites, each with double sofa bed, microwave, fridge, coffeemaker, TV, hair dryer, and safe. The suites aren't lavish, but they're clean and contemporary, with muted deep-purple and beige tones. Extra bathroom counter space is especially convenient for larger families. The heated pool is large and has plenty of lounge chairs and moderate landscaping. A kiddie pool, whirlpool, and

7888 W. Irlo Bronson
Memorial Hwy.
Kissimmee
☎ 407-390-9888 or
888-390-9888
clarionsuites
kissimmee.com

poolside bar complete the courtyard. Other amenities include an arcade and a gift shop. But Maingate's big plus is its location next door to a shopping center with about everything a family could need. There, you'll find 10 dining options, including Outback Steakhouse, Red Lobster, Subway, T.G.I. Friday's, and Chinese, Italian, and Japanese eateries; a Winn-Dixie Marketplace; a liquor store; a bank; a dry cleaner; and a tourist-information center with park passes for sale, among other services. All this is a short walk from your room.

Gaylord Palms Hotel and Convention Center ★★★★½

Rate per night $144–$289. **Pool** ★★★★. **Fridge in room** Yes. **Shuttle to parks** Yes (Disney only). **Maximum number of occupants per room** 4. **Special comments** Probably the closest you'll get off-World to Disney-level extravagance. Resort fee of $20/day.

6000 W. Osceola Pkwy.
Kissimmee
☎ 407-586-2000
gaylordpalms.com

THIS DECIDEDLY UPSCALE RESORT has a colossal convention facility and caters strongly to business clientele, but it's still a nice (if pricey) family resort. Hotel wings are defined by the three themed, glass-roofed atriums they overlook. Key West's design is reminiscent of island life in the Florida Keys; Everglades is an overgrown spectacle of shabby swamp chic, complete with piped-in cricket noise and a robotic alligator; and the immense, central St. Augustine harks back to Spanish Colonial Florida. Lagoons, streams, and waterfalls cut through and connect all three, and walkways and bridges abound. A fourth wing, Emerald Bay Tower, overlooks the Emerald Plaza shopping and dining area of the St. Augustine atrium. These rooms are the nicest and the most expensive, and they're mostly used by convention-goers. Though rooms have fridges and alarm clocks with CD players (as well as other perks such as high-speed Internet access), the rooms themselves really work better as retreats for adults than for kids. However, children will enjoy wandering the themed areas, playing in the family pool (with water-squirting octopus). In-room child care is provided by Kid's Nite Out (see page 75).

Orange Lake Resort ★★★★½

Rate per night $69–$289. **Pools** ★★★★. **Fridge in room** Yes. **Shuttle to parks** Yes (fee varies depending on destination). **Maximum number of occupants per room** Varies. **Special comments** This is a time-share property, but if you rent directly through the resort (as opposed to the sales office), you can avoid time-share sales pitches.

8505 W. Irlo Bronson
Memorial Hwy.
Kissimmee
☎ 407-239-0000 or
800-877-6522
orangelake.com

YOU COULD SPEND YOUR ENTIRE VACATION never leaving this property, about 6–10 minutes from the Disney theme parks. From its 10 pools and two mini–water parks to its golfing opportunities (36 holes of championship greens plus two nine-hole executive courses), Orange Lake offers an extensive menu of amenities and recreational opportunities. If you tire of lazing by the pool, try waterskiing, wakeboarding, tubing, fishing, or other activities on the 80-acre lake. There's also a live alligator show, exercise programs, organized competitive sports and games, arts-and-crafts sessions, and miniature golf. Activities don't end when the sun goes down. Karaoke, live music, a Hawaiian luau, and movies at the resort cinema are some of the evening options.

The 2,412 units are tastefully decorated and comfortably furnished, ranging from suites and studios to three-bedroom villas, all containing fully equipped kitchens. If you'd rather not cook on vacation, try one of the seven restaurants scattered across the resort: two cafés, three grills, one pizzeria, and a fast-food eatery. Babysitters are available to come to your villa, accompany your family on excursions, or take your children to attractions for you.

Radisson Resort Orlando-Celebration ★ ★ ★ ★

Rate per night $70–$250. **Pool** ★★★★½. **Fridge in room** Yes. **Shuttle to parks** Yes (Disney only). **Maximum number of occupants per room** 5. **Special comments** $12.50/day resort fee; kids age 10 and younger eat free with a paying adult at Mandolin's restaurant.

2900 Parkway Blvd.
Kissimmee
☎ 407-396-7000 or
800-634-4774
radissonorlando
resort.com

THE POOL ALONE IS WORTH A STAY HERE, but the Radisson Resort gets high marks in all areas. The free-form pool is huge, with a waterfall and waterslide surrounded by palms and flowering plants, plus a smaller heated pool, two whirlpools, and a kiddie pool. Other outdoor amenities include two lighted tennis courts, sand volleyball, a playground, and jogging areas. Kids can also blow off steam at the arcade, while adults might visit the fitness center. Rooms are elegant, featuring Italian furnishings and marble baths. They're of ample size and include minibar (some rooms), coffeemaker, TV, iron and board, hair dryer, and safe. Dining options include Mandolin's for breakfast (buffet) and dinner, and a 1950s-style diner serving burgers, sandwiches, shakes, and Pizza Hut pizza, among other fare. A sports lounge with a 6-by-11–foot TV offers nighttime entertainment. Guest services can help with tours, park passes, car rental, and babysitting. While there are no children's programs per se, there are plenty of activities such as face painting by a clown, juggling classes, bingo, and arts and crafts at the pool.

GETTING A GOOD DEAL ON A ROOM OUTSIDE WALT DISNEY WORLD

UNABLE TO COMPETE WITH Disney resorts for convenience or perks, out-of-World hotels lure patrons with bargain rates. The extent of the bargain depends on the season, day of the week, and local events. Here are tips and strategies for getting a good deal on a room outside Walt Disney World.

1. ORLANDO MAGICARD This discount program is sponsored by Visit Orlando. Cardholders are eligible for discounts of 12–50% at about 50 hotels. The Magicard is also good for discounts at some area attractions, three dinner theaters, museums, performing-arts venues, restaurants, shops, and more. Valid for up to six persons, the card isn't available for larger groups or conventions.

To obtain a free Magicard and a list of participating hotels and attractions, call ☎ 800-643-9492 or 407-363-5872. On the Web, go to **orlandoinfo.com/magicard;** the Magicard and accompanying brochure can be printed from a personal computer. If you miss getting one before you leave home, obtain one at the Convention and Visitors Bureau Information Center at 8723 International Dr. When you call for your Magicard, also request the *Official Vacation Guide.*

2. *HOTELCOUPONS.COM FLORIDA GUIDE* This book of coupons for lodging statewide is free in many restaurants and motels on main highways leading to Florida. Because most travelers make reservations before leaving home, picking up the book en route doesn't help much. To view it online or sign up for a free monthly e-guide, visit **hotelcoupons.com.** For a hard copy ($3 for handling, $5 if shipped to Canada), call ☎ 800-222-3948 Monday–Friday, 8 a.m.–5 p.m. Eastern time.

3. HOTEL SHOPPING ONLINE The secret to shopping on the Internet is . . . shopping. When we're really looking for a deal, we scour sites such as the ones below for unusually juicy hotel deals that meet our criteria (location, quality, price, amenities).

OUR FAVORITE ONLINE HOTEL RESOURCES
mousesavers.com Best site for hotels in Disney World
hotelcoupons.com Self-explanatory
floridakiss.com Primarily US 192–Kissimmee area hotels
orlandoinfo.com Good info; not user-friendly for booking
orlandovacation.com Great rates for condos and home rentals

If we find a hotel that fills the bill, we check it out at other websites and comparative travel search engines such as **Kayak** (**kayak .com**) and **Mobissimo** (**mobissimo.com**) to see who has the best rate. (As an aside, Kayak used to be purely a search engine but now sells travel products, raising the issue of whether products not sold by Kayak are equally likely to come up in a search. Mobissimo, on the other hand, only links potential buyers to provider websites.) Your initial shopping effort should take about 15–20 minutes, faster if you can zero in quickly on a particular hotel.

Next, armed with your insider knowledge of hotel economics, call the hotel or have your travel agent call. Start by asking about specials. If there are none, or if the hotel can't beat the best price you've found on the Internet, share your findings and ask if the hotel can do better. Sometimes you'll be asked for proof of the rate you've discovered online—to be prepared for this, go to the site and enter the dates of your stay, plus the rate you've found to make sure it's available. If it is, print the page with this information and have it handy for your travel agent or for when you call the hotel.

4. IF YOU MAKE YOUR OWN RESERVATION Always phone the hotel directly and ask about specials before you inquire about corporate rates. Don't hesitate to bargain, but do it before you check in. If you're buying a hotel's weekend package, for example, and want to extend your stay, you can often obtain at least the corporate rate for the extra days.

 Bob: Always call the hotel in question, not the hotel chain's national 800 number.

CONDOMINIUMS AND VACATION HOMES

VACATION HOMES ARE FREESTANDING, while condominiums are essentially one- to three-bedroom accommodations in a larger building housing a number of similar units. In a condo, if something goes wrong, someone will be on hand to fix the problem. Vacation homes rented from a property-management company likewise will have someone to come to the rescue, though responsiveness tends to vary vastly from company to company. If you rent directly from an owner, correcting problems is often more difficult, particularly when the owner doesn't live in the same area as the rental home.

Because condos tend to be part of large developments (frequently time-shares), amenities such as swimming pools, playgrounds, game arcades, and fitness centers often rival those found in the best hotels. In a vacation home, all the amenities are contained in the home (though in planned developments there may be community amenities available as well). Depending on the specific home, you might find a small swimming pool, hot tub, two-car garage, family room, game room, and even a home theater. Features found in both condos and vacation homes include full kitchens, laundry rooms, TVs, DVD players, and frequently stereos. Time-shares are clones when it comes to furniture and decor, but single-owner condos and vacation homes are furnished and decorated in a style that reflects the taste of the owner. Vacation homes very rarely afford interesting views (though some overlook lakes or natural areas), while condos, especially the high-rise variety, sometimes offer exceptional ones.

The Price Is Nice

The best deals in lodging in the Walt Disney World area are vacation homes and single-owner condos. Prices range from about $65 a night for two-bedroom condos and town homes to $200–$500 a night for three- to seven-bedroom vacation homes. Forgetting about taxes to keep the comparison simple, let's compare renting a vacation home to staying at one of Disney's Value resorts. A family of two parents, two teens, and two grandparents would need three hotel rooms at Disney's All-Star Resorts. At the lowest rate obtainable, that would run you $85 per night, per room, or $255 total. Rooms are 260 square feet each, so you'd have a total of 780 square feet. Each room has a private bath and TV.

Renting at the same time of year from **All Star Vacation Homes** (no relation to Disney's All-Star Resorts), you can stay at a 2,053-square-foot, four-bedroom, three-bath vacation home with a private pool 3 miles from Walt Disney World for $269—not quite as economical as Disney's Value resorts, but plenty of value all the same: With four bedrooms, each of the teens can have his or her own room. Further, for the dates we checked, All Star Vacation Homes was running a special in which they threw in a free rental car with a one-week home rental.

Location, Location, Location

The best vacation home is one that is within easy commuting distance of the theme parks. If you plan to spend some time at SeaWorld and the Universal parks, you'll want something just to the northeast of Walt Disney World (between the World and Orlando). If you plan to spend most of your time in the World, the best selection of vacation homes is along US 192 to the south of the park.

To get the most from a vacation home, you need to be close enough to commute in 20 minutes or less to your Walt Disney World destination. This proximity will allow for naps, quiet time, swimming, and dollar-saving meals you prepare yourself. Though traffic and road conditions are as important as the distance from a vacation home to your Disney destination, we recommend a home no farther than 5 miles away in areas northeast of Walt Disney World and no farther than 4.5 miles away in areas south of the park.

Recommended Websites

The only practical way to shop for a rental home is on the Web. Problem is, there are so many owners, rental companies, and individual homes to choose from that you could research yourself into a stupor. The best websites provide the following:

- Ease of navigation
- The ability to browse without having to log in or divulge personal information
- Photos and in-depth descriptions of individual homes
- Overview maps or text descriptions that reflect how distant specific homes or developments are from Walt Disney World
- The ability to book the specific rental home of your choice on the site
- A prominently displayed phone number for non-Internet bookings and questions

After checking out dozens upon dozens of sites, we narrowed our recommendations to the following:

All Star Vacation Homes (**allstarvacationhomes.com**) is easily the best of the sites run by vacation-home management companies, with plenty of photographs and details about featured homes. Properties are within either 4 miles of Walt Disney World or 3 miles of Universal. **#1 Dream Homes** (**floridadreamhomes.com**) also has a good reputation for customer service.

Vacation Rental by Owner (vrbo.com) is a nationwide vacation-homes listings service that puts prospective renters in direct contact with owners of rental homes. The site is straightforward and lists a large number of rental properties in Celebration, Disney's planned community situated about 8–10 minutes from the theme parks. Two similar listings services with good websites are **Vacation Rentals 411 (vacationrentals411.com)** and **Last Minute Villas (lastminutevillas.net)**.

Orlando's Finest Vacation Homes (orlandosfinest.com) represents both homeowners and management companies. It's not quite as comprehensive as sites such as All Star Vacation Homes, but friendly sales agents can help you fill in the blanks.

Visit Orlando (visitorlando.com) is the way to go when it comes to shopping for time-shares (click "Places to Stay" on the home page), because you can bypass these developments' notoriously high-pressure sales pitches. The site also lists hotels and vacation homes.

We frequently receive letters from readers extolling the virtues of renting a condo or vacation home. This endorsement from a New Jersey family of five is typical:

> *I cannot stress enough how important it is if you have a large family (more than two kids) to rent a house for your stay! . . . We stayed at Windsor Hills Resort, which I booked through* **globalresorthomes** **.com** . . . *It took us about 10 minutes to drive there in the a.m., and we had no traffic issues at all. We had a brand-new four-bedroom, four-bathroom house with our own pool. . . . All for $215 a night! This was in October, but rates never climb above $300, even in the high season. We loved getting away from the hubbub of Disney and relaxing back at the house in "our" pool.*

HOW *to* CHILDPROOF *a* HOTEL ROOM

SMALL CHILDREN UP TO 3 YEARS OLD (and sometimes older) can wreak mayhem—if not outright disaster—in a hotel room. Chances are you're pretty experienced when it comes to spotting potential dangers, but just in case you need a refresher course, here's what to look for.

Begin by checking for hazards that you can't fix yourself: balconies, chipping paint, cracked walls, sharp surfaces, shag carpeting, and windows that can't be secured shut. If you encounter anything that you don't like or is too much of a hassle to fix, ask for another room.

If you use a crib supplied by the hotel, make sure that the mattress is firm and covers the entire bottom of the crib. The mattress cover, if there is one, should fit tightly. Slats should be 2½ inches (about the width of a soda can) or less apart. Test the drop sides to ensure that they work properly. Check for sharp edges, along with chipping paint and other potentially toxic substances. Wipe down surfaces with disinfectant. Finally, position the crib away from drapery cords, heaters, wall sockets, and air conditioners.

A Monteno, Illinois, mom offers this suggestion:

> *You can request bed rails at the Disney resorts. Our 2½-year-old was too big for the pack-and-play; the bed rails worked perfectly for us.*

If your infant can turn over, we recommend changing him or her on a pad on the floor. Likewise, if you have a child seat of any sort, place it where it cannot be knocked over, and always strap your child in.

If your child can roll, crawl, or walk, you should bring about eight electrical outlet covers and some cord to tie cabinets shut and to bind drape cords and the like out of reach. Check for appliances, lamps, ashtrays, ice buckets, and anything else that your child might pull down on him- or herself. Have the hotel remove coffee tables with sharp edges, and both real and artificial plants that are within your child's reach. Round up items from tables and countertops such as matchbooks, courtesy toiletries, and drinking glasses, and store them out of reach.

If the bathroom door can be accidentally locked, cover the locking mechanism with duct tape or a doorknob cover. Use the security chain or upper latch on the room's entrance door to ensure that your child doesn't open it without your knowledge.

Inspect the floor and remove pins, coins, and other foreign objects that your child might find. Don't forget to check under beds and furniture. *Tip:* Crawl around the room on your hands and knees in order to see possible hazards from your child's perspective.

If you rent a suite or a condo, you'll have more territory to childproof and will have to stuff like cleaning supplies, a stove, a refrigerator, cooking utensils, and low cabinet doors, among other things. Sometimes the best option is to seal off the kitchen with a safety gate.

PART FOUR

DINING

DINING OPTIONS ABOUND BOTH IN AND OUT of Walt Disney World, and if you're so inclined, there are a lot of ways to save big bucks while keeping your crew nourished and happy.

EATING *outside* WALT DISNEY WORLD

1. A CAR HELPS Access to restaurants outside of Walt Disney World can really cut the cost of your overall vacation, but you need to have wheels. If you eat only your evening meal outside the World, the savings will more than pay for a rental car.

2. PLENTY OF CHOICES Eating outside of Walt Disney World doesn't relegate you to dining in lackluster restaurants. The range of choices is quite broad and includes elegant dining options, as well as familiar chain restaurants and local family eateries.

3. DISCOUNTS ARE EVERYWHERE Visitor magazines and booklets containing discount coupons to dozens of out-of-the-World restaurants are available everywhere except in Walt Disney World. The coupons are good at a broad selection of eateries, ranging from burger joints to some of the best restaurants in the area. Though coupon booklets and freebie visitor mags are pretty much everywhere, the mother lode can be found at the **Visit Orlando Official Visitor Center** at 8723 International Dr., Ste. 101, at the corner of Austrian Row, open 8:30 a.m.–6:30 p.m.; ☎ 407-363-5872. Here you'll find copies of every magazine and booklet available. The center also sells slightly discounted tickets to the theme parks. Also see **visitorlando.com.** The **Kids Eat Free Card** may be a good investment if you have young children and plan to eat off Disney property frequently. It provides free kids' meals at more than 50 restaurants in the Orlando area. To see a full listing, visit **kidseatfree card.com.** Each $20 card is valid for one child age 11 or younger and requires that the child be accompanied by one adult paying for a full price entrée.

You can save money at some Disney World–area restaurants by purchasing discounted gift certificates from **restaurant.com.** Most certificates are for a specific amount (usually $25) at a discounted price (usually $10). The certificates do not expire and can be printed at home. You can only use one certificate per restaurant per month (but that means you could use one certificate at each restaurant during your vacation). Occasionally there are other restrictions, so be sure to read the information provided on the site carefully. Some restaurants require you to buy a certain number of entrées, for instance. Note that restaurants occasionally drop out of the program, so call the restaurant before you go to reconfirm that it is still participating. If a restaurant is no longer a participant, you can change the certificate for another restaurant by contacting the site's customer service.

BUFFETS AND MEAL DEALS OUTSIDE WALT DISNEY WORLD

BUFFETS, RESTAURANT SPECIALS, and discount dining abound in the area surrounding Walt Disney World, especially on US 192 (known locally as Irlo Bronson Memorial Highway) and along International Drive. The local visitor magazines, distributed free at non-Disney hotels, among other places, are packed with advertisements and discount coupons for seafood feasts, Chinese buffets, Indian buffets, and breakfast buffets, as well as specials for everything from lobster to barbecue. For a family trying to economize, some of the come-ons are mighty sweet. But are these places any good? Is the food fresh, tasty, and appealing? Are the restaurants clean and inviting? Armed with little more than a roll of Tums, the *Unofficial* research team tried all the eateries that advertise heavily in the free tourist magazines. Here's what we discovered.

CHINESE SUPER BUFFETS If you've ever tried preparing Chinese food, especially a stir-fry, you know that split-second timing is required to avoid overcooking. So it should come as no big surprise that Chinese dishes languishing on a buffet lose their freshness and flavor in a hurry.

For the past few editions of this guide, we were able to find several Chinese buffets that were better than the rest and that we felt comfortable recommending. Unfortunately, however, our endorsements seem to be the kiss of death: We return the next year to discover that quality has slipped precipitously. We attempted to find a new buffet to replace the ones we deleted from the guide, and we can tell you that wasn't fun work. At the end of the day, **Ichiban Buffet** (5269 W. Irlo Bronson Memorial Highway; ☎ 407-396-6668; **ichibanfl.com**); **Dragon Court Chinese Buffet & Sushi Bar** (12384 S. Apopka–Vineland Road, just after FL 535 turns 90 degrees to the west; ☎ 407-238-9996; **dragon courtorlando.com**); and **Ace Plus Chinese Buffet** (8701 W. Irlo Bronson Memorial Hwy.; ☎ 407-390-7588; **acepluschinesebuffet.com**) are the only Asian buffets we've elected to list. Ichiban, with Japanese, Chinese, and American offerings, is the pick of the litter. Dragon Court is friendly and low-key with a faithful local clientele and a good selection of mainly Chinese dishes. Ace Plus is a good choice if you're staying near where West Irlo Bronson intersects the FL 429 toll road.

INDIAN BUFFETS Indian food works better on a buffet than Chinese food; in fact, it actually improves as the flavors marry. In the Disney

World area, most Indian restaurants offer a buffet at lunch only—not too convenient if you're spending your day at the theme parks. If you're out shopping or taking a day off, these Indian buffets are worth trying:

AASHIRWAD INDIAN CUISINE 5748 International Dr., at the corner of International Drive and Kirkman Road; ☎ 407-370-9830; **aashirwadrestaurant.com**

PUNJAB INDIAN RESTAURANT 7451 International Dr.; ☎ 407-352-7887; **punjabindianrestaurant.com**

SOUTH AMERICAN BUFFETS A number of these have sprung up along International Drive. The best of these is **Café Mineiro** (6432 International Dr.; ☎ 407-248-2932; **cafemineiroorlando.com**), a Brazilian steak house north of Sand Lake Road. The Argentinean churrasco specialties at **The Knife** (12501 FL 535; ☎ 321-395-4892; **thekniferestaurant.com**) are worth a try as well.

SEAFOOD AND LOBSTER BUFFETS These affairs don't exactly fall under the category of inexpensive dining. The main draw (no pun intended) is all the lobster you can eat. The problem is that lobsters, like Chinese food, don't wear well on a steam table. After a few minutes on the buffet line, they make better tennis balls than dinner. If, however, there's someone in the kitchen who knows how to steam a lobster, and if you grab your lobster immediately after a fresh batch has been brought out, it'll probably be fine. There are three lobster buffets on US 192 and another two on International Drive. Although all five do a reasonable job, we prefer **Boston Lobster Feast** (6071 W. Irlo Bronson Memorial Hwy.; ☎ 407-396-2606; and 8731 International Dr., five blocks north of the Convention Center; ☎ 407-248-8606; **bostonlobsterfeast.com**). Both locations are distinguished by a vast variety of seafood in addition to the lobster. The International Drive location is cavernous and insanely noisy, which is why we prefer the Irlo Bronson location, where you can actually have a conversation over dinner. The International Drive location has ample parking, while parking places are in short supply at the Irlo Bronson restaurant. At about $38 for early birds (4–6 p.m.) and $43 after 6 p.m., dining is expensive at both locations.

SALAD BUFFETS The most popular of these in the Walt Disney World area is **Sweet Tomatoes** (6877 S. Kirkman Rd., ☎ 407-363-1616; 12561 S. Apopka–Vineland Rd., ☎ 407-938-9461; 3236 Rolling Oaks Blvd., off US 192 near the FL 429 western entrance to Walt Disney World, ☎ 407-966-4664; **sweettomatoes.com**). During lunch and dinner, you can expect a line out the door, but fortunately one that moves fast. The buffet features prepared salads and an extensive array of ingredients for building your own. In addition to the rabbit food, Sweet Tomatoes offers a variety of soups, a modest pasta bar, a baked-potato bar, an assortment of fresh fruit, and ice-cream sundaes. Dinner runs $12 for adults, $8 for children ages 6–12, and $5 for children ages 3–5. Lunch costs $10 for adults, $6 for children ages 6–12, and $4 for children ages 3–5.

Where to Eat outside Walt Disney World

AMERICAN

JOHNNIE'S HIDEAWAY 12551 FL 535, Orlando; ☎ 407-827-1111; **talkofthetown restaurants.com/johnnies.html;** moderate to expensive. Seafood and steaks, with an emphasis on Florida cuisine.

THE RAVENOUS PIG★ 1234 N. Orange Ave., Winter Park; ☎ 407-628-2333; **theravenouspig.com;** moderate–expensive. New American cuisine with an award-winning menu that changes frequently, with seasonal ingredients.

BARBECUE

BUBBALOU'S BODACIOUS BAR-B-QUE 5818 Conroy Rd., Orlando (near Universal Orlando); ☎ 407-295-1212; **bubbalous.com;** inexpensive. Tender, smoky barbecue; tomato-based "killer" sauce.

4 RIVERS SMOKEHOUSE 1047 S. Dillard St., Winter Garden; ☎ 407-474-8377; **4rsmokehouse.com;** inexpensive. Award-winning beef brisket; fried pickles, cheese grits, fried okra, and collard greens.

CHINESE

MING'S BISTRO★ 1212 Woodward St., Orlando; ☎ 407-898-9672; inexpensive. Authentic Chinese, including dim sum, crispy roast pork, and roast duck.

CUBAN/SPANISH

COLUMBIA 649 Front St., Celebration; ☎ 407-566-1505; **columbiarestaurant.com;** moderate. Cuban/Spanish creations such as paella and the 1905 salad.

FRENCH

LE COQ AU VIN★ 4800 S. Orange Ave., Orlando; ☎ 407-851-6980; **lecoqauvin restaurant.com;** moderate–expensive. Country French cuisine in a relaxed atmosphere. Reservations suggested.

INDIAN

MEMORIES OF INDIA 7625 Turkey Lake Rd., Orlando; ☎ 407-370-3277; **memoriesofindiacuisine.com;** inexpensive–moderate. Classic tandoori dishes, samosas, *tikka masala,* and Sunday Champagne brunch with buffet.

RAGA 7559 W. Sand Lake Rd., Orlando; ☎ 407-985-2900; **ragarestaurant.com;** moderate. Blend of Indian, Pakistani, and Middle Eastern cuisines prepared with locally sourced ingredients.

ITALIAN

BICE ORLANDO RISTORANTE Loews Portofino Bay, 5601 Universal Blvd., Orlando; ☎ 407-503-1415; **orlando.bicegroup.com;** expensive. Authentic Italian; great wines.

ANTHONY'S COAL-FIRED PIZZA 8031 Turkey Lake Rd., Orlando; ☎ 407-363-9466; **anthonyscoalfiredpizza.com;** inexpensive. Pizza, eggplant, pasta, beer and wine.

JAPANESE/SUSHI

AMURA 7786 W. Sand Lake Rd., Orlando; ☎ 407-370-0007; **amura.com;** moderate. A favorite sushi bar for locals. The tempura is popular too.

HANAMIZUKI 8255 International Dr., Orlando; ☎ 407-363-7200; **hanamizuki.us;** moderate–expensive. Usually filled with Japanese visitors; pricey but authentic.

NAGOYA SUSHI 7600 Dr. Phillips Blvd., Ste. 66, in the very rear of The Marketplace at Dr. Phillips; ☎ 407-248-8558; **nagoyasushi.com;** moderate. A small, intimate restaurant with great sushi and an extensive menu.

*20 minutes or more from Walt Disney World

MEXICAN

CANTINA LAREDO 800 Via Dellagio Way, Orlando; ☎ 407-345-0186; **cantinalaredo. com;** moderate–expensive. Authentic Mexican in an upscale atmosphere.

CHEVYS FRESH MEX 12547 FL 535, Lake Buena Vista; ☎ 407-827-1052; **chevys.com;** inexpensive–moderate. Across from the FL 535 entrance to WDW.

EL PATRON 12167 S. Apopka–Vineland Rd., Orlando; ☎ 407-238-5300; **elpatronrestaurantcantina.com;** inexpensive. Family-owned restaurant serving freshly prepared Mexican dishes. Full bar.

MOE'S SOUTHWEST GRILL 7541-D W. Sand Lake Rd., Orlando; ☎ 407-264-9903; **moes.com;** inexpensive. Dependable southwestern fare.

TAQUITOS JALISCO 1041 S. Dillard St., Winter Garden; ☎ 407-654-0363; inexpensive. Low-key. Flautas, chicken mole, fajitas, hearty burritos, good vegetarian.

SEAFOOD

BONEFISH GRILL 7830 W. Sand Lake Rd., Orlando; ☎ 407-355-7707; **bonefish grill.com;** moderate. Casual setting along busy Restaurant Row on Sand Lake Road. Choose your fish; then choose a sauce to accompany. Also has steaks and chicken.

CELEBRATION TOWN TAVERN 721 Front St., Celebration; ☎ 407-566-2526; **thecelebrationtowntavern.com;** moderate. Popular hangout for locals, with New England–style seafood. Clam chowder is a big hit.

STEAK/PRIME RIB

BULL & BEAR Waldorf Astoria Orlando, 14200 Bonnet Creek Resort Ln., Orlando; ☎ 407-597-5500; **waldorfastoriaorlando.com/dining/bullandbear;** expensive. Classic steakhouse with a clubby ambience. Steaks, seafood, lamb chops, and more.

TEXAS DE BRAZIL 5259 International Dr., Orlando; ☎ 407-355-0355; **texasdebrazil.com;** expensive. All-you-can-eat Brazilian-style *churrascaria*. Ribs, filet mignon, chicken, lamb, and salad bar. Kids ages 3–5 eat for $5, ages 6–12 for half price.

VITO'S CHOP HOUSE 8633 International Dr., Orlando; ☎ 407-354-2467; **vitoschophouse.com;** moderate. Upscale meat house with a taste of Tuscany.

THAI

RED BAMBOO 6803 S. Kirkman Rd. at International Dr., Orlando; ☎ 407-226-8997; **redbamboothai.com;** moderate. Acclaimed by Orlando dining critics for its authentic Thai dishes. Delicious vegetarian options; impressive wine list.

*20 minutes or more from Walt Disney World

BREAKFAST AND ENTRÉE BUFFETS Most chain steak houses in the area, including **Ponderosa, Sizzler,** and **Golden Corral,** offer entrée buffets. Among them, they have 18 locations in the Walt Disney World area. All serve breakfast, lunch, and dinner. At lunch and dinner, you get the buffet when you buy an entrée, usually a steak; breakfast service is a straightforward buffet (that is, you aren't obligated to buy an entrée). As for the food, it's chain-restaurant quality but decent all the same. Prices are a bargain, and you can get in and out at lightning speed—important at breakfast when you're trying to get to the theme parks early. Some locations offer lunch and dinner buffets at a set price without your having to buy an entrée.

Though you can argue about which chain serves the best steak, **Golden Corral** wins the buffet contest hands-down, with at least twice as many offerings as its three competitors (visit **goldencorral.com** and click "Find a Restaurant" for Orlando locations). While buffets at Golden Corral and Ponderosa are pretty consistent from location to location, the buffets at the different Sizzlers vary a good deal. Our pick of the Sizzlers is the one at 7602 W. Irlo Bronson Memorial Hwy. (☎ 407-397-0997). In addition to the steak houses, area **Shoney's** also offer breakfast, lunch, and dinner buffets. Local freebie visitor magazines are full of discount coupons for all of the previous restaurants.

MEAL DEALS Discount coupons are available for a wide range of restaurants, including some wonderful upscale-ethnic places such as **Ming Court** (Chinese; 9188 International Dr., Orlando; ☎ 407-351-9988; **ming-court.com**).

A meat eater's delight is the Feast for Four at **Sonny's Real Pit Bar-B-Q.** For $40 per family of four, you get sliced pork and beef plus chicken, ribs, your choice of three sides (choose from beans, slaw, fries, among others), garlic bread or corn bread, and soft drinks or tea, all served family-style. The closest Sonny's location to Walt Disney World and Universal is at 7423 S. Orange Blossom Trail in Orlando (☎ 407-859-7197; **sonnysbbq.com.**) No coupons are available (or needed) for Sonny's, but they're available for the other "meateries."

A meatery to approach with caution is **Western Sizzlin's Wood Grill Buffet** (11701 International Dr.; ☎ 407-778-4844), whose ubiquitous ads tantalizingly depict steak, ribs, and the like. In point of fact, none of these items are available for lunch, and we advise calling ahead to see what's available for dinner.

COUPONS Find discounts and two-for-one coupons for many of the restaurants mentioned in freebie visitor guides available at most hotels outside of Walt Disney World. The **Orlando–Orange County Official Visitors Center** (8723 International Dr.; ☎ 407-363-5872; open daily, 8:30 a.m.–6:30 p.m., except Christmas) offers a treasure trove of coupons and free visitor magazines. On the Internet, check out **coupons alacarte.com** and **orlandocoupons.com** for printable coupons.

DINING *in* WALT DISNEY WORLD

ONCE YOU COULD HAVE JOKED that a chapter about dining in Walt Disney World was an oxymoron. Whatever else it was (and it was many wonderful things), Disney World was no gourmet paradise. For the most part, in fact, the restaurants were as much entertainment as the rest of Disney World: Then and now, fast-food joints feature character decor, and the waitstaff at the Epcot pavilions sport native costumes.

Over the years, however, Disney's food-and-beverage department has not only vastly expanded but has succeeded in upgrading the full-service restaurants around the World. Now there are 9 or 10 first-class restaurants and perhaps an equal number of B+ establishments. The wine lists have been seriously improved and expanded (there's even a wine bar, **Martha's Vineyard,** at the Yacht & Beach Club).

Of course, if the average parents roaming Walt Disney World were primarily concerned with pleasing their palates, the hottest dinner ticket in the parks wouldn't be the *Hoop-Dee-Doo Musical Revue.* In fact, if you want to know what Disney World visitors really like, look at the numbers: Every year, they consume 1.6 million turkey legs, nearly 10 million hamburgers, 7.7 million hot dogs, 46 million sodas, and 5 million bags of popcorn.

So for many families, food is a secondary consideration, but if you do care about dining out on your vacation or you'd like to experiment with different cuisines, *The Unofficial Guide to Walt Disney World,* a.k.a. the "Big Book," includes detailed reviews of the sit-down establishments in the World.

 Liliane: One thing parents should be aware of is that both full- and counter-service restaurants at Walt Disney World serve very substantial portions. You can easily put aside parts of dinners for lunches the next day (if you have a fridge in your room), split an entrée, or load up at lunch and go light on dinner.

"WAITER, THESE PRICES ARE GIVING ME HEARTBURN!"

INCREASES IN DISNEY'S TICKET COSTS are always sure to grab headlines, but most people haven't noticed that Disney's restaurant prices rise about as fast. For example, while the cost of a one-day theme park ticket has increased about 20% since 2010, the average entrée price at Le Cellier has gone from around $28 to over $39—an increase of 41%. Plus, Disney levies a "dining surcharge" during the summer and other busy times of year. Factoring in the surcharge, an adult breakfast at The Crystal Palace has increased almost 43% during the same time.

You might need a stiff drink after seeing those menu prices, but alcohol is no bargain either. While the average bottle of wine in WDW costs three times as much as retail, some wines have much higher markups. For example, a $6 bottle of Placido Pinot Grigio costs $39 in Epcot and various Disney resort lounges—six-and-a-half times as much as the retail price. If you rent a car and eat dinner each day at non-Disney restaurants, you'll save enough to more than pay for the rental cost.

This comment from a New Orleans mom spells it out:

> *Disney keeps pushing prices up and up. For us, the sky is NOT the limit. We won't be back.*

ADVANCE RESERVATIONS: WHAT'S IN A NAME?

DISNEY TINKERS CEASELESSLY with its restaurant-reservations policy. When you call, your name and essential information are taken as if you were making an honest-to-goodness reservation for the restaurant on the date and time you requested. Though they're called Advance Reservations, most reservations at Disney World don't guarantee you a table at a specific time, as they would at your typical hometown restaurant. The Disney rep usually explains that you'll be seated ahead of walk-ins—that is, those who do not have Advance Reservations.

GETTING AN ADVANCE RESERVATION AT POPULAR RESTAURANTS

DINNER AT THE MAGIC KINGDOM'S **Be Our Guest** restaurant, in New Fantasyland, and the 8 a.m. breakfast slots at **Cinderella's Royal Table,** in Cinderella Castle, are the two hardest-to-get reservations in Walt Disney World. Why? Be Our Guest has the best food in the park, awesome atmosphere, and good word of mouth; Cinderella's Royal Table is Disney's tiniest character restaurant, accommodating only about 130 diners at a time. You'll have to hustle to secure an Advance Reservation at these places.

 Bob: The $10 penalty fee for skipping an Advance Reservation at many Disney restaurants has reduced no-shows to as few as 2% during especially busy times of year.

The easiest and fastest way to get a reservation is go to **disneyworld.disney.go.com /dining** starting at 6 a.m. Eastern time, a full hour before phone reservations open. To familiarize yourself with how the site works, try it out a couple of days before you actually need to make reservations. You'll also save time by setting up an account online before your 180-day booking window, making sure to enter any credit-card information needed to guarantee your reservations. If you live in California and have to get up at 3 a.m. Pacific time to make a reservation, Disney couldn't care less.

Disney's website is usually within a few seconds of the official time as determined by the U.S. Naval Observatory or the National Institute of Standards and Technology, accessible online at **time.gov.** Using this site, synchronize your computer to the second the night before your 180-day window opens.

Early on the morning you want to make reservations, take a few minutes to type the date of your visit into a word processor in MM/DD/YYYY format (for example, 11/16/2014 for November 16, 2014). Select the date and copy it to your computer's clipboard by pressing the Ctrl and C keys simultaneously (Command-C on Mac) or right-clicking your mouse and selecting "Copy"). This will save you from having to type in the date when the site comes online.

Next, start trying Disney's website about 3 minutes before 6 a.m. You'll see a text box where you can specify the date of your visit. Click the text box and press Ctrl-A, then Ctrl-V (substitute *Command* for *Ctrl* on Mac) to paste the date; then press the tab key on your keyboard. (You can also click on the blue calendar icon to flip through a month-by-month calendar, or you can select the entire date in the text box, right-click your mouse, and select "Paste," but these are slower.) You'll also see a place to specify the time of your meal and your party size; you can fill these in ahead of time, too.

Above the "Party Size" widget is a text box with the words "Search within Dining." Start typing your restaurant name in that text box. As

Advance Reservations: The Official Line

YOU CAN RESERVE THE FOLLOWING up to 180 days in advance:

AFTERNOON TEA AND CHILDREN'S PROGRAMS at the Grand Floridian Resort & Spa

ALL DISNEY TABLE-SERVICE RESTAURANTS and character-dining venues

FANTASMIC! **DINING PACKAGE** at Disney's Hollywood Studios

HOOP-DEE-DOO MUSICAL REVUE at Fort Wilderness Resort & Campground

MICKEY'S BACKYARD BBQ at Fort Wilderness Resort & Campground

SPIRIT OF ALOHA DINNER SHOW at the Polynesian Resort

Guests staying at Walt Disney World resorts—these do *not* include the Swan, the Dolphin, Shades of Green, or the hotels of the Downtown Disney Resort Area—can book their dining 180 days before their arrival date and can book dining reservations for their entire length of stay (up to 10 days).

soon as you start typing, the website will start guessing which restaurant you want and offer a list of suggestions. It's faster if you just type a few letters—*bog* or *cin* are enough for the site to know you mean Be Our Guest and Cinderella's Royal Table, respectively. Click on the desired restaurant in the list of suggestions. Finally, click "Find a Table" or hit the Enter key on your keyboard—both submit your request to CDRS.

If your date isn't yet available, a message will appear saying "There is a problem searching for reservations at this time" or something similar. If this happens, refresh the browser page and start over. If you don't see an error message, however, the results returned will tell you whether your restaurant has a table available.

Bear in mind that while you're typing, other guests are trying to make Advance Reservations, too, so you want the transaction to go down as quickly as possible. Flexibility on your part counts—it's much harder to get a seating for a large group, so give some thought to breaking your group into numbers that can be accommodated at tables for four. Also make sure that you have your credit card out where you can read it.

All Advance Reservations for Cinderella's Royal Table character meals, the *Fantasmic!* Dining Package, the *Hoop-Dee-Doo Musical Revue*, the *Spirit of Aloha Dinner Show*, and *Mickey's Backyard BBQ* require complete prepayment with a credit card at the time of the booking. The name on the booking can't be changed after the Advance Reservation is made. Reservations may be canceled, with the deposit refunded in full, by calling ☎ 407-WDW-DINE at least 24 hours (Cindy's) or 48 hours (*Fantasmic!* and the dinner shows) before seating time.

While many readers have been successful using our strategies, some have not:

Advance Reservations: The Unofficial *Scoop*

BECAUSE DISNEY CHARGES a $10-per-person no-show penalty at many popular restaurants, some of those restaurants' no-show rates have dropped almost to zero. The penalty ensures that serious diners have some chance to get into Disney's better restaurants.

These days you'll need to reserve only a few breakfast venues in advance most times of the year. The most popular of these is **Cinderella's Royal Table** at the Magic Kingdom. If you don't care what time you eat, you'll need to call about 10 weeks out to get in for breakfast. If you're visiting during a holiday or peak season, or you want a specific time such as 8 a.m., you'll need to call a full 180 days in advance. If Cindy's is unavailable, we recommend **'Ohana** at the Polynesian Resort, which can be booked as little as a week before your trip.

Likewise, only a handful of restaurants require lunch reservations. The most popular is Epcot's **Le Cellier Steakhouse,** in the Canada Pavilion, which fills up about three months in advance; Cinderella's Royal Table, which fills up during about the same time frame; and **Akershus Royal Banquet Hall** in the Norway Pavilion, which fills up about 7–10 weeks out.

Except for **Be Our Guest Restaurant** at the Magic Kingdom, for which reservations are snapped up as soon as they're available, dinner reservations are generally easy to get within 60 days at most locations, as long as you're not particular about the time you eat. (If that's critical to your family's happiness, click or call 180 days in advance.)

I got up extra-early 180 days before our trip to get Thanksgiving reservations at Le Cellier for my husband's birthday. Even though I logged on to Disney's website right at 6 a.m., by the time I got done typing and clicking the only table that was available was for 8:40 p.m.—too late for our children, and we would have missed IllumiNations.

On most days, a couple hundred users slam Disney's computer system within milliseconds of one another. With this volume, a 20th of a second or less can make the difference between getting a table and not getting one. As it happens, there are variables beyond your control. One is the number of computers through which your request passes before it reaches Disney's reservation system. The explanation—explained in excruciating detail in the Big Book—is rather technical, but the same principle applies whether you're trying to get dining reservations online with Disney or concert seats through Ticketmaster.

If you don't have access to a computer at 6 a.m. on the morning you need to make reservations, Disney's phone agents begin taking calls at 7 a.m. Eastern time. Call ☎ 407-WDW-DINE and follow the prompts to speak to a live person. You may still get placed on hold if call volume is higher than usual, and you'll be an hour behind the early birds with computers. Still, you'll be well ahead of those who couldn't make it up before sunrise.

Also, if you're on the Disney Dining Plan and you want to book the *Fantasmic!* package, Cinderella's Royal Table, or one the dinner shows, you may be better off reserving by phone. The online system may not recognize your table-service credits, but you can book and pay with a credit card and then call ☎ 407-WDW-DINE after 7 a.m. and have them credit the charge for the meal back to your card (a potential hassle if you get an uncooperative cast member). When you get to Walt Disney World, you'll use credits from your dining plan to "pay" for the meal. (Sometimes the online system has glitches and shows no availability; in this case, call after 7 a.m. to confirm if the online system is correct.)

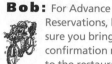

Bob: For Advance Reservations, be sure you bring your confirmation number to the restaurant.

If You Still Can't Get an Advance Reservation

If you insist on a meal at a specific restaurant but can't get an Advance Reservation, go to the restaurant on the day you wish to dine and try for a table as a walk-in (most full-service restaurants take walk-ins between 2:30 and 4:30 p.m.). This is a long shot, though it's possible during the least busy times of year. There's also a fair shot at success on cold or rainy days during busier seasons, when there's a good chance of no-shows. If you try to walk in then, your chances are best during the last hour of serving.

Landing an Advance Reservation for Cinderella's Royal Table at dinner is somewhat easier than for breakfast or lunch, but the price is a whopping $53 for adults and $34 for children ages 3–9. As at the other two meals, five photos of your group, a photo of Cinderella Castle, and a Cinderella-themed photo holder are included in the price—like it or not. If you're unable to lock up a table for breakfast or lunch, a dinner reservation will at least get your children inside the castle.

Canceling an Advance Reservation

Disney charges a per-person penalty fee if you fail to show up for an Advance Reservation at a character meal or Disney Signature restaurant, or if you cancel within 24 hours of the meal. Happily, you won't be penalized at all as long as at least one person in your party shows up. A $10 no-show penalty is enforced at the following restaurants: **Akershus Royal Banquet Hall, Artist Point, California Grill, Cape May Cafe, Le Cellier Steakhouse, Chef Mickey's, Cítricos, The Crystal Palace, Flying Fish Cafe, Garden Grill Restaurant, Hollywood & Vine, The Hollywood Brown Derby, Jiko—The Cooking Place, Narcoossee's, 1900 Park Fare, 'Ohana, Tusker House Restaurant,** and **Yachtsman Steakhouse.** At **Victoria & Albert's,** it's $25 for the main dining room, $50 for the Queen Victoria Room and Chef's Table (the latter two also require 48 hours' notice to cancel an Advance Reservation).

DRESS

DRESS IS INFORMAL at most theme park restaurants, but Disney has a "business casual" dress code for some of its resort restaurants: khakis, dress slacks, jeans, or dress shorts with a collared shirt for men and capris, skirts, dresses, jeans, and dress shorts for women. Restaurants with this dress code are **Jiko—The Cooking Place** at Animal Kingdom Lodge & Villas, the **Flying Fish Cafe** at the BoardWalk, the **California Grill** at the Contemporary Resort, **Monsieur Paul** at Epcot's France Pavilion, **Cítricos** and **Narcoossee's** at the Grand Floridian Resort & Spa, **Artist Point** at Wilderness Lodge & Villas, **Yachtsman Steakhouse** at the Yacht Club Resort, **Todd English's bluezoo** and **Shula's Steak House** at the Dolphin, and **Il Mulino New York Trattoria** at the Swan. **Victoria & Albert's** at the Grand Floridian is the only Disney restaurant that requires men to wear a jacket to dinner.

Also, be aware that smoking is banned at all restaurants and lounges on Walt Disney World property. Diners who puff must feed their nicotine fix outdoors—and in the theme parks, that might also mean going to a designated smoking area.

FOOD ALLERGIES AND SPECIAL REQUESTS

IF YOU HAVE FOOD ALLERGIES or observe some specific type of diet (such as eating kosher), make your needs known when you make your Advance Reservations. For more information, e-mail **specialdiets @disneyworld.com** or visit **tinyurl.com/wdwspecialdiets.**

A Phillipsburg, New Jersey, mom reports her family's experience:

My 6-year-old has many food allergies. When making my Advance Reservations, I indicated these to the clerk. When we arrived at the restaurants, the staff was already aware of my child's allergies and assigned our table a chef who double-checked the list of allergies with us. The chefs were very nice and made my son feel very special.

A Charlotte, North Carolina, mom offers this handy tip:

A website called **AllergyEats** (**allergyeats.com/disney**) *is a lifesaver. Put in your allergies and your park, and it shows you what you can eat.*

A FEW CAVEATS

BEFORE YOU BEGIN EATING your way through the World, you need to know:

1. Theme park restaurants rush their customers in order to make room for the next group of diners. Dining at high speed may appeal to a family with young, restless children, but for people wanting to relax, it's more like eating in a pressure chamber than fine dining.

2. Disney restaurants have comparatively few tables for parties of two, and servers are generally disinclined to seat two guests at larger tables. If you're a duo, you might have to wait longer—sometimes much longer—to be seated.

3. At full-service Disney restaurants, an automatic gratuity of 18% is added to your tab—even at buffets where you get your own food.

4. If you're dining in a theme park and cost is an issue, make lunch your main meal. Entrées are similar to those on the dinner menu, but prices are significantly lower.

5. Disney adds a surcharge of $4 per adult and $2 per child to certain popular restaurants during weeks of peak attendance, including Presidents Day, Spring Break, Easter, mid-December–New Year's Eve, and every day from early June to early August. The following restaurants participate in the gouging: **Akershus Royal Banquet Hall** (Princess Storybook Dining), **Biergarten, Boma— Flavors of Africa** (breakfast and dinner), **Cape May Cafe** (breakfast and dinner buffet), **Chef Mickey's** (breakfast and dinner), **Cinderella's Royal Table, The Crystal Palace, Garden Grill Restaurant, Hollywood & Vine** (Play 'n Dine character buffets), *Liberty Tree Tavern* (dinner), **1900 Park Fare** (Supercalifragilistic Breakfast and Cinderella's Happily Ever After Dinner), **'Ohana** (breakfast and dinner), the *Spirit of Aloha Dinner Show,* **Trail's End Restaurant** at Fort Wilderness (an exception: $2 extra for adults and $1 for kids), and **Tusker House Restaurant.**

WALT DISNEY WORLD RESTAURANT CATEGORIES

IN GENERAL, FOOD AND BEVERAGE offerings at Walt Disney World are defined by service, price, and convenience.

FULL-SERVICE RESTAURANTS Full-service restaurants are in all Disney resorts (except the All-Star Resorts, Art of Animation, Port Orleans French Quarter, and Pop Century) and all major theme parks, Downtown Disney Marketplace, and Downtown Disney West Side. Disney operates most of the restaurants in the theme parks and its hotels, while contractors or franchisees operate the restaurants in hotels of the Downtown Disney Resort Area (DDRA), the Swan and Dolphin resorts, and some in Disney's Animal Kingdom, Epcot, the BoardWalk, and Downtown Disney Marketplace–West Side. Advance Reservations (see page 143) are recommended for most full-service restaurants except those in the DDRA. The restaurants accept American Express, Carte Blanche, Diners Club, Japan Credit Bureau, MasterCard, and Visa.

BUFFETS AND FAMILY-STYLE RESTAURANTS Many of these have Disney characters in attendance, and most have a separate children's menu featuring dishes such as hot dogs, burgers, chicken nuggets, pizza, macaroni and cheese, and spaghetti and meatballs. In addition to the buffets, several restaurants serve a family-style, all-you-can-eat, fixed-price meal.

Advance Reservations are required for character buffets and recommended for all other buffets and family-style restaurants. Most major credit cards are accepted.

If you want to eat a lot but don't feel like standing in yet another line, then consider one of the all-you-can-eat family-style restaurants. These feature platters of food brought to your table in courses by a server. You can eat as much as you like—even go back to a favorite appetizer after you finish the main course. The food tends to be a little better than what you'll find on a buffet line.

The table on page 150 lists buffets and family-style restaurants (where you can belly up for bulk loading) at Walt Disney World.

FOOD COURTS Featuring a collection of counter-service eateries under one roof, food courts can be found at the Moderate resorts (Coronado

Walt Disney World Buffets and Family-Style Restaurants

RESTAURANT	LOCATION	CUISINE	MEALS SERVED	CHAR-ACTERS
Akershus Royal Banquet Hall	Epcot	American (B), Norwegian (L, D)	B, L, D	Yes
Biergarten	Epcot	German	L, D	No
Boma—Flavors of Africa	Animal Kingdom Lodge	African (D), American (B)	B, D	No
Cape May Café	Beach Club Resort	American	B, D	Yes (B)
Captain's Grille	Yacht Club Resort	American	B*, L, D	No
Chef Mickey's	Contemporary Resort	American	B, D	Yes
Cinderella's Royal Table	The Magic Kingdom	American	B*, L, D	Yes
The Crystal Palace	The Magic Kingdom	American	B, L, D	Yes
The Garden Grill	Epcot	American	D	Yes
Garden Grove	Swan	American	B****, L, D****	Yes (B**)
Hollywood & Vine	Disney's Hollywood Studios	American	B, L, D	Yes (B, L)
Hoop-Dee-Doo Musical Revue	Fort Wilderness	American	D	No
LakeView Restaurant	Wyndham LBV Resort	American	B****, D	Yes (B***)
Liberty Tree Tavern	The Magic Kingdom	American	L, D*	No
Mickey's Backyard BBQ	Fort Wilderness	American	D	Yes
1900 Park Fare	Grand Floridian	American	B, D	Yes
'Ohana	Polynesian Resort	Polynesian	B, D	Yes (B)
Spirit of Aloha Dinner Show	Polynesian Resort	American	D	No
Trail's End Restaurant	Fort Wilderness	American	B****, L, D****	No
Tusker House Restaurant	Disney's Animal Kingdom	African (L, D), American (B)	B, L, D	Yes (B, L)
Whispering Canyon Café	Wilderness Lodge	American	B, L, D	No

    *   Serves family-style meals only at the meal(s) indicated.

  **   Character-breakfast buffet served only on weekends.

 ***   Character-breakfast buffet served three times a week.

**** Serves buffet-style meals only at the meal(s) indicated.

Springs, Caribbean Beach, Port Orleans) and Value resorts (All-Star, Art of Animation, and Pop Century). (The closest thing to a food court at the theme parks is **Sunshine Seasons** at Epcot; see below and page 166.) Advance Reservations are neither required nor available at these restaurants.

COUNTER SERVICE Counter-service fast food is available in all theme parks and at Downtown Disney Marketplace, the BoardWalk, and Downtown Disney West Side. The food compares in quality with Captain D's, McDonald's, or Taco Bell but is more expensive, though often served in larger portions.

FAST CASUAL Somewhere between burgers and formal dining are the establishments in Disney's "fast casual" category, including three in the theme parks: **Tomorrowland Terrace Restaurant** in the Magic Kingdom, **Sunshine Seasons** in Epcot, and **Studio Catering Co.** in Disney's Hollywood Studios. Fast-casual restaurants feature menu choices a cut above what you'd normally see at a typical counter-service location. At Sunshine Seasons, for example, chefs will prepare grilled salmon on an open cooking surface while you watch, or you can choose from rotisserie chicken or pork, tasty noodle bowls, or large sandwiches made with artisanal breads. Entrées cost about $2 more on average than traditional counter service, but the variety and food quality more than make up for the difference.

VENDOR FOOD Vendors abound at the theme parks, Downtown Disney Marketplace, Downtown Disney West Side, and the BoardWalk. Offerings include popcorn, ice-cream bars, churros (Mexican pastries), soft drinks, bottled water, and (in theme parks) fresh fruit. Prices include tax; many vendors are set up to accept credit cards, charges to your room at a Disney resort, and the Disney Dining Plan. Others take only cash (look for a sign near the cash register).

HARD CHOICES

DINING DECISIONS WILL DEFINITELY affect your Walt Disney World experience. If you're short on time and you want to see the theme parks, avoid full service. Ditto if you're short on funds. If you do want full service, arrange Advance Reservations—again, they won't actually reserve you a table, but they can minimize your wait.

Integrating Meals into the *Unofficial Guide* Touring Plans

Arrive before the park of your choice opens. Tour expeditiously, using your chosen plan (taking as few breaks as possible), until about 11 or 11:30 a.m. Once the park becomes crowded around midday, meals and other breaks won't affect the plan's efficiency. If you intend to stay in the park for evening parades, fireworks, or other events, eat dinner early enough to be finished in time for the festivities.

Character Dining

A number of restaurants, primarily those that serve all-you-can-eat buffets and family-style meals, offer character dining. At character meals, you pay a fixed price and dine in the presence of one to five Disney characters who circulate throughout the restaurant, hugging children (and sometimes adults), posing for photos, and signing autographs. Character breakfasts, lunches, and dinners are served at restaurants in and out of the theme parks.

FAST FOOD IN THE THEME PARKS

BECAUSE MOST MEALS DURING a Disney World vacation are consumed on the run while touring, we'll tackle counter-service and vendor foods first. Plentiful in all theme parks are hot dogs, hamburgers, chicken sandwiches, salads, and pizza. They're augmented by special items that relate to the park's theme or the part of the park you're touring. In Epcot's Germany, for example, counter-service bratwurst and beer are sold. In Frontierland in the Magic Kingdom, vendors sell smoked turkey legs. Counter-service prices are fairly consistent from park to park.

Getting your act together in regard to counter-service restaurants in the parks is more a matter of courtesy than necessity. Rude guests rank fifth among reader complaints. A mother from Fort Wayne, Indiana, points out that indecision can be as maddening as outright discourtesy, especially when you're hungry:

> *Every fast-food restaurant has menu signs the size of billboards, but do you think anybody reads them? People still don't have a clue what they want when they finally get to the counter. If by some miracle they've managed to choose between the hot dog and the hamburger, they then fiddle around another 10 minutes deciding what size Coke to order. Folks, PULEEEZ get your orders together ahead of time!*

A North Carolina reader on counter-service food lines:

Many counter-service registers serve two queues each, one to the left and one to the right of each register. People are not used to this and will instinctively line up in one queue per register, typically on the right side, leaving the left vacant. We had register operators wave us up to the front several times to start a left queue instead of waiting behind others on the right.

Healthful Food at Walt Disney World

 Liliane: Look for the **Mickey Check** icon on healthy menu items such as fresh fruit and low-fat milk.

One of the most commendable developments in food service at Disney World has been the introduction of healthier foods and snacks. Health-conscious choices are available at most fast-food counters and even vendors. All the major theme parks have fruit stands, for example.

Cutting Your Dining Time at the Theme Parks

Even if you confine your meals to vendor and counter-service fast food, you lose a lot of time getting food in the theme parks. Here are some ways to minimize the time you spend hunting and gathering:

1. Eat breakfast before you arrive. Restaurants outside the World offer some outstanding breakfast specials. Plus, some hotels furnish small refrigerators in their guest rooms, or you can rent a fridge or bring a cooler. If you can get by on cold cereal, rolls, fruit, and juice, this will save a ton of time.

2. After a good breakfast, buy snacks from vendors in the parks as you tour, or stuff some snacks in a fanny pack.

3. All theme park restaurants are busiest between 11:30 a.m. and 2:15 p.m. for lunch and 6 and 9 p.m. for dinner. For shorter lines and faster service, don't eat during these hours, especially 12:30–1:30 p.m.

4. Many counter-service restaurants sell cold sandwiches. Buy a cold lunch minus drinks before 11:30 a.m., and carry it in small plastic bags until you're ready to eat (within an hour or so of purchase). Ditto for dinner. Buy drinks at the appropriate time from any convenient vendor.

5. Most fast-food eateries have more than one service window. Regardless of the time of day, check the lines at all windows before queuing. Sometimes a window that's staffed but out of the way will have a much shorter line or none at all. Note, however, that some windows may offer only certain items.

6. If you're short on time and the park closes early, stay until closing and eat dinner outside Disney World before returning to your hotel. If the park stays open late, eat dinner about 4 or 4:30 p.m. at the restaurant of your choice. You should sneak in just ahead of the dinner crowd.

Tips for Saving Money on Food

Every time you buy a soda at the theme parks, it's going to set you back about $3, and everything else from hot dogs to salad is comparably high. You can say, "Oh well, we're on vacation," and pay the exorbitant prices, or you can plan ahead and save big bucks.

THE COST OF COUNTER-SERVICE FOOD	
BAGEL OR MUFFIN	$2.79
BROWNIE	$3.29
BURRITO	$7.09–$8.99
CAKE OR PIE	$3.79
CEREAL WITH MILK	$3.19–$3.99
CHEESEBURGER WITH FRIES	$9.39–$9.99
CHICKEN-BREAST SANDWICH (grilled)	$8.99–$10.95
CHICKEN NUGGETS WITH FRIES	$8.69
CHILDREN'S MEAL	$5.99
CHIPS	$2.69
COOKIES	$2.39
FISH (fried) **BASKET WITH FRIES**	$7.99–$10.95
FRENCH FRIES	$2.79
FRUIT (whole)	$1.49
FRUIT CUP/FRUIT SALAD	$3.59
HOT DOG	$6.99 (basket), $8.99 (gourmet)
ICE CREAM/FROZEN NOVELTIES	$3.49
NACHOS WITH CHEESE	$3.99–$7.69
PB&J SANDWICH	$2.49 (à la carte), $5.99 (kids' meal)
PIZZA (personal)	$6.79–$9.49
POPCORN	$3.50–$5.25
PRETZEL	$3.99–$4.75
SALAD (ENTRÉE)	$5.99–$10.99
SALAD (SIDE)	$3.99
SMOKED TURKEY LEG	$9.49
SOUP/CHILI	$2.99–$8.49
SUB/DELI SANDWICH	$5.99–$10.59
TACO SALAD	$7.89–$8.59
VEGGIE BURGER	$7.99

THE COST OF COUNTER-SERVICE DRINKS		
DRINKS	**SMALL**	**LARGE**
BEER	$5.50–$8.00	$7.99–$12.00
BOTTLED WATER	$1.50	$2.50
LATTE (one size)	$3.99	$3.99
COFFEE (one size)	$2.19	$2.19
FLOAT/MILKSHAKE/SUNDAE (one size)	$4.49–$6.95	$4.49–$6.95
FRUIT JUICE	$2.59	$2.89
HOT TEA AND COCOA (one size)	$2.19	$2.19
MILK	$1.69	$2.39
SOFT DRINKS, ICED TEA, AND LEMONADE	$2.59	$2.99

Refillable souvenir mugs cost $15.49 (free refills) at Disney resorts and $10 at water parks. Each person on a Disney Dining Plan gets a free mug, refillable only at his/her Disney resort.

For comparison purposes, let's say that a family of two adults and two teens arrives at Walt Disney World on Sunday afternoon and departs for home the following Saturday after breakfast. During that period the family eats six breakfasts, five lunches, and six dinners. What those meals cost depends on where and what they eat. They could rent a condo and prepare all of their own meals, but they didn't travel all the way to Walt Disney World to cook. So let's be realistic and assume that they'll eat their evening meals out—which is what most families do, because, among other reasons, they're too tired to think about cooking.

That leaves breakfast and lunch to contend with. Here are just a few sensible options for our hypothetical family. Needless to say, there are dozens of other combinations.

1. Eat breakfast in their room out of their cooler or fridge and prepare sandwiches and snacks to take to the theme parks in their hip packs. Carry water bottles or rely on drinking fountains for water. Cost: $130 for family of four for six days (does not include dinners or food purchased on travel days).

2. Eat breakfast in their room out of their cooler or fridge, carry snacks in their hip packs, and buy lunch at Disney counter-service restaurants. Cost: $315 for family of four for six days (does not include dinners or food purchased on travel days).

3. Eat breakfast at their hotel restaurant, buy snacks from vendors, and eat lunch at Disney counter-service restaurants. Cost: $650 for family of four for six days (does not include dinners or food purchased on travel days).

In case you're wondering, these are the foods on which we've based our grocery costs for those options where breakfast, lunch, and/ or snacks are prepared from the cooler:

BREAKFAST Cold cereal (choice of two), breakfast pastries, bananas, orange juice, milk, and coffee.

LUNCH Cold cuts or peanut butter and jelly sandwiches, condiments (mayo, mustard, and such), boxed juice, and apples.

SNACKS Packaged cheese or peanut butter crackers, boxed juice, and trail mix (combination of M&M's, nuts, raisins, and so on).

If you opt to buy groceries, you can stock up on food for your cooler at the Publix at either the intersection of International Drive and US 192 or at the intersection of Reames Road and FL 535. There's also a Winn-Dixie on Apopka–Vineland Road, about a mile north of Crossroads Shopping Center.

 Liliane: If you're an Entertainment Club member, don't forget to take your card and coupons for Orlando. Publix currently offers $5 off any purchase over $50.

Projected costs for snacks purchased at the theme parks are based on drinks (coffee or sodas) twice a day and popcorn once each day. Counter-service-meal costs assume basic fare (hot dogs, burgers, fries, and a drink). Hotel breakfast expenses assume eggs, bacon, and toast or pancakes with bacon and juice, milk, or coffee.

DISNEY DINING SUGGESTIONS

BELOW ARE SUGGESTIONS for dining at each of the major theme parks. If you are interested in trying a theme-park full-service restaurant, be aware that the restaurants continue to serve after the park's official closing time. We showed up at the Hollywood Brown Derby just as Disney's Hollywood Studios closed at 8 p.m. We were seated almost immediately and enjoyed a leisurely dinner while the crowds cleared out. Don't worry if you are depending on Disney transportation: Buses, boats, and monorails run 1–2 hours after the parks close.

The Magic Kingdom

Of the park's six full-service restaurants, **Be Our Guest** (dinner) in New Fantasyland is the best, followed by **Liberty Tree Tavern** in Liberty Square and **The Plaza Restaurant** on Main Street. **Cinderella's Royal Table** in the castle and **The Crystal Palace** on Main Street serves a decent-but-expensive buffet chaperoned by Disney characters. Avoid **Tony's Town Square Restaurant** on Main Street.

AUTHORS' FAVORITE COUNTER-SERVICE RESTAURANTS

Be Our Guest (lunch)   *New Fantasyland*
Columbia Harbour House   *Liberty Square*

These two restaurants offer the most variety within the Magic Kingdom. Be Our Guest serves a tasty tuna Niçoise salad (with seared tuna), a grilled-ham-and-cheese sandwich that's better than you'd expect, and a juicy braised-pork entrée. (It's also the first restaurant in the Kingdom to serve alcohol.) Columbia Harbour House's offerings include lobster rolls, grilled salmon, and a delicious hummus sandwich on multigrain bread. Otherwise, the Magic Kingdom's fast-food eateries are undistinguished. They're also about twice as expensive as McDonald's, for about the same quality. On the positive side, portions are large, sometimes large enough for children to share.

Epcot

Since the beginning, dining has been an integral component of Epcot's entertainment product. World Showcase has many more restaurants than attractions, and Epcot has added bars, tapas-style eateries, and full-service restaurants faster than any park in memory.

For the most part, Epcot's restaurants have always served decent food, though the World Showcase restaurants have occasionally been timid about delivering honest representations of their host nations' cuisine. That seems to be changing faster in some areas (Mexico) than others (Morocco), but we're hopeful that we see a trend. It's still true that the less adventuresome diner can find steak and potatoes on virtually every menu, but the same kitchens will serve up the real thing for anyone willing to ask.

Many Epcot restaurants are overpriced, most conspicuously **Monsieur Paul** (France) and **Coral Reef Restaurant** (The Seas). Representing decent value with their combination of attractive ambience and well-prepared food are **Via Napoli** (Italy), **Biergarten** (Germany), and **La Hacienda de San Angel** (Mexico). Biergarten (along with **Restaurant Marrakesh** in Morocco) also features live entertainment.

AUTHORS' FAVORITE COUNTER-SERVICE RESTAURANTS

Les Halles Boulangerie Patisserie *France*	Sunshine Seasons *The Land*
Sommerfest *Germany*	Tangierine Cafe *Morocco*

Les Halles Boulangerie Patisserie sells pastries, sandwiches, and quiches. The pastries don't compare to what you' find in Paris, but the sandwiches are as close to actual French street food—in taste, size, and price—as you'll get anywhere in Epcot. (We had one of those *Ratatouille* flashback scenes while eating one, only ours was in the Marais.) Another favorite is the chicken-and-lamb *shawarma* platter at Morocco's **Tangierine Cafe.** Besides juicy lamb, it comes with some of the best tabbouleh we've tasted in Florida.

In addition to these, we recommend the following ethnic counter-service specialties:

GERMANY Sommerfest for bratwurst and Beck's beer	
JAPAN Katsura Grill for noodle dishes, teriyaki, and tempura	
NORWAY Kringla Bakeri Og Kafe for pastries, open-face sandwiches, and Carlsberg beer (our favorite)	
UNITED KINGDOM Rose & Crown Pub for Guinness, Harp, and Bass beers	

Disney's Animal Kingdom

Because touring the Animal Kingdom takes less than a day, crowds are heaviest 9:30 a.m.–3:30 p.m. Expect a mob at lunch and thinner crowds at dinner. We recommend you tour early after a good breakfast, and then eat a very late lunch or graze on vendor food. If you tour later in the day, eat lunch before you arrive, and then enjoy dinner in or out of the theme park.

Bob: Don't expect a broad choice of exotic dishes at Animal Kingdom.

Animal Kingdom offers a lot of counter-service fast food, along with **Tusker House,** a buffet-style restaurant, and **Yak & Yeti,** a table-service restaurant, in Asia. You'll find plenty of traditional Disney-theme-park food—hot dogs, hamburgers, and the like—but even the fast food is superior to typical Disney fare. The third restaurant in the Animal Kingdom is the **Rainforest Cafe,** with entrances both inside and outside the theme park (you don't have to purchase theme-park admission, in other words, to eat at the restaurant). Unlike the Rainforest Cafe at the Downtown Disney Marketplace, the Animal Kingdom branch accepts Advance Reservations.

AUTHORS' FAVORITE COUNTER-SERVICE RESTAURANTS

Flame Tree Barbecue *Discovery Island*
Yak & Yeti Local Food Cafés *Asia*

Liliane's Top 10 Disney World Snacks

FOLLOWING IS A TOP-10 LIST of particularly decadent or unusual snacks available at WDW. We've omitted the usual funnel cakes, popcorn, and ice cream available anywhere. Also absent are the truly bizarre snacks, such as the squid treats sold at the Mitsukoshi Department Store in the Japan Pavilion at Epcot's World Showcase. These are the goodies worth scouring the parks and resorts for, in ascending order:

10. Kaki Gori at the Japan Pavilion, Epcot World Showcase A little on the sweet side but lighter than ice cream, the shaved ice at this small stand comes in such unique flavors as honeydew melon, strawberry, and tangerine. And at $3.50, it's a bargain.

9. Turkey legs Available at every theme park, these must come from 85-pound turkeys because they're huge, not to mention extra-juicy and flavorful. Grab some napkins and go primal on one of these bad boys, and don't worry about the stares you might attract—they're all just jealous.

8. Tie-Dyed Cheesecake at Disney's Pop Century Resort A colorful and delicious treat. Part red-velvet cake and part cheesecake, the dessert is so popular that many discussion boards offer recipes such as this one: **tinyurl .com/tie-dyedcheesecake.**

7. Les Halles Boulangerie Patisserie at the France Pavilion, Epcot World Showcase There are simply no words to adequately describe the pastries at this revamped bakery. Try the frangipane or the Napoleon. Oh, did we mention the apple tart, the crème brûlée, and the chocolate mousse?

6. Cadbury chocolate bars at the United Kingdom Pavilion, Epcot World Showcase If you've never had a genuine English Cadbury bar, you just don't know what you're missing.

5. Milkshakes from Beaches & Cream at the Beach Club Resort Hand-dipped, thick, and creamy. When was the last time you sported a milkshake mustache? For large crowds, or large appetites, try the Kitchen Sink: a huge sundae consisting of mountains of ice cream and toppings that is actually served in a kitchen sink.

4. Selma's cookies at the BoardWalk Oddly enough, these are available at the candy store, Seashore Sweets, rather than at the BoardWalk Bakery (go figure), but they're worth tracking down for their rich, buttery, homemade taste.

3. Ghirardelli Soda Fountain and Chocolate Shop at Downtown Disney Marketplace Everything is good, and the atmosphere has a sophisticated ice-cream-shop–plus–coffee-bar vibe. *Very* San Fran.

2. Zebra Domes at Animal Kingdom Lodge Offered as a dessert on the Boma buffet, they're also available at the Mara food court, on the lower level of the resort near the pool. They consist of a layer of sponge cake topped with chocolate mousse, and then covered in white- and dark-chocolate ganache stripes. Fun and yum rolled into one!

And the number-one snack at Walt Disney World is . . .

1. Two words: Dole Whip! Available in Adventureland at the Magic Kingdom, a Dole Whip is a soft-serve pineapple–ice cream dream.

(P.S.: Bob has a favorite snack, too. Keep reading to find it!)

We like Flame Tree Barbecue for its waterfront dining pavilions, and Yak & Yeti Local Food Cafes (just outside the full-service Yak & Yeti) for casual Asian dishes from egg rolls to crispy honey chicken. The sit-down Yak & Yeti also serves above-average dishes from China, Thailand, Vietnam, and Japan.

Disney's Hollywood Studios

Dining at Disney's Hollywood Studios is more interesting than in the Magic Kingdom and less ethnic than at Epcot. The Studios has five restaurants where Advance Reservations are recommended: the **Hollywood Brown Derby, 50's Prime Time Café, Sci-Fi Dine-In Theater Restaurant, Mama Melrose's Ristorante Italiano,** and the **Hollywood & Vine** buffet. The upscale Brown Derby is by far the best restaurant at the Studios. For simple Italian food, including pizza, Mama Melrose's is fine. Just don't expect anything fancy. At the Sci-Fi Dine-In, you eat in little cars at a simulated drive-in movie of the 1950s. Though you won't find a more entertaining restaurant in Walt Disney World, the food is quite disappointing. Somewhat better is the 50's Prime Time Café, where you sit in Mom's kitchen of the 1950s and scarf down meat loaf while watching clips of vintage TV sitcoms. It's a hoot, and the food is pretty good, too. The best way to experience either restaurant is to stop in for dessert or a drink 2:30–4:30 p.m. Hollywood & Vine features singing and dancing characters from *Disney Junior* during breakfast and lunch.

AUTHORS' FAVORITE COUNTER-SERVICE RESTAURANTS

ABC Commissary *Echo Lake*   Pizza Planet *Streets of America*
Backlot Express *Echo Lake*   Toluca Legs Turkey Company *Sunset Boulevard*

READERS' COMMENTS ABOUT WALT DISNEY WORLD DINING

EATING IS A POPULAR TOPIC AMONG *Unofficial Guide* readers. In addition to participating in our annual restaurant survey, many readers like to share their thoughts with us. The following comments are representative of those we receive.

A reader from Glendale, Illinois, had a positive experience with Disney food, writing:

In general, we were pleasantly surprised. I expected it to be over-priced, generally bad, and certainly unhealthy. There were a lot of options, and almost all restaurants (including counter service) had generally good food and some healthy options. It's not the place to expect fine cuisine—and it's certainly overpriced—but if you understand the parameters, you can eat quite well.

We've received consistent raves for Boma—Flavors of Africa:

Please stop telling everyone how wonderful Boma is, because I love it so much there and I don't want everyone to know the secret as it's already difficult to get a table! Prime rib and Zebra Domes—yum!

A Lombard, Illinois, mom underscores the need to make Advance Reservations:

> *Please stress that if you want a "normal" dining hour at a specific restaurant, call them 90 or 60 days in advance—IT IS WORTH IT! One reservation I wanted to change about two weeks before our arrival date, and I had a choice of dinner times of either 7:45 or 9 p.m. (not feasible with little ones).*

A Greenwood, Indiana, family had this to say:

> *The food was certainly expensive, but contrary to many of the views expressed in the* Unofficial Guide, *we all thought the quality was excellent. Everything we had, from chicken strips and hot dogs in the parks to dinner at the Coral Reef, tasted great and seemed very fresh.*

A family from Youngsville, Louisiana, got a leg up on other guests:

> *The best thing we ate were the smoked turkey legs.*

A mom from Aberdeen, South Dakota, writes:

> *When we want great food, we'll be on a different vacation. Who wants to waste fun time with the kids at a sit-down restaurant when you know the food will be mediocre anyway?*

On the topic of saving money, a Seattle woman offered this:

> *For those wanting to save a few bucks (or in some cases several bucks), we definitely suggest eating outside WDW for as many meals as possible. To keep down our costs, we ate a large breakfast before leaving the hotel, had a fast-food lunch in the park, a snack later to hold us over, and then ate a good dinner outside the park. Several good restaurants in the area have excellent food at reasonable prices, notably Café Tu Tu Tango and Ming [Court], both on International Drive. We also obtained the* Entertainment Book *for Orlando, which offers 50% off meals all over town.*

COUNTER-SERVICE RESTAURANT MINI-PROFILES

TO HELP YOU FIND PALATABLE FAST-SERVICE FOOD that suits your taste, we have developed mini-profiles of Walt Disney World theme-park counter-service restaurants. The restaurants are listed alphabetically by theme park.

The restaurants profiled on the following pages are rated for quality and portion size (self-explanatory), as well as for value. The value rating ranges A–F as follows:

A	=	Exceptional value, a real bargain
B	=	Good value
C	=	Fair value, you get exactly what you pay for
D	=	Somewhat overpriced
F	=	Significantly overpriced

THE MAGIC KINGDOM

Aloha Isle

QUALITY Excellent   VALUE B+   PORTION Medium   LOCATION Adventureland
READER-SURVEY RESPONSES   98% 🖐   2% 🖐   DISNEY DINING PLAN?   No

Selections Soft-serve ice cream; ice-cream floats; fresh pineapple spears; chips; juice, bottled water, coffee, tea.

Comments The pineapple Dole Whip soft-serve is a must-try.

Be Our Guest Restaurant

QUALITY Excellent   VALUE B+   PORTION Medium   LOCATION New Fantasyland
READER-SURVEY RESPONSES   92% 🖐   8% 🖐   DISNEY DINING PLAN?   Yes

Selections Tuna Niçoise salad; *croque monsieur;* carved-turkey and roast-beef sandwiches; braised pork with bacon mashed potatoes; veggie quiche; quinoa salad. Kids' meals include carved turkey sandwich, pulled pork, a tasty meatloaf, or pasta with marinara sauce.

Comments The best counter-service restaurant in the Magic Kingdom, and one of the best in all of Disney World. Our favorite lunch selections are the seared-tuna Niçoise salad and the *croque monsieur* sandwich. The tuna, slightly peppery, is served on a bed of greens with chilled green beans, potatoes, olives, peppers, and tomatoes and topped with a hard-poached egg. The croque monsieur is a grown-up version of grilled ham and cheese, with carved ham, Gruyère cheese, and béchamel sauce and *pommes frites* on the side. Be Our Guest's full-service dinner (reviewed in the Big Book) is excellent as well.

Note: Lines for lunch start forming as early as 9:30 a.m. Expect at least a 30-minute wait if you go between 11 a.m. and 1 p.m. Because the restaurant is so popular, Fastpass is sometimes offered for faster seating at lunch. Disney is also said to be testing advance ordering for lunch via its My Disney Experience mobile app.

Casey's Corner

QUALITY Fair   VALUE B   PORTION Medium   LOCATION Main Street, U.S.A.
READER-SURVEY RESPONSES   81% 🖐   19% 🖐   DISNEY DINING PLAN?   Yes

Selections Hot dogs, corn-dog nuggets, fries, and brownies.

Comments The hot dogs are frequently lukewarm and the buns stale. The Chicago-style dog, topped with tomato slices, dill pickle, Chicago-style relish, and banana peppers, is the best of the bunch.

Columbia Harbour House

QUALITY Good   VALUE B   PORTION Medium   LOCATION Liberty Square
READER-SURVEY RESPONSES   90% 🖐   10% 🖐   DISNEY DINING PLAN?   Yes

Selections Healthful options such as grilled salmon with couscous and broccoli and the Lighthouse Sandwich with hummus and broccoli slaw. Other choices: fried fish and shrimp; lobster rolls; chicken nuggets; child's plate with macaroni and cheese, PB&J sandwich, chicken nuggets, or tuna salad with grapes; New England clam chowder; vegetarian chili; coleslaw; garden salad; chocolate cake, apple crisp, strawberry yogurt.

Comments No trans fats in the fried items, and the soups and sandwiches are a cut above most fast-food fare.

Cosmic Ray's Starlight Cafe

QUALITY Good	VALUE B	PORTION Large	LOCATION Tomorrowland
READER-SURVEY RESPONSES	83% 👍	17% 👎	DISNEY DINING PLAN? Yes

Selections Rotisserie chicken and ribs; burgers (and vegetarian burgers); hot dogs; Greek salad; chicken, turkey and vegetable sandwiches; chicken-noodle soup; chili-cheese fries; strawberry yogurt for dessert. Kosher choices available by request.

Comments Big, noisy place. Inside tables usually available. Plenty of options. Generous toppings bar.

Friar's Nook

QUALITY Good	VALUE B	PORTION Medium–large	LOCATION Fantasyland
READER-SURVEY RESPONSES	81% 👍	19% 👎	DISNEY DINING PLAN? Yes

Selections Hot dogs, teriyaki chicken nuggets, veggies and chips with hummus, freshly made potato chips, lemonade slush.

Comments Part of the Fantasyland expansion.

Gaston's Tavern

QUALITY Good	VALUE C	PORTION Medium	LOCATION New Fantasyland
READER-SURVEY RESPONSES	85% 👍	15% 👎	DISNEY DINING PLAN? Yes

Selections Roast pork shank (the porcine equivalent of the giant turkey leg), hummus with chips, cinnamon rolls, LeFou's Brew (a frozen apple-juice-and-toasted-marshmallow-flavored drink).

Comments Clever setting with lots of fun details for fans of *Beauty and the Beast*'s villain-in-chief. The menu is really limited, though, and that makes Gaston's difficult to recommend.

Golden Oak Outpost

QUALITY Good	VALUE B+	PORTION Medium–large	LOCATION Frontierland
READER-SURVEY RESPONSES	81% 👍	19% 👎	DISNEY DINING PLAN? Yes

Selections Chicken nuggets; fried-chicken-breast sandwiches; fries; chocolate cake, carrot cake, and cookies.

Comments Entrées are served with apple slices or french fries.

The Lunching Pad

QUALITY Good	VALUE B–	PORTION Medium	LOCATION Tomorrowland
READER-SURVEY RESPONSES	86% 👍	14% 👎	DISNEY DINING PLAN? Yes

Selections Sweet cream-cheese pretzel, frozen sodas.

Comments The frozen carbonated drinks—cola, cherry, blue raspberry—are a treat in summer's heat.

Pecos Bill Tall Tale Inn & Cafe

QUALITY Good	VALUE B	PORTION Medium–large	LOCATION Frontierland
READER-SURVEY RESPONSES	84% 👍	16% 👎	DISNEY DINING PLAN? Yes

Selections One-third-pound Angus cheeseburgers; barbecue-pork sandwiches; veggie burgers; chicken sandwich; Southwest chicken salad; taco salad; chili; child's plate with burger or salad with grilled chicken and child's beverage; fries and chili-cheese fries; strawberry yogurt and carrot cake.

Comments Garnish your burger at the fixin's station.

The Pinocchio Village Haus

QUALITY Fair	VALUE C	PORTION Medium	LOCATION Fantasyland
READER-SURVEY RESPONSES 82% 👍 16% 👎		DISNEY DINING PLAN? Yes	

Selections Personal pizzas; chicken nuggets; fries; Caesar salad with chicken; meatball sub sandwiches; Mediterranean salad; kids' meals of pizza, mac and cheese, or PB&J.

Comments An easy stop for families in Fantasyland, but it's usually crowded. Consider Columbia Harbour House and Pecos Bill Tall Tale Inn & Cafe, both only a few minutes' walk away (and tastier, too).

Tomorrowland Terrace Restaurant *(open seasonally)*

QUALITY Fair	VALUE C	PORTION Medium–large	LOCATION Tomorrowland
READER-SURVEY RESPONSES 81% 👍 19% 👎		DISNEY DINING PLAN? Yes	

Selections One-third-pound Angus bacon cheeseburger; fried-chicken sandwich; chicken nuggets; pasta alone or with shrimp or chicken; lobster roll; beef-and-blue-cheese salad; citrus shrimp salad; chocolate cake, carrot cake, or yogurt for dessert.

Comments The ancient kitchen wasn't designed for much more than keeping food warm, making the food lackluster. That's a shame, because we like the setting better than Cosmic Ray's. Stick to nuggets or salads and avoid the pasta.

Tortuga Tavern *(open seasonally)*

QUALITY Fair	VALUE B	PORTION Medium–large	LOCATION Adventureland
READER-SURVEY RESPONSES 85% 👍 15% 👎		DISNEY DINING PLAN? Yes	

Selections Beef taco salad; chicken Caesar salad; beef nachos; chicken, beef, or vegetarian burritos; quesadillas and PB&J sandwiches for kids.

Comments Large, shaded eating area. Generous toppings bar with tomatoes, lettuce, cheese, and salsa.

EPCOT

L'Artisan des Glaces

QUALITY Excellent	VALUE C	PORTION Large	LOCATION France
READER-SURVEY RESPONSES Too new to rate		DISNEY DINING PLAN? Yes	

Selections Flavors change but can include vanilla, chocolate, mint chocolate, pistachio, hazelnut, profiterole, caramel with salt, cherry, white chocolate with coconut, and coffee ice creams. Sorbet flavors can include strawberry, mango, melon, lemon, pomegranate, and mixed berry. Over-21s can enjoy two scoops in a martini glass, topped with a shot of Grand Marnier, rum, or whipped cream–flavored vodka.

Comments The ice creams are better than you'd expect in a theme park. Our profiterole sample had chunks of chocolate-covered cookie pieces, and our white chocolate–coconut had fresh shaved coconut in it.

La Cantina de San Angel

QUALITY Good	VALUE B	PORTION Medium–large	LOCATION Mexico
READER-SURVEY RESPONSES 84% 👍 16% 👎		DISNEY DINING PLAN? Yes	

Selections Chicken or beef tacos, nachos, cheese empanadas, guacamole and chips, churros and frozen fruit pops, margaritas.

Comments The Cantina is a popular spot for a quick meal, with 150 covered outdoor seats.

Crêpes des Chefs de France

QUALITY Excellent	VALUE B+	PORTION Medium	LOCATION France
READER-SURVEY RESPONSES	78%	22%	DISNEY DINING PLAN? No

Selections Crepes filled with chocolate, strawberry preserves, or sugar; ice cream; specialty beer (Kronenbourg 1664); espresso.
Comments These crepes rate high—even with French guests.

Electric Umbrella Restaurant

QUALITY Fair–good	VALUE B–	PORTION Medium	LOCATION Innoventions East
READER-SURVEY RESPONSES	70%	10%	DISNEY DINING PLAN? Yes

Selections Meatball subs, Angus bacon cheeseburgers; mushroom-and-Swiss burgers; veggie flatbread; Caesar salad; child's plate with cheeseburger or mac and cheese; cheesecake, no-sugar-added brownies.
Comments World Showcase has more-interesting fast food.

Fife & Drum Tavern

QUALITY Fair	VALUE C	PORTION Large	LOCATION United States
READER-SURVEY RESPONSES	89%	11%	DISNEY DINING PLAN? Yes

Selections Turkey legs, popcorn, pretzels, ice cream, frozen slushes, beer.
Comments Better for a drink or a quick snack than an actual meal. Seating is available in and around the Liberty Inn, behind the Fife & Drum.

Katsura Grill

QUALITY Good	VALUE B	PORTION Small–medium	LOCATION Japan
READER-SURVEY RESPONSES	90%	10%	DISNEY DINING PLAN? Yes

Selections Udon noodles with beef and tempura shrimp; chicken, beef, or salmon teriyaki; edamame; sushi; miso soup; green tea; green-tea ice cream and cheesecake; Kirin beer, sake, and plum wine.
Comments Pleasant gardens and outdoor seating a little off the World Showcase promenade offer a nice respite, but seating is limited.

Kringla Bakeri Og Kafe

QUALITY Good–excellent	VALUE B	PORTION Small–medium	LOCATION Norway
READER-SURVEY RESPONSES	94%	6%	DISNEY DINING PLAN? Yes

Selections Pastries and cakes; rice cream; sandwiches (club, ham-and-apple, roast beef, salmon-and-egg); green salad; espresso, cappuccino, and imported beers (Carlsberg beer for $7.50).
Comments Delicious and different, but pricey. Try the rice cream (not a typo, by the way). Shaded outdoor seating.

Les Halles Boulangerie Patisserie

QUALITY Good	VALUE A	PORTION Small–medium	LOCATION France
READER-SURVEY RESPONSES	95%	5%	DISNEY DINING PLAN? Yes

Selections Niçoise or lyonnaise salads, ham-and-cheese sandwiches, turkey BLT, chicken-breast sandwich, smoked-pork-sausage sandwich, quiches, salads, soups, pastries.
Comments The pastries are fine, but the sandwiches are excellent. For a Parisian experience, eat a baguette while walking around the pavilion.

Open for breakfast. Usually crowded starting at lunch and throughout the day. Now with indoor seating and a few shaded outside tables.

Liberty Inn

QUALITY Fair	VALUE C	PORTION Medium	LOCATION United States
READER-SURVEY RESPONSES 74% 👍 26% 👎		DISNEY DINING PLAN? Yes	

Selections Burger topped with pulled pork; 6-ounce New York strip with red-wine butter, roasted potatoes, and fresh broccoli; hot dogs; veggie burgers; chicken nuggets; grilled-chicken flatbread or Caesar salad; chili; child's plate of grilled chicken, pasta with marinara, cheeseburger, or mac and cheese. For dessert, apple pie, brownies, and peach cobbler.

Comments Try the New York strip, a relative bargain at $10.69. Kosher items also available.

Lotus Blossom Cafe

QUALITY Fair	VALUE C	PORTION Medium	LOCATION China
READER-SURVEY RESPONSES 81% 👍 19% 👎		DISNEY DINING PLAN? Yes	

Selections Pork and vegetable egg rolls, pot stickers, veggie stir-fry, Hong Kong–style vegetable curry (chicken optional), sesame chicken salad, shrimp fried rice, orange chicken, beef-noodle soup bowl, caramel ginger or lychee ice cream, plum wine, Tsingtao beer.

Comments Middling, overpriced Chinese food.

Promenade Refreshments

QUALITY Fair	VALUE C	PORTION Large	LOCATION World Showcase Promenade
READER-SURVEY RESPONSES 86% 👍 14% 👎		DISNEY DINING PLAN? Yes	

Selections Hot dogs, popcorn, pretzels, ice cream, beer.

Comments Best for a quick snack. Seating is limited to nonexistent—be prepared to walk and chew.

Refreshment Outpost

QUALITY Good	VALUE B–	PORTION Small	LOCATION Between Germany and China
READER-SURVEY RESPONSES 88% 👍 12% 👎		DISNEY DINING PLAN? Yes	

Selections Hot dogs, soft-serve in a waffle cone, floats and sundaes, coffee or tea, draft Safari Amber beer ($6.75).

Comments Mainly prepackaged food for a quick drink or snack.

Refreshment Port

QUALITY Good	VALUE B–	PORTION Medium	LOCATION World Showcase
READER-SURVEY RESPONSES 86% 👍 14% 👎		DISNEY DINING PLAN? Yes	

Selections Fried shrimp, fried-chicken sandwich, chicken nuggets, frozen Bacardi mojito, iced lattes, soft-serve.

Comments Fun tastes for nibbling and sipping as you begin your walk around World Showcase.

Rose & Crown Pub

QUALITY Good	VALUE C+	PORTION Medium	LOCATION United Kingdom
READER-SURVEY RESPONSES 98% 👍 2% 👎		DISNEY DINING PLAN? No	

Selections Fish-and-chips; Scotch egg (hard-boiled, wrapped in sausage, and deep-fried); corned-beef sandwiches; English Bulldog (split sausage stuffed with mashed potatoes, bacon, and Irish Cheddar); British cheese plate; Guinness, Harp, and Bass beers, as well as other spirits.

Comments The attractions here are the pub atmosphere and the draft beer. Outside the pub is Yorkshire County Fish Shop (see below), which serves food to go.

Sommerfest

QUALITY Good	VALUE B–	PORTION Medium	LOCATION Germany
READER-SURVEY RESPONSES 100% 👍 0% 👎		DISNEY DINING PLAN? Yes	

Selections Bratwurst and frankfurter sandwiches with kraut; soft pretzels; apple strudel; Black Forest cake; cheesecake; German wine and beer.

Comments Tucked in the entrance to the Biergarten restaurant, Sommerfest is hard to find from the street. Very limited seating. A good place to grab a cold brew and bratwurst.

Sunshine Seasons

QUALITY Excellent	VALUE A	PORTION Medium	LOCATION The Land
READER-SURVEY RESPONSES 92% 👍 8% 👎		DISNEY DINING PLAN? Yes	

Selections Comprises the following four areas: (1) wood-fired grills and rotisseries, with rotisserie half-chicken or slow-roasted pork chop and wood-grilled fish with seasonal vegetables; (2) sandwich shop with made-to-order sandwiches such as oak-grilled veggie flatbread, Reuben panini, and turkey-and-cheese on focaccia; (3) Asian shop, with noodle bowls and various stir-fry combos; (4) soup-and-salad shop, with soups made daily and unusual creations such as seared tuna-noodle salad and roasted-beet-and-goat-cheese salad. Breakfast includes the usual suspects: pastries, bacon, eggs, and the like.

Comments One of the best counter-service spots in Epcot. The breakfast panini with eggs, bacon, roast pork, and cheese is an *Unofficial* favorite.

Tangierine Cafe

QUALITY Good	VALUE B	PORTION Medium	LOCATION Morocco
READER-SURVEY RESPONSES 91% 👍 9% 👎		DISNEY DINING PLAN? Yes	

Selections Chicken and lamb *shawarma;* hummus; tabbouleh; lentil salad; couscous salad; chicken, lamb, and falafel wraps; marinated olives; child's hamburger or chicken tenders with carrot sticks and apple slices; Moroccan wine and beer; baklava.

Comments No belly dancers as at Restaurant Marrakesh, but the food here is authentic. The best seating is at the outdoor tables.

Yorkshire County Fish Shop

QUALITY Good	VALUE B+	PORTION Medium	LOCATION United Kingdom
READER-SURVEY RESPONSES 93% 👍 7% 👎		DISNEY DINING PLAN? Yes	

Selections Fish-and-chips, shortbread, Bass Ale draft and Harp Lager.

Comments There's usually a line for the crisp, hot fish-and-chips at this convenient fast-food window attached to the Rose & Crown Pub (see full-service profile on page 488). Outdoor seating overlooks the lagoon.

DISNEY'S ANIMAL KINGDOM

Flame Tree Barbecue

QUALITY Excellent	VALUE B–	PORTION Large	LOCATION Discovery Island
READER-SURVEY RESPONSES 95% 👍 5% 👎		DISNEY DINING PLAN? Yes	

Selections Half-slab St. Louis–style ribs; smoked half-chicken; smoked-pork sandwiches; barbecue-chicken salad; fruit plate with honey yogurt; child's plate of baked chicken drumstick, hot dog, or PB&J sandwich; french fries, coleslaw, and onion rings; Key lime or chocolate mousse; Safari Amber beer, Bud Light, and wine.

Comments One of our favorites for lunch. Try the covered gazebo overlooking the water.

Kusafiri Coffee Shop and Bakery

QUALITY Good	VALUE B	PORTION Medium	LOCATION Africa
READER-SURVEY RESPONSES 93%	7%	DISNEY DINING PLAN? Yes	

Selections Fruit turnovers, Danish and other pastries, muffins, croissants, bagels with cream cheese, cookies, brownies, cake, fruit cups, yogurt, coffee, cocoa, and juice.

Comments An early-morning sugar rush on the way to Kilimanjaro Safaris.

Pizzafari

QUALITY Fair	VALUE B	PORTION Medium	LOCATION Discovery Island
READER-SURVEY RESPONSES 81%	19%	DISNEY DINING PLAN? Yes	

Selections Cheese, pepperoni, and veggie personal pizzas served with Caesar salad; Italian sandwich; Caesar salad with chicken; chicken-and-veggie pasta salad. Kids' choices include mac and cheese, turkey sandwich, cheese pizza, or PB&J. Chocolate mousse or cheesecake for dessert. Beer and wine available.

Comments A favorite with children, but the pizza is unimpressive.

Restaurantosaurus

QUALITY Good	VALUE B+	PORTION Medium–large	LOCATION DinoLand U.S.A.
READER-SURVEY RESPONSES 85%	15%	DISNEY DINING PLAN? Yes	

Selections Angus bacon cheeseburgers; chicken nuggets; grilled-veggie sub; mac-and-cheese hot dog; chicken BLT salad; grilled-chicken sandwich; kids' turkey wrap, cheeseburger, or PB&J.

Comments Good burger-toppings bar.

Royal Anandapur Tea Company

QUALITY Good	VALUE B	PORTION Medium	LOCATION Asia
READER-SURVEY RESPONSES 94%	6%	DISNEY DINING PLAN? No	

Selections Wide variety of hot and iced teas; lattes; coffee, espresso, and cappuccino; pastries.

Comments Halfway between Expedition Everest and Kali River Rapids, this is the kind of small, eclectic, Animal Kingdom–specific food stand that you wish other parks had. Offers nine loose-leaf teas from Asia and Africa, some organic, and many of which can be made either hot or iced. Pastries violate the "never eat anything larger than your head" rule, but everyone knows that doesn't apply when you're on vacation.

Tamu Tamu Eats & Refreshments

QUALITY Good	VALUE C	PORTION Large	LOCATION Africa
READER-SURVEY RESPONSES 90%	10%	DISNEY DINING PLAN? Yes	

Selections For breakfast: egg, ham, and cheese flatbread; French-toast sticks; yogurt; fruit salad. For lunch and dinner: quinoa salad; roasted-chicken-salad sandwich; pulled-beef sandwich; fruit salad.

Comments Seating is behind the building and could easily be overlooked.

Yak & Yeti Local Food Cafes

QUALITY Fair	VALUE B	PORTION Large	LOCATION Asia
READER-SURVEY RESPONSES	91% 👍	9% 👎 DISNEY DINING PLAN?	Yes

Selections Crispy honey chicken with steamed rice, sweet-and-sour chicken, beef lo mein, Mandarin chicken salad, Asian chicken sandwiches, egg rolls, chicken fried rice. Kids' menu includes chicken bites or a cheeseburger with applesauce and carrots.

Comments The crispy honey chicken is the best choice.

DISNEY'S HOLLYWOOD STUDIOS

ABC Commissary

QUALITY Fair	VALUE B–	PORTION Medium–large	LOCATION Echo Lake
READER-SURVEY RESPONSES	74% 👍	26% 👎 DISNEY DINING PLAN?	Yes

Selections Asian salads; chicken bleu sandwiches; Angus cheeseburgers; shrimp platter; seafood platter; couscous, quinoa, and arugula salad; child's chicken nuggets, cheeseburger, or turkey sandwich; chocolate mousse; no-sugar-added strawberry parfait; wine and beer.

Comments Indoors, centrally located, but hard to find. Offers kosher meals. One of the lowest-rated counter-service places in the theme parks.

Backlot Express

QUALITY Fair	VALUE C	PORTION Medium–large	LOCATION Echo Lake
READER-SURVEY RESPONSES	82% 👍	18% 👎 DISNEY DINING PLAN?	Yes

Selections Cheeseburgers with fries or carrot sticks, Southwest salad with chicken, grilled turkey and cheese, chicken nuggets, hot dogs, grilled-vegetable sandwiches, desserts. For children, chicken nuggets or grilled-veggie sandwich. Soft drinks and beer.

Comments A big dining space that's often overlooked. Great burger-fixin's bar. Indoor and outdoor seating.

Catalina Eddie's

QUALITY Fair	VALUE B	PORTION Medium–large	LOCATION Sunset Boulevard
READER-SURVEY RESPONSES	68% 👍	32% 👎 DISNEY DINING PLAN?	Yes

Selections Cheese and pepperoni pizzas, hot Italian deli sandwiches, salads, and chocolate fudge cake.

Comments The lowest-rated counter-service restaurant in the park. Seldom crowded. Go figure.

Fairfax Fare

QUALITY Fair	VALUE B	PORTION Medium–large	LOCATION Sunset Boulevard
READER-SURVEY RESPONSES	78% 👍	22% 👎 DISNEY DINING PLAN?	Yes

Selections Breakfast: egg-and-cheese English muffins, pastries, cereal, yogurt, and fruit. Lunch: barbecue chicken and ribs; pulled-pork sandwiches; "designer" hot dogs with gourmet toppings; salad with tomato, roasted corn, peppers, cheese, and tortillas; chocolate and carrot cake.

Comments Like Charo on *The Love Boat,* the mac-and-cheese–truffle-oil hot dog is a standout in a sea of forgettable supporting players. Ask to have your bun warmed before your dog is served.

Min and Bill's Dockside Diner

QUALITY Fair	VALUE C	PORTION Small–medium	LOCATION Echo Lake
READER-SURVEY RESPONSES	97% 👍	3% 👎	DISNEY DINING PLAN? Yes

Selections Italian sausage, chicken Caesar sandwiches, frankfurters on a pretzel roll, shakes and soft drinks, chips and cookies, beer.

Comments The highest rated counter-service restaurant in the Studios. The hot dog in a pretzel roll is genius, and although the menu is very limited, all of the sandwiches are good.

Pizza Planet

QUALITY Good	VALUE B+	PORTION Medium	LOCATION Streets of America
READER-SURVEY RESPONSES	78% 👍	22% 👎	DISNEY DINING PLAN? Yes

Selections Cheese, pepperoni, and vegetarian pizzas; meatball subs; salads; child's meatball sub and cheese pizza; cookies and cupcakes.

Comments *The* pizza place at the Studios.

Rosie's All-American Cafe

QUALITY Fair	VALUE C	PORTION Medium	LOCATION Sunset Boulevard
READER-SURVEY RESPONSES	76% 👍	24% 👎	DISNEY DINING PLAN? Yes

Selections Cheeseburgers; veggie burgers; chicken nuggets; soups; child's turkey sandwich or chicken nuggets with carrot sticks or applesauce; apple pie and chocolate cake.

Comments Backlot Express is a better option for similar fare.

Starring Rolls Cafe

QUALITY Good	VALUE B	PORTION Small–medium	LOCATION Sunset Boulevard
READER-SURVEY RESPONSES	94% 👍	6% 👎	DISNEY DINING PLAN? Yes

Selections Deli sandwiches, sushi, pastries and desserts, coffee.

Comments Open for breakfast. Slowest counter service in the Studios.

Studio Catering Co.

QUALITY Good	VALUE B	PORTION Small–medium	LOCATION Streets of America
READER-SURVEY RESPONSES	88% 👍	22% 👎	DISNEY DINING PLAN? Yes

Selections Grilled-veggie sandwiches, grilled-turkey clubs, buffalo chicken sandwiches, pressed Tuscan deli sandwiches, chicken Caesar wraps, sloppy joes, Greek salad. PB&J, veggie sandwich, or chicken nuggets for kids. The adjacent High Octane Refreshments serves cocktails, including a variety of margaritas.

Comments Good place for a break while your kids enjoy the Honey, I Shrunk the Kids Movie Set Adventure. Shady outside seating.

Toluca Legs Turkey Company

QUALITY Good	VALUE B	PORTION Medium–large	LOCATION Sunset Boulevard
READER-SURVEY RESPONSES	88% 👍	22% 👎	DISNEY DINING PLAN? Yes

Selections Smoked turkey legs; bottled soda and beer.

Comments For fans of the giant turkey legs.

DISNEY'S FULL-SERVICE RESTAURANTS: A QUICK ROMP AROUND THE WORLD

DISNEY RESTAURANTS OFFER AN EXCELLENT (though expensive) opportunity to introduce young children to the variety and excitement of ethnic food. No matter how formal a restaurant appears, the staff is accustomed to wiggling, impatient, and often boisterous children. **Les Chefs de France** at Epcot, for example, may be the nation's only French restaurant where most patrons wear shorts and T-shirts and at least two dozen young diners are attired in basic black . . . mouse ears.

Liliane: Young children are the rule, not the exception, at Disney World restaurants.

Almost all Disney restaurants offer children's menus, and all have booster seats and high chairs. They understand how tough it may be for kids to sit for an extended period of time, and waiters will supply little ones with crackers and rolls and serve your dinner much faster than in comparable restaurants elsewhere. Letters from readers suggest that being served too quickly is much more common than having a long wait.

In **Epcot,** preschoolers most enjoy the **Biergarten** in Germany, **San Angel Inn** in Mexico, and **Coral Reef** at The Seas with Nemo & Friends Pavilion in Future World. The Biergarten combines a rollicking and noisy atmosphere with good basic food, including roast chicken and German sausages; a German oompah band entertains. Children often have the opportunity to participate in Bavarian dancing. San Angel Inn is in the Mexican village marketplace. From the table, children can watch boats on Gran Fiesta Tour drift beneath a smoking volcano. With a choice of chips, tacos, and other familiar items, picky children usually have no difficulty finding something to eat. Be aware that the service is sometimes glacially slow. Coral Reef, with tables beside windows looking into The Seas' aquarium, offers a colorful mealtime diversion for all ages. If your kids don't eat fish, Coral Reef also serves beef and chicken. The downside is that the food is extremely expensive. For a more affordable splurge, forget lunch or dinner and drop in during off-hours for one of the Coral Reef's decadent desserts. The San Angel Inn is likewise overpriced but not in the same league as Coral Reef. The Biergarten offers reasonable value, plus good food.

Be Our Guest Restaurant and **Cinderella's Royal Table,** both in Fantasyland, are the hot tickets in the Magic Kingdom, but reservations are often well-nigh-impossible to get. (At present, there are no characters at Be Our Guest.) Interestingly, other Magic Kingdom full-service restaurants hold little appeal for children. For the best combination of food and entertainment, book a character meal at **The Crystal Palace.** From a strictly foodie standpoint, we think the best kids' fare is at the **Liberty Tree Tavern,** and it's easy to book, too.

At **Disney's Hollywood Studios,** all ages enjoy the atmosphere and entertainment at the **Sci-Fi Dine-In Theater Restaurant** and the **50's Prime Time Café.** Unfortunately, the Sci-Fi's food is close to dismal except for dessert, and the Prime Time's is uneven. Theme aside, children enjoy the character meals at **Hollywood & Vine,** and the pizza at **Mama Melrose's** never fails to please.

The three full-service restaurants at Disney's Animal Kingdom are

Tusker House Restaurant (actually a buffet); **Rainforest Cafe,** a great favorite of children; and **Yak & Yeti Restaurant.**

As you've undoubtedly noticed by now, Disney World is a trend-savvy place, and every market share has its niche. But Disney World is also about stars, fantasies, and meeting characters. So if you've become habituated to wood-fired pizza, the **California Grill** atop the Contemporary Resort will oblige. Great sushi can be had at **Teppan Edo** at Japan in Epcot and at **Kimonos** in the Swan. The best and biggest steaks are at **Shula's Steak House** in the Dolphin, **Le Cellier Steakhouse** in the Canada Pavilion, or **Yachtsman Steakhouse** at the Yacht Club, albeit way overpriced. **Kouzzina** is a family-style eatery at Disney's BoardWalk that features celebrity chef Cat Cora's Mediterranean-style recipes. In Italy **Via Napoli,** an authentic Neapolitan pizzeria, features wood-burning ovens and imports water from a source that most resembles the water in Naples, Italy, home of some of the world's best pizza dough. The 300-seat pizzeria is inspired by the Naples 45 pizzeria on East 45th Street in New York City and has both indoor and outdoor dining. In Mexico, the counter-service **La Cantina de San Angel** and the full-service **La Hacienda de San Angel** (dinner only) offer a combined 400 seats with alfresco seating for lunch and a perfect place for viewing *IllumiNations,* the nightly Epcot fireworks spectacular. **La Cava de Tequila,** a tequila-and-tapas joint, is a place you're never gonna see unless you can find somewhere to park your under-18s.

The **Planet Hollywood** at Downtown Disney (teens love it) famously belongs to and has memorabilia from the likes of Demi Moore, Bruce Willis, and Sylvester Stallone; plus, the planet-shaped building is a perfect counterpoint to Epcot's Spaceship Earth. The West Side has two celebrity-connected restaurant-nightclubs: **House of Blues,** part of the chain of New Orleans–style music halls–restaurants once partly owned by surviving Blues Brother Dan Aykroyd; and **Bongos,** a Cuban-flavored café created by Gloria Estefan and her husband, Emilio.

Not only film and sports stars but also the Food Network and food-magazine stars have been enlisted in the Disney World parade. Paul Bocuse was one of the eponymous **Chefs de France** who designed the menu for that restaurant and, most recently, **Monsieur Paul** in Epcot (and now that the building actually has a kitchen rather than hauling in food from outside commissaries, it does them much more credit). Boston star chef Todd English created **bluezoo** for the Dolphin. California's Wolfgang Puck is so celebrity-kitchen-conscious that the TV monitors at **Wolfgang Puck Grand Cafe** on the West Side show not sports or movies but the cooks at work, a fad English has also adopted.

Celebrity status notwithstanding, neither Puck's café nor the Estefans' Bongos has drawn much praise from diners, though bluezoo is very good (but also quite adult). House of Blues, surprisingly enough, has done much better with its Louisiana-inspired fare and gospel brunch.

If your kids haven't had their fill of robotic crocodiles, Abraham Lincolns, singing parrots, and the like, **T-REX** and **Rainforest Cafe** will serve up all they can handle. T-REX features animatronic dinosaurs and an occasional woolly mammoth, while Rainforest Cafe is stuffed with jungle critters. Both of course have gift shops. There are not one but two super-trendy Rainforest Cafe branches, one at Downtown Disney Marketplace and a supertheatrical version at the entrance to Disney's Animal Kingdom, where the decor and animatronic elephants make it fit right into the scenery there. Not surprisingly in a place where the sky "rains" and the stars flicker overhead, more thought went into naming the dishes than perfecting the recipes.

If your kids prefer dinosaurs to pachyderms, try T-REX, which is located within spitting distance of the Rainforest Cafe and operated by the same folks. The food is better than Rainforest, and children go nuts about being surrounded by a life-size animatronic brontosaurus, triceratops, and such.

In fact, although the official guides to Walt Disney World describe various restaurants as *delicious, delectable,* and *delightful,* the truth is that only perhaps a dozen of the nearly 100 full-service establishments are first-rate. And some of the most disappointing restaurants, in general, are the often attractive but commissary-bland ethnic kitchens.

Though a blessing in disguise to many children and picky eaters of all ages, most of the "ethnic" food at Walt Disney World is Americanized, or rather homogenized, especially at Epcot, where visitors from so many countries, as well as the United States, tend to have preconceived notions of egg rolls and enchiladas. **Teppan Edo** in the Japan Pavilion happens to be one of the better restaurants in the World, with pretty good teppanyaki (and good tempura next door)—but it specializes in a particularly Westernized form of Japanese cuisine, first produced in New York only about 30 years ago. **Nine Dragons Restaurant** in the China Pavilion serves satisfying dim sum along with handmade noodles (taffy-pulled out in the dining room), a respectable five-spiced fish, and crisp vegetables. The **San Angel Inn** in the Mexico Pavilion is associated with the famous Debler family of Mexico City. **Les Chefs de France** and **Monsieur Paul,** the brainchildren of master chefs Paul Bocuse, the late Gaston Lenôtre, and Roger Vergé, are serious dining destinations. Kids will love meeting Remy, star of Disney's *Ratatouille,* who visits the tables at Les Chefs de France in animatronic form. When making your reservation, check his schedule with a cast member.

Liliane loves meeting the princesses at Norway's **Akershus Royal Banquet Hall,** but Bob finds the buffet stodgy, smoky, and cheese- and mayonnaise-heavy. (If smoked meats are your thing, he thinks the smoked turkey legs from the outdoor vendors are far better.)

Among the places the culinary staff actually recommends (off the record) are the classic-continental prix-fixe **Victoria & Albert's** at the Grand Floridian, where you pay $200 a head to have every waitress introduce herself as Vicky and all the waiters as Al; the **Flying Fish Cafe; Artist Point; Jiko; Sanaa; Cítricos;** and the ultra-chic **California Grill.**

Another thing: A lot of the food at Disney World, particularly the fast food, is not what you'd describe as healthy. (Funnel cakes? Happy Meals?) But this is an area that the parks have started to address. **Artist's**

Palette at Saratoga Springs Resort and **Sunshine Seasons** in the Land Pavilion at Epcot are "fast casual" spots where the food is freshly prepared, often when you order it, but can be carried out or taken to nearby tables. At Sunshine Seasons, there are four different fully staffed kitchens, one preparing entrée salads with seared tuna or roasted beets with goat cheese, as well as soups du jour; another stir-frying veggies and preparing Asian noodle soup; a third wood-grilling chicken and beef to be wrapped in grilled flatbread or salmon with pesto; and a fourth preparing deluxe focaccia sandwiches. Artist's Palette offers everything from French toast to individual wood-grilled pizzas to gourmet-prepared entrées for carryout. Try the **Turf Club Bar & Grill** next door for roasted and grilled specialties.

Bob: OK, because you've been good, I'll tell you the one junk food to blow your calorie budget on: In Epcot's France Pavilion, there's a cart that sells bags of cinnamon-glazed pecans and almonds. Don't say we never spoil you.

Beyond that, there are fruit stands and juice bars scattered around, veggie sandwiches, wraps, rotisserie chicken, soft pretzels as well as the deceptively simple popcorn, baked potatoes (not, frankly, prepared with the apparent care of the turkey legs but about a tenth of the calories and salt), as well as the frozen fruit bars in the ice-cream freezers and frozen yogurt or smoothies at the ice-cream shops. Yes, it's hard, especially with all those fudge and cookie stands practically pelting you with sugary goodness as you saunter past, but stick to your guns. Look for the fruit markets in Liberty Square in the Magic Kingdom, on Sunset Boulevard in Disney's Hollywood Studios, and at the Harambe Village marketplace in Disney's Animal Kingdom.

MAGIC YOUR WAY DINING PLANS

DISNEY OFFERS DINING PLANS to accompany its Magic Your Way lodging packages (see page 115). They're available to all Disney resort guests except those staying at the Swan, the Dolphin, the hotels of the Downtown Disney Resort Area, and Shades of Green. Guests must also purchase a Magic Your Way package from Disney (not through an online reseller), have Annual Passes, or be members of the Disney Vacation Club (DVC) to participate in the plan. Except for DVC members, a three-night minimum stay is typically also required. Overall cost is determined by the number of nights you stay at a Disney resort.

MAGIC YOUR WAY PLUS DINING PLAN For each member of your group, for each night of your stay at a Walt Disney World resort, the basic dining plan provides one counter-service meal, one full-service meal, and one snack at participating Disney dining locations and restaurants, including room service at some resorts (type "Disney Dining Plan Locations 2013 [or 2014]" into your favorite Internet search engine to find sites with the entire list). For guests age 10 and up, the price is $59–$60 per night; for guests ages 3–9, the price is $19–$20 per night, tax included (prices vary seasonally). Children younger than age 3 eat free from an adult's plate.

The counter-service meal includes a main course (sandwich, dinner salad, pizza, or the like), dessert, and nonalcoholic drink, or a complete combo meal (a main course and a side—think burger and fries), dessert, and nonalcoholic drink, including tax. The full-service sit-down meals include a main course, dessert, a nonalcoholic drink, and tax. If you're dining at a buffet, the full-service meal includes the buffet, a nonalcoholic drink, and tax. The snack includes items normally sold from carts or small stands throughout the parks and resorts: ice cream, popcorn, soft drinks, fruit, chips, apple juice, and the like. In addition, the plan includes one refillable drink mug per person, per package, eligible for refills only at counter-service locations in your Disney resort. (Ever the penny-pincher, Disney is currently testing mugs with RFID chips to prevent illicit refills and to cut off resort guests after midnight on their checkout day.)

For instance, if you're staying for three nights, each member of your party will be credited with three counter-service meals, three full-service meals, and three snacks. All those meals will be put into an individual meal account for each person in your group. Meals in your account can be used on any combination of days, so you're not required to eat every meal every day. Thus, you can skip a full-service meal one day and have two on another day.

Top-of-the-line restaurants, dubbed **Disney Signature Restaurants** in the plan, along with all the dinner shows, count as two full-service meals. If you dine at one of these locations, two full-service meals will be deducted from your account for each person dining.

In addition to the preceding, the dining plan comes with several other important rules:

- Everyone staying in the same resort room must participate in the plan.
- Children ages 3–9 must order from the kids' menu, if one is available. This rule is occasionally not enforced at Disney's counter-service restaurants, enabling older children to order from the regular (adult) menu.
- In-room minibars are not included in the plan.
- A full-service meal can be breakfast, lunch, or dinner. The greatest savings occur when you use your full-service-meal allocations for dinner.
- The meal plan expires at midnight **on the day you check out** of the Disney resort. **Unused meals are nonrefundable.**
- The dining plan is occasionally unavailable when using certain room-only discounts.
- The full-service meal does not include an appetizer.
- While tax is included, gratuities are not.

QUICK-SERVICE DINING PLAN This plan includes meals, snacks, and nonalcoholic drinks at most counter-service eateries in Walt Disney World. The cost is $40 per night for guests age 10 and older, $16 per night for kids ages 3–9, tax included (no seasonal pricing). The plan includes two counter-service meals and one snack per day, plus the aforementioned refillable drink mug. The economics of the plan are difficult to justify unless you're drinking gallons of soda or coffee.

MAGIC YOUR WAY DELUXE DINING PLAN This one offers a choice of full-service or counter-service meals for three meals a day at any participating restaurant. In addition to the three meals a day, the plan also includes two snacks per day, appetizers, and a refillable drink mug. The Deluxe Plan costs $103–$104 per night for guests age 10 and older, and $29–$30 per night for kids ages 3–9, tax included (prices vary seasonally).

In addition to food, all the plans include deal-sweeteners such as a free round of miniature golf, a certificate for a 5-by-10-inch print from Disney's PhotoPass, a sort of two-for-one certificate for use of Sea Raycers watercraft, a commemorative luggage tag, and such.

MAGIC YOUR WAY PREMIUM PACKAGE Along with park tickets and lodging, you get breakfast, lunch, and dinner (including two snacks per day plus gratuities and one refillable resort drink mug per person), character meals, and dinner shows; unlimited golf, tennis, fishing excursions, and water sports; select theme park tours; Cirque du Soleil show tickets; unlimited use of child-care facilities—everything you can think of except for alcoholic beverages. The Premium Package costs $189 for adults and $139 for kids ages 3–9 (tax included) in addition to the cost of the standard Magic Your Way travel package.

MAGIC YOUR WAY PACKAGE The favorite of high rollers who want to prepay for everything they might desire while at Walt Disney World, the Platinum Package gets you lodging; park tickets; breakfast, lunch, and dinner in full-service restaurants; unlimited golf, tennis, boating, and recreation; unlimited dinner shows and character breakfasts; primo Cirque du Soleil seats; private in-room child care *and* unlimited use of child-care facilities; personalized itinerary planning; the Richard Petty Ride-Along Experience; a balloon ride at Characters in Flight in Downtown Disney; a spa treatment; a fireworks cruise; admission to select tours; and (here's the kicker) nightly turndown service! Everything you can think of, in other words, except alcoholic beverages. Per diem prices (including tax) for the Platinum Package are $249 for adults and $180 for kids in addition to the cost of a standard Magic Your Way package—but anyone who buys this package doesn't give a Goofy fart what the prices are anyway.

Things to Consider When Evaluating the Plus Dining Plan

If you prefer to always eat at counter-service restaurants, you'll be better off with the Quick-Service plan. Other poor candidates for the Plus plan include finicky eaters, light eaters, families who can't agree on restaurants, and those who can't get reservations at their first- or second-choice sit-down restaurants. It's usually not cost-effective during the holidays or summer either. In addition, if you have children age 10 and older, be sure that they can eat an adult-size dinner at a sit-down restaurant every night; if not, you'd probably come out ahead just paying for everyone's meals without the plan.

Disney ceaselessly tinkers with the dining plans' rules, meal definitions, and participating restaurants. For example, it's possible (though not documented) to exchange a sit-down-meal credit for a counter-service meal, though doing this even once can negate any savings you get from using a plan in the first place. Any Magic Your Way package that includes table-service dining can be upgraded—for a fee—to a Wine and Dine Plan, which includes one wine entitlement per night, per room.

In addition to obsessively tinkering with the plan and raising the prices, Disney also constantly cuts benefits. When the dining plan was first introduced, it included an appetizer and gratuity for each full-service meal, making it a pretty good deal; by our estimate, savings of up to 13% per person per day were possible in some of Disney's best restaurants. As a result, the dining plan was one of the most requested of Disney's package add-ons.

Alas, with the initial success of the plan, Disney saw an opportunity to make more money. In 2008, Disney stopped covering appetizers and gratuities, increasing the cost of a full-service meal by at least 15–18% for the tip alone, and an additional 15–20% per appetizer per person. Some of the pricier entrées were modified or eliminated from menus.

If you opt for the plan, keep in mind that skipping a single full-service meal during a visit of five or fewer days can mean the difference between saving and losing money. In our experience, having a scheduled sit-down meal for every day of a weeklong vacation can be mentally exhausting, especially for kids and teens. One option might be to schedule a meal at a Disney Signature restaurant, which requires two full-service credits. Because you have a full dinner credit for the day you check out, and because it's not likely that you'll still be around for dinner, you have an extra credit to use during your stay to dine in a signature restaurant without skipping a full-service meal one night.

Many of the most popular restaurants are fully booked as soon as their reservation window opens, so book your restaurants as soon as possible. Then decide whether the dining plan makes economic sense.

If you're making reservations at restaurants in Disney hotels other than your own, a car allows you to easily access all the participating restaurants. When you use the Disney transportation system, dining at the various Disney-resort restaurants can be a logistical nightmare. Those without a car may want to weigh the immediate services of a taxi (typically at $10–$12 each way across Disney property, versus a 50- to 75-minute trip on Disney transportation each way.

For an in-depth discussion of the various plans, including number-crunching (and even algebra!), visit **touringplans.com** (click "Dining" on the home page, then "Disney Dining Plan").

Readers who try the Disney dining plans have varying experiences. A St. Louis family of three comments:

We got the dining plan and would never do it again. Far too expensive, far too much food, and then you have to tip on top of the expense. Much easier to buy what you want, where and when you want.

From a Midwestern reader:

We could almost relate our dining experience to that of a person who receives food stamps—very restricted and always at the mercy of someone else for food selection.

A Belmont, Massachusetts, dad likes the Quick-Service Dining Plan:

If you intend to eat Disney food, the counter-service meal plan is a good option. We didn't want the full plan because the restaurants seemed overpriced, and the necessity of reservations months in advance seemed crazy and a bar to flexibility. You get two counter-service meals (entrée/combo, dessert, drink) and two snacks (food item or drink) per person as part of the plan, and even though kids' meals are cheaper, there is no distinction when you order—kids can order (more-expensive) adult meals.

But a reader from The Woodlands, Texas, laments that the plan has altered the focus of her vacation:

For me, the dining plan has taken a lot of the fun out of going to Disney World. Now, dining for each day must be planned months in advance unless one is to eat just hot dogs, pizza, and other walk-up items. I want to have fun. I don't want to be locked into a tight schedule, always worrying about where we need to be when it's time to eat, and I don't want to eat when I'm not hungry just because I have a reservation somewhere. As heretical as it may sound, I'm actually less inclined to go to WDW now.

A mom from Orland Park, Illinois, comments on the difficulty of getting Advance Reservations:

It's impossible to get table reservations anywhere good—the restaurants that are available are available for a reason. We found ourselves taking whatever was open and were unhappy with every sit-down meal we had, except for lunch at Liberty Tree Tavern. I don't enjoy planning my day exclusively around eating at a certain restaurant at a certain time, but that is what you must do six months in advance if you want to eat at a good sit-down restaurant in Disney. That is ridiculous.

In a similar vein, a San Jose, California, reader says that guests who are not on the dining plan need to know how it has affected obtaining Advance Reservations:

The Disney Dining Plan has almost eliminated any chance of spontaneity when visiting any of the sit-down restaurants. When planning 90 days out for the off-season, I was told by the Disney rep to make all my Advance Reservations then because the restaurants are booked by people on the dining plan. In fact, I was told that most of the sit-down restaurants don't even take walk-ins anymore. Sure enough, even though I was well over 90 days away from my vacation, a lot of my restaurant choices were unavailable. I had to rearrange my entire schedule to fit the open slots at the restaurants I didn't want to miss.

On a positive note, many readers report that Disney cast members are much more knowledgeable about the dining plan these days than in the past. A Washington, D.C.–area couple writes:

> The kinks are worked out, and everyone at the parks we talked to seemed to get it, but we still spent $40 or more at most sit-down dinners on drinks and tips.

A mum from Sutton Coldfield, England, warns that toddlers fall through the cracks:

> We were traveling with two 6-year-olds and a 2-year-old. My youngest did not qualify for the dining plan, which worked well in the buffet-style restaurants where he could eat free. However, if you eat in a full-service restaurant and your 2-year-old is eating off the menu, there's no infant option—you have to pay for a child's meal.

A Land O' Lakes, Florida, dad bumped into this problem:

> We had some trouble with our Deluxe Dining Plan being "invalidated" after checkout, though it was supposed to be valid until midnight of our checkout date. That was annoying, since calls to the resort were needed to verify the meals left on our passes for The Crystal Palace and for some snacks later.

The dining plan left a family of five from Nashville, Tennessee, similarly dazed and confused:

> What was annoying was the inconsistency. You can get a 16-ounce chocolate milk on the kids' plan, but only 8 ounces of white milk at many places. At Earl of Sandwich, you can get 16 ounces of either kind. A pint of milk would count as a snack (price $1.52), but they wouldn't count a quart of milk (price $1.79) because it wasn't a single serving. However, in Animal Kingdom, my husband bought a water-bottle holder (price $3.75) and used a snack credit.

Reader Tips for Getting the Most Out of the Plan

A mom from Radford, Virginia, shares the following:

> Warn people to eat lunch early if they have dinner reservations before 7 p.m. Disney doesn't skimp on food—if you eat a late lunch, you WILL NOT be hungry for dinner.

A mom from Brick Township, New Jersey, found that the dining plan streamlined her touring:

> We truly enjoyed our Disney trip, and this time we purchased the Dining Plan. This was great for the kids because we did a character-dining experience every day. This helped us in the parks because we didn't have to wait in line to see the characters. Instead, we got all of our autographs during our meals.

A Saskatoon, Saskatchewan, father of three says it's important to be vigilant when it comes to the outdoor food vendors:

*We had a problem with a vendor who charged us meal service for
each of the ice cream bars we purchased. This became evident at our
final sit-down meal, when we didn't have any meal vouchers left.*
Check the receipts after every purchase!

CHARACTER DINING

ALL THE RAGE AT WALT DISNEY WORLD for more than a decade,
character dining combines a meal with meeting the characters. The characters circulate throughout the meal, stopping at each table to sign autographs, pose for photos, and lavish attention on mostly adoring (but
sometimes stupefied) children. For a detailed description of this Disney
ritual, see pages 250–258.

WALT DISNEY WORLD DINNER THEATERS

SEVERAL DINNER-THEATER SHOWS play each night at Walt Disney World, and unlike other Disney dining venues, they make hard reservations instead of Advance Reservations, meaning you must guarantee
your reservation ahead of time with a credit card. You'll receive a confirmation number and be told to pick up your tickets at a Disney-hotel
Guest Relations desk. Unless you cancel your tickets at least 48 hours
before your reservation time, your credit card will still be charged the
full amount. Dinner-show reservations can be made 180 days in
advance; call ☎ 407-939-3463.

Hoop-Dee-Doo Musical Revue

Pioneer Hall, Fort Wilderness Campground

Showtimes 4, 6:15, and 8:30 p.m. nightly. **Cost** $59–$68 adults, $30–$35 children ages
3–9. Prices include tax and gratuity. **Discounts** Seasonal. **Type of seating** Tables of
various sizes to fit the number in each party, set in an Old West–style dance hall. **Menu**
All-you-can-eat barbecue ribs, fried chicken, corn, and strawberry shortcake. **Vegetarian alternative** On request (at least 24 hours in advance). **Beverages** Unlimited beer,
wine, sangria, and soft drinks.

SIX WILD WEST PERFORMERS arrive by stagecoach (sound effects only) to
entertain the crowd inside Pioneer Hall. There isn't much of a plot, just
corny jokes interspersed with song or dance. The humor is of the *Hee Haw*
ilk, but it's presented enthusiastically.

Audience participation includes sing-alongs, hand clapping, and a
finale that uses volunteers to play parts on stage. Performers are accompanied by a banjo player and pianist who also play quietly while the food
is being served. The fried chicken and corn on the cob are good, the ribs a
bit tough though tasty.

Traveling to Fort Wilderness and absorbing the rustic atmosphere of Pioneer Hall augments the adventure. For repeat Disney World visitors, an
annual visit to the revue is a tradition of sorts. Plus, warts and all, the revue
is all Disney, and for some folks that's enough. The fact that performances
sell out far in advance gives the experience a special aura. To make reservations for the *Hoop-Dee-Doo Musical Revue*, call as soon as you're certain of
the dates of your visit. The earlier you call, the better your seats will be.

If you go to *Hoop-Dee-Doo*, allow plenty of driving time (about an
hour) to get there. Or do as this California dad suggests:

To go to the Hoop-Dee-Doo Musical Revue, *take the boat from the Magic Kingdom rather than any bus. This is contrary to the "official" directions. The boat dock is a short walk from Pioneer Hall in Fort Wilderness, while the bus goes to the main Fort Wilderness parking lot, where one has to transfer to another bus to Pioneer Hall.*

Boat service may be suspended during thunderstorms, so if it's raining or it looks like it's about to rain, Disney will provide bus service from the parks.

Mickey's Backyard BBQ

Fort Wilderness Campground

Showtimes Thursday and Saturday at 5, 6:30, and 7 p.m. **Cost** $57 adults, $33 children ages 3–9. Prices include tax and gratuity. **Type of seating** Picnic tables. **Menu** Baked chicken, barbecue pork ribs, burgers, hot dogs, corn, beans, mac and cheese, salads and slaw, bread, and watermelon and ice-cream bars for dessert. **Vegetarian alternatives** On request. **Beverages** Unlimited beer, wine, lemonade, and iced tea.

SITUATED ALONG BAY LAKE and held in a covered pavilion, *Mickey's Backyard BBQ* features Mickey, Minnie, Chip 'n' Dale, and Goofy, along with a country band and line dancing. Though the pavilion gets some breeze off Bay Lake, we recommend going during the spring or fall, if possible. The food is pretty good, as is, fortunately, the insect control.

The easiest way to get to the barbecue is to take a boat from the Magic Kingdom or from one of the Disney resorts on the Magic Kingdom monorail. Give yourself at least 45 minutes if you plan to arrive by boat. Ferry service may be suspended during thunderstorms, so if it's raining or it looks like it's about to rain, Disney will provide bus service from the parks.

Spirit of Aloha Dinner Show

Disney's Polynesian Resort

Showtimes Tuesday–Saturday, 5:15 and 8 p.m. **Cost** $59–$72 adults, $30–$37 children ages 3–9. Prices include tax and gratuity. **Discounts** Seasonal. **Type of seating** Long rows of tables, with some separation between individual parties. The show is performed on an outdoor stage, but all seating is covered. Ceiling fans provide some air movement, but it can get warm, especially at the early show. **Menu** Tropical fruit, roasted chicken, island pork ribs, mixed vegetables, rice, and pineapple bread; chicken tenders, PB&J sandwiches, mac and cheese, and hot dogs are also available for children. **Vegetarian alternative** On request. **Beverages** Beer, wine, and soft drinks.

THIS SHOW FEATURES South Seas–island native dancing followed by an all-you-can-eat "Polynesian-style" meal. The dancing is interesting and largely authentic, and the dancers are attractive though definitely PG-rated in the Disney tradition. We think the show has its moments and the meal is adequate, but neither is particularly special.

The show follows (tenuously) the common "girl leaves home for the big city, forgets her roots, and must rediscover them" theme. The story, however, never really makes sense as anything other than a slender thread between musical numbers. Our show lasted for more than 2 hours and 15 minutes.

The food does little more than illustrate how difficult it must be to prepare the same meal for hundreds of people simultaneously. The roasted chicken is better than the ribs, but neither is anything special. We conditionally recommend *Spirit of Aloha* for special occasions, when the people celebrating get to go on stage. But go to the early show and get dessert somewhere else in the World.

WALT DISNEY WORLD RESTAURANTS: RATED AND RANKED

STAR RATING The star rating represents the entire dining experience: style, service, and ambience, in addition to taste, presentation, and quality of food. Five stars is the highest rating and indicates that the restaurant offers the best of everything. Four-star restaurants are above average, and three-star restaurants offer good, though not necessarily memorable, meals. Two-star restaurants serve mediocre fare, and one-star restaurants are below average. Our star ratings don't correspond to ratings awarded by AAA, Mobil, Zagat, or other restaurant reviewers.

★★★★★	Exceptional value, a real bargain
★★★★	Good value
★★★	Fair value, you get exactly what you pay for
★★	Somewhat overpriced
★	Significantly overpriced

COST RANGE The next rating tells how much a complete meal will cost. We include a main dish with vegetable or side dish and a choice of soup or salad. Appetizers, desserts, drinks, and tips aren't included. We've rated the cost as inexpensive, moderate, or expensive.

Inexpensive	$15 or less per person
Moderate	$15–$30 per person
Expensive	More than $30 per person

QUALITY RATING The food quality is rated on a scale of one to five stars, five being the best rating attainable. The quality rating is based on the taste, freshness of ingredients, preparation, presentation, and creativity of food served. There is no consideration of price. If you are a person who wants the best food available and cost is not an issue, you need look no further than the quality ratings.

VALUE RATING If, on the other hand, you are looking for both quality and value, then you should check the value rating, expressed as stars.

Walt Disney World Restaurants by Cuisine

CUISINE	LOCATION	OVERALL RATING	COST	QUALITY RATING	VALUE RATING
AFRICAN					
JIKO— THE COOKING PLACE	Animal Kingdom Lodge/Jambo House	★★★★½	Exp	★★★★½	★★★½
BOMA— FLAVORS OF AFRICA	Animal Kingdom Lodge/Jambo House	★★★★	Exp	★★★★	★★★★½
TUSKER HOUSE RESTAURANT	Animal Kingdom	★½	Mod	★	★★
AMERICAN					
CALIFORNIA GRILL (reopens 2013)	Contemporary	★★★★½	Exp	★★★★½	★★★
THE HOLLYWOOD BROWN DERBY	DHS	★★★★	Exp	★★★★	★★★
ARTIST POINT	Wilderness Lodge	★★★½	Exp	★★★★	★★★
CAPE MAY CAFÉ	Beach Club	★★★½	Mod	★★★½	★★★★
WHISPERING CANYON CAFÉ	Wilderness Lodge	★★★	Mod	★★★½	★★★★
CAPTAIN'S GRILLE	Yacht Club	★★★	Mod	★★★½	★★★
THE CRYSTAL PALACE	Magic Kingdom	★★★	Mod	★★★½	★★★
HOUSE OF BLUES	Downtown Disney	★★★	Mod	★★★½	★★★
50'S PRIME TIME CAFÉ	DHS	★★★	Mod	★★★	★★★
LIBERTY TREE TAVERN	Magic Kingdom	★★★	Mod	★★★	★★★
CINDERELLA'S ROYAL TABLE	Magic Kingdom	★★★	Exp	★★★	★★
OLIVIA'S CAFE	Old Key West	★★★	Mod	★★★	★★
T-REX	Downtown Disney	★★★	Mod	★★	★★
THE WAVE . . . OF AMERICAN FLAVORS	Contemporary	★★★	Mod	★★	★★
ESPN CLUB	BoardWalk	★★½	Mod	★★★	★★★
ESPN WIDE WORLD OF SPORTS CAFE	ESPN Wide World of Sports Complex	★★½	Mod	★★★	★★★
HOLLYWOOD & VINE	DHS	★★½	Mod	★★★	★★★
1900 PARK FARE	Grand Floridian	★★½	Mod	★★★	★★★
CHEF MICKEY'S	Contemporary	★★½	Exp	★★★	★★★
BOATWRIGHTS DINING HALL	Port Orleans	★★½	Mod	★★★	★★
GRAND FLORIDIAN CAFE	Grand Floridian	★★½	Mod	★★★	★★
BEACHES & CREAM SODA SHOP	Beach Club	★★½	Inexp	★★½	★★½
SPLITSVILLE	Downtown Disney	★★½	Mod	★★½	★★
PLANET HOLLYWOOD	Downtown Disney	★★½	Mod	★★	★★
RAINFOREST CAFE	Animal Kingdom and Downtown Disney	★★½	Mod	★★	★★

Walt Disney World Restaurants by Cuisine (cont'd)

CUISINE	LOCATION	OVERALL RATING	COST	QUALITY RATING	VALUE RATING
GARDEN GROVE	Swan	★★	Mod	★★★	★★
SCI-FI DINE-IN THEATER RESTAURANT	DHS	★★	Mod	★★½	★★
GARDEN GRILL RESTAURANT	Epcot	★★	Exp	★★	★★★
BIG RIVER GRILLE & BREWING WORKS	BoardWalk	★★	Mod	★★	★★
THE FOUNTAIN	Dolphin	★★	Mod	★★	★★
THE PLAZA RESTAURANT	Magic Kingdom	★★	Mod	★★	★★
TURF CLUB BAR & GRILL	Saratoga Springs	★★	Mod	★★	★★
TRAIL'S END RESTAURANT	Fort Wilderness Resort	★★	Mod	★★	★★
WOLFGANG PUCK GRAND CAFE	Downtown Disney	★★	Exp	★½	★½
LAKEVIEW RESTAURANT	Wyndham LBV	★★	Mod	★	★★★
TUSKER HOUSE RESTAURANT	Animal Kingdom	★½	Mod	★	★★
MAYA GRILL	Coronado Springs	★	Mod	★	★
BUFFET					
BOMA— FLAVORS OF AFRICA	Animal Kingdom Lodge	★★★★	Exp	★★★★	★★★★½
CAPE MAY CAFÉ	Beach Club	★★★½	Mod	★★★½	★★★★
THE CRYSTAL PALACE	Magic Kingdom	★★★	Mod	★★★½	★★★
AKERSHUS ROYAL BANQUET HALL	Epcot	★★★	Exp	★★★	★★★★
HOLLYWOOD & VINE	DHS	★★½	Mod	★★★	★★★
1900 PARK FARE	Grand Floridian	★★½	Mod	★★★	★★★
CHEF MICKEY'S	Contemporary	★★½	Exp	★★★	★★★
GARDEN GROVE	Swan	★★	Mod	★★★	★★
BIERGARTEN	Epcot	★★	Exp	★★	★★★★
TRAIL'S END RESTAURANT	Fort Wilderness Resort	★★	Mod	★★	★★
TUSKER HOUSE RESTAURANT	Animal Kingdom	★½	Mod	★	★★
CHINESE					
NINE DRAGONS RESTAURANT	Epcot	★★★	Mod	★★★	★★
CUBAN					
BONGOS CUBAN CAFE	Downtown Disney	★★	Mod	★★	★★
ENGLISH					
ROSE & CROWN DINING ROOM	Epcot	★★★	Mod	★★★½	★★

Walt Disney World Restaurants by Cuisine (cont'd)

CUISINE	LOCATION	OVERALL RATING	COST	QUALITY RATING	VALUE RATING
FRENCH					
MONSIEUR PAUL	Epcot	★★★★	Exp	★★★★½	★★★
BE OUR GUEST RESTAURANT	Magic Kingdom	★★★★	Exp	★★★★	★★★★
LES CHEFS DE FRANCE	Epcot	★★★	Exp	★★★	★★★
GERMAN					
BIERGARTEN	Epcot	★★	Exp	★★	★★★★
GLOBAL					
PARADISO 37	Downtown Disney	★★½	Inexp	★★★	★★★
GOURMET					
VICTORIA & ALBERT'S	Grand Floridian	★★★★★	Exp	★★★★★	★★★★
INDIAN/AFRICAN					
SANAA	Animal Kingdom Villas–Kidani Village	★★★★	Exp	★★★★	★★★★
IRISH					
RAGLAN ROAD IRISH PUB & RESTAURANT	Downtown Disney	★★★★	Mod	★★★½	★★★
ITALIAN					
TUTTO ITALIA RISTORANTE	Epcot	★★★★	Exp	★★★★	★★★
VIA NAPOLI	Epcot	★★★★	Mod	★★★½	★★★
ANDIAMO ITALIAN BISTRO & GRILLE	Hilton	★★★	Exp	★★★	★★★
IL MULINO NEW YORK TRATTORIA	Swan	★★★	Exp	★★★	★★
MAMA MELROSE'S RISTORANTE ITALIANO	DHS	★★½	Mod	★★★	★★
TONY'S TOWN SQUARE RESTAURANT	Magic Kingdom	★★½	Mod	★★★	★★
JAPANESE/SUSHI					
KIMONOS	Swan	★★★★	Mod	★★★★½	★★★
KONA ISLAND SUSHI BAR	Polynesian	★★★★	Mod	★★★★	★★★★
TEPPAN EDO	Epcot	★★★½	Exp	★★★★	★★★
TOKYO DINING	Epcot	★★★	Mod	★★★★	★★★
BENIHANA	Hilton	★★★	Mod	★★★½	★★★
MEDITERRANEAN					
KOUZZINA BY CAT CORA	BoardWalk Inn	★★★★	Mod	★★★★	★★★★

Walt Disney World Restaurants by Cuisine (cont'd)

CUISINE	LOCATION	OVERALL RATING	COST	QUALITY RATING	VALUE RATING
CÍTRICOS	Grand Floridian	★★★½	Exp	★★★★½	★★★
FRESH MEDITERRANEAN MARKET	Dolphin	★★½	Mod	★★½	★★
MEXICAN					
LA HACIENDA DE SAN ANGEL	Epcot	★★★	Exp	★★★½	★★½
SAN ANGEL INN	Epcot	★★★	Exp	★★	★★
MOROCCAN					
RESTAURANT MARRAKESH	Epcot	★★	Mod	★★½	★★
NORWEGIAN					
AKERSHUS ROYAL BANQUET HALL	Epcot	★★★	Exp	★★★	★★★★
POLYNESIAN/PAN-ASIAN					
KONA ISLAND SUSHI BAR	Polynesian	★★★★	Mod	★★★★	★★★★
'OHANA	Polynesian	★★★	Mod	★★★½	★★★
KONA CAFE	Polynesian	★★★	Mod	★★★	★★★★
YAK & YETI RESTAURANT	Animal Kingdom	★★	Exp	★★½	★★
AVU AVU	Buena Vista Palace	★★	Mod	★★	★★★
SEAFOOD					
NARCOOSSEE'S	Grand Floridian	★★★★½	Exp	★★★½	★★
FLYING FISH CAFÉ	BoardWalk	★★★★	Exp	★★★★	★★★
ARTIST POINT	Wilderness Lodge	★★★½	Exp	★★★★	★★★
TODD ENGLISH'S BLUEZOO	Dolphin	★★★	Exp	★★★	★★
FULTON'S CRAB HOUSE	Downtown Disney	★★½	Exp	★★★½	★★
SHUTTERS AT OLD PORT ROYALE	Caribbean Beach	★★	Mod	★★½	★★
STEAK					
SHULA'S STEAK HOUSE	Dolphin	★★★★	Exp	★★★★	★★
LE CELLIER STEAKHOUSE	Epcot	★★★½	Exp	★★★½	★★★
YACHTSMAN STEAKHOUSE	Yacht Club	★★★	Exp	★★★½	★★
SHUTTERS AT OLD PORT ROYALE	Caribbean Beach	★★	Mod	★★½	★★

PART FIVE

DISNEY BOOT CAMP:
Basic Training for World-Bound Families

The **BRUTAL TRUTH** *about* **FAMILY VACATIONS**

IT HAS BEEN SUGGESTED THAT THE PHRASE *family vacation* is a bit of an oxymoron. This is because you can never take a vacation from the responsibilities of parenting if your children are traveling with you. Though you leave your work and normal routine far behind, your children require as much attention, if not more, when traveling as they do at home.

Parenting on the road is an art. It requires imagination and organization. Think about it: You have to do all the usual stuff (feed, dress, bathe, supervise, teach, comfort, discipline, put to bed, and so on) in an atmosphere where your children are hyperstimulated, without the familiarity of place and the resources you take for granted at home. Although it's not impossible—and can even be fun—parenting on the road is not something you want to learn on the fly, particularly at Walt Disney World.

The point we want to drive home is that preparation, or the lack thereof, can make or break your Walt Disney World vacation. Believe us, you do *not* want to leave the success of your expensive Disney vacation to chance. But don't confuse chance with good luck. Chance is what happens when you fail to prepare. Good luck is when preparation meets opportunity.

Your preparation can be organized into several categories, all of which we will help you undertake. Broadly speaking, you need to prepare yourself and your children mentally, emotionally, physically, organizationally, and logistically. You also need a basic understanding of Walt Disney World and a well-considered plan for how to go about seeing it.

MENTAL *and* EMOTIONAL PREPARATION

THIS IS A SUBJECT THAT WE WILL TOUCH on here and return to many times in this book. Mental preparation begins with realistic expectations about your Disney vacation and consideration of what each adult and child in your party most wants and needs from their Walt Disney World experience. Getting in touch with this aspect of planning requires a lot of introspection and good, open family communication.

DIVISION OF LABOR

TALK ABOUT WHAT YOU AND YOUR PARTNER NEED and what you expect to happen on the vacation. This discussion alone can preempt some unpleasant surprises mid-trip. If you are a two-parent family, do you have a clear understanding of how the parenting workload is to be distributed? We have seen some distinctly disruptive misunderstandings in two-parent households where one parent is (pardon the legalese) the primary caregiver. Often, the other parent expects the primary caregiver to function on vacation as she (or he) does at home. The primary caregiver, on the other hand, is ready for a break. She expects her partner to either shoulder the load equally or perhaps even assume the lion's share so she can have a *real* vacation. However you divide the responsibility, of course, is up to you. Just make sure you negotiate a clear understanding *before* you leave home.

TOGETHERNESS

ANOTHER DIMENSION TO CONSIDER is how much togetherness seems appropriate to you. For some parents, a vacation represents a rare opportunity to really connect with their children, to talk, exchange ideas, and get reacquainted. For others, a vacation affords the time to get a little distance, to enjoy a round of golf while the kids are participating in a program organized by the resort.

At Walt Disney World you can orchestrate your vacation to spend as much or as little time with your children as you desire, but more about that later. The point here is to think about your and your children's preferences and needs concerning your time together. A typical day at a Disney theme park provides the structure of experiencing attractions together, punctuated by periods of waiting in line, eating, and so on, which facilitate conversation and sharing. Most attractions can be enjoyed together by the whole family, regardless of age ranges. This allows for more consensus and less dissent when it comes to deciding what to see and do. For many parents and children, however, the rhythms of a Walt Disney World day seem to consist of passive entertainment experiences alternated with endless discussions of where to go and what to do next. As a mother from Winston-Salem, North Carolina, reported:

Our family mostly talked about what to do next with very little shar-
ing or discussion about what we had seen. [The conversation] was
pretty task oriented.

Two observations: First, fighting the crowds and keeping the family moving along can easily escalate into a pressure-driven outing.
Having an advance plan or itinerary eliminates moment-to-moment
guesswork and decision making, thus creating more time for savoring and connecting. Second, external variables such as crowd size,
noise, and heat, among others, can be so distracting as to preclude any
meaningful togetherness. These negative impacts can be moderated,
as previously discussed, by your being selective concerning the time
of year, day of the week, and time of day you visit the theme parks.
The bottom line is that you can achieve the degree of connection and
togetherness you desire with a little advance planning and a realistic
awareness of the distractions you will encounter.

LIGHTEN UP

PREPARE YOURSELF MENTALLY to be a little less compulsive on
vacation about correcting small behavioral deviations and pounding
home the lessons of life. Certainly, little Mildred will have to learn eventually that it's very un-Disney-like to take off her top at the pool. But
there's plenty of time for that later. So what if Matt eats hamburgers for
breakfast, lunch, and dinner every day? You can make him eat peas and
broccoli when you get home and are in charge of meal preparation
again. Roll with the little stuff, and remember when your children act
out that they are wired to the max. At least some of that adrenaline is
bound to spill out in undesirable ways. Coming down hard will send an
already frayed little nervous system into orbit.

SOMETHING FOR EVERYONE

IF YOU TRAVEL WITH AN INFANT, TODDLER, or any child who
requires a lot of special attention, make sure that you have some
energy and time remaining for your other children. In the course of
your planning, invite each child to name something special to do or
see at Walt Disney World with mom or dad
alone. Work these special activities into
your trip itinerary. Whatever else, if you
commit, write it down so that you don't
forget. Remember, a casually expressed
willingness to do this or that may be perceived as a promise by your children.

Liliane: Try to schedule some time alone
with each of your chil-
dren, if not each day,
then at least a couple
of times during the trip.

WHOSE IDEA WAS THIS, ANYWAY?

THE DISCORD THAT MANY VACATIONING FAMILIES experience
arises from the kids being on a completely different wavelength from
mom and dad. Parents and grandparents are often worse than children
when it comes to conjuring up fantasy scenarios of what a Walt Disney

World vacation will be like. A Disney vacation can be many things, but believe us when we tell you that there's a lot more to it than just riding Dumbo and seeing Mickey.

In our experience, most parents and nearly all grandparents expect children to enter a state of rapture at Walt Disney World, bouncing from attraction to attraction in wide-eyed wonder, appreciative beyond words of their adult benefactors. What they get, more often than not, is not even in the same ballpark. Preschoolers will, without a doubt, be wide-eyed, often with delight but also with a general sense of being overwhelmed by noise, crowds, and Disney characters as big as tool sheds.

 Liliane: Short forays to the parks interspersed with naps, swimming, and quiet activities such as reading to your children will go a long way toward keeping things on an even keel.

We have substantiated through thousands of interviews and surveys that the best part of a Disney vacation for a preschooler is the hotel swimming pool. With some grade-schoolers and pre-driving-age teens you get near-manic hyperactivity coupled with periods of studied nonchalance. This last, which relates to the importance of being cool at all costs, translates into a maddening display of boredom and a "been there, done that" attitude. Older teens are frequently the exponential version of the younger teens and grade-schoolers, except without the manic behavior.

Liliane: The more information your children have before arriving at Walt Disney World, the less likely they will be to act out.

As a function of probability, you may escape many—but most likely not all—of the aforementioned behaviors. Even in the event that they are all visited on you, however, take heart, there are antidotes.

For preschoolers keep things light and happy by limiting the time you spend in the theme parks. The most critical point is that the overstimulation of the parks must be balanced by adequate rest and more mellow activities. For grade-schoolers and early teens, moderate the hyperactivity and false apathy by enlisting their help in planning the vacation, especially by allowing them to take a leading role in determining the itinerary for days at the theme parks. Being in charge of specific responsibilities that focus on the happiness of other family members also works well. One reader, for example, turned a 12-year-old liability into an asset by asking him to help guard against attractions that might frighten his 5-year-old sister.

Knowledge enhances anticipation and at the same time affords a level of comfort and control that helps kids understand the big picture. The more they feel in control, the less they will act out of control.

DISNEY, KIDS, AND SCARY STUFF

DISNEY ATTRACTIONS, BOTH RIDES AND SHOWS, are adventures. They focus on themes common to adventures: good and evil, life

Continued on page 194

Small-Child Fright-Potential Chart

This is a quick reference to identify attractions to be wary of, and why. The chart represents a generalization, and all kids are different. It relates specifically to kids ages 3–7. On average, children at the younger end of the range are more likely to be frightened than children in their sixth or seventh year.

THE MAGIC KINGDOM

SORCERERS OF THE MAGIC KINGDOM Loud but not frightening.

MAIN STREET, U.S.A.

MAIN STREET VEHICLES Not frightening in any respect.

WALT DISNEY WORLD RAILROAD Not frightening in any respect.

ADVENTURELAND

ENCHANTED TIKI ROOM A thunderstorm, loud volume level, and simulated explosions frighten some preschoolers.

JUNGLE CRUISE Moderately intense, some macabre sights. A good test attraction for little ones.

PIRATES OF THE CARIBBEAN Slightly intimidating queuing area; intense boat ride with gruesome (though humorously presented) sights and a short, unexpected slide down a flume.

THE MAGIC CARPETS OF ALADDIN Much like Dumbo. A favorite of young children.

SWISS FAMILY TREEHOUSE May not be suitable for kids who are afraid of heights.

FRONTIERLAND

BIG THUNDER MOUNTAIN RAILROAD Visually intimidating from outside, with moderately intense visual effects. The roller coaster is wild enough to frighten many adults, particularly seniors. Switching-off option provided (see page 245).

COUNTRY BEAR JAMBOREE Not frightening in any respect.

FRONTIERLAND SHOOTIN' ARCADE Frightening to children who are scared of guns.

SPLASH MOUNTAIN Visually intimidating from outside, with moderately intense visual effects. The ride culminates in a 52-foot plunge down a steep chute. Switching-off option provided (see page 245).

TOM SAWYER ISLAND AND FORT LANGHORN Some very young children are intimidated by dark walk-through tunnels that can be easily avoided.

LIBERTY SQUARE

THE HALL OF PRESIDENTS Not frightening, but boring for young ones.

THE HAUNTED MANSION Name raises anxiety, as do sounds and sights of waiting area. Intense attraction with humorously presented macabre sights. The ride itself is gentle.

LIBERTY BELLE RIVERBOAT Not frightening in any respect.

FANTASYLAND

DUMBO THE FLYING ELEPHANT A tame midway ride; a great favorite of most young children.

THE BARNSTORMER May frighten some preschoolers.

ENCHANTED TALES WITH BELLE Not frightening in any respect.

IT'S A SMALL WORLD Not frightening in any respect.

MAD TEA PARTY Midway-type ride can induce motion sickness in all ages.

THE MANY ADVENTURES OF WINNIE THE POOH Frightens a small percentage of preschoolers.

PETER PAN'S FLIGHT Not frightening in any respect.

PRINCE CHARMING REGAL CARROUSEL Not frightening in any respect.

SEVEN DWARFS MINE TRAIN Not open at press time.

UNDER THE SEA: JOURNEY OF THE LITTLE MERMAID Animatronic octopus character frightens some preschoolers.

TOMORROWLAND

ASTRO ORBITER Visually intimidating from the waiting area, but the ride is relatively tame.

BUZZ LIGHTYEAR'S SPACE RANGER SPIN Dark ride with cartoonlike aliens. May frighten some preschoolers.

MONSTERS, INC. LAUGH FLOOR May frighten a small percentage of preschoolers.

SPACE MOUNTAIN Very intense roller coaster in the dark; the Magic Kingdom's wildest ride and a scary roller coaster by any standard.
Switching-off option provided (see page 245).

STITCH'S GREAT ESCAPE! Very intense. May frighten children age 9 and younger. Switching-off option provided (see page 245).

TOMORROWLAND SPEEDWAY Noise of waiting area slightly intimidates preschoolers; otherwise, not frightening.

TOMORROWLAND TRANSIT AUTHORITY PEOPLEMOVER Not frightening in any respect.

WALT DISNEY'S CAROUSEL OF PROGRESS Not frightening in any respect.

EPCOT

FUTURE WORLD

IMAGINATION!: *CAPTAIN EO* Extremely intense visual effects and loudness frighten many young children.

INNOVENTIONS EAST AND WEST Not frightening in any respect.

JOURNEY INTO IMAGINATION WITH FIGMENT Loud noises and unexpected flashing lights startle younger children.

THE LAND: *THE CIRCLE OF LIFE* Not frightening in any respect.

THE LAND: LIVING WITH THE LAND Not frightening in any respect.

THE LAND: SOARIN' May frighten kids age 7 and younger, or anyone with a fear of heights. Otherwise a very mellow ride.

MISSION: SPACE Extremely intense space-simulation ride that has been known to frighten guests of all ages. Preshow may also frighten some children. Switching-off option provided (see page 245).

THE SEAS—THE SEAS WITH NEMO & FRIENDS Very sweet but may frighten some toddlers.

THE SEAS: MAIN TANK AND EXHIBITS Not frightening in any respect.

THE SEAS: *TURTLE TALK WITH CRUSH* Not frightening in any respect.

Small-Child Fright-Potential Chart (continued)

EPCOT (continued)

FUTURE WORLD (continued)

SPACESHIP EARTH Dark, imposing presentation intimidates a few preschoolers.

TEST TRACK Intense thrill ride may frighten guests of any age. Switching-off option provided (see page 245).

UNIVERSE OF ENERGY: *ELLEN'S ENERGY ADVENTURE* Dinosaur segment frightens some preschoolers; visually intense, with some intimidating effects.

WORLD SHOWCASE

CANADA: *O CANADA!* Not frightening, but audience must stand.

CHINA: *REFLECTIONS OF CHINA* Not frightening in any respect.

FRANCE: *IMPRESSIONS DE FRANCE* Not frightening in any respect.

GERMANY Not frightening in any respect.

ITALY Not frightening in any respect.

JAPAN Not frightening in any respect.

MEXICO: GRAN FIESTA TOUR Not frightening in any respect.

MOROCCO Not frightening in any respect.

NORWAY: MAELSTROM Visually intense in parts. Ride ends with a plunge down a 20-foot flume. A few preschoolers are frightened.

UNITED KINGDOM Not frightening in any respect.

UNITED STATES: *THE AMERICAN ADVENTURE* Not frightening in any respect.

DISNEY'S ANIMAL KINGDOM

THE OASIS Not frightening in any respect.

RAFIKI'S PLANET WATCH Not frightening in any respect.

DISCOVERY ISLAND

THE TREE OF LIFE/*IT'S TOUGH TO BE A BUG!* Very intense and loud, with special effects that startle viewers of all ages and potentially terrify little kids.

CAMP MINNIE-MICKEY

FESTIVAL OF THE LION KING A bit loud, but otherwise not frightening.

AFRICA

KILIMANJARO SAFARIS A "collapsing" bridge and the proximity of real animals make a few young children anxious.

PANGANI FOREST EXPLORATION TRAIL Not frightening in any respect.

WILDLIFE EXPRESS TRAIN Not frightening in any respect.

ASIA

EXPEDITION EVEREST Can frighten guests of all ages. Switching-off option provided (see page 245).

FLIGHTS OF WONDER Swooping birds alarm a few small children.

KALI RIVER RAPIDS Potentially frightening and certainly wet for guests of all ages. Switching-off option provided (see page 245).

MAHARAJAH JUNGLE TREK Some children may balk at the bat exhibit.

DINOLAND U.S.A.

THE BONEYARD Not frightening in any respect.

DINOSAUR High-tech thrill ride rattles riders of all ages. Switching-off option provided (see page 245).

PRIMEVAL WHIRL A beginner roller coaster. Most children age 7 and older will take it in stride. Switching-off option provided (see page 245).

THEATER IN THE WILD/FINDING NEMO—THE MUSICAL Not frightening in any respect, but loud.

TRICERATOP SPIN A midway-type ride that will frighten only a small percentage of younger children.

DISNEY'S HOLLYWOOD STUDIOS

HOLLYWOOD BOULEVARD

THE GREAT MOVIE RIDE Intense in parts, with very realistic special effects and some visually intimidating sights. Frightens many preschoolers.

SUNSET BOULEVARD

FANTASMIC! Terrifies some preschoolers.

ROCK 'N' ROLLER COASTER The wildest coaster at Walt Disney World. May frighten guests of any age. Switching-off option provided (see page 245).

THEATER OF THE STARS/BEAUTY AND THE BEAST—LIVE ON STAGE Not frightening in any respect.

THE TWILIGHT ZONE TOWER OF TERROR Visually intimidating to young children; contains intense and realistic special effects. The plummeting elevator at the ride's end frightens many adults as well as kids. Switching-off option provided (see page 245).

ECHO LAKE

THE AMERICAN IDOL EXPERIENCE At times, the singing may frighten anyone.

INDIANA JONES EPIC STUNT SPECTACULAR! An intense show with powerful special effects, including explosions, but young kids generally handle it well.

STAR TOURS—THE ADVENTURES CONTINUE Extremely intense visually for all ages; too intense for children under age 8. Switching-off option provided (see page 245).

STREETS OF AMERICA

HONEY, I SHRUNK THE KIDS MOVIE SET ADVENTURE Not scary (though oversized).

JIM HENSON'S MUPPET-VISION 3-D Intense and loud, but not frightening.

LIGHTS, MOTORS, ACTION! EXTREME STUNT SHOW Super stunt spectacular; intense with loud noises and explosions, but not threatening in any way.

STUDIO BACKLOT TOUR Sedate and not intimidating except for Catastrophe Canyon, where an earthquake and a flash flood are simulated. Prepare younger children for this part of the tour.

Small-Child Fright-Potential Chart (continued)

DISNEY'S HOLLYWOOD STUDIOS (continued)

PIXAR PLACE

TOY STORY MANIA! Dark ride may frighten some preschoolers.

MICKEY AVENUE

THE LEGEND OF CAPTAIN JACK SPARROW Skeletons, monsters, and shooting can frighten small children.

WALT DISNEY: ONE MAN'S DREAM Not frightening in any respect.

ANIMATION COURTYARD

DISNEY JUNIOR—LIVE ON STAGE! Not frightening in any respect.

THE MAGIC OF DISNEY ANIMATION Not frightening in any respect.

VOYAGE OF THE LITTLE MERMAID Some children are creeped out by Ursula.

Continued from page 189

and death, beauty and the grotesque, fellowship and enmity. As you sample the attractions at Walt Disney World, you transcend the spinning and bouncing of midway rides to thought-provoking and emotionally powerful entertainment. All of the endings are happy, but the adventures' impact, given Disney's gift for special effects, often intimidates and occasionally frightens young children.

There are rides with burning towns and ghouls popping out of their graves, all done with a sense of humor, provided you're old enough to understand the joke. And bones. There are bones everywhere: human bones, cattle bones, dinosaur bones, even whole skeletons. There's a stack of skulls at the headhunter's camp on the Jungle Cruise, a platoon of skeletons sailing ghost ships in Pirates of the Caribbean, and a haunting assemblage of skulls and skeletons in The Haunted Mansion. Skulls, skeletons, and bones punctuate Peter Pan's Flight and Big Thunder Mountain Railroad. In the Animal Kingdom, there's an entire children's playground made up exclusively of giant bones and skeletons.

Bob: Before lining up for any attraction, check out our description of it and see our Small-Child Fright-Potential Chart on pages 190–194.

Monsters and special effects at Disney's Hollywood Studios are more real and sinister than those in the other theme parks. If your child has difficulty coping with the ghouls of The Haunted Mansion, think twice about exposing him or her to machine-gun battles, earthquakes, and the creature from *Alien* at the Studios.

One reader tells of taking his preschool children on Star Tours:

We took a 4-year-old and a 5-year-old, and they had the *^%#! scared out of them at Star Tours. We did this first thing in the morning, and it took hours of Tom Sawyer Island and Small World to get back to normal.

Our kids were the youngest by far in Star Tours. I assume that other adults had more sense or were not such avid readers of your book. Preschoolers should start with Dumbo and work up to the Jungle Cruise in late morning, after being revved up and before getting hungry, thirsty, or tired. Pirates of the Caribbean is out for preschoolers. You get the idea.

At Walt Disney World, anticipate the almost inevitable emotional overload of your young children. Be sensitive, alert, and prepared for practically anything, even behavior that is out of character for your child at home. Most young children take Disney's macabre trappings in stride, and others are easily comforted by an arm around the shoulder or a squeeze of the hand. Parents who know that their children tend to become upset should take it slow and easy, sampling more benign adventures, gauging reactions, and discussing with the children how they felt about what they saw.

Liliane: You know I scream a lot on roller coasters, but did you know that I don't leave my feet on the floor during the *It's Tough to Be a Bug!* 3-D show at the Animal Kingdom? Well, now you know I do not like bugs, and they sting too; they do, they do.

Some Tips

1. START SLOW AND WARM UP Although each major theme park offers several fairly nonintimidating attractions that you can sample to determine your child's relative sensitivity, the Magic Kingdom is probably the best testing ground. At the Magic Kingdom, try Buzz Lightyear's Space Ranger Spin in Tomorrowland, Peter Pan's Flight in Fantasyland, and the Jungle Cruise in Adventureland to measure your child's reaction to unfamiliar sights and sounds. If your child takes these in stride, try Pirates of the Caribbean. Try the Astro Orbiter in Tomorrowland, the Mad Tea Party in Fantasyland, or The Barnstormer also in Fantasyland to observe how your child tolerates certain ride speeds and motions.

Do not assume that because an attraction is a theater presentation it will not frighten your child. Trust us on this one. An attraction does not have to be moving to trigger unmitigated, panic-induced hysteria. Rides such as the Big Thunder Mountain Railroad and Splash Mountain may look scary, but they do not have even one-fiftieth the potential for terrorizing children as do theater attractions such as *Stitch's Great Escape!*

2. BE ATTUNED TO PEER AND PARENT PRESSURE Sometimes young children will rise above their anxiety in an effort to please parents or siblings. This doesn't necessarily indicate a mastery of fear, much less enjoyment. If children leave a ride in apparently good shape, ask if they would like to go on it again (not necessarily now, but sometime). The response usually will indicate how much they actually enjoyed the experience. There's a big difference between having a good time and just mustering the courage to get through.

3. ENCOURAGE AND EMPATHIZE Evaluating a child's capacity to handle the visual and tactile effects of Walt Disney World requires

Liliane: While there is no certain way to know what will scare your kids or what will garner a big smile, many rides are so intense that they can even eat adults. I make a huge detour around The Twilight Zone Tower of Terror or Space Mountain, but I can't get enough of Star Tours, Mission: SPACE, and Kali River Rapids—and I have survived the Mad Tea Party and Expedition Everest. Parents know their children best. I do remember braving The Twilight Zone Tower of Terror once because I felt that I could not deprive my then-10-year-old just because I was a chicken. I didn't let on that this was not my cup of tea. My prayers to exit the attraction were answered when he asked me shyly if we could ask a cast member to get out. The request was granted instantly by both me and the cast member.

patience, understanding, and experimentation. Each of us, after all, has our own demons. If a child balks at or is frightened by a ride, respond constructively. Let your children know that lots of people, adults and children, are scared by what they see and feel. Help them understand that it's OK if they get frightened and that their fear doesn't lessen your love or respect. Take pains not to compound the discomfort by making a child feel inadequate; try not to undermine self-esteem, impugn courage, or ridicule. Most of all, don't induce guilt by suggesting the child's trepidation might be ruining the family's fun. It is also sometimes necessary to restrain older siblings' taunting or teasing.

A visit to Walt Disney World is more than just an outing or an adventure for a young child. It's a testing experience, a sort of controlled rite of passage. If you help your little one work through the challenges, the time can be immeasurably rewarding and a bonding experience for you both.

The Fright Factor

Of course, each youngster is different, but there are eight attraction elements that alone or combined can push a child's buttons:

1. NAME OF THE ATTRACTION Young children will naturally be apprehensive about something called The Haunted Mansion or The Twilight Zone Tower of Terror.

2. VISUAL IMPACT OF THE ATTRACTION FROM OUTSIDE Big Thunder Mountain Railroad and Splash Mountain look scary enough to give even adults second thoughts, and they visually terrify many young children.

3. VISUAL IMPACT OF THE INDOOR QUEUING AREA Pirates of the Caribbean's caves and dungeons and The Haunted Mansion's "stretch rooms" can frighten kids even before they board the ride.

4. INTENSITY OF THE ATTRACTION Some attractions are overwhelming, inundating the senses with sights, sounds, movement, and even smell. *It's Tough to Be a Bug!* in the Animal Kingdom, for example, combines loud sounds, lights, smoke, animatronic insects, and 3-D cinematography to create a total sensory experience. For some preschoolers, this is two or three senses too many.

5. VISUAL IMPACT OF THE ATTRACTION ITSELF Sights in various attractions range from falling boulders to lurking buzzards, from grazing dinosaurs to attacking white blood cells. What one child calmly absorbs may scare the bejeebers out of another.

6. DARK Many Disney World attractions operate indoors in the dark. For some children, darkness alone triggers fear. A child who is frightened on one dark ride (The Haunted Mansion, for example) may be unwilling to try other indoor rides.

7. THE RIDE ITSELF; THE TACTILE EXPERIENCE Some rides are wild enough to cause motion sickness, to wrench backs, and to discombobulate patrons of any age.

8. LOUD The sound levels in some attractions and live shows are so loud that younger children flip out even though the general content of the presentation is quite benign. For toddlers and preschoolers especially, it's good to have a pair of earplugs handy.

Liliane: My first roller coaster experience ever was with my son. We rode The Barnstormer. I screamed his ears off. Next I took a ride with you-know-who: Bob. He tricked me into riding The Incredible Hulk Coaster at Universal's Islands of Adventure. One cannot print what I said to him. (*Editor's note:* Bob is still deaf in one ear.)

Disney Orientation Course

We receive many tips from parents telling how they prepared their young children for the Disney experience. A common strategy is to acquaint children with the characters and stories behind the attractions by reading Disney books and watching Disney videos at home. A more direct approach is to watch videos that show the attractions. A Lexington, Kentucky, mom reports:

> My timid 7-year-old daughter and I watched rides and shows on You-Tube, and we cut out all the ones that looked too scary.

You can also order a free **Walt Disney World Vacation Planning DVD** by clicking on "Free Vacation Planning DVD" at the **disneyworld .com** home page or by calling ☎ 407-w-DISNEY (934-7639). As a YouTube supplement, it gives your kids an adequate sense of what they'll see. Allow at least one month for delivery. For more immediate gratification, you can also watch the **Travel Channel**'s Disney World specials on iTunes.

A MAGICAL TIME FOR MOM AND DAD

OK, LILIANE WRITING HERE. Because Bob's idea of a romantic evening is watching *Monday Night Football* on the sofa with his honey instead of sitting in his La-Z-Boy, I'm going to tackle this subject solo.

Let's face it: We all know that moms and dads deserve some special time. But the reality on the ground is that the kids come first. And when the day is over, mom and dad are way too tired to think about having a special evening alone. It's difficult enough to catch a movie or go out for a romantic dinner in our hometowns, so how realistic is a romantic parents' night out while on vacation at Walt Disney World?

The answer is: No planning, no romance! With a little magic and some advance preparation, you can make it happen. Here we offer a few suggestions.

Staying at a hotel that offers great kids' programs is a big plus. Consider signing up small children for a half-day program with lunch or dinner while you enjoy your resort. Go to the pool and read a book, and then have a meal in calm and peace. Rent a bike, a boat, or just take off outside the World. This is also a great opportunity to enjoy the thrill rides you passed up when you were busy worshipping at the altar of Dumbo.

PREPARING YOUR CHILDREN TO MEET THE CHARACTERS

ALMOST ALL DISNEY CHARACTERS ARE QUITE LARGE; several, like Baloo, are huge! Young children don't expect this and can be intimidated if not terrified. Discuss the characters with your children before you go. If there is a high school or college with a costumed mascot nearby, arrange to let your kids check it out. If not, then Santa Claus or the Easter Bunny will do.

On the first encounter at Walt Disney World, don't thrust your child at the character. Allow the little one to deal with this big thing from whatever distance feels safe to him or her. If two adults are present, one should stay near the youngster while the other approaches the character and demonstrates that it's safe and friendly. Some kids warm to the characters immediately; some never do. Most take a little time and several encounters.

Ian: Tell kids in advance that head-piece characters don't talk.

There are two kinds of characters: "furs," or those whose costumes include face-covering headpieces (including animal characters and such humanlike characters as Captain Hook), and "face characters," those for whom no mask or headpiece is necessary. These include Tiana, Mary Poppins, Ariel, Jasmine, Aladdin, Cinderella, Belle, Snow White, Merida, and Prince Charming, among others.

Only face characters speak. Headpiece characters don't make noises of any kind. Because cast members couldn't possibly imitate the distinctive cinema voice of the character, Disney has determined that it's more effective to keep them silent. Lack of speech notwithstanding, headpiece characters are very warm and responsive and communicate very effectively with gestures. Disney is currently testing new technology that will allow headpiece characters to speak. It is assumed that the technology is a portable version of that used in *Turtle Talk with Crush* at Epcot,

Liliane: If a character appears to be ignoring your child, ask the character's handler to get its attention.

where an animated turtle converses in real time with audience members. A less advanced option is a menu-driven selection of recorded phrases such as, "Hi, I'm Mickey," or "What's your name?"

Some character costumes are cumbersome and give cast members very poor visibility. (Eye holes frequently are in the mouth of the costume or even on the neck or chest.) This means characters are somewhat clumsy and have limited sight. Children who approach the character from the back or side may not be noticed, even if the child touches the character. It's possible in this situation for the character to accidentally step on the child or knock him or her down. It's best for a child to approach a character from the front, but occasionally not even this works. Duck characters (such as Donald, Daisy, and Uncle Scrooge), for example, have to peer around their bills.

It's OK for your child to touch, pat, or hug the character. Understanding the unpredictability of children, the character will keep his feet very still, particularly refraining from moving backward or sideways. Most characters will sign autographs or pose for pictures.

Another great way to show young kids how the characters appear in the parks is to rent or buy a *Disney SingAlong Songs* DVD (you can also find excerpts on YouTube). These programs show Disney characters interacting with real kids. At a minimum, the videos will give your kids a sense of how big the Disney characters are. The best two are *Flik's Musical Adventure SingAlong Songs at Disney's Animal Kingdom* and *Campout SingAlong Songs at Walt Disney World. It's a Small World SingAlong Songs— Disneyland Fun* is a third offering, but then there's THAT SONG. No sense turning your brain to mush before even leaving home.

Bob: If your child wants to collect character autographs, it's a good idea to carry a pen the width of a Magic Marker. Costumes make it exceedingly difficult for characters to wield a pen, so the bigger the writing instrument, the better. Unfortunately, a few characters, such as Buzz Lightyear, can't sign autographs at all.

ROLE-PLAYING

ESPECIALLY FOR YOUNGER CHILDREN, role-playing is a great way to inculcate vital lessons concerning safety, contingency situations,

and potential danger. Play "What would you do if?" for a variety of scenarios, including getting lost, being approached by strangers, getting help if Mommy is sick, and so on. Children have incredible recall when it comes to role-playing with siblings and parents, and are much more likely to respond appropriately in an actual situation than they will if the same information is presented in a lecture.

PHYSICAL PREPARATION

YOU'LL FIND THAT SOME PHYSICAL CONDITIONING, coupled with a realistic sense of the toll that Walt Disney World takes on your body, will preclude falling apart in the middle of your vacation. As one of our readers put it, "If you pay attention to eat, heat, feet, and sleep, you'll be OK."

As you contemplate the stamina of your family, it's important to understand that somebody is going to run out of steam first, and when they do, the whole family will be affected. Sometimes a cold drink or a snack will revive the flagging member. Sometimes, however, no amount of cajoling or treats will work. In this situation it's crucial that you recognize that the child, grandparent, or spouse is at the end of his or her rope. The correct decision is to get them back to the hotel. Pushing the exhausted beyond their capacity will spoil the day for them—and you.

Accept that stamina and energy levels vary and be prepared to administer to members of your family who poop out. One more thing: no guilt trips. "We've driven a thousand miles to take you to Disney World and now you're going to ruin everything!" is not an appropriate response.

THE AGONY OF THE FEET

HERE'S A LITTLE FACTOID TO CHEW ON: If you spend a day at Epcot and visit both sections of the park, you will walk 5–9 miles! The walking, however, will be nothing like a 5-mile hike in the woods. At Epcot (and the other Disney parks as well) you will be in direct sunlight most of the time, will have to navigate through huge jostling crowds, will be walking on hot pavement, and will have to endure waits in line between bursts of walking. The bottom line, if you haven't figured it out, is that Disney theme parks (especially in the summer) are not for wimps!

Bob: If your children (or you, for that matter) do not consider it cool to wear socks, get over it! Bare feet, whether encased in Nikes, Weejuns, Docksides, or Birkenstocks, will turn into lumps of throbbing red meat if you tackle a Disney park without socks.

Though most children are active, their normal play usually doesn't condition them for the exertion of touring a Disney theme park. We recommend starting a program of family walks six weeks or more before your trip. A Pennsylvania mom who did just that offers the following:

We had our 6-year-old begin walking with us a bit every day one month before leaving—when we arrived [at Walt Disney World], her little legs could carry her and she had a lot of stamina.

The first thing you need to do, immediately after making your hotel reservation, is to get thee to a "footery." Take the whole family to a shoe store and buy each member the best pair of walking, hiking, or running shoes you can afford. Wear exactly the kind of socks to try on the shoes that you will wear when using them. Do not under any circumstances attempt to tour Walt Disney World shod in sandals, flip-flops, loafers, or any kind of high heel or platform shoe.

Liliane: Be sure to give your kids adequate recovery time between training walks (48 hours will usually be enough), however, or you'll make the problem worse.

Good socks are as important as good shoes. When you walk, your feet sweat like a mule in a peat bog, and moisture increases friction. To minimize friction, wear a pair of SmartWool or Coolmax hiking socks, available at most outdoor retail (camping equipment) stores. To further combat moisture, dust your feet with some antifungal powder.

All right, now you've got some good shoes and socks. The next thing to do is to break the shoes in. You can accomplish this painlessly by wearing the shoes in the course of normal activities for about three weeks.

Once the shoes are broken in, it's time to start walking. The whole family will need to toughen up their feet and build endurance. As you begin, remember that little people have little strides, and though your

6-year-old may create the appearance of running circles around you, consider that (1) he won't have the stamina to go at that pace very long, and (2) more to the point, he probably has to take two strides or so to every one of yours to keep up when you walk together.

Start by taking short walks around the neighborhood, walking on pavement, and increasing the distance about a quarter of a mile on each outing. Older children will shape up quickly. Younger children should build endurance more slowly and incrementally. Increase distance until you can manage a 6- or 7-mile hike without requiring CPR. And remember, you're not training to be able to walk 6 or 7 miles just once; at Walt Disney World you will be hiking 5–9 miles or more almost *every day*. So unless you plan to crash after the first day, you've got to prepare your feet to walk long distances for three to five consecutive days.

Let's be honest and admit up front that not all feet are created equal. Some folks are blessed with really tough feet, whereas the feet of others sprout blisters if you look at them sideways. Assuming that there's nothing wrong with either shoes or socks, a few brisk walks will clue you in to what kind of feet your family have. If you have a tenderfoot in your family, walks of incrementally increased distances will usually toughen up his or her feet to some extent. For those whose feet refuse to toughen, your only alternative is preventive care. After several walks, you will know where your tenderfoot tends to develop blisters. If you can anticipate where blisters will develop, you can cover sensitive spots in advance with moleskin (a friction-resistant adhesive dressing) or a blister bandage.

Bob: If your child is age 8 or younger, we recommend regular foot inspections whether he or she understands the hot-spot idea or not. Even the brightest and most well-intentioned child will fail to sound off when distracted.

When you initiate your walking program, teach your children to tell you if they feel a hot spot on their feet. This is the warning that a blister is developing. If your kids are too young, too oblivious, too preoccupied, or don't understand the concept, your best bet is to make regular foot checks. Have your children remove their shoes and socks and present their feet for inspection. Look for red spots and blisters, and ask if they have any places on their feet that hurt.

Liliane: If you have a child who will physically fit in a stroller, rent one, no matter how well conditioned your family is.

During your conditioning, and also at Walt Disney World, carry a foot emergency kit in your day pack or hip pack. The kit should contain gauze, Betadine antibiotic ointment, an assortment of Band-Aid Advanced Healing Blister Bandages, a sewing needle or some such to drain blisters, as well as matches or a lighter to sterilize the needle. An extra pair of dry socks and foot powder are optional.

If you discover a hot spot, dry the foot and cover the spot immediately with a blister bandage. If you find that a blister has fully or partially developed, first air out and dry the foot. Next, using your sterile needle, drain the fluid, but do not remove the top skin. Clean the area with antiseptic cleaner and place a blister bandage over the blister. If you do not have blister bandages, do not try to cover the hot spot or blister with regular Band-Aid bandages. Regular ones slip and wad up.

A stroller will provide the child the option of walking or riding, and, if he collapses, you won't have to carry him. Even if your child hardly uses the stroller at all, it serves as a convenient rolling depository for water bottles and other stuff you may not feel like carrying. Strollers at Walt Disney World are covered in detail on pages 258–260.

SLEEP, REST, AND RELAXATION

OK, WE KNOW THAT THIS SECTION is about physical preparation *before you go,* but this concept is so absolutely critical that we need to tattoo it on your brain right now.

Physical conditioning is important but is *not* a substitute for adequate rest. Even marathon runners need recovery time. If you push too hard and try to do too much, you'll either crash or, at a minimum, turn what should be fun into an ordeal. Rest means plenty of sleep at night, naps during the afternoon on most days, and planned breaks in your vacation itinerary. And don't forget that the brain needs rest and relaxation as well as the body. The stimulation inherent in touring a Disney theme park is enough to put many children and some adults into system overload. It is imperative that you remove your family from this unremitting assault on the senses, preferably for part of each day, and do something relaxing and quiet like swimming or reading.

The theme parks are huge; don't try to see everything in 1 day. Tour in early morning and return to your hotel around 11:30 a.m. for lunch, a swim, and a nap. Even during off-season, when the crowds are smaller and the temperature more pleasant, the size of the major theme parks will exhaust most children under age 8 by lunchtime. Return to the park in late afternoon or early evening and continue touring. A family from Texas underlines the importance of naps and rest:

Despite not following any of your "tours," we did follow the theme of visiting a specific park in the morning, leaving midafternoon for either a nap back at the room or a trip to the pool, and then returning to one of the parks in the evening. On the few occasions when we skipped your advice, I was muttering to myself by dinner. I can't tell you what I was muttering . . .

When it comes to naps, this mom does not mince words:

One last thing for parents of small kids—take the book's advice and get out of the park and take the nap, take the nap, TAKE THE NAP! Never in my life have I seen so many parents screaming at, ridiculing, or slapping their kids. (What a vacation!) Walt Disney World is overwhelming for kids and adults. Even though the rental strollers recline for sleeping, we noticed that most of the toddlers and preschoolers didn't give up and sleep until 5 p.m., several hours after the fun had worn off, and right about the time their parents wanted them to be awake and polite in a restaurant.

A mom from Rochester, New York, was equally adamant:

You absolutely must rest during the day. Kids went 8 a.m.–9 p.m. in the Magic Kingdom. Kids did great that day, but we were all completely worthless the next day. Definitely must pace yourself. Don't ever try to do two full days of park sightseeing in a row. Rest during the day. Go to a water park or sleep in every other day.

If you plan to return to your hotel in midday and would like your room made up, let housekeeping know.

DEVELOPING *a* GOOD PLAN

ALLOW YOUR CHILDREN TO PARTICIPATE in the planning of your time at Walt Disney World. Guide them diplomatically through the options, establishing advance decisions about what to do each day and how the day will be structured. Begin with your trip *to* Walt Disney World, deciding what time to depart, who sits by the window, whether to stop for meals or eat in the car, and so on. For the Walt Disney World part of your vacation, build consensus for wake-up call, bedtime, and building naps into the itinerary, and establish ground rules for eating, buying refreshments, and shopping. Determine the order for visiting the different theme parks and make a list of must-see attractions. To help you with filling in the blanks of your days, and especially to prevent you from spending most of your time standing in line, we offer a number of field-tested touring plans. The plans are designed to minimize your waiting time at each park by providing step-by-step itineraries that route you counter to the flow of traffic. The plans are explained in detail on pages 228–234.

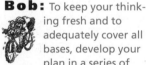

Bob: To keep your thinking fresh and to adequately cover all bases, develop your plan in a series of family meetings no longer than 30 minutes each. You'll discover that all members of the family will devote a lot of thought to the plan both in and between meetings. Don't try to anticipate every conceivable contingency, or you'll end up with something as detailed and unworkable as the tax code.

Generally it's better to just sketch in the broad strokes on the master plan. The detail of what to do when you actually arrive at the park can be decided the night before you go or with the help of one of our touring plans once you get there. Above all, be flexible. One important caveat, however: Make sure you keep any promises or agreements that you make when planning. They may not seem important to you, but they will to your children, who will remember for a long, long time that you let them down.

The more that you can agree to and nail down in advance, the less potential you'll have for disagreement and confrontation once you arrive. Because children are more comfortable with the tangible than the conceptual, and also because they sometimes have short memories, we recommend typing up all of your decisions and agreements and providing a copy to each child. Create a fun document, not a legalistic one. You'll find that your children will review it in anticipation of all the things they will see and do, will consult it often, and will even read it to their younger siblings.

By now you're probably wondering what one of these documents looks like, so here's a sample. Incidentally, this itinerary reflects the preferences of its creators, the Langston family, and is not meant to be offered as an example of an ideal itinerary. It does, however, incorporate many of our most basic and strongly held recommendations, such as setting limits and guidelines in advance, getting enough rest, getting to the theme parks early, touring the theme parks in shorter visits with naps and swimming in between, and saving time and money by having a cooler full of food for breakfast. As you will see, the Langstons go pretty much full-tilt without much unstructured time and will probably be exhausted by the time they get home, but that's their choice. One more thing—the Langstons visited Walt Disney World in late June, when all of the theme parks stay open late.

THE GREAT WALT DISNEY WORLD EXPEDITION

COCAPTAINS Mary and Jack Langston

TEAM MEMBERS Lynn and Jimmy Langston

EXPEDITION FUNDING The main Expedition Fund will cover everything except personal purchases. Each team member will receive $40 for souvenirs and personal purchases. Anything above $40 will be paid for by team members with their own money.

EXPEDITION GEAR Each team member will wear an official expedition T-shirt and carry a hip pack.

PREDEPARTURE Jack makes priority seating arrangements at Walt Disney World restaurants. Mary, Lynn, and Jimmy make up trail mix and other snacks for the hip packs.

Notice that the Langstons' itinerary on pages 206–207 provides minimal structure and maximum flexibility. It specifies which park the family will tour each day without attempting to nail down exactly what the family will do there. No matter how detailed your itinerary is, be prepared for surprises at Walt Disney World, both good and bad. If an unforeseen event renders part of the plan useless or impractical, just roll with it. And always remember that it's your itinerary; you created it, and you can change it. Just try to make any changes the result of family discussion, and be especially careful not to scrap an element of the plan that your children perceive as something you promised them.

Routines That Travel

If when at home you observe certain routines—for example, reading a book before bed or having a bath first thing in the morning—try to

Continued on page 208

Langston Family Itinerary

DAY 1: FRIDAY

6:30 p.m.	Dinner
After dinner	Pack car
10 p.m.	Lights out

DAY 2: SATURDAY

7 a.m.	Wake up!
7:15 a.m.	Breakfast
8 a.m.	Depart Chicago for Hampton Inn, Chattanooga; Confirmation # DE56432; Lynn rides shotgun
About noon	Stop for lunch; Jimmy picks restaurant
7 p.m.	Dinner
9:30 p.m.	Lights out

DAY 3: SUNDAY

7 a.m.	Wake up!
7:30 a.m.	Depart Chattanooga for Walt Disney World, Port Orleans Resort–Riverside; confirmation # L124532; Jimmy rides shotgun
About noon	Stop for lunch; Lynn picks restaurant
5 p.m.	Check in, buy park admissions, and unpack
6–7 p.m.	Mary and Jimmy shop for breakfast food for cooler
7:15 p.m.	Dinner at Boatwright's at Port Orleans Riverside
After dinner	Walk along Bonnet Creek
10 p.m.	Lights out

DAY 4: MONDAY

7 a.m.	Wake up! Cold breakfast from cooler in room
8 a.m.	Depart room to catch bus for Epcot
Noon	Lunch at Epcot
1 p.m.	Return to hotel for swimming and a nap
5 p.m.	Return to Epcot for touring, dinner, and *IllumiNations*
9:30 p.m.	Return to hotel
10:30 p.m.	Lights out

DAY 5: TUESDAY

7 a.m.	Wake up! Cold breakfast from cooler in room
7:45 a.m.	Depart room to catch bus for Disney's Hollywood Studios
Noon	Lunch at Studios
2:30 p.m.	Return to hotel for swimming and a nap
6 p.m.	Drive to dinner at cafe at Wilderness Lodge
7:30 p.m.	Return to Studios via car for touring and *Fantasmic!*
10 p.m.	Return to hotel
11 p.m.	Lights out

DAY 6: WEDNESDAY	
ZZZZZZ!	Lazy morning—sleep in!
10:30 a.m.	Late-morning swim
Noon	Lunch at Riverside Mill Food Court at Port Orleans
1 p.m.	Depart room to catch bus for Animal Kingdom; tour until park closes
8 p.m.	Dinner at Rainforest Cafe at Animal Kingdom
9:15 p.m.	Return to hotel via bus
10:30 p.m.	Lights out
DAY 7: THURSDAY	
6 a.m.	Wake up! Cold breakfast from cooler in room
6:45 a.m.	Depart via bus for early entry at Magic Kingdom
11:30 a.m.	Return to hotel for lunch, swimming, and a nap
4:45 p.m.	Drive to Contemporary for dinner at Chef Mickey's
6:15 p.m.	Walk from the Contemporary to the Magic Kingdom for more touring, fireworks, and parade
11 p.m.	Return to Contemporary via walkway or monorail; get car and return to hotel
11:45 p.m.	Lights out
DAY 8: FRIDAY	
8 a.m.	Wake up! Cold breakfast from cooler in room
8:40 a.m.	Drive to Blizzard Beach water park
Noon	Lunch at Blizzard Beach
1:30 p.m.	Return to hotel for nap and packing
4 p.m.	Revisit favorite park or do whatever we want
Dinner	When and where we decide
10 p.m.	Return to hotel
10:30 p.m.	Lights out
DAY 9: SATURDAY	
7:30 a.m.	Wake up!
8:30 a.m.	After fast-food breakfast, depart for Executive Inn, Nashville; confirmation # SD234; Lynn rides shotgun
About noon	Stop for lunch; Jimmy picks restaurant
7 p.m.	Dinner
10 p.m.	Lights out
DAY 10: SUNDAY	
7 a.m.	Wake up!
7:45 a.m.	Depart for home after fast-food breakfast; Jimmy rides shotgun
About noon	Stop for lunch; Lynn picks restaurant
4:30 p.m.	Home sweet home!

Continued from page 205

incorporate these familiar activities into your vacation schedule. They will provide your children with a sense of security and normalcy.

Maintaining a normal routine is especially important with toddlers, as a mother of two from Lawrenceville, Georgia, relates:

> *The first day, we tried an early start, so we woke the children (ages 2 and 4) and hurried them to get going. BAD IDEA with toddlers. This put them off schedule for naps and meals the rest of the day. It is best to let young ones stay on their regular schedule and see Disney at their own pace, and you'll have much more fun.*

We offer a Sleepyhead Touring Plan for each park, perfect for families like this reader's.

LOGISTIC PREPARATION

WHEN WE RECENTLY LAUNCHED into our spiel about good logistic preparation for a Walt Disney World vacation, a friend from Indianapolis said, "Wait, what's the big deal? You pack clothes, a few games for the car, then go!" So OK, we confess, that will work, but life can be sweeter and the vacation smoother (as well as less expensive) with the right gear.

CLOTHING

LET'S START WITH CLOTHES. We recommend springing for vacation uniforms. Buy for each child several sets of jeans (or shorts) and T-shirts, all matching, and all the same. For a one-week trip, as an example, get each child three or so pairs of khaki shorts, three or so light yellow T-shirts, three pairs of SmartWool or Coolmax hiking socks.

Liliane: Give your teens the job of coming up with the logo for your shirts. They will love being the family designers.

What's the point? First, you don't have to play fashion designer, coordinating a week's worth of stylish combos. Each morning the kids put on their uniform. It's simple, it's time-saving, and there are no decisions to make or arguments about what to wear. Second, uniforms make your children easier to spot and keep together in the theme parks. Third, the uniforms give your family, as well as the vacation itself, some added identity. You might even go so far as to create a logo for the trip to be printed on the shirts.

When it comes to buying your uniforms, we have a few suggestions. Purchase well-made, durable shorts or jeans that will serve your children well beyond the vacation. Buy short-sleeve T-shirts in light colors for warm weather or long-sleeve, darker-colored T-shirts for cooler weather. We suggest that you purchase your colored shirts from a local screen-printing company. You can select from a wide choice of colors not generally available in retail clothing stores and will not have to worry about finding the sizes you need. Plus, the shirts will cost a fraction of what a clothing retailer would charge. All-cotton shirts are a little cooler and more comfortable in hot, humid weather; polyester-cotton blends dry a bit faster if they get wet.

LABELS A great idea, especially for younger children, is to attach labels with your family name, hometown, the name of your hotel, the dates of your stay, and your mobile number inside the shirt. For example:

Carlton Family of Frankfort, KY; Port Orleans Riverside
May 5–12; 502-555-2108

Instruct your smaller children to show the label to an adult if they get separated from you. Elimination of the child's first name (which most children of talking age can articulate in any event) allows you to order labels that are all the same, that can be used by anyone in the family, and that can also be affixed to such easily lost items as caps, hats, jackets, hip packs, ponchos, and umbrellas. If fooling with labels sounds like too much of a hassle, check out "When Kids Get Lost" (pages 260–263) for some alternatives.

TEMPORARY TATTOOS An easier and trendier option is a temporary tattoo with your child's name and your phone number. Unlike labels, ID bracelets, or wristbands, the tattoos cannot fall off or be lost. Temporary tattoos last about two weeks, won't wash or sweat off, and are not irritating to the skin. They can be purchased online from **SafetyTat** at **safetytat.com,** or from **Tattoos With A Purpose** at **tattooswithapurpose .com.** Special tattoos are available for children with food allergies or cognitive impairment such as autism.

DRESSING FOR COOLER WEATHER Central Florida experiences temperatures all over the scale from November through March, so it could be a bit chilly if you visit during those months. Our suggestion is to layer: For example, a breathable, waterproof or water-resistant windbreaker over a light, long-sleeved polypropylene shirt over a long-sleeved T-shirt. As with the baffles of a sleeping bag or down coat, it is the air trapped between the layers that keeps you warm. If all the layers are thin, you won't be left with something bulky to cart around if you want to pull one or more off. Later in this section, we'll advocate wearing a hip pack. Each layer should be sufficiently compactible to fit easily in that hip pack, along with whatever else is in it.

ACCESSORIES

I (BOB) WANTED TO CALL THIS PART "Belts and Stuff," but Liliane (who obviously spends a lot of time at Macy's) thought "Accessories" put a finer point on it. In any event, we recommend pants for your children with reinforced elastic waistbands that eliminate the need to wear a belt (one less thing to find when you're trying to leave). If your children like belts or want to carry an item suspended from their belts, buy them military-style 1-inch-wide web belts at any Army/Navy surplus or camping-equipment store. The belts weigh less than half as much as leather, are cooler, and are washable.

SUNGLASSES The Florida sun is so bright and the glare so blinding that we recommend sunglasses for each family member. For children and adults of all ages, a good accessory item is a polypropylene eyeglass strap for spectacles or sunglasses. The best models have a little device for adjusting the amount of slack in the strap. This allows your child to comfortably hang sunglasses from his or her neck when indoors or, alternately, to secure them fast to his or her head while experiencing a fast ride outdoors.

HIP PACKS AND WALLETS Unless you are touring with an infant or toddler, the largest thing anyone in your family should carry is a hip pack, or fanny pack. Each adult and child should have one. They should be large enough to carry at least a half-day's worth of snacks, as well as other items deemed necessary (lip balm, bandanna, antibacterial hand gel, and so on), and still have enough room left to stash a hat, poncho, or light windbreaker. We recommend buying full-size hip packs as opposed to small, child-size hip packs at outdoor retailers. The packs are light; can be made to fit any child large enough to tote a hip pack; have slip-resistant, comfortable, wide belting; and will last for years.

Bob: Unless you advise the front desk to the contrary, all Disney resort room keys can be used for park admission and as credit cards. They are definitely something you don't want to lose. Our advice is to void the charge privileges on your preteen children's cards, and then collect them and put them together someplace safe when not in use.

Do not carry billfolds or wallets, car keys, park tickets, or room keys in your hip packs. We usually give this advice because hip packs are vulnerable to thieves (who snip them off and run), but pickpocketing and theft are not all that common at Walt Disney World. In this instance, the advice stems from a tendency of children to inadvertently drop their wallet in the process of rummaging around in their hip packs for snacks and other items.

Liliane: Equip each child with a big bandanna. Although bandannas come in handy for wiping noses, scouring ice cream from chins and mouths, and dabbing sweat from the forehead, they can also be tied around the neck to protect from sunburn.

You should weed through your billfold and remove to a safe place anything that you will not need on your vacation (family photos, local library card, department store credit cards, business cards, and so on). In addition to having a lighter wallet to lug around, you will decrease your exposure in the event that your wallet is lost or stolen. When we're working at Walt Disney World, we carry a small profile billfold with a driver's license, a credit card, our Disney resort room key, and a small amount of cash. Think about it: You don't need anything else.

DAY PACKS We see a lot of folks at Walt Disney World carrying day packs (that is, small, frameless backpacks) and/or water bottle belts that strap around the waist. Day packs might be a good choice if you plan to carry a lot of camera equipment or if you need to carry baby supplies on your person. Otherwise, try to travel as light as possible. Packs are hot, cumbersome, not very secure, and must be removed every time you get on a ride or sit down for a show. Hip packs, by way of contrast, can simply be rotated around the waist from your back to your abdomen if you need to sit down. Additionally, our observation has been that the contents of one day pack can usually be redistributed to two or so hip packs.

CAPS Caps protect young eyes from damaging ultraviolet rays, but the lifespan of a child's hat is usually pretty short. Simply put, kids pull caps on and off as they enter and exit attractions, restrooms, and restaurants, and . . . big surprise, they lose them. In fact, they lose them by the thousands. You could provide a ball cap for every Little Leaguer in America from the caps that are lost at Walt Disney World each summer.

If your children are partial to caps, there is a device sold at ski and camping supply stores that might increase the likelihood of the cap returning home with the child. Essentially, it's a short, light cord with little alligator clips on both ends. Hook one clip to the shirt collar and the other to the hat. It's a great little invention. Bob uses one when he skis in case his ball cap blows off.

RAINGEAR Rain in central Florida is a fact of life, although persistent rain day after day is unusual (it is the Sunshine State, after all!). Our suggestion is to check out The Weather Channel or weather forecasts on the Internet for three or so days before you leave home to see if there are any major storm systems heading for central Florida. Weather forecasting has improved to the extent that predictions concerning systems and fronts four to seven days out are now pretty reliable. If it appears that you might see some rough weather during your visit, you're better off bringing raingear from home. If, however, nothing big is on the horizon weather-wise, you can take your chances.

We at the *Unofficial Guide* usually do not bring raingear. Scattered thundershowers are more the norm than are prolonged

Liliane: If your kids are little and don't mind a hairdo change, consider getting them a short haircut before you leave home. Not only will they be cooler and more comfortable, but—especially with your girls—you'll save them (and yourselves) the hassle of tangles and about 20 minutes of foo-fooing a day. Don't try this with your confident teen or preteen, though. Braids will do the trick for girls, and your Mick Jagger in the party will be grateful for the bandanna or sports headband, unless of course the hair is meant to keep the monsters and dinosaurs out of sight!

periods of rain. At Walt Disney World, the ponchos that are available in seemingly every retail shop sell for about $10. If you insist on bringing raingear, however, any dollar store has them for exactly that: $1! In the theme parks, a surprising number of attractions and queuing areas are under cover, so we prefer to travel light.

If you do find yourself in a big storm, however, you'll want to have both a poncho and an umbrella. As one *Unofficial* reader put it:

> *Umbrellas make the rain much more bearable. When rain isn't beating down on your ponchoed head, it's easier to ignore.*

Another advantage of buying ponchos before you leave home is that you can choose the color. At Walt Disney World all the ponchos are clear, and it's quite a sight when 30,000 differently clad individuals suddenly transform themselves into what looks like an army of really big larvae. If your family is wearing blue ponchos, they'll be easier to spot.

And consider this tip from a Memphis, Tennessee, mom:

> *Scotchgard your shoes. The difference is unbelievable.*

MISCELLANEOUS ITEMS

MEDICATION Some parents of hyperactive children on medication discontinue or decrease the child's normal dosage at the end of the school year. If you have such a child, be aware that Walt Disney World might overly stimulate him or her. Consult your physician before altering your child's medication regimen. Also, if your child has attention deficit disorder, remember that especially loud sounds can drive him or her right up the wall. Unfortunately, some Disney theater attractions are almost unbearably loud.

SUNSCREEN Overheating and sunburn are among the most common problems of younger children at Walt Disney World. Carry and use full-spectrum sunscreen of SPF 30 or higher. Be sure to put some on children in strollers, even if the stroller has a canopy. Some of the worst cases of sunburn we've seen were on the exposed foreheads and feet of toddlers and infants in strollers. To avoid overheating, rest regularly in the shade or in an air-conditioned restaurant or show.

Liliane: Often little ones fall asleep in their strollers (hallelujah!). Bring a large lightweight cloth to drape over the stroller to cover your child from the sun. A few clothespins will keep it in place.

WATER BOTTLES Don't count on keeping young children hydrated with soft drinks and stops at water fountains. Long lines may hamper buying refreshments, and fountains may not be handy. Furthermore, excited children may not realize or tell you that they're thirsty or hot. We recommend renting a stroller for children age 6 and younger and carrying plastic bottles of water. Plastic squeeze bottles with caps run about $3 in all major parks. You can save oodles of money by buying your own water outside the parks (Disney allows you to bring water to the parks). If you are staying in a rental home, freeze the water and use it to keep sandwiches cool. By the time you are thirsty, the water should be just right to quench your thirst.

Respect for the Sun

Health and science writer **Avery Hurt** sheds some light on the often confusing products and methods for avoiding sunburn. Here's the basic advice from the medical experts.

CHOOSE A SUNSCREEN THAT IS CONVENIENT FOR YOU TO USE. Some prefer sprays, others lotions. The form of sunscreen doesn't matter as much as the technique of applying it.

Apply sunscreen a half hour before going out, and be sure to get enough on you. One ounce per application is recommended—that means a full shot glass worth each time you apply. The 1-ounce amount was calculated for average adults in swimsuits; an average 7-year-old will probably take two-thirds of an ounce (20 cc). It's a good idea to measure that ounce in your hands at home so you will be familiar with what an ounce looks in your palms. It really is far more sunscreen than you tend to think.

Be sure and get a generous covering on all exposed skin. Then reapply (another full shot glass) every two hours or after swimming or sweating. No matter what it says on the label, no sunscreen is waterproof, and water resistance is limited. And none of them last all day.

There is very little difference in protection between 30 or so SPF and 45 or 50 or greater. There is no need to spend more for higher SPF numbers. In fact, it is much safer to choose a lower (and typically less expensive) SPF (as long as it is at least 30) and apply it more often. However, do be sure to choose a product that has broad-spectrum coverage, meaning that it filters out both UVA and UVB rays. As long as the SPF is at least 30 and offers broad-spectrum protection, one brand can serve the whole family. There's no need to pay extra for special formulas made for children.

It is best to keep babies under 6 months old covered and out of the sun. However, the American Academy of Pediatrics condones a small amount of sunscreen on vulnerable areas, such as the nose and chin, when you have your baby out. Be very careful to monitor your baby even if he is wearing a hat and sitting under an umbrella.

Use a lip balm with an SPF of 15 and reapply often to your own lips and those of your kids. Again, the brand is less important than choosing something that you will use—and remembering to use it.

Sunglasses are also a must. Too much sun exposure can contribute to age-related macular degeneration (among other things). Not all sunglasses filter out damaging rays. Be sure to choose shades (for adults and kids) that have 99% UV protection. Large lenses and wraparound styles might not look as cool, but they offer much better protection. You may have to spend a little more to be sure you are getting adequate protection, but you don't want to skimp on this.

If you do slip up and get a burn, cool baths, aloe gels, and ibuprofen (or for adults, aspirin) usually help ease the suffering. Occasionally sunburns can be as dangerous in the short term as they are in the long term. If you or your child experience nausea, vomiting, high fever, severe pain, confusion, or fainting, seek medical care immediately.

COOLERS AND MINI-FRIDGES If you drive to Walt Disney World, bring two coolers: a small one for drinks in the car and a large one for the hotel room. If you fly and rent a car, stop and purchase a large Styrofoam cooler, which can be discarded at the end of the trip. Refrigerators in all Disney resort rooms are free of charge. If you arrive at your room and there is no refrigerator, call housekeeping and request one. Along with free fridges, coffeemakers have also been added in the rooms.

Coolers and mini-fridges allow you to have breakfast in your hotel room, store snacks and lunch supplies to take to the theme parks, and supplant expensive vending machines for snacks and beverages at the hotel. To keep the contents of your cooler cold, we suggest freezing a 2-gallon milk jug full of water before you head out. In a good cooler, it will take the jug five or more days to thaw. If you buy a Styrofoam cooler in Florida, you can use bagged ice and ice from the ice machine at your hotel. Even if you have to rent a mini-fridge, you will save a bundle of cash, as well as significant time, by reducing dependence on restaurant meals and expensive snacks and drinks purchased from vendors.

FOOD-PREP KIT If you plan to make sandwiches, bring along your favorite condiments and seasonings from home. A good travel kit will

Liliane: About two weeks before I arrive at WDW, I always ship a box to my hotel containing food, plastic cutlery, and toiletries, plus pretty much any other consumables that might come in handy during my stay. If you fly, this helps avoid baggage fees and problems with liquid restrictions for carry-on luggage.

include mayonnaise, ketchup, mustard, salt and pepper, and packets of sugar or artificial sweetener. Also bring some plastic knives and spoons, paper napkins, plastic cups, and a box of ziptop plastic bags. For breakfast you will need some plastic bowls for cereal. Of course, you can buy this stuff in Florida, but you probably won't consume it all, so why waste the money? If you drink bottled beer or wine, bring a bottle opener and corkscrew.

ENERGY BOOSTERS Kids get cranky when they're hungry, and when that happens, your entire group has a problem. Like many parents you might, for nutritional reasons, keep a tight rein on snacks available to your children at home. At Walt Disney World, however, maintaining energy and equanimity trumps between-meal snack discipline. For maximum zip and contentedness, give your kids snacks containing complex carbohydrates (fruits, crackers, nonfat energy bars, and the like) *before* they get hungry or show signs of exhaustion. You should avoid snacks that are high in fats and proteins because these foods take a long time to digest and will tend to unsettle your stomach if it's a hot day.

Bob enthusiastically recommends **Clif Shot Bloks,** chewable cubes that replaces electrolytes in the body. They're light, come in several different flavors (all tasty), and don't melt even on the hottest days. Bob uses them when needed on mountain bike rides. They really work wonders.

ELECTRONICS Regardless of your children's ages, always bring a nightlight. Flashlights are also handy for finding stuff in a dark hotel room after the kids are asleep. If you are big coffee drinkers and if you drive, bring along a coffeemaker if it's not included in your room.

Smartphones, tablets, digital music players with headphones, and electronic games are often controversial gear for a family outing. We recommend compromise. Headphones allow kids to create their own space even when they're with others, and that can be a safety valve. That said, try to agree before the trip on some headphone parameters, so you don't begin to feel as if they're being used to keep other family members and the trip itself at a distance.

POWERING UP Speaking of smart devices, their use has become standard in the parks. In addition to taking photos, guests also use apps to check on waiting lines and score seats at restaurants. All that technology comes at a price: dead batteries. You spend all day using your phone to e-mail photos to Great-Aunt Fern, but at the end of the day, you can't find the missing members of your party because you don't have enough power to place a call or even send a text. Having experienced the problem firsthand, Liliane has a few suggestions:

First, bring an extra charged battery, and always, *always* bring the charging cable.

You can drop off your phone to be charged at any Guest Relations desk in any park. While they've usually got cords and plugs for most phones, it helps to bring yours along. You'll be issued a claim check to pick up your phone, which will be done charging in an hour or two.

Six charging stations are also available at the new **D-Zone,** near the *Tangled*-themed bathrooms in New Fantasyland in the Magic Kingdom. They're built into the faux-wood posts near the seating area.

You can also recharge at the Baby Care Centers in the parks and at restrooms. Charging policies at restaurants vary—our experience has been that the upscale places will fuss about a request, while the counter-service places don't mind.

Here are a few good choices during lunch- or dinnertime: In the Magic Kingdom, several tables at the **Columbia Harbour House** (especially upstairs) are near electrical outlets. At **Pecos Bill Tall Tale Inn and Cafe,** a table opposite the condiments station is next to a power outlet. At Disney's Hollywood Studios, don't count on the sit-down restaurants; rather, head for the **Backlot Express,** which has lots of tables nestled next to power outlets. At Epcot, you'll find outlets at **Sunshine Seasons** and **Electric Umbrella,** as well as in the single-rider line at **Soarin',** which is good for a quick 5- or 10-minute charge. At Animal Kingdom, try outlets at **Pizzafari** or **Tusker House.**

For a rundown of additional charging locations in the parks, charging etiquette, and tips for extending your device's battery life, go to **blog.touringplans.com** and type "phone charging" in the search box.

DON'T FORGET THE TENT *Bob here:* This is not a joke, and it has nothing to do with camping. When my daughter was preschool-age, I about went crazy trying to get her to sleep in a shared hotel room. She was accustomed to having her own room at home and was hyperstimulated

whenever she traveled. I tried makeshift curtains and room dividers and even rearranged the furniture in a few hotel rooms to create the illusion of a more private, separate space for her. It was all for naught. It wasn't until she was around 4 years old and I took her camping that I seized on an idea that had some promise. She liked the cozy, secure, womblike feel of a backpacking tent and quieted down much more readily than she ever had in hotel rooms. So the next time the family stayed in a hotel, he pitched his backpacking tent in the corner of the room. In she went, nested for a bit, and fell asleep.

Since the time of my daughter's childhood, there has been an astounding evolution in tent design. Responding to the needs of climbers and paddlers who often have to pitch tents on rocks (where it's impossible to drive stakes), tent manufacturers developed a broad range of tents with self-supporting frames that can be erected virtually anywhere without ropes or stakes. Affordable and sturdy, many are as simple to put up as opening an umbrella. So, if your child is too young for a room of his or her own, or you can't afford a second hotel room, try pitching a small tent. Modern tents are self-contained, with floors and an entrance that can be zipped up (or not) for privacy but cannot be locked. Kids appreciate having their own space and enjoy the adventure of being in a tent, even one set up in the corner of a hotel room. Sizes range from children's play tents with a 2- to 3-foot base to models large enough to sleep two or three husky teens. Light and compact when stored, a two-adult-size tent in its own storage bag (called a stuff sack) will take up about one-tenth or less of a standard overhead bin on a commercial airliner. Another option for infants and toddlers is to drape a sheet over a portable crib or playpen to make a tent.

"THE BOX" *Bob again:* On one memorable Walt Disney World excursion when my children were young, we started each morning with an immensely annoying, involuntary scavenger hunt. Invariably, seconds before our scheduled departure to the theme park, we discovered that some combination of shoes, billfolds, sunglasses, hip packs, or other necessities were unaccountably missing. For the next 15 minutes we would root through the room like pigs hunting truffles in an attempt to locate the absent items. Now I don't know about your kids, but when my kids lost a shoe or something, they always searched where it was easiest to look, as opposed to where the lost article was most likely to be. I would be jammed under a bed feeling around, while my children stood in the middle of the room intently inspecting the ceiling. As my friends will tell you, I'm as open to a novel theory as the next guy, but we never did find any shoes on the ceiling. Not once. Anyway, here's what I finally did: I swung by a liquor store and mooched a big empty box. From then on, every time we returned to the room, I had the kids deposit shoes, hip packs, and other potentially wayward items in the box. After that the box was off-limits until the next morning, when I doled out the contents.

PLASTIC GARBAGE BAGS   On two attractions, the **Kali River Rapids** raft ride in Animal Kingdom and **Splash Mountain** in the Magic Kingdom, you are certain to get wet and possibly soaked. If it's really hot and you don't care, then fine. But if it's cool or you're just not up for a soaking, bring a large plastic trash bag to the park. By cutting holes in the top and on the sides, you can fashion a sack poncho that will keep your clothes from getting wet. On the raft ride, you will also get your feet wet. If you're not up for walking around in squishy, soaked shoes, bring a second, smaller plastic bag to wear over your feet while riding.

SUPPLIES FOR INFANTS AND TODDLERS

BASED ON RECOMMENDATIONS from hundreds of *Unofficial Guide* readers, here's what we suggest you carry with you when touring with infants and toddlers:

- A disposable diaper for every hour you plan to be away from your hotel room
- A plastic (or vinyl) diaper wrap with Velcro closures
- A cloth diaper or kitchen towel to put over your shoulder for burping
- Two receiving blankets: one to wrap the baby, one to lay the baby on or to drape over you when you nurse
- Ointment for diaper rash
- Moistened towelettes such as Wet Ones
- Prepared formula in bottles if you are not breast-feeding
- A washable bib, baby spoon, and baby food if your infant is eating solids
- For toddlers, a small toy for comfort and to keep them occupied during attractions

Baby Care Centers at the theme parks will sell you just about anything that you forget or run out of. As with all things Disney, prices will be higher than elsewhere, but at least you won't need to detour to a drugstore in the middle of your touring day.

TIPS FOR PREGNANT MOTHERS

LET'S FACE IT: A visit to Walt Disney World is not the ideal vacation for an expecting mom, but we also know that quite a lot of pregnant moms visit the World every year. The most important advice for pregnant moms is to take it easy. If you travel by car or plane, make sure you prepare your schedule in such a manner that you have plenty of rest. Don't stay on your feet all day; stick to a healthy, balanced diet; but most of all don't skip meals; and drink plenty of fluids. Keep the dining options flexible; morning sickness or sudden aversions or preferences to food can be dealt with easily if you don't make reservations and go for whatever you feel like eating. Always carry some snacks and bottled water with you. A plastic bag folded in your pocket in case you feel unwell takes no space but gives peace of mind. You also should discuss your upcoming Walt Disney World visit with your physician. He or she will certainly have valuable tips.

Comfortable clothes are a must, and so are well-worn-in supporting shoes. You may consider getting a maternity support belt to keep your back from hurting. If you're using a special pillow at night to support your belly, don't forget to bring it with you. If you do not have enough space for it in your suitcase, consider shipping one ahead in a care box. Of course the hotel will provide you with extra pillows if needed.

Maternity bathing suit: If you don't own one, purchase a maternity bathing suit; you will be glad you did. A relaxing afternoon at the pool or a float down the lazy river in the water parks is wonderful.

At the parks take frequent breaks; put your legs up! The Baby Care Centers also welcome expectant moms, and you can sit and relax in a pleasant atmosphere. Go back to the hotel for a nap during the day, and plan a day away from the parks. Go splurge and have a massage; your back and feet will be grateful. Sleep is precious, so don't overdo it; a good night of sleep is better than all the fireworks in the sky.

Heed the warnings! Here is a short list of rides that are absolutely not suitable for expecting moms: **Big Thunder Mountain Railroad; DINOSAUR; Expedition Everest; Kali River Rapids; Kilimanjaro Safaris; Mission: SPACE; Rock 'n' Roller Coaster; Star Tours; Space Mountain; Splash Mountain; Test Track; Tomorrowland Speedway;** and **The Twilight Zone Tower of Terror.** Remember, this is just a short list; use your own best judgment.

A word about the water parks: Obviously, experiencing the offerings of **Crush 'n' Gusher** at Typhoon Lagoon or barreling down **Summit Plummet** at Blizzard Beach is ill-advised if you're in the family way, but the water parks offer great lazy rivers and pools, as well as shady beaches where you can relax and let the rest of your group enjoy the wild things.

Tips for Nursing Mothers

Baby Care Centers are available at all Walt Disney World parks, and nursing mothers will not have difficulty finding a comfortable, clean, and pleasant place to take care of their infants. In addition to breast-feeding rooms equipped with rocking chairs and love seats, the child-care facilities have sinks for washing and a room with toys and videos for your older children. Should you need diapers, baby clothes, children's medicines, and other small necessities, Disney has those items available right there for a fee.

Here are some tips to remember when visiting:

- Getting there by plane: Remember to nurse your child at takeoff and landing. It helps to open the baby's ears and also eliminates discomfort due to pressure changes.

- Nurse your infant at the first sign of hunger. You and the baby will be calmer, and you will attract much less attention if you feed the baby before he or she gets fussy and screams at the top of his or her lungs.

- Wear comfortable clothes. While you can access the Baby Care Centers at any time, there is nothing wrong with nursing your infant in a calm, shady spot anywhere at Walt Disney World or at the pool of your hotel. A dress with buttons in the front and a small baby blanket to put over your shoulder will do the trick. A large T-shirt that allows the baby to nurse "from under" is another option. In case you feel self-conscious, remember that Florida was the first state to protect breast-feeding in public by law in 1993.

- Pick a quiet place to nurse your baby.

- Adequate rest is another must. Schedule several breaks into your day and go back to the hotel for a nap.

- Make sure you plan regular healthy meals. A nursing mom, much like an expecting mother, has increased nutritional needs. In addition to eating a well-balanced diet and drinking plenty of fluids, it is always a good idea to take along some snacks.

- It is hot in Florida, and while it is important for all visitors to drink lots of water, it is crucial for nursing moms, so stay hydrated!

- Schedule a down day into your trip. If you have older children, let dad take them to the park while you stay behind with the baby. A day of rest works wonders.

- If you plan on a parent's evening out, consider pumping milk for later use or supplementing breast milk with a bottle of formula.

- Nursing is exhausting, and so is touring Walt Disney World. Fatigue can reduce milk flow. Get enough rest and don't stay up past your bedtime. The night of a nursing mom is already short. Leave the park whenever you feel tired and get enough sleep.

- A bath and a massage calm most fussy babies and are good for mom too.

We also suggest reading *Baby Massage: A Practical Guide to Massage and Movement for Babies and Infants*, by Peter Walker.

REMEMBERING *Your* TRIP

1. Purchase a notebook for each child and spend some time each evening recording the events of the day. If your children have trouble getting motivated or don't know what to write about, start a discussion; otherwise, let them write or draw whatever they want to remember from the day's events.

2. Collect mementos along the way and create a treasure box in a small tin or cigar box. Months or years later, it's fun to look at postcards, pins, seashells, or ticket stubs to jump-start a memory.

3. Add inexpensive postcards to your photographs to create an album; then write a few words on each page to accompany the images.

4. Give each child a disposable camera to record his or her version of the trip. One 5-year-old snapped an entire series of photos that never showed anyone above the waist—his view of the world and the photos were priceless.

5. Nowadays, many families travel with a camcorder or make videos with their smartphones/tablets, though we recommend using one sparingly—parents end up viewing the trip through the lens rather than being in the moment. If you must, take your device of choice along, but record only a few moments of major sights (too much is boring anyway). And let the kids record and narrate. On the topic of narration, speak loudly so as to be heard over the not insignificant background noise of the parks. Make use of lockers at all of the parks when the recorder becomes a burden or when you're going to experience an attraction that might damage it or get it wet. Unless you've got a waterproof camcorder or smart device, leave it behind on Splash Mountain, Kali River Rapids, and any other ride where water is involved.

6. Another inexpensive way to record memories is a palm-size voice recorder. Let all family members describe their experiences. Hearing a small child's voice years later is so endearing, and those recorded descriptions will trigger an album's worth of memories, far more focused than what many novices capture on video.

Bob: Liliane will throw a party at the least provocation— Groundhog Day, National Tulip Day, Bless the Reptiles Day, you name it. But scheduling a wingding the weekend before you go to Disney World is to me like holding an Easter-egg hunt in a cattle stampede—just a little too much going on to add one more thing.

Finally, when it comes to taking photos and collecting mementos, don't let the tail wag the dog. You're not going to Disney World to build the biggest scrapbook in history. Or as this Houston mom put it:

Tell your readers to get a grip on the photography thing. We were so busy shooting pictures that we kind of lost the thread.

HOW TO HAVE FUN BEFORE AND AFTER YOUR VISIT—OR, THINGS THAT BOB WOULD NEVER DO

PREPARING FOR YOUR Walt Disney World vacation is important, but it is equally important to have a good time. Doing so before you leave is yet another way to get the whole family involved.

The weekend before your departure, plan a party for all who are going to Walt Disney World. Pick a Disney movie the entire family will enjoy and plan a meal in front of the TV. A chocolate cake or cookies shaped like the famous mouse head will be a guaranteed success and add to the fun. This is the perfect time to go over the must-see list and reiterate the dos and dont's.

A similar event can be planned upon your return, when it is time to share the pictures and maybe even the movie you made during your visit to Walt Disney World.

Liliane: Don't forget to send Bob an invitation.

Great Websites

Arts and crafts and party tips: **disney.go.com/create**

Some serious cooking: **magicalkingdoms.com/wdw/recipes**

Recommended Books:

The Disney Party Handbook by Alison Boteler

The Disney Bakery by Adrienne Berofsky

TRIAL RUN

IF YOU GIVE THOUGHTFUL CONSIDERATION to all areas of mental, physical, organizational, and logistical preparation discussed in this chapter, what remains is to familiarize yourself with Walt Disney World itself, and of course, to conduct your field test. Yep, that's right, we want you to take the whole platoon on the road for a day to see if you are combat ready. No joke, this is important. You'll learn who poops out first, who is prone to developing blisters, who has to pee every 11 seconds, and given the proper forum, how compatible your family is in terms of what you like to see and do.

For the most informative trial run, choose a local venue that requires lots of walking, dealing with crowds, and making decisions on how to spend your time. Regional theme parks and state fairs are your best bets, followed by large zoos and museums. Devote the whole day. Kick off the morning with an early start, just like you will at Walt Disney World, paying attention to who's organized and ready to go and who's dragging his or her butt and holding up the group. If you have to drive an hour or two to get to your test venue, no big deal. You'll have to do some commuting at Walt Disney World too. Spend the whole day, eat a couple meals, and stay late.

Don't bias the sample (that is, mess with the outcome) by telling everyone you are practicing for Walt Disney World. Everyone behaves differently when they know they are being tested or evaluated. Your objective is not to run a perfect drill but to find out as much as you can about how the individuals in your family, as well as the family as a group, respond to and deal with everything they experience during the day. Pay attention to who moves quickly and who is slow; to

WDW transportation planners use the latest technology when planning new development of bus routes.

who is adventuresome and who is reticent; to who keeps going and who needs frequent rest breaks; to who sets the agenda and who is content to follow; to who is easily agitated and who stays cool; to who tends to dawdle or wander off; to who is curious and who is bored; to who is demanding and who is accepting. You get the idea.

Discuss the findings of the test run with your spouse the next day. Don't be discouraged if your test day wasn't perfect; few (if any) are. Distinguish between problems that are remediable and problems that are intrinsic to your family's emotional or physical makeup (no amount of hiking, for example, will toughen up some people's feet).

Establish a plan for addressing remediable problems (further conditioning, setting limits before you go, trying harder to achieve family consensus, whatever) and develop strategies for minimizing or working around problems that are a fact of life (waking sleepyheads 15 minutes early, placing moleskin on likely blister sites before setting out, packing familiar food for the toddler who balks at restaurant fare). If you are an attentive observer, a fair diagnostician, and a creative problem solver, you'll be able to work out a significant percentage of the problems you're likely to encounter at Walt Disney World before you ever leave home.

PART SIX

GET *in the* BOAT, MEN!

THE ABOVE IS NOT A *JEOPARDY!* ANSWER, but if it were, the question would be this: "What did George Washington say to his soldiers before they crossed the Delaware?" We share this historical aside as our way of sounding the alarm, blowing the bugle, or whatever. It's time to move beyond preparation and practice and to leap into action. Walt Disney World, here we come! Get in the boat, men—and women!

READY, SET, TOUR!
Some Touring Considerations

HOW MUCH TIME IS REQUIRED TO SEE EACH PARK?

THE MAGIC KINGDOM AND EPCOT offer such a large number of attractions and special live-entertainment options that it is impossible to see everything in a single day, with or without a midday break. For a reasonably thorough tour of each, allocate a minimum of one and a half days and preferably two days. The Animal Kingdom and Disney's Hollywood Studios can each be seen in a day, although planning on a day and a half allows for a more relaxed visit.

WHICH PARK TO SEE FIRST?

THIS QUESTION IS LESS ACADEMIC than it appears, especially if your party includes children or teenagers. Children who see the Magic Kingdom first expect the same type of entertainment at the other parks. At Epcot, they're often disappointed by the educational orientation and serious tone (many adults react the same way). Disney's Hollywood Studios offers some wild action along with family-friendly stage shows and attractions. Children may not find Animal Kingdom as exciting as the Magic Kingdom or DHS, because animals can't be programmed to entertain on cue.

First-time visitors should see Epcot first; you'll be able to enjoy it without having been preconditioned to think of Disney entertainment as solely fantasy or adventure.

See Disney's Animal Kingdom second. Like Epcot, it's educational, but its live animals provide a change of pace.

Next, see Disney's Hollywood Studios, which helps all ages transition from the educational Epcot and Animal Kingdom to the fanciful Magic Kingdom. Also, because DHS is smaller, you won't walk as much or stay as long. Save the Magic Kingdom for last.

If you can't postpone the Magic Kingdom without a major revolt, at least see Epcot first. Adult orientation notwithstanding, there's lots that children 7 and up will love, younger children not so much. Be sure to participate in the Agent P and Kidcot programs, described in Part 8. They'll be the highlight of your child's day. If seeing Mickey is your kid's top priority, be advised that you can see him in each of the major theme parks. Any cast member can tell you where to find him.

OPERATING HOURS

THE DISNEY WORLD WEBSITE publishes preliminary park hours 180 days in advance, but schedule adjustments can happen at any time, including the day of your visit. Check **disneyworld.com** or call ☎ 407-824-4321 for the exact hours before you arrive. Off-season, parks may be open as few as 8 hours (9 a.m.–5 p.m.). At busy times (particularly holidays), they may operate 8 a.m.–2 a.m.

OFFICIAL OPENING VERSUS REAL OPENING

WHEN YOU CALL, you're given "official hours." Sometimes, parks open earlier. If the official hours are 9 a.m.–9 p.m., for example, Main Street in the Magic Kingdom might open at 8:30 a.m., and the remainder of the park at 9 a.m.

Disney surveys local hotel reservations, estimates how many visitors to expect on a given day, and opens the theme parks early to avoid bottlenecks at parking facilities and ticket windows, as well as to absorb crowds as they arrive.

Rides and attractions shut down at approximately the official closing time. Main Street in the Magic Kingdom remains open 30 minutes to an hour after the rest of the park has closed.

THE RULES

SUCCESSFUL TOURING OF THE MAGIC KINGDOM, Animal Kingdom, Epcot, or Disney's Hollywood Studios hinges on five rules:

1. Determine in Advance What You Really Want To See

What rides and attractions appeal most to you? Which additional rides and attractions would you like to experience if you have some time left? What are you willing to forgo?

To help you set your touring priorities, we describe each theme park and its attractions later in this book. In each description, we include the author's evaluation of the attraction and the opinions of Walt Disney World guests expressed as star ratings. Five stars is the best possible rating.

Finally, because attractions range from midway-type rides and horse-drawn trolleys to colossal, high-tech extravaganzas, we have developed a hierarchy of categories to pinpoint an attraction's magnitude:

SUPER HEADLINERS The best attractions the theme park has to offer. Mind-boggling in size, scope, and imagination. Represents the cutting edge of modern attraction technology and design.

HEADLINERS Full-blown, multimillion-dollar, full-scale themed adventures and theater presentations. Modern in technology and design and employing a complete range of special effects.

MAJOR ATTRACTIONS Themed adventures on a more modest scale but incorporating state-of-the-art technologies. Or, larger-scale attractions of older design.

MINOR ATTRACTIONS Midway-type rides, small dark rides (cars on a track, zigzagging through the dark), small theater presentations, transportation rides, and elaborate walk-through attractions.

DIVERSIONS Exhibits, both passive and interactive. Includes playgrounds, video arcades, and street theater.

Though not every Walt Disney World attraction fits neatly into these descriptions, the categories provide a comparison of attractions' size and scope. Remember that bigger and more elaborate doesn't always mean better. Peter Pan's Flight, a minor attraction in the Magic Kingdom, continues to be one of the park's most beloved rides. Likewise, for many young children, no attraction, regardless of size, surpasses Dumbo.

2. Arrive Early! Arrive Early! Arrive Early!

This is the single most important key to efficient touring and avoiding long lines. First thing in the morning, there are no lines and fewer people. The same four rides you experience in 1 hour in early morning can take as long as 3 hours after 10:30 a.m. Eat breakfast before you arrive; don't waste prime touring time sitting in a restaurant.

The earlier a park opens, the greater your advantage. This is because most vacationers won't rise early and get to a park before it opens. Fewer people are willing to make an 8 a.m. opening than a 9 a.m. opening. If you visit during midsummer, arrive at the turnstile 30–40 minutes before opening. During holiday periods, arrive 45–60 minutes early.

3. Avoid Bottlenecks

Crowd concentrations and/or faulty crowd management cause bottlenecks. Avoiding bottlenecks involves being able to predict where, when, and why they occur. Concentrations of hungry people create bottlenecks at restaurants during lunch and dinner. Concentrations of

people moving toward the exit at closing time create bottlenecks in gift shops en route to the gate. Concentrations of visitors at new and popular rides and at rides slow to load and unload create bottlenecks and long lines. To help you get a grip on which attractions cause bottlenecks, we've developed a Bottleneck Scale with a range of 1–10. If an attraction ranks high on the Bottleneck Scale, try to experience it during the first 2 hours the park is open. The scale is included in each attraction profile in Parts Seven through Eleven.

The best way to avoid bottlenecks, however, is to use one of our field-tested touring plans available in clip-out form complete with a map on pages 453–478. The plans will save you as much as 4½ hours of standing in line in a single day.

4. Go Back to Your Hotel for a Rest in the Middle of the Day

You may think we're beating the dead horse with this midday nap thing, but if you plug away all day at the theme parks, you'll understand how the dead horse feels. No joke; resign yourself to going back to the hotel in the middle of the day for swimming, reading, and a snooze.

5. Let Off Steam

Time at a Disney theme park is extremely regimented for younger children. Often held close for fear of losing them, they are ushered from line to line and attraction to attraction throughout the day. After a couple of hours of being on such a short leash, it's not surprising that they're in need of some physical freedom and an opportunity to discharge that pent-up energy. As it happens, all of the major theme parks except Epcot offer some sort of elaborate, creative playground perfect for such a release. Be advised that each playground (or plaza) is fairly large, and it's pretty easy to misplace a child while they're exploring. All children's playgrounds, however, have only one exit, so although your kids might get lost within the playground, they cannot wander off into the rest of the park without passing through the single exit (usually staffed by a Disney cast member).

Liliane: If you can't calm them—dunk them. Whenever my son was too wound up to nap or go to bed at night, I took him to the pool—water works wonders.

YOUR DAILY ITINERARY

PLAN EACH DAY in three blocks:

1. Early morning theme park touring

2. Midday break

3. Late-afternoon and evening theme park touring

Choose the attractions that interest you most and check their bottleneck ratings along with what time of day we recommend you visit. If your children are 8 years old or younger, review the attraction's fright-potential rating. Use one of our touring plans or work out a step-by-step plan of your own and write it down. Experience attractions with a high bottleneck rating as early as possible, transitioning to attractions with ratings of 6–8 around midmorning. Plan on departing the park for your midday break by 11:30 a.m. or so.

Bob: We strongly recommend deferring parades, stage shows, and other productions until the afternoon/evening.

For your late-afternoon and evening touring block, you do not necessarily have to return to the same theme park. If you have purchased one of the Disney admission options that allow you to "park-hop"—that is, visit more than one theme park on a given day—you may opt to spend the afternoon/evening block somewhere different. In any event, as you start your afternoon/evening block, see attractions with low bottleneck ratings until about 5 p.m. After 5 p.m., any attraction with a rating of 1–7 is fair game. If you stay into the evening, try attractions with ratings of 8–10 during the hour just before closing.

In addition to attractions, each theme park offers a broad range of special live entertainment events. In the morning, concentrate on the attractions. For the record, we regard live shows that offer five or more daily performances a day (except for street entertainment) as attractions. Thus, *Indiana Jones* at Disney's Hollywood Studios is an attraction, as is *Festival of the Lion King* at the Animal Kingdom. *IllumiNations* at Epcot or the parades at the Magic Kingdom, on the other hand, are live entertainment events. A schedule of live performances is listed in the *Times Guide* available at the entrance of each park. When planning your day, also be aware that major live events draw large numbers of guests from the attraction lines. Thus, a good time to see an especially popular attraction is during a parade or other similar event.

TOURING PLANS

OUR TOURING PLANS ARE STEP-BY-STEP GUIDES for seeing as much as possible with a minimum of standing in line. They're designed to help you avoid crowds and bottlenecks on days of moderate-to-heavy attendance. On days of lighter attendance (see "When To Go to Walt Disney World," pages 46–49), the plans will still save time, but they won't be as critical to successful touring. *Unofficial Guide* touring plans, it seems, have side effects. As two readers attest, the plans can fan the embers of love and help you impress your friends. First from a 30-something mother of two from Oconomowoc, Wisconsin:

Liliane: Don't get obsessed with the touring plans. It's your vacation, after all. You can amend or even scrap the plans if you want.

> *My husband was a bit doubtful about using a touring plan, but on our first day at Magic Kingdom, when we had done all of the Fantasyland attractions and ridden Splash Mountain twice before lunch, he looked at me with amazement and said, "I've never been so attracted to you."*

And from a young Gardner, Massachusetts, reader:

I went with my school for the Magic Music Days. I've been to Disney World before several times, and my parents have always used the guide. I looked crazy to my friends, with my huge book marked and well-worn and a stack of clip-out touring plans in my hand. The group that traveled around with me were amazed, commenting that it seemed like we were in front of a huge crowd. As soon as we left a ride we had walked on with no wait minutes before, there'd be a line of 15–20 minutes! Thank you for helping me impress my friends!

What You Can Realistically Expect from the Touring Plans

The best way to see as much as possible with the least amount of waiting is to arrive early. Several of our touring plans require that you be on hand when the park opens. Because this is often difficult and sometimes impossible for families with young children or nocturnal teens, we've developed additional touring plans for families who get a late start. You won't see as much as with the early-morning plans, but you'll see significantly more than visitors without a plan.

Variables That Will Affect the Success of the Touring Plans

The plans' success will be affected by how quickly you move from ride to ride; when and how many refreshment and restroom breaks you take; when, where, and how you eat meals; and your ability (or lack thereof) to find your way around. Smaller groups almost always move faster than larger groups, and parties of adults generally cover more ground than families with young children. Switching off (see page 245), also known as "The Baby Swap" or child swapping, among other things, inhibits families with little ones from moving expeditiously among attractions.

Along with dining breaks, the appearance of a Disney character usually stops a touring plan in its tracks. While some characters stroll the parks, it's equally common that they assemble in a specific venue where families queue up for photos and autographs. Meeting characters, posing for photos, and getting autographs can burn hours of touring time.

Liliane: Character meals are another way to collect autographs and might be something you could promise your avid collector in exchange for a full day of touring when the signature hunt is off.

If your kids collect character autographs, you need to anticipate these interruptions by including character greetings when creating your online touring plans, or else negotiate some understanding with your children about when you'll collect autographs. Note that queues for autographs, especially in the Magic Kingdom and Disney's Animal Kingdom, are sometimes as long as the queues for major attractions. The only time-efficient ways to collect autographs are to use Fastpass+ where available or to line up at the character-greeting areas first thing in the morning. Early morning is also the best time to experience popular attractions, so you may have some tough choices to make.

While we realize that following the touring plans isn't always easy, we nevertheless recommend continuous, expeditious touring until around noon. After noon, breaks and diversions won't affect the plans significantly.

A multigenerational family from Aurora, Ohio, wonders how to know if you are on track or not, writing:

> It seems like the touring plans were very time-dependent, yet there were no specific times attached to the plan outside of the early morning. On more than one day, I often had to guess as to whether we were on track. Having small children and a grandparent in our group, we couldn't move at a fast pace.

There is no objective measurement for being on track. Each family's or touring group's experience will differ to some degree. Regardless of whether your group is large or small, fast or slow, the sequence of attractions in the touring plans will allow you to enjoy the greatest number of attractions in the least possible amount of time. Two quickly moving adults will probably take in more attractions in a specific time period than will a large group made up of children, parents, and grandparents. However, given the characteristics of the respective groups, each will maximize their touring time and experience as many attractions as possible.

What To Do if You Lose the Thread

If unforeseen events interrupt a plan:

1. If you're following a touring plan in our **Lines** app (**touringplans.com /lines**), just press "Optimize" when you're ready to start touring again. Lines will figure out the best possible plan for the remainder of your day.

2. If you're following a printed touring plan, skip a step on the plan for every 20 minutes' delay. For example, if you lose your wallet and spend an hour hunting for it, skip three steps and pick up from there.

3. Forget the plan and organize the remainder of the day using the standby wait times listed in Lines.

What to Expect When You Arrive at the Parks

Because most touring plans are based on being present when the theme park opens, you need to know about opening procedures. Disney transportation to the parks begins 1½–2 hours before official opening. The parking lots open at around the same time.

Each park has an entrance plaza outside the turnstiles. Usually, you're held there until 30 minutes before the official opening time, when you're admitted. What happens next depends on the season and the day's crowds.

1. **STANDARD OPENING PROCEDURES** For the Magic Kingdom, Epcot, and Disney's Animal Kingdom, you'll usually be confined to a small section of the park until official opening time. At the Magic Kingdom, you might be admitted to Main Street, U.S.A.; at Disney's Animal Kingdom, to The Oasis;

and at Epcot, to Future World Plaza behind Spaceship Earth. A human wall of Disney cast members keeps you there until opening, when the wall speed-walks you back to the headliner attractions (to prevent anyone from running or getting trampled). At the Studios, the entire park is usually open and you're free to start touring immediately.

2. **HIGH-ATTENDANCE DAYS** When large crowds are expected, you'll usually be admitted through the turnstiles up to 30 minutes before official opening, and the entire park will be operating.

3. **VARIATIONS** Sometimes Disney will run a variation of those two procedures. In this, you'll be permitted through the turnstiles and find that one or several specific attractions are open early. At Epcot, Spaceship Earth and sometimes Test Track or Soarin' will be operating. At Animal Kingdom, you may find it's Kilimanjaro Safaris and Expedition Everest. At Disney's Hollywood Studios, look for Tower of Terror, Toy Story Mania!, and/or Rock 'n' Roller Coaster. The Magic Kingdom almost never runs a variation. Instead, you'll usually encounter number 1, or occasionally 2.

HOW TO FIND THE TOURING PLAN THAT'S BEST FOR YOU

THE DIFFERENT TOURING PLANS FOR EACH PARK are described in the chapter pertaining to that park. The descriptions will tell you for whom (for example, teens, parents with preschoolers, grandparents, and so on) or for what situation (such as sleeping late or enjoying the park at night) the plans are designed. The actual touring plans are located on pages 453–478 at the back of the book. Each plan includes a numbered map of the park in question to help you find your way around. Clip the plan of your choice out of the book by cutting along the line indicated and take it with you to the park.

Will the Plans Continue to Work Once the Secret Is Out?

Yes! First, all the plans require that a patron be there when a park opens. Many Disney World patrons simply won't get up early while on vacation. Second, less than 2% of any day's attendance has been exposed to the plans—too few to affect results. Last, most groups tailor the plans, skipping rides or shows according to taste.

How Frequently Are the Touring Plans Revised?

We revise them every year, and updates are always available at **touring plans.com.** Most complaints we receive come from readers using out-of-date editions of the *Unofficial Guide.* Even if you're up-to-date, though, be prepared for surprises. Opening procedures and showtimes may change, for example, and you can't predict when an attraction might break down.

"Bouncing Around"

Some readers object to crisscrossing a theme park as our touring plans sometimes require. A woman from Decatur, Georgia, told us she "got dizzy from all the bouncing around." Believe us, we empathize.

We've worked hard over the years to eliminate the need to crisscross a theme park in our touring plans. (In fact, our customized software can minimize walking instead of waiting in line, if that's important to you.) Occasionally, however, it's possible to save a lot of time in line with a few extra minutes of walking.

The reasons for this are varied. Sometimes a park is designed intentionally to require walking. In the Magic Kingdom, for example, the most popular attractions are positioned as far apart as possible—in the north, east, and west corners of the park—so that guests are more evenly distributed throughout the day. Other times, you may be visiting just after a new attraction has opened that everyone wants to try. In that case, a special trip to visit the new attraction may be required earlier in the day than normal, in order to avoid longer waits later. And live shows, especially at the Studios, sometimes have performance schedules so at odds with each other (and the rest of the park's schedule) that orderly touring is impossible.

If you want to experience headliner attractions in one day without long waits, you can see those first (requires crisscrossing the park), use Fastpass+ (if available), or hope to squeeze in visits during parades and the last hour the park is open (may not work).

Touring Plans and the Obsessive-Compulsive Reader

We suggest sticking to the plans religiously, especially in the mornings, if you're visiting during busy times. The consequence of touring spontaneity in peak season is hours of standing in line. When using the plans, however, relax and always be prepared for surprises and setbacks.

If you find your type-A brain doing cartwheels, reflect on the advice of a woman from Trappe, Pennsylvania:

> I had planned for this trip for two years and researched it by use of guidebooks, computer programs, videotapes, and information received from WDW. On night three of our trip, I ended up taking an unscheduled trip to the emergency room. When the doctor asked what seemed to be the problem, I responded, "I don't know, but I can't stop shaking, and I can't stay here very long because I have to get up in a couple hours to go to Disney's Hollywood Studios." Diagnosis: an anxiety attack caused by my excessive itinerary.

Touring Plan Rejection

Some folks don't respond well to the regimentation of a touring plan. If you encounter this problem with someone in your party, roll with the punches as this Maryland couple did:

> The rest of the group was not receptive to the use of the touring plans. I think they all thought I was being a little too regimented about planning this vacation. Rather than argue, I left the touring plans behind as we ventured off for the parks. You can guess the outcome. We took our camcorder with us and watched the movies when

we returned home. About every 5 minutes or so there's a shot of us all gathered around a park map trying to decide what to do next.

A reader from Royal Oak, Michigan, ran into trouble by not getting her family on board ahead of time:

The one thing I will suggest is if one member of the family is doing most of the research and planning (like I did), that they communicate what the book/touring plans suggest. I failed to do this and it led to some, shall we say, tense moments between my husband and me on our first day. However, once he realized how much time we were saving, he understood why I was so bent on following the plans.

Finally, note that our mobile app, **Lines,** can be used to find attractions with low wait times, even if you're not using a structured touring plan.

Touring Plans for Low-Attendance Days

We receive a number of letters each year similar to the following one from Lebanon, New Jersey:

The guide always assumed there would be large crowds. We had no lines. An alternate tour for low-traffic days would be helpful.

There are, thankfully, still days on which crowds are low enough that a full-day touring plan isn't needed. However, some attractions in each park bottleneck even if attendance is low:

MAGIC KINGDOM Space Mountain, Splash Mountain, The Many Adventures of Winnie the Pooh, Enchanted Tales with Belle, Peter Pan's Flight, and the Seven Dwarfs Mine Train

EPCOT Test Track and Soarin'

DISNEY'S ANIMAL KINGDOM Kilimanjaro Safaris and Expedition Everest

DHS Rock 'n' Roller Coaster, The Twilight Zone Tower of Terror, and Toy Story Mania!

For this reason, we recommend that you follow a touring plan at least through the first five or six steps. If you're pretty much walking onto every attraction, scrap the remainder of the plan. Alternatively, you can see the attractions above immediately after the park is open, or use Fastpass+.

Extra Magic Hours and the Touring Plans

If you're a Disney resort guest and use your morning Extra Magic Hours privileges, complete your early-entry touring before the general public is admitted and position yourself to follow the touring plan. When the public is admitted, the park will suddenly swarm. A Wilmington, Delaware, mother advises:

The early-entry times went like clockwork. We were finishing up the Great Movie Ride when Disney's Hollywood Studios opened to the public, and we had to wait in line quite a while for Voyage of the Little Mermaid, which sort of screwed up everything thereafter. Early-opening

attractions should be finished up well before regular opening time so you can be at the plan's first stop as early as possible.

In the Magic Kingdom, the attractions open for early entry are located in Fantasyland and Tomorrowland. At Epcot, they're in the Future World section. At Disney's Animal Kingdom, they're in DinoLand U.S.A., Asia, Discovery Island, and Africa. At Disney's Hollywood Studios, they're dispersed. Practically speaking, see any attractions on the plan that are open for early entry, crossing them off as you do. If you finish all early-entry attractions and have time left before the general public is admitted, sample early-entry attractions not included in the plan. Stop touring about 10 minutes before the rest of the public is admitted, and position yourself for the first attraction on the plan that wasn't open for early entry. During early entry in the Magic Kingdom, for example, you can almost always experience Peter Pan's Flight and Under the Sea: Voyage of the Little Mermaid in Fantasyland, plus Space Mountain and Buzz Lightyear's Space Ranger Spin in Tomorrowland. As official opening nears, go to the boundary between Fantasyland and Liberty Square and be ready to blitz Splash and Big Thunder mountains according to the touring plan when the rest of the park opens.

Evening Extra Magic Hours, when a designated park remains open for Disney resort guests 2 hours beyond normal closing time, have less effect on the touring plans than early entry in the morning. Parks are almost never scheduled for both early entry and evening Extra Magic Hours on the same day. Thus a park offering evening Extra Magic Hours will enjoy a fairly normal morning and early afternoon. It's not until late afternoon, when park hoppers coming from the other theme parks descend, that the late-closing park will become especially crowded. By that time, you'll be well toward the end of your touring plan.

FASTPASS AND FASTPASS+

DISNEY INTRODUCED THE FASTPASS ride-reservation system in 1999 as a way to moderate the high wait times at some of its headliner attractions. A new version of this system, called **Fastpass+,** should roll out across the parks in 2013 and will (eventually) replace the old system entirely. Fastpass and Fastpass+ are available free to all park guests, even if you're not staying at a Disney resort.

Fastpass+ adds features such as the ability to make ride reservations months in advance, and more attractions to use it on. It also limits how many Fastpasses you can obtain per day and per attraction.

Because the introduction of Fastpass+ has already been delayed for more than a year, it's possible that Disney will run both Fastpass and Fastpass+ concurrently while they work out the kinks. To cover both bases, the next section describes the existing system in detail. The section after describes Fastpass+, including what's being retained from the original system and new features that are being introduced.

Fastpass Attractions at Walt Disney World

MAGIC KINGDOM	• The Barnstormer • Big Thunder Mountain • Buzz Lightyear's Space Ranger Spin • Dumbo • Jungle Cruise	• Peter Pan's Flight • Seven Dwarfs Mine Train** • Space Mountain • Splash Mountain • Town Square Theater (Mickey, Princesses Meet-and-Greets) • Under the Sea: Journey of the Little Mermaid • Winnie the Pooh
EPCOT	• *Captain EO** • Living with the Land* • Maelstrom	• Mission: SPACE • Soarin' • Test Track
ANIMAL KINGDOM	• DINOSAUR • Expedition Everest	• Kali River Rapids • Kilimanjaro Safaris • Primeval Whirl
DHS	• Rock 'n' Roller Coaster • Star Tours—The Adventures Continue	• Toy Story Mania! • Twilight Zone Tower of Terror • *Voyage of the Little Mermaid**

* Available seasonally; ** opens 2014

Fastpass v1.0

Here's how it works: Your park map and signage at attractions tell you which attractions are included. Participating attractions have a regular line and a Fastpass line. A sign at the entrance tells how long the wait is in the regular line. If you don't mind the wait, hop in line. If it seems too long, insert your admission ticket into a Fastpass machine; it'll give you an appointment time to return and ride later in the day. When you return at the designated time, enter the Fastpass line and proceed with minimal waiting to the attraction's preshow or boarding area.

Fastpass can save you a lot of waiting by distributing guests at designated attractions throughout the day. This is accomplished by providing an incentive—a shorter wait—for guests willing to put off experiencing the attraction until later in the day. The system also, in effect, imposes a penalty—standby status—on those who don't use it. However, spreading out guest arrivals sometimes decreases the wait for standby guests as well.

Fastpass doesn't eliminate the need to arrive early at a theme park. Because each park offers a limited number of Fastpass attractions, you still need an early start to avoid long lines at non-Fastpass attractions. Plus, there's a limited supply of Fastpasses available for each attraction on any day. If you don't arrive at a given theme park until midafternoon, you might find that all Fastpasses are gone. When it's available, though, it's great for those who like to sleep late or who choose an afternoon or evening at the parks on their arrival day. It also allows you to postpone wet rides, such as Kali River Rapids at Disney's Animal Kingdom or Splash Mountain at the Magic Kingdom, until a warmer time of day.

OBTAINING A FASTPASS   You can ordinarily obtain a Fastpass anytime after a park opens (some attractions are a little tardy getting their Fastpass system up), but the Fastpass return lines don't usually begin operating until 35–90 minutes after opening.

When you obtain a Fastpass, you can be assured of a period of time between when you receive your Fastpass and when you report

back. The interval can be as short as 30 minutes or as long as 3–7 hours, depending on park attendance and the attraction's popularity and hourly capacity. Generally, the earlier in the day you obtain a Fastpass, the shorter the interval before your return window. If the park opens at 9 a.m. and you obtain a Fastpass for Splash Mountain at 9:25 a.m., your appointment for returning to ride would be 10–11 a.m. or 10:10–11:10 a.m. The exact time will be determined by how many other guests have obtained Fastpasses before you.

To more effectively distribute guests over the day, Fastpass machines bump the 1-hour return period back a few minutes for a set number of passes issued (usually about 6% of the attraction's hourly capacity). For example, when Splash Mountain opens at 9 a.m., the first 125 people to obtain a Fastpass may get a 9:40–10:40 a.m. return window. The next 125 guests are issued Fastpasses with a 9:45–10:45 a.m. window. And so it goes, with the time window dropping back 5 minutes for every 125 guests. The fewer guests who obtain Fastpasses for an attraction, the shorter the interval between receipt of your pass and the return window. Conversely, the more guests issued Fastpasses, the longer the interval. If an attraction is exceptionally popular and/or its hourly capacity is relatively small, the return window might be pushed back to park closing time. When this happens, the Fastpass machines shut down and a sign is posted indicating that all Fastpasses are gone for the day. It's not unusual, for example, for Soarin' at Epcot to have exhausted its Fastpasses by 1 p.m. or for Toy Story Mania! at the Studios to have distributed all available Fastpasses by 11 a.m.

Liliane: Rides routinely exhaust their daily Fastpass supply, but shows almost never do. The standby line almost always requires less waiting.

So why not just run around the park first thing in the morning, collecting Fastpasses for every attraction? Because Disney won't let you. To keep guests from abusing the system, Disney requires them to wait a certain amount of time between obtaining passes. That time span varies based on the attraction and time of year, but it's usually either the beginning of your Fastpass return time or 2 hours, whichever comes first. The actual time is usually printed near the bottom of your most recent pass. Also, you don't have to use your most recent Fastpass before getting another—the Fastpass computer monitors only the distribution of passes, ignoring whether or when a pass is used.

Let's say, for example, you get a Fastpass for Toy Story Mania! at 9 a.m. and the return-time window is 10:05–11:05 a.m. You should be able to get another Fastpass for any attraction (including Toy Story Mania!) at 10:05 a.m. Alternatively, if you get a Fastpass for the same attraction at 10 a.m. and the return-time window is 4:05–5:05 p.m., you should be able to get another Fastpass for any attraction (including Toy Story Mania!) around noon.

RETURNING TO RIDE Disney officially enforces the ride return time printed on the Fastpass. If your return time for Space Mountain is between 8:05 a.m. and 9:05 a.m., then Disney expects you to return between those times to ride. *Unofficially,* Disney will usually allow you to show up 5 minutes early or up to 15 minutes late and still use the pass (8 a.m.–9:20 a.m. in our example). If you arrive late to the Fastpass line because of a lengthy meal, ride breakdown, or other unforeseen circumstance, you can explain the issue to the cast member working the line, and he or she will decide whether you can still use your pass.

When the cast member has validated your Fastpass, you'll enter a line marked FASTPASS RETURN that routes you more or less directly to the boarding or preshow area. Each person in your party must have his own Fastpass and be ready to show it at the entrance of the Fastpass return line. Before you enter the boarding area or theater, another cast member will collect your Fastpass.

Cast members are instructed to minimize waits for Fastpass holders. Thus, if the Fastpass return line suddenly becomes inundated (something that occurs by chance), cast members will intervene to shorten the line. As many as 25 Fastpass holders will be admitted for each standby guest until the Fastpass line is reduced to an acceptable length.

WHEN TO USE FASTPASS Except as discussed below, there's no reason to use Fastpass during the first 30–40 minutes a park is open. Lines for most attractions are manageable then, and it's the only time of day when Fastpass attractions exclusively serve those in the regular line.

Using Fastpass requires two trips to the same attraction: one to obtain the pass and another to use it. You must invest time to obtain the pass, then interrupt your touring later to backtrack in order to use it. The additional time, effort, and touring modification are justified only if you can save more than 30 minutes.

 Bob: Although Fastpass usually eliminates 85% or more of the wait you'd experience in the standby line, you can still expect a short wait—usually less than 15 minutes and frequently less than 10 minutes.

Eight Fastpass attractions build lines so quickly in the morning that failing to queue up within the first 6 or so minutes of operation will all but guarantee a long wait: Soarin' and Test Track at Epcot;

Expedition Everest and Kilimanjaro Safaris at Disney's Animal Kingdom; Space Mountain at the Magic Kingdom; and Rock 'n' Roller Coaster, Toy Story Mania!, and The Twilight Zone Tower of Terror at Disney's Hollywood Studios. With these, you should race directly to the attractions when the park opens or obtain a Fastpass. (Given that Seven Dwarfs Mine Train at the Magic Kingdom is certain to be a Fastpass attraction when it opens in 2014, our advice above will apply to it as well.)

Another three Fastpass attractions—Splash Mountain, Winnie the Pooh, and Peter Pan's Flight in the Magic Kingdom—develop long queues within 30–50 minutes of park opening. If you can make your way to them before the wait becomes intolerable, lucky you. Otherwise, your options are Fastpass or a long time waiting in line.

At a number of Fastpass attractions, the time gap between getting your pass and returning to ride can range from 3–7 hours. If you think you might want to use Fastpass on the following attractions, obtain it before 11 a.m.:

MAGIC KINGDOM	Buzz Lightyear's Space Ranger Spin	Peter Pan's Flight	7 Dwarfs Mine Train	Space Mountain	Splash Mountain	Winnie the Pooh
EPCOT	Mission: SPACE	Soarin'	Test Track			
ANIMAL KINGDOM	Expedition Everest					
DHS	Rock 'n' Roller Coaster	Toy Story Mania!				

In case you're wondering how Fastpass waits compare with waits in the standby line, here's what we observed at Space Mountain during spring break on a day when the park opened at 9 a.m. From 9 to 10 a.m., both sides of Space Mountain served standby guests (there are two identical roller coasters in the Space Mountain building). At 10 a.m., the entire right side was cleared and became dedicated to Fastpass. At 10:45 a.m., the posted standby wait time was 45 minutes, for Fastpass only 10 minutes. At 1:45 p.m., the posted standby wait time was 1 hour, with 10 minutes for Fastpass. These observations document the benefit of Fastpass and, interestingly, also reveal shorter waits in the regular line than those observed at the same time of day before the advent of Fastpass.

TRICKS OF THE TRADE It's possible to acquire a second Fastpass before you use the first one (and sooner than 2 hours after getting it). Disney's computer system looks only at when the Fastpass return-time window starts, not whether you've actually used the Fastpass. At press time, the maximum wait between obtaining Fastpasses at Animal Kingdom was only 1 hour, versus 2 hours at the Magic Kingdom, Epcot, and DHS.

Also at press time, several Magic Kingdom Fastpass attractions were disconnected from the rest of the park's Fastpass system. Machines at Fantasyland's Dumbo and Barnstormer attractions and Main Street's Mickey Mouse meet-and-greet will give you Fastpasses even if you've just obtained them for other attractions. Thus, you could get Fast-passes for Space Mountain, Dumbo, The Barnstormer, and the Mickey meet-and-greet as fast as you can walk between those attractions. This situation may change, so check **touringplans.com** for the latest news.

Another tip: Obtain Fastpasses for all members of your party, including those who are too short, too young, or simply not interested in riding, as this family of four recommends:

> *Utilize the Fastpasses of people in your group who don't want to ride. Our 6-year-old didn't want to ride anything rough. All four of us got Fastpasses for each ride. When the 6-year-old didn't want to ride, my husband and I took turns riding with the 12-year-old. It was our version of the Fastpass child swap, and the 12-year-old got double rides.*

A reader from Kettle Falls, Washington, shares his technique:

> *When I went to a park, I headed for my favorite ride and got in the standby line while I sent my companion to get us Fastpasses. So we were able to ride twice with almost no wait.*

Our wait-times app, **Lines,** will show you which Fastpass attractions still have passes available and when we estimate they'll run out. See Lines in action before you go at **touringplans.com/lines.**

Fastpass+

Disney's next-gen version of Fastpass hadn't launched at publication of this edition, but it had gone through enough rounds of small-scale guest testing for us to form a general sense of how it's supposed to work.

One major change to the existing system is that Fastpass+ users will be able to select their own return-time windows for attractions. For example, Big Thunder Mountain Railroad may display a list of 1-hour time windows (1–2 p.m., 2–3 p.m., etc.) for you to choose from. This solves the problem of not being able to use Fastpasses whose return times end up in the middle of meals or naps—an important consideration, because Disney enforces those return-time windows.

Another new feature of the Fastpass+ initiative is the ability to make Fastpass reservations in advance—we hear it's around 60 days ahead, but the actual number hasn't been set yet. In the current Fast-pass system, you obtain Fastpasses when you get into the park by walking to the attraction's Fastpass kiosk. With Fastpass+, you'll be able to **Liliane:** You won't be able to use Fastpass and Fastpass+ at the same time.

reserve in advance through the Disney World website and the My Disney Experience app. You'll need an existing Disney resort reservation or a theme park ticket in hand to do this. If you buy your admission the day you arrive at the parks or you want to change your Fastpass selections when you're in the park, you'll (eventually) be able to use the app or new in-park computer terminals to make reservations.

Also in the plans, we're told, is a hard limit on the number of daily Fastpass+ reservations you can have. The rumor is that when Fastpass+

rolls out across the four parks, each guest will be limited to between two and four passes per day, depending on park and crowd conditions. We also hear that guests will get fewer Fastpass+ reservations on the busiest 5–15% of park operating days, depending on the park.

This is a significant constraint for *Unofficial Guide* readers, who report using 8–10 regular Fastpasses per day in the Magic Kingdom simply by knowing the rules and doing the walking.

Why does Disney need to limit the number of Fastpasses+ available? Because guests who use Fastpass are more satisfied with their trip, so Disney wants more guests using it. But the number of guests who can use Fastpass+ in a given day is a function of the number of rides that offer Fastpass, their hourly capacity, and how long the park is open.

Take the Magic Kingdom: When the Seven Dwarfs Mine Train opens, the park should have around 13 Fastpass-enabled attractions. Combined, those 13 should be able to give rides to about 19,000 people per hour. Assume two-thirds of that capacity is allocated to Fastpass and the other third to standby riders. Over the course of a 12-hour day, that works out to around 152,000 Fastpass spots available on those rides.

About 49,000 people visit the Magic Kingdom on an average day. If there are 152,000 Fastpass spots available, each person can have three Fastpasses before all of the spots are taken.

However, if 75,000 people visit the Magic Kingdom during the same 12-hour day, they can have only two Fastpasses each before all the spots are taken. At 75,000 people, Disney could keep the park open longer, but it would take an 18-hour day (say, 8 a.m.–2 a.m.) to guarantee three Fastpasses per guest. And keeping the park open costs money.

Another way of making more Fastpasses available is to add Fastpass to more attractions. Today, Disney's four parks have about 30 Fastpass-enabled attractions, and our latest information is that Disney will up this number to around 50. Attractions such as The Haunted Mansion and Pirates of the Caribbean in the Magic Kingdom, Spaceship Earth at Epcot, and The Great Movie Ride at Disney's Hollywood Studios should eventually have Fastpass lines. In addition, Disney will use Fastpass for more character greetings, and to reserve some of the best viewing spots for the parks' afternoon and evening parades and fireworks.

"NO FASTPASS FOR YOU!" In addition to limiting the number of Fastpasses you can obtain, Disney seems likely to prevent some guests from obtaining certain combinations of Fastpasses. Under the old system, any guest willing to do the walking could obtain Fastpasses for Space Mountain, Splash Mountain, and Big Thunder Mountain on the same day; the same guest could obtain three Fastpasses for Space Mountain, too.

That looks likely to change with Fastpass+. While the rules haven't been finalized, most scenarios we've seen only allow guests to obtain one Fastpass per attraction, per day. If you want to ride Space Mountain twice, one of those rides will have to use the standby line.

Disney also seems ready to limit the combinations of Fastpasses you can have, preventing some guests from using Fastpass on the park's headliner attractions. Again, while the rules haven't been finalized, we're hearing that Disney's computer systems may enforce different rules depending on whether you're staying off-site or at a Value, Moderate, or Deluxe Disney resort. Here's how these rules might shake out at the Magic Kingdom:

TYPE OF HOTEL GUEST VS. NUMBER OF FASTPASSES FOR MAGIC KINGDOM HEADLINERS	
Off-site/day guest: None	Disney Moderate Resort: 2
Disney Value Resort: 1	Disney Deluxe Resort: 3

To prevent class warfare, we hear Disney's computer systems won't even *hint* at the distinctions among hotel guests. You'll simply be presented a list of available Fastpass+ opportunities, without further explanation.

Disney may also allocate more Fastpasses to guests staying at higher-priced hotels. For example, Grand Floridian guests may get five passes, while guests of other Deluxe resorts get three or four.

We've not heard yet how Disney Vacation Club members will fit into this scheme. We hear Annual Pass holders may get an allotment of Fastpass+ reservations every 90 days or so, but we don't know whether these folks will be subject to any Fastpass restrictions.

Further, guests who book last-minute vacations may see their Fastpass allocations or choices reduced. In one proposal we've heard, guests who book 60 days in advance get a full allotment of Fastpasses: three or four for the Magic Kingdom and two or three for the other parks. Guests who book 45 days in advance may be guaranteed only three and two, respectively, while guests who book 30 days in advance may have just two and one. And because an attraction's Fastpass availability is limited by its hourly rider capacity, those who book last-minute trips may find that Fastpasses are no longer available at their favorite attractions.

Clearly, these new rules are designed to do three things: persuade you to stay at a Disney resort, encourage you to book your trip well in advance, and tell Disney exactly where you plan to be every day— pretty much the same three things the Disney Dining Plan is designed to do. These three things not only increase Disney's revenue but also decrease its operating expenses, because Disney will be able to adjust its staffing levels at each park based on how many people have made Fastpass+ reservations. More importantly, with the promise of lower wait times when you book ahead, Disney hopes you'll spend more time at its parks rather than make last-minute trips to Universal or other parks.

HOW FASTPASS+ WILL AFFECT YOUR WAITS IN LINE When Fastpass+ is fully implemented, we think the average *Unofficial Guide* reader who arrives at park opening and follows a touring plan should expect to wait about the same amount of time in line as with the old Fastpass system.

Increasing the number of Fastpass+ attractions and allowing guests to choose their Fastpass+ reservation times should help distribute crowds more evenly throughout the park. That should reduce the wait times at some attractions and increase the waits elsewhere.

Limiting the number of Fastpasses a guest can obtain, however, or the rides at which they can be obtained, will tend to increase wait times at some attractions, mostly headliners, because the standby line will be the only option for riding. The question is whether the reduced wait times at some attractions with Fastpass+ will outweigh the increased times at the headliners.

As we've already stated, adding Fastpass+ to more attractions will reduce waits in line for Fastpass+ guests at those attractions. The new Fastpass+ attractions, however, are not usually the ones with the highest waits, thereby limiting some of the potential benefit. For example, standby waits at The Great Movie Ride typically peaked at around 30 minutes during Christmas 2012, with posted waits of around 20 minutes for much of the day. Guests using Fastpass+ at The Great Movie Ride can still expect to wait a few minutes to board, so the average time saved using Fastpass+ probably tops out at around 15 minutes for most of the day, and even less during slower times of the year.

Also, because some ride capacity will have to be reserved for Fastpass+ guests, waits should increase slightly for standby guests at these new Fastpass+ attractions. And because of the new Fastpass+ limits, most guests will use the standby line at most attractions.

Waits should also increase slightly for guests visiting each park's headliner attractions, virtually all of which already have Fastpass. Most of this increase owes to two factors: (1) the new Fastpass+ rule restricting the number of passes you can get for a park's headliner attractions, which prevents you from saving time at all of a park's headliners; and (2) the enforcement of Fastpass return times, which began in 2012 and requires you to use the Fastpass during its specified return window instead of accumulating passes for later use. Together, our computer simulations estimate that these changes will add 4–7 minutes to the average standby wait at headliner attractions.

We expect very small increases in standby waits at secondary attractions, probably on the order of a minute or so per ride, due to more even crowd distribution throughout the park. Some of that will be offset by the use of Fastpass+ at these secondary attractions. Again, having a touring plan should help you avoid most of these increases.

BLOWBACK More bodies in beds at Disney resorts aside, Fastpass+ is a complicated system that rescinds certain privileges enjoyed by all Disney World guests since 1999. The end result, except for a few fortunate Disney resort guests, is that it will take more time to see less with Fastpass+. Humans respond negatively, sometimes angrily, when something of value is taken from them. We expect Disney to endure backlash on Fastpass+ eclipsing that which it's received regarding its ever-escalating ticket, dining, and hotel prices. Compromising a guest's time and quality of experience is more personal than gouging on elective expenditures like food and lodging.

A WORD ABOUT DISNEY THRILL RIDES

READERS OF ALL AGES should try to be open-minded about Disney "thrill rides." In comparison with those at other theme parks, the Disney attractions are quite tame, with more emphasis on sights, atmosphere, and special effects than on the motion, speed, or feel of the ride. While we suggest you take Disney's pre-ride warnings seriously, we can tell you that guests of all ages report enjoying rides such as Tower of Terror, Big Thunder Mountain, and Splash Mountain.

A Washington State reader sums up the situation well:

> When I thought of Big Thunder Mountain and Space Mountain, what came to mind was gigantic hills, upside-down loops, huge vertical drops, etc. I actually hate roller coasters, especially the unpleasant sensation of a long drop, and I have never taken a ride that loops you upside down.
>
> In fact, the Disney thrill rides are all tame in comparison. There are never any long and steep hills (except Splash Mountain, and it's there for anyone to see, so you have informed consent going on the ride). I was able to build up courage to go on all of them, and the more I rode them, the more I enjoyed them.

Seniors who experience Disney thrills generally enjoy the smoother rides such as Splash Mountain, Big Thunder Mountain, and Tower of Terror and tend to dislike jerkier attractions. This letter from a Gig Harbor, Washington, woman is typical:

> I am a senior woman of small stature and good health. I am writing my comments on Space Mountain, Splash Mountain, Big Thunder Mountain, and Star Tours. My experience is that all of the rides, with the exception of Star Tours, were wonderful rides. Star Tours is too jerky and fast, the music is too loud, and I found it to be unacceptable.

Notwithstanding this letter, most comments we receive from seniors about Star Tours are positive. The Rock 'n' Roller Coaster and Expedition Everest, however, are a different story. Both are serious coasters that share more in common with Revenge of the Mummy at Universal Studios than they do with Space Mountain or Big Thunder Mountain.

Mission: SPACE, a high-tech simulation ride at Epcot, is a toss-up (pun intended). It's a smooth ride, but it absolutely has the potential to make you sick. After many guest incidents, Disney made half of the ride a tamer, no-spin experience—one that's less likely to launch your lunch.

HEIGHT REQUIREMENTS

A NUMBER OF ATTRACTIONS REQUIRE children to meet minimum height and age requirements. If you have children too short or too young to ride, you have several options, including switching off (described on

Attraction and Ride Restrictions

THE MAGIC KINGDOM

Big Thunder Mountain Railroad	40" minimum height
Seven Dwarfs Mine Train	(not open at press time)
Space Mountain	44" minimum height
Splash Mountain	40" minimum height
Stitch's Great Escape!	40" minimum height
Tomorrowland Speedway	32" to ride, 54" to drive unassisted

EPCOT

Mission: SPACE	44" minimum height
Soarin'	40" minimum height
Sum of All Thrills	48" minimum height, 54" for inversions
Test Track	40" minimum height

DISNEY'S ANIMAL KINGDOM

DINOSAUR	40" minimum height
Expedition Everest	44" minimum height
Kali River Rapids	38" minimum height
Primeval Whirl	48" minimum height

DISNEY'S HOLLYWOOD STUDIOS

Honey, I Shrunk the Kids Movie Set Adventure	10 yrs. maximum recommended age
Rock 'n' Roller Coaster	48" minimum height
Star Tours—The Adventures Continue	40" minimum height
The Twilight Zone Tower of Terror	40" minimum height

BLIZZARD BEACH WATER PARK

Chair Lift	32" minimum height
Downhill Double Dipper slide	48" minimum height
Slush Gusher slide	48" minimum height
Summit Plummet slide	48" minimum height
T-Bar (in Ski Patrol Training Camp)	60" maximum height
Tike's Peak children's area	48" maximum height

TYPHOON LAGOON WATER PARK

Bay Slides	60" minimum height
Crush 'n' Gusher	48" minimum height
Humunga Kowabunga slide	48" minimum height
Ketchakiddee Creek children's area	48" maximum height
Shark Reef saltwater reef swim *unless accompanied by adult:*	10 years minimum age
Wave Pool	*Adult supervision required*

DISNEYQUEST

Buzz Lightyear's AstroBlasters	51" minimum height
CyberSpace Mountain	51" minimum height
Mighty Ducks Pinball Slam	48" minimum height
Pirates of the Caribbean—Battle for Buccaneer Gold	35" minimum height

page 245). Although the alternatives may resolve some practical and logistical issues, be forewarned that your smaller children might nonetheless be resentful of their older (or taller) siblings who qualify to ride. A mom from Virginia bumped into just such a situation, writing:

> You mention height requirements for rides but not the intense sibling jealousy this can generate. Frontierland was a real problem in that respect. Our very petite 5-year-old, to her outrage, was stuck hanging around while our 8-year-old went on Splash Mountain and Big Thunder Mountain with Grandma and Granddad, and the nearby alternatives weren't helpful (too long a line for rafts to Tom Sawyer Island, etc.). If we had thought ahead, we would have left the younger kid with one of the grown-ups for another roller-coaster ride or two and then met up later at a designated point.

The reader makes a valid point, though in practical terms splitting the group and meeting up later can be more complicated than she might imagine. If you choose to split up, ask the Disney greeter at the entrance to the attraction(s) with height requirements how long the wait is. Tack 5 minutes for riding onto the anticipated wait, and then add 5 or so minutes to exit and reach the meeting point for an approximate sense of how long the younger kids (and their supervising adult) will have to do other stuff. Our guess is that even with a long line for the rafts, the reader would have had more than sufficient time to take her daughter to Tom Sawyer Island while the sib rode Splash Mountain and Big Thunder Mountain Railroad with the grandparents. For sure she had time to tour the Swiss Family Treehouse in adjacent Adventureland.

WAITING-LINE STRATEGIES FOR ADULTS WITH YOUNG CHILDREN

CHILDREN HOLD UP BETTER through the day if you minimize the time they spend in lines. Arriving early and using our touring plans immensely reduces waiting. Here are additional ways to reduce stress for children:

1. LINE GAMES Wise parents anticipate restlessness in line and plan activities to reduce the stress and boredom. In the morning, have waiting children discuss what they want to see and do during the day. Later, watch for and count Disney characters or play simple guessing games such as 20 Questions. Lines move continuously, so games requiring pen and paper are impractical. The holding area of a theater attraction, however, is a different story. Here, tic-tac-toe, hangman, drawing, and coloring make the time fly by. As an alternative we've provided a trivia game for each park, developed by Walt Disney World trivia guru Lou Mongello, author of *The Walt Disney World Trivia Book, Volumes 1 and 2*; see **intrepidtraveler.com**.

2. SWITCHING OFF Several attractions have minimum height and/or age requirements. Some couples with children too small or too young forgo these attractions, while others take turns riding. Missing some of

Disney's best rides is an unnecessary sacrifice, and waiting in line twice for the same ride is a tremendous waste of time.

ATTRACTIONS WHERE SWITCHING OFF IS COMMON	
THE MAGIC KINGDOM	**DISNEY'S ANIMAL KINGDOM**
Big Thunder Mountain Railroad	DINOSAUR
Seven Dwarfs Mine Train	Expedition Everest
Space Mountain	Kali River Rapids
Splash Mountain	Primeval Whirl
Stitch's Great Escape!	
EPCOT	**DISNEY'S HOLLYWOOD STUDIOS**
Mission: SPACE	Rock 'n' Roller Coaster
Test Track	Star Tours—The Adventures Continue
	The Twilight Zone Tower of Terror

Instead, take advantage of "switching off," also known as "The Baby Swap" or "The Rider Swap" (or "The Baby/Rider Switch"). To switch off, there must be at least two adults. Adults and children wait in line together. When you reach a cast member, say you want to switch off. The cast member will allow everyone, including young children, to enter the attraction. When you reach the loading area, one adult rides while the other exits with the kids. Then the riding adult disembarks and takes charge of the children while the other adult rides. A third member of the party, either an adult or an older child, can ride twice, once with each switching-off adult, so that the switching-off adults don't have to ride alone.

On most Fastpass attractions, Disney handles switching off somewhat differently. When you tell the cast member that you want to switch off, he or she will issue you a special "rider exchange" Fastpass good for three people. One parent and the nonriding child (or children) will at that point be asked to leave the line. When those riding reunite with the waiting adult, the waiting adult and two other persons from the party can ride using the special Fastpass. This system eliminates confusion and congestion at the boarding area while sparing the nonriding adult and child the tedium and physical exertion of waiting in line.

3. COMBINING THE FASTPASS SYSTEM WITH SWITCHING OFF We expect Disney to replace Fastpass with Fastpass+ in late 2013 or early 2014 (see page 234). While the old system is in place, you can incorporate Fastpasses into switching off in order to secure passes for multiple attractions at the same time. This is of enormous benefit for larger groups.

In the Fastpass system, each ticket is limited to one Fastpass at a time. The holder of the Fastpass for one attraction may not acquire a Fastpass for a second attraction until the return window indicated on the original Fastpass has begun. Only then can a ticket-holder

seek a Fastpass for a second attraction, but the "rider exchange" is a game-changer for those who are serious about time efficiency.

Because the rider-exchange pass can be used by the adult holding it as well as by three companions, this yields a "four for the price of one" scenario in terms of Fastpass currency.

Depending on size and number of ticket-bearers, this strategy has the potential to hold Fastpasses for as many as five attractions at any given time while still maintaining the ability to get the entire group on each attraction with a single swap. This mass Fastpass acquisition is accomplished by dividing the group's tickets for Fastpasses at different attraction kiosks, but the maximum number of attractions a party can exploit in this way diminishes as the size of the group increases.

Using the strategy to its fullest, a family of two adults and four ticket-bearing children, one of whom is unable or unwilling to ride, can divide their tickets into five groups. One ticket would be used to obtain a Fastpass at Attraction A, another to get a Fastpass at Attraction B. The pattern would continue for acquiring tickets for Attractions C, D, and E simultaneously. With the attraction of the earliest Fastpass time stamp designated Attraction A, an adult wielding the Fastpass for that attraction would request a rider-exchange pass by approaching the cast member at the standby entrance. After securing the exchange pass and giving it to the waiting adult, the riding adult would use his Fastpass to board the ride. Once he rejoins his party, the second adult—accompanied by the three kids who are riding—would present the switch-off pass to the cast member at the Fastpass Return entrance. All four family members would be permitted to enter the Fastpass lane for the ride, while the first adult would remain with the nonriding child. Upon the return of the second group, the same procedure could be followed for the remaining four Fastpass attractions without the family having to wait an extended period for the assigned time-frames.

This scenario may seem unappealing, as it would require an adult who was always willing to ride solo as well as some serious team cooperation in gathering Fastpasses from all corners of the park. For that reason, we see dividing the group's tickets into thirds and using them for three different attractions as a more reasonable option, provided the number of riders in the party doesn't exceed six. *Note:* We don't expect this loophole to survive the transition to Fastpass+. Use it while you can.

4. LAST-MINUTE COLD FEET If your young child gets cold feet just before boarding a ride where there's no age or height requirement, you usually can arrange a switch-off with the loading attendant. (This happens frequently in Pirates of the Caribbean's dungeon waiting area.)

No law says you have to ride. If you reach the boarding area and someone is unhappy, tell an attendant you've changed your mind and you'll be shown the way out.

5. CATCH-22 AT TOMORROWLAND SPEEDWAY Though Tomorrowland Speedway is a great treat for young children, they're required to be 54 inches tall in order to drive unassisted. Few children age 6 and younger measure up, so the ride is essentially withheld from the very age group that would most enjoy it. To resolve this catch-22, go on the ride with your small child. The attendants will assume that you will drive. After getting into the car, shift your child over behind the steering wheel. From your position, you will still be able to control the foot pedals. Children will feel like they're really driving, and because the car travels on a self-guiding track, there's no way they can make a mistake while steering.

CHARACTER ANALYSIS

THE LARGE, FRIENDLY COSTUMED VERSIONS of Mickey, Minnie, Donald, Goofy, and others—known as Disney characters—provide a link between Disney animated films and the theme parks. To people emotionally invested, the characters in Disney films are as real as next-door neighbors, never mind that they're just drawings on plastic. In recent years, theme park personifications of the characters also have become real to us. It's not just a person in a mouse costume we see; it is Mickey himself. Similarly, meeting Goofy or Snow White in Fantasyland is an encounter with a celebrity, a memory to be treasured.

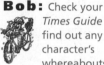 **Bob:** Check your *Times Guide* to find out any character's whereabouts in the parks.

While Disney animated-film characters number in the hundreds, only about 250 have been brought to life in costume. Of these, fewer than a fifth mix with guests; the others perform in shows or parades. Originally confined to the Magic Kingdom, characters are now found in all major theme parks and at Disney Deluxe resorts that host character meals.

CHARACTER WATCHING

CHARACTER WATCHING HAS BECOME A PASTIME. Families once were content to meet a character occasionally. They now pursue them relentlessly, armed with autograph books and cameras. Some characters are only rarely seen, so character watching has become character collecting. (To cash in on character collecting, Disney sells autograph books throughout the World.) Mickey, Minnie, and Goofy seem to be everywhere. But some characters, such as the Queen of Hearts and Friar Tuck, seldom come out, and quite a few appear only in parades or stage shows. Other characters appear only in a location consistent with their starring role. The Fairy Godmother is often near Cinderella Castle in Fantasyland, while Buzz Lightyear appears close to his eponymous attraction in Tomorrowland.

A Brooklyn dad complains that character collecting has gotten out of hand:

This year, when we took our youngest child (who is now 8 years old), he had already seen his siblings' collection and was determined to outdo them. However, rather than random meetings, the characters are now available practically all day long at different locations, according to a printed schedule, which our son was old enough to read. We spent more time standing in line for autographs than we did for the most popular rides!

A family from Birmingham, Alabama, found some benefit in their children's pursuit of characters:

We had no idea we'd be caught up in this madness, but after my daughters grabbed your guidebook to get Pocahontas to sign it (we had no blank paper), we quickly bought a Disney autograph book and gave in. It was actually the highlight of their trip, and my son even got into the act by helping get places in line for his sisters. They LOVED looking for characters. It was an amazing, totally unexpected part of our visit.

"THEN SOME CONFUSION HAPPENED" Children sometimes become lost at character encounters. Usually, there's a lot of activity around a character, with both adults and children touching it or posing for pictures. Most commonly, Mom and Dad stay in the crowd while Junior approaches the character. In the excitement and with the character moving around, Junior heads in the wrong direction to look for Mom and Dad. In the words of a Salt Lake City mom: "Milo was shaking hands with Dopey one minute, then some confusion happened and Milo was gone."

Bob: Our advice for parents with preschoolers is to stay with the kids when they meet characters, stepping back only to take a quick picture.

CHARACTER DINING: WHAT TO EXPECT

BECAUSE OF THE INCREDIBLE POPULARITY of character dining, reservations can be hard to come by if you wait until a couple of months before your vacation to book your choices. What's more, if you want to book a character meal, you must provide Disney with a credit-card number. Your card will be charged $10 *per person* if you no-show or cancel your reservation less than 24 hours in advance; you may, however, reschedule with no penalty. See "Getting an Advance Reservation at Popular Restaurants" (page 144) for the full story.

At very popular character meals like the breakfast at Cinderella's Royal Table, you're required to make a for-real reservation and guarantee it with a for-real deposit.

Liliane: Even with Advance Reservations, expect to wait 10–20 minutes to be seated.

Character meals are bustling affairs held in hotels' or theme parks' largest full-service restaurants. Character breakfasts offer a fixed menu served individually, family-style, or on a buffet. The typical breakfast includes scrambled eggs; bacon, sausage, and ham; hash browns; waffles or French toast; biscuits, rolls, or pastries; and fruit. With family-style service, the meal is served in large skillets or platters at your table. The character breakfast at Akershus Royal Banquet Hall, for example, is served family-style and consists of typical breakfast fare such as eggs, bacon and sausage, and Danish pastries. Seconds (or thirds) are free. Buffets offer much the same fare, but you fetch it yourself.

Character dinners range from a set menu to buffets to ordering off the menu. Character-dinner buffets, such as those at 1900 Park Fare at the Grand Floridian and Chef Mickey's at the Contemporary Resort, separate the kids' fare from the grown-ups', though everyone is free to eat from both lines. Typically, the children's buffet includes hamburgers, hot dogs, pizza, fish sticks, chicken nuggets, macaroni and cheese, and peanut-butter-and-jelly sandwiches. Selections at the adult buffet usually include prime rib or other carved meat, baked or broiled Florida seafood, pasta, chicken, an ethnic dish or two, vegetables, potatoes, and salad.

At all meals, characters circulate around the room while you eat. During your meal, each of the three to five characters present will visit your table, arriving one at a time to cuddle the kids (and sometimes the adults), pose for photos, and sign autographs. Keep autograph books (with pens) handy and cameras or mobile phones at the ready. For the best photos, adults should sit across the table from their children. Seat the children where characters can easily reach them. If a table is against a wall, for example, adults should sit with their backs to the wall and children on the aisle.

Servers generally don't rush you to leave after you've eaten—you can stay as long as you wish to enjoy the characters. Remember, however, that lots of eager kids and adults are waiting not so patiently to be admitted.

"Casting? There's been a mistake. We were supposed to get the Assorted Character Package with one Mickey, one Goofy, one Donald . . . "

When To Go

Attending a character breakfast usually prevents you from arriving at the theme parks in time for opening. Because early morning is best for touring and you don't want to burn daylight lingering over breakfast, we suggest the following:

1. Schedule your in-park character breakfast for the first seating if the park opens at 9 a.m. or later. You'll be admitted to the park before other guests (admission is still required) through a special line at the turnstiles. Arrive early to be among the first parties seated.

2. Go to a character dinner or lunch instead of breakfast. It'll be a nice break.

3. Schedule the last seating for breakfast. Have a light snack such as cereal or bagels before you head to the parks for opening, hit the most popular attractions until 10:15 or so, and then head to brunch. The buffet should keep you fueled until dinner, especially if you eat another light snack in the afternoon.

4. Go on your arrival or departure day. The day you arrive and check in is usually good for a character dinner. Settle at your hotel, swim, then dine with the characters. This strategy has the added benefit of exposing your children to the characters before chance encounters at the parks. Some children, moreover, won't settle down to enjoy the parks until they have seen Mickey. Departure day also is good for a character meal. Schedule a character breakfast on your check-out day before you head for the airport or begin your drive home.

5. Go on a rest day. If you plan to stay five or more days, you'll probably take a day or half-day from touring to rest or do something else. These are perfect days for a character meal.

How To Choose a Character Meal

Many readers ask for advice about character meals. This question from a Waterloo, Iowa, mom is typical:

> Are all character breakfasts pretty much the same, or are some better than others? How should I go about choosing one?

Liliane: If you've secured Advance Reservations for a character meal, I say roll out the costume chest. Dress up your little one—from princess to pirate, anything goes.

In fact, some are better, sometimes much better. When we evaluate character meals, we look for these things:

1. **THE CHARACTERS** The meals offer a diverse assortment of characters. Select a meal that features your kids' favorites. Check out our Character-Meal Hit Parade chart (see pages 254–255) to see which characters are assigned to each meal. Most restaurants stick with the same characters. Even so, check the lineup when you call to make Advance Reservations.

2. **ATTENTION FROM THE CHARACTERS** At all character meals, characters circulate among guests, hugging children, posing for pictures, and signing autographs. How much time a character spends with you and your children depends primarily on the ratio of characters to guests. The more characters and fewer guests, the better. Because many character meals never fill to capacity, the character-to-guest ratios found in our Character-Meal Hit Parade chart (see pages 254–255) have been adjusted to reflect an average attendance. Even

so, there's quite a range. The best ratio is at Cinderella's Royal Table, where there's approximately one character to every 26 guests.

The worst ratio is theoretically at the Swan Resort's Garden Grove, where there could be as few as 1 character for every 198 guests. We say "theoretically," however, because in practice there are far fewer guests at the Garden Grove than at character meals in Disney-owned resorts, and often more characters. During one recent meal, friends of ours were literally the only guests in the restaurant for breakfast and had to ask the characters to leave them alone to eat.

3. **THE SETTING** Some character meals are in exotic settings. For others, moving the event to an elementary-school cafeteria would be an improvement. Our chart rates each meal's setting with the familiar scale of zero (worst) to five (best) stars. Two restaurants, Cinderella's Royal Table in the Magic Kingdom and The Garden Grill Restaurant in the Land Pavilion at Epcot, deserve special mention. Cinderella's Royal Table is on the first and second floors of Cinderella Castle in Fantasyland, offering guests a look inside the castle. The Garden Grill is a revolving restaurant overlooking several scenes from the Living with The Land boat ride. Also at Epcot, the popular Princesses Character Breakfast is held in the castlelike Akershus Royal Banquet Hall. Though Chef Mickey's at the Contemporary Resort is rather sterile in appearance, it affords a great view of the monorail running through the hotel. Themes and settings of the remaining character-meal venues, while apparent to adults, will be lost on most children.

4. **THE FOOD** Although some food served at character meals is quite good, most is average (palatable but nothing to get excited about). In variety, consistency, and quality, restaurants generally do a better job with breakfast than with lunch or dinner (if served). Some restaurants offer a buffet, while others opt for one-skillet family-style service, in which all hot items are served from the same pot or skillet. To help you sort it out, we rate the food at each character meal in our chart using the five-star scale.

5. **THE PROGRAM** Some larger restaurants stage modest performances where the characters dance, head a parade around the room, or lead songs and cheers. For some guests, these activities give the meal a celebratory air; for others, they turn what was already mayhem into absolute chaos. Either way, the antics consume time the characters could spend with families at their table.

6. **NOISE** If you want to eat in peace, character meals are a bad choice. That said, some are much noisier than others. Our chart gives you an idea of what to expect.

7. **WHICH MEAL** Although breakfasts seem to be most popular, character lunches and dinners are usually more practical because they don't interfere with early-morning touring. During hot weather, a character lunch can be heavenly.

8. **COST** Dinners cost more than lunches and lunches more than breakfasts. Prices for meals (except at Cinderella Castle) vary only about $10 from the least expensive to the most expensive restaurant. Breakfasts run $21–$53 for adults and $11–$34 for kids ages 3–9. For character lunches, expect to pay

Continued on page 256

Character-Meal Hit Parade

1. CINDERELLA'S ROYAL TABLE   MAGIC KINGDOM

- **MEALS SERVED DAILY** Breakfast, lunch, and dinner   • **SETTING** ★★★★
- **CHARACTERS** Cinderella, Fairy Godmother, Aurora, Belle, Jasmine, Snow White
- **TYPE OF SERVICE** Fixed menu   • **FOOD VARIETY & QUALITY** ★★★
- **NOISE LEVEL** Quiet   • **CHARACTER–GUEST RATIO** 1:26

2. AKERSHUS ROYAL BANQUET HALL   EPCOT

- **MEALS SERVED** Breakfast, lunch, and dinner   • **SETTING** ★★★★
- **CHARACTERS** 4–6 characters chosen from Alice, Ariel, Belle, Jasmine, Mary Poppins, Mulan, Sleeping Beauty, Snow White
- **TYPE OF SERVICE** Family-style and menu (all you care to eat)
- **FOOD VARIETY & QUALITY** ★★★½
- **NOISE LEVEL** Quiet   • **CHARACTER–GUEST RATIO** 1:54

3. CHEF MICKEY'S   CONTEMPORARY

- **MEALS SERVED** Breakfast, dinner   • **SETTING** ★★★
- **CHARACTERS** Mickey, Minnie, Donald, Goofy, Pluto (sometimes Chip 'n' Dale)
- **TYPE OF SERVICE** Buffet
- **FOOD VARIETY & QUALITY** breakfast ★★★ dinner ★★★½
- **NOISE LEVEL** Loud   • **CHARACTER–GUEST RATIO** 1:56

4. THE CRYSTAL PALACE   MAGIC KINGDOM

- **MEALS SERVED** Breakfast, lunch, and dinner   • **SETTING** ★★★
- **CHARACTERS** Pooh, Eeyore, Piglet, Tigger
- **TYPE OF SERVICE** Buffet
- **FOOD VARIETY & QUALITY** breakfast ★★½   lunch and dinner ★★★
- **NOISE LEVEL** Very loud
- **CHARACTER–GUEST RATIO** breakfast 1:67 lunch and dinner 1:89

5. 1900 PARK FARE   GRAND FLORIDIAN

- **MEALS SERVED** Breakfast, dinner   • **SETTING** ★★★
- **CHARACTERS** *Breakfast:* Mary Poppins, Alice, Mad Hatter, Pooh *Dinner:* Cinderella, Prince Charming, Lady Tremaine, the two stepsisters
- **TYPE OF SERVICE** Buffet
- **FOOD VARIETY & QUALITY** breakfast ★★★ dinner ★★★½
- **NOISE LEVEL** Moderate
- **CHARACTER–GUEST RATIO** breakfast 1:54 dinner 1:44

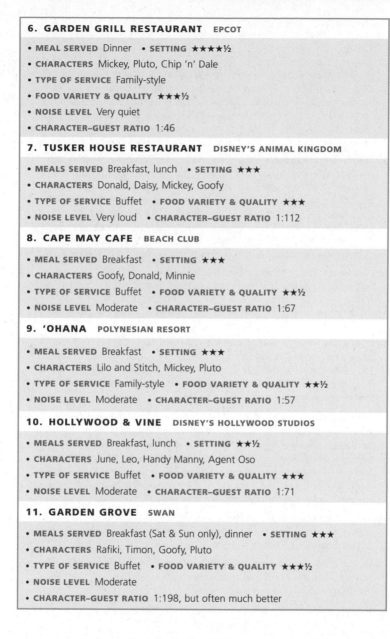

6. GARDEN GRILL RESTAURANT EPCOT

- **MEAL SERVED** Dinner • **SETTING** ★★★★½
- **CHARACTERS** Mickey, Pluto, Chip 'n' Dale
- **TYPE OF SERVICE** Family-style
- **FOOD VARIETY & QUALITY** ★★★½
- **NOISE LEVEL** Very quiet
- **CHARACTER–GUEST RATIO** 1:46

7. TUSKER HOUSE RESTAURANT DISNEY'S ANIMAL KINGDOM

- **MEALS SERVED** Breakfast, lunch • **SETTING** ★★★
- **CHARACTERS** Donald, Daisy, Mickey, Goofy
- **TYPE OF SERVICE** Buffet • **FOOD VARIETY & QUALITY** ★★★
- **NOISE LEVEL** Very loud • **CHARACTER–GUEST RATIO** 1:112

8. CAPE MAY CAFE BEACH CLUB

- **MEAL SERVED** Breakfast • **SETTING** ★★★
- **CHARACTERS** Goofy, Donald, Minnie
- **TYPE OF SERVICE** Buffet • **FOOD VARIETY & QUALITY** ★★½
- **NOISE LEVEL** Moderate • **CHARACTER–GUEST RATIO** 1:67

9. 'OHANA POLYNESIAN RESORT

- **MEAL SERVED** Breakfast • **SETTING** ★★★
- **CHARACTERS** Lilo and Stitch, Mickey, Pluto
- **TYPE OF SERVICE** Family-style • **FOOD VARIETY & QUALITY** ★★½
- **NOISE LEVEL** Moderate • **CHARACTER–GUEST RATIO** 1:57

10. HOLLYWOOD & VINE DISNEY'S HOLLYWOOD STUDIOS

- **MEALS SERVED** Breakfast, lunch • **SETTING** ★★½
- **CHARACTERS** June, Leo, Handy Manny, Agent Oso
- **TYPE OF SERVICE** Buffet • **FOOD VARIETY & QUALITY** ★★★
- **NOISE LEVEL** Moderate • **CHARACTER–GUEST RATIO** 1:71

11. GARDEN GROVE SWAN

- **MEALS SERVED** Breakfast (Sat & Sun only), dinner • **SETTING** ★★★
- **CHARACTERS** Rafiki, Timon, Goofy, Pluto
- **TYPE OF SERVICE** Buffet • **FOOD VARIETY & QUALITY** ★★★½
- **NOISE LEVEL** Moderate
- **CHARACTER–GUEST RATIO** 1:198, but often much better

Continued from page 253

$26–$57 for adults and $15–$36 for kids. Dinners are $36–$67 for adults and $14–$41 for children. Little ones ages 2 years and younger eat free. The meals at the high end of the price range are at Cinderella's Royal Table in the Magic Kingdom and Akershus Royal Banquet Hall at Epcot. The reasons for the sky-high prices: (1) Cinderella's Royal Table is small but in great demand and (2) the prices at Cinderella's and Akershus include a set of photos of your group taken by a Disney photographer. Whereas photos at other venues are optional, at Cindy's and Akershus you don't have a say in the matter.

9. ADVANCE RESERVATIONS Disney makes Advance Reservations for character meals 180 days before you wish to dine (Disney resort guests can reserve 190 days out, or 10 additional days in advance); moreover, Disney resort guests can make Advance Reservations for all meals during their stay. Advance Reservations for most character meals are easy to obtain even if you call only a couple of weeks before you leave home. Meals at Cinderella's Royal Table and Be Our Guest are another story. For these two, you'll need our strategy (see Part Four), as well as help from Congress and the Pope.

10. "FRIENDS" For some venues, Disney has stopped specifying characters scheduled for a particular meal. Instead, they say it's a given character "and friends"—for example, "Pooh and friends," meaning Eeyore, Piglet, and Tigger, or some combination thereof, or "Mickey and friends" with some assortment chosen among Minnie, Goofy, Pluto, Donald, Daisy, Chip, and Dale.

11. THE BUM'S RUSH Most character meals are leisurely affairs, and you can usually stay as long as you want. An exception is Cinderella's Royal Table in the Magic Kingdom. Because Cindy's is in such high demand, the restaurant does everything short of pre-chewing your food to move you through, as this European mother of a 5-year-old can attest:

We dined a lot, did three character meals and a few signature restaurants, and every meal was awesome except for lunch with Cinderella in the castle. While I'd often read it wouldn't be a rushed affair, it was exactly that. We had barely sat down when the appetizers were thrown on our table, the princesses each spent just a few seconds with our daughter—almost no interaction—and the side dishes were cold. We were out of there within 40 minutes and felt very stressed. Considering the price for the meal, I cannot recommend it.

12. BOYS To answer a common reader question, most character meals featuring Disney princesses include some element to appeal to the young roughnecks. A Texas mom shares her experience:

We ate at Cinderella's Royal Table for lunch, and my sons were made to feel very welcome. They loved the swords they received and have enjoyed "fight-ing off the dragons" with them.

(Presumably, "fighting off the dragons" did not occur during the meal. Princesses are sticklers for decorum, after all.)

Boosting Sales of Mementos and Souvenirs

Usually when Disney sees a horse carrying moneybags, it rides the beast until it drops. Disney's latest scheme of bundling photos in the price of character meals at Cinderella's Royal Table extends to Akershus Royal Banquet Hall at Epcot. Adding photos of your group taken by a Disney photographer is Disney's justification for raising the price of the character meals by about 60%. Disney insists that you are getting the photos at a bargain price. This is well and good if you're in the market, but if buying photos was not in your plans, well, they gotcha. It's a matter of some conjecture how far Disney will run with this idea. Maybe next year the price will be $200 and include fanciful medieval costumes for your entire party (charges for the changing room and locker to store your street clothes not included).

Getting an Advance Reservation at Cinderella's Royal Table

Once upon a time, breakfast was the only character meal at Cinderella Castle in the Magic Kingdom. Reservations for every table were gone within minutes of becoming available each morning. Disney responded to this popularity by adding character lunches and dinners—and jacking up the price to almost $60 per adult. As a result, it's now much easier to get into Cinderella's Royal Table for some meals during your stay. Also, the opening of the wildly popular Be Our Guest restaurant in the new Fantasyland has taken a lot of pressure off Cindy's. If you're visiting during peak periods or you've got to have a reservation at a specific, popular time, see our Advance Reservation tips starting on page 144.

DISNEY'S ROYAL ALTERNATIVES If you're unwilling to fund Cinderella's shoe habit or you simply weren't able to get an Advance Reservation before young Ariel graduates from college, rest assured there are other venues that will feed you in the company of princesses.

Akershus Royal Banquet Hall, in the Norway Pavilion of Epcot's World Showcase, serves family-style breakfast, lunch, and dinner. Ariel, Cinderella, Snow White, and Belle are regulars. Entrees are a combination of traditional buffet fare and the occasional Scandinavian dish.

Dinner at the Grand Floridian's **1900 Park Fare** features the whole crew from Cinderella, including Lady Tremaine and the stepsisters (breakfast is a character buffet with Pooh and friends). At $42 per adult and $21 for children age 9 and under, this is a far more economical option for diners wishing to get their princess on, and the stepsisters are an absolute hoot. This meal is also a little more boy-friendly if you're entertaining a mixed crowd. Finally, remember that your princess may be feeding off your own excitement over eating in the Castle—she might be just as happy with a plastic crown purchased in the gift shop and a burger from Cosmic Ray's.

Liliane: The character meals at Akershus are my all-time favorite. There are plenty of princesses, I love the food, and a keepsake picture with one of the princesses is included in the price of the meal.

OTHER CHARACTER EVENTS

A CAMPFIRE AND SING-ALONG are held nightly (times vary with the season) near the Meadow Trading Post and Bike Barn at **Fort**

Wilderness Resort & Campground. Chip 'n' Dale lead the songs, and a Disney film is shown. The program is free and open to Disney resort guests (☎ 407-824-2900). Another character encounter at Fort Wilderness is **Mickey's Backyard BBQ,** held seasonally on Thursday and Saturday. See page 180 for details.

▮▮ STROLLERS

STROLLERS ARE AVAILABLE for rent at all four theme parks and the Downtown Disney area (single stroller, $15 per day with no deposit, $13 per day for the entire stay; double stroller, $31 per day with no deposit, $27 per day for the entire stay; stroller rentals at Downtown Disney require a $100 credit card deposit; double strollers not available at Downtown Disney). Strollers are welcome at Blizzard Beach and Typhoon Lagoon, but no rentals are available. With multiday rentals, you can skip the rental line entirely after your first visit—just head over to the stroller-handout area, show your receipt, and you'll be wheeling out of there in no time. If you rent a stroller at the Magic Kingdom and you decide to go to Epcot, Disney's Animal Kingdom, or Disney's Hollywood Studios, turn in your Magic Kingdom stroller and present your receipt at the next park. You'll be issued another stroller at no additional charge.

With Disney pricing its own stroller rentals so high, several Orlando companies have sprung up, able to undercut Disney's prices, provide more comfortable strollers, and deliver them to your hotel. Most of the larger companies offer the same stroller models (the Baby Jogger City Mini Single, for example), so the primary differences between the companies are price and service.

Liliane: Rental strollers are too large for all infants and many toddlers. If you plan to rent a stroller for your infant or toddler, bring pillows, cushions, or rolled towels to buttress him in.

To rate stroller companies, we had mom and *Unofficial Guide* researcher Scarlett Litton, along with **touringplans.com** blogger Shelley Caran, rent the same strollers from each company, use the strollers in the parks, and return them. Our evaluation covers the overall experience, from the ease with which the stroller was rented to the delivery of the stroller, its condition upon arrival, and the return process.

Baby Wheels Orlando (☎ 800-510-2480; **babywheelsorlando .com**) had the best combination of price and service. Upon request, Baby Wheels will include a rain cover and beverage cooler free—both of which are useful during Florida's summer months. A one-day rental is $30, three nights are $40, and five nights are $48. Thus, the break-even point for using Baby Wheels Orlando instead of Disney is four nights. Drop-off and pickup went without incident, and customer service is excellent.

We also recommend **Orlando Stroller Rentals, LLC** (☎ 800-281-0884; **orlandostrollerrentals.com**), which is slightly more expensive (rain covers, for instance, are $10 instead of free) and whose strollers have a few more miles on them. The service is excellent, though.

Another important matter is protection against the sun. Liliane always used a stroller with an adjustable canopy and also had lightweight pieces of cloth handy to protect her child from the sun. You can use anything for that purpose; a receiving blanket works well. Liliane used clothespins and safety pins to attach the pieces to the canopy.

Strollers are a must for infants and toddlers, but we've observed many sharp parents renting strollers for somewhat older children (up to age 5 or so). The stroller prevents parents from having to carry children when they sag and provides a convenient place to carry water and snacks.

A family from Tulsa, Oklahoma, recommends springing for a double stroller:

We rent a double for baggage room or in case the older child gets tired of walking.

If you go to your hotel for a break and intend to return to the park, leave your rental stroller by an attraction near the park entrance, marking it with something personal, such as a bandanna. When you return, your stroller will be waiting.

Bringing your own stroller is permitted. However, only collapsible strollers are allowed on monorails, parking-lot trams, and buses. Your stroller is unlikely to be stolen, but mark it with your name.

Having her own stroller was indispensable to a Mechanicsville, Virginia, mother of two toddlers:

How I was going to manage to get the kids from the parking lot to the park was a big worry for me before I made the trip. I didn't read anywhere that it was possible to walk to the entrance of the parks instead of taking the tram, so I wasn't sure I could do it.

I found that for me personally, since I have two kids aged 1 and 2, it was easier to walk to the entrance of the park from the parking lot with the kids in (my own) stroller than to take the kids out of the stroller, fold the stroller (while trying to control the two kids and associated gear), load the stroller and the kids onto the tram, etc. No matter where I was parked, I could always just walk to the entrance. It sometimes took awhile, but it was easier for me.

An Oklahoma mom, however, reports a bad experience with bringing her own stroller:

> *The first time we took our kids, we had a large stroller (big mistake). It is so much easier to rent one in the park. The large (personally owned) strollers are nearly impossible to get on the buses and are a hassle at the airport. I remember feeling dread when a bus pulled up that was even semifull of people. People look at you like you have a cage full of live chickens when you drag heavy strollers onto the bus.*

STROLLER WARS Sometimes strollers disappear while you're enjoying a ride or show. Disney staff will often rearrange strollers parked outside an attraction. This may be done to tidy up or to clear a walkway. Don't assume that your stroller is stolen because it isn't where you left it. It may be neatly arranged a few feet away—or perhaps more than a few feet away.

Sometimes, however, strollers are taken by mistake or ripped off by people not wanting to spend time replacing one that's missing. Don't be alarmed if yours disappears. You won't have to buy it, and you'll be issued a new one.

Bob: Don't try to lock your stroller to a fence, post, or anything else at WDW. You'll get in big trouble.

You'd be surprised at how many people are injured by strollers pushed by parents who are aggressive or in a hurry. Given the number of strollers, pedestrians, and tight spaces, mishaps are inevitable on both sides. A simple apology and a smile are usually the best remediation.

WHEN KIDS GET LOST

IF ONE OF YOUR CHILDREN gets separated from you, don't panic. All things considered, Walt Disney World is about the safest place to get lost we can think of. Disney cast members are trained to watch for seemingly lost kids, and because children become detached from parents so frequently in the theme parks, cast members know exactly what to do.

If you lose a child in the Magic Kingdom, report it to a Disney employee, and then check at the Baby Care Center and at City Hall, where lost-children logs are kept. At Epcot, report the loss, then check at the Baby Care Center in the Odyssey Center. At Disney's Hollywood Studios, report the loss at the Guest Service Building, at the entrance end of Hollywood Boulevard. At Disney's Animal Kingdom, go to the Baby Care Center in Discovery Island. Paging isn't used, but in an emergency, an "all-points bulletin" can be issued throughout the park(s) via internal communications. If a Disney employee encounters a lost child, he or she will take the child immediately to the park's Baby Care Center.

As comforting as this knowledge is, however, it's nevertheless scary when a child turns up missing. Fortunately, circumstances surrounding a child becoming lost are fairly predictable and, for the most part, are also preventable.

Sew a label into each child's shirt that states his or her name, your name, the name of your hotel, and if you have one, your cell phone number. Accomplish the same thing by writing the information on a strip of masking tape.

Other than just blending in, children tend to become separated from their parents under remarkably similar circumstances:

Bob: We suggest that children younger than age 8 be color-coded by dressing them in vacation uniforms with distinctively colored T-shirts or equally eye-catching apparel.

1. **PREOCCUPIED SOLO PARENT** In this situation, the party's only adult is preoccupied with something like buying refreshments, loading the camera, or using the restroom. Junior is there one second and gone the next.

2. **THE HIDDEN EXIT** Sometimes parents wait on the sidelines while two or more young children experience a ride together. Parents expect the kids to exit in one place and, lo and behold, the youngsters pop out somewhere else. Exits from some attractions are distant from the entrances. Make sure you know exactly where your children will emerge before letting them ride by themselves. If in doubt, ask a cast member.

3. **AFTER THE SHOW** At the end of many shows and rides, a Disney staffer will announce, "Check for personal belongings and take small children by the hand." When dozens, if not hundreds, of people leave an attraction simultaneously, it's surprisingly easy for parents to lose contact with their children unless they have them directly in tow.

4. **RESTROOM PROBLEMS** Mom tells 6-year-old Tommy, "I'll be sitting on this bench when you come out of the restroom." Three possibilities: One, Tommy exits through a different door and becomes disoriented (Mom may not know there's another door). Two, Mom decides she also will use the restroom, and Tommy emerges to find her gone. Three, Mom pokes around in a shop while keeping an eye on the bench but misses Tommy when he comes out.

If you can't find a companion- or family-accessible restroom, make sure there's only one exit. The restroom on a passageway between Frontierland and Adventureland in the Magic Kingdom is the all-time worst for disorienting visitors. Children and adults alike have walked in from the Adventureland side and walked out on the Frontierland side (and vice versa). Adults realize quickly that something is wrong. Children, however, sometimes fail to recognize the problem. Designate a distinctive meeting spot and give clear instructions: "I'll meet you by this flagpole. If you get out first, stay right here." Have your child repeat the directions back to you.

5. **PARADES** There are many parades and shows at which the audience stands. Children tend to jockey for a better view. By moving a little this way and that, the child quickly puts distance between you before either of you notices.

6. MASS MOVEMENTS Be on guard when huge crowds disperse after fireworks or a parade, or at park closing. With 20,000–40,000 people at once in an area, it's very easy to get separated from a child or others in your party. Use extra caution after the evening parade and fireworks in the Magic Kingdom, *Fantasmic!* at Disney's Hollywood Studios, or *IllumiNations* at Epcot. Families should have specific plans for where to meet if they get separated.

7. CHARACTER GREETINGS Activity and confusion are common when the Disney characters appear, and children can slip out of sight. See "Then Some Confusion Happened" on page 250.

8. GETTING LOST AT DISNEY'S ANIMAL KINGDOM It's especially easy to lose a child in Animal Kingdom, particularly at the Oasis entryway, on the Maharajah Jungle Trek, and on the Pangani Forest Exploration Trail. Mom and Dad will stop to observe an animal. Junior stays close for a minute or so, and then, losing patience, wanders to the exhibit's other side or to a different exhibit.

9. LOST . . . IN THE ZONE More often than you'd think, kids don't realize they're lost. They are so distracted that they sometimes wander around for quite a while before they notice that their whole family has mysteriously disappeared. Fortunately, Disney cast members are trained to look out for kids who have zoned out and will either help them find their family or deposit them at the Baby Care Center.

LILIANE'S TIPS FOR KEEPING TRACK OF YOUR BROOD

ON A GOOD DAY, it's possible for Liliane to lose a cantaloupe in her purse. Thus challenged, she works overtime developing ways to hang on to her possessions, including her child. Here's what she has to say:

I've seen parents write their cell phone numbers on a child's leg with a felt-tip marker . . . effective but crude. Before you resort to that, or perhaps a cattle brand, consider some of the tips I've busted my brain dreaming up. My friends—some much ditzier than I—have used them with great success.

- On your very first day in the parks, teach your kids how to recognize a Disney cast member by pointing out the Disney name tags that they all wear. Instruct your children to find someone with such a name tag if they get separated from you.

- Same-colored T-shirts for the whole family will help you gather your troops in an easy and fun way. You can opt for just a uniform color or go the extra mile and have the T-shirts printed with a logo such as "The Brown Family's Assault on the Mouse." You might also include the date or the year of your visit. Your imagination is the limit. Light-colored T-shirts can even be autographed by the Disney characters.

- Clothing labels are great, of course. If you don't sew, buy labels that you can iron on the garment. If you own a cell phone, be sure to include the number on the label. If you do not own a cell phone, put in the phone number of the hotel where you'll be staying. Another option is a custom-made temporary tattoo with all the pertinent info. They're cheap, last two weeks, don't wash off, and solve the problem of having to sew or iron a label on every garment. (They can be purchased online at **safetytat.com** or **tattooswitha purpose.com**.)

- In pet stores you can have name tags printed for a very reasonable price. These are great to add to necklaces and bracelets or attach to your child's shoelace or belt loop.

- When you check into the hotel, take a business card of the hotel for each member in your party, especially those old enough to carry wallets and purses.

- Always agree on a meeting point before you see a parade, fireworks, and nighttime spectacles such as *IllumiNations* and *Fantasmic!* Make sure the meeting place is in the park (as opposed to the car or someplace outside the front gate).

- If you have a digital camera or cell phone camera, you may elect to take a picture of your kids every morning. If they get lost, the picture will show what they look like and what they are wearing.

- If all the members of your party have cell phones, it's easy to locate each other. Be aware, however, that the ambient noise in the parks is so loud that you probably won't hear your cell phone ring. Your best bet is to carry your phone in a front pants pocket and to program the phone to vibrate. If any of your younger kids carry cell phones, secure the phones with a strap. Even better, send text messages.

- Save key tags and luggage tags for use on items you bring to the parks, including your stroller, diaper bag, and backpack or hip pack.

- Don't underestimate the power of the permanent marker, such as a Sharpie. They are great for labeling pretty much anything. Mini-Sharpies are sold as clip-ons and are great for collecting character autographs. The Sharpie will also serve well for writing down the location of your car in the parking lot. (Bob suggests on my son's forehead.)

A word about keeping track of your park-admission passes: One minute you have them, the next you don't. The passes (which for Disney hotel guests also serve as a credit card and room key) are precious. They are also your key to obtaining Fastpasses and this, typically, is how they get lost. I have tried many ways of keeping track of my passes, but my all-time favorite is a clear badge-holder that you wear around your neck. It's perfect for holding admission passes, room keys, and some cash; best of all it is completely waterproof, and you can wear the case in the pool or at the water parks.

Tests of the new MagicBand admission wristbands demonstrate that they're difficult, but not impossible, to lose. Most adults will be fine, but slender children without much articulation between the forearm and wrist need to wear the band more tightly. If you're worried about the band slipping off, ask for an RFID card instead (see page 68).

PART SEVEN

The MAGIC KINGDOM

OPENED IN 1971, the Magic Kingdom was the first of Walt Disney World's four theme parks to be built. Many of the attractions found here are originals from that park opening, and a few—including Cinderella Castle, Pirates of the Caribbean, and Splash Mountain—have helped define the basic elements of theme-park attractions the world over. Indeed, the Magic Kingdom is undoubtedly what most people think of when Walt Disney World is mentioned.

Much of the Magic Kingdom was built by the same Disney team that built Disneyland two decades earlier. The remarkable achievement isn't that Disney could build a second, equally compelling theme park, but rather that it could do so on a much larger scale while keeping the fine details that make visiting a Disney park such an immersive experience.

At the Magic Kingdom, stroller, wheelchair, and ECV/ESV rentals are to the right of the train station, and lockers are on the station's ground floor. On your left as you enter Main Street is City Hall, the center for information, lost and found, guided tours, and entertainment schedules. Automated tellers (ATMs) are underneath the Main Street railroad station, near the Transportation and Ticket Center (TTC), near City Hall, near the Frontierland shooting gallery, near Pinocchio Village Haus in Fantasyland, and inside the Tomorrowland Arcade. Down Main Street and left around the central hub (toward Adventureland) are the Baby Care Center and a first-aid post. Disney no longer has pet-care facilities adjacent to the park, but the Best Friends Pet Resort across from Disney's Port Orleans Resort will provide a comfortable home away from home for Fido, Frisky, and all their pet pals.

If you don't already have a handout park map, get one at City Hall. The handout lists all attractions, shops, and eateries; provides helpful information about first aid, baby care, and assistance for the disabled; and gives tips for good photos. It also lists times for the day's special events, live entertainment, Disney character parades, concerts, and other activities. Additionally, it tells when and where to find Disney characters.

The guide map is supplemented by a daily entertainment schedule known as the *Times Guide,* which provides info on special Disney character appearances, shows and performances, parades, and street entertainment. It also identifies attractions that operate on a schedule different from normal park hours of operation. If you are lodging at a Walt Disney World resort hotel and the park is operating on an Extra Magic Hour evening schedule, make sure you also pick up the Extra Magic Hours "Evenings" flyer, which lists the attractions that are open late. All members of your party need to present a resort ID and theme-park ticket to participate in Extra Magic Hours.

Main Street ends at a central hub from which branch the entrances to the other five sections of the Magic Kingdom: Adventureland, Frontierland, Liberty Square, Fantasyland, and Tomorrowland.

In this and the following three chapters, we rate the individual attractions at each of the four major Disney theme parks. The authors' ratings, as well as ratings according to age group, are given on a scale of zero to five stars—the more stars, the better the attraction. The authors' rating is from the perspective of an adult. The authors, for example, might rate a ride such as Dumbo much lower than the age group for which the ride is intended, in this case, children. This rating, therefore, will more closely approximate how another adult will experience the attraction than how your children will like it. The bottleneck rating ranges 1–10; the higher the rating, the more congested the attraction. In general, try to experience attractions with a high bottleneck rating early in the morning (that is, 8–10:30 a.m.) before the park gets crowded, or late in the day when the crowd has diminished.

With the opening of the Seven Dwarfs Mine Train in 2014, the Magic Kingdom will complete the Fantasyland expansion begun in 2010. The first phase of New Fantasyland opened in 2012 with attractions and restaurants that quickly joined the Magic Kingdom's must-do list. Parents with small children race each morning to *Enchanted Tales with Belle,* an interactive stage show and character greeting, the way that teens head for Space Mountain. Families will line up for an hour or more to eat lunch at the new Be Our Guest restaurant, which serves the best food in the Magic Kingdom (dinner requires Advance Dining Reservations 180 days before your visit). We expect the Seven Dwarfs Mine Train to be a huge hit when it opens.

We've updated our Magic Kingdom touring plans to include all of the Magic Kingdom's new attractions and new traffic patterns. As with anything, things may change. Check **touringplans.com** for the latest developments and touring plan updates.

MAGIC KINGDOM FASTPASS LOOPHOLES

WE EXPECT DISNEY TO ROLL OUT its new Fastpass+ ride reservation system (see page 234) to replace the existing Fastpass in late 2013 or early 2014. While the old Fastpass system is still in place, there are a few quirks available in the Magic Kingdom for savvy readers to exploit. The Fastpass machines at the Mickey Mouse character greeting on Main

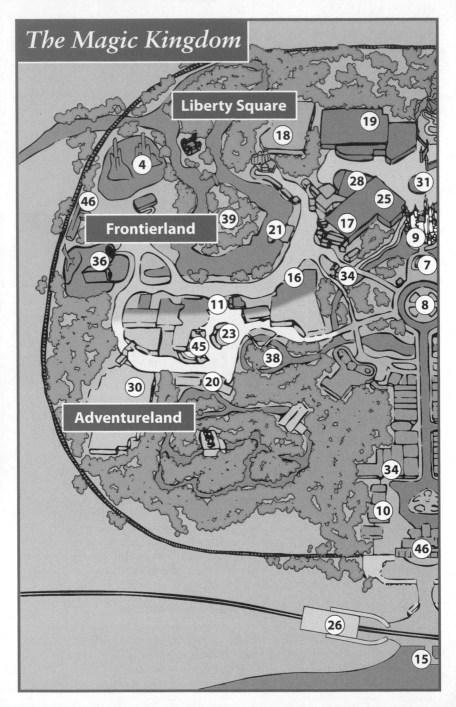

The Magic Kingdom

Liberty Square

Frontierland

Adventureland

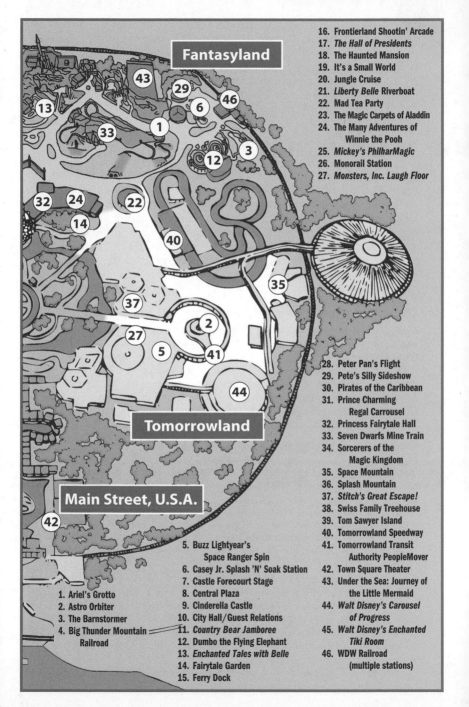

Fantasyland

Tomorrowland

Main Street, U.S.A.

16. Frontierland Shootin' Arcade
17. *The Hall of Presidents*
18. The Haunted Mansion
19. It's a Small World
20. Jungle Cruise
21. *Liberty Belle* Riverboat
22. Mad Tea Party
23. The Magic Carpets of Aladdin
24. The Many Adventures of
    Winnie the Pooh
25. *Mickey's PhilharMagic*
26. Monorail Station
27. *Monsters, Inc. Laugh Floor*

28. Peter Pan's Flight
29. Pete's Silly Sideshow
30. Pirates of the Caribbean
31. Prince Charming
    Regal Carrousel
32. Princess Fairytale Hall
33. Seven Dwarfs Mine Train
34. Sorcerers of the
    Magic Kingdom
35. Space Mountain
36. Splash Mountain
37. *Stitch's Great Escape!*
38. Swiss Family Treehouse
39. Tom Sawyer Island
40. Tomorrowland Speedway
41. Tomorrowland Transit
    Authority PeopleMover
42. Town Square Theater
43. Under the Sea: Journey of
    the Little Mermaid
44. *Walt Disney's Carousel
    of Progress*
45. *Walt Disney's Enchanted
    Tiki Room*
46. WDW Railroad
    (multiple stations)

5. Buzz Lightyear's
   Space Ranger Spin
6. Casey Jr. Splash 'N' Soak Station
7. Castle Forecourt Stage
8. Central Plaza
9. Cinderella Castle
10. City Hall/Guest Relations
11. *Country Bear Jamboree*
12. Dumbo the Flying Elephant
13. *Enchanted Tales with Belle*
14. Fairytale Garden
15. Ferry Dock

1. Ariel's Grotto
2. Astro Orbiter
3. The Barnstormer
4. Big Thunder Mountain
   Railroad

Street, and at Dumbo and the Barnstormer in Fantasyland, are disconnected from the rest of the Fastpass system. This means that it's possible to get a Fastpass for all three of these attractions just as fast as you can walk between them, and you can get another Fastpass for any other Magic Kingdom attraction immediately before or after too. Our computerized touring plans know of these loopholes. Disney can change these Fastpass settings at will, so there's no guarantee they'll work forever.

MAIN STREET, U.S.A.

BEGIN AND END YOUR VISIT ON MAIN STREET, which may open 30 minutes before and closes 30 minutes–1 hour after the rest of the park. It is easy to get sidetracked when entering Main Street, as this Disney-fied turn-of-the-19th-century small town street is lovely, with exceptional attention to detail. But remember: Time is of the essence, and the rest of the park is waiting to be discovered. The same goes for the one and only Cinderella Castle. Stick with your touring plan and return to Cinderella Castle and Main Street after you've experienced the must-dos on your list.

Character Greetings *(Fastpass)* ★★

Meet Mickey, Minnie, and other Disney characters throughout the day at the Town Square Theater on Main Street, to your right as you enter the park. Other characters may also be available. Check the *Times Guide* for details. If the wait to meet Mickey or the princesses appears long, you can obtain Fastpasses to schedule your visit. As mentioned earlier, Fastpasses for the character greeting venue are disconnected to the system, meaning that obtaining a Fastpass to see Mickey doesn't affect your ability to obtain additional Fastpasses.

Sorcerers of the Magic Kingdom ★★★

APPEAL BY AGE   PRESCHOOL ★★★½   GRADE SCHOOL ★★★★½   TEENS ★★★★
YOUNG ADULTS ★★★★   OVER 30 ★★★★   SENIORS ★★★

What it is Interactive game in which players must defeat villains spread around different lands. **Scope and scale** Minor attraction. **Fright potential** Loud but not frightening. **Bottleneck rating** 7. **When to go** Before 11 a.m. or after 8 p.m. **Special comments** Long lines to play. **Authors' rating** Great idea; ★★★. **Duration of presentation** About 2 minutes per step, 4 or 5 steps per game. **Probable waiting time per step** 10–15 minutes.

Sorcerers of the Magic Kingdom combines aspects of role-playing games such as Dungeons and Dragons with Disney characters and theme park attractions. Your objective is to help the wizard Merlin keep evildoers from taking over the Magic Kingdom. Merlin sends you on adventures in different parts of the park to fight these villains. Each land hosts a different adventure within the game, and there are different villains in each adventure.

The game is played with a set of trading cards—similar to baseball cards or Magic: The Gathering cards—with a different Disney character on each card. Each character possesses special properties that help it fight certain villains. Pick up the cards (free), plus a map showing where in the park you can play the game, at either the Fire Station on Main Street, U.S.A., or across from Sleepy Hollow Refreshments in Liberty Square.

You'll need your park ticket to pick up your first set of cards and start the game. One card, known as your key, is special because it links you to your game. You'll need to present your key card when you pick up a set of cards to start your next adventure.

When you pick up your first set of cards, you'll view an instructional video explaining how to use them and the object of the game. Then you'll be sent to another location in another land to start your first adventure. Each location in the park is associated with a unique symbol such as an eye or a feather. Look for these symbols on the map to find the best route to your starting point.

Each adventure consists of four or five stops in a particular land. At each stop, another story will play on a computer screen, outlining what your villain is trying to do. Merlin will ask you to cast a spell, using your character cards, to stop the villain. Hold one or more of your cards up to the video display to cast your spell. Cameras in the display read your card, deploy the spell, and show you the results.

The game has three levels: easy, medium, and hard. The easy version is the default and is appropriate for small children; holding up any one of your character cards is enough to defeat any villain. In more-advanced levels of the game, you need to display two or more character cards in specific combinations to defeat a particular villain. Different card combinations produce different spells, and only some spells work on certain characters in those advanced levels.

The audio at each step holds clues to which cards you should use against advanced villains. For example, if a villain says something like "Don't toy with me!" then you should look for cards with characters that are toys, such as the *Toy Story* characters; references to "being spotted" suggest using cards with characters from *101 Dalmatians;* and so on.

The game launched with an initial series of around 70 unique cards; you can obtain 5 new ones per day. Don't worry if you play more than once and end up with duplicate cards—a brisk trading market exists within the park, and it's fairly easy to find someone to trade with. Disney plans to issue new card series over time. On special event nights, such as Mickey's Not So Scary Halloween Party, a commemorative card is available in addition to the regular five-card package.

Sorcerers is fun and was immediately popular with guests. You'll probably encounter a line of five to ten people ahead of you at each portal, especially if you play during the afternoon. One complete adventure should take about 30–60 minutes to play, depending on how crowded the park is. If the line to pick up cards is too long at the Main Street Fire Station, try the Liberty Square distribution point.

A Pirate's Adventure: Treasures of the Seven Seas ★★

What it is Interactive game in which players take on the role of a pirate in an attempt to save Adventureland. **Scope and scale** Minor attraction. **Fright potential** Loud but not frightening. **Bottleneck rating** 7. **When to go** Before 11 a.m. or after 8 p.m. **Special comments** Long lines to play. **Authors' rating** Great idea but could be more interactive; ★★. **Duration of presentation** About 4 minutes per step, 4 or 5 steps per game. **Probable waiting time per step** 10–15 minutes.

Guests begin their journey at an old Cartography Shop (formerly the Crow's Nest store near Golden Oak Outpost) that has been converted into a central hub for adventurers to help locate missing treasures. Guests are given a talisman (an RFID card) that will help them on their journey. Players use the talisman to activate a screen that will assign them one of five different missions: Guardian's Curse, Blackbeard, Heads You Lose, Haven Defense, and The King's Ransom. Map and talisman in hand, guests are sent off to find their first location.

On their adventure, guests interact with Captain Jack Sparrow's famous compass and come in contact with things such as a parrot, an oyster, and a bobcat spirit, as well as a cannon and a treasure chest. If there are no lines, it takes approximately 20 minutes to complete all of the tasks in each mission. Guests may complete as many missions as they wish.

The game is much less interactive than Sorcerers of the Magic Kingdom and does not come with any trading cards. The game is geared toward younger kids, but like the Sorcerers of the Magic Kingdom, it will take out a big chunk of touring time, especially if you play during the later part of the day, as one adventure can take up 30–60 minutes to play.

Walt Disney World Railroad ★★½

APPEAL BY AGE PRESCHOOL ★★★★½ GRADE SCHOOL ★★★★ TEENS ★★★
YOUNG ADULTS ★★★★   OVER 30 ★★★★   SENIORS ★★★★

What it is Scenic railroad ride around perimeter of the Magic Kingdom and transportation to Frontierland and Fantasyland. **Scope and scale** Minor attraction. **Fright potential** Not frightening in any respect. **Bottleneck rating** 6. **When to go** Anytime; closed during parades. **Special comment** Main Street is usually the least congested station. **Authors' rating** Plenty to see; ★★½. **Duration of ride** About 20 minutes for a complete circuit. **Average wait in line per 100 people ahead of you** 8 minutes. **Assumes** Two or more trains operating. **Loading speed** Moderate.

Thumbs Up for the Whole Family

Later in the day when you need a break, this full-circuit ride will give you and your feet 20 minutes of rest. You cannot take your rental stroller on the train, but if you get off short of a complete circuit, you can get a free replacement. Folding strollers are allowed aboard. Be advised that the railroad shuts down immediately preceding and during parades.

■┃ ADVENTURELAND

THE FIRST LAND TO THE LEFT OF MAIN STREET, Adventureland combines an African safari theme with an old New Orleans/ Caribbean atmosphere.

Jungle Cruise *(Fastpass)* ★★★

APPEAL BY AGE PRESCHOOL ★★★★ GRADE SCHOOL ★★★★ TEENS ★★★½
YOUNG ADULTS ★★★★   OVER 30 ★★★★   SENIORS ★★★★

What it is Outdoor safari-themed boat ride adventure. **Scope and scale** Major attraction. **Fright potential** Moderately intense, some macabre sights; a good test attraction for little ones. **Bottleneck rating** 10. **When to go** Before 10:30 a.m., the last 2 hours the park is open, or use Fastpass. **Authors' rating** An enduring Disney masterpiece; ★★★. **Duration of ride** 8–9 minutes. **Average wait in line per 100 people ahead of you** 3½ minutes. **Assumes** 10 boats operating. **Loading speed** Moderate.

You have to put things into perspective to truly enjoy this ride and realize that it once was a super-headliner attraction at the Magic Kingdom. It still is a relaxing and enjoyable boat ride, but it won't capture the fascination of the high-tech savvy youngsters of the new millennium.

Thumbs Up for the Whole Family

DISNEY DISH WITH JIM HILL

NEMO AND FRIENDS WON'T LIKE THIS One of the ideas being considered for Jungle Cruise is a new show scene where your ship wanders into piranha-infested waters. At that point, I'm thinking it would probably be a good time to keep your hands and arms inside the boat.

Magic Carpets of Aladdin ★★½

APPEAL BY AGE PRESCHOOL ★★★★½ GRADE SCHOOL ★★★★ TEENS ★★★
YOUNG ADULTS ★★★ OVER 30 ★★★ SENIORS ★★★

What it is Elaborate midway ride. **Scope and scale** Minor attraction. **Fright potential** Much like Dumbo; a favorite of most younger children. **Bottleneck rating** 10. **When to go** Before 11 a.m. or after 7 p.m. **Authors' rating** An eye-appealing children's ride; ★★½. **Duration of ride** 1½ minutes. **Average wait in line per 100 people ahead of you** 16 minutes. **Loading speed** Slow.

For parents with preschoolers, there's no way out—like Dumbo, it is a must. Try to get your kids to ride in the first 30 minutes the park is open or just before park closing. Beware, the ride has a spitting camel positioned to spray jets of water on riders. The magic-carpet vehicles are rider-controlled, so you can fly your magic carpet up, down, or pitch forward or backward. The front-seat control is for up and down, while the backseat control pitches the carpet forward or backward. Sweet, but oh-so-slow loading. One more tip: Jasmine and Aladdin are often on hand for meeting and greeting.

Of course the ride is inspired by the 1992 Disney movie *Aladdin*. Did you know that Robin Williams is the voice of the Genie?

Movie Tip

Pirates of the Caribbean ★★★★★

APPEAL BY AGE PRESCHOOL ★★★½ GRADE SCHOOL ★★★★ TEENS ★★★★½
YOUNG ADULTS ★★★★½ OVER 30 ★★★★½ SENIORS ★★★★½

What it is Indoor pirate-themed adventure boat ride. **Scope and scale** Headliner. **Fright potential** Slightly intimidating queuing area; intense boat ride with gruesome (though humorously presented) sights and a short, unexpected slide down a flume. **Bottleneck rating** 7. **When to go** Before 11 a.m. or after 7 p.m. **Special comment** Frightens some young children. **Authors' rating** Disney Audio-Animatronics at their best; not to be missed; ★★★★★. **Duration of ride** About 7½ minutes. **Average wait in line per 100 people ahead of you** 1½ minutes. **Assumes** Both waiting lines operating. **Loading speed** Fast.

Yo ho, yo ho, a pirate's life for me! This indoor ride cruises through a series of sets depicting a pirate raid on a Caribbean port. It has been a favorite for decades, but with the release of *Pirates of the Caribbean: The Curse of the Black Pearl* (2003), *Pirates of the Caribbean: Dead Man's Chest* (2006), *Pirates of the Caribbean: At World's End* (2007), and *Pirates of the Caribbean: On Stranger Tides* (2011), the popularity of the ride has soared to new heights. Oh yeah, the films' protagonist, Captain Jack Sparrow, has joined the attraction's animatronic cast. A must for all young pirates is *Captain Jack Sparrow's Pirate Tutorial,* which takes place several times a day next to the Pirates of the Caribbean ride. Check the daily entertainment schedule (*Times Guide*) and arrive 15 minutes in advance if you want your little buccaneer to have a chance of joining the ranks of Captain Jack Sparrow and his faithful companion Mack.

DISNEY DISH WITH JIM HILL

I WILL NOT TALK . . . WITHOUT MY AGENT It's kind of a tradition that each *Pirates of the Caribbean* film features at least one scene from the theme park attractions. The rumor for *Pirates 5* is that we'll see Carlos (the mayor) being dunked in the well. What secrets are the pirates trying to extract from the mayor? We'll all find out when the movie debuts in July 2015.

When you're entering the ride's line, you can look through the bars in the jail cells and see guns, barrels, and skeletons. The scariest part is when there's a cannon fight between the pirate's boat and the town. And Davy Jones looks kind of creepy.

Hannah

Movie Tip

For all fans of the *Pirates of the Caribbean* movies, rent the movies before you go to Walt Disney World. They're a blast.

Swiss Family Treehouse ★★★

APPEAL BY AGE	PRESCHOOL ★★★½	GRADE SCHOOL ★★★½	TEENS ★★★
YOUNG ADULTS ★★★		OVER 30 ★★★	SENIORS ★★★

Thumbs Up for the Whole Family

What it is Outdoor walk-through tree house. **Scope and scale** Minor attraction. **Fright potential** Not frightening in any respect. **Bottleneck rating** 6. **When to go** Before 11:30 a.m. or after 5 p.m. **Special comment** Requires climbing a lot of stairs. **Authors' rating** A visual delight; ★★★. **Duration of tour** 10–15 minutes. **Average wait in line per 100 people ahead of you** 7 minutes.

This king of all tree houses is perfect for the 10-and-under crowd. Though a minor attraction, it's a great place to expend pent-up energy. Parents might be inclined to sit across the walkway and watch their aspiring Tarzans, but in truth the tree house is fun for adults too.

It's pretty fun to look at it, but my sister and I thought it was expendable. However, if you're over 30 years old, you'll probably really appreciate it.

Shelton

Movie Tip

Swiss Family Robinson is a 1960 film adaptation of the Johann David Wyss novel and was the inspiration for the Swiss Family Treehouse.

Walt Disney's Enchanted Tiki Room ★★★

APPEAL BY AGE	PRESCHOOL ★★★½	GRADE SCHOOL ★★★½	TEENS ★★★
YOUNG ADULTS ★★★½		OVER 30 ★★★½	SENIORS ★★★½

What it is Audio-animatronic Pacific Island musical theater show. **Scope and scale** Minor attraction. **Fright potential** Young children might be frightened by the thunder and lightning storm, plus the theater is at times plunged into utter darkness. **Bottleneck rating 4. When to go** Before 11 a.m. or after 3:30 p.m. **Special comment** Frightens some preschoolers. **Authors' rating** Very, very unusual; ★★★. **Duration of show** 15½ minutes. **Preshow** Talking birds. **Probable waiting time** 15 minutes.

The *Tiki* birds are a great favorite of the 8-and-under age set. The outright absurdity of the whole concept saves the show for older patrons. If you can look beyond the cheese, it is actually hilariously funny. The air-conditioned theater is a great place to cool off and rest your feet.

FRONTIERLAND

FRONTIERLAND ADJOINS ADVENTURELAND as you move clockwise around the Magic Kingdom. The focus is on the Old West, with stockade-type structures and pioneer trappings.

Big Thunder Mountain Railroad *(Fastpass)* ★★★★

APPEAL BY AGE PRESCHOOL ★★★★	GRADE SCHOOL ★★★★½	TEENS ★★★★½
YOUNG ADULTS ★★★★½	OVER 30 ★★★★½	SENIORS ★★★★

What it is Tame, Western-mining-themed roller coaster. **Scope and scale** Headliner. **Fright potential** Visually intimidating from outside, with moderately intense visual effects; the roller coaster is wild enough to frighten many adults, particularly seniors. **Bottleneck rating 9. When to go** Before 10 a.m., in the hour before closing, or use Fastpass. **Special comments** Must be 40" tall to ride; children younger than age 7 must ride with an adult. Switching-off option provided (see page 245). **Authors' rating** Great effects; relatively tame roller coaster; not to be missed; ★★★★. **Duration of ride** Almost 3½ minutes. **Average wait in line per 100 people ahead of you** 2½ minutes. **Assumes** 5 trains operating. **Loading speed** Moderate–fast.

Zooming on a runaway train around a mountain and through a deserted mining town is Disney at its best (if only one could concentrate on the scenery). The ride is rough, and if you do not like roller coasters, this one is going to remind you why. A recent refurbishment added air-conditioning and interactive props to the queue and spruced up these first-rate examples of Disney creativity: a realistic mining town, geysers, swinging possums, petulant buzzards, and the like. Ride after dark if you can. Regardless of when you ride, seats in the back offer a better experience.

Watch out on this one. Sitting in the back jerks me around too much. If you go in the front or the middle, you'll have a smoother ride. It has a lot of dips but no flips because it is more like a wooden roller coaster.

Ian

Hannah

I was not feeling the love the first time I went on this. You always feel like you're going to hit your head on one rock or another, and there are a lot of twists and turns. Eventually, I liked the bumps and how high the ride went, so I went on it again with my dad.

My whole family loved the falling rocks and earthquakes. DO NOT duck right near the end. There is a very low rock, which looks like it will hit your head. I ducked, and I got whiplash because there is then a sudden 5-foot drop. It's very small but very quick.

Shelton

Country Bear Jamboree ★★★

APPEAL BY AGE PRESCHOOL ★★★½ GRADE SCHOOL ★★★½ TEENS ★★★
YOUNG ADULTS ★★★ OVER 30 ★★★ SENIORS ★★★★

What it is Audio-animatronic country hoedown theater show. **Scope and scale** Major attraction. **Fright potential** Not frightening in any respect. **Bottleneck rating 6. When to go** Anytime. **Authors' rating** A Disney classic; ★★★. **Duration of show** 11 minutes. **Probable waiting time** This attraction is not that popular and has a relatively small capacity. On a busy day, noon–5:30 p.m., your waiting time will average 10–20 minutes.

A charming cast of audio-animatronic bears sings and stomps in a Western-style hoedown. Recent editing has cut a few minutes from the show, quickening its pace somewhat. Most songs remain the same, though, and *Country Bear Jamboree* has run for so long that the geriatric bears are a step away from assisted living. Reader comments tend to echo the need for something new. From a Sandy Hook, Connecticut, mom:

> *I know they consider it a classic, and kids always seem to love it, but could they PLEASE update it after half a century?*

 Kids will love watching *The Country Bears,* a live-action film produced by Walt Disney Pictures based loosely on the *Country Bear Jamboree* show. It was Disney's first movie based on a ride or attraction, released in 2002, almost a year before *Pirates of the Caribbean: The Curse of the Black Pearl.*

Frontierland Shootin' Arcade ★½

APPEAL BY AGE PRESCHOOL ★★ GRADE SCHOOL ★★★★ TEENS ★★★½
YOUNG ADULTS ★★½ OVER 30 ★★★ SENIORS ★★★

What it is Electronic shooting gallery. **Scope and scale** Diversion. **Fright potential** Not frightening in any respect. **When to go** Whenever convenient. **Special comment** Costs $1 per play. **Authors' rating** Very nifty shooting gallery; ★½.

Shooters get around 30 shots per $1 play. The rifles are set so that each shot must be followed by a short delay before the next shot is fired. This prevents small children from accidentally using all 30 shots in 5 seconds. It's barely noticeable for adults. Bring quarters; it's big-time fun.

Splash Mountain *(Fastpass)* ★★★★★

APPEAL BY AGE PRESCHOOL† ★★★★ GRADE SCHOOL ★★★★½ TEENS ★★★★½
YOUNG ADULTS ★★★★★ OVER 30 ★★★★½ SENIORS ★★★★½

† Many preschoolers are too short to meet the height requirement. Among preschoolers who actually ride, most give the attraction high marks.

What it is Indoor/outdoor water-flume adventure ride. **Scope and scale** Super-headliner. **Fright potential** Visually intimidating from outside, with moderately intense visual effects. The ride, culminating in a 52-foot plunge down a steep chute, is somewhat hair-raising for all ages. **Bottleneck rating 10. When to go** As soon as the park opens, during afternoon or evening parades, just before closing, or use Fastpass. **Special comments** Must be 40" tall to ride; children younger than 7 must ride with an adult. Switching-off option provided (see page 245). **Authors' rating** A wet winner; not to be missed; ★★★★★. **Duration of ride** About 10 minutes. **Average wait in line per 100 people ahead of you** 3½ minutes. **Assumes** Operating at full capacity. **Loading speed** Moderate.

Lose Things   Wet   Scary

Zip-a-dee-doo-dah, are we having fun yet, my-o-my, did we get wet! The 0.5-mile ride through swamps, caves, and backwoods bayous is wonderful. Based on the 1946 Disney film *Song of the South,* the log flume ride takes you through Uncle Remus's tales of Br'er Rabbit. Three small drops lead up to the big one, a five-story drop at 40 mph.

Way too cool! If you want to feel what it's like to go over a waterfall, sit in the front, but I prefer the back. I think you get wetter. Get as many big people sitting in front of you as you can. They weigh down the boat and make the biggest splash.

Ian

You get really wet on this ride, and there are a lot of surprises! When you get in, the seats are going to be really wet.

Hannah

I don't know why people complain about getting wet. You really don't get all that wet. My sister and I were in the front row, and my sister even complained that she didn't get wet enough!

Shelton

Unavailable in the United States, *Song of the South* will become public domain in 2039, and Disney might re-release the movie before they lose the rights to it. If you're interested in the history of this controversial movie, check out **songofthesouth.net.**

Movie Tip

Tom Sawyer Island and Fort Langhorn ★★★

APPEAL BY AGE **PRESCHOOL** ★★★½ **GRADE SCHOOL** ★★★½ **TEENS** ★★★★
YOUNG ADULTS ★★★ **OVER 30** ★★★½ **SENIORS** ★★★½

What it is Outdoor walk-through exhibit/rustic playground. **Scope and scale** Minor attraction. **Fright potential** Not frightening in any respect. **Bottleneck rating** 4. **When to go** Midmorning through late afternoon. **Special comment** Closes at sunset. **Authors' rating** The place for rambunctious kids; ★★★.

This is a great place for kids age 5 and up to unwind. The wildest and most uncooperative youngster will relax after exploring caves and climbing around in an old fort. While it is also a great place for a picnic, there is no food, so bring your own. Access to the island is by raft with a (usually short) wait both coming and going. Plan to give your kids at least 20 minutes on the island. Left to their own devices, they would likely stay all day.

Thumbs Up for the Whole Family

The caves were interesting. It may sound like a little kid's playground, but I think it's worth a look for all ages.

Shelton

I thought this was really cool because I like adventurous stuff like the rope bridges. There's also a playground. You take a boat across the lake to get there.

Hannah

LIBERTY SQUARE

LIBERTY SQUARE RE-CREATES COLONIAL AMERICA at the time of the American Revolution. The architecture is Federal or Colonial. The Liberty Tree, a live oak that's more than 130 years old, lends dignity and grace to the setting.

The Hall of Presidents ★ ★ ★

APPEAL BY AGE	PRESCHOOL ★★½	GRADE SCHOOL ★★★	TEENS ★★★½
YOUNG ADULTS ★★★★		OVER 30 ★★★★	SENIORS ★★★★½

Thumbs Up for the Whole Family

What it is Audio-animatronic historical theater presentation. **Scope and scale** Major attraction. **Fright potential** Not frightening in any respect. **Bottleneck rating** 4. **When to go** Anytime. **Authors' rating** Impressive and moving; ★★★. **Duration of show** Almost 23 minutes. **Probable waiting time** Lines for this attraction look awesome but are usually swallowed up as the theater exchanges audiences. Your wait will probably be the remaining time of the show that's in progress when you arrive. It would be exceptionally unusual not to be admitted to the next show.

Disney immortalizes the presidents of the United States with their own audio-animatronic counterparts. In 2009 Disney added Barack Obama and revamped the entire show, which includes narration by Morgan Freeman and a speech by George Washington. The Father of Our Country joins Presidents Lincoln and Obama as the only chief executives with speaking parts. Although the show is revamped roughly every decade, the presentation remains strongly inspirational and patriotic and highlights milestones in American history. *The Hall of Presidents* is a very moving show for Americans and features one of Disney's best and most ambitious audio-animatronic efforts. The show is definitely a must-see for adults. Kids will fidget or fall asleep.

Shelton

Not very interesting, but I thought the presidents were real actors. Very realistic and kind of creepy is what we thought.

Did you know that famous Western actor Royal Dano is the voice of President Lincoln? Dano was also the voice of Lincoln for Disney's *Great Moments with Mr. Lincoln* program, first presented at the 1964–1965 World's Fair in New York.

Liliane

The Haunted Mansion ★ ★ ★ ★

APPEAL BY AGE	PRESCHOOL ★★★½	GRADE SCHOOL ★★★★	TEENS ★★★★½
YOUNG ADULTS ★★★★½		OVER 30 ★★★★½	SENIORS ★★★★½

What it is Haunted-house dark ride. **Scope and scale** Major attraction. **Fright potential** The name raises anxiety, as do the sounds and sights of the waiting area. An intense attraction with humorously presented macabre sights, the ride itself is gentle. **Bottleneck rating** 8. **When to go** Before 11 a.m. or the last 2 hours the park is open. **Special comment** Frightens some very young children. **Authors' rating** Some of Walt Disney World's best special effects; not to be missed; ★★★★. **Duration of ride** 7-minute ride plus a 1½-minute preshow. **Average wait in line per 100 people ahead of you** 2½ minutes. **Assumes** Both "stretch rooms" operating. **Loading speed** Fast.

Dark   Scary

Don't let the apparent spookiness of the old-fashioned Haunted Mansion put you off. This is one of the best attractions in the Magic Kingdom (and, in fact, one that seems to get a few new twists each year). It's not scary, except in the sweetest of ways, but it will remind you of the days before ghost stories gave way to slasher flicks. The Haunted Mansion takes less than 10 minutes to ride, preshow included, but you may have to do it more than once—it's jam-packed with visual puns, special effects, Hidden Mickeys, and really lovely Victorian-spooky sets.

It's freaky, man. One time I almost chickened out. Real people in costumes stare you down. There's lots of weird stuff going on, like eyes in paintings on the wall following you and a lady's face inside a crystal ball. At the end, a ghost rides in the car with you. Read the funny tombstones before you go in.

Ian

Liberty Belle Riverboat ★★½

| APPEAL BY AGE | PRESCHOOL ★★★½ | GRADE SCHOOL ★★★ | TEENS ★★★ |
| YOUNG ADULTS ★★★½ | OVER 30 ★★★½ | | SENIORS ★★★★ |

Thumbs Up for the Whole Family

What it is Outdoor scenic boat ride. **Scope and scale** Major attraction. **Fright potential** Not frightening in any respect. **Bottleneck rating** 4. **When to go** Anytime. **Authors' rating** Slow, relaxing, and scenic; ★★½. **Duration of ride** About 16 minutes. **Average wait to board** 10–14 minutes.

This fully narrated 16-minute trip is relaxing and offers great photo ops. It's a good choice also at night when the boat and the attractions along the waterfront are lighted. Did you know that the *Liberty Belle* Riverboat runs on a track hidden just below the water?

DISNEY DISH WITH JIM HILL

SERVICE WITH A SCOWL The Imagineers see the Magic Kingdom slowly running out of space to build new rides, shows, and attractions. So as a long-term (like 20-year) solution, one of their ideas is to fill in the Rivers of America to make developable land. The *Liberty Belle* riverboat would be converted to Madame Medusa's, a Disney villain–themed restaurant.

FANTASYLAND

FANTASYLAND IS DIVIDED into three distinct sections. Directly behind Cinderella Castle and set on a snowcapped mountain is **Beast's Castle,** part of a *Beauty and the Beast*–themed area. Most of this section holds dining and shopping, such as the **Be Our Guest** restaurant; **Gaston's Tavern,** a small quick-service restaurant; and a gift shop. Outside Beast's Castle is **Belle's Village.** Nestled inside lush and beautifully decorated grounds, with gardens, meadows, and waterfalls, is Maurice's Cottage, where *Enchanted Tales with Belle* brings back the popular interactive storytelling session between Belle and park guests. In front of Gaston's Tavern, the centerpiece fountain features a larger-than-life statue of Gaston and LeFou. Strolling around the village is Gaston himself, willingly posing for pictures.

Liliane: The only way to visit Beast's Castle is by eating at the Be Our Guest restaurant. Dinner reservations are fully booked months in advance, and the line for the counter-service lunch often forms as soon as the park opens.

The far-right corner of Fantasyland—including **Dumbo, The Barnstormer** kiddie coaster, and the Fantasyland train station—is called **Storybook Circus** as an homage to Disney's *Dumbo* film. These are low-capacity amusement-park rides appropriate for younger children. Also located here is **Pete's Silly Sideshow,** a meet and greet where guests interact with The Great Goofini (Goofy as a stunt pilot), The Astounding Donaldo (Donald as a snake charmer), Minnie Magnifique (Minnie as a circus star), and Madame Daisy Fortuna (Daisy as a fortune teller).

The middle of the new Fantasyland territory holds the headliners, including **Under the Sea: Journey of the Little Mermaid** and **Seven Dwarfs Mine Train.** Placing these in the middle of the new land should allow good traffic flow either to the left (toward Beast's Castle) for dining, to the right for attractions geared to smaller children, or back to the original part of Fantasyland for classic attractions such as **Peter Pan's Flight** and **The Many Adventures of Winnie the Pooh.** Finally, don't miss the new *Tangled*-themed restrooms and outdoor seating area (with phone charging stations) near Peter Pan and **It's A Small World.**

These changes increased the number of guests heading to Fantasyland, which was already one of the most crowded lands in the Magic Kingdom. The good news is that the new attractions and restaurants are well designed to handle crowds. The ride vehicles in Under the Sea: Journey of the Little Mermaid, for example, admit riders almost continuously throughout the day, at a rate of around 2,000 per hour—about the same number of riders that Space Mountain serves per hour. And because the overall size of Fantasyland has doubled, crowds have more room to spread out.

We've updated our Magic Kingdom touring plans to reflect the latest developments with all the attractions. As with any construction project, plans may change. Check **touringplans.com** for the latest developments and touring plan updates.

Ariel's Grotto ★★★

APPEAL BY AGE	PRESCHOOL ★★★★½	GRADE SCHOOL ★★★★	TEENS ★★★
YOUNG ADULTS ★★★½	OVER 30 ★★★½		SENIORS ★★★½

What it is Character greeting venue. **Scope and scale** Minor attraction. **Fright potential** Not frightening in any respect. **Bottleneck rating** 8. **When to go** Before 10:30 a.m. or the last 2 hours the park is open. **Authors' rating** Not as themed as other character greetings; ★★★. **Duration of experience** Maybe 30–90 seconds. **Average wait in line per 100 people ahead of you** 45 minutes. **Queue speed** Slow.

As part of the Fantasyland expansion, Ariel has an elaborate new home next to the Under the Sea: Journey of the Little Mermaid ride. Located in the base of the seaside cliffs under Prince Eric's castle, Ariel (in mermaid form) greets guests from a seashell throne. The queue isn't as detailed as other character greeting venues in the park.

The meet and greet sometimes closes an hour before the rest of the park. The greeting area is set up almost as if to encourage guests to linger with Ariel, which keeps the line long. The queue isn't air-conditioned, which is surprising for something that's supposed to store fish.

The Barnstormer *(Fastpass)* ★★

APPEAL BY AGE	PRESCHOOL ★★★★	GRADE SCHOOL ★★★★	TEENS ★★★
YOUNG ADULTS ★★★	OVER 30 ★★★		SENIORS ★★★

What it is Small roller coaster. **Scope and scale** Minor attraction. **Fright potential** A children's coaster; frightens some preschoolers. **Bottleneck rating** 9. **When to go** Before 11 a.m., during parades, the last 2 hours the park is open, or use Fastpass. **Special comment** Must be 35" tall to ride. **Authors' rating** Great for little ones but not worth the wait for adults; ★★. **Duration of ride** About 53 seconds. **Average wait in line per 100 people ahead of you** 7 minutes. **Loading speed** Slow.

Remember that the height requirement for this ride is 35 inches. If you want to see how your child handles riding coasters, The Barnstormer is the perfect testing ground.

Yours truly screamed big-time from start to end (thankfully it only lasted a minute), and no way would I let the apple of my eye ride alone unless he or she is 6 years or older.

Liliane is a gentle and sensitive soul. Most kids experience rides wilder than The Barnstormer on their tricycles. When I heard Liliane wailing like a banshee on this dinky coaster, I thought that her appendix must have ruptured.

Casey Jr. Splash 'N' Soak Station

Casey Jr., the circus train from *Dumbo,* hosts an absolutely drenching experience outside the Fantasyland Train Station in the Storybook Circus area. Expect a cadre of captive circus beasts to spray water on you in this elaborate water play area. It puts all other theme park splash areas to soaking shame and is a marvel to watch. Bring a change of clothes and a big towel.

Dumbo the Flying Elephant *(Fastpass)* ★ ★ ★

APPEAL BY AGE	PRESCHOOL ★ ★ ★ ★ ½	GRADE SCHOOL ★ ★ ★ ★	TEENS ★ ★ ★
YOUNG ADULTS ★ ★ ★ ½	OVER 30 ★ ★ ★ ½		SENIORS ★ ★ ★

What it is Disney-fied midway ride. **Scope and scale** Minor attraction. **Fright potential** A tame midway ride; a favorite of most young children. **Bottleneck rating** 10. **When to go** Before 10:30 a.m., in the last 2 hours the park is open, or use Fastpass. **Authors' rating** Attractive children's ride; ★ ★ ★. **Duration of ride** 1½ minutes. **Average wait in line per 100 people ahead of you** 5 minutes. **Loading speed** Slow.

Making sure your child gets his fill of this tame, happy children's ride is what mother love is all about. The 90-second ride is hardly worth the long lines, unless, of course, you're under 7 years old. The attraction's capacity was doubled with the addition of a second ride, a clone of the first. The revamped Dumbo also includes a covered queue with interactive elements (read: things your kids can play with to pass the time in line). When entering the attraction, guests receive a pager, and kids can play in the air-conditioned playground area until it is time to ride. This is a major improvement, but we still recommend that you ride Dumbo within the first 30 minutes the park is open or use Fastpass.

If you have not seen *Dumbo* (first released in 1941 and winner of an Academy Award for original music score), you have an elephant-size gap in your Disney education. Watch the movie, fun for all ages, when you get home.

Movie Tip

Enchanted Tales with Belle ★ ★ ★ ★

APPEAL BY AGE	PRESCHOOL ★ ★ ★ ★ ½	GRADE SCHOOL ★ ★ ★ ★ ½	TEENS ★ ★ ★ ½
YOUNG ADULTS ★ ★ ★ ★	OVER 30 ★ ★ ★ ★		SENIORS ★ ★ ★ ★

What it is Interactive character show. **Scope and scale** Minor attraction. **Fright potential** Not frightening in any respect. **Bottleneck rating** 10. **When to go** As soon as the park opens or the last 2 hours the park is open. **Authors' rating** The prettiest meet and greet in the park; ★★★★. **Duration of presentation** About 20 minutes. **Average wait in line per 100 people ahead of you** 10 minutes. **Queue speed** Slow.

A multiscene *Beauty and the Beast* experience takes guests into Maurice's workshop, through a magic mirror, and into Beast's library, where the audience shares a story with Belle. You discover the attraction by walking into the living room of Maurice's Cottage, where you see mementos tracing Belle's childhood, including her favorite books, and lines drawn on one wall showing how fast Belle grew every year.

From there you'll enter Maurice's workshop at the back of the cottage. Covering every inch of the floor, walls, and ceiling, you'll find an assortment of odd wood gadgets that Maurice has been working on. Take a moment to look around, and then focus your attention on the mirror to the left of the door from which you entered.

Soon enough, the room gets dark and the mirror begins to sparkle. Through magic and some really good carpentry skills, the mirror turns into a full-size doorway, through which guests enter into a wardrobe room. Once in the wardrobe room, the attraction's premise is explained: you're supposed to re-enact the story of *Beauty and the Beast* for Belle on her birthday, and guests are chosen to act out key parts in the play.

Once the parts are chosen, everyone walks into the castle's library and takes seats. Cast members explain how the play will take place and introduce Belle, who gives a short speech about how thrilled she is for everyone to be there. The play is acted out within a few minutes, and all of the actors get a chance to take photos with Belle and receive a small bookmark as a memento (sorry, only for those who were chosen to act in the play). A separate PhotoPass card is given to those who take photos with Belle.

For the relative few who get to act in the play, it's a chance to interact with Belle in a way that isn't possible in other character encounters. We also like how Disney "stages" guests in the cottage, workshop, and wardrobe rooms—it's an efficient way to handle the wait in line, and it keeps guests from getting bored. As with all new attractions inside the new Fantasyland area, *Enchanted Tales with Belle* is very popular. On busy days the waiting time in the queue leading up to Maurice's Cottage can be 1–2 hours.

It's a Small World ★★★

APPEAL BY AGE	PRESCHOOL ★★★★½	GRADE SCHOOL ★★★★	TEENS ★★★
YOUNG ADULTS ★★★½	OVER 30 ★★★½		SENIORS ★★★★

Thumbs Up for the Whole Family

What it is World brotherhood–themed indoor boat ride. **Scope and scale** Major attraction. **Fright potential** Not frightening in any respect. **Bottleneck rating** 7. **When to go** Before 11 a.m., during parades, or after 7 p.m. **Authors' rating** Exponentially "cute"; ★★★. **Duration of ride** Approximately 11 minutes. **Average wait in line per 100 people ahead of you** 3½ minutes. **Assumes** Busy conditions with 30 or more boats operating. **Loading speed** Fast.

Small boats carry visitors on a tour around the world, with singing and dancing dolls showcasing the dress and culture of each nation. Totally rehabbed in

2005, Small World is one of Disney's oldest entertainments. Did you know that the ride originated at the 1964 New York World's Fair? If you listen closely, you will realize that the theme song is actually sung in numerous languages as your boat is carried from one continent to the next. Of course, there's no escaping the brain-numbing little tune. You'll go home with it lodged in your brain like a bullet, and just when you think you've repressed it, the song will resurface without warning to torture you some more.

This ride is why MP3 players were invented. Just put on your headphones and listen to Velvet Revolver all the way through the ride. The Small World song won't bother you a bit. Promise.

Ian

I must be immune to the tune. I love the ride and would not miss riding It's a Small World anytime I visit.

Liliane

DISNEY DISH WITH JIM HILL

DLROW LLAMS A S'TI To improve traffic flow through this part of Fantasyland, Disney swapped the location of Small World's entrance and exit. This small change has alleviated much of the traffic issue on this side of park, making it easier to handle people and stroller parking.

Mad Tea Party ★★

APPEAL BY AGE   PRESCHOOL ★★★★½   GRADE SCHOOL ★★★★½   TEENS ★★★★
YOUNG ADULTS ★★★½   OVER 30 ★★★½   SENIORS ★★½

What it is Midway-type spinning ride. **Scope and scale** Minor attraction. **Fright potential** Low, but this type of ride can induce motion sickness in all ages. **Bottleneck rating** 9. **When to go** Before 11 a.m. or after 5 p.m. **Special comment** You can make the teacups spin faster by turning the wheel in the center of the cup. **Authors' rating** Fun but not worth the wait; ★★. **Duration of ride** 1½ minutes. **Average wait in line per 100 people ahead of you** 7½ minutes. **Loading speed** Slow.

Queasy

It's a party, and a mad one at that. Prepare yourself for a whirling adventure inside a giant teacup (also known as the human centrifuge). Teenagers love to lure adults into the spinning teacups and then turn the wheel in the middle (making the cup spin faster) until the adults are plastered against the sides and on the verge of throwing up. The only sane way to experience this ride with teenagers is, paradoxically, to put them in straitjackets so they can't spin the wheel. We're dying to try this. Volunteers, anyone?

My son loves this ride, and so do I. I'll take the Mad Tea Party over Big Thunder Mountain any day. Plus, it's good training for experiencing Mission: SPACE at Epcot.

Liliane

Researchers at NASA determined that you're less likely to experience motion sickness if you don't ride on an empty stomach.

Movie Tip

The Mad Tea Party is inspired by the unusual tea party scene in the 1951 Disney adaptation of Lewis Carroll's *Alice in Wonderland*. Did you know that the voice of Alice, British voice actress and schoolteacher Kathryn Beaumont, is also the voice of Wendy in *Peter Pan*?

The Many Adventures of Winnie the Pooh
(Fastpass) ★★★½

APPEAL BY AGE PRESCHOOL ★★★★½ GRADE SCHOOL ★★★★ TEENS ★★★½
YOUNG ADULTS ★★★½   OVER 30 ★★★½   SENIORS ★★★★

Thumbs Up for the Whole Family

What it is Indoor track ride. **Scope and scale** Minor attraction. **Fright potential** Not frightening in any respect. **Bottleneck rating** 8. **When to go** Before 10 a.m., the last hour the park is open, or use Fastpass. **Authors' rating** Cute as the Pooh bear himself; ★★★½. **Duration of ride** About 4 minutes. **Average wait in line per 100 people ahead of you** 4 minutes. **Loading speed** Moderate.

This ride is a romp through the Hundred-Acre Wood on a blustery day. The visuals are gentle and charming without being saccharine. The Many Adventures of Winnie the Pooh is a perfect test to assess how your very young children will react to the indoor, so-called dark rides. Pooh's Fastpass machines have been located over at *Mickey's PhilharMagic* during the Fantasyland construction. No word as to whether they'll move back when construction is done in 2014.

Movie Tip

The ride is based on a 1977 Disney animated feature, *The Many Adventures of Winnie the Pooh.* The movie and Winnie the Pooh books are perfect for very young children. Did you know that Paul Winchell won a Grammy for his voicing of Tigger? Other Disney roles of Paul Winchell include parts in *The Aristocats* as a Chinese cat and *The Fox and the Hound* as Boomer the woodpecker. He also lends his voice to evil Gargamel in *The Smurfs* TV show (not the movie).

Mickey's PhilharMagic ★★★★

APPEAL BY AGE PRESCHOOL ★★★★ GRADE SCHOOL ★★★★½ TEENS ★★★★½
YOUNG ADULTS ★★★★½   OVER 30 ★★★★½   SENIORS ★★★★½

What it is 3-D movie. **Scope and scale** Major attraction. **Fright potential** Some preschoolers may be scared at first, but taking off the 3-D glasses tones down the effect. **Bottleneck rating** 6. **When to go** Before 11 a.m. or during parades. **Authors' rating** Not to be missed; a masterpiece; ★★★★. **Duration of show** About 12 minutes. **Probable waiting time** 12–25 minutes.

A real stunner, *Mickey's PhilharMagic* combines three fabulous ideas: Mickey and Donald mix and meet with latter-day Disney stars such as Aladdin, Jasmine, Ariel, the Beast's pantry servants (such as Lumiere and Mrs. Potts), and Simba; it employs a form of computer-enhanced 3-D video technology that is truly impressive (it's the first time most of these characters have been digitally animated, which will make them more "flexible," so to speak, in the future); and the whole shebang is projected on a 150-foot-wide, 180-degree screen. *Mickey's PhilharMagic* even employs some of those famous Disney scent effects and turns the old sorcerer's apprentice trick back on Mickey.

You want to duck when corks and other things come flying out at you. I loved the part with Aladdin, when they were flying on their magic carpet. It felt very real!
Shelton

Peter Pan's Flight *(Fastpass)* ★★★★

APPEAL BY AGE PRESCHOOL ★★★★½ GRADE SCHOOL ★★★★½ TEENS ★★★½
YOUNG ADULTS ★★★★   OVER 30 ★★★★   SENIORS ★★★★

What it is Indoor track ride. **Scope and scale** Minor attraction. **Fright potential** Not frightening in any respect. **Bottleneck rating** 8. **When to go** First or last 30 minutes the park is open, or use Fastpass. **Authors' rating** Happy, mellow, and well done; ★★★★. **Duration of ride** A little more than 3 minutes. **Average wait in line per 100 people ahead of you** 5½ minutes. **Loading speed** Moderate–slow.

Thumbs Up for the Whole Family

Take a snort of pixie dust and off you go soaring over London and on to Never Land.

Disney's animated film version of Peter Pan is, of course, the inspiration for this wonderful ride. While the original is easy to find, the sequel, *Return to Never Land,* is not. Try to get a copy at a library or find a used one at **amazon.com** and reunite with Peter, Wendy, Tinker Bell, Mr. Smee, the Lost Boys, and Captain Hook. But most of all: Don't grow up.

Movie Tip

Pete's Silly Sideshow ★★★½

| APPEAL BY AGE | PRESCHOOL ★★★★½ | GRADE SCHOOL ★★★★½ | TEENS ★★★½ |
| YOUNG ADULTS ★★★★ | | OVER 30 ★★★★ | SENIORS ★★★ |

What it is Character greeting venue. **Scope and scale** Minor attraction. **Fright potential** Not frightening in any respect. **Bottleneck rating** 8. **When to go** Before 11 a.m. or in the last 2 hours the park is open. **Authors' rating** Well-themed with unique character costumes; ★★★½. **Duration of experience** 7 minutes per character. **Average wait in line per 100 people ahead of you** 25 minutes. **Queue speed** Slow.

Pete's Silly Sideshow is a circus-themed character greeting area in the Storybook Circus part of Fantasyland. The characters' costumes are distinct from the ones normally used around the parks. Characters available include Goofy as The Great Goofini, Donald Duck as The Astounding Donaldo, Daisy Duck as Madame Daisy Fortuna, and Minnie Mouse as Minnie Magnifique. The sideshow opens 45 minutes later than the rest of the park and closes an hour before the rest of the park on non–Extra Magic Hour days. The queue is indoor and air-conditioned. Note that there is one queue for the male characters (Goofy and Donald) and a second queue for the female characters (Minnie and Daisy). You can meet two characters at once but must line up twice to meet all four.

Prince Charming Regal Carrousel ★★★

| APPEAL BY AGE | PRESCHOOL ★★★★½ | GRADE SCHOOL ★★★★ | TEENS ★★★ |
| YOUNG ADULTS ★★★ | | OVER 30 ★★★½ | SENIORS ★★★½ |

What it is Merry-go-round. **Scope and scale** Minor attraction. **Fright potential** Not frightening in any respect. **Bottleneck rating** 7. **When to go** Anytime. **Special comment** Adults enjoy the beauty and nostalgia of this ride. **Authors' rating** A beautiful children's ride; ★★★. **Duration of ride** About 2 minutes. **Average wait in line per 100 people ahead of you** 5 minutes. **Loading speed** Slow.

It is a long wait, but the beauty of the carousel (formerly known as Cinderella's Golden Carrousel) captures everyone. The carousel, built in 1917, was discovered in New Jersey, where it was once part of an amusement park. It is beautifully maintained and especially magical at night when all the lights are on. Check out your children's delighted expressions as the painted ponies go up and down.

Princess Fairytale Hall ★★

What it is Character greeting venue. **Scope and scale** Minor attraction. **Fright potential** Not frightening in any respect. **Bottleneck rating** 9. **When to go** Before

10:30 a.m. or after 4:30 p.m. **Authors' rating** You want princesses? We got 'em; ★★. **Duration of experience** About 7–10 minutes (estimated). **Average wait in line per 100 people ahead of you** 35 minutes (estimated). **Queue speed** Slow.

DISNEY DISH WITH JIM HILL

THE PSYCHIC PRINCESSES NETWORK Princess Fairytale Hall is set to blow some little girls' minds. Thanks to new radio-frequency-identification (RFID) technology being installed all over the parks, a carefully hidden, out-of-the-way prompter will feed the Disney princesses all sorts of information about guests' daughters—info that Mom or Dad shared with WDW reserva-tionists ahead of time. Activated by a Fastpass+ wristband, RFID will supply princesses with not only a girl's name, but also perhaps her pet's name, her favorite food or color, and maybe even the last ride she experienced. This is Disney magic at a whole new level, thanks to some pretty pricey technology.

Scheduled to open in late 2013 on the site of Snow White's Scary Adventures, Fairytale Hall is the central location for meeting Disney's princesses in the Magic Kingdom. The meeting-and-greeting process will work similar to other Magic Kingdom meet and greets: The princesses occupy a greeting room where 15–20 guests are admitted at a time. They're allowed about 7–10 minutes, long enough for a photo, autograph, and a hug from each princess. It's possible that Fairytale Hall will offer Fastpass.

Seven Dwarfs Mine Train *(opens spring 2014)*

Thumbs Up for the Whole Family

What it is Dark ride and indoor/outdoor coaster combo. **Scope and scale** Super-headliner. **Fright potential** Marginally wild ride, dark scenes, and special effects may frighten children age 7 and younger. **Bottleneck rating** 10. **When to go** As soon as the park opens or use Fastpass. **Duration of ride** About 4 minutes. **Average wait in line per 100 people ahead of you** 4 minutes. **Loading speed** Fast.

In the pantheon of Disney coasters, Seven Dwarfs Mine Train is supposed to fit somewhere between The Barnstormer and Big Thunder Mountain Railroad. That is, it's geared to older grade-school kids who have been on amusement park rides before. There are no loops, inversions, or rolls in the track, and no massive hills or steep drops; the Mine Train's trick is that your ride vehicle's seats swing side to side as you go through turns. And—what a coincidence!—Disney has designed a curvy track with steep turns. An elaborate indoor section shows the dwarfs' underground operation. The exterior design includes waterfalls, forests, and landscaping and is meant to join together all of the surrounding Fantasyland's various locations, including France and Germany. Forget hidden

---

DISNEY DISH WITH JIM HILL

THE HIGH PRICE OF HEIGH-HO Disney took a spare-no-expense approach to construction of this family coaster. For example, the main show scene is in a cavern where the dwarfs start to sing their signature song, and the cavern's ceiling is a $5 million piece of custom steel. It's a good thing these guys own a diamond mine.

Mickeys—Seven Dwarfs needs a hidden Charlemagne. We expect Mine Train to have long lines throughout the day. If your vacation won't be complete without a comprehensive tour of Fantasyland, see Mine Train first, then Barnstormer, Dumbo, and Under the Sea. Mine Train should have Fastpass; if it does, use it if the line exceeds 30 minutes.

Under the Sea: Journey of the Little Mermaid
(Fastpass) ★★★½

APPEAL BY AGE PRESCHOOL ★★★★½ GRADE SCHOOL ★★★★ TEENS ★★★½
YOUNG ADULTS ★★★★   OVER 30 ★★★★   SENIORS ★★★½

What it is Dark ride retelling the film's story. **Scope and scale** Major attraction. **Fright potential** Evil Ursala and dark effects frighten children under 7 years of age. **Bottleneck rating** 8. **When to go** Before 10:30 a.m., the last 2 hours the park is open, or use Fastpass. **Authors' rating** Colorful, but most effects are too simple for an attraction this big; ★★★½. **Duration of ride** 5½ minutes. **Average wait in line per 100 people ahead of you** 3 minutes. **Loading speed** Fast.

Under The Sea takes riders through almost a dozen scenes retelling the story of *The Little Mermaid* film, this time with Audio-Animatronics, video effects, and a vibrant 3-D set the size of a small theater.

Guests board a clam-shell-shaped ride vehicle running along a continuously moving track (similar to The Haunted Mansion's). Once you're on board, the ride descends "underwater" past Ariel's grotto and to King Triton's undersea kingdom. The most detailed animatronic is Ursula the octopus, and she's a beauty. Other scenes hit the film's highlights, including Ariel meeting Prince Eric, her deal with Ursula to become human, and, of course, the happy couple at the end.

While Fantasyland is under construction, Under the Sea's Fastpass machines are located at *Mickey's PhilharMagic.*

I am disappointed! The ride feels very much like a clone of The Seas with Nemo & Friends at Epcot. The interactive queuing area is whimsical, but who wants to be stuck in a queuing area? Disney could do much better with this ride, much better!

Liliane

▌ TOMORROWLAND

TOMORROWLAND IS A MIX OF RIDES and experiences relating to the technological development of humankind and what life will be like in the future. When Disney overhauled Tomorrowland a few years back, it bailed on trying to predict how the future might appear, opting instead for a timeless, retro Buck Rogers look.

Keep an eye out for PUSH, the talking trash can of Tomorrowland. Kids love PUSH and delight in the opportunity to talk trash with the real thing.

Astro Orbiter ★★

APPEAL BY AGE PRESCHOOL ★★★★ GRADE SCHOOL ★★★½ TEENS ★★★½
YOUNG ADULTS ★★★   OVER 30 ★★★   SENIORS ★★½

What it is Buck Rogers–style rockets revolving around a central axis. **Scope and scale** Minor attraction. **Fright potential** Visually intimidating waiting area for a relatively tame ride. **Bottleneck rating** 10. **When to go** Before 11 a.m. or the last hour the park is open. **Special comment** This attraction is not as innocuous as it appears. **Authors' rating** Not worth the wait; ★★. **Duration of ride** 1½ minutes. **Average wait in line per 100 people ahead of you** 13½ minutes. **Loading speed** Slow.

Queasy

Parents, beware! If you are prone to motion sickness, this ride a) spins round and round; b) is faster than Dumbo; and c) for added "fun," a joystick lets you raise and lower the rocket throughout your 1½-minute journey. We like to ride the Astro Orbiter at night. The combination of lighting and the view are spectacular.

I don't have a fear of heights, but I get scared when something that's moving up and down is leaning outward like it's going to dump you out. It's very scary for me.
Shelton

Buzz Lightyear's Space Ranger Spin *(Fastpass)* ★★★★

APPEAL BY AGE PRESCHOOL ★★★★½ GRADE SCHOOL ★★★★½ TEENS ★★★★
YOUNG ADULTS ★★★★   OVER 30 ★★★★   SENIORS ★★★★

What it is Combination space travel–themed indoor ride and shooting gallery. **Scope and scale** Minor attraction. **Fright potential** Dark ride with cartoonlike aliens may frighten some preschoolers. **Bottleneck rating** 8. **When to go** First or last hour the park is open. **Authors' rating** A real winner! ★★★★. **Duration of ride** About 4½ minutes. **Average wait in line per 100 people ahead of you** 3 minutes. **Loading speed** Fast.

Once you get the hang of it, you'll come back for more, to infinity and beyond.

Totally awesome! I earned my Space Ranger Wings on my first ride. Use the joystick to spin and set up your shots, but don't spin too much because that uses up time and energy. Always aim and never stop shooting, especially at the big alien targets. Those are the ones with lots of arms and legs, and four eyes. They get you the most points.
Ian

Movie
Tip

The ride is based on the space-commando character Buzz Lightyear from the 1995 Disney-Pixar feature *Toy Story*. Did you know that Tom Hanks and Tim Allen are the voices of Woody and Buzz?

You'll see Zurg in jail at the end of the ride. Little kids can squeeze through the bars and pretend that they're in jail too.
Hannah

Monsters, Inc. Laugh Floor ★★★½

APPEAL BY AGE PRESCHOOL ★★★½ GRADE SCHOOL ★★★★½ TEENS ★★★★
YOUNG ADULTS ★★★★   OVER 30 ★★★★   SENIORS ★★★★

What it is Interactive animated comedy routines. **Scope and scale** Major attraction. **Fright potential** Not much is frightening, but they are monsters, after all. **Bottleneck rating** 8. **When to go** Before 11 a.m. or after 4 p.m. **Special comment** Audience members may be asked to participate in skits. **Author's rating** Good concept; jokes are hit-and-miss; ★★★½. **Duration of show** About 15 minutes including pre-show. **Probable waiting time** 25 minutes.

We learned in Disney-Pixar's *Monsters, Inc.* that children's screams could be converted into electricity, which was used to power a town inhabited by monsters. During the film, the monsters discovered that children's laughter was an even better source of energy. In this attraction, the monsters have set up a comedy club to capture as many laughs as possible. Mike Wazowski, the one-eyed character from the film, emcees the club's three comedy acts. Each consists of an animated monster (most not seen in the film) trying out various bad puns, knock-knock jokes, and Abbott and

Costello–like routines. Using the same cutting-edge technology as Epcot's popular *Turtle Talk with Crush,* behind-the-scenes Disney employees voice the characters and often interact with audience members during the skits. As with any comedy club, some performers are funny and some are not. A good thing about this attraction is that Disney has shown a willingness to try new routines and jokes, so the show should remain fresh to repeat visitors. A Sioux Falls, South Dakota, mom is a big fan:

> *The Laugh Floor was great. It's amazing how the on-screen characters inter-act with the audience—I got picked on twice without trying. This should def-initely be seen; plus, kids are able to text jokes to Roz.*

The show is based on the 2001 Pixar film *Monsters, Inc.,* starring Billy Crystal (voice) in the role of Mike Wazowski. It won an Oscar for best song.

Space Mountain *(Fastpass)* ★★★★

| APPEAL BY AGE† | PRESCHOOL ★★½ | GRADE SCHOOL ★★★★ | TEENS ★★★★★ |
| YOUNG ADULTS ★★★★½ | | OVER 30 ★★★★½ | SENIORS ★★★½ |

† Some preschoolers love Space Mountain; others are frightened. The sample size of senior citizens who experienced this ride was too small to develop an accurate rating.

What it is Roller coaster in the dark. **Scope and scale** Super-headliner. **Fright potential** Very intense roller coaster in the dark; the Magic Kingdom's wildest ride and a scary roller coaster by any standard. **Bottleneck rating** 10. **When to go** When the park opens or use Fastpass. **Special comments** Great fun and action; much wilder than Big Thunder Mountain Railroad. Must be 44" tall to ride; children younger than age 7 must be accompanied by an adult. Switching-off option provided (see page 245). **Authors' rating** An unusual roller coaster with excellent special effects; not to be missed; ★★★★. **Duration of ride** Almost 3 minutes. **Average wait in line per 100 people ahead of you** 3 minutes. **Assumes** Two tracks, one dedicated to Fastpass riders, dispatching at 21-second intervals. **Loading speed** Moderate–fast.

Space Mountain is one of the zippiest (and darkest) rides in Walt Disney World, lasting just under 3 minutes and including numerous abrupt turns and plummets. So those with neck or back problems or vertigo should probably skip it. However, this ride achieves "only" about 28 mph, a leisurely pace by 21st-century standards.

Space Mountain involves sudden blackouts, as do many thrill rides at Disney World. Those who suffer from claustrophobia (Liliane), tend to panic in the dark (Liliane), or have vision problems with extremes of light and darkness (Liliane) should avoid this attraction. Plunged into darkness and bouncing around like a marble in a spittoon, many warmly recall Space Mountain as the longest 3 minutes of their lives. Your kids will love it.

Space Mountain goes through regular refurbishments to add effects and maintain ride quality. Past improvements include new lighting and interactive games in the queue to help pass the time in line. In 2010 a new soundtrack accented high-octane music with sounds of speeding rocket ships and other intergalactic occurrences. It may just be from hearing asteroids whiz past your vehicle, but we think the new ride is slightly faster than it was.

If you're not sure that you are brave enough to ride Space Mountain, you can always take the Tomorrowland Transit Authority PeopleMover and watch the actual ride in action before you get in line.

I dream of riding Space Mountain at the pace of Spaceship Earth in Epcot. At last, I would be able to enjoy the twinkling lights.

Liliane

All of the people screaming sort of scared me at first. I did like all the flashing lights and the astronaut stuff. Look for the giant chocolate-chip cookies flying by on the ceiling when you're in line.

Hannah

Stitch's Great Escape! ★★

APPEAL BY AGE	PRESCHOOL ★★½	GRADE SCHOOL ★★½	TEENS ★★½
YOUNG ADULTS ★★½		OVER 30 ★★	SENIORS ★★½

What it is Theater-in-the-round sci-fi adventure show. **Scope and scale** Major attraction. **Fright potential** Frightens children of all ages; must be 40" tall. **Bottleneck rating** 6. **When to go** Before 11 a.m. or after 6 p.m.; try during parades. **Authors' rating** A cheap coat of paint on a broken car; ★★. **Duration of show** About 12 minutes. **Preshow** About 6 minutes. **Probable waiting time** 12–35 minutes.

Dark   Loud   Scary

Disney's press release touting *Stitch* as a child-friendly attraction was about as accurate as Lehman Brothers bookkeeping. You are held in your seat by overhead restraints and subjected to something weird clambering around you and whispering to you in a theater darker than a stack of black cats. Enough to scare the pants off many kids age 8 and younger.

Not fair! I love Stitch but agree with parents of young children who have complained about how scary the show is, especially because the overhead restraint prevents you from leaving your seat to comfort your child if need arises. Preteens and up, however, will enjoy the wicked fun of the show. All I could think of was the Pink Floyd song "Comfortably Numb": "Is there anybody in there?"

Liliane

Movie Tip

Skip the show, but do not discount the movie. *Lilo & Stitch* (released in 2002) is a great family movie. The Hawaiian culture of 'Ohana, which in Hawaiian means "extended family" including friends, is the cornerstone philosophy of this wonderful flick. The movie reminds children about the importance of good behavior and points out to adults that there is good inside every child, no matter how rotten he or she may behave at times.

This should be scrapped. My dad thought it was mediocre, but everyone else hated it.

Shelton

Tomorrowland Speedway ★★

APPEAL BY AGE	PRESCHOOL ★★★★	GRADE SCHOOL ★★★★	TEENS ★★★½
YOUNG ADULTS ★★½		OVER 30 ★★★	SENIORS ★★½

What it is Drive-'em-yourself miniature cars. **Scope and scale** Major attraction. **Fright potential** Not frightening in any respect. **Bottleneck rating** 9. **When to go** Before 10 a.m. or in the last 2 hours the park is open. **Special comment** Must be 54" tall to drive unassisted. **Authors' rating** Boring for adults; great for preschoolers; ★★. **Duration of ride** About 4¼ minutes. **Average wait in line per 100 people ahead of you** 4½ minutes. **Assumes** 285-car turnover every 20 minutes. **Loading speed** Slow.

The sleek cars and racetrack noise will get your younger kids hopped up to ride this extremely prosaic attraction. The minimum height requirement of 54 inches means that the younger (or shorter) set will have to ride with an adult. We suggest that you work the accelerator and brakes and let your future Kasey Kahne steer the car. Unless the sibling is willing to hand over the steering wheel, resist the urge to dispatch your little one with a taller sibling. The loading and unloading speed is excruciatingly slow, and the attraction offers hardly any protection from the sun.

What I like about this ride is you don't have to be 16 years old to drive! Dude, you have total control . . . well, almost. Pretend that you're an Indy car driver like Sam Hornish Jr. Turn the steering wheel, put your foot on the gas, and even hit the brakes . . . just like a go-cart. Sweet!

Ian

Tomorrowland Transit Authority PeopleMover ★★★

APPEAL BY AGE	PRESCHOOL ★★★★	GRADE SCHOOL ★★★★	TEENS ★★★½
YOUNG ADULTS ★★★★		OVER 30 ★★★★	SENIORS ★★★★

Thumbs Up for the Whole Family

What it is Scenic tour of Tomorrowland. **Scope and scale** Minor attraction. **Fright potential** Not frightening in any respect. **Bottleneck rating** 3. **When to go** During hot, crowded times of day (11:30 a.m.–4:30 p.m.). **Special comment** A good way to check out the Fastpass line at Space Mountain. **Authors' rating** Scenic, relaxing, informative; ★★★. **Duration of ride** 10 minutes. **Average wait in line per 100 people ahead of you** 1½ minutes. **Assumes** 39 trains operating. **Loading speed** Fast.

There is never a line, and the ride is ideal for taking a break. It's also a great way to see Tomorrowland all aglow at night. The route gives a sneak preview of Buzz Lightyear's Space Ranger Spin, and you can check on those screams emanating from Space Mountain. Most of the time cast members will let you ride several times in a row without having to get off. This last thing, according to many moms, makes the ride a great option for nursing.

It's good because you don't have to scream at anything, and there are no hills.

Hannah

Walt Disney's Carousel of Progress ★★★

APPEAL BY AGE	PRESCHOOL ★★★½	GRADE SCHOOL ★★★½	TEENS ★★★½
YOUNG ADULTS ★★★★		OVER 30 ★★★★	SENIORS ★★★★

What it is Audio-animatronic theater production. **Scope and scale** Major attraction. **Fright potential** Not frightening in any respect. **Bottleneck rating** 4. **When to go** Anytime. **Authors' rating** Nostalgic, warm, and happy; ★★★. **Duration of show** 21 minutes. **Preshow** Documentary on the attraction's long history. **Probable waiting time** Less than 10 minutes.

DISNEY DISH WITH JIM HILL

A PRAIRIE HOME-OF-THE-FUTURE COMPANION As annual attendance continues to drop at *Walt Disney's Carousel of Progress,* the Imagineers have been fretting about what to do with this theater-go-round presentation. The attraction, last updated in 1994, is sorely in need of makeover, but whom could Disney get to replace the late, great Jean Shepherd as the narrator of this show? Some at WDI have proposed recruiting another radio legend, Garrison Keillor, to be the new voice of Father. So far, however, no one's responded to all those letters sent from Lake Buena Vista to Lake Wobegon asking Keillor to come take a ride on Walt's nearly 50-year-old *Carousel.*

A piece of Disney history not to be missed. The attraction offers a nostalgic look at how technology and electricity have changed the lives of an audio-animatronic family over several generations.

My dad forced us all to see it, and we're glad he did. It was very good!

Shelton

LIVE ENTERTAINMENT
and PARADES *in the*
MAGIC KINGDOM

IT'S IMPOSSIBLE TO TAKE IN ALL THE MANY LIVE entertainment offerings at the Magic Kingdom in a single day. To experience both the attractions and the live entertainment, we recommend that you allocate at least two days to this park. In addition to parades, stage shows, and fireworks, check the daily entertainment schedule (*Times Guide*) or ask a cast member about concerts in Fantasyland, the Flag Retreat at Town Square, and the appearances of the various bands, singers, and street performers that roam the park daily. WDW live-entertainment guru Steve Soares usually posts the Magic Kingdom's performance schedule about a week in advance at **wdwent.com**.

Following is a short list of daily events with special appeal for families with children:

CASTLE FORECOURT STAGE The 20-minute *Dream-Along with Mickey* live show features Mickey, Minnie, Donald, Goofy, and a peck of princesses and other secondary characters, plus human backup dancers, in a show built around the premise that—*quelle horreur!*—Donald doesn't

FAVORITE EATS IN MAGIC KINGDOM		
LAND	**SERVICE LOCATION**	**FOOD ITEM**
MAIN STREET		
Main Street Bakery	Homemade goodies & crisped-rice treats	
ADVENTURELAND		
Tortuga Tavern	Quesadillas for kids	
FANTASYLAND		
Friar's Nook	Fries	
Pinocchio Village Haus	Mac and cheese & pizza	
FRONTIERLAND		
Pecos Bill Tall Tale Inn & Café	Burgers & great fixin's station	
LIBERTY SQUARE		
Columbia Harbour House	Soup & sandwiches	
Sleepy Hollow	Funnel cake	
TOMORROWLAND		
Cosmic Ray's Starlight Café	Rotisserie chicken, ribs, & kosher choices	
The Lunching Pad	"Designer" dogs, pretzels, & frozen soda	

believe in the power of dreams. Crisis is averted through a frenetic whirlwind of song and dance.

MERIDA MEET AND GREET AT THE FAIRYTALE GARDEN The garden, formerly the site of *Storytime with Belle* and the *Tangled* play and greet, is a small outdoor theater. It received a Scottish Highlands–inspired makeover and

Liliane: While meeting Merida is a real treat, the wait time makes for some very cranky kids.

is now the home of Merida, the strong-willed heroine from *Brave*. The new setting has an area in which those waiting to meet Merida can get archery lessons and participate in other activities until it's their turn to meet Merida. The activity targets the under-5 age group.

If you plan on meeting Merida, arrive at least 20–30 minutes early to the staging area. Once the area is at capacity (about 20 children and parents), cast members rope it off. Be forewarned that the entire experience will take a whole hour out of your day. The play and greet takes place six to eight times a day; check the daily entertainment schedule (*Times Guide*) for showtimes.

AFTERNOON PARADE Usually staged at 3 p.m., this parade features floats and marching Disney characters. A new afternoon parade is introduced every year or two. While some of the elements, such as the Disney characters, remain constant, the theme, music, and float design change. Seasonal parades round up the mix.

Liliane: A parade is a parade, or is it? While Disney tinkers with everything—the theme, the music, and the floats—one thing has been constant: the parade is shrinking! If Disney really wants return visitors, and I know they do, the new parade better be good!

The new Disney Festival of Fantasy Parade will come to the Magic Kingdom in spring 2014. The parade will include new floats based on the stories of *The Little Mermaid, Sleeping Beauty, Dumbo, Pinocchio, Peter Pan, Tangled,* and *Brave*. It will feature a brand-new original soundtrack with songs from Disney films in addition to a parade theme song. Disney Festival of Fantasy will replace the current Celebrate a Dream Come True parade.

EVENING PARADE Evening parade performances vary by season, happening as often as twice a night during the busy times of year, to two or three times a week during the less busy seasons. We rate the evening parade as not to be missed.

The Main Street Electrical Parade (MSEP) is the current nightly cavalcade at the Magic Kingdom. Its soundtrack, "Baroque Hoedown," is a synthesizer-heavy testament to what prog rock might have been with access to modern technology and antidepressants. In our opinion, the

Bob: Fastpass+ may be available for premium viewing spots for the afternoon and evening parades.

Magic Kingdom's nighttime parade is always the best in Walt Disney World, and the Electrical Parade is the standard against which everything else is judged. Disney is known to swap out parades (MSEP replaced SpectroMagic in 2010) and may do so at any time. If you're at Disney World while MSEP is running, make a special trip to see it.

MOVE IT! SHAKE IT! CELEBRATE IT! PARADE Starting at the train station end of Main Street, U.S.A., and working toward the central hub, this short walk incorporates about a dozen guests with a handful of floats, Disney characters, and entertainers. Music is provided by one of Disney's latest artists, and there's a good amount of interaction between the entertainers and the crowd.

PARADES Parades at the Magic Kingdom are full-fledged spectaculars with dozens of Disney characters and amazing special effects. An outstanding new afternoon parade is introduced every year or two; while some elements such as the Disney characters remain constant, the theme, music, and float design change. Always check your entertainment schedule (*Times Guide*) to make sure what parade is happening when, as well as the guide map for the parade route.

Remember, parades disrupt traffic, and it is nearly impossible to move around the park when one is going on. Parades also draw thousands of guests away from the attractions, making parade time the perfect moment to catch your favorite attraction with a shorter line. Finally, be advised that the Walt Disney World Railroad shuts down during parades.

The best place to view a parade is the upper platform of the Walt Disney Railroad station, but you will have to stake out your position 30–45 minutes before the event. Try also, especially on rainy days, the covered walkway between Liberty Tree Tavern and The Diamond Horseshoe Saloon on the border of Liberty Square and Frontierland.

FLAG RETREAT At 5 p.m. daily at Town Square (railroad-station end of Main Street). Sometimes performed with great fanfare and college marching bands, sometimes with a smaller Disney band.

MAGIC KINGDOM BANDS Banjo, Dixieland, steel drum, marching, and fife-and-drum bands play daily throughout the park.

CAPTAIN JACK SPARROW'S PIRATE TUTORIAL
Sign up with Captain Jack Sparrow and his crewman Mack for a hilarious pirate one-on-one. Check your *Times Guide* for the scheduled daily encounters and meet the Johnny Depp look-alike right across the street from the Pirates of the Caribbean ride. The lucky chosen buccaneers are taught how to be pirates and receive an honorary pirate certificate at the end of the show.

Liliane: Chances of being picked as an apprentice pirate are good at most shows, so don't push your kid in front of Jack and Mack. Dressing up for the part helps, however.

Liliane: The show is wonderful for little wannabe pirates and grown-ups alike and draws quite a crowd, especially ladies. I signed up for the pirate's life in a jiffy.

TINKER BELL'S FLIGHT This nice special effect in the sky above Cinderella Castle heralds the beginning of the fireworks show (when the park is open late).

WISHES **FIREWORKS SHOW** The nightly fireworks show starts just after Tinker Bell's flight in the sky above Cinderella Castle. The fireworks are synchronized to music from beloved Disney films.

View the fireworks from the upper platform of the railroad station. This vantage point also provides an easy path to the park exit when the fireworks are over. Our favorite spot, if we intend to remain in the park after the fireworks, is between Plaza Restaurant on Main Street and the Tomorrowland Terrace area to its right (if you're facing the castle).

A very special spot to view the fireworks is atop the nearby Contemporary Resort at the California Grill. Once the fireworks begin, the restaurant dims its lights and broadcasts the music from the show.

Liliane: If all you want is a serene spot to watch the fireworks or the Bay Lake and Seven Seas Lagoon Floating Electrical Pageant, you do not need to spend big bucks. The gardens of the Grand Floridian are perfect for the fireworks, and the beach of the Polynesian Resort does the trick for the electrical pageant.

CELEBRATE THE MAGIC In one of the most imaginative shows yet, videos and special effects are set to music and projected nightly on Cinderella Castle. The effects are tremendous: in one vignette, the entire castle becomes a kaleidoscope of brightly colored Mickeys and Donalds; in another, flames appear throughout the castle's windows to emulate a scene from the Pirates of the Caribbean ride. Best of all, Disney regularly updates the show's content to keep it fresh. While the show's soundtrack is excessively sentimental, the visuals more than make up for it. We rate this as not to be missed.

FIREWORKS CRUISE For a different view, you can watch the fireworks from the Seven Seas Lagoon aboard a chartered pontoon boat. The charter comes with a price (about $350 for up to 10 people and includes chips and drinks), of course. Your Disney captain will take you for a little cruise and then position the boat in a perfect place to watch the fireworks. For an additional cost, you can arrange for more substantial food items through the catering department. Life jackets are provided, but wearing them is at your discretion. To reserve, call 407-WDW-PLAY 180 days prior to your visit. Similar charters are available for viewing *IllumiNations* at Epcot.

BAY LAKE AND SEVEN SEAS LAGOON FLOATING ELECTRICAL PAGEANT Performed at nightfall at about 9 p.m. most of the year on Seven Seas Lagoon and Bay Lake, this pageant is the perfect culmination of a wonderful day. You have to leave the Magic Kingdom to see this floating electric light show. Take the monorail to the Polynesian Resort, get the kids a snack and yourself a drink, and walk to the end of the pier to watch the show. Pure magic, less the crowds. You can also watch the show at the Grand Floridian at 9:15 p.m. and at the Contemporary at 10:05 p.m.

MICKEY'S HALLOWEEN AND CHRISTMAS PARTIES The Magic Kingdom hosts special after-hours, holiday-themed events in September,

October, November, and December, celebrating Halloween and Christmas. These events require separate admission (see pages 50–58 for details) and can sell out. Space doesn't permit us to cover these events in the book, but we have full details—including photos, best days to go, touring advice, and more—at **blog.touringplans.com.** Search for "Halloween Party" or "Christmas Party" to see the coverage.

EXIT STRATEGIES

LEAVING THE PARK AFTER EVENING PARADES and fireworks is no small matter. Huge throngs depart the Magic Kingdom after parades, after fireworks, and at closing. Trust us, with small children, you don't want to be among them. The best strategy for avoiding the mass exodus is to view both fireworks and parades from the upper platform of the railroad station at the Town Square end of Main Street. As soon as the performance concludes, beat feet to the park exits. If you remain in the park after the fireworks and parades, don't wait until closing time to leave. On a busy day give yourself a 30- to 40-minute cushion.

Another strategy for beating the masses out of the park (if your car is in the TTC lot) is to watch the early parade and then leave before the fireworks begin. Line up for the ferry instead of the monorail. A ferry departs about every 8–10 minutes. Try to catch the ferry that will be crossing Seven Seas Lagoon while the fireworks are in progress. The best vantage point is on the top deck to the right of the pilothouse. Your chances are about 50/50 of catching it just right. If you are in front of the line for the ferry and you don't want to board the boat that's loading, stop at the gate and let people pass you. You'll be the first to board the next boat.

MAGIC KINGDOM TOURING PLANS

Bob: Don't worry that other people will be following the plans and render them useless. Fewer than 2 in every 100 people in the park will have been exposed to this information.

OUR STEP-BY-STEP TOURING PLANS are field-tested, independently verified itineraries that will keep you moving counter to the crowd flow and allow you to see as much as possible in a single day with minimum time wasted in line.

We developed many of these plans when preparing to visit the Magic Kingdom with our own children (ages 2–8). Some plans offer a midday break of at least 3 hours back at your hotel. It's debatable whether the kids will need the nap more than you, but you'll thank us later, we promise.

If you have just one day to spend in the Magic Kingdom, our single-day plans will allow you to see the best attractions for kids while avoiding crowds and long waits in line. If you're looking for a more relaxed, less structured tour of the park, try the one-and-a-half, two-day, or Sleepyhead plans. These alternatives have less backtracking. The Sleepyhead plans assume that you'll get to the park around 11 a.m., so they're great for mornings when you don't feel like getting out of bed early.

We recommend eating lunch outside of the Magic Kingdom. If you find yourself ahead of schedule, however, consider sending one member of your party to get in line for lunch at Fantasyland's Be Our Guest restaurant. Be Our Guest has the best food in the Magic Kingdom and is one of the most difficult places to get into in Walt Disney World (reservations are not accepted for lunch, but Fastpass+ might be available). Our other favorites in the park are the Columbia Harbour House in Liberty Square, Pecos Bill's in Frontierland, and Cosmic Ray's in Tomorrowland.

Liliane: Switching off allows adults to enjoy the more adventuresome attractions while keeping the group together.

The different touring plans are described below. The descriptions will tell you for whom (for example, tweens, parents with preschoolers, grandparents, and so on) or for what situation (such as sleeping late) the plans are designed. The actual touring plans are located on pages 453–461. Each plan includes a numbered map of the park to help you find your way around. The plan's steps include advice for Disney's current Fastpass system. When Disney switches to the new Fastpass+ system, refer to the detailed notes at the bottom of each plan. Those notes show the approximate start of the Fastpass return window for each Fastpass obtained in the plan, and the order in which you should try to obtain Fastpass+ reservations if they're limited.

For example, the Magic Kingdom Happy Family touring plan's Fastpass+ priority order is Under the Sea, Pooh, Buzz, Barnstormer, and Dumbo. Thus, you should try to obtain Fastpass+ reservations for Under the Sea first, then Winnie the Pooh, then Buzz Lightyear, and so on, until you run out of Fastpass+ opportunities. If you can't get Fastpass+ reservations for the exact time shown on the plan, get as close as possible. Remember that you can customize any plan and any Fastpass+ reservations you get on our website, **touringplans.com.**

MAGIC KINGDOM HAPPY FAMILY ONE-DAY TOURING PLAN This is a one-day touring plan that includes something for everyone in the family: small children, tweens (children ages 8–12), teenagers, parents, and seniors. The plan keeps the entire family together for most of the day, plus lunch and dinner. A midday break is integrated into the day's touring.

The plan includes the new Fantasyland attractions for the whole family, such as the Seven Dwarfs Mine Train (opens 2014) and Under the Sea: Journey of the Little Mermaid, as well as classics popular with small children. For older kids and teenagers, we recommend thrill rides such as Space Mountain and Big Thunder Mountain, with both groups getting back together when each is done.

MAGIC KINGDOM ONE-DAY TOURING PLAN FOR GRANDPARENTS WITH SMALL CHILDREN The attractions in this touring plan are generally those rated at least three stars (out of five) by both seniors and small children, plus a handful of senior-friendly attractions that children just love. Specifically designed to minimize walking, this plan also includes a midday break of at least 3 hours, assuming lunch around noon and dinner around 6 p.m. Skip the Swiss Family Treehouse if you'd like to leave a little earlier for lunch, and skip *Monsters, Inc. Laugh Floor* if you'd like to extend your midday break a little longer but still want to see the evening parade and fireworks.

To convert this itinerary into a two-day plan, see the Fantasyland and Frontierland attractions on day one, and the Tomorrowland, Adventureland, and character greetings on day two. An alternative strategy is to do steps 1–9 on the morning of day one, and steps 10–23 during the afternoon and evening of day two.

MAGIC KINGDOM ONE-DAY TOURING PLAN FOR TWEENS AND THEIR PARENTS A one-day plan for parents with children ages 8–12, it includes most attractions rated three stars and higher by this age group and sets aside ample time for lunch and dinner.

MAGIC KINGDOM TWO-DAY TOURING PLAN FOR PARENTS WITH SMALL CHILDREN This is a two-day touring plan designed specifically to eliminate extra walking and backtracking. It is a comprehensive touring plan of the Magic Kingdom and includes nearly every child-friendly attraction in the park. The plan features long midday breaks for rest and naps outside the park.

MAGIC KINGDOM TWO-DAY SLEEPYHEAD TOURING PLAN FOR PARENTS WITH SMALL CHILDREN Another version of the two-day touring plan described above, this plan allows families with young children to sleep in, arrive at the park in the late morning, and still see the very best attractions in the Magic Kingdom over two days. The plan uses Fastpass to reduce your waits at the most popular attractions, including Seven Dwarfs Mine Train, Peter Pan's Flight, Buzz Lightyear's Space Ranger Spin, the Jungle Cruise, and Splash Mountain.

PARENT'S MAGIC KINGDOM TOURING PLAN—ONE AFTERNOON AND ONE FULL DAY This day-and-a-half plan works perfectly if you're arriving in Orlando late in the morning of your first vacation day and can't wait to start touring. It also works great for families who want to sleep in one morning after spending a full day in the Magic Kingdom the day before.

The attractions in these plans are the same as those found in the standard one-day plans for parents with small children, so these day-and-a-half itineraries also work as relaxed versions of those plans. Both plans employ Fastpass and take advantage of lower evening crowds to visit other popular attractions. The plans should work well during the more crowded times of the year.

PRELIMINARY INSTRUCTIONS FOR ALL MAGIC KINGDOM TOURING PLANS

ON DAYS OF MODERATE-TO-HEAVY ATTENDANCE, follow your chosen touring plan exactly, deviating only:

1. When you aren't interested in an attraction it lists. For example, the plan may tell you to go to Tomorrowland and ride Space Mountain, a roller coaster. If you don't enjoy roller coasters, skip this step and proceed to the next.

2. When you encounter a very long line at an attraction the touring plan calls for. Crowds ebb and flow at the park, and an unusually long line may have gathered at an attraction to which you're directed. For example, you arrive at The Haunted Mansion and find extremely long lines. It's possible that this is a temporary situation caused by several hundred people arriving en masse from a recently concluded performance of *The Hall of Presidents* nearby. If this is the case, skip The Haunted Mansion and go to the next step, returning later to retry.

WHAT TO DO IF YOU GET OFF-TRACK

IF UNFORESEEN EVENTS interrupt a plan:

1. If you're following a touring plan in our mobile app Lines (**touringplans.com /lines**), just press the "Optimize" button when you're ready to start touring again. Lines will figure out the best possible plan for the remainder of your day.

2. If you're following a printed touring plan, skip one step on the plan for every 20 minutes' delay. For example, if you lose your wallet and spend an hour hunting for it, skip three steps and pick up from there.

3. Forget the plan and organize the remainder of the day using the standby wait times listed in the Lines app.

BEFORE YOU GO

1. Call ☎ 407-824-4321 or check **disneyworld.com** the day before you go to check the official opening time.

2. Purchase admission before you arrive.

3. Familiarize yourself with park-opening procedures (described on page 230) and reread the touring plan you've chosen so that you know what you're likely to encounter.

MAGIC KINGDOM TRIVIA QUIZ

By Lou Mongello

1. **What is the name of Sonny Eclipse's (unseen) backup group at Cosmic Ray's Starlight Café?**
   a. The Space Cadets   **c.** Space Angels
   b. The Sun Bonnets   **d.** Cranium Commandos

2. **What is the name of the riverboat at Liberty Square?**
   a. *Joe Fowler*   **c.** *Liberty Belle*
   b. *Mark Twain*   **d.** *Lily Belle*

3. **What is the name of Mike Wazowski's nephew in *Monsters, Inc. Laugh Floor*?**
   a. Roz   **c.** Bob
   b. Henry   **d.** Marty

4. Where in the Magic Kingdom can you find a dog named Nana?

a. *The Hall of Presidents*　　**c.** *Walt Disney's Carousel of Progress*

b. The Haunted Mansion　　**d.** Peter Pan's Flight

5. In what scene can you find a bride in The Haunted Mansion?

a. The ballroom　　**c.** The attic

b. The séance room　　**d.** The graveyard

6. The number on the front of *The Hall of Presidents* building represents:

a. The year Walt Disney World opened

b. The current year

c. The year America gained its independence

d. The year the Constitution was ratified

7. The narrator on the Liberty Square riverboat is:

a. Mark Twain　　**c.** Prince Naveen

b. Ben Franklin　　**d.** Paul Revere

8. About how many leaves can you find on the Swiss Family Treehouse?

a. 3,000　　**c.** 300,000

b. 30,000　　**d.** 3,000,000

9. At the end of *Mickey's PhilharMagic,* how does Mickey wake up Donald?

a. Blowing a trumpet in his face　　**c.** Tickling him

b. Grabbing his feet　　**d.** Banging a drum

10. The Main Street Electrical Parade features a float based on a character from which of these movies:

a. *Pete's Dragon*　　**c.** *The Incredibles*

b. *The Sword in the Stone*　　**d.** *101 Dalmations*

Answers can be found on page 434.

Trivia content courtesy of Lou Mongello, author of *Walt Disney World Trivia Books (Volumes I and II),* as well as the *Audio Guides to WDW.* Mongello is also the host and producer of WDW Radio (**wdwradio.com**) and is the publisher of *Celebrations* magazine (**celebrationspress.com**). Dream Team Project (**dreamteamproject.org**), which Mongello founded, helps raise money for the Make-A-Wish Foundation of America to send seriously ill children and their families to Walt Disney World.

PART EIGHT

EPCOT

EDUCATION, INSPIRATION, AND CORPORATE IMAGERY are the focus at Epcot, the most adult of the Walt Disney World theme parks. What it gains in taking a futuristic, visionary, and technological look at the world, it loses, just a bit, in warmth, happiness, and charm. Some people find the attempts at education to be superficial; others want more entertainment and less education. Most visitors, however, are in between, finding plenty of amusement *and* information alike.

Epcot's theme areas are distinctly different. Future World combines Disney creativity and major corporations' technological resources to examine where humankind has come from and where we're going. World Showcase features landmarks, cuisine, and culture from almost a dozen nations and is meant to be a sort of permanent World's Fair.

So you thought that the Magic Kingdom was big? Epcot is more than twice as large as the Magic Kingdom, so unless one day is all you have, plan on spending two days at Epcot to savor all it has to offer. While Epcot, unlike the Magic Kingdom, does not stand out as a natural for kids, rest assured that families can have as much fun at Epcot as at any of the other theme parks.

Now for the practical stuff: Future World always opens first; that is where you start your day. While most of Future World's attractions stay open until the entire park closes, a few close around 7 p.m. most of the year. If you are lodging at a Disney hotel, consider visiting when the park offers morning or evening Extra Magic Hours. Once you arrive, pick up a park map and the daily entertainment schedule (*Times Guide*). If you are a Disney hotel guest and the park offers morning or evening Extra Magic Hours, grab the flyer that lists all the attractions open during the additional hours. If you intend to stay for Extra Magic Hours in the evening, each member of your party will need to have his or her resort ID.

Stroller, wheelchair, and ECV/ESV rentals are available inside the main entrance to the left, toward the rear of the Entrance Plaza. For storage lockers, turn right at Spaceship Earth. The Baby Care Center

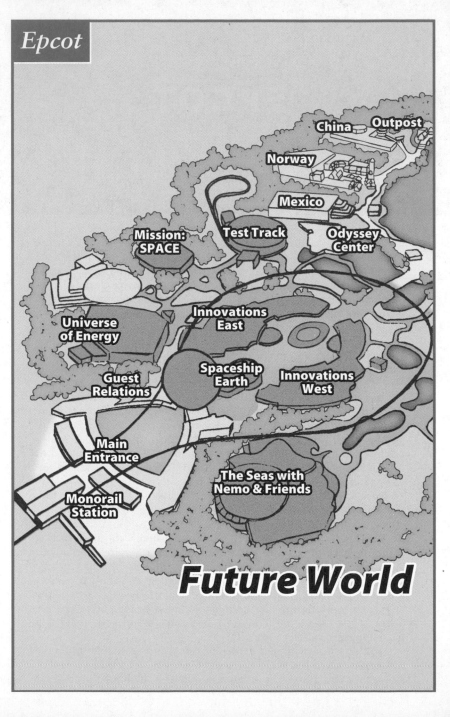

Epcot

China

Outpost

Norway

Mexico

Mission: SPACE

Test Track

Odyssey Center

Universe of Energy

Innovations East

Guest Relations

Spaceship Earth

Innovations West

Main Entrance

Monorail Station

The Seas with Nemo & Friends

Future World

is on the World Showcase side of the Odyssey Center complex, to the rear of Test Track. At the same location are first-aid and lost-persons services. For a live-entertainment schedule and dining reservations, stop at Guest Relations to the left of Spaceship Earth. Lost and found is located at the main entrance. Banking services (ATMs) are available outside the main entrance, on the Future World Bridge, and in World Showcase at the Germany Pavilion. Disney no longer has pet-care facilities adjacent to the park, but the Best Friends Pet Resort across from Disney's Port Orleans Resort will provide a comfortable home away from home for Fido, Frisky, and all their pet pals.

KIDCOT FUN STOPS

THIS PROGRAM, DESIGNED TO MAKE EPCOT more interesting for younger visitors, is basically a movable feast of simple arts and crafts projects. Tables are set up at some locations in Future World and at each pavilion in World Showcase. The tables are staffed by cast members who discuss their native country with the children and engage them in a craft project. Look for the brightly colored Kidcot signs. Participation is free. For a memento and to augment the experience, you can purchase a World Showcase Passport for your children. The passports are sold for $10 at most stores throughout Epcot. As you visit the different lands, cast members at the Kidcot stations will stamp the passport. If your child is really interested in different lands, Guest Relations offers free fact sheets for each country.

Children as young as age 3 will enjoy the Kidcot Fun Stops. If you do not want to spring for the passport, the Disney folks will be happy to stamp an autograph book or just about anything else, including your child's forehead.

FUTURE WORLD

Innoventions East and West ★★★½

APPEAL BY AGE	PRESCHOOL ★★★★	GRADE SCHOOL ★★★★	TEENS ★★★½
YOUNG ADULTS ★★★		OVER 30 ★★★½	SENIORS ★★★½

What it is Static and hands-on exhibits relating to products and technologies of the near future. **Scope and scale** Major diversion. **Fright potential** Not frightening in any respect. **Bottleneck rating** 8. **When to go** On your second day at Epcot or after seeing all major attractions. **Special comments** Most exhibits demand time and participation to be rewarding; not much gained here by a quick walk-through. **Authors' rating** Vastly improved; ★★★½.

Innoventions—a huge, busy collection of walk-through, hands-on exhibits—consists of two huge, crescent-shaped, glass-walled structures separated by a central plaza. Exhibits, many of which are changed each year, demonstrate such products as virtual-reality games, high-definition TV, voice-activated appliances, future cars, medical diagnostic equipment, and Internet applications. Each of the major exhibit areas is sponsored by a different manufacturer or research lab, emphasizing the effect of the products or technology on daily living. The most popular Innoventions attraction is an arcade of video and simulator games. One of the coolest exhibits, however, is the demonstration area for the Segway Human Transporter, the much-publicized two-wheeled vehicle that makes riders look as if they're standing on top of a push lawn mower. Another feature, the Sum of All Thrills, is a design-your-own roller-coaster simulator. Guests have three vehicle options: bobsled, roller coaster, or jet aircraft. It's possible to program actual loops into both the coaster and jet course, and the robot arm will swing you upside down! Hit Sum of All Thrills before 10:30 a.m. or after 5 p.m.

The newer exhibits are certainly more compelling, but they require waiting in line to be admitted. Because the theater at each exhibit is quite small, you often wait as long for an Innoventions infomercial as for a real attraction elsewhere in the park. We observed a wide range of reactions by visitors to the exhibits and can suggest only that you form your own opinion. We suggest skipping exhibits with waits of more than 10 minutes or experiencing them first thing in the morning when there are no lines.

This is a great place for parents to abandon their teenagers—at least for a while—to enjoy a meal of escargot at Bistro de Paris in France.

Liliane

Whoa! You gotta check out the e-mail postcards. Star in your own cartoon and e-mail it to all your friends. The best is in Innoventions. I put myself in an alien movie and landed on Mars! On the way home, we couldn't wait to get there to see it on our computer. A very cool souvenir—and it's free.

Ian

Spaceship Earth ★★★★

APPEAL BY AGE	PRESCHOOL ★★★★	GRADE SCHOOL ★★★★	TEENS ★★★★
YOUNG ADULTS ★★★★½		OVER 30 ★★★★	SENIORS ★★★★½

Thumbs Up for the Whole Family

What it is Educational dark ride through past, present, and future. **Scope and scale** Headliner. **Fright potential** Dark and imposing presentation intimidates a few preschoolers. **Bottleneck rating** 7. **When to go** Before 10 a.m. or after 4 p.m. **Special comment** If lines are long when you arrive, try again after 4 p.m. **Authors' rating** One of Epcot's best; not to be missed; ★★★★. **Duration of ride** About 16 minutes. **Average wait in line per 100 people ahead of you** 3 minutes. **Loading speed** Fast.

This ride spirals through the 18-story interior of Epcot's premier landmark, taking guests through audio-animatronic scenes depicting mankind's development in communications from cave painting to the Internet. It's actually more fun than it sounds and is carried off with a lot of humor. Spaceship Earth draws crowds like a magnet first thing in the morning because it is so close to the park entrance.

I hate this ride because it's boring. Most of these people didn't have cars or TV or anything we have today.

Hannah

CLUB COOL

ATTACHED TO THE FOUNTAIN SIDE OF INNOVENTIONS WEST is a sort of international soda fountain called Club Cool. The exhibit provides free unlimited samples of soft drinks from around the world.

Kids will love to fill their own tasting cups and move from one sampling station to the next. Mix lemon, water, and honey and you get Kinley, popular in Israel. In Mozambique Krest Ginger Ale is in; in China a drink based on watermelon is highly popular. The Japanese recommend the nutrition and health benefits of a vitamin drink, and the Italians are in love with a beverage that could chalk up great sales as an emetic in the U.S. VegitaBeta, anyone? Club Cool also lives up to its name; it is cool inside and makes for a good meeting place.

Club Cool is my favorite place to go when I'm thirsty, and the drinks are FREE. You can have as much as you want, soft drinks that is, from all over the world. Some are pretty yucky, but some are pretty good. Give it a try and see what you think. Coke from China is not bad.

Ian

THE SEAS WITH NEMO & FRIENDS PAVILION

THE SEAS IS HOME TO ONE OF AMERICA'S top marine aquariums, a ride, an interactive animated film, and a number of first-class educational exhibits. Featuring characters from the animated feature *Finding Nemo*, it brings some whimsy and much-needed levity to what was heretofore educationally brilliant but somewhat staid. Before the makeover, The Seas (or The Living Seas, as it was previously known) was a snoozer for children. Now it ranks near the top of the kids' list.

The Seas Main Tank and Exhibits ★★★½

APPEAL BY AGE PRESCHOOL ★★★½ GRADE SCHOOL ★★★½ TEENS ★★★★
YOUNG ADULTS ★★★★ OVER 30 ★★★★ SENIORS ★★★★

Thumbs Up for the Whole Family

What it is A huge saltwater aquarium, plus exhibits on oceanography, ocean ecology, and sea life. **Scope and scale** Major attraction. **Fright potential** Not frightening in any respect. **Bottleneck rating** 7. **When to go** Before 11:30 a.m. or after 5 p.m. **Authors' rating** An excellent marine exhibit; ★★★½. **Average wait in line per 100 people ahead of you** 3½ minutes. **Loading speed** Fast.

Take a *Finding Nemo*–themed ride to Sea Base to start your discovery of The Seas' main tank and exhibits. Watch scientists and divers conduct actual marine experiments in the main tank, containing fish, mammals, and crustaceans in a simulation of an ocean ecosystem. Visitors can observe the activity through windows below the surface (including inside the Coral Reef Restaurant). Children will be enchanted to discover the substantial fish population and the many exhibits offered. With the addition of *Turtle Talk with Crush* and The Seas with Nemo & Friends, The Seas has been transformed from a Future World backwater into one of Epcot's most popular venues. We recommend experiencing the ride and *Turtle Talk* in the morning before the park gets crowded, saving the excellent exhibits for later.

The Seas with Nemo & Friends ★★★

APPEAL BY AGE PRESCHOOL ★★★½ GRADE SCHOOL ★★★★ TEENS ★★★½
YOUNG ADULTS ★★★½ OVER 30 ★★★½ SENIORS ★★★★

What it is Ride through a tunnel in The Seas' main tank. **Scope and scale** Major attraction. **Fright potential** Not frightening in any respect. **Bottleneck rating** 7. **When to go** Before 11 a.m. or after 5 p.m. **Authors' rating** Educational *and* fun;

★★★. **Duration of ride** 4 minutes. **Average wait in line per 100 people ahead of you** 3½ minutes. **Loading speed** Fast.

Upon entering The Seas, you proceed to the loading area, where you'll be made comfortable in a "clamobile" for your journey through the aquarium. The technology used makes it seem as if the animated characters are swimming with the live fish. Meet characters from *Finding Nemo,* such as Mr. Ray, and help Dory, Bruce, Marlin, Squirt, and Crush find Nemo. This cool ride attracts lots of the lovable clown fish's fans, so ride early.

Clamobiles! This ride is fun because it shows real fish and real dolphins, and sometimes real scuba divers! I still get really cautious when I see real sharks, but they can't break the glass and attack you.

Hannah

See *Finding Nemo* prior to your visit if you have not already. You will not soon forget this superb family movie that won the 2004 Oscar for best animated feature. Did you know that Alexander Gould, who gives his voice to little Nemo, is also the voice behind Bambi in the Disney animated sequel *Bambi II*? And stay tuned for *Finding Dory* (2015), a sequel to *Finding Nemo* that brings back Ellen DeGeneres as the voice of the adorable, forgetful blue fish Dory.

Turtle Talk with Crush ★★★★

APPEAL BY AGE	PRESCHOOL ★★★★½	GRADE SCHOOL ★★★★½	TEENS ★★★★
YOUNG ADULTS ★★★★	OVER 30 ★★★★		SENIORS ★★★★

What it is An interactive animated film. **Scope and scale** Minor attraction. **Fright potential** Not frightening in any respect. **Bottleneck rating** 9. **When to go** Before 11 a.m. or after 3 p.m. **Special comments** Get there early to avoid long lines; a real spirit lifter. **Authors' rating** Amazing technology; ★★★★. **Duration of show** 17 minutes. **Probable waiting time** 10–20 minutes before 11 a.m. and after 5 p.m.; as much as 40–60 minutes during the more crowded part of the day.

Thumbs Up for the Whole Family

This interactive theater show starring the 153-year-old surfer turtle from *Finding Nemo* starts like a typical Disney theme-park movie but quickly turns into an interactive encounter, as Crush begins conversations with guests in the audience. Not to be missed! It's unusual to wait more than one or two shows to get in. If you find long lines in the morning, try back after 3 p.m., when more of the crowd has moved on to World Showcase.

I like this show a lot. Don't miss it. You actually feel as if you're in the movie *Finding Nemo*. *Turtle Talk* comes alive when Crush swims up on the movie screen and talks to people. I mean really talks to people. He saw me raise my hand and—Dude!—he said my name and we had a conversation. I don't know how they do it. It was great.

Ian

THE LAND PAVILION

THE LAND IS A HUGE PAVILION containing three attractions and two restaurants. When the pavilion was originally built, its emphasis was on farming, but now it focuses on environmental concerns. Dry as that sounds, kids really enjoy The Land's attractions, especially Soarin', a thrill ride where the operative word is *thrill,* not *terror.* The Land Pavilion is a great place to grab a fast-food lunch. If you're here to see the attractions, however, stay away during mealtimes, as the place is super crowded.

The Circle of Life ★★★½

APPEAL BY AGE	PRESCHOOL ★★★	GRADE SCHOOL ★★★½	TEENS ★★★
YOUNG ADULTS ★★★		OVER 30 ★★★	SENIORS ★★★½

What it is Film exploring man's relationship with his environment. **Scope and scale** Minor attraction. **Fright potential** Not frightening in any respect. **Bottleneck rating** 5. **When to go** Anytime. **Authors' rating** Highly interesting and enlightening; ★★★½. **Duration of show** About 20 minutes. **Probable waiting time** 10–15 minutes.

The Swahili saying *hakuna matata* ("don't worry") does not apply to this movie. On the contrary, Simba, Pumbaa, and Timon from Disney's animated feature *The Lion King* offer a sugarcoated lesson on how to protect and care for the environment.

Did you know that Elton John wrote the music to the song "Hakuna Matata"?

Movie
Tip

Living with the Land *(Fastpass seasonally)* ★★★★

APPEAL BY AGE	PRESCHOOL ★★★½	GRADE SCHOOL ★★★★	TEENS ★★★★
YOUNG ADULTS ★★★★		OVER 30 ★★★★	SENIORS ★★★★

Thumbs Up for the Whole Family

What it is Indoor boat-ride adventure through the past, present, and future of US farming and agriculture. **Scope and scale** Major attraction. **Fright potential** Not frightening in any respect, but loud. **Bottleneck rating** 9. **When to go** Before 11 a.m. or after 1 p.m. **Authors' rating** Interesting and fun; not to be missed; ★★★★. **Duration of ride** About 14 minutes. **Average wait in line per 100 people ahead of you** 3 minutes. **Assumes** 15 boats operating. **Loading speed** Moderate.

DISNEY DISH WITH JIM HILL

GOOD NEWS: OUR HEALTH PLAN COVERS BENADRYL The next time you ride Living with the Land, remember that all plants need to be pollinated before they bear fruit. Disney can't let a million bees fly around inside the pavilion, so everything here is hand-pollinated by a Disney cast member.

This boat ride through four experimental growing areas is inspiring and educational. Kids like seeing the giant pumpkins and hearing about the tomato tree that produced 32,000 tomatoes. Teens will be fascinated by the imaginative ways to grow crops—without soil, hanging in the air, and even on a space station. A lot of the fruits and vegetables grown here are served to guests in the restaurants at Epcot.

I like the gardening part and looking at the fruits and vegetables. They need to make Living with the Land into a rock song.

Hannah

Soarin' *(Fastpass)* ★★★★½

APPEAL BY AGE	PRESCHOOL ★★★★½	GRADE SCHOOL ★★★★★	TEENS ★★★★½
YOUNG ADULTS ★★★★½		OVER 30 ★★★★★	SENIORS ★★★★★

What it is Flight simulation ride. **Scope and scale** Super-headliner. **Fright potential** Frightens almost no one who meets the minimum height requirements. **Bottleneck rating** 10. **When to go** First 30 minutes the park is open or use Fastpass. **Special comments** Entrance on the lower level of The Land Pavilion. May induce motion sickness; must be 40" tall to ride; switching-off option provided (see page 245). **Authors' rating** Exciting and mellow at the same time; not to be missed; ★★★★½. **Duration**

of ride 5½ minutes. **Average wait in line per 100 people ahead of you** 4 minutes. **Assumes** 2 concourses operating. **Loading speed** Moderate.

DISNEY DISH WITH JIM HILL

 SOARIN' OVER . . . SHANGHAI For a while now, the Imagineers have been rumored to be working on a new ride film for Soarin', the original of which debuted at Disney California Adventure in 2001. As it turns out, the rumors are true— but the film is slated to premiere at Shanghai Disneyland when it opens in December 2015. What's more, the film will be China-specific, built around IMAX HD footage captured during low-level flyovers of such landmarks as the Great Wall, the Forbidden City, and the Three Gorges Dam. As for a stateside Soarin' movie, word around WDI is to look for it in 2016.

This is the closest to hang gliding you will come without trying the real thing. Once airborne, you are flying over California with IMAX-quality images projected all around you, while a flight simulator moves your hang glider in sync with the movie. The experience is extremely mellow and nonthreatening. Any child (or adult) who meets the 40-inch minimum height requirement will love Soarin'. If you opt for Fastpass, make sure to get one before lunch, as there may not be any passes left after 12:30 p.m. As a matter of fact, Liliane had to be rescued by her son during one of her visits, as a mob of gone-wild guests nearly ran her over on her way to the Fastpass machine. Gaming stations have been added to keep visitors entertained while waiting in line.

> It's a ride, but you don't really move that much. There's a huge movie screen in front of you. You go past an orange farm in the ride, and it starts to smell like oranges. It's a good thing you don't go near any wet dogs!
> Hannah

 Now I know what it feels like to be a kite. Fly high into the clouds and soar like a bird! It's like you have a front-row seat to see the world. You feel the wind in your face and smell the oranges as you fly over the trees. I'll never forget flying through the golf course when all of a sudden—oh, dude!—a golf ball whooshed by my head.
Ian

IMAGINATION! PAVILION

THIS MULTIATTRACTION PAVILION is situated on the west side of Innoventions West and down the walk from The Land. Outside is an "upside-down" waterfall and one of our favorite Future World landmarks, the "jumping water," a fountain that hops over the heads of unsuspecting passersby.

> When it's hot, all I want to do is wear my swim trunks and get wet. One of the best places is outside of the Imagination! Pavilion. They have dancing waters skipping through the air. I like to follow where the water is flying and let it splash my face. Another place to get wet is near Test Track. Water shoots up from the ground. It's fun!
> Ian

Captain EO ★ ★ ★

APPEAL BY AGE	PRESCHOOL ★★½	GRADE SCHOOL ★★★	TEENS ★★★
YOUNG ADULTS ★★★		OVER 30 ★★★	SENIORS ★★★

What they are 3-D film with special effects. **Scope and scale** Headliner. **Fright potential** Extremely intense visual effects and loudness frighten young children.

308 PART 8 EPCOT

Bottleneck rating 8. **When to go** Anytime. **Special comments** Adults should not be put off by the sci-fi theme or rock music. The high decibels frighten some young children. **Authors' rating** ★★★. **Duration of show** About 17 minutes. **Preshow** 8 minutes. **Probable waiting time** 15 minutes.

In response to Michael Jackson's death in 2009, Disney brought back his 3-D space-themed musical film *Captain EO* for a "limited engagement" in its theme parks. *Captain EO* originally ran here 1986–1994. A very loud soundtrack has a propensity to frighten small kids.

The ultimate music video stars the late Michael Jackson. Directed by Francis Ford Coppola, this 3-D space fantasy is augmented by lasers, fiber optics, cannons, and a host of other special effects in the theater, as well as by some audience participation. There's not much of a story, but there's plenty of music and dancing performed by some of the most unlikely creatures ever to shake a tail feather. If nothing else, *Captain EO* reminds us that music videos once contained more than young urbanites dancing in clubs or five ill-dressed, unshaven guys whining onstage.

Young children will be frightened at times. If, however, they want to see the show, I recommend letting them watch first without the 3-D glasses and with earplugs.

Liliane

Journey into Imagination with Figment ★★½

APPEAL BY AGE	PRESCHOOL ★★★★	GRADE SCHOOL ★★★½	TEENS ★★★
YOUNG ADULTS ★★★½		OVER 30 ★★★	SENIORS ★★★

What it is Dark fantasy-adventure ride. **Scope and scale** Major attraction wannabe. **Fright potential** Frightens a small percentage of preschoolers. **Bottleneck rating** 6. **When to go** Anytime. **Authors' rating** Vacuous; ★★½. **Duration of ride** About 6 minutes. **Average wait in line per 100 people ahead of you** 2 minutes. **Loading speed** Fast.

"One little spark of inspiration is at the heart of all creation," croons the ever-popular Figment, as he takes you on a tour of the zany Imagination Institute with the help of your five senses. Young children will love the little purple dragon, but grown-ups and teens will be mildly amused (and probably bored) at best.

Mission: SPACE *(Fastpass)* ★★★★

APPEAL BY AGE	PRESCHOOL ★★★½	GRADE SCHOOL ★★★★½	TEENS ★★★★
YOUNG ADULTS ★★★★		OVER 30 ★★★★	SENIORS ★★★½

What it is Space flight simulation ride. **Scope and scale** Super-headliner. **Fright potential** Intense thrill ride may frighten guests of any age. Switching-off option provided (see page 245). **Bottleneck rating** 9. **When to go** First or last hour the park is open, or use Fastpass. **Special comments** Not recommended for pregnant women or people prone to motion sickness; must be 44" tall to ride; a gentler, non-spinning version is also available. **Authors' rating** Impressive; ★★★★. **Duration of ride** About 5 minutes plus preshow. **Average wait in line per 100 people ahead of you** 4 minutes.

In this attraction, you join three other guests in a four-man crew to fly a space mission. Each guest plays a role (commander, pilot, navigator, or engineer) and is required to perform certain functions during the flight. A cleverly conceived, technological marvel, Mission: SPACE made national news when, in separate incidents, two guests died after riding it. While neither of the deaths were linked to the attraction (the victims had unknown preexisting conditions), the negative publicity caused many guests to skip it entirely. In response, Disney has added a less stressful non-spinning version of Mission: SPACE. If you want to experience the spinning version of the ride, join the orange team, and if you prefer to check it out without those pesky g-forces, join the green team.

Liliane

Follow the orange brick road; it's much more fun. The ride is too intense for little ones and people prone to motion sickness, but grade-schoolers, teens, and brave moms and dads will love it! And don't worry about the job assignments. Do you really think Disney is going to let you meddle around with its multimillion-dollar high-tech toys?

Movie Tip

The host during your expedition is Gary Sinise, known for his roles in the space flicks Apollo 13 and Mission to Mars.

The "Mom, I Can't Believe It's Disney!" Fountain ★★★★

**APPEAL BY AGE   PRESCHOOL ★★★★★   GRADE SCHOOL ★★★★★
TEENS ★★★★   YOUNG ADULTS ★★★★   OVER 30 ★★★★   SENIORS ★★★★★**

What it is Combo fountain/shower. **Scope and scale** Diversion. **Fright potential** Not frightening in any respect. **Bottleneck rating** 2. **When to go** When it's hot. **Special comment** Secretly installed by Martians during *IllumiNations*. **Authors' rating** Yes! ★★★★.

Thumbs Up for the Whole Family

On a broiling Florida day, when you think you might suddenly combust, fling yourself into the fountain and dance, skip, sing, jump, splash, stick your toes down the spouts, or catch the water in your mouth! Toddlers and preschoolers, along with hippies, especially love the fountain. We know that your kids will be right in the middle of this thing before your brain sounds the alert. Our advice: Pack a pair of dry shorts and turn the kids loose. Make sure that they don't go into the fountain with sneakers, as wet sneakers are a recipe for blisters.

Test Track *(Fastpass)* ★★★½

**APPEAL BY AGE   PRESCHOOL ★★★★   GRADE SCHOOL ★★★★½   TEENS ★★★★½
YOUNG ADULTS ★★★★½   OVER 30 ★★★★½   SENIORS ★★★★**

What it is Automobile test-track simulator ride. **Scope and scale** Super-headliner. **Fright potential** Intense thrill ride may frighten guests of any age. Switching-off option provided (see page 245). **Bottleneck rating** 10. **When to go** First 30 minutes the park is open, just before closing, or use Fastpass. **Special comment** Must be 40" tall to ride. **Authors' rating** Good but not worth a 40-minute or longer wait; ★★★½. **Duration of ride** About 4 minutes. **Average wait in line per 100 people ahead of you** 4½ minutes. **Loading speed** Moderate–fast.

Rough   Scary

Refurbished in 2012, Test Track's new presentation takes you through the process of designing a new vehicle and then "testing" your car in a high-speed drive through and around the pavilion. After hearing about automobile design, you enter the Chevrolet Design Studio to create your own concept car. Using a large touch-screen interface (like a giant iPad), groups of up to three guests drag their fingers to design their car's body, engine, wheels, trim, and color. The computer screen reflects each design decision's impact on four performance characteristics: capability, efficiency, responsiveness, and power. For example, designing a large truck with a huge V-8 engine increases the car's capability and power but drastically reduces its efficiency. Next, you board a six-seat ride vehicle, attached to a track on the ground, for an actual drive through Chevrolet's test track. The vehicle's tests include braking maneuvers, cornering, and acceleration, culminating in a spin around the outside of the pavilion at speeds of up to 65 miles per hour. Most guests figure out quickly that absolutely nothing in their car's design has any effect whatsoever on their ride experience: designing a fuel-sipping electric hybrid results in the exact same sensations as a monster truck with huge tires. Although Test Track got a sleek new look, it's still a challenge to keep the attraction running, especially in humid or wet conditions. Test Track is a favorite attraction of teens. If nobody in your family wants to join you on the ride and you don't have a Fastpass, join the single-rider line. It moves much faster.

Man, this is about as scary as driving with my older sister! The ride is pretty cool, especially driving in a car that nearly wipes out and hits a truck. The best time is when you hit the speed track outside and rip around an oval like you're a NASCAR driver.

Shelton

I love fast things, and this was more than fast! You ride in a really cool car on what looks like a real road. There's no radio, but it's a convertible, and I like convertibles!

Hannah

It was pretty fun but not as exciting as I thought it would be. The thought of going 65 miles an hour was amazing, but you might as well get in a convertible and go down the highway. There is a Kidcot Fun Stop at Test Track where those too short to ride can occupy themselves with arts and crafts. When the temperature's boiling, try the neighboring Cool Wash misting station.

Liliane

Universe of Energy: *Ellen's Energy Adventure* ★★★★

APPEAL BY AGE   PRESCHOOL ★★★½   GRADE SCHOOL ★★★½   TEENS ★★★½
YOUNG ADULTS ★★★½   OVER 30 ★★★½   SENIORS ★★★½

What it is Combination ride/theater presentation about energy. **Scope and scale** Major attraction. **Fright potential** Dinosaur segment frightens some preschoolers; visually intense, with some intimidating effects. **Bottleneck rating** 7. **When to go** Anytime. **Special comment** Don't be dismayed by long lines; 580 people enter the pavilion each time the theater changes audiences. **Authors' rating** The most unique theater in Walt Disney World; ★★★★. **Duration of presentation** About 26½ minutes. **Preshow** 8 minutes. **Probable waiting time** 14 minutes.

Join Ellen DeGeneres and Bill Nye, the science guy, who star in this 26-minute presentation about energy. Visitors are seated in what appears to be an ordinary theater. After a short film, the theater seats divide into six 97-passenger traveling cars that glide among swamps and through a prehistoric forest full of animatronic dinosaurs. The ride itself is smooth and not scary at all, though some children are frightened by the dinosaurs.

Scary

Ellen DeGeneres lent her voice to the role of Dory, a fish with short-term memory loss, in the animated Disney-Pixar film *Finding Nemo*.

Movie
Tip

■ WORLD SHOWCASE

WORLD SHOWCASE, EPCOT'S SECOND THEME AREA, is an ongoing World's Fair encircling a picturesque, 40-acre lagoon. The cuisine, culture, history, and architecture of almost a dozen countries are permanently displayed in individual national pavilions spaced along a 1.2-mile promenade. Pavilions replicate familiar landmarks and street scenes from the host countries. Until the Fantasyland expansion is complete, the best places to see characters are in Epcot. Mulan and Musha appear regularly in China; Snow White in Germany; Mickey in the United States; Donald in Mexico; Pinocchio in Italy; Alice and Mary Poppins in the United Kingdom; Marie, Remy, Belle, and the Beast in France; and Aladdin, Jasmine, and the Genie in Morocco. Now moving clockwise around the World Showcase promenade, here are the nations represented and their attractions.

Agent P's World Showcase Adventure ★ ★ ★ ★

APPEAL BY AGE PRESCHOOL ★ ★ ★ ½ **GRADE SCHOOL** ★ ★ ★ ½ **TEENS** ★ ★ ★ ★
YOUNG ADULTS ★ ★ ★ ½ **OVER 30** ★ ★ ★ ½ **SENIORS** ★ ★ ★

What it is Interactive scavenger hunt in select World Showcase pavilions. **Scope and scale** Minor attraction. **Fright potential** Not frightening in any respect. **Bottleneck rating** 1. **When to go** Anytime. **Authors' rating** Fun activity, especially for return visitors. It's best experienced if your group has at least two pairs; ★ ★ ★ ★. **Duration of experience** Allow 30 minutes per adventure.

What used to be the Kim Possible World Showcase Adventure game has been transformed into a *Phineas and Ferb*–themed adventure game called Agent P's World Showcase Adventure. Guests will help Agent P foil the evil plans of Dr. Doofenshmirtz and his various Inators. The Agent P game is similar to the Kim Possible version as guests become agents and use a "high-tech secret agent device" to search for clues. Different cases are available in Mexico, France, Germany, Norway, Japan, China, and the United Kingdom. Why the change? Well, *Kim Possible* had not been on the air for a while, and for Disney, capitalizing on the popularity of a current show such as *Phineas and Ferb* is a great way to get younger kids excited to explore World Showcase, which can be a chore for any parent visiting Epcot.

As with Kim Possible, the game is included with park admission; however, be prepared to leave credit card information for the secret agent device that players are issued to experience the interactive elements of the game.

MEXICO PAVILION

A PRE-COLUMBIAN PYRAMID dominates the architecture of this exhibit. Inside you will find authentic and valuable artifacts, a village scene complete with restaurant, and the Gran Fiesta boat ride. Don't miss Mariachi Cobre, the 12-piece Mexican band entertaining daily in front of the pyramid. The meet and greet for Donald Duck fans is outside on the right-hand side of the Mexico Pavilion.

SPANISH 101	
HELLO: Hola	**Pronunciation:** *Oh-la*
GOODBYE: Adios	**Pronunciation:** *Ah-dee-ohs*
THANK YOU: Gracias	**Pronunciation:** *Grah-see-ahs*
MICKEY MOUSE: El Ratón Miguelito	**Pronunciation:** *El Rah-tone Mee-gell-lee-toe*

Gran Fiesta Tour Starring the Three Caballeros ★★½

APPEAL BY AGE	PRESCHOOL ★★★★	GRADE SCHOOL ★★★★	TEENS ★★★
YOUNG ADULTS ★★★½		OVER 30 ★★★	SENIORS ★★★½

What it is Indoor scenic boat ride. **Scope and scale** Minor attraction. **Fright potential** Not frightening in any respect. **Bottleneck rating** 5. **When to go** Before noon or after 5 p.m. **Authors' rating** New role for classic Disney characters; ★★½. **Duration of ride** About 7 minutes (plus 1½-minute wait to disembark). **Average wait in line per 100 people ahead of you** 4½ minutes. **Assumes** 16 boats in operation. **Loading speed** Moderate.

Thumbs Up for the Whole Family

Gran Fiesta Tour's story line features Donald Duck, José Carioca (a parrot), and Panchito (a Mexican charro rooster) from the 1944 Disney film *The Three Caballeros;* the story has our heroes racing to Mexico City for a gala reunion performance. Guests are treated to detailed scenes done in eye-catching colors.

NORWAY PAVILION

SURROUNDING A COURTYARD is an assortment of traditional Scandinavian buildings, including a replica of the 14th-century Akershus Castle, now home to princess-hosted character meals. The major attraction is the boat ride Maelstrom.

NORWEGIAN 101	
HELLO: God dag	**Pronunciation:** *Good dagh*
GOODBYE: Ha det	**Pronunciation:** *Hah deh*
THANK YOU: Takk	**Pronunciation:** *Tahk*
MICKEY MOUSE: Mikke Mus	**Pronunciation:** *Mikeh Moose*

It is hard to say no to the mouthwatering pastries at Kringla Bakeri Og Kafe in Norway. It is my favorite stop at the end of the day to pick up the next day's breakfast.

Liliane

Maelstrom *(Fastpass)* ★★★

APPEAL BY AGE	PRESCHOOL ★★★½	GRADE SCHOOL ★★★½	TEENS ★★★½
YOUNG ADULTS ★★★★		OVER 30 ★★★½	SENIORS ★★★½

What it is Indoor adventure boat ride. **Scope and scale** Major attraction. **Fright potential** Dark; visually intense in parts. Ride ends with a plunge down a 20-foot flume. **Bottleneck rating** 9. **When to go** Before 1 p.m., after 7 p.m., or use Fastpass. **Authors' rating** Too short but has its moments; ★★★. **Duration of ride** 4½ minutes, followed by a 5-minute film with a short wait in between; about 14 minutes for the ride and show combo. **Average wait in line per 100 people ahead of you** 4 minutes. **Assumes** 12 or 13 boats operating. **Loading speed** Fast.

Board a dragon-headed ship for a voyage through the fabled seas of Viking history and legends with brave trolls, rocky gorges (fjords), and a storm at sea. Sounds dangerous? The ride can be intense at times, but the only hold-your-breath moment is when your boat descends a 20-foot slide. The rather short ride is followed by a 5-minute film on Norway, but if you don't want to see the film, you will be given the opportunity to exit before it begins.

CHINA PAVILION

THERE IS NO RIDE AT THE CHINA PAVILION, but the majestic half-size replica of the Temple of Heaven in Beijing will surely make it into your photo album. See *Reflections of China,* an impressive film about the people and natural beauty of China. Children will enjoy the regularly scheduled performances of Chinese acrobats. Check your entertainment schedule (*Times Guide*) for showtimes. The China Pavilion is also home to Mulan, who holds court here outside most of the time, or inside the Temple of Heaven during inclement weather.

CHINESE (MANDARIN) 101	
HELLO: Ni hao	**Pronunciation:** *Knee how*
GOODBYE: Zai jian	**Pronunciation:** *Zy jehn*
THANK YOU: Xiè xie	**Pronunciation:** *Chi-eh chi-eh*
MICKEY MOUSE: Mi Lao Shu	**Pronunciation:** *Me Lah-oh Su*

Reflections of China ★★★½

APPEAL BY AGE	PRESCHOOL ★★	GRADE SCHOOL ★★★	TEENS ★★★½
YOUNG ADULTS ★★★½		OVER 30 ★★★★	SENIORS ★★★★

What it is Film about the Chinese people and country. **Scope and scale** Major attraction. **Fright potential** Not frightening in any respect. **Bottleneck rating** 4. **When to go** Anytime. **Special comment** Audience stands throughout performance. **Authors' rating** This beautifully produced film was introduced in 2003; ★★★½. **Duration of presentation** About 14 minutes. **Probable waiting time** 10 minutes.

GERMANY PAVILION

GERMAN 101	
HELLO: Hallo	**Pronunciation:** *Hall-o*
GOODBYE: Auf wiedersehen	**Pronunciation:** *Ow-f veeh-der-zain*
THANK YOU: Danke	**Pronunciation:** *Dan-keh*
MICKEY MOUSE: Micky Maus	**Pronunciation:** *Me-key Mouse*

THE GERMANY PAVILION DOES NOT HAVE RIDES. The main focus is Biergarten, a full-service (reservations suggested) restaurant serving German food and beer. Yodeling, folk dancing, and oompah-band music are regularly performed during mealtimes. Be sure to check out the large, elaborate model railroad located just beyond the restrooms as you walk from Germany toward Italy. Snow White will sign autographs at the well just as you reach the Germany Pavilion.

Ian

Biergarten German restaurant: The best party I ever went to. My dad liked the beer band, and so did I. They shouted, "Ticky tocky, ticky tocky!" and we yelled back, "Oy, oy, oy!" (whatever that means). Everybody raised their beer glasses, sang songs, and did goofy dances. I think I had one too many root beers.

Liliane

The Germany Pavilion is the perfect place to introduce your kids to a great snack: Gummibaerchen (gummy bears), my favorite candy.

ITALY PAVILION

THE ENTRANCE TO ITALY is marked by an 83-foot-tall campanile (bell tower) intended to mirror the tower in St. Mark's Square in Venice. Left of the campanile is a replica of the 14th-century Doge's Palace.

Streets and courtyards in the Italy Pavilion are among the most realistic in the World Showcase. You really feel as if you're in Italy. Because there's no film or ride, tour any time.

ITALIAN 101	
HELLO: Buon giorno	Pronunciation: Bon jor-no
GOODBYE: Ciao (informal)	Pronunciation: Chow
THANK YOU: Grazie	Pronunciation: Grah-zee-eh
MICKEY MOUSE: Topolino	Pronunciation: To-po-lee-no

I don't know how they do this, but I couldn't stop watching. A lady statue comes alive and messes with people. She stands perfectly still in front of Italy. When people have their pictures taken next to her, she moves and does crazy things to them. My family laughed a lot, but I was too chicken to go up to her.

Ian

UNITED STATES PAVILION

THE UNITED STATES PAVILION is an imposing brick structure reminiscent of Colonial Philadelphia and is home to a very moving and patriotic, albeit sanitized, retrospective of US history. Street entertainment outside includes the Voices of Liberty choral ensemble and the Spirit of America Fife & Drum Corps, among others. Across the plaza is the America Gardens Theatre, Epcot's premier venue for concerts and stage shows.

The American Adventure ★★★★

APPEAL BY AGE	PRESCHOOL ★★	GRADE SCHOOL ★★★	TEENS ★★★½
YOUNG ADULTS ★★★½	OVER 30 ★★★★		SENIORS ★★★★½

Thumbs Up for the Whole Family

What it is Patriotic mixed-media and audio-animatronic theater presentation on US history. **Scope and scale** Headliner. **Fright potential** Not frightening in any respect. **Bottleneck rating** 6. **When to go** Anytime. **Authors' rating** Disney's best historic/patriotic attraction; not to be missed; ★★★★. **Duration of presentation** About 29 minutes. **Preshow** Voices of Liberty chorale singing. **Probable waiting time** 25 minutes.

The 29-minute multimedia show is narrated by animatronic Mark Twain and Ben Franklin. *The American Adventure* reminds you of a contest: Tell us everything you love about America in 30 minutes or less. Only four female figures are among the 12 personified ideals around the theater, one of them representing the rather ambiguous "tomorrow" by virtue of holding a baby. The North American continent seemingly does not exist prior to the landing of the *Mayflower.*

JAPAN PAVILION

THE FIVE-STORY, BLUE-ROOFED PAGODA, inspired by a 17th-century shrine in Nara, sets this pavilion apart. A hill garden behind it encompasses waterfalls, rocks, flowers, lanterns, paths, and rustic bridges. There are no attractions unless you count the huge Japanese retail venue. Not to be missed, though, are the Matsuriza Taiko drummers. The drums can often be heard throughout the World Showcase, but you need to be up close to see the graceful way the drums are played. Another absolute must is to watch Miyuki create animals or flowers from very hot, soft dough that hardens when it cools. Of the current 15 Japanese candy artists, Miyuki is the only woman trained in this 250-year-old art. Check the *Times Guide* for scheduled performances.

JAPANESE 101	
HELLO: Konnichiwa	Pronunciation: *Ko-nee-chee wah*
GOODBYE: Sayonara	Pronunciation: *Sigh-yo-nah-ra*
THANK YOU: Arigato	Pronunciation: *Ah-ree-gah-to*
MICKEY MOUSE: Mikki Mausu	Pronunciation: *Mikkee Mou-su*

MOROCCO PAVILION

THE BUSTLING MARKET, WINDING STREETS, lofty minarets, and stuccoed archways re-create the romance and intrigue of Marrakech and Casablanca. Attention to detail makes Morocco one of the most exciting World Showcase pavilions. And while there are no attractions, do not miss Mo'Rockin!, a group blending rhythms from around the globe—including Middle Eastern, African, Spanish, and American sounds. The Morocco Pavilion is also home to Jasmine, Aladdin, and Genie. Get the autograph books ready! A new restaurant, Spice Road Table, opens in late 2013 and should provide tasty tapas-style Mediterranean dishes and excellent views of *IllumiNations.* Expect large crowds.

ARABIC 101	
HELLO: Salaam alekoum	Pronunciation: *Sah-lahm ah-leh-koom*
GOODBYE: Ma'salama	Pronunciation: *Mah sah-lah-mah*
THANK YOU: Shoukran	Pronunciation: *Shoe-krah-n*
MICKEY MOUSE: Mujallad Miki	Pronunciation: *Muh-jahl-lahd Me-key*

FRANCE PAVILION

WELCOME AND BIENVENUE to Paris, Eiffel Tower, and all. There is not much to do for the kids here, but you won't have any trouble luring them into Les Halles Boulangerie Patisserie for a scrumptious French pastry. Givenchy, the famed French perfume empire, opened a shop at the France Pavilion and is the only retail location in the United States offering the full line of Givenchy makeup and skin-care products, as well as a large selection of Givenchy fragrances. Belle, Beast, and Aurora are regularly found here for picture opportunities and autographs. Character appearances are intermittent, so check the *Times Guide*.

FRENCH 101	
HELLO: Bonjour	**Pronunciation:** *Bon-jure*
GOODBYE: Au revoir	**Pronunciation:** *Oh reh-vwa*
THANK YOU: Merci	**Pronunciation:** *Maer-si*
MICKEY MOUSE: Mickey	**Pronunciation:** *Mee-keh*

Impressions de France ★★★½

APPEAL BY AGE	PRESCHOOL ★★½	GRADE SCHOOL ★★★½	TEENS ★★★½
YOUNG ADULTS ★★★★		OVER 30 ★★★★	SENIORS ★★★★½

What it is Film essay on the French people and country. **Scope and scale** Major attraction. **Fright potential** Not frightening in any respect. **Bottleneck rating** 7. **When to go** Anytime. **Authors' rating** Exceedingly beautiful film; not to be missed; ★★★½. **Duration of presentation** About 18 minutes. **Probable waiting time** 15 minutes (at suggested times).

France, here I come! This truly lovely 18-minute movie will make you want to pack your suitcase. An added bonus is that the showing is *très civilizé*, as you get to sit down and rest your weary feet.

UNITED KINGDOM PAVILION

A BLEND OF ARCHITECTURE ATTEMPTS to capture Britain's city, town, and rural atmospheres. One street alone has a thatched-roof cottage, four-story timber-and-plaster building, pre-Georgian plaster building, formal Palladian exterior of dressed stone, and a city square with a Hyde Park bandstand (whew!). There are no attractions, but don't miss the British Revolution! The band performs the greatest UK hits from the Beatles to the music of Led Zeppelin and The Who. Alice in Wonderland and Mary Poppins greet their fans outside the little English cottage, while Winnie the Pooh, Tigger, and Eeyore appear at the Toy Soldier shop.

Liliane

If your child loves Mary Poppins, your best chance to meet her is here.

CANADA PAVILION

CANADA'S CULTURAL, NATURAL, AND architectural diversity is reflected in this large and impressive pavilion. Older kids will be interested in the 30-foot-tall totem poles that embellish an American Indian village. Canada is also home to a sort of punk-Celtic-country band called Off Kilter—yes, the lead singer wears a kilt—that performs in front of the showcase entrance. Check your entertainment schedule (*Times Guide*) for performance times.

O Canada! ★★★½

| APPEAL BY AGE | PRESCHOOL ★★★ | GRADE SCHOOL ★★★½ | TEENS ★★★½ |
| YOUNG ADULTS ★★★½ | | OVER 30 ★★★★ | SENIORS ★★★★ |

What it is Film essay on the Canadian people and their country. **Scope and scale** Major attraction. **Fright potential** Not frightening in any respect. **Bottleneck rating** 5. **When to go** Anytime. **Special comment** Audience stands during performance. **Authors' rating** Makes you want to catch the first plane to Canada! ★★★½. **Duration of presentation** About 15 minutes. **Probable waiting time** 9 minutes.

O Canada! showcases Canada's natural beauty and population diversity and demonstrates the immense pride that Canadians have in their country. A film starring Martin Short features clips of Canada's stunning landscape, all the way from Swift Current to Moose Jaw. (Just kidding, eh. From Prince Edward Island to Vancouver.) Visitors leave the theater through Victoria Gardens, which was inspired by the famed Butchart Gardens of British Columbia.

Cast members often run a preshow quiz on Canadian trivia outside the theater before the show. Here are some helpful tips: Canada's capital is Ottawa; its $1 coin is nicknamed the Loonie, after the bird engraved on it; and the $2 coin is the Toonie—not, unfortunately, the Doubloonie.

This large-capacity attraction (guests must stand) gets fairly heavy late-morning attendance, as Canada is the first pavilion encountered as one travels counterclockwise around World Showcase Lagoon.

LIVE ENTERTAINMENT *at* EPCOT

IN FUTURE WORLD

KIDS WILL LOVE THE CREW of drumming janitors (The JAMMitors), as well as the Krystos gymnasts in alien attire and the dancing fountains show in the plaza between the Innoventions East and West buildings.

Combine a rest break with a little fun. Let your kids experience one of the special talking water fountains at Epcot (located outside the Mouse Works shop, behind Innoventions West; between Innoventions and *Honey, I Shrunk the Audience* or *Captain EO* in the Imagination Pavilion; and next to the play fountain between Future World and World Showcase). For a hilarious chat, seek out PUSH the talking trash can at the Electric Umbrella Restaurant in Innoventions East.

Liliane

AROUND THE WORLD SHOWCASE

STREET PERFORMANCES IN AND AROUND the World Showcase are what set live entertainment at Epcot apart from the other Disney

FAVORITE EATS AT EPCOT

LAND | SERVICE LOCATION | FOOD ITEM

THE SEAS PAVILION

Coral Reef Restaurant* | Food with a view—fish menu. The aquarium will keep the kids happy for quite some time.

THE LAND PAVILION

Sunshine Seasons | Healthy choices—our all-time favorite

MEXICO

La Cantina de San Angel | Children's plate with burrito, chips, & beverage

NORWAY

Kringla Bakeri Og Kafe | Salmon sandwiches & pastries

CHINA

Lotus Blossom Café | Beef & chicken rice bowls, vegetable lo mein, & egg rolls

GERMANY

Sommerfest | Bratwurst & frankfurter with kraut & apple strudel

ITALY

Tutto Italia* | Reasonable pasta & kids' menu

UNITED STATES

Liberty Inn | If you are craving all-American food

JAPAN

Katsura Grill | Beef & chicken teriyaki

MOROCCO

Tangierine Café | *Shawarma,* hummus, couscous, & kids' meals; outdoor seating

FRANCE

Crêpes des Chefs de France | Crêpes & espresso

Les Halles Boulangerie Patisserie | Croissants, chocolate mousse, & yummy sandwiches on baguettes

UNITED KINGDOM

The Tea Caddy | You must have an English Cadbury bar once in your life.

* *table service only—Advance Reservations highly recommended*

theme parks. A strolling mariachi group can be found in Mexico; street actors in Italy; a fife-and-drum corps or The Voices of Liberty in the United States; traditional songs, drums, and dances in Japan; street comedy and British rock in the United Kingdom; white-faced mimes in France; and bagpipes and Celtic bands in Canada, among other performances. Check your entertainment schedule *(Times Guide)* for performance times. Some restaurants get in on the act too. You can dine among singing waiters in Italy, enjoy Oktoberfest entertainment in Germany, and see belly dancing in Morocco. WDW live-entertainment guru Steve Soares usually posts the Epcot performance schedule about a week in advance at **wdwent.com**.

AMERICA GARDENS THEATRE

THE AMERICA GARDENS THEATRE, an amphitheater on the lagoon across from the United States Pavilion, features pop (and oldies pop) musical acts throughout much of the year, as well as Epcot's popular Candlelight Processional for the Christmas holidays. Showtimes are listed on a board outside the exits and in the daily *Times Guide*.

ILLUMINATIONS

A NIGHTLY CAPSTONE EVENT AT EPCOT called *IllumiNations* features a program of music, fireworks, erupting fountains, special lighting, and laser technology performed on World Showcase Lagoon. This enchanting and ambitious show (it tells the history of the universe starting with the Big Bang) is well worth keeping the kids up late. The best places to view the show are from the lakeside veranda of La Hacienda at the Mexico Pavilion, Spice Road Table in Morocco (opens late 2013), or Rose & Crown Pub at the United Kingdom Pavilion. Come early and relax with a drink or snack. The drawback is, you guessed it, that you will have to claim this spot at least 90 minutes before *IllumiNations*.

For other great viewing spots, check out our "Where to View *IllumiNations*" map. Note that the boat dock opposite Germany may be exposed to a lot of smoke from the fireworks because of Epcot's prevailing winds.

IllumiNations is the climax of every day at Epcot, so keep in mind that once the show is over, you will be leaving the park and so will almost everybody else. For suggested exit strategies, see below.

For a really good view of the show, you can charter a pontoon boat for about $350. Captained by a Disney cast member, the boat holds up to 10 guests. Your captain will take you for a little cruise and then position the boat in a perfect place to watch *IllumiNations*. For more information, call ☎ 407-WDW-PLAY.

IllumiNations ★ ★ ★ ★ ½

APPEAL BY AGE	PRESCHOOL ★★★½	GRADE SCHOOL ★★★★	TEENS ★★★★½
YOUNG ADULTS ★★★★½	OVER 30 ★★★★½		SENIORS ★★★★½

What it is Nighttime fireworks and laser show at World Showcase Lagoon. **Scope and scale** Super-headliner. **Fright potential** Not frightening in any respect. **When to go** Stake out viewing position 20–40 minutes before showtime. **Special comments** Showtime is listed in the daily entertainment schedule on the handout park map. Audience stands during performance. **Authors' rating** Epcot's most impressive entertainment event; ★★★★½. **Duration of show** About 18 minutes.

Bob: Disney may soon offer Fastpasses to reserve prime viewing spots for *IllumiNations*.

EXIT STRATEGIES

MORE GROUPS GET SEPARATED AND MORE CHILDREN lost after *IllumiNations* than at any other time. Make sure that you have preselected a meeting point in the Epcot entrance area, such as the

Where to View IllumiNations

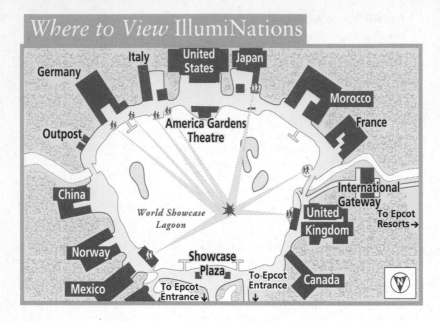

fountain just inside the main entrance. Warn your group not to leave
through the exit turnstiles until everyone is reunited.

- If you are staying at the Swan, Dolphin, Yacht & Beach Club Resorts,
  or BoardWalk Inn & Villas, watch *IllumiNations* from somewhere
  between Italy and the United Kingdom, and exit the park through
  the International Gateway between France and the United Kingdom. You can walk or take a boat back to your hotel.

- If you have a car in the Epcot lot, find a viewing spot at the Future
  World end of World Showcase Lagoon (Showcase Plaza) and leave
  immediately after *IllumiNations* ends. The problem is not the traffic in
  the parking lot—it actually moves pretty well—it's making your way
  to, and finding, your car. Make sure that you write down or take a
  picture of where you are parked—this is not the time to rely on your
  memory. If you are parked near the entrance, skip the tram and walk.
  If you walk, watch your children closely and hang on to them for all
  you're worth. The parking lot is pretty wild at this time of night.

EPCOT TOURING PLANS

OUR STEP-BY-STEP TOURING PLANS are field-tested, independently
verified itineraries that will keep you moving counter to the crowd flow
and allow you to see as much as possible in a single day with minimum
time wasted in line. We present three Epcot one-day touring plans specifically geared toward visiting with children. We also offer, and recommend,

a two-day touring plan that is much more relaxing and far less tiring. Touring Epcot is much more strenuous and demanding than touring the other theme parks. Epcot requires about twice as much walking. And, unlike the Magic Kingdom, Epcot has no effective in-park transportation—wherever you want to go, it's always quicker to walk. Our plans will help you avoid crowds and bottlenecks on days of moderate to heavy attendance, but they can't shorten the distance you have to walk. (Wear comfortable shoes.) On days of lighter attendance, when crowd conditions aren't a critical factor, the plans will help you organize your tour.

As a group, the *Unofficial Guide* research staff loves Epcot. Because we spend so much time there, we really wanted our small children to enjoy it too. The challenge was figuring out how to get the kids connected to the theme or presentation at each pavilion, especially in Future World. Let's face it—even with Test Track and Sum of All Thrills, a 7-year-old is only going to take so much talk about hydroponic vegetables, nuclear fission, or communication systems before tuning out.

The key for us was to brief our children on what they were likely to see in each attraction and then tie it back to something they could relate to in their everyday lives. During the tour of the greenhouse in Living with the Land, for example, we made a game of finding foods they like. (They have cocoa beans—chocolate—so we think that covers almost everyone.) While riding Test Track, we asked our daughter to figure out which parent's driving was most like the ride's. Epcot's Future World attractions can be a lot more palatable to young children if they're engaged and prepared going in. It's all about presentation.

The different touring plans are described below. The descriptions will tell you for whom (for example, tweens, parents with preschoolers, and so on) or for what situation (such as sleeping late) the plans are designed. The actual touring plans are located on pages 462–466. Each plan includes a numbered map of the park to help you find your way around. The plan's steps include advice for Disney's current Fastpass system. When Disney switches to the new Fastpass+ system, refer to the detailed notes at the bottom of each plan. Those notes show the approximate start of the Fastpass return window for each Fastpass obtained in the plan, and the order in which you should try to obtain Fastpass+ reservations if they're limited.

EPCOT ONE-DAY TOURING PLAN FOR PARENTS WITH SMALL CHILDREN This plan is designed for parents of children ages 3–8 who wish to see the very best age-appropriate attractions in Epcot. Every attraction has a rating of at least three stars (out of five) from preschool and grade-school children surveyed by the *Unofficial Guide*. Special advice is provided for touring the park with small children. The plan keeps walking and backtracking to a minimum.

EPCOT ONE-DAY SLEEPYHEAD TOURING PLAN FOR PARENTS WITH SMALL CHILDREN A relaxed plan that allows families with small children to sleep late and still see the highlights of Epcot. The plan begins around 11 a.m., sets aside ample time for lunch, and includes the very best child-friendly attractions in the park. The plan also points out where Fastpass can best be used.

EPCOT ONE-DAY TOURING PLAN FOR TWEENS AND THEIR PARENTS A one-day touring plan for parents with children ages 8–12. It includes attractions rated three stars and higher by this age group, and it sets aside ample time for lunch and dinner.

PARENT'S EPCOT TOURING PLAN—ONE AFTERNOON AND ONE FULL DAY This touring plan is for families who want to tour Epcot comprehensively over two days. Day one uses early-morning touring opportunities. Day two begins in the afternoon and continues until closing.

BEFORE YOU GO

1. Call ☎ 407-824-4321 or check **disneyworld.com** the day before you go to verify the official opening time.

2. Make reservations at the Epcot full-service restaurant(s) of your choice up to 180 days in advance of your visit.

EPCOT TRIVIA QUIZ
By Lou Mongello

1. In what World Showcase pavilion can you meet Donald Duck?
  a. United States   **c.** United Kingdom
  b. Germany   **d.** Mexico

2. In Soarin', what U.S. state do you soar over?
  a. Florida   **c.** Texas
  b. California   **d.** The entire nation

3. *Captain EO* is played by which of these famous stars?
  a. Michael Jordan   **c.** Robin Williams
  b. Michael Jackson   **d.** Joe Jonas

4. What country is found between Germany and the United States?
  a. France   **c.** Japan
  b. Morocco   **d.** Italy

5. What is the largest pavilion at Epcot?
  a. The Seas with Nemo & Friends   **c.** Universe of Energy
  b. Mission: SPACE   **d.** The Land

6. How many different international pavilions can be found in Epcot?
  a. 7   **c.** 11
  b. 9   **d.** 13

7. What is unique about the waterfalls outside the Imagination! Pavilion?
  a. They flow upwards.   **c.** They are holograms.
  b. The water is purple.   **d.** They flow only at night.

8. What does EPCOT stand for?
   a. Employee Paychecks Come On Tuesday
   b. Every Person Comes Out Tired
   c. Experimental Prototype Community of Tomorrow
   d. Economic Private City of Orlando Taxation

9. Kids of all ages can participate in an adventure through World Showcase based on which Disney Channel show?
   a. *Phineas and Ferb*   c. *Kim Possible*
   b. *Wizards of Waverly Place*   d. *The Replacements*

10. The Gran Fiesta Tour features Donald and:
   a. Daisy and Goofy.   c. Pepe and Pancho.
   b. José Carioca and Panchito. d. José Carioca and Marco.

11. What color are Figment's eyes?
   a. Red   c. Yellow
   b. Orange   d. Green

12. In the Universe of Energy, what does Ellen nickname her college roommate?
   a. Jumpin' Judy   c. Smarty Pants
   b. Stupid Judy   d. Einstein

Answers can be found on page 434.

PART NINE

DISNEY'S ANIMAL KINGDOM

WITH ITS LUSH FLORA, winding streams, meandering paths, and exotic setting, Disney's Animal Kingdom is a stunningly beautiful theme park. The landscaping alone conjures images of a rain forest, veld, and even formal gardens. Add to this loveliness a population of more than 1,700 animals, replicas of Africa's and Asia's most intriguing architecture, and a diverse array of singularly original attractions, and you have the most unique of all Walt Disney World theme parks. The Animal Kingdom's seven sections, or "lands," are Oasis, Discovery Island, DinoLand U.S.A., Camp Minnie-Mickey, Africa, and Asia. Rafiki's Planet Watch is touted as a land by Disney but doesn't really qualify as such in our eyes.

On Discovery Island, behind the Creature Comforts Shop, is the Baby Care Center with supplies, changing tables, and a quiet place to nurse, as well as a first-aid center. Garden Gate Gifts at the main entrance and Duka La Filimu in Africa will save the day if you run out of memory cards or other camera supplies.

At the entrance plaza, ticket kiosks front the main entrance. To your right before the turnstiles, you'll find an ATM. Passing through the turnstiles, wheelchair and stroller rentals (at Garden Gate Gifts) are to your right. Guest Relations—the park headquarters for information, handout park maps, entertainment schedules, missing persons, and lost and found—is to the left. Lockers are just inside the main entrance to the left. Disney no longer has pet-care facilities adjacent to the park, but the Best Friends Pet Resort across from Disney's Port Orleans Resort will provide a comfortable home away from home for Puff, Killer, Snarky, and all their pet pals.

While having a car is the best way to get around at Walt Disney World, the Animal Kingdom is somewhat of an exception. If you are staying at a Disney resort, we suggest that you use Disney transportation, as the Animal Kingdom parking lot often opens only 15 minutes before the park, causing lots of long lines and frustrations for drivers.

The park is arranged somewhat like the Magic Kingdom. The lush, tropical Oasis serves as Main Street, funneling visitors to Discovery

Island at the center of the park. Discovery Island is the park's retail and dining center. From Discovery Island, guests can access the respective theme areas: Africa, Camp Minnie-Mickey, Asia, and DinoLand U.S.A. Rafiki's Planet Watch is accessed from Africa.

Extra Magic Hours are offered to guests lodging at the Disney hotels. However, our testing has shown that the early-entry program doesn't really save you any time waiting in line. In addition, Evening Magic Hours are currently not offered.

Kilimanjaro Safaris and Pangani Forest Exploration Trail close about 30–60 minutes before sunset. Thus, as days get shorter with the change of seasons, the attractions close earlier in the day. In the fall, when the clocks are rolled back, Disney closes animal exhibits as early as 4:45 p.m. During slower or colder times of the year, Disney may delay the daily opening of Kali River Rapids in Asia, as well as the Boneyard playground, the Wildlife Express Train, and Conservation Station.

Big plans are in the works for the Animal Kingdom! In March 2012 Disney announced that it will build a theme-park "land" based on the movie *Avatar* to open in 2018, with construction starting in 2013. Disney bought exclusive rights to use elements from the 2009 blockbuster and from sequels due out in 2014 and 2015, so it seems clear that Disney follows the approach Universal took with the phenomenally successful Wizarding World of Harry Potter. Because the project is still in the early design phase, it remains to be seen if the *Avatar*-themed land will also feature food and merchandise based on items found in the films.

The OASIS

THOUGH THE FUNCTIONAL PURPOSE of the oasis is to funnel guests to the center of the park, it also sets the stage and gets you into the right mood to enjoy Animal Kingdom. The Oasis immediately envelops you in an environment that is replete with choices. There is not one broad thoroughfare but rather multiple paths. Each will deliver you to Discovery Island at the center of the park, but which path you choose and what you see along the way is up to you. The natural-habitat zoological exhibits are primarily designed for the comfort and well-being of the animals. A sign will identify the animal(s) in each exhibit, but there's no guarantee that the animals will be immediately visible. Because most habitats are large and provide ample terrain for the occupants to hide, you must linger and concentrate, looking for small movements in the vegetation. The Oasis is a place to linger and appreciate, and although this is exactly what the designers intended, it will be largely lost on Disney-conditioned guests who blitz through at warp speed to queue up for the big attractions. If you are a blitzer in the morning, plan to spend some time in The Oasis on your way out of the park. The Oasis usually closes 30–60 minutes after the rest of the park.

We thought the animals were very cool. But don't get too close to the spoonbills. One squawked at me!

Shelton

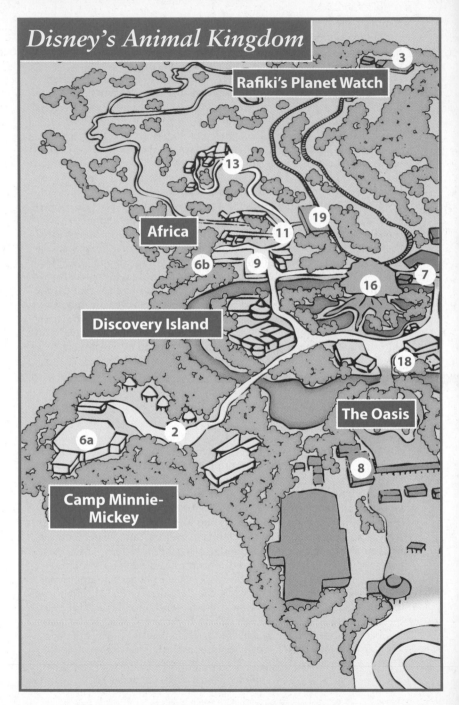

Disney's Animal Kingdom

Rafiki's Planet Watch

Africa

Discovery Island

The Oasis

Camp Minnie-Mickey

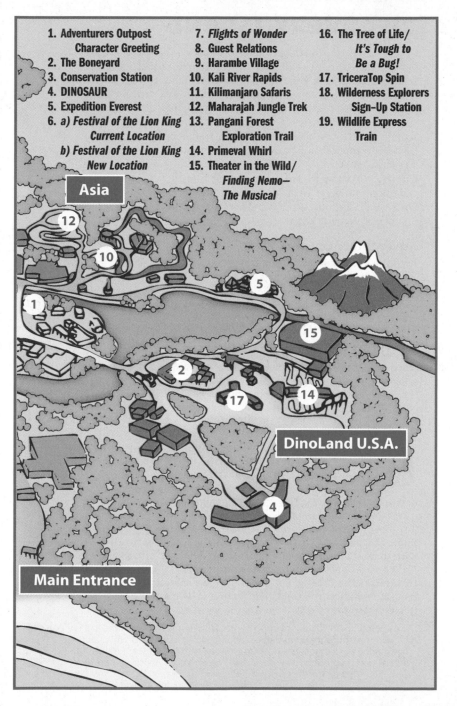

1. Adventurers Outpost Character Greeting
2. The Boneyard
3. Conservation Station
4. DINOSAUR
5. Expedition Everest
6. a) *Festival of the Lion King* Current Location
   b) *Festival of the Lion King* New Location
7. *Flights of Wonder*
8. Guest Relations
9. Harambe Village
10. Kali River Rapids
11. Kilimanjaro Safaris
12. Maharajah Jungle Trek
13. Pangani Forest Exploration Trail
14. Primeval Whirl
15. Theater in the Wild/ *Finding Nemo— The Musical*
16. The Tree of Life/ *It's Tough to Be a Bug!*
17. TriceraTop Spin
18. Wilderness Explorers Sign-Up Station
19. Wildlife Express Train

Asia

DinoLand U.S.A.

Main Entrance

DISCOVERY ISLAND

DISCOVERY ISLAND IS AN ISLAND of tropical greenery and whimsical equatorial African architecture, executed in vibrant hues of teal, yellow, red, and blue. Connected to the other lands by bridges, the island is the hub from which guests can access the park's various theme areas. Discovery Island is the park's central shopping, dining, and services headquarters. It is here that you will find the first-aid and Baby Care centers. For the best selection of Disney trademark merchandise, try the Island Mercantile shop. Counter-service food and snacks, but no full-service restaurants, are available. In addition to several wildlife exhibits, Discovery Island's Tree of Life hosts the film *It's Tough to Be a Bug!* A new meet and greet with Mickey and Minnie opened in May 2013 at Discovery Island; the all-new indoor Adventurers Outpost is located in the former Beastly Bazaar.

Adventurers Outpost

An indoor (and air-conditioned) character greeting location for Mickey and Minnie Mouse, Adventurers Outpost is decorated with photos, memorabilia, and souvenirs from the two's various world travels. There are two greeting rooms here, with two identical sets of characters.

The Tree of Life/*It's Tough to Be a Bug!* ★★★★

APPEAL BY AGE	PRESCHOOL ★★★½	GRADE SCHOOL ★★★★	TEENS ★★★★
YOUNG ADULTS ★★★★		OVER 30 ★★★★	SENIORS ★★★★

What it is 3-D theater show. **Scope and scale** Major attraction. **Fright potential** Very intense and loud, with special effects that startle viewers of all ages and potentially terrify young children. **Bottleneck rating** 9. **When to go** Anytime. **Special comment** The theater is inside the tree. **Authors' rating** Zany and frenetic; ★★★★. **Duration of show** Approximately 8 minutes. **Probable waiting time** 12–20 minutes.

Before entering the show, take a close look at The Tree of Life, the remarkable home of this 3-D movie. The primary icon and focal point of the Animal Kingdom, the tree features a trunk with high-relief carvings depicting 325 animals.

It's Tough to Be a Bug! is a zany, cleverly conceived, but very intense 3-D show housed below The Tree of Life. For starters, the show is about bugs, and bugs always rank high on the ick-factor scale. That, coupled with some startling special effects and a very loud soundtrack, make *It's Tough to Be a Bug!* a potential horror show for the age-7-and-under crowd. Tread cautiously, but don't write off the attraction. You can prepare by watching the animated feature *A Bug's Life* before you leave home—many of the characters are the same.

The closing lines of the show tipped me off when it was announced that "honorary bugs (read: audience members) remain seated while all the lice, bedbugs, maggots, and cockroaches exit first." In plain English, this means that if you don't like bugs crawling on you, even simulated ones, keep your feet off the floor. And thanks to Disney ingenuity, the bugs sting too—they do, they do.

Liliane

CAMP MINNIE-MICKEY

THIS LAND WAS DESIGNED TO BE THE DISNEY characters' Animal Kingdom headquarters. It once boasted two theater attractions, as well as character trails that led to meet and greets for Disney characters. Currently, only one attraction, the *Festival of the Lion King* show, remains, and it will be moved to a new theater in the Africa section of the park. Once vacant, Camp Minnie-Mickey, along with some adjoining acreage, will be incorporated into the new *Avatar*-themed land.

DISNEY DISH WITH JIM HILL

ANIMAL KINGDOM SINGS THE (*AVATAR*) BLUES James Cameron never does anything small. So when work begins on the building that will be the centerpiece of Animal Kingdom's forthcoming *Avatar* "land," expect to see one truly massive structure looming over the trees on the west side of the park. If all goes according to plan, the Imagineers will make use of the hi-def digital-projection system that powers the Magic Kingdom's *Celebrate the Magic* to make it appear as if clouds are moving across the surface of Pandora.

Festival of the Lion King ★★★★

APPEAL BY AGE   PRESCHOOL ★★★★½   GRADE SCHOOL ★★★★½   TEENS ★★★★½   YOUNG ADULTS ★★★★½   OVER 30 ★★★★½   SENIORS ★★★★½

What it is Theater-in-the-round stage show. **Scope and scale** Major attraction. **Fright potential** A bit loud, but otherwise not frightening in any respect. **Bottleneck rating** 9. **When to go** Before 11 a.m. or after 4 p.m. **Special comment** Performance times are listed in the handout park map or *Times Guide*. **Authors' rating** Upbeat and spectacular; not to be missed; ★★★★. **Duration of show** 30 minutes. **Probable waiting time** 20–35 minutes.

Fantastic pageantry, dazzling costumes, a mini–Broadway show, and air-conditioning too. *Festival of the Lion King* at the Animal Kingdom was the precursor of the Broadway production of *The Lion King*. *The Festival of the Lion King* will be moved to a new location in the Africa section of the park in the near future.

This was one of my favorite things I did on the whole trip. It was cool how they put us on teams.

Shelton

Try to score front-row seats. Kids are invited to play musical instruments and join the performance.

Liliane

The show is based on the animated feature *The Lion King,* a must-see movie. Did you know that James Earl Jones, the voice behind Mufasa (father of Simba), is also the voice behind Darth Vader in *Star Wars?*

Movie Tip

Wilderness Explorers ★★★★

What it is Park-wide scavenger hunt/puzzle-solving adventure game. **Scope and scale** Diversion. **Fright potential** Not frightening in any respect. **Bottleneck rating** 6. **When to go** Sign up first thing in the morning and complete activities throughout the day. **Authors' rating** Ties in well to the park's strengths; ★★★★. **Duration of experience** Collecting all 32 badges takes 3–5 hours, which can be done over several days.

Wilderness Explorers is an interactive game based on Russell's Boy Scout-esque troop from the movie *Up*, in which you earn badges (stickers) by traveling around the park to complete predefined activities. When you register for the game (near the bridge from the Oasis to Discovery Island), you'll be given instructions and a map showing the park location for each task to be completed. Tasks include solving a puzzle, going on a scavenger hunt, or learning about a culture. There's lots of interaction with cast members, who have been specially trained for this game. Also, the cast members are able to tailor the activities based on the age of the child playing: small children might get an explanation about what deforestation means, for example, while older kids may have to figure out why tigers have stripes. The game is aimed at ages 7–10 but will appeal to all members of the family. Like Agent P's World Showcase Adventure, Wilderness Explorers integrates well into its park. Activities are spread out through the park, including areas to which many guests never venture. You have to ride specific attractions to earn certain badges, so using Fastpass for those will save some time.

■┃ AFRICA

AFRICA IS THE LARGEST OF THE ANIMAL KINGDOM'S lands, and guests enter through Harambe, Disney's idealized and immensely sanitized version of a modern, rural African town. A market (with modern cash registers), a sit-down buffet, limited counter service, and snack stands are available.

Kilimanjaro Safaris *(Fastpass)* ★★★★★

APPEAL BY AGE PRESCHOOL ★★★★½ GRADE SCHOOL ★★★★½ TEENS ★★★★½
YOUNG ADULTS ★★★★½   OVER 30 ★★★★½   SENIORS ★★★★½

Thumbs Up for the Whole Family

What it is Truck ride through an African wildlife reservation. **Scope and scale** Super-headliner. **Fright potential** A "collapsing" bridge and the proximity of real animals make a few young children anxious. **Bottleneck rating** 10. **When to go** As soon as the park opens, in the 2 hours before closing, or use Fastpass. **Authors' rating** Truly exceptional; ★★★★★. **Duration of ride** About 20 minutes. **Average wait in line per 100 people ahead of you** 4 minutes. **Assumes** Full-capacity operation with 18-second dispatch interval. **Loading speed** Fast.

Off you go in an open safari vehicle through a simulated African savanna, looking for hippos, zebras, giraffes, lions, and rhinos. Many readers have asked us whether fewer animals are visible from Kilimanjaro Safaris around lunchtime than at park opening, out of concern that the animals might be less active in the midday heat. To help answer that question, we sent a team of researchers to ride continuously during 1 week in the summer and had them count the number of animals visible at different times of day. We subdivided our counting into large animals (elephants, hippos, and lions, for example), small (deer and other ungulates), and birds. Our results indicate that you'll probably see the same number of animals regardless of when you visit. This finding is almost certainly due to Disney's deliberate placement of water, food, and shade near the safari vehicles.

There are animals here that I've never heard of. It was cool to discover new animals, learn about them, and see what they look like. I didn't know how big a baby giraffe really is!

Hannah

Winding through the safari is Disney's Wild Africa Trek, a behind-the-scenes walking tour of the Animal Kingdom that takes you into several of Kilimanjaro Safaris' animal enclosures.

Pangani Forest Exploration Trail ★★★★

APPEAL BY AGE   PRESCHOOL ★★★★   GRADE SCHOOL ★★★★   TEENS ★★★★
YOUNG ADULTS ★★★★   OVER 30 ★★★★   SENIORS ★★★★½

What it is Walk-through zoological exhibit. **Scope and scale** Major attraction. **Fright potential** Not frightening in any respect. **Bottleneck rating** 9. **When to go** Before 10 a.m. and after 2:30 p.m. **Authors' rating ★★★★**. **Duration of tour** About 20–25 minutes.

The Pangani Forest Exploration Trail is lush, beautiful, and jammed to the gills with people much of the time. This is particularly unpleasant if you have to wiggle your way through with a stroller. Walk the trail before 11 a.m. or after 2:30 p.m.

If you are more into the wildlife than the thrill rides, head to Kilimanjaro Safaris as soon as the park opens and get a Fastpass. Early in the morning, the return window will be short—just long enough, in fact, for an uncrowded, leisurely tour of the Pangani Forest Exploration Trail before you go on safari.

Rafiki's Planet Watch

Rafiki's Planet Watch is not a "land" and not really an attraction either. Our best guess is that Disney uses the name as an umbrella for Conservation Station, the petting zoo, and the environmental exhibits accessible from Harambe via the Wildlife Express train. Presumably, Disney hopes that invoking Rafiki (a beloved character from *The Lion King*) will stimulate guests to make the effort to check out things in this far-flung corner of the park. As for your kids seeing Rafiki, don't bet on it. The closest likeness we've seen here is a two-dimensional wooden cutout.

I think we went to this, but I'm not sure. It wasn't very memorable.

Shelton

Conservation Station and Affection Section ★★★

APPEAL BY AGE   PRESCHOOL ★★★½   GRADE SCHOOL ★★★★   TEENS ★★★½
YOUNG ADULTS ★★★   OVER 30 ★★★½   SENIORS ★★★½

What it is Behind-the-scenes walk-through educational exhibit and petting zoo. **Scope and scale** Minor attraction. **Fright potential** Not frightening in any respect.

Bottleneck rating 6. **When to go** Anytime. **Special comment** Opens 30 minutes after rest of park. **Authors' rating** ★★★.

This is the Animal Kingdom's veterinary and conservation headquarters. Guests can meet wildlife experts, observe some of the ongoing projects, and learn about the operations of the park. A rehabilitation area for injured animals, a nursery for recently born or hatched critters, and a petting zoo are included. Conservation Station is interesting, but you have to invest a little effort, and it helps to be inquisitive. Because it's so removed from the rest of the park, you'll never bump into Conservation Station unless you take the train round-trip from Harambe. There's a lot going on in and around Conservation Station in the morning, as a university biologist from Springfield, Missouri, attests:

> At Animal Kingdom, if you get to Rafiki's [Planet Watch and Conservation Station] between 10 a.m. and noon, you can see the vet techs actually doing some routine procedures as they maintain the health of the animals. Our aspiring 7-year-old vet LOVED visiting with the technician. She spent 20 minutes asking her all kinds of questions.

Habitat Habit!

Located on the pedestrian path between the train station and Conservation Station, and listed on the park maps as an attraction, Habitat Habit! consists of a tiny collection of signs (about coexistence with wildlife) and a few cotton-top tamarins. To call it an attraction is absurd.

Wildlife Express Train ★★

APPEAL BY AGE	PRESCHOOL ★★★½	GRADE SCHOOL ★★★½	TEENS ★★★
YOUNG ADULTS ★★★		OVER 30 ★★★½	SENIORS ★★★½

What it is Scenic railroad ride to Rafiki's Planet Watch and Conservation Station. **Scope and scale** Minor attraction. **Fright potential** Not frightening in any respect. **Bottleneck rating** 7. **When to go** Anytime. **Special comment** Opens 30 minutes after the rest of the park. **Authors' rating** Ho hum; ★★. **Duration of ride** About 5–7 minutes one way. **Average wait in line per 100 people ahead of you** 9 minutes. **Loading speed** Moderate.

Take the train only if you have small kids who would really enjoy the Affection Section petting zoo at Rafiki's Planet Watch. If you have a future veterinarian in your family, it is also well worth checking out the behind-the-scenes exhibits at Conservation Station.

ASIA

CROSSING THE ASIA BRIDGE FROM DISCOVERY ISLAND, you enter Asia through the village of Anandapur, a veritable collage of Asian themes inspired by the architecture and ruins of India, Thailand, Indonesia, and Nepal.

Expedition Everest *(Fastpass)* ★★★★½

APPEAL BY AGE PRESCHOOL ★★★	GRADE SCHOOL ★★★★½	TEENS ★★★★★
YOUNG ADULTS ★★★★★	OVER 30 ★★★★★	SENIORS ★★★★

What it is High-speed roller coaster through Mount Everest. **Scope and scale** Super-headliner. **Fright potential** Frightens guests of all ages. **Bottleneck rating** 8. **When to go** Before 9:30 a.m., after 3 p.m., or use Fastpass. **Special comments** Contains some of the park's most stunning visual elements. Must be 44" tall to ride. **Authors' rating** ★★★★½. **Duration of ride** 4 minutes. **Average wait in line per 100 people ahead of you** Just under 4 minutes. **Assumes** 2 tracks operating. **Loading speed** Moderate–fast.

Lose Things   Scary

As you enjoy one of the most spectacular panoramas in Walt Disney World, you wish this expedition would never end. But you get over that in a hurry as the train starts whirring through the guts of Disney's largest man-made mountain (not only the largest in Florida, but it also beats out Mount Petty Poot Poot in Kansas by 2 feet). After a high-speed encounter with a large, smelly (and often AWOL) yeti and a dead stop at the top of the mountain, the 50-mph chase continues backward. The ride is very smooth and rich both in visuals and special effects. The backward segment is one of the most creative and exciting 20 seconds in roller-coaster annals.

I think it's cool because there are a lot of big hills. There's a yeti, and he tries to eat you. If you're a big screamer like me, you'll probably just close your eyes and open your mouth.

Hannah

Flights of Wonder ★★★★

APPEAL BY AGE	PRESCHOOL ★★★★	GRADE SCHOOL ★★★★½	TEENS ★★★★
YOUNG ADULTS ★★★★		OVER 30 ★★★★½	SENIORS ★★★★½

Thumbs Up for the Whole Family

What it is Stadium show about birds. **Scope and scale** Major attraction. **Fright potential** Swooping birds startle some younger children. **Bottleneck rating** 6. **When to go** Anytime. **Special comment** Performance times are listed in the handout park map or *Times Guide*. **Authors' rating** Unique; ★★★★. **Duration of show** 30 minutes. **Probable waiting time** 20–30 minutes.

Humorously presented, the show is ideal for kids. Don't expect parrots riding unicycles though. *Flights of Wonder* is about the natural talents and characteristics of various bird species. If your child is comfortable with you sitting a few rows behind, encourage him or her to take a seat in the up-front "for kids only" section. When the show is over, stick around and talk to the bird trainers and meet the feathery cast of the show up close and personal. It is a great opportunity to ask questions and take pictures. *Flights of Wonder* plays at the stadium located near the Asia Bridge on the walkway between Asia and Africa. Though the stadium is covered, it's not air-conditioned; thus, early-morning and late-afternoon performances are more comfortable. To ensure finding a seat, arrive about 10–15 minutes before showtime.

Kali River Rapids *(Fastpass)* ★★★½

APPEAL BY AGE	PRESCHOOL ★★★★	GRADE SCHOOL ★★★★½	TEENS ★★★★½
YOUNG ADULTS ★★★★		OVER 30 ★★★★	SENIORS ★★★★

What it is White-water raft ride. **Scope and scale** Headliner. **Fright potential** Potentially frightening and certainly wet for guests of all ages. **Bottleneck rating** 9. **When to go** First or last hour the park is open, or use Fastpass. **Special comments**

Must be 38" tall to ride; guaranteed to get wet; opens 30 minutes after the rest of the park. Switching-off option provided (see page 245). **Authors' rating** Short but scenic; ★★★½. **Duration of ride** About 5 minutes. **Average wait in line per 100 people ahead of you** 5 minutes. **Loading speed** Moderate.

The ride itself is tame and allows you to take in the outstanding scenery as you drift through a dense rain forest, past waterfalls and temple ruins. There are neither big drops nor terrifying rapids waiting to swallow the raft and riders. The foregoing information notwithstanding, Disney still manages to drench you. Nonriding park guests will take great pleasure squirting water at the rafters from above. The water-squirting elephant stations are a great consolation prize for young ones who do not meet the 38-inch height requirement.

Don't wear anything fancy because you're going to get soaked.

If you ride early in the morning or on a cool day, use raingear and make sure that your shoes stay dry. Touring in wet clothes is unpleasant, and walking all day in soaked sneakers is a recipe for blisters.

Liliane   Hannah

Maharajah Jungle Trek ★★★★

APPEAL BY AGE   PRESCHOOL ★★★★   GRADE SCHOOL ★★★★   TEENS ★★★★
YOUNG ADULTS ★★★★   OVER 30 ★★★★   SENIORS ★★★★½

What it is Walk-through zoological exhibit. **Scope and scale** Headliner. **Fright potential** Some children may balk at the bat exhibit. **Bottleneck rating** 5. **When to go** Anytime. **Special comment** Opens 30 minutes after the rest of the park. **Authors' rating** A standard-setter for natural habitat design; ★★★★. **Duration of tour** About 20–30 minutes.

The Jungle Trek is less congested than the Pangani Forest Exploration Trail and is a good choice for midday touring. Tigers, gibbons, bats, and birds are waiting to be discovered along a path winding through the fabulous ruins of the maharajah's palace.

The bat enclosure is outstanding and my favorite section of the trek. This is the opportunity to increase your knowledge, from Batman to Dracula, of these mysterious mammals.

Liliane

◧ DINOLAND U.S.A.

THIS MOST TYPICALLY DISNEY of the Animal Kingdom's lands is a cross between an anthropological dig and a quirky roadside attraction. Accessible via the bridge from Discovery Island, DinoLand U.S.A. is home to a children's play area, a nature trail, a 1,500-seat amphitheater, and DINOSAUR, one of the Animal Kingdom's three thrill rides. Children ages 4–12 will feel right at home at DinoLand U.S.A. *Finding Nemo—The Musical* is shown at the Theater in the Wild.

The Boneyard ★★★½

APPEAL BY AGE   PRESCHOOL ★★★★½   GRADE SCHOOL ★★★★½   TEENS ★★★½
YOUNG ADULTS ★★½   OVER 30 ★★★   SENIORS ★★★

What it is Elaborate playground. **Scope and scale** Diversion. **Fright potential** Not frightening in any respect. **Bottleneck rating** 5. **When to go** Anytime. **Special comment** Opens 30 minutes after the rest of the park. **Authors' rating** Stimulating fun for children; ★★★½.

It's playtime! The Boneyard is an elaborate playground for kids age 12 and younger and is a great place for them to let off steam and get dirty (or at least sandy). The playground equipment consists of skeletal replicas of triceratops, Tyrannosaurus rex, Brachiosaurus, and the like. In addition, there are climbing mazes, as well as sandpits, where little ones can scrounge around for bones and fossils.

The Boneyard can get very hot in the scorching Florida sun, so make sure that your kids are properly hydrated and protected against sunburn. The playground is huge and parents might lose sight of a small child. Fortunately, however, there's only one entrance and exit. Your little ones are going to love the Boneyard, so resign yourself to staying awhile.

DINOSAUR *(Fastpass)* ★ ★ ★ ½

APPEAL BY AGE	PRESCHOOL ★★½	GRADE SCHOOL ★★★½	TEENS ★★★★½
YOUNG ADULTS ★★★★		OVER 30 ★★★★	SENIORS ★★★½

What it is Motion-simulator dark ride. **Scope and scale** Super-headliner. **Fright potential** High-tech thrill ride rattles riders of all ages. **Bottleneck rating** 8. **When to go** Before 10:30 a.m., after 4:30 p.m., or use Fastpass. **Special comments** Must be 40" tall to ride. Switching-off option provided (see page 245). **Authors' rating** ★★★★½. **Duration of ride** 3½ minutes. **Average wait in line per 100 people ahead of you** 3 minutes. **Assumes** Full-capacity operation with 18-second dispatch interval. **Loading speed** Fast.

Here you board a time capsule to return to the Jurassic age in an effort to bring back a live dinosaur before a meteor hits the Earth and wipes them out. The bad guy in this epic is the little-known carnotaurus, an evil-eyed, long in the tooth, Tyrannosaurus rex–type fellow. A combination track ride and motion simulator, DINOSAUR is not for the fainthearted. You get tossed and pitched around in the dark with pesky dinosaurs jumping out at you. DINOSAUR has left many an adult weak-kneed. Most kids under age 9 find it terrifying.

DINOSAUR is an absolute no-no for preschoolers and any child easily frightened. The carnotaurus, unlike Barney and Figment, did not make my favorite dino list.
Liliane

It doesn't really go up any hills, and it didn't make me scream, but it scared my cousin half to death when she was 4. Even if you're 5 or 6, the dinosaurs might scare you.
Hannah

I love the story line, which is thick and detailed and not thin, like the stories for some other rides. I love the part where you just barely escape and you go under a carnotaurus's belly!
Shelton

Primeval Whirl *(Fastpass)* ★ ★ ★

APPEAL BY AGE	PRESCHOOL ★★★½	GRADE SCHOOL ★★★★	TEENS ★★★★
YOUNG ADULTS ★★★½		OVER 30 ★★★½	SENIORS ★★★

What it is Small coaster. **Scope and scale** Minor attraction. **Fright potential** Scarier than it looks. **Bottleneck rating** 9. **When to go** During the first hour the park is open, in the hour before park closing, or use Fastpass. **Special comments** Must be 48" tall to ride. Switching-off option provided (see page 245). **Authors' rating** Wild Mouse on steroids; ★★★. **Duration of ride** Almost 2½ minutes. **Average wait in line per 100 people ahead of you** 4½ minutes. **Loading speed** Slow.

Scary   Rough   Queasy

This is a tricky little coaster with short drops, curves, and tight loops. As if that's not enough, the coaster cars also spin. The problem is that unlike with the evil teacups, guests cannot control the spinning. Complete spins are fun, but watch out for the screeching-stop half-spins.

Theater in the Wild/*Finding Nemo–The Musical* ★★★★

APPEAL BY AGE	PRESCHOOL ★★★★½	GRADE SCHOOL ★★★★½	TEENS ★★★★
YOUNG ADULTS ★★★★½		OVER 30 ★★★★½	SENIORS ★★★★½

Thumbs Up for the Whole Family

What it is Open-air venue for live stage shows. **Scope and scale** Major attraction. **Fright potential** Not frightening in any respect. **Bottleneck rating** 6. **When to go** Anytime. **Special comment** Performance times are listed in the handout park map or *Times Guide*. **Authors' rating** ★★★★. **Duration of show** 30 minutes. **Probable waiting time** About 30 minutes.

Based on the Disney/Pixar animated feature, *Finding Nemo—The Musical* is an elaborate stage show headlining puppets, dancing, acrobats, and special effects. *Finding Nemo* is arguably the most elaborate live show in any Disney World theme park. A few scenes, such as one in which Nemo's mom is eaten (!!!), may be too intense for some very small children. Some of the mid-show musical numbers slow the pace, so the main concern for parents is whether the kids can sit still for an entire show. With that in mind, we advise parents to catch an afternoon performance after seeing the rest of Animal Kingdom.

To get a seat, show up 20–25 minutes in advance for morning and late-afternoon shows and 30–35 minutes in advance for shows scheduled noon–4:30 p.m. Access to the theater is via a relatively narrow pedestrian path; if you arrive as the previous show is letting out, you will feel like a salmon swimming upstream.

When the line is very long, don't assume that you will get into the next show just by queuing up. Disney cast members monitor the line; ask them if you are likely to get into the next show.

Liliane

TriceraTop Spin ★★

APPEAL BY AGE	PRESCHOOL ★★★★½	GRADE SCHOOL ★★★★	TEENS ★★★
YOUNG ADULTS ★★½		OVER 30 ★★★	SENIORS ★★★½

What it is Hub-and-spoke midway ride. **Scope and scale** Minor attraction. **Fright potential** May frighten preschoolers. **Bottleneck rating** 9. **When to go** Before noon or after 3 p.m. **Authors' rating** Dumbo's prehistoric forebear; ★★. **Duration of ride** 1½ minutes. **Average wait in line per 100 people ahead of you** 10 minutes. **Loading speed** Slow.

Instead of Dumbo, you get Dino spinning around a central axis. The ride is fun for young children, but this slow loader is infamous for inefficiency and long waits.

FAVORITE EATS AT ANIMAL KINGDOM

LAND | SERVICE LOCATION | FOOD ITEM

DISCOVERY ISLAND

Flame Tree Barbecue | Ribs & chicken with beans
Pizzafari | Pizza & chicken Caesar salad, breadsticks

AFRICA

Tamu Tamu | Tandoori chicken salad and milk shakes
Tusker House Restaurant** | Marrakech couscous with roasted veggies
Donald's Safari Breakfast at Tusker House is a character breakfast including
Donald, Daisy, Goofy, and Mickey. All-you-can-eat buffet, 8 a.m.–10:30 a.m.

ASIA

Royal Anandapur Tea Company | Teas & specialty coffees
Yak & Yeti** | Shaoxing steak & shrimp

DINOLAND U.S.A.

Restaurantosaurus | Kid's cheeseburger comes with choice of two sides
(grapes, carrot sticks, or applesauce) & choice of 1% milk, bottled water,
or apple juice

OUTSIDE ENTRANCE

Rainforest Cafe* | Breakfast, lunch, & dinner in a tropical rain forest set-
ting with a huge saltwater aquarium, gorillas going wild once in a while, &
simulated thunderstorms. The place to take the kids if you want to sit down!
They'll love you for it—cross my heart, and hope to die.

* *table service only*   ** *counter- and table service available*

Tusker House is my favorite. It has a lot of choices,
and there are always a lot of people there because the food is good.
You can get cinnamon rolls here as big as a stuffed animal!

Hannah

LIVE ENTERTAINMENT
at ANIMAL KINGDOM

STAGE SHOWS are performed daily at the Animal Kingdom; check your
entertainment schedule (*Times Guide*) for showtimes. Street performers
can be found most of the time at in Harambe, Africa; Anandapur, Asia;
and at Camp Minnie-Mickey. For an updated listing of live entertainment
at Animal Kingdom, check out Steve Soares's website **wdwent.com.**

LOOK WHO'S TALKING At The Oasis, don't miss introducing your kids
to **Wes Palm,** the talking palm tree who pokes fun at unsuspecting guests.
At Conservation Station have a chat with **Pipa,** the recycling trash can.

Though Wes Palm and Pipa will have you roaring with laughter,
DiVine will leave you speechless. A perfect fusion between fantasy
and reality, DiVine is an artist in a garb half-vine and half-creeping
plant. She blends perfectly with the foliage at the Animal Kingdom
and is only noticeable when she moves (which can be quite startling if
you're not aware of her presence). DiVine travels around the park but
seems to love the path between Asia and Africa. The silent graceful-
ness of her movements and the serenity of her demeanor are totally

captivating. If you don't encounter her, ask a cast member where she can be found. There is a video of DiVine on **youtube.com.**

ANIMAL ENCOUNTERS Throughout the day, Disney staff conduct impromptu short lectures on specific animals at the park. Look for a cast member in safari garb holding a bird, reptile, or small mammal.

GOODWILL AMBASSADORS A number of Asian and African natives are on hand throughout the park. Both gracious and knowledgeable, they are delighted to discuss their countries. Look for them in Harambe and along the Maharajah Jungle Trek in Asia. They can also be found near the main entrance and at The Oasis.

KIDS' DISCOVERY CLUB Activity stations offer kids ages 4–8 a structured learning experience as they tour Animal Kingdom. Set up along walkways in six themed areas, Discovery Club stations are manned by cast members who supervise a different activity at each station. A souvenir logbook is available at no charge and will be stamped at each station when the child completes a craft or exercise. Kids enjoy collecting the stamps and completing logbook puzzles while in attraction lines.

AFTERNOON PARADE Mickey's Jammin' Jungle Parade features characters from *The Lion King* and other Disney stories. The parade begins and ends near the entrance to Camp Minnie-Mickey. From the Camp Minnie-Mickey entrance, the route goes counterclockwise around Discovery Island and over the bridge to Asia (the parade doesn't enter DinoLand at all). Once over the Asia bridge, the parade turns left and heads for Africa, where it turns left again at the Dawa Bar in the village of Harambe, crosses the bridge to Discovery Island, and heads back to Camp Minnie-Mickey.

The walking path between Africa and Asia has small cutouts that offer good views of the parade and excellent sun protection. Most guests scramble to Camp Minnie-Mickey, the starting point of the parade, and leave this area as soon as the parade crosses over the bridge to Discovery Island. Because most guests don't realize that the parade returns, few are on hand when the parade rumbles through the second time en route to going offstage. Therefore, if you make your way to Camp Minnie-Mickey about 20 minutes after the parade time listed in the *Times Guide*, you'll be able to score a super vantage point at the last minute. In the future, Disney may set aside certain "premium" parade viewing locations for Fastpass+ guests.

ANIMAL KINGDOM TOURING PLANS

OUR STEP-BY-STEP TOURING PLANS ARE FIELD-TESTED, independently verified itineraries that will keep you moving counter to the crowd flow. The plans will also allow you to see as much as possible in a single day with minimum time wasted in line. With an early start, you can take in all the attractions at the Animal Kingdom in a single day, even when traveling with young children.

If you are not interested in an attraction listed on the touring plan, just skip that step and proceed to the next one. Should you encounter a very long line at an attraction the touring plan calls for, skip the attraction and go to the next step, returning later to retry. The use of Fastpass is factored into the touring plans. When Disney switches to the new Fastpass+ system, refer to the detailed notes at the bottom of each plan. Those notes show the approximate start of the Fastpass return window for each Fastpass obtained in the plan, and the order in which you should try to obtain Fastpass+ reservations if they're limited. *Festival of the Lion King*'s venue may move from Camp Minnie-Mickey to Africa; check the park map when you arrive to find the show's location.

The different touring plans are described below. The descriptions will tell you for whom (for example, tweens, parents with preschoolers, and so on) or for what situation (such as sleeping late) the plans are designed. The actual touring plans are located on pages 467–470. Each plan includes a numbered map of the park to help you find your way around.

ANIMAL KINGDOM ONE-DAY TOURING PLAN FOR PARENTS WITH SMALL CHILDREN This plan is designed for parents of children ages 3–8 who wish to see the very best age-appropriate attractions in the Animal Kingdom. Every attraction has a rating of at least three stars (out of five) from preschool and grade-school children surveyed by the *Unofficial Guide*. Special advice is provided for touring the park with small children, including restaurant recommendations. The plan keeps walking and backtracking to a minimum, with no crisscrossing of the park.

ANIMAL KINGDOM ONE-DAY SLEEPYHEAD TOURING PLAN FOR PARENTS WITH SMALL CHILDREN A relaxed plan that allows families with small children to sleep late and still see the highlights of the Animal Kingdom. The plan begins around 11 a.m., sets aside ample time for lunch, and includes the very best child-friendly attractions in the park.

ANIMAL KINGDOM ONE-DAY TOURING PLAN FOR TWEENS AND THEIR PARENTS A one-day plan for parents with children ages 8–12. It includes every attraction rated three stars and higher by this age group and sets aside ample time for lunch.

ANIMAL KINGDOM ONE-DAY HAPPY FAMILY TOURING PLAN A plan for families of all ages. Includes time-saving tips for teens and adults visiting the Animal Kingdom's thrill rides, as well as age-appropriate attractions for parents with small children. The entire family stays together as much as possible (including lunch), but this plan allows groups with different interests to explore their favorite attractions without having everyone wait around.

BEFORE YOU GO

1. Call ☎ 407-824-4321 or check **disneyworld.com** before you go for the park's operating hours.

2. Purchase your admission prior to arrival.

DISNEY'S ANIMAL KINGDOM TRIVIA QUIZ

By Lou Mongello

1. Who are the proprietors of DinoRama?
   - **a.** Mickey and Minnie
   - **b.** Wes Palm and Dr. Seeker
   - **c.** Chester and Hester
   - **d.** Freddy the Yeti

2. Disney spends more than $1.7 million yearly on what for Disney's Animal Kingdom?
   - **a.** Worms
   - **b.** Manure
   - **c.** Transportation costs to import new animals from overseas
   - **d.** Plant food

3. About how many branches are on The Tree of Life?
   - **a.** 500
   - **b.** 3,000
   - **c.** 1,000
   - **d.** 8,000

4. What are the ride vehicles in DINOSAUR called?
   - **a.** Jurassic Jeeps
   - **b.** Time Rovers
   - **c.** XP-37s
   - **d.** Omnimovers

5. What land in Disney's Animal Kingdom has the greatest number of attractions?
   - **a.** Discovery Island
   - **b.** Asia
   - **c.** Africa
   - **d.** DinoLand U.S.A.

6. Which of these attractions is the largest in all of Walt Disney World?
   - **a.** Maharajah Jungle Trek
   - **b.** Kilimanjaro Safaris
   - **c.** Pangani Forest Exploration Trail
   - **d.** Primeval Whirl

7. What attraction's ride vehicles are known as Steam Donkeys?
   - **a.** Wildlife Express Train
   - **b.** Expedition Everest
   - **c.** Kali River Rapids
   - **d.** Kilimanjaro Safaris

8. Where can you find Guano Joe?
   - **a.** Pangani Forest Exploration Trail
   - **b.** Rafiki's Planet Watch
   - **c.** Maharajah Jungle Trek
   - **d.** *Flights of Wonder*

9. As you enter Disney's Animal Kingdom, what is the first land that you reach?
   - **a.** Africa
   - **b.** Discovery Island
   - **c.** The Oasis
   - **d.** Harambe Village

10. About how many different food items are available in Walt Disney World?
    - **a.** 400
    - **b.** 3,000
    - **c.** 1,600
    - **d.** 6,000

Answers can be found on page 434.

PART TEN

DISNEY'S HOLLYWOOD STUDIOS

ABOUT HALF OF DISNEY'S HOLLYWOOD STUDIOS is set up as a theme park. The other half is off-limits except by guided tour. Though modest in size, the Studios' open-access areas are confusingly arranged (a product of the park's hurried expansion in the early 1990s). As at the Magic Kingdom, you enter the park and pass down a main street, only this time it's Hollywood Boulevard of the 1920s and 1930s. Though the park is largely organized by street names rather than by "lands," the easiest way to navigate it is by landmarks and attractions using the park map.

After Disney severed its relationship with MGM in 2008, the park formerly known as Disney–MGM Studios was renamed Disney's Hollywood Studios. Though the attraction lineup is essentially unchanged, the vision for the park going forward is to develop themes and attractions based on Pixar films and characters. The use of Hollywood in the park's name represents a more generic reference to moviemaking. In popular usage, however, many folks drop the Hollywood entirely, referring to the park simply as Disney Studios or The Studios.

While it is true that Disney's Hollywood Studios educates and entertains, what it does best is promote. Self-promotion of Disney films and products was once subtle and in context but is now blatant, inescapable, and distracting. Although most visitors are willing to forgive Disney its excesses, Studios veterans will lament the changes and remember how good it was when education was the park's goal instead of the medium.

Guest Relations, on your left as you enter, serves as the park headquarters and information center, similar to City Hall in the Magic Kingdom. Go there for a schedule of live performances, lost persons, package pickup, lost and found (on the right side of the entrance), general information, or in an emergency. If you haven't received a map of the Studios, get one here. To the right of the entrance are locker, stroller, and wheelchair rentals.

A Baby Care Center is located at Guest Relations, and Oscar's sells baby food and other necessities. Camera supplies for those precious

Disney's Hollywood Studios

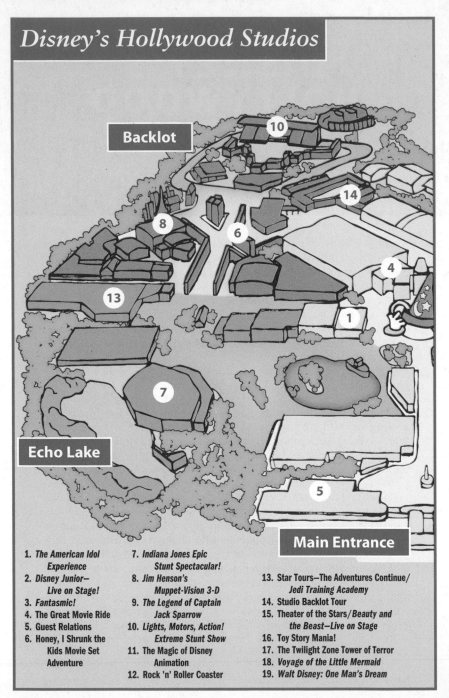

Backlot

Echo Lake

Main Entrance

1. *The American Idol Experience*
2. *Disney Junior— Live on Stage!*
3. *Fantasmic!*
4. The Great Movie Ride
5. Guest Relations
6. Honey, I Shrunk the Kids Movie Set Adventure
7. *Indiana Jones Epic Stunt Spectacular!*
8. *Jim Henson's Muppet-Vision 3-D*
9. *The Legend of Captain Jack Sparrow*
10. *Lights, Motors, Action! Extreme Stunt Show*
11. The Magic of Disney Animation
12. Rock 'n' Roller Coaster
13. Star Tours—The Adventures Continue/ Jedi Training Academy
14. Studio Backlot Tour
15. Theater of the Stars/*Beauty and the Beast—Live on Stage*
16. Toy Story Mania!
17. *The Twilight Zone Tower of Terror*
18. *Voyage of the Little Mermaid*
19. *Walt Disney: One Man's Dream*

moments can be purchased at The Darkroom on the right side of Hollywood Boulevard, just past Oscar's. Oddly enough the closest ATM is located outside the park to the right of the turnstiles. Disney no longer has pet-care facilities adjacent to the park, but the Best Friends Pet Resort across from Disney's Port Orleans Resort will provide a comfortable home away from home for Fido, Frisky, and all their pet pals.

Guests enter the park on Hollywood Boulevard, a palm-lined street reminiscent of the famous Hollywood main avenue of the 1930s. The best way to navigate is to decide what you really want to see and go for it! If you want the whole enchilada, it can be done in one day. But, as with the other parks, this is best accomplished by using one of our touring plans.

Architecture on Hollywood Boulevard is streamlined modern with Art Deco embellishments. Most service facilities are here, interspersed with eateries and shops. Merchandise includes Disney trademark items, Hollywood and movie-related souvenirs, and one-of-a-kind collectibles obtained from studio auctions and estate sales. Hollywood characters and roving performers entertain on the boulevard.

Sunset Boulevard, evoking the 1940s, is a major component of DHS. The first right off Hollywood Boulevard, Sunset Boulevard provides another venue for dining, shopping, and street entertainment.

The American Idol Experience ★★★★

APPEAL BY AGE	PRESCHOOL ★★½	GRADE SCHOOL ★★★★	TEENS ★★★★½
YOUNG ADULTS ★★★½		OVER 30 ★★★★	SENIORS ★★★★

What it is Theme-park version of the popular TV show, with guests doing the singing. **Scope and scale** Major attraction. **Fright potential** Some of the singing would frighten Frankenstein. **Bottleneck rating** 5. **When to go** Anytime. **Special comments** All shows except the finale last 20 minutes; the finale can last around 40. **Authors' rating** Even if you don't watch the show, you'll find someone to cheer for; ★★★★. **Duration of show** About 20–30 minutes. **When to arrive** 25–30 minutes before showtime.

Based on the successful *American Idol* television show, *The American Idol Experience* is your chance to showcase your karaoke abilities to the world. Your path to stardom goes something like this: Potential singers of all ages will select a song and audition in front of a live judge. Most singers will receive a "thanks for auditioning" message from the judge, but a handful will be selected to perform in the attraction's next stage show, held several times per day. During the show, contestants repeat their songs in front of a live audience of theme-park guests. As with *American Idol*, three judges (Disney cast members here) provide feedback. Don't worry that your operatic rendition of "Achy Breaky Heart" will meet with critical disdain. For the most part, the Disney panel uses humor to tell you not to quit your day job. Audience members vote to decide the winner. During the last show of the night, all of the winners from throughout the day meet for one final competition. The winner of that show receives a front-of-the-line pass for the next season's audition of *American Idol* in their local city. The last show of the day offers (ostensibly) the best talent but is twice the length of the daytime shows. If you don't want to commit to the entire show inside the auditorium, the final show (usually around 7 p.m.) can be viewed from outside on a Jumbotron screen. This is a wise option (as is catching one of the daytime shows) for those who have to leave for a dinner reservation or line up early for *Fantasmic!*

Beauty and the Beast—Live on Stage/ Theater of the Stars ★ ★ ★ ★

APPEAL BY AGE	PRESCHOOL ★★★★½	GRADE SCHOOL ★★★★½	TEENS ★★★½
YOUNG ADULTS ★★★★		OVER 30 ★★★★½	SENIORS ★★★★½

What it is Live musical, featuring Disney characters; performed in an open-air theater. **Scope and scale** Major attraction. **Fright potential** Not frightening in any respect. **Bottleneck rating** 5. **When to go** Anytime; evenings are cooler. **Special comment** Performances are listed in the daily *Times Guide*. **Authors' rating** Excellent; ★★★★. **Duration of show** 25 minutes. **Preshow** Sometimes. **Probable waiting time** 20–30 minutes.

DISNEY DISH WITH JIM HILL

THIS COULD GET HAIRY WDW Entertainment is looking to ease this 20-plus-year-old musical out of the 1,500-seat Theater of the Stars and bring in an all-new production based on 2010's *Tangled*. Among the ideas being considered to bring this film to life as a musical is turning the backmost wall of the set into a massive video screen. This is a staging technique previously used on the Disney Cruise Line, but never for a show inside a Disney theme park.

Join Cogsworth, Lumiere, Chip, and Mrs. Potts as they help Belle to break the spell. This 25-minute musical stage show of Disney's *Beauty and the Beast* feature will charm everybody. The show is popular, so show up 30 minutes early to get a seat.

> The decor and the costumes, the actors and the music: Everything is in perfect harmony. Little girls fond of Belle will want to have that ball gown, and young boys will be eager to teach that mean Gaston a lesson!

Liliane

Disney Junior—Live on Stage! ★ ★ ★ ★

APPEAL BY AGE	PRESCHOOL ★★★★½	GRADE SCHOOL ★★★½	TEENS ★★★
YOUNG ADULTS ★★½		OVER 30 ★★★	SENIORS ★★★

What it is Live show for children. **Scope and scale** Minor attraction. **Fright potential** Not frightening in any respect. **Bottleneck rating** 8. **When to go** Per the daily entertainment schedule. **Special comment** Audience sits on the floor. **Authors' rating** A must for families with preschoolers; ★★★★. **Duration of show** 20 minutes. **Probable waiting time** 30 minutes.

The show features characters from the Disney Channel's *Mickey Mouse Clubhouse, Jake and the Never Land Pirates, Doc McStuffins,* and *Sofia the First,* plus other Disney Channel characters. *Disney Junior* uses elaborate puppets instead of live characters on stage. A simple plot serves as the platform for singing, dancing, some great puppetry, and a great deal of audience participation. The characters, who ooze love and goodness, rally throngs of tots and preschoolers to sing and dance along with them. All the jumping, squirming, and high-stepping is facilitated by having the audience sit on the floor so that kids can spontaneously erupt into motion when the mood strikes. Even for adults without children, it's a treat to watch the tykes rev up. If you have a younger child in your party, all the better: Just stand back and let the video roll. For preschoolers, *Disney Junior* will be the highlight of their day, as a Thomasville, North Carolina, mom attests:

> *[The show] was fantastic! My 3-year-old loved it. The children danced, sang, and had a great time.*

Disney Junior is the third iteration of the stage show since 2007. All three versions replaced live characters with puppets, a fact that has left some parents less than thrilled. These comments from a Virginia Beach, Virginia, couple are typical:

> *We were disappointed with the [show]. This did not consist of live characters, and I think the level of excitement from the kids was lower because of this. I mean, the kids enjoyed it, but you would think they would be more excited when it's a show with some of their favorite characters.*

The show is staged in a huge building to the right of the Animation Tour. Show up at least 25 minutes before showtime. Once inside, pick a spot on the floor and take a breather until the performance begins.

The Great Movie Ride ★ ★ ★ ½

APPEAL BY AGE	PRESCHOOL ★ ★ ★	GRADE SCHOOL ★ ★ ★ ½	TEENS ★ ★ ★ ½
YOUNG ADULTS ★ ★ ★ ½		OVER 30 ★ ★ ★ ★ ½	SENIORS ★ ★ ★ ★

What it is Movie-history indoor adventure ride. **Scope and scale** Headliner. **Fright potential** Intense in parts, with very realistic special effects and some visually intimidating sights. **Bottleneck rating** 8. **When to go** Before 11 a.m. or after 8 p.m. **Special comment** Elaborate, with several surprises. **Authors' rating** Unique; ★ ★ ★ ½. **Duration of ride** About 19 minutes. **Average wait in line per 100 people ahead of you** 2 minutes. **Assumes** All trains operating. **Loading speed** Fast.

DISNEY DISH WITH JIM HILL

ONE SET OF THEME PARK RIGHTS TO RULE THEM ALL For the past few years, both Disney and Universal have been wooing *Lord of the Rings* director Peter Jackson in hopes of getting the theme park rights to his high-grossing trilogy of films. WDI wants to use the cinematic versions of J. R. R. Tolkien's characters to update a scene in The Great Movie Ride, whereas Universal is looking to use the films as a springboard for a brand-new "land" at Islands of Adventure, done in the highly detailed style of The Wizarding World of Harry Potter. Jackson, to his credit, has reportedly postponed making any decisions on this issue until he finishes production of his two-part *Hobbit* movie.

Inside the re-creation of Hollywood's Chinese Theater awaits a trip down memory lane. From *Casablanca* to *Raiders of the Lost Ark,* classic movies are showcased in this ride through some of the movies' most memorable sets. Young movie buffs might be flipped out along the way (*Alien* is one of the movies represented), but the wonderful Munchkins from *The Wizard of Oz* scene will make up for it—the Wicked Witch of the North notwithstanding.

I've only seen some of these movies, so I like how it's not just a ride, but a hostess who tells you about the movies, like if it's a Western or something. There's the yellow-brick road from *The Wizard of Oz*, and the Munchkins sing "Follow the Yellow Brick Road."

Hannah

Honey, I Shrunk the Kids Movie Set Adventure ★★½

APPEAL BY AGE	PRESCHOOL ★★★★½	GRADE SCHOOL ★★★★½	TEENS ★★★½
YOUNG ADULTS ★★★		OVER 30 ★★★	SENIORS ★★★

What it is Small but elaborate playground. **Scope and scale** Diversion. **Fright potential** Everything is oversize, but nothing is scary. **Bottleneck rating** 8. **When to go** Before 11 a.m. or after dark. **Special comment** Opens 1 hour later than the rest of the park. **Authors' rating** Great for young children, more of a curiosity for adults; ★★½. **Average wait in line per 100 people ahead of you** 20 minutes.

This elaborate playground appeals particularly to kids age 11 and younger. Tunnels, slides, rope ladders, and oversize props offer lots of playtime fun. However, the place is too small to accommodate all the children who would like to play, and supervision inside the jam-packed and poorly ventilated playground can be trying. Last but not least, kids play as long as parents allow, so be prepared for this stop to take a big chunk of time out of your touring day. If you visit during the warmer months and want your children to experience the playground, get them in and out before 11 a.m. By late morning, this attraction is way too hot and crowded for anyone to enjoy. A mom from Tolland, Connecticut, found the playground exasperating:

We let the kids hang out at [Honey, I Shrunk the Kids] because we thought it would be relaxing. NOT! You have three choices here: (1) Let your kids go anywhere and hope that if they try to get out without your permission, someone will stop them. Also hope that someone else will help your kids if they get caught up in the exhibit. (2) Go everywhere with your kids—this takes a lot of stamina and some athleticism. If you care about appearances, this could be a problem because you look pretty stupid coming down those slides. (3) Try to visually keep track of your kids. This is impossible, so you will be either on the edge of or in the middle of an anxiety attack the whole time you are there.

Indiana Jones Epic Stunt Spectacular! ★★★★

APPEAL BY AGE	PRESCHOOL ★★★½	GRADE SCHOOL ★★★★	TEENS ★★★★½
YOUNG ADULTS ★★★★½		OVER 30 ★★★★	SENIORS ★★★★½

What it is Movie-stunt demonstration and action show. **Scope and scale** Headliner. **Fright potential** An intense show with powerful special effects, including explosions. Presented in an educational context that young children generally handle well. **Bottleneck rating** 8. **When to go** First two shows or last show. **Special comment** Performance times posted on a sign at the entrance to the theater. **Authors' rating** Done on a grand scale; ★★★★. **Duration of show** 30 minutes. **Preshow** Selection of "extras" from audience. **Probable waiting time** None.

Professional stunt men and women demonstrate dangerous stunts with a behind-the-scenes look at how it is done. Most kids handle the show well. The show always needs a few "extras." To be chosen from the audience, arrive early, sit down front, and display unmitigated enthusiasm. Unfortunately "victims" must be 18 years old and up.

An amazing show with fiery explosions and nonstop action. Did you know that the folks at Disney have a vault filled with sound-effects ranging from gunshots to magical twinkles? When a show is created, they pick and choose from this treasure chest and upload the sounds into their state-of-the-art computerized mixing table. *Liliane*

Huh? What's a magical twinkle sound like? But now that I think about it, I sure remember the noise my innards made after eating about a dozen magical twinkles.

Those were Twinkies, Mr. Tiki-Birdbrain! *Liliane*

Jedi Training Academy ★★★★

APPEAL BY AGE PRESCHOOL ★★★★½ GRADE SCHOOL ★★★★½ TEENS ★★★½
YOUNG ADULTS ★★★½ OVER 30 ★★★★ SENIORS ★★★½

What it is Outdoor stage show. **Scope and scale** Minor attraction. **Fright potential** It does involve battle with Darth Vader, but the good guys always win; children typically love it. **Bottleneck rating** 8. **When to go** First two shows of the day. **Special comment** Volunteers from the audience go on stage to fight Darth Vader. **Authors' rating** A treat for young *Star Wars* lovers; ★★★★. **Duration of show** About 20 minutes. **When to arrive** 15 minutes before showtime.

Jedi Training Academy is to the left of the Star Tours building entrance, opposite Backlot Express. Young Skywalkers-in-training are taught the ways of The Force and do battle against Darth Vader. If all this sounds too intense, it's not—Storm Troopers provide comic relief and, just as in the movies, the Jedi always wins. Space is limited and kids ages 4–12 must register early in the day to make it into the show. To register see a cast member at the ABC Sound Studio building (near Star Tours). From a Windham, New Hampshire, mother of three:

> [Concerning] the sign-up process for Jedi Training Academy, I'm guessing many young families will have to choose between racing to Toy Story Mania to ride or get Fastpasses (or both) or racing to sign up for Jedi Training Academy (children MUST be present at sign up). We hopped on Toy Story, grabbed a few Fastpasses for later, and then crossed the park to sign up for Jedi Training Academy. By the time we got there, we were pushed to the 2:20 p.m. show. Not bad, but it certainly eliminates the possibility of leaving the park for a nap after lunch.

A father of two boys from Ontario did a divide and conquer:

> To see both Toy Story Mania and Jedi Training, I suggest having one parent take the kids to sign up for Jedi Training (kids need to be present), while the other parent runs for Toy Story Fastpasses.

Jim Henson's Muppet-Vision 3-D ★★★★½

APPEAL BY AGE PRESCHOOL ★★★★ GRADE SCHOOL ★★★★½ TEENS ★★★★
YOUNG ADULTS ★★★★½ OVER 30 ★★★★ SENIORS ★★★★½

What it is 3-D movie starring the Muppets. **Scope and scale** Major attraction. **Fright potential** Intense and loud but not frightening. **Bottleneck rating** 8. **When to go** Anytime. **Authors' rating** Uproarious; not to be missed; ★★★★½. **Duration of show** 17 minutes. **Preshow** Muppets on television. **Probable waiting time** 12 minutes.

Kermit, Miss Piggy, and the rest of the gang will lift your spirits as they unleash their hilarious mayhem. Because adults tend to associate Muppet characters with the children's show *Sesame Street,* many bypass this attraction. Big mistake. *Muppet-Vision 3-D* operates on several planes, and there's as much here for oldsters as for

Thumbs Up for the Whole Family

youngsters. The presentation is intense and sometimes loud, but most preschoolers handle it well. If your child is a little scared, encourage him to watch without the 3-D glasses at first.

The Legend of Captain Jack Sparrow ★★½

| APPEAL BY AGE | PRESCHOOL ★★★ | GRADE SCHOOL ★★★½ | TEENS ★★★½ |
| YOUNG ADULTS ★★★½ | | OVER 30 ★★★ | SENIORS ★★★ |

What it is Interactive film. **Scope and scale** Minor attraction. **Fright potential** Skeletons, monsters, and shooting can frighten small children. **Bottleneck rating** 8. **When to go** After dinner. **Authors' rating** Promising technology, but not much story; ★★½. **Duration of presentation** Around 10 minutes. **Probable waiting time** 20–30 minutes.

This walk-through, interactive attraction takes guests through pirate adventures, including a confrontation with skeleton pirates, singing mermaids, and a summoning of the squidlike Kraken. Virtually all of the presentation takes place in a room designed like a pirate's cave lair. Animatronic figures and other props are placed around the room and used throughout the show. A talking skull, recognizable from the Magic Kingdom's Pirates of the Caribbean attraction, serves as a narrator for each scene. Finally, an impressive holographic Jack Sparrow takes guests through a pirate oath, cementing their commitment to kidnapping, ransacking, and not-giving-a-hoot-ing.

   Legend may not open until late morning or noon; check the *Times Guide.* Because it's next to Toy Story Mania!, *Jack Sparrow* tends to draw guests who have either just finished riding or who have balked at getting in Toy Story's long line. If the wait for *Sparrow* is more than 20 minutes, try later in the day.

Lights, Motors, Action! Extreme Stunt Show ★★★½

| APPEAL BY AGE PRESCHOOL ★★★★ | GRADE SCHOOL ★★★★½ | TEENS ★★★★½ |
| YOUNG ADULTS ★★★★ | OVER 30 ★★★★½ | SENIORS ★★★★ |

What it is Auto stunt show. **Scope and scale** Headliner. **Fright potential** Loud with explosions but not scary. **Bottleneck rating** 5. **When to go** Anytime. **Authors' rating** Good stunt work, slow pace; ★★★½. **Duration of show** 33 minutes. **Preshow** Selection of audience "volunteers." **When to arrive** 25–30 minutes before showtime.

Loud

This show features cars and motorcycles in a blur of chases, crashes, jumps, and explosions. The secrets behind the special effects are explained after each stunt sequence. The show runs about 30 minutes, and small children may become restless. Teens, however, will be gobsmacked.

Liliane

The stunts and the special effects are fabulous but less would be more.

The Magic of Disney Animation ★ ★ ½

APPEAL BY AGE   PRESCHOOL ★ ★ ★ ½   **GRADE SCHOOL** ★ ★ ★ ★   **TEENS** ★ ★ ★ ★
YOUNG ADULTS ★ ★ ★ ★ ½   **OVER 30** ★ ★ ★ ★ ½   **SENIORS** ★ ★ ★ ★

What it is Overview of Disney Animation process with limited hands-on demonstrations. **Scope and scale** Minor attraction. **Fright potential** Not frightening in any respect. **Bottleneck rating** 7. **When to go** Anytime. **Special comment** Opens 1 hour later than the rest of the park. **Authors' rating** Not as good as previous renditions; ★ ★ ½. **Duration of presentation** 20 minutes. **Preshow** Gallery of animation art in waiting area. **Average wait in line per 100 people ahead of you** 7 minutes.

The consolidation of Disney Animation at the Burbank, California, studio has left this attraction without a story to tell. A shadow of its former self, the attraction doesn't warrant waiting in line. Guests learn very little about animation. The only interesting part, especially for children, is Animation Academy, an optional stop after the presentation. Here, kids and grown-ups alike can draw their own cartoon with the help of an animator. (Space is limited and on a first-come, first-serve basis.) The compelling presentation provides a good idea of how difficult hand-drawn animation is. Children who need more time or assistance with their drawing may become frustrated. The third part of this attraction is a character meet and greet. Guests can meet Mickey as the sorcerer's apprentice from *Fantasia*, and usually one of the latest Disney characters—currently Wreck-It Ralph. Check *Times Guide* for hours of appearance.

Rock 'n' Roller Coaster *(Fastpass)* ★ ★ ★ ★

APPEAL BY AGE   PRESCHOOL ★ ★   **GRADE SCHOOL** ★ ★ ★ ★ ½   **TEENS** ★ ★ ★ ★ ★
YOUNG ADULTS ★ ★ ★ ★ ★   **OVER 30** ★ ★ ★ ★ ½   **SENIORS** ★ ★ ★ ½

What it is Rock music–themed roller coaster. **Scope and scale** Headliner. **Fright potential** Extremely intense for all ages; the ride is one of Disney's wildest. **Bottleneck rating** 10. **When to go** First 30 minutes the park is open, or use Fastpass. **Special comments** Must be 48" tall to ride; children younger than age 7 must ride with an adult. Switching-off option provided (see page 245). **Authors' rating** Not to be missed; ★ ★ ★ ★. **Duration of ride** Almost 1½ minutes. **Average wait in line per 100 people ahead of you** 2½ minutes. **Assumes** All trains operating. **Loading speed** Moderate–fast.

Dark   Lose Things   Rough   Queasy   Scary

Aerosmith once did a tour called Route of All Evil, and the notorious ride at the Studios will make good on fans' expectations. Loops, corkscrews, and drops that make Space Mountain seem like the Jungle Cruise is what to expect and what is delivered—pronto. You will be launched from 0 to 57 miles per hour in less than 3 seconds, and by the time you enter the first loop, you'll be pulling five g's. By comparison, that is two more g's than astronauts experienced at liftoff on a space shuttle. A good strategy for riding Rock 'n' Roller Coaster, Toy Story Mania, and Tower of Terror with minimum waits is to rush to get Fastpasses for Toy Story Mania first thing after opening, and then line up for Rock 'n' Roller Coaster. Save Tower of Terror for last. If the standby line at Rock 'n' Roller Coaster is more than 30 minutes, consider using the single-rider line. Or skip Rock 'n' Roller Coaster for now, ride Toy Story Mania, and pick up Fastpasses for Rock 'n' Roller Coaster when you can.

Liliane

Aerosmith describes this ride best in one of their songs: "Living on the Edge."

Star Tours: The Adventures Continue *(Fastpass)* ★ ★ ★ ★

APPEAL BY AGE PRESCHOOL ★ ★ ★ **GRADE SCHOOL** ★ ★ ★ ½ **TEENS** ★ ★ ★ ½
YOUNG ADULTS ★ ★ ★ ½ **OVER 30** ★ ★ ★ ½ **SENIORS** ★ ★ ★ ★

What it is Indoor space flight–simulation ride. **Scope and scale** Headliner. **Fright potential** Extremely intense visually for all ages; too intense for children under age 8. Likely to cause motion sickness. Switching-off option provided (see page 245). **Bottleneck rating** 8. **When to go** Before 10 a.m., after 6 p.m., or use Fastpass. **Special comments** Expectant mothers and anyone prone to motion sickness are advised against riding. Must be 40" tall to ride. **Authors' rating** Not to be missed; ★ ★ ★ ★. **Duration of ride** About 7 minutes. **Average wait in line per 100 people ahead of you** 5 minutes. **Assumes** All simulators operating. **Loading speed** Moderate–fast.

  Based on the *Star Wars* movie series, the ride, overhauled in 2011 and based on the pod racing scene from *Star Wars Episode 1: The Phantom Menace,* uses 3-D special effects and interactive elements. The ride has lots of dips, turns, twists, and climbs as your vehicle goes through an intergalactic version of the chariot race in *Ben-Hur.* Characters from the prequel films released 1999–2005 were included in the makeover. The ride has more than 50 combinations of scenes!!

Rough   Queasy   Scary

Movie Tip

Every year (mid-May to mid-June) Walt Disney World hosts four *Star Wars* weekends. Celebrities from the saga and fans converge at the park in celebration of George Lucas's epic series. Even Mickey turns into a Jedi and joins Ewoks, Jawas, and Wookies for a ride to a galaxy far, far away. *Star Wars* weekends are a must for any and all *Star Wars* fans.

Liliane   Oh, no! We're caught in a tractor beam!

Streets of America ★ ★ ★

APPEAL BY AGE PRESCHOOL ★ ★ ½ **GRADE SCHOOL** ★ ★ ★ ½ **TEENS** ★ ★ ★ ½
YOUNG ADULTS ★ ★ ★ ½ **OVER 30** ★ ★ ★ ½ **SENIORS** ★ ★ ★ ★

What it is Walk-through back lot movie set. **Scope and scale** Diversion. **Fright potential** Not frightening in any respect. **Bottleneck rating** 1. **When to go** Anytime. **Authors' rating** Interesting, with great detail; ★ ★ ★. **Probable waiting time** None.

There is never a wait to enjoy the Streets of America; save your visit here until you have seen those attractions that develop long lines. During the Christmas season, Streets of America are decorated with millions of Christmas lights and serve as a backdrop for the Osborne Family Spectacle of Lights.

Studio Backlot Tour ★ ★ ★ ★

APPEAL BY AGE PRESCHOOL ★ ★ ★ **GRADE SCHOOL** ★ ★ ★ ½ **TEENS** ★ ★ ★
YOUNG ADULTS ★ ★ ★ ½ **OVER 30** ★ ★ ★ ½ **SENIORS** ★ ★ ★ ½

What it is Combination tram and walking tour of modern film and video production. **Scope and scale** Headliner. **Fright potential** Sedate and nonintimidating except for Catastrophe Canyon, where an earthquake and flash flood are simulated. Prepare younger children for this part of the tour. **Bottleneck rating** 6. **When to go** Before noon or after 5 p.m. **Special comment** Use the restroom before getting in line. **Authors' rating** Educational and fun; not to be missed; ★ ★ ★ ★. **Duration of tour** About 35 minutes. **Preshow** A video before the special effects segment and another video in the tram boarding area. **Probable waiting time** Usually less than 10 minutes.

Loud

About two-thirds of Disney's Hollywood Studios was once a film and television facility. The tour is an absolute must. Special effects are explained with demonstrations of rain and a naval battle. Next, visitors board a tram that takes them through wardrobe and craft shops, where costumes, sets, and props are designed. The tour continues through the back lot, where western canyons exist side by side with New York City brownstones. The tour's highlight is Catastrophe Canyon, an elaborate special-effects movie set where a thunderstorm, earthquake, oilfield fire, and a flash flood are simulated. Prepare young children for Catastrophe Canyon, as the rattling earthquake and the sudden flood shake the tram, and yes, if you are sitting on the left side facing the canyon, you will get wet. Disney often chooses four volunteers to be part of the special effects demonstration. You must be in the very front of the line to get a chance to be part of the naval battle scene. Or if you are at the end of the line, you can stay behind and ask to be part of the next showing.

Toy Story Mania! *(Fastpass)* ★★★★½

**APPEAL BY AGE   PRESCHOOL ★★★★½   GRADE SCHOOL ★★★★★   TEENS ★★★★★
YOUNG ADULTS ★★★★★   OVER 30 ★★★★★   SENIORS ★★★★½**

What it is 3-D ride through indoor shooting gallery. **Scope and scale** Headliner. **Fright potential** Not frightening in any respect. **Bottleneck rating** 10. **When to go** As soon as the park opens or use Fastpass (if available). **Authors' rating** ★★★★½. **Duration of ride** About 6½ minutes. **Average wait in line per 100 people ahead of you** 6½ minutes. **Loading Speed** Fast.

This is an interactive shooting gallery much like Buzz Lightyear's Space Ranger Spin, but in Toy Story Mania! your vehicle passes through a totally virtual midway, with booths offering such games as the ring toss and ball throw. You use a cannon on your ride vehicle to play as you move along from booth to booth. The pull-string cannon takes advantage of computer-graphic image technology to toss rings, shoot balls, and even throw eggs and pies. Each game booth is manned by a *Toy Story* character who is right beside you in 3-D glory cheering you on. In addition to 3-D imagery, you experience vehicle motion, wind, and water spray. The ride begins with a training round to familiarize you with the nature of the games and then continues through a number of games that count for score, in which you compete against your riding mate. The technology has the ability to self-adjust the level of difficulty, and there are plenty of easy targets for small children to reach. *Tip:* Let the pull-string retract all the way back into the cannon before pulling it again.

Toy Story Mania! is the hottest ticket in the park and stays packed all day. Ride first thing after the park opens or use Fastpass. Regarding the latter, pick up your Fastpasses before 11 a.m. or they may be exhausted for the day. Following are reports from readers. First from a Cold Spring, New York, mom:

> There was a 20-minute wait just for Fastpasses as soon as the park opened, and by 11 [a.m.] Fastpasses were gone for the day. Thanks to the DIS forums I was aware of how popular the ride was though, so I got Fastpasses for it first, then followed the touring plan, and everything fell into place nicely.

A Nashville, Tennessee, mom shared this:

Toy Story Mania! was swamped by the time we got to it, still fairly early in the day. We had to resort to getting some of the last Fastpasses, and it elongated our day to wait until our [return] time came up. But, oh my gosh, what fun! It was worth the wait!

An Ontario, Canada, mom observed:

By 10 a.m. the line was 50 minutes long and we got Fastpasses for 2 in the afternoon. At 2 p.m. the line was 80 minutes and there were no more Fast-passes left.

From an Evansville, Indiana, mom:

We immediately went to Toy Story Mania! and found a HUGE line for the ride. We figured we'd be smart and get a Fastpass. Turns out the HUGE line WAS the Fastpass line! The FP return time was already at 12:45. Unfortu-nately we had to skip this ride due to the long wait.

Toy Story Mania! has become the biggest bottleneck in Disney World, surpassing even Test Track at Epcot. The only way to get aboard without a horrendous wait is to be one of the first through the turnstiles when the park opens and zoom to the attraction. Another alternative is to obtain Fastpasses for Toy Story Mania! as soon as the park opens, and then back-track to ride the Rock 'n' Roller Coaster and Tower of Terror. Expect long queues at the Fastpass kiosks. If you decide to get Fastpasses, spare your family the extra legwork and dispatch the fittest member to get Fastpasses for all while you get in line to ride Tower of Terror or Rock 'n' Roller Coaster. If you have a cell phone, text your location in line to the brave warrior getting the Fastpasses and reunite to ride together.

The Twilight Zone Tower of Terror *(Fastpass)* ★★★★★

APPEAL BY AGE PRESCHOOL ★★½ GRADE SCHOOL ★★★★ TEENS ★★★★½
YOUNG ADULTS ★★★★★ OVER 30 ★★★★½ SENIORS ★★★★

What it is Sci-fi–themed indoor thrill ride. **Scope and scale** Super-headliner. **Fright potential** Visually intimidating to young children; contains intense and realistic spe-cial effects. The plummeting elevator at the ride's end frightens many adults. Switching-off option provided (see page 245). **Bottleneck rating** 10. **When to go** First or last 30 minutes the park is open, or use Fastpass. **Special comment** Must be 40" tall to ride. **Authors' rating** Walt Disney World's best attraction; not to be missed; ★★★★★. **Duration of ride** About 4 minutes plus preshow. **Average wait in line per 100 people ahead of you** 4 minutes. **Assumes** All elevators operating. **Loading speed** Moderate.

Another ride that gives you surprises. I like it when you go up and think you're going to stay up but end up zooming down. There's a part of the ride where it looks like you're in outer space, and then it turns back into the hotel.

Hannah

Dark   Rough   Scary

And suddenly the cable went *snap.* If riding a capricious elevator in a haunted hotel sounds like fun to you, this is your ride. Erratic yet thrill-ing, the Tower of Terror is an experience to savor. The Tower has great potential for terrifying young children and rattling more mature visitors. Random ride-and-drop sequences make the attraction wilder and keep you guessing about when, how far, and how many times the elevator drops. We suggest that you use teenagers in your party as experimental probes. If they report back that they really, really liked the

Tower of Terror, run as fast as you can in the opposite direction. Tower of Terror is one of the hottest tickets in the park. If you're up to it, experience the ride first thing in the morning or use Fastpass.

The part where you get up and then suddenly start moving through the floor is cool. I did not see that coming. I consider it a thrill ride for people who don't like thrill rides. You can easily trick someone into going on it.

Shelton

Voyage of the Little Mermaid ★★★★

APPEAL BY AGE	PRESCHOOL ★★★½	GRADE SCHOOL ★★★★	TEENS ★★★½
YOUNG ADULTS ★★★★		OVER 30 ★★★★	SENIORS ★★★★

Thumbs Up for the Whole Family

What it is Musical stage show featuring characters from the Disney movie *The Little Mermaid*. **Scope and scale** Major attraction. **Fright potential** Ursula the sea witch may frighten preschoolers. **Bottleneck rating** 10. **When to go** Before 9:45 a.m. or just before closing. **Authors' rating** Romantic, lovable, and humorous in the best Disney tradition; not to be missed; ★★★★. **Duration of show** 15 minutes. **Preshow** Taped ramblings about the decor in the preshow holding area. **Probable waiting time** Before 9:30 a.m., 10–30 minutes; after 9:30 a.m., 35–70 minutes.

This most tender and romantic stage show is a winner, appealing to every age. Once inside the theater, the audience is transported into the wonderful underwater world of Ariel and her friends. Very young children might be frightened by Ursula the sea witch (she is actually a puppet standing 12 feet tall).

Because it's well done and located at a busy pedestrian intersection, *Voyage of the Little Mermaid* plays to capacity crowds all day. When the theater doors open, pick a row of seats, and let 6–10 people enter the row ahead of you. The strategy is twofold: to obtain a good seat and be near the exit.

The scary characters like the eels just show up on the side—they don't come out at you. Ariel's hair is really, really bright red.

Hannah

Walt Disney: One Man's Dream ★★★

APPEAL BY AGE	PRESCHOOL ★★½	GRADE SCHOOL ★★★½	TEENS ★★★★
YOUNG ADULTS ★★★★		OVER 30 ★★★★½	SENIORS ★★★★½

What it is Tribute to Walt Disney. **Scope and scale** Minor attraction. **Fright potential** Not frightening in any respect. **Bottleneck rating** 2. **When to go** Anytime. **Authors' rating** Excellent! ★★★ and about time. **Duration of presentation** 25 minutes. **Preshow** Disney memorabilia. **Probable waiting time** For film, 10 minutes.

One Man's Dream is a long-overdue tribute to Walt Disney. The attraction consists of an exhibit area showcasing Disney memorabilia, followed by a film documenting Disney's life. Teens and adults, especially those old enough to remember Walt Disney, will enjoy this homage to the man behind the Mouse!

My son, who graduated as a cinematographer from Florida State University film school, used to take me to this attraction during every visit, and today, when visiting, he still sees the show in what he calls "paying tribute to the man who started it all." Hands off! Don't even think of packing this gem off!

Liliane

LIVE ENTERTAINMENT *at* DISNEY'S HOLLYWOOD STUDIOS

THE STUDIOS LIVE ENTERTAINMENT includes theater shows, musical acts, roaming bands of street performers, and *Fantasmic!*, a nighttime water, fireworks, and laser show that draws rave reviews. Of these, the theater shows, musical acts, and street performers are generally as good or better than comparable acts found at the other Disney theme parks. You can read on for the details, but we'd be remiss if we didn't tell you to catch a show of Mulch, Sweat, and Shears, a group of landscaping "brothers" who form a rock-and-roll cover band playing everything from AC/DC to Journey. Guests standing near the front may be invited into the act.

Liliane: Disney's Hollywood Studios is the only Disney World park without an interactive game. I vote for a *Star Wars*–themed game with trading cards and all.

AFTERNOON PARADE "We regularly and carefully review the entertainment offerings in our parks and make adjustments as part of our normal course of business." This is how Disney announced in April 2013 that it was canning the daily afternoon parade Pixar Pals Countdown to Fun along with Disney Channel Rocks! With no replacement announced in the near future, the question is why? I doubt that Disney listened to Liliane's complaints about the parade, which never made it high on her top things to do at The Studios. And while rumors include anything from cost-cutting measures to expansion of the park for a new Cars Land or Star Wars Land, nobody really knows. We know one thing, though— admission prices are on the rise and guests expect an afternoon parade. Sooner or later Disney will have to come up with a replacement.

MULCH, SWEAT, & SHEARS—LIVE IN CONCERT Known as Los Lawn Boys outside of Hollywood Studios, this Central Florida rock act plays in the park under the name Mulch, Sweat, & Shears. The 30-minute show takes place several times during the day, except on Wednesdays, in front of the giant sorcerer's hat. Check *Times Guide* for performance times, and rock on!

Liliane: Wait a minute; I never said to cancel the afternoon parade entirely! I suggest that Disney comes up with a better one pronto. There is simply no such thing as a Disney theme park without a parade!

DISNEY CHARACTERS Find characters in front of the sorcerer's hat, in front of the Magic of Disney Animation building, the Cars Meet and Greet (near Mama Melrose's on Streets of America), in the Animation Courtyard, and along Pixar Place. Characters from *Monsters, Inc.* can sometimes be found near the Backlot Tour. Times and locations for character appearances are listed in the *Times Guide*.

STREET ENTERTAINMENT With the possible exception of Epcot's World Showcase Players, the Studios has the best collection of roving street

FAVORITE EATS AT DISNEY'S HOLLYWOOD STUDIOS
LAND | SERVICE LOCATION | FOOD ITEM
ECHO LAKE
ABC Commissary | Chicken nuggets with fruit or veggies **Backlot Express** | Great burgers & fixin's
STREETS OF AMERICA
Pizza Planet | THE place for pizza **Sci-Fi Dine-In Theater*** | It's not about the food (dismal) but about eating in a vintage convertible car watching old sci-fi movie previews. Teens love it! Great place to cool off.
SUNSET BOULEVARD
Studio Catering Co. | Good place for a break while your kids check out Honey, I Shrunk the Kids playground

* *table service only*

performers in all of Walt Disney World. Appearing primarily on Hollywood and Sunset Boulevards, the cast of characters includes Hollywood stars and wannabes, their agents, film directors, and gossip columnists, as well as police officers and Hollywood public-works crews.

The performers are not shy about asking you to join in their skits, and you may be asked anything from explaining why you came to "Hollywood" all the way to reciting a couple of lines in one of the directors' new films. If you're looking for a spot to rest and a bit of entertainment, grab a drink and seek out these performers.

Fantasmic! ★★★★★

What it is Mixed-media nighttime spectacular. **Scope and scale** Super-headliner. **Fright potential** Loud and intense with fireworks and some scary villains, but most young children like it. **Bottleneck rating** 9. **When to go** Check *Times Guide* for schedule; if two shows are offered, the second is less crowded. **Special comment** Disney's best nighttime event. **Authors' rating** Not to be missed; ★★★★★. **Duration of show** 25 minutes. **Probable waiting time** 50–90 minutes for a seat; 35–40 minutes for standing room.

Loud   Scary

Until 2009, *Fantasmic!* was staged nightly and always played to a full house. Presumably as a cost-containment measure, Disney has cut performances to two evenings a week, or three nights a week during busier times. As you might imagine, trying to cram seven nights of capacity crowds into two nights is not working very well, as a reader from Sandwich, Illinois, reports:

> The reduction in Fantasmic! shows per week is ridiculous to me. The Studios is an absolute ghost town on nights it doesn't show and packed to capacity on nights when it does! There has to be a happy medium.

Nonetheless, *Fantasmic!* is far and away the most unique outdoor spectacle ever attempted in any theme park and a must-see for the whole family. Starring Mickey Mouse in his role as the sorcerer's apprentice from *Fantasia,* the production uses lasers, images projected on a shroud of mist, dazzling fireworks, lighting effects, and powerful music. *Fantasmic!* has the potential to frighten young children. Prepare your children for the show, and make sure that they know that in addition to all the favorite Disney characters, the maleficent dragon and the evil Jafar will make appearances. To give you an idea, just picture this: The evil Jafar turns into a cobra 100 feet long and 16 feet high. Rest assured, however, that during the final parade your kids will cheer on Cinderella and Prince Charming, Belle, Snow White, Ariel and Prince Eric, Jasmine and Aladdin, Donald Duck, Minnie, and Mickey. You can alleviate the fright factor somewhat by sitting back a bit. Also, if you are seated in the first 12 rows, you will get sprayed with water at times.

The theater is huge, but so is the popularity of the show. If there are two performances, the second show will almost always be less crowded. If you attend the first (or only) scheduled performance, show up at least 1 hour in advance. If you opt for the second show, arrive 50 minutes early. Plan to use that time for a picnic. Bring food and drinks and something to entertain the younger kids. If you forget to bring munchies, not to worry; there are food concessions in the theater. As a cost-cutting measure, since 2009 Disney has staged **Liliane:** In light of the skyrocketing admission price to the parks, I vote to reinstall *Fantasmic!* as a nightly performance now! Seriously, you did it before, and yes, you can do it again.
Fantasmic! on only two nights a week. This makes it almost impossible to see the show without lining up 90 minutes to 2 hours in advance. Yes, *Fantasmic!* is a great show, but is it worth a 2-hour wait?

Unless you buy a *Fantasmic!* dinner package, you will not have reserved seats, so arrive early for best choice. Try to sit in the middle three or four sections, a bit off-center. Disney has experimented with using Fastpass for reserved seating for *Fantasmic!,* and we expect this to become a regular offering. Check Disney's website or park map for availability. Finally, understand that you are out of luck if *Fantasmic!* is canceled due to weather or other circumstances.

Fantasmic! Dinner Packages

Three restaurants offer a ticket voucher for the members of your dining party to enter *Fantasmic!* via a special entrance and sit in a reserved section of seats. The package consists of a buffet at Hollywood & Vine, or a fixed-price dinner at Mama Melrose's Ristorante Italiano or The Hollywood Brown Derby (full-service restaurants). You can call ☎ 407-WDW-DINE up to 180 days in advance and request the *Fantasmic!* dinner package. This is a real reservation and must be guaranteed by a credit card at the time of booking. There's a 48-hour cancellation policy.

Included in the package are fixed-price menus as follows; respective prices are for adults and kids ages 3–9: *Hollywood & Vine:* dinner, $30–$40/$15–$20; *The Hollywood Brown Derby:* lunch and dinner, $50–$57/$15–$20; *Mama Melrose's:* lunch and dinner, $35–$40/$15–$20. Nonalcoholic drinks and tax are included; park admission and gratuity are not. Please note that prices fluctuate according to season, so call ☎ 407-WDW-DINE if you want to know exactly what the dinner charge will be for a particular date. Please note that if there are two scheduled performances in one night, the lunch package will only grant you reserved seating for the first performance.

Allow a minimum of 2 hours to eat. You will receive the vouchers (tickets for the show) at the restaurant. After dinner, report to the *Fantasmic!* sign on Hollywood Boulevard next to Oscar's (just inside the front entrance to the park) no later than 35 minutes prior to showtime. A cast member will collect the vouchers and escort you to the reserved section. If *Fantasmic!* is canceled for any reason, such as weather, technical problems, and the like, you will not receive a refund. However, you can Guest Relations to receive a voucher for another (next) performance. The problem is that this only works if you are still in town when *Fantasmic!* is on next and if you are willing to pay another admission to the Studios. If you're still around and have a Park Hopper, go for it!

EXIT STRATEGIES

EXITING THE STUDIOS at the end of the day following *Fantasmic!* is not nearly as difficult as leaving Epcot after *IllumiNations*. We recommend that you take it easy and make your way out of the park after the first wave of guests has departed. Pick a spot inside the park and give instructions that nobody is to go through the turnstiles before the group is reunited. Most important, latch on to your kids.

DISNEY'S HOLLYWOOD STUDIOS TOURING PLANS

OUR STEP-BY-STEP TOURING PLANS ARE FIELD-TESTED, independently verified itineraries that will keep you moving counter to the crowd flow and allow you to see as much as possible in a single day with a minimum of time wasted in line.

The different touring plans are described on the opposite page. The descriptions will tell you for whom (for example, tweens, parents with preschoolers, and so on) or for what situation (such as sleeping late) the plans are designed. The actual touring plans are on pages 471–474 and include a numbered map of the park to help you find your way around.

You can take in all the attractions at the Disney's Hollywood Studios in one day, even when traveling with young children. If you are not interested in an attraction listed on the touring plan, just skip that attraction and proceed to the next step. Likewise, should you encounter a very long line at an attraction, skip it. Use of Fastpass is factored into the touring plans. When Disney switches to the new Fastpass+ system, refer to the detailed notes at the bottom of each plan. Those notes show the approximate start of the Fastpass return window for each Fastpass obtained in the plan, and the order in which you should try to obtain Fastpass+ reservations if they're limited.

DISNEY'S HOLLYWOOD STUDIOS ONE-DAY TOURING PLAN FOR PARENTS WITH SMALL CHILDREN This plan is designed for parents of children ages 3–8 who wish to see the very best age-appropriate attractions and shows in Disney's Hollywood Studios. Every attraction has a rating of at least three stars (out of five) from preschool and grade-school children surveyed by the *Unofficial Guide*. The plan includes a midday break outside the park so families can rest, relax, and regroup. The plan keeps walking and backtracking to a minimum, with no criss-crossing of the park.

DISNEY'S HOLLYWOOD STUDIOS ONE-DAY SLEEPYHEAD TOURING PLAN FOR PARENTS WITH SMALL CHILDREN A relaxed plan that allows families with small children to sleep late and still see the highlights of Disney's Hollywood Studios. The plan begins around 11 a.m., sets aside ample time for lunch and dinner, and includes the very best child-friendly attractions and shows in the park. Special advice is provided for touring the park with small children. The plan points out where Fastpass can best be used.

DISNEY'S HOLLYWOOD STUDIOS ONE-DAY TOURING PLAN FOR TWEENS AND THEIR PARENTS A one-day plan for parents with children ages 8–12. It includes every attraction rated three stars and higher by this age group and sets aside ample time for lunch and dinner.

DISNEY'S HOLLYWOOD STUDIOS ONE-DAY HAPPY FAMILY TOURING PLAN A one-day itinerary for multigenerational families, this plan allows teens and older children to experience the Studios' thrill rides while parents and small children visit more age-appropriate attractions. The family stays together most of the day, including lunch and dinner, and each attraction in the plan is rated three stars or higher.

BEFORE YOU GO

1. Call ☎ 407-824-4321 or visit **disneyworld.com** to verify the park's operating hours.

2. Buy your admission before arriving.

3. Make lunch and dinner Advance Reservations or reserve the *Fantasmic!* dinner package (if desired) before you arrive by calling ☎ 407-WDW-DINE.

4. The schedule of live entertainment changes from week to week and even from day to day. Review the daily *Times Guide* handout, available free throughout Disney's Hollywood Studios.

DISNEY'S HOLLYWOOD STUDIOS TRIVIA QUIZ
By Lou Mongello

1. In *Muppet-Vision 3-D,* Sam the Eagle states that the finale will be "A Salute to All Nations but Mostly . . . ":
   a. America
   b. Muppets
   c. Florida
   d. Walt Disney World

2. What is the name of the hotel featuring The Twilight Zone Tower of Terror?
   a. Hollywood Tower Hotel   c. Hightower Hotel
   b. Hollywood Hills Hotel   d. The Sunset Hotel

3. At the end of *Muppet-Vision 3-D*, what "crashes" through the screen?
   a. A monorail   c. A fire engine
   b. An animal   d. Dumbo

4. What color are your 3-D glasses in Toy Story Mania!?
   a. Yellow   c. Blue
   b. Black   d. Purple

5. What band is featured in Rock 'n' Roller Coaster?
   a. The Jonas Brothers   c. U2
   b. Aerosmith   d. Guns N' Roses

6. The Mr. Potato Head figure in the queue for Toy Story Mania! is able to:
   a. Remove his ear   c. Walk up stairs
   b. Tip his hat   d. Moonwalk

7. How many people disappear in the elevator of The Twilight Zone Tower of Terror?
   a. 0   c. 5
   b. 1   d. 7

8. Many Walt Disney World attractions are based on movies, but which of these attractions had a movie made about it after it opened at Disney's Hollywood Studios?
   a. *Muppet-Vision 3-D*   c. The Great Movie Ride
   b. The Twilight Zone Tower of Terror   d. *Fantasmic!*

9. The giant replica of a *Star Wars* vehicle outside the Star Tours attraction is:
   a. A landspeeder   c. An AT-AT walker
   b. A Star Destroyer   d. A probe droid

10. What is the name of the dinosaur that is also an ice-cream stand?
    a. Deeno   c. Diner-Saur
    b. Gertie   d. Hector

11. What animals make up the orchestra in *Muppet-Vision 3-D*?
    a. Penguins   c. Frogs
    b. Rats   d. Bunnies

Answers can be found on page 434.

PART ELEVEN

UNIVERSAL ORLANDO and SEAWORLD

■ UNIVERSAL ORLANDO

UNIVERSAL ORLANDO HAS TRANSFORMED into a complete destination resort, with two theme parks, three hotels, and a shopping, dining, and entertainment complex. A system of roads and two multistory parking facilities are connected by moving sidewalks to **CityWalk,** a shopping, dining, and nighttime-entertainment complex that also serves as a gateway to the **Universal Studios Florida** and **Islands of Adventure** theme parks.

LODGING AT UNIVERSAL ORLANDO

UNIVERSAL CURRENTLY HAS THREE OPERATING resort hotels. The 750-room **Portofino Bay Hotel** is set on an artificial bay with an Italian coastal town theme. The 650-room **Hard Rock Hotel** is an ultracool Hotel California replica, with contemporary design and a hip, friendly attitude. The 1,000-room, Polynesian-themed **Loews Royal Pacific Resort** is sumptuously decorated and richly appointed. All three are excellent hotels; the Portofino and the Hard Rock are on the pricey side, and the Royal Pacific ain't exactly cheap. The 1,800-room **Cabana Bay Beach Hotel** (opens 2014), with rates of $119 and up, will be a less expensive alternative to Universal's three existing hotels. With a 1950s and '60s Florida beachfront hotel theme, the Cabana Bay will be split evenly between suites sleeping up to six people and standard hotel rooms.

ARRIVING AT UNIVERSAL ORLANDO

THE UNIVERSAL ORLANDO COMPLEX can be accessed from eastbound I-4 by taking Exit 75A and turning left at the top of the ramp onto Universal Boulevard. Traveling westbound on I-4, use Exit 74B and then turn right on Hollywood Way. Entrances are also off Kirkman Road to the east, Turkey Lake Road to the north, and Vineland Road to the west. Universal Boulevard connects the International Drive area to Universal via an overpass bridging I-4. Turkey Lake and Vineland Roads are particularly good alternatives when I-4 is gridlocked. Once on-site, you will be directed to park in one of two multitiered parking garages. Parking runs $15 for cars and $20 for RVs. From the garages, (sometimes) moving sidewalks deliver you to the Universal CityWalk venue described earlier; it takes about 8–20 minutes to get from the garages to the parks. From CityWalk, you can access the main entrances of both Universal Studios Florida and Islands of Adventure theme parks.

UNIVERSAL ORLANDO ADMISSION		
	ADULTS	CHILDREN (3–9)
One-Day, One-Park Pass	$100.13	$93.74
One-Day, Two-Park Pass	$138.47	$132.08
Two-Day, Two-Park Pass	$177.85	$167.20

Given that it's hard to find your car among 20,000 other cars, we strongly recommend that you write down or take a picture of the name and number of your section, level, and row. Sections are named for movies such as *Jurassic Park, King Kong,* and so on. The first numeral of the number following the section name tells you what deck level you're on and the remaining numbers specify the row. So if a sign tells you that you're on King Kong 410, you're in the King Kong section on the fourth floor in row 10.

Universal offers one-day, two-day, three-day, and four-day passes for one park or two parks, as well as annual passes for both parks. Passes can be obtained in advance on the phone with your credit card at ☎ 800-711-0080 or **universalorlando.com.** Prices above include tax and fees.

Be sure to check Universal's website for seasonal deals and specials. You can save as much as 25% by buying your tickets in advance on Universal's website. A five-park, 14-day pass called the Orlando Flex Ticket allows unlimited entry to Universal Studios, Islands of Adventure, SeaWorld, Aquatica, and Wet 'n Wild and costs about $305 for adults and $285 for children (ages 3–9), plus tax. A six-park, 14-day pass called the Orlando Flex Ticket Plus provides unlimited entry to Universal Studios, Islands of Adventure, SeaWorld, Aquatica, Wet 'n Wild, and Busch Gardens for about $345 for adults and $325 for children, plus tax. The six-park ticket includes a free shuttle to Busch Gardens. At Undercover Tourist, a reputable wholesaler, you can obtain the Flex tickets at substantial savings. Visit **undercovertourist.com.** New is the VIP Experience, a 5- to 6-hour guided tour of Universal Studios, which includes behind-the-scenes visits to closed sets and the movie-studio back lot. At the price of $299 plus tax, the VIP Experience includes escorted priority access to all rides, shows, and attractions, plus lunch in a VIP dining room. Buy online or call ☎ 818-622-8477.

The main Universal Orlando information number is ☎ 407-363-8000. Reach Guest Services at ☎ 407-224-4233, or schedule a character lunch at **universalorlando.com.** The numbers for lost and found are ☎ 407-224-4244 (Universal Studios) and 407-224-4245 (IOA).

UNIVERSAL EXPRESS

Like Disney's Fastpass, Universal Express is a system whereby a guest can experience an attraction with little or no waiting. Unlike Fastpass, Universal Express is not free; two versions are available, both of which require you to cough up more money beyond your park admission:

Universal Express is available to all guests at Universal hotels. Guests at Universal hotels can access the Universal Express lines by simply flashing their hotel keys. This can be especially valuable during peak season. This perk far surpasses any accorded to guests of Disney resorts.

Guests not staying at a Universal hotel can purchase the **Universal Express Plus** pass, which starts at $20–$70 (depending on the season) and provides line-cutting privileges at each Universal Express attraction at a given park. You can purchase Universal Express Plus online, at the park's ticket windows just outside the front gates, or in the parks. Once in the Studios, Universal Express Plus is available at NickStuff or Sahara Traders. Inside Islands of Adventure, you can buy Express Plus at Jurassic Outfitters, Toon Extra, and the Marvel Alterniverse Store. Universal Express Plus is available online up to 8 months in advance. You must know what date you plan on using Universal Express Plus because different dates have different prices.

The Plus feature is good for only one day at one park (in other words, no park-hopping) and for one ride only on each participating attraction. The number of Plus passes is limited each day, and they can sell out. Increase your chances of securing passes by buying and printing them from home from Universal's website. More than 90% of rides and shows are included in the Universal Express program, a much higher percentage than those included in the Fastpass program at the Disney parks. A two-park Express Plus ticket is also available starting at $36, in addition to a valid two-park access ticket.

When we tested Express Plus one recent summer, we discovered that Universal employees very rarely scrutinize the Express Plus card and that we could use the card several times on most attractions as long as we waited 15 minutes or so between attempts. Although there's a bar code on the pass, it was never scanned, nor did we see any scanning devices at the entrances of the attractions.

Be aware that neither Gringotts Wizarding Bank at Universal Studios nor Harry Potter and the Forbidden Journey at Islands of Adventure are Universal Express attractions. However, Universal hotel guests are eligible to enter The Wizarding World of Harry Potter in either park 1 hour before the park opens to the public.

IS UNIVERSAL EXPRESS PLUS WORTH IT?

THE ANSWER DEPENDS ON THE SEASON you visit, hours of park operation, and crowd levels. Because The Wizarding World of Harry Potter: Diagon Alley is new, crowd levels are expected to increase dramatically at Studios. In the Studios, only two attractions, Hollywood Rip Ride Rockit and Gringotts Wizarding Bank, might be difficult to ride without waiting an unacceptable length of time. However, if you arrive 30 minutes before park opening and use our touring plan (see page 475), you should experience them with a minimal wait, though with Gringotts, a minimal wait might exceed an hour unless you use the single-rider line.

Islands of Adventure is a different story because of the lack of high-capacity theater shows at IOA to siphon off crowds (one show at IOA compared to six shows at the Studios). Using our touring plan will cut your wait to a minimum, so our advice is to try it first. The beauty of Universal Express Plus is that you can purchase it in the park if waits for the rides become intolerable. A father from Snellville, Georgia, did the math and discovered that it was cheaper for his family to stay at a Universal resort than buy Universal Express:

> The benefits of that [Universal Resort] room key alone can be worth the price, with early entry to the Wizarding World and unlimited Express Pass use at both parks. We got a room at the Royal Pacific Resort for $349 on a Saturday night, which allowed us to use Universal Express Saturday and Sunday. The room cost $43.63 per person per day, while an Express Pass this same weekend would have cost $55.99 per person per day, and we still would have had to pay for a hotel.

UNIVERSAL MEAL DEALS

AT UNIVERSAL STUDIOS try the breakfast at Café La Bamba with characters from Universal's Superstar Parade. Guests can interact with minions from *Despicable Me* and *SpongeBob SquarePants*, and even get an autograph from Dora and Diego. Later in the day, you get special VIP viewing access to Universal's Superstar Parade. The private viewing area is near the bus stop by Revenge of the Mummy and Finnegan's. The breakfast costs $25 for adults and $11 for kids. After purchasing your dining experience online, you must call ☎ 407-224-7554 up to 24 hours before arriving to confirm your table. Separate park admission is required.

ONE-PARK MEAL DEAL With your Universal Meal Deal ticket, enjoy as much food as you would like all day long at participating Meal Deal locations in one park only. Meal includes one entrée and one dessert. Food service ends 30 minutes before theme-park closing time; children under age 9 must eat from a kid's menu. Guests will receive a wristband in exchange for the Meal Deal coupon at the first participating restaurant they visit in the park. Costs (before tax) for adults are $22, $11 for kids.

TWO-PARK MEAL DEAL With your Universal Meal Deal ticket, enjoy as much food as you would like all day long at participating Meal Deal locations in both parks. Guests receive a wristband in exchange for the Meal Deal coupon at the first participating restaurant they visit that day in cither park. Costs for adults are $26 and $13 for children.

ONE-DAY MEAL DEAL SOUVENIR CUP This ticket entitles you to one day of unlimited soft-drink fountain beverages at all participating Meal Deal locations at either Universal Studios Florida OR Islands of Adventure. Cost is $11 for all ages. Add an extra day for $9 at the participating Coca-Cola freestyle locations.

CITYWALK MEAL AND MOVIE DEAL This deal includes a ticket to any movie playing at the Universal Cineplex and a meal from a limited menu at participating CityWalk restaurants. The meal includes one entrée and a coffee, tea, or soft drink. This combination costs $22 for all ages. Buy your Meal and Movie Deal tickets at the CityWalk Guest Services ticket window or at all Destination Universal locations, or call a CityWalk sales coordinator at ☎ 407-224-2691. Additional charges apply for IMAX, IMAX 3-D, and 3-D movies.

UNIVERSAL'S CINEMATIC SPECTACULAR **DINING EXPERIENCE** First have dinner at Lombard's Seafood Grille; choose from an array of entrées, including fresh seafood, pasta, sandwiches, and more. Afterward, enjoy a spectacular view of *Universal's Cinematic Spectacular* nighttime show in an exclusive area at the restaurant's waterfront boardwalk. The experience is available for $45 per adult and $13 per child. After reserving and purchasing your dining experience online, you must call ☎ 407-224-7554 up to 24 hours before arriving to confirm your table. Separate theme park admission is required.

UNIVERSAL DINING PLAN This plan is available exclusively to guests who book their vacation with Universal. Guests will receive one counter-service meal (entrée and nonalcoholic beverage), one table-service meal (entrée, dessert, and nonalcoholic beverage), one snack (from a cart or counter-service location), and one additional beverage (from a cart or counter-service location) each day. Select CityWalk locations and all in-park dining locations, except those in The Wizarding World of Harry Potter: London Street, participate. Gratuity is not included, and no substitutions may be made. Eligible menu items and restaurants are indicated by a Universal Dining Plan logo. Price per day is $46 for adults and $18 for children. To book your vacation package with the Universal Dining Plan, visit **universalorlando.com**.

UNIVERSAL, KIDS, AND SCARY STUFF

ALTHOUGH THERE'S PLENTY FOR YOUNGER CHILDREN to enjoy at the Universal parks, the majority of the attractions have the potential for wigging out kids less than 8 years of age. At Universal Studios Florida, forget Hollywood Rip Ride Rockit, Revenge of the Mummy, *TWISTER . . . Ride It Out, Disaster!,* Men in Black Alien Attack, Transformers: The Ride, Gringotts Wizarding Bank, and *Terminator 2: 3-D.* The Simpsons Ride is not too scary but very intense and rough. At Islands of Adventure, watch out for The Incredible Hulk Coaster, Doctor Doom's Fearfall, The Amazing Adventures of Spider-Man, the Jurassic Park River Adventure, Harry Potter and the Forbidden Journey, Dragon Challenge, and Poseidon's Fury. Popeye & Bluto's Bilge-Rat Barges is wet and wild, but younger children handle it well. Dudley Do-Right's Ripsaw Falls is a toss-up, to be considered only if your kids like water-flume rides. *The Eighth Voyage of Sindbad* stunt show includes some explosions and startling special effects, but once again, children tolerate it well. Nothing else should pose a problem.

Child swap (or switching-off) at Universal is similar to Disney's version. The entire family goes through the whole line together before being split into riding and nonriding groups near the loading platform. The nonriding parent and child(ren) wait in a special room, usually with some sort of entertainment (for example, Forbidden Journey at IOA shows the first 20 minutes of the first *Harry Potter* film on a loop), a place to sit down, and sometimes restrooms with a changing table. At any theme park, the best tip we can give is to talk to the greeter in front of the attraction to see what you're supposed to do.

THE BLUE MAN GROUP

UNIVERSAL STUDIO'S Sharp Aquos Theater, near CityWalk, is home to the Blue Man Group. Tickets for shows start at $69 for adults and $29 for children ages 3–9 and can be purchased online or at the Universal box office; tickets purchased at the box office are $15 more. Upon presenting a valid International Student Identity Card, students can purchase tickets for $30. The show can be accessed from inside or outside the Universal Studios theme park. We recommend seats at least 15 rows back from the stage. In 2012 the exciting show received a makeover. Universal and Stanton's production company poured upward of $5 million into new music, staging, and high-resolution special effects, as well as a new interactive finale for the 90-minute show. In a funny tribute to contemporary communications, the Blue Man Group interacts with a giant GI-Pad. The investment signals a five-year extension of Blue Man Group's partnership with the theme park. Combo tickets for one or both parks including the Blue Man Group show are also available at **universalorlando.com**.

UNIVERSAL STUDIOS FLORIDA

UNIVERSAL STUDIOS FLORIDA OPENED IN JUNE 1990. At that time, it was almost four times the size of Disney's Hollywood Studios (which has since expanded to become the larger of the two parks), with much more of the facility accessible to visitors. Like its sister facility in Hollywood, Universal Studios Florida is spacious, beautifully landscaped, meticulously clean, and delightfully varied in its entertainment. Rides are exciting and innovative and, as with many Disney rides, focus on familiar and/or beloved movie characters or situations.

Universal Studios Florida is laid out in a P configuration, with the rounded part of the P extending disproportionately out from the stem. Beyond the main entrance, a wide boulevard stretches past several shows and rides to the park's New York section. Branching off this pedestrian thoroughfare to the right are five streets that access other areas of the studios and intersect a promenade circling a large lake.

The park is divided into seven sections: Production Central, New York, Hollywood, Springfield USA, Woody Woodpecker's KidZone,

World Expo, and The Wizarding World of Harry Potter London Street and Diagon Alley. Where one section begins and another ends is blurry, but no matter. Guests orient themselves by the major rides, sets, and landmarks and refer, for instance, to "New York," "the waterfront," "over by E. T.," or "by Mel's Diner."

The park offers all standard services and amenities, including stroller and wheelchair rentals, lockers, diaper-changing and infant-nursing facilities, car assistance, and foreign-language assistance. Most of the park is accessible to disabled guests, and TDDs are available for the hearing impaired. Almost all services are in the Front Lot, just inside the main entrance.

DISNEY'S HOLLYWOOD STUDIOS *versus* UNIVERSAL STUDIOS FLORIDA

DISNEY'S HOLLYWOOD STUDIOS (DHS) and Universal Studios Florida are direct competitors. Because both are large and expensive and they take at least 1 day to see, some guests must choose one park over the other. In the summer of 1999, Universal launched its second major theme park, Universal's Islands of Adventure, which competes directly with Disney's Magic Kingdom. (Universal Studios Florida theme park, Islands of Adventure theme park, the three Universal hotels, and the CityWalk complex are collectively known as Universal Orlando.)

Both Disney's Hollywood Studios and Universal Studios Florida draw their themes and inspiration from film and television. Both offer movie- and TV-themed rides and shows, some of which are just for fun, while others provide an educational, behind-the-scenes introduction to the cinematic arts.

 Bob: One-third of Disney's Hollywood Studios is off-limits to guests—except by guided tour— while most of Universal Studios Florida is open to exploration.

Unlike Disney's Hollywood Studios, Universal Studios Florida's open area includes the entire back lot, where guests can walk at leisure among movie sets. Because almost all of it is open to the public, the crowding and congestion so familiar at Disney's Hollywood Studios are largely mitigated. Universal Studios has plenty of elbow room.

Both parks include film and television-production studios. Guests are more likely, however, to see a movie, commercial, or television production in progress at Universal Studios than at Disney's Hollywood Studios. On most days, production crews will be shooting on the Universal back lot in full view of guests who care to watch.

Amazingly, and to the visitor's advantage, each park offers a completely different product mix, so there is little or no redundancy for

Continued on page 372

Universal Orlando

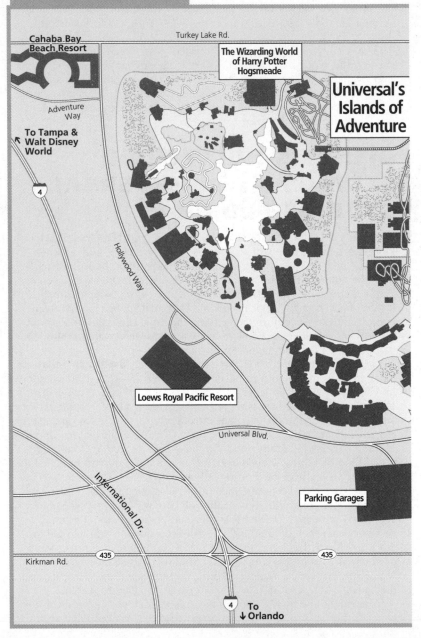

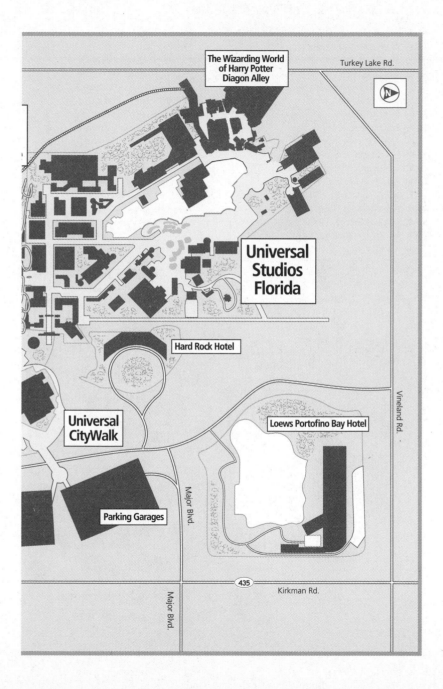

The Wizarding World
of Harry Potter
Diagon Alley

Turkey Lake Rd.

Universal
Studios
Florida

Hard Rock Hotel

Universal
CityWalk

Loews Portofino Bay Hotel

Vineland Rd.

Parking Garages

Major Blvd.

435

Kirkman Rd.

Major Blvd.

Universal Studios Florida

1. *Animal Actors on Location*
2. *Beetlejuice's Graveyard Revue*
3. *The Blues Brothers*
4. *A Day in the Park with Barney*
5. Despicable Me
6. *Disaster!*
7. *E.T. Adventure*
8. *Fear Factor Live*
9. *Fievel's Playland*
10. Gringotts Wizarding Bank
11. Hogwarts Express
12. Hollywood Rip Ride Rockit
13. Kang & Kodos' Twirl 'n' Hurl
14. *Lucy—A Tribute*
15. Men in Black Alien Attack
16. Revenge of the Mummy
17. *Shrek 4-D*
18. The Simpsons Ride
19. *Terminator 2: 3-D*
20. Transformers: The Ride 3-D
21. *TWISTER . . . Ride It Out*
22. *Universal's Cinematic Spectacular* (seasonal)
23. *Universal Orlando's Horror Make-Up Show*
24. Woody Woodpecker's Nuthouse Coaster, Curious George Goes to Town

Parade Route: ·············

To Universal's
← Islands of
Adventure

New York

Production Central

16

2

5th Ave. 3

57th St.

7th Ave.   7th Ave.

20

8th Ave.

12

5

17

Plaza-of-the-Stars

South St.

Nickelodeon Way

14

Rodeo Dr.

Hollywood-Blvd.

23

19

Hollywood

Main Entrance

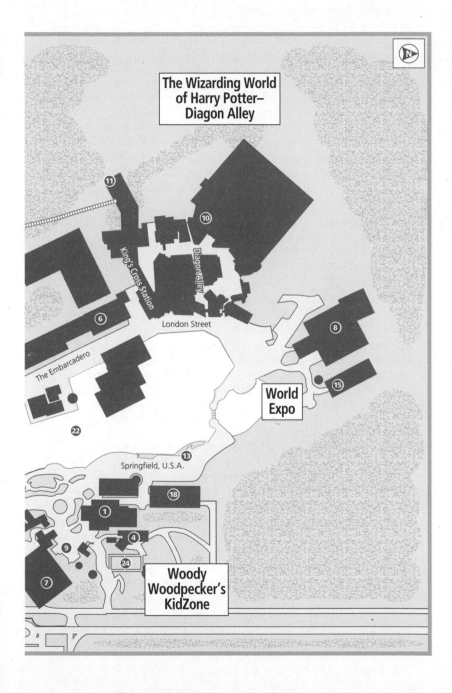

The Wizarding World
of Harry Potter–
Diagon Alley

King's Cross Station

Diagon Alley

London Street

The Embarcadero

World
Expo

Springfield, U.S.A.

Woody
Woodpecker's
KidZone

Continued from page 367

a person who visits both. Disney's Hollywood Studios and Universal Studios Florida each provide good exposure to the cinematic arts. Disney's Hollywood Studios over the years has turned several of its better tours into infomercials for Disney films. At Universal, you can still learn about postproduction, soundstages, set creation, and special effects without being bludgeoned by promotional hype.

We recommend trying one of the studios. If you enjoy one, you'll probably enjoy the other. If you have to choose, consider the following:

1. TOURING TIME If you tour efficiently, it takes about 8–10 hours to see Disney's Hollywood Studios (including a lunch break). Because Universal Studios Florida contains more rides and shows, touring, including one meal, takes about 9–12 hours.

2. CONVENIENCE If you're lodging along International Drive, I-4's northeast corridor, the Orange Blossom Trail (US 441), or in Orlando, Universal Studios Florida is closer. If you're lodging along US 27 or FL 192 or in Kissimmee or Walt Disney World, Disney's Hollywood Studios is more convenient.

3. ENDURANCE Universal Studios Florida requires more walking than Disney's Hollywood Studios, but it is also much less congested, so the walking is easier. Both parks offer wheelchairs and disabled access.

4. COST Both parks cost about the same for one-day admission, food, and incidentals, though Universal admission can be purchased in combo packages that include discounted passes to SeaWorld, Busch Gardens, and/or Wet 'n Wild. When Disney instituted the multiday Magic Your Way admission system in which you pay extra for park-hopping privileges, admissions to the minor parks, and the no-expiration pass option, Universal was quick to follow. However, multiday one-park passes are significantly less at Universal. Park-hopping (or "park to park" in Universal parlance) passes are comparable to Disney. In this category, the one admission where Universal seriously underprices Disney is for one-day park-hopping passes, which are about $25 less at Universal than at Disney. As at Disney, passes expire 13 days after first use.

5. BEST DAYS TO GO In order, Mondays, Sundays, and Saturdays are best to visit Universal Studios Florida and Islands of Adventure. The best day to visit DHS depends on whether *Fantasmic!* is playing and on the Extra Magic Hours rotation. Expressed differently, it changes from week to week. Daily crowd forecasts are available at **touringplans.com**.

6. WHEN TO ARRIVE For Disney's Hollywood Studios, arrive with your ticket in hand 30–40 minutes before official opening time. For Universal Studios, arrive with your admission already purchased about 35–45 minutes before official opening time. Arrive 45–55 minutes before official opening time if you need to purchase admission.

7. YOUNG CHILDREN Both DHS and Universal Studios Florida are relatively adult entertainment offerings. By our reckoning, half the rides and shows at DHS and about two-thirds at Universal Studios have a significant potential for frightening young children.

8. FOOD For counter-service, Universal Studios has a decided edge. Disney's Hollywood Studios full-service restaurants are marginally better.

9. LOCKERS Universal has instituted a mandatory locker system at its big thrill rides. Bags and other items must be placed in lockers outside the attractions. Lockers are free for the first hour, and then $3 for each half hour after that, with a $20 maximum.

The locker banks are easy to find; each bank has a small computer in the center. When the sun is bright, the screen is almost impossible to read, so have someone block the sun or use a different computer. After selecting your language, press your thumb onto the keypad and have your fingerprints scanned. We've seen people walk off cursing at this step, having repeated it over and over with no success. Most patrons press their thumb down too hard. The computer cannot read your thumbprint if it's squished onto the scanner, so take a deep breath and just lightly place your thumb on the designated spot.

After your thumb scans, you will receive a locker number. Write it down! When you return from your ride, go to the same kiosk machine, enter your locker number, and scan your thumb again. At Guest Services, family-size lockers are available for $8 for the entire day, but remember that only the person who scanned his or her thumb can open it.

UNIVERSAL STUDIOS FLORIDA ATTRACTIONS

Animal Actors on Location (Universal Express) ★★★

APPEAL BY AGE	PRESCHOOL ★★★★	GRADE SCHOOL ★★★★	TEENS ★★★
YOUNG ADULTS ★★★		OVER 30 ★★★	SENIORS ★★★★

What it is Animal tricks and comedy show. **Scope and scale** Major attraction. **Fright potential** Not frightening in any respect. **Bottleneck rating** 4. **When to go** After you have experienced all rides. **Authors' rating** Cute li'l critters; ★★★. **Duration of show** 20 minutes. **Probable waiting time** 25 minutes.

> Successful touring of Universal Studios with young children is absolutely possible, and this show is a must-see!

Liliane

This show integrates video segments with live sketches, jokes, and animal tricks performed onstage. Live animals, some of which are veterans of television and movies, take part, and kids are invited to participate. Where else can you get the chance to hold an 8-foot albino reticulated python in your lap? Check the daily entertainment schedule for showtimes.

Beetlejuice's Graveyard Revue
(Universal Express) ★★★½

What it is Rock-and-roll stage show. **Scope and scale** Almost major attraction. **Fright potential** Costumes and loud noises scare the under-7 crowd. **Bottleneck rating** 2. **When to go** At your convenience. **Authors' rating** Outrageous; ★★★½. **Duration of show** 18 minutes. **Probable waiting time** None.

Loud

This high-powered rock-and-roll stage show stars Beetlejuice, Frankenstein, the Bride of Frankenstein, Wolfman, and Dracula. Mercifully, this attraction is under cover. If you have small children, tell them beforehand that it is a live show with "monsters," but that they are all really very funny and totally nice, albeit a little loud. Rock on!

The show is based on the popular movie *Beetlejuice*, which won an Oscar in 1989 for Best Makeup.
Movie Tip

The Blues Brothers ★★★½

What it is Blues concert. **Scope and scale** Diversion. **Fright potential** Not frightening in any respect. **Bottleneck rating** 1. **When to go** Scheduled showtimes. **Special comment** A party in the street. **Authors' rating** ★★★½. **Duration of presentation** 12 minutes.

An impromptu concert featuring live singing and saxophone playing with a background track. The concert is a great pick-me-up, and the short run time keeps the energy high.

A Day in the Park with Barney (Universal Express)
★★★★

What it is Live character stage show. **Scope and scale** Major children's attraction. **Fright potential** Toddlers may balk at Barney's size. **Bottleneck rating** 4. **When to go** Anytime. **Authors' rating** Great hit with preschoolers; ★★★★. **Duration of show** 20 minutes plus preshow and character greeting. **Probable waiting time** 15 minutes.

Liliane

I love you, and you love me. This show should be a top priority if you have little ones.

Barney, the purple dinosaur of public-television fame, leads a sing-along with the help of the audience and sidekicks Baby Bop and BJ. A short preshow gets the kids lathered up before they enter Barney's Park (the theater). Interesting theatrical effects include wind, falling leaves, clouds and stars in the simulated sky, and snow. After the show, Barney exits momentarily to allow parents and children to gather along the stage. He then returns and moves from child to child, hugging each and posing for photos. If your child likes Barney, this show is a must. It's happy and upbeat, and the character greeting that follows is the best organized we've seen in any theme park. There's no line and no fighting for Barney's attention. Just relax by the rail and await your hug.

Despicable Me ★★★★

APPEAL BY AGE	PRESCHOOL ★★★★	GRADE SCHOOL ★★★★	TEENS ★★★★
YOUNG ADULTS ★★★★		OVER 30 ★★★★	SENIORS ★★★★

What it is Motion simulator 3-D ride. **Scope and scale** Major attraction. **Fright potential** Ride is wild and jerky but not frightening. **Bottleneck rating** 10. **When to go** First hour after park opening or after 5 p.m. **Special comment** Expect long waits in line. **Authors' rating ★★★★. Duration of ride** 5 minutes. **Average wait in line per 100 people ahead of you** 7 minutes. **Assumes** All simulators in use. **Loading speed** Moderate.

Rough   Queasy

This motion-simulator system premiered as the Funtastic World of Hanna-Barbera when the park opened in 1990; was used again in Jimmy Neutron's Nicktoon Blast, which replaced the former in 2003; and was retained for the attraction's third incarnation as Despicable Me.

As with the former attractions, the Despicable Me ride involves the motion simulators moving and reacting in sync with a cartoon projected on an IMAX-like screen. Though the simulators have been updated, the most significant upgrade is incorporated in the projection system, which employs high-definition 3-D digital technology. The story line combines elements from the animated movie *Despicable Me,* starring Gru, the villain, along with his adopted daughters and his diminutive yellow minions.

All new attractions draw large crowds, and Despicable Me is not any different. Compounding the crowding is the ride's location just inside the main entrance. Be aware that the simulators cause motion sickness in a very small percentage of riders. Stationary seating is available for those prone to motion sickness and for children less than 40 inches tall.

Disaster! (Universal Express) ★★★★

APPEAL BY AGE	PRESCHOOL ★★★	GRADE SCHOOL ★★★★	TEENS ★★★★
YOUNG ADULTS ★★★★		OVER 30 ★★★★	SENIORS ★★★★

What it is Combination theater presentation and adventure ride. **Scope and scale** Major attraction. **Fright potential** Special effects frighten those age 8 and under. **Bottleneck rating** 7. **When to go** In the morning or late afternoon. **Special comment** May frighten young children. **Authors' rating** Shaken, not stirred; **★★★★. Duration of presentation** 20 minutes. **Probable waiting time** 18 minutes. **Loading speed** Moderate.

Liliane

Yours truly was recruited for a part in *Mutha Nature.* I am so happy that the movie is shown only once!

Yep, I saw that movie. Liliane starred as the earthquake.

Loud   Scary

Disaster! is an updated version of *Earthquake: The Big One.* Guests are recruited for roles in a film called *Mutha Nature,* directed by an overbearing and conceited director. After the recruiting, the audience enters a soundstage where a number of scenes are filmed starring the guests/volunteers. If you ever wondered about special effects, this is the show to see. Next, guests board a faux subway where they experience a simulated earthquake. For younger children the earthquake is pretty intense. Older kids will love it! Following the quake, while the subway returns to the station, guests view a finished cut of *Mutha Nature* that incorporates all the soundstage shots.

E. T. Adventure *(Universal Express)* ★★★½

**APPEAL BY AGE   PRESCHOOL ★★★★   GRADE SCHOOL ★★★★   TEENS ★★★
YOUNG ADULTS ★★★   OVER 30 ★★★★   SENIORS ★★★★**

Thumbs Up for the Whole Family

What it is Indoor adventure ride based on the *E. T.* movie. **Scope and scale** Major attraction. **Fright potential** Too intense for some preschoolers. **Bottleneck rating** 8. **When to go** Before noon; before 10 a.m. if you have small children. **Authors' rating** A happy reunion; ★★★½. **Duration of ride** 4½ minutes. **Average wait in line per 100 people ahead of you** 5 minutes. **Loading speed** Moderate.

Guests aboard a bicycle-like conveyance escape with E. T. from earthly law enforcement officials and then journey to E. T.'s planet. The attraction is similar to Peter Pan's Flight at the Magic Kingdom but is longer and has more elaborate special effects. Make sure that you give the attendant your name—we recommend that you just state your name; don't try to spell it—and relish the end of the ride as E. T. will personalize his good-bye message. Lines build quickly after 10 a.m., and waits can be more than 2 hours on busy days. Ride in the morning or late afternoon.

Very cute. Liliane wants to phone home . . .

Liliane

Movie Tip

E. T. is based on Steven Spielberg's film *E. T.: The Extra-Terrestrial*—a great family movie that won four Oscars in 1982.

Fear Factor Live (Universal Express) ★★★★

**APPEAL BY AGE   PRESCHOOL ½   GRADE SCHOOL ★★   TEENS ★★★★
YOUNG ADULTS ★★★   OVER 30 ★★★   SENIORS ★½**

What it is Live version of the gross-out-stunt television show on NBC. **Scope and scale** Headliner. **Fright potential** Stuff of nightmares. **Bottleneck rating** 6. **When to go** Six to eight shows daily; crowds are smallest at the first and second-to-last shows. **Authors' rating** Great fun if you love the TV show; ★★★★. **Duration of show** 30 minutes. **Probable waiting time** 25 minutes.

Fear Factor Live is a live stage show in which up to six volunteers compete for one prize by doing dumb and yucky things such as swimming with eels and eating bugs. The show is really payback for adults; adolescents will enjoy watching mom squirm during the icky parts. For children age 8 and under, *Fear Factor Live* is nightmare material. Whether you participate or simply watch, this show will keep your innards in an uproar. *Fear Factor Live* has recently returned to network television.

Fievel's Playland ★★★★

**APPEAL BY AGE   PRESCHOOL ★★★★   GRADE SCHOOL ★★★★
TEENS —   YOUNG ADULTS —   OVER 30 —   SENIORS —**

What it is Children's play area with waterslide. **Scope and scale** Minor attraction. **Fright potential** Not frightening in any respect. **Bottleneck rating** 1. **When to go** Anytime. **Authors' rating** A much-needed attraction for preschoolers; ★★★★. **Probable waiting time** 20–30 minutes for the waterslide; otherwise, no waiting.

This is a great playground that features ordinary household items repro-
duced on a giant scale, seen as a mouse would experience them. Preschoolers and grade-schoolers can climb nets, walk through a huge boot, splash
in a sardine-can fountain, seesaw on huge spoons, and climb onto a cow
skull. Most of the playground is reserved for preschoolers, but a waterslide/
raft ride is open to all ages. There's almost no waiting in line here, and you
can stay as long as you want. Younger children love the oversize items, and
there's enough to keep teens and adults busy while little ones cut loose.
The waterslide/raft ride is open to everyone but is extremely slow loading
and carries only 300 riders per hour. With an average wait of 20–30 minutes, we don't think the 16-second ride is worth the trouble, and, yes, you
will get soaked.

> Fievel's Playland is another must for a successful visit to Universal
> Studios with small children. The playground is themed after the 1991
> Steven Spielberg movie *Fievel Goes West*. Young children will
> love to identify with the tales of Fievel Mousekewitz.

Liliane

Hollywood Rip Ride Rockit *(Universal Express)* ★★★★

What it is Super-high-tech roller coaster. **Scope and scale** Headliner. **Fright potential** Frightening for all ages. **Bottleneck rating** 9. **When to go** Immediately after
park opening. **Special comments** Expect long waits in line; must be 51" tall to ride.
Authors' rating ★★★★. **Duration of ride** 2½ minutes. **Average wait in line per
100 people ahead of you** 6–8 minutes. **Loading speed** Fast.

Rough   Queasy

Opened in the summer of 2009, Hollywood Rip Ride
Rockit has some features that we've never seen before.
Let's start with the basics: Rip Ride Rockit is a sit-down
X-Car coaster that runs on a 3,800-foot steel track, with
a maximum height of 167 feet and a top speed of 65 mph. X-Car vehicles
are more maneuverable than most other kinds and use less restrictive
restraints, making for an exhilarating ride.

You ascend—vertically—at 11 feet per second to crest the 17-story-tall
first hill, the highest point reached by any roller coaster in Orlando. The
drop is almost vertical, too, and launches you into Double Take, a loop
inversion in which you begin on the inside of the loop, twist to the outside
at the top (so you're upright), and then twist back inside the loop for the
descent. Double Take stands 136 feet tall, and its loop is 103 feet in diam-
eter at its widest point. You next hurl (not that hurl—it comes later) into
a stretch of track shaped like a musical treble clef. As on Double Take, the
track configuration on Treble Clef is a first.

The ride starts in the Production Central area; weaves into the New York
area near *TWISTER,* popping out over the heads of guests in the square
below; and then storms out and over the lagoon separating Universal Studios from Islands of Adventure. Each row is outfitted with color-changing
LEDs and high-end audio and video technology for each seat. Like the Rock
'n' Roller Coaster at Disney's Hollywood Studios, this coaster features a
musical soundtrack. With Rip Ride Rockit, however, you can choose the
genre of music you want to hear as you ride: classic rock, country, disco,

pop, or rap. After the ride, Universal flogs a digital-video "rip" of your ride, complete with the soundtrack you chose, that you can upload to websites such as YouTube.

The incentive for me to try out this thingy has not been invented. Therefore, Bob, stop asking me to ride the monster. The answer is NO.

Liliane

Liliane, I'm still half-deaf from the last roller coaster I rode with you.

Kang and Kodos Twirl n Hurl ★★½

APPEAL BY AGE	PRESCHOOL ★★★★	GRADE SCHOOL ★★★	TEENS ★★★
YOUNG ADULTS ★★★		OVER 30 ★★★	SENIORS ★★

What it is Spinner ride. **Scope and scale** Minor attraction. **Fright potential** Like Dumbo only louder. **Bottleneck rating** 10. **When to go** After the Simpsons Ride. **Special comment** Expect *long* waits in line. **Authors' rating** A touching remembrance; ★★½. **Duration of ride** 1½ minutes. **Average wait in line per 100 people ahead of you** 21 minutes.

Queasy

The Twirl n Hurl is primarily eye candy for Springfield USA (where the Simpsons live) section of the park that was added to create a theme area around the Simpsons Ride. Think of it as Dumbo with a quirky sense of humor. Kang and Kodos are tentacled aliens who hold pictures of Simpson characters for you to blast away at with a ray gun as you ride in a little flying saucer (who thinks this stuff up?). All the while Kang is exhorting you (loudly) to destroy Springfield and making insulting comments about humans. Preschoolers enjoy the ride while older kids crack up over the insulting narration.

Lucy—A Tribute ★★★

APPEAL BY AGE	PRESCHOOL ★	GRADE SCHOOL ★★	TEENS ★★
YOUNG ADULTS ★★★		OVER 30 ★★★	SENIORS ★★★

What it is Walk-through tribute to Lucille Ball. **Scope and scale** Diversion. **Fright potential** Not frightening in any respect. **Bottleneck rating** 0. **When to go** Anytime. **Authors' rating** A touching remembrance; ★★★.

This museumlike exhibit spotlights the life and career of comedienne Lucille Ball. See Lucy during the hot, crowded midafternoon or on your way out of the park.

The well-deserved tribute is not for young children, and most teenagers will lack a frame of reference. As for me: "I love Lucy."

Liliane

Men in Black Alien Attack (*Universal Express*) ★★★★½

APPEAL BY AGE	PRESCHOOL †	GRADE SCHOOL ★★★★★	TEENS ★★★★★
YOUNG ADULTS ★★★★★		OVER 30 ★★★★★	SENIORS ★★★★

† Due to height requirement, sample size too small for an accurate rating.

What it is Interactive dark thrill ride. **Scope and scale** Super-headliner. **Fright potential** Dark and intense; frightens many children age 10 and under. **Bottleneck rating** 9. **When to go** In the morning after Revenge of the Mummy. **Special comments** May induce motion sickness; must be 42" tall to ride. Switching-off option provided (see page 245). **Authors' rating** Buzz Lightyear on steroids; not to be missed; ★★★★½. **Duration of ride** 2½ minutes. **Average wait in line per 100 people ahead of you** 5 minutes. **Loading speed** Moderate–fast.

Based on the movie of the same name, the story line has you volunteering as a Men in Black (MIB) trainee. After an introduction warning that aliens "live among us" and articulating MIB's mission to round them up, Zed expands on the finer points of alien spotting and familiarizes you with your training vehicle and your weapon, an alien "zapper." Following this, you load up and are dispatched on an innocuous training mission that immediately deteriorates into a situation where only you are in a position to prevent aliens from taking over the universe. Now, if you saw the movie, you understand that the aliens are mostly giant exotic bugs and cockroaches and that zapping the aliens involves exploding them into myriad, gooey body parts. Thus, the meat of the ride (no pun intended) consists of careening around Manhattan in your MIB vehicle and shooting aliens. Each of the 120 or so alien figures has sensors that activate special effects and respond to your zapper. Aim for the eyes and keep shooting until the aliens' eyes turn red. To avoid a long wait, hotfoot it to MIB immediately after riding Mummy in the first 30 minutes the park is open.

> Bugs are everywhere. The ride is really fun, especially if you have seen the movie. Can't wait to go back and shoot some aliens.

Ian

Revenge of the Mummy *(Universal Express)* ★★★★½

APPEAL BY AGE	PRESCHOOL ★★	GRADE SCHOOL ★★★★	TEENS ★★★★★
YOUNG ADULTS ★★★★½		OVER 30 ★★★★	SENIORS ★★★½

What it is Combination dark ride and roller coaster. **Scope and scale** Super-headliner. **Fright potential** Scary for all ages. **Bottleneck rating** 8. **When to go** The first hour the park is open or after 6 p.m. **Special comment** Must be 48" tall to ride; switching-off option provided (see page 245). **Authors' rating** Killer! ★★★★½. **Duration of ride** 4 minutes. **Average wait in line per 100 people ahead of you** 7 minutes. **Loading speed** Moderate.

Revenge of the Mummy is an indoor dark ride based on the *Mummy* flicks, where guests fight off "deadly curses and vengeful creatures" while flying through Egyptian tombs and other spooky places on a high-tech roller coaster. The special effects are cutting-edge, integrating the best technology from such attractions as *Terminator 2: 3-D* and Spider-Man (the ride). The ride begins slowly, passing through various chambers, including one where flesh-eating scarab beetles descend on you. Suddenly your vehicle stops, and then drops backward and rotates. Next thing you know, you're shot at high speed up the first hill of the roller coaster. Though it's a wild ride by anyone's definition, the emphasis remains as much on the visuals, robotics, and special effects as on the ride itself. Note that the Mummy's queue contains enough scary stuff to frighten small children all on its own.

> The mummy scared the willies out of me. This one is definitely not for young children.

Liliane

Shrek 4-D *(Universal Express)* ★★★★½

APPEAL BY AGE   PRESCHOOL ★★★   GRADE SCHOOL ★★★★★   TEENS ★★★★★
YOUNG ADULTS ★★★★★   OVER 30 ★★★★★   SENIORS ★★★★★

What it is 3-D movie. **Scope and scale** Headliner. **Fright potential** Loud but not frightening. Preshow area is a little macabre. **Bottleneck rating** 7. **When to go** The first hour the park is open or after 4 p.m. **Authors' rating** Warm, fuzzy mayhem; ★★★★½. **Duration of show** 20 minutes. **Probable waiting time** 16 minutes.

This attraction is a real winner. It's irreverent, frantic, laugh-out-loud funny, and iconoclastic. In contrast to Disney's *It's Tough to Be a Bug!,* *Shrek 4-D* doesn't generally frighten children under age 7.

> Take off the 3-D glasses if it is all too scary, and consider earplugs.
> Did you know that Shrek in German means "the scare"?

Liliane

The Simpsons Ride *(Universal Express)* ★★★★

APPEAL BY AGE   PRESCHOOL —   GRADE SCHOOL ★★★★   TEENS ★★★★
YOUNG ADULTS ★★★★   OVER 30 ★★★★   SENIORS ★★★½

What it is Mega-simulator ride. **Scope and scale** Super-headliner. **Fright potential** Visuals not scary but very wild ride. **Bottleneck rating** 9. **When to go** First thing after park opening. **Special comments** Must be 40" tall to ride; not recommended for pregnant women or people prone to motion sickness. Switching-off option provided (see page 245). **Authors' rating** Despicable Me with attitude; ★★★★. **Duration of ride** 4⅓ minutes. **Average wait in line per 100 people ahead of you** 5 minutes. **Loading speed** Moderate.

Rough   Queasy

Two preshows involve Simpsons characters speaking sequentially on different video screens in the queue. Their comments help define the characters for guests who are unfamiliar with the TV show. The attraction is a simulator ride, similar to Star Tours at Disney's Hollywood Studios and Despicable Me at Universal, but with a larger screen more like that of Soarin' at Epcot. The attraction takes a wild and humorous poke at thrill rides, dark rides, and live shows. Like the show on which it's based, The Simpsons Ride definitely has an edge—and more than a few wild hairs. Like *Shrek 4-D,* it operates on several levels. There will be jokes and visuals that you'll get but will fly over your children's heads—and most assuredly vice versa. You can expect large crowds all day.

> The ride is a long way from being tame. Skip it if you're an expectant
> mom or prone to motion sickness. Several families we interviewed
> found the humor a little too adult for their younger children.

Street Scenes ★★★★★

APPEAL BY AGE   PRESCHOOL ★★   GRADE SCHOOL ★★★★★   TEENS ★★★★★
YOUNG ADULTS ★★★★★   OVER 30 ★★★★★   SENIORS ★★★★★

What it is Elaborate outdoor sets for making films. **Scope and scale** Diversion. **Fright potential** Not frightening in any respect. **Bottleneck rating** 0. **When to go** Anytime. **Special comment** You'll see most sets without special effort as you tour the park. **Authors' rating** One of the park's great assets; ★★★★★.

Unlike at Disney's Hollywood Studios, all Universal Studios Florida's back-lot sets are accessible for guest inspection. You'll see most as you walk through the park. Enjoy a New York City street, San Francisco's waterfront, a New England coastal town, Rodeo Drive, and Hollywood Boulevard. The sets make for great photo ops!

Terminator 2: 3-D *(Universal Express)* ★★★★

APPEAL BY AGE	PRESCHOOL ★★★	GRADE SCHOOL ★★★★	TEENS ★★★★
YOUNG ADULTS ★★★★★		OVER 30 ★★★★★	SENIORS ★★★★

What it is 3-D thriller mixed-media presentation. **Scope and scale** Super-headliner. **Fright potential** Intense; will frighten children age 7 and under. **Bottleneck rating** 7. **When to go** After 3:30 p.m. **Special comments** The nation's best theme-park theater attraction; very intense for some preschoolers and grade-schoolers. **Authors' rating** Furiously paced high-tech experience; not to be missed; ★★★★. **Duration of show** 20 minutes, including an 8-minute preshow. **Probable waiting time** 20–40 minutes.

The attraction, like the films, is all action, and you really don't need to understand much. What's interesting is that it uses 3-D film and a theater full of sophisticated technology to integrate the real with the imaginary. Images seem to move in and out of the film, not only in the manner of traditional 3-D but also in actuality. Remove your 3-D glasses momentarily and you'll see that the guy on the motorcycle is actually onstage. *Terminator 2: 3-D* has been eclipsed a bit by newer attractions such as Revenge of the Mummy, Hollywood Rip Ride Rockit, and Despicable Me. We suggest that you save *Terminator* and other theater presentations until you have experienced all of the rides. Families with young children should know that the violence characteristic of the *Terminator* movies is largely absent from the attraction. There's suspense and action but not much blood and guts.

Transformers: The Ride 3-D ★★★★★

APPEAL BY AGE	PRESCHOOL ★★★	GRADE SCHOOL ★★★★★	TEENS ★★★★★
YOUNG ADULTS ★★★★★		OVER 30 ★★★★★	SENIORS ★★★★

What it is Multisensory 3-D dark ride. **Scope and scale** Super-headliner. **Fright potential** Loud, intense, and violent: prepare 7-and-unders by previewing a movie trailer before you visit. **Bottleneck rating** 10. **When to go** The first 30 minutes the park is open or after 4 p.m. **Special comment** Must be 40" tall to ride; children 40–48" must be accompanied by a rider 14 years or older; single-rider line is available. **Authors' rating** ★★★★★. **Duration of ride** 4½ minutes. **Average wait in line per 100 people ahead of you** 4½ minutes. **Loading speed** Moderate–fast.

Hasbro's Transformers—those toy robots from the 1980s that you turned and twisted into trucks and planes—have been, er, transformed into director Michael Bay's blockbuster movie trilogy and then to a theme park attraction befitting their pop-culture idols. Recruits to this cybertronic war enlist by entering the N.E.S.T. Base (headquarters of the heroic Autobots and their human allies). Inside, in the queue, video monitors catch you up on the backstory. Basically, the Decepticon baddies are after the Allspark, source of cybernetic sentience. Your job is to safeguard the shard. The vastly annoying top villain, Megatron, and his pals Starscream and Devastator threaten the mission, but don't worry, you have Sideswipe and Bumblebee on the bench to back you up. The plot amounts to little more than a giant game of keep-away, and the uninitiated will likely be unable to tell one meteoric mass of metal from another, but you'll be too dazzled by the debris whizzing by to notice. The ride's mix of detailed set pieces and high-tech video projections bring these colossi to life in one very intense and immersive thrill ride.

If you visit before Harry's debut in spring 2013, ride immediately after park opening. After Harry opens, follow our touring plan to minimize waits. The single-rider line will get you on board faster, but you'll miss all the cool show elements of the regular queue. Finally, it's difficult to focus on the fast-moving imagery from the front row; center seats in the second and third rows provide the best perspective.

The Supply Vault, also known as the Transformers gift shop, opened in March 2013. Transformer characters Optimus Prime, Bumblebee, and Megatron appear regularly on the streets of Universal Studios.

TWISTER . . . Ride It Out *(Universal Express)* ★★★½

APPEAL BY AGE	PRESCHOOL ★★	GRADE SCHOOL ★★★★	TEENS ★★★★
YOUNG ADULTS ★★★★		OVER 30 ★★★★	SENIORS ★★★

What it is Theater presentation featuring special effects from the movie *Twister*. **Scope and scale** Major attraction. **Fright potential** Will frighten children age 7 and under. **Bottleneck rating** 7. **When to go** Should be your first show after experiencing all rides. **Special comment** High potential for frightening young children. **Authors' rating** Gusty; ★★★½. **Duration of show** 15 minutes. **Probable waiting time** 20 minutes.

Loud   Scary

Twister combines an elaborate set and special effects, climaxing with a five-story-tall simulated tornado created by circulating 2 million cubic feet of air per minute. The wind, pounding rain, and freight-train sound of the tornado are deafening, and the entire presentation is exceptionally intense. Schoolchildren are mightily impressed, while younger children are terrified and overwhelmed. Unless you want the kids hopping in your bed whenever they hear thunder, try this attraction yourself before taking your kids.

Universal Orlando's Horror Make-Up Show
(Universal Express) ★★★½

APPEAL BY AGE	PRESCHOOL ★★★	GRADE SCHOOL ★★★★	TEENS ★★★★
YOUNG ADULTS ★★★★		OVER 30 ★★★★	SENIORS ★★★★

Thumbs Up for the Whole Family

What it is Theater presentation on the art of makeup. **Scope and scale** Major attraction. **Fright potential** Gory but not frightening. **Bottleneck rating** 6. **When to go** After you have experienced all rides. **Special comment** May upset young children. **Authors' rating** A gory knee-slapper; ★★★½. **Duration of show** 25 minutes. **Probable waiting time** 20 minutes.

Lively, well-paced look at how makeup artists create film monsters, realistic wounds, severed limbs, and other unmentionables. Exceeding most guests' expectations, the *Horror Make-Up Show* is the sleeper attraction at Universal. Its humor and tongue-in-cheek style transcend the gruesome effects, and most folks (including preschoolers) take the blood and guts in stride. It usually isn't too hard to get into.

Woody Woodpecker's Nuthouse Coaster and Curious George Goes to Town ★★★

APPEAL BY AGE	PRESCHOOL ★★★★	GRADE SCHOOL —	TEENS —
YOUNG ADULTS —	OVER 30 —		SENIORS —

What it is Interactive playground and kid's roller coaster. **Scope and scale** Minor attraction. **Fright potential** Not frightening in any respect. **Bottleneck rating** 5. **When to go** Anytime. **Special comment** Must be 36" tall to ride coaster. **Authors' rating** A good place to turn the kids loose; ★★★.

The KidZone consists of Woody Woodpecker's Nuthouse Coaster and an interactive playground called Curious George Goes to Town. The child-size roller coaster is small enough for kids, though its moderate speed might unnerve some smaller children. The Curious George playground exemplifies the Universal obsession with wet stuff; in addition to innumerable spigots, pipes, and spray guns, two giant roof-mounted buckets periodically dump a *thousand gallons* of water on unsuspecting visitors below. Kids who want to stay dry can mess around in the foam-ball playground, also equipped with chutes, tubes, and ball blasters. The playground is creatively designed and a great place for kids to cut loose after being in tow all day.

Liliane

Have the kids wear a bathing suit under their clothes so they can enjoy the water features. Simpler still, let the 4-and-unders frolic in their underwear (bring an extra pair).

THE WIZARDING WORLD OF HARRY POTTER: DIAGON ALLEY

WHEN UNIVERSAL OPENED The Wizarding World of Harry Potter at Islands of Adventure, it created a paradigm shift in the Disney–Universal theme park rivalry. Not only did Universal trot out some groundbreaking ride technology, but it also demonstrated that it could trump Disney's most distinctive competence: the creation of infinitely detailed and totally immersive themed areas. To say that The Wizarding World was a game-changer is an understatement of the first order.

It was immediately obvious that Universal would build on its Potter franchise success—but how and where? Universal's not sitting on 27,000-plus acres like Disney, so real estate was at a premium. If Potterville was going to grow, something else had to go. Conventional wisdom suggested the Wizarding World expansion would gobble up the Lost Continent section of Islands of Adventure, and that may happen yet. But looking at the ledger, it was clear that the older Universal Studios theme park could use a boost. Concurring, we remember sitting at the foot of the escalators monitoring traffic coming from the parking garages. For every guest who tacked right, toward the Studios, 15 made a beeline for IOA and Harry Potter.

It just so happened that a substantial chunk of turf at the Studios was occupied by the aging JAWS ride and its contiguous Amity themed area. The space would allow for substantial development;

plus, its isolated location—in the most remote corner of the park—was conducive to creating a totally self-contained area where Potter themes could be executed absent any distraction from neighboring attractions. In short, it was perfect.

So how would the new Potter area tie in to the original at IOA? And what Harry Potter literary icons could be exploited? It was pretty clear that a new suburb of Hogsmeade wasn't going to cut it. Turns out the answer was virtually shouting from the pages of the Harry Potter novels, which observe a clear dichotomy of place—plots originate in London and then unfold at distant Hogwarts.

Three London sites figure prominently in the Potter saga: the house where Harry once lived with his adoptive family; Diagon Alley, a secret part of London that is a sort of sorcerers' shopping mall; and the King's Cross railroad station, where wizarding students embark for the train trip to Hogwarts. There wasn't much to milk from Harry's house, but Diagon Alley and the train station brimmed with possibilities.

Following much deliberation and consultation with Warner Bros. and author J. K. Rowling, the final design called for a London-waterfront street scene flanking Universal Studios Lagoon. The detailed facades, anchored by the **King's Cross** railroad station on the left and including **Grimmauld Place** and **Wyndham's Theatre,** recall West London scenes from the books and movies. **Diagon Alley,** secreted behind the London street scene, is accessed through a secluded entrance in the middle of the facade. Like Hogsmeade at IOA, Diagon Alley will feature shops and restaurants in addition to three attractions and live entertainment.

Expanding The Wizarding World into Universal Studios will offer about two-and-a-half times the pedestrian space of the original at IOA. Where approximately 4,500 people have Hogsmeade stretched to the max, Diagon Alley will accommodate almost 8,000. But with only one high-capacity ride (**Gringotts Wizarding Bank**), along with an enlarged version of the **Ollivanders** wand-shop experience in Hogsmeade and the **Hogwarts Express** train connecting the two Wizarding Worlds, what are all these people going to do? The answer: shop (and eat) 'til they drop. Research shows that Hogsmeade visitors are nuts about the wizardy shops. Diagon Alley, aside from the train and headliner ride, will be the planet's wackiest mall. In the attraction department, many Potter faithful speculated about rides based on the Weasley flying car or the double-decker flying Knight Bus, but they were thinking small. Universal once again came out swinging for the fences. As before with Harry Potter and the Forbidden Journey, the headliner attraction for the expansion will be high-tech and cutting-edge—and once again a dark ride, but this time of the roller coaster genre. The labyrinthine passages and caverns of Gringotts, the financial institution of choice for the wizarding set, will be the setting of the plot-driven 3-D dark ride–coaster.

Though the Gringotts attraction is Diagon Alley's headliner, the most creative element in the two-park Potter domain is the Hogwarts Express, which re-creates the train trip from London to Hogwarts and vice versa. Serving as both an attraction and transportation between

the Studios and IOA, the Express unifies the two disparately located
Wizarding Worlds into a continuous whole.

Diagon Alley in Detail

Liliane: I want to sneak into the Wizarding World through the Leaky Cauldron pub. OK, I'll take the Hogwarts Express.

Guests access Diagon Alley in two ways: From the
Universal Studios entrance, take the first right turn
onto Rodeo Drive; then, across from Mel's Diner,
take the promenade clockwise or counterclockwise
around the lagoon to the London-waterfront area.
From The Wizarding World of Harry Potter: Hogsmeade at IOA, take
the Hogwarts Express to London King's Cross Station in the Studios.

Having arrived at the London area, enter Diagon Alley from approximately the center of the building facades comprising the waterfront. As
in the books and movies, Diagon Alley is ordinarily reserved for wizards and the like, and inaccessible to Muggles (garden-variety humans).
The entrance is secret, so entering The Wizarding World entails a transitional experience—and the endless queue of Muggles in shorts and
flip-flops will leave little doubt where that experience begins.

Once admitted, look down the alley to the rounded facade of **Gringotts Wizarding Bank.** An animatronic dragon inspired by *Harry Potter
and the Deathly Hallows: Part 2* perches atop the bank's dome. To your
left, the **Leaky Cauldron** is the area's flagship restaurant, supplemented
by **Florean Fortescue's Ice Cream Parlour,** down the alley and around
the corner. Shops include **Weasleys' Wizard Wheezes,** a joke shop;
Wiseacre's Wizarding Equipment, for scales, celestial charts, telescopes,
globes, and hourglasses; and **Madam Malkin's Robes for All Occasions,**
selling school uniforms and dress robes for wizards and witches. In general, Diagon Alley's stores will be somewhat larger and more plentiful
than the tiny shops over in Hogsmeade, but don't expect Walmart.

Intersecting Diagon Alley near Gringotts is **Knockturn Alley,** where
the Harry Potter bad guys hang out. Mostly a covered walk-through
area, it features some show elements in the faux shop windows among
other things. Shops include **Borgin and Burkes,** which sells objects
from the dark side of magic according to the Potter canon.

Gringotts Wizarding Bank *(opens 2014)*

What it is Super-high-tech roller coaster and dark ride. **Scope and scale** Super-
headliner. **Fright potential** All scary elements are heaped on this one, though the ride
itself is less intense than Forbidden Journey at IOA. **Bottleneck rating** 10+. **When to
go** Immediately after park opening. **Special comment** Expect lengthy waits in line.
Duration of ride 4½ minutes. **Average waiting time in line per 100 people
ahead of you** 4 minutes. **Loading speed** Fast.

Owned and operated by goblins, Gringotts is the only bank in the world
of wizards. Known for its cavernous lobby and halls, multilayered twisting
passages, and dim lighting, the bank exudes spookiness. The theme park
adaptation, a dark ride, is the centerpiece of Diagon Alley. Like Forbidden Journey, Gringotts incorporates a substantial part of the overall experience into the queue. You enter through the bank's lobby, where you're
critically appraised by glowering animatronic goblins. Then you board

Gringotts' internal transportation system—two-car coaster trains, each holding 24 people—for a tour of the bank. Along the way, you encounter holographic images of Harry, Ron, and Hermione, who are at loggerheads with some pesky Death Eaters. At midpoint you run afoul of the dragon that winds up on Gringotts roof.

The ride is similar to Spider-Man at IOA in that elaborate sets are seamlessly integrated with high-resolution 3-D film. Similarly, the ride borrows a page from Revenge of the Mummy, also at Universal Studios, in that it operates on a steel coaster track engineered by Premier Rides of Baltimore. As with the Mummy, sometimes the ride is slow, with an emphasis on visuals and special effects, and fast and wild at other times. Unlike Harry Potter and the Forbidden Journey at IOA, Gringotts was designed to be less intense (read: less nauseating) and therefore more appealing to families. Accordingly, it has fewer height, weight, and size restrictions. (For a peek at Gringotts as depicted in *Harry Potter and the Deathly Hallows: Part 2*, and a few hints at the ride's story line, search for "Escape from Gringotts" on YouTube.)

Gringotts Bank is the pot of gold at the end of Universal's rainbow that a kazillion crazed guests are racing toward. If you're a Universal resort guest and you qualify for early entry, use it. Otherwise, arrive at the turnstiles, admission in hand, 35–45 minutes before park opening and be ready to haul butt. If you arrive by train from IOA, make Gringotts your first stop. If you don't mind breaking up your group, using the singles line always cuts wait time.

Hogwarts Express *(opens 2014)*

What it is Transportation attraction. **Scope and scale** Super-headliner. **Fright potential** Potter villains and spirit creatures menace the train. **Bottleneck rating** 10+. **When to go** Immediately after park opening. **Special comment** Two-park ticket required to enter Islands of Adventure **Duration of ride** 4 minutes. **Average waiting time in line per 100 people ahead of you** 7 minutes. **Loading speed** Moderate.

Part of the genius of creating Diagon Alley at the Studios is that it will be connected to Hogsmeade at IOA by the Hogwarts Express, just as in the novels and films. The Hogsmeade Village station will be situated within the footprint of the Dragon Challenge roller coaster and will provide pedestrian access to Hogsmeade and IOA's Lost Continent themed area. On days of low-to-average attendance, disembarking guests will be allowed directly into Hogsmeade, less than a minute's walk away. On days of heavy attendance, they'll be directed to The Lost Continent, where they'll have to either queue to enter Hogsmeade or obtain a free timed-entry ticket to visit The Wizarding World at a specified time. The same situation prevails in the Studios at London King's Cross Station. Arriving guests will be admitted directly to Diagon Alley unless attendance is extremely heavy, in which case they'll exit the station onto the London waterfront, where they can either queue or pick up a timed-entry ticket.

Along your Hogwarts Express journey, you'll see moving images projected in the windows of the car—say, the Scottish countryside passing outside your window—rather than the park's backstage areas. There will be different presentations coming and going, and in addition to pastoral scenery there will be surprises, challenges, and threats en route, augmented by special effects in the cars.

Though we expect Universal to be tweaking the train's operational protocols even after opening in the summer of 2014, here are some educated guesses about how it will work:

Not everyone in one or the other park will be able to experience the train because its carrying capacity is relatively small and the track can only accommodate two trains, each moving in a different direction and passing one another in the middle of the journey. This leaves Universal with a few options.

First, because using the train for a one-way trip involves park-hopping, one-way passengers will need a valid two-park ticket. If the Express is limited to one-way travel, it will stir up a hornet's nest because guests will certainly want to use their one-park pass for a round-trip. If both one-way and round-trip options are offered, riders in queue will be separated into one-way and round-trip lines.

Or, for simplicity of operation, to allow more guests to experience the train, and as a strong incentive to sell more two-park passes, it's more likely that no direct round-trips will be offered. The train would be limited to guests with two-park tickets, and disembarking passengers would have to enter the second park and, if desired, queue again for their return trip.

Another alternative is for the trains to run on a schedule, with guests holding two-park tickets to book, at an additional fee, specific departures for both outbound and return. This would reduce the number of guests per day experiencing the train but could also be a good moneymaker, with some itinerary packages including restaurant meals at the destination as well as appointment times for headliner attractions. We think such scheduled, reserved departures will be part of the mix, but that the trains will run between scheduled departures serving guests without reservations.

There's a capacity-versus-authenticity issue front and center with the Hogwarts Express—and if you know J. K. Rowling's reputation for perfectionism where adaptations of her books are concerned, you know the sticky wicket this presented for Universal. The train cars from the films and novels are divided into private compartments that seat six, but replicating those compartments would mean fewer seats and longer loading times (and longer queues, too). Happily, Universal was able to strike a balance between practicality and verisimilitude.

At IOA, Universal set up a backstory to explain why Muggles could visit Hogwarts. In short, the Muggles visit is a one-time event—on "a day frozen in time"—coinciding with the day that the Dragon Challenge (from *Harry Potter and the Goblet of Fire*) is being held. All the Potter bad guys, including Voldemort, Death Eaters, and Dementors, are mustering their powers to wreak havoc on the tournament, among other things. Anyway, the background is important only to explain why Dumbledore ordered special railroad cars to better protect the Muggles heading to and from The Wizarding World: these cars, unlike the iconic ones from the movies and books, will hold a lot of Muggles. All of this will be explained as you wait to board, so you won't be crestfallen about not riding in the cool cars that Harry, Ron, and Hermione rode in the movies. A detail truer to the Potter canon: You'll walk "through" a brick wall at King's Cross to access Platform 9¾.

Universal was somehow surprised by a survey that showed guests considered the Hogwarts Express an attraction rather than merely transportation connecting the two parks. This "revelation" threw the creative team into a tizzy about how they could increase the capacity of the train—a task made all the more difficult because the stations and track were already under construction and designed to handle only two cars in each direction carrying guests. Plans are still very much up in the air, the current strategy being basically to open the Express on schedule and see what happens. If capacity is totally inadequate relative to demand, the smart money's on taking the Express out of service for a year or so to redesign it.

No matter how things shake out, low capacity and high demand will make the Hogwarts Express the toughest ticket in both Universal parks. Assuming that not all departures will require reservations, make the train your first attraction of the day. If, for example, Diagon Alley is your top priority of the day, enter Islands of Adventure as early as possible and line up at the Hogsmeade Village station for the train to London King's Cross. The earlier you arrive at King's Cross, the more likely you'll be admitted directly to Diagon Alley.

Ollivanders *(opens 2014)*

What it is Combination wizarding demonstration and shopping op. **Scope and scale** Major attraction. **Fright potential** Special effects may startle 6-and-unders. **Bottleneck rating** 10. **When to go** After riding Gringotts Bank. **Special comment** Audience stands. **Duration of presentation** 6 minutes. **Average waiting time in line per 100 people ahead of you** 7 minutes.

Ollivanders, located in Diagon Alley in the books and films, somehow sprouted a branch location in Hogsmeade at IOA (see page 402). Potter purists pointed out this misplacement, but the wand shop stayed and became one of the most popular features of The Wizarding World. It also became a horrendous bottleneck, with long lines where guests roasted in an unshaded queue. In The Wizarding World: Diagon Alley, Ollivanders will assume its rightful place, and with much larger digs. At IOA, only 24 guests at a time can experience the little drama where wands choose a wizard (rather than the other way around). At the Studios, the shop will have three separate choosing chambers, turning it from a popular curiosity into an actual attraction. As for the IOA location, there's no indication that it will close when Diagon Alley opens.

If your young 'un is selected to test-drive a wand, be forewarned that you'll have to buy it if you want to take it home.

Touring Strategy

The Wizarding World of Harry Potter: Diagon Alley will be the queen of the hop in the theme park world in 2014 and beyond. Because of the crowds, experiencing Diagon Alley without interminable waits will be a challenge—if you visited The Wizarding World of Harry Potter: Hogsmeade during its first three years at IOA, you know what we mean. Hogsmeade opened with three rides and Ollivanders; now it has four rides including the train plus the wand shop. As discussed earlier, Diagon Alley has another Ollivanders and only two rides, one of which, Hogwarts Express, it shares with Hogsmeade in IOA. Because only half of each day's total train passengers can board at the Studios station, Diagon Alley in essence has only one-and-a-half rides, plus Ollivanders and the various shops, to entertain the expected masses. It's gonna be crazy.

Once again, Universal resort guests will be admitted an hour before the general public. This is a tremendous perk if you're staying on Universal property, but you'll still be competing with thousands of other resort guests, so arrive at least 30 minutes before early entry starts. If you're a day guest, Diagon Alley will already be packed when you arrive. As at IOA, except on days of moderate-to-low attendance, we expect Universal to distribute timed-entry tickets specifying when you can visit. The earlier you obtain your ticket, the sooner you'll be admitted to Diagon Alley. Once admitted, however, you'll still have to wait for the attractions. It remains imperative, therefore, that you arrive at the Studios' turnstiles 35–45 minutes before opening.

Timed-entry tickets will possibly be available near the Studios entrance, but the most likely distribution points will be to either side of the London-waterfront area. Circling the lagoon clockwise to the waterfront is shorter, but it's also the route we expect about 70% of guests will take. Hustling to the waterfront counterclockwise may require more footwork, but the ticket-distribution point on that side will probably be less busy.

On the upside, the rush to Diagon Alley will diminish crowds and waits at other attractions. The downside to that upside: Those who can't enter Diagon Alley right away will spread to nearby attractions, particularly *Disaster!,* Men in Black Alien Attack, and to a lesser extent The Simpsons Ride and Revenge of the Mummy. Diagon Alley spillover will affect wait times at these attractions all day, so try to experience them as early as possible.

In addition to guests flocking to Diagon Alley from the Studios entrance, we estimate that about 96 passengers will arrive from IOA's Hogsmeade Village Station every 7–8 minutes on the Hogwarts Express—which we think will be an even tougher ticket than Gringotts. Heading first to The Wizarding World: Hogsmeade and lining up for the Express may be the best way to experience the train plus the coaster–dark ride in the least amount of time. Hogsmeade won't be hit with a morning inundation comparable to that of the Studios, so waits for the train should be less onerous. Also, especially early in the day, disembarking train passengers are more likely to be admitted directly into Diagon Alley.

LIVE ENTERTAINMENT *at* UNIVERSAL STUDIOS

IN ADDITION TO THE SHOWS profiled earlier, Universal offers a wide range of street entertainment. Costumed comic-book and cartoon characters (Shrek, Donkey, SpongeBob SquarePants, and Woody

FAVORITE EATS AT UNIVERSAL STUDIOS
LAND | SERVICE LOCATION | FOOD ITEM
PRODUCTION CENTRAL
Classic Monsters Cafe | Chicken, salads, & fresh fruit
NEW YORK
Finnegan's Bar & Grill | Irish pub, frequently with live music (table service only)
Louie's Italian Restaurant | Pasta
SAN FRANCISCO
Richter's Burger Co. | Burgers
WORLD EXPO
International Food & Film Festival | Asian food & ice cream
WOODY WOODPECKER'S KIDZONE
KidZone Pizza Company | Pizza
HOLLYWOOD
Mel's Drive-In | Old-fashioned root beer float

Woodpecker) roam the park for photo ops, along with movie star look-alikes, plus the Frankenstein monster, who can be said to be neither. The handout park map has a section called "Character Zones" that provides times and places for character appearances and shows. Musical acts include Blues Brothers impersonators dancing and singing in the New York section of the park.

In 2012 Universal Studios introduced the Disney-like Universal's Superstar Parade, which features dancers and performers, four large and elaborate floats inspired by cartoons and animated features, and a mixed bag of street-prowling Universal characters. The parade stops twice for a highly choreographed ensemble number. Though impressive in its scope and coordination, the performance is nigh impossible to take in from any given viewing spot. The same floats are trotted out individually at various times of day for mini-shows and character meet and greets.

The parade begins at the gate between Louie's Italian Restaurant, in the New York section of the park, and *Beetlejuice's Graveyard Revue* in the San Francisco section. From there it proceeds along Fifth Avenue past Revenge of the Mummy. At the end of Fifth Avenue the parade takes a left onto Plaza of the Stars and heads toward the front of the park, where it makes another left onto Hollywood Boulevard, from whence it disappears backstage across from Mel's Diner. The best viewing spots are along Fifth Avenue on the front steps of faux buildings in the New York set.

Cinematic Spectacular–100 Years of Movie Memories
★ ★ ★ ½

What it is Fireworks, dancing fountains, and movies. **Scope and scale** Major attraction. **Fright potential** Loud and intense with fireworks and some scary villains, but most young children like it. **Bottleneck rating** 9. **When to go** Only staged in the evening. **Authors' rating** Not to be missed; ★★★★★. **Duration of show** 17 minutes.

Cinematic Spectacular is Universal Studios' nighttime event, shown on the lagoon in the middle of the park. The presentation, a celebration of the last 100 years of Universal movies, is built around three large water screens that are flanked by colorful fountains (roughly similar to Disneyland's *World of Color*—check YouTube for an idea). During the 17-minute show, montages of various movie genres are projected onto water screens. Enhanced by the colorful fountains, special water effects, fireworks, and Morgan Freeman's narration, the clips form an entertaining show. Because the Studios is bordered by residential areas across Turkey Lake Road, don't expect fireworks of similar magnitude to Epcot's *IllumiNations* or the Magic Kingdom's ground-shaking *Wishes* fireworks spectacular.

Reviews have been generally either mixed or positive. This mother of two had a positive experience:

> *My family really enjoyed the show. It didn't have the same emotional impact as [Disney's] Wishes, but it was entertaining. There were so many great movies we hadn't thought about in ages! I wouldn't make a special trip to see it, but it was great to have a night event to end the day. We will definitely stay for the Cinematic Spectacular on our next trip.*

UNIVERSAL STUDIOS FLORIDA TOURING PLANS

UNIVERSAL STUDIOS FLORIDA ONE-DAY TOURING PLAN (page 475)

THIS PLAN IS FOR ALL VISITORS and works regardless of whether Diagon Alley is open. If a ride or show is listed that you don't want to experience, skip that step and proceed to the next. Move quickly from attraction to attraction, and if possible, don't stop for lunch until around Step 11. Minor street shows occur at various times and places throughout the day; check the daily schedule for details.

THE BEST OF UNIVERSAL ORLANDO IN ONE DAY (pages 477–478)

THIS PLAN IS FOR GUESTS with a two-park pass who wish to see the highlights of Universal Studios and Islands of Adventure in a single day. It assumes that Universal hotel guests will be allowed into both parks an hour before day guests. The plan uses Hogwarts Express to get from IOA to USF; you'll walk back to IOA in the evening. Finally, a one-day, two-park plan doesn't leave time for sit-down meals, so snack as you go along.

UNIVERSAL'S ISLANDS
of ADVENTURE

WHEN UNIVERSAL'S ISLANDS OF ADVENTURE theme park opened in 1999, it provided Universal with enough critical mass to actually compete with Disney. Doubly interesting is that the second Universal park is pretty much just for fun—in other words, a direct competitor to Disney's Magic Kingdom, the most-visited theme park in the world.

And though Universal played second fiddle to Disney for many years, times have changed: Universal's Islands of Adventure is a state-of-the-art park competing with a Disney park that is more than 35 years old and has not added a new super-headliner attraction for many years prior to launching new Fantasyland attractions in 2012 and 2013.

The year 2010 was Islands of Adventure's coming-out party. In one of the greatest seismic shifts in theme park history, Universal secured the rights to build a Harry Potter–themed area within the park. Harry P. is possibly the only fictional character extant capable of trumping Mickey Mouse, and Universal has gone all out, under J. K. Rowling's watchful and exacting eye, to create a setting and attractions designed to be the envy of the industry.

If you're having trouble sizing up how big a deal The Wizarding World is, you need only to check the discussion boards of any website associated with Orlando, theme parks, Harry Potter, Daniel Radcliffe, J. K. Rowling, or dozens of other tenuously related topics. What you're likely to see is a billion or so postings like this:

> *OMG I CAN'T WAIT!!!!!!!!! I wuz just lking 4 Harry Potter stuff & I saw a link 2 this!! SQUEEEEEEE!!!!*

Disney and Universal officially downplay their fierce competition, pointing out that any new theme park or attraction makes central Florida a more marketable destination. Behind closed doors, however, it's a Pepsi versus Coke–type rivalry that will keep both companies working hard to gain a competitive edge. The good news, of course, is that all this translates into better and better attractions for you to enjoy.

BEWARE OF THE WET AND WILD

ALTHOUGH WE HAVE DESCRIBED Universal's Islands of Adventure as a direct competitor to the Magic Kingdom, there is one major qualification you should be aware of. Whereas most Magic Kingdom attractions are designed to be enjoyed by guests of any age, attractions at Islands of Adventure are largely created for an under-40 population. The roller coasters at Universal are serious with a capital "s," making Space Mountain and Big Thunder Mountain look about as tough as Dumbo. In fact, seven out of the nine top attractions at Islands are thrill rides, and of

Liliane: Consider yourself warned: Several attractions at Islands of Adventure will drench you to the bone.

these, there are three that not only scare the bejabbers out of you but also drench you with water.

For families, there are three interactive playgrounds, as well as six rides, that young kids will enjoy. Of the thrill rides, only the two in Toon Lagoon (described later) are marginally appropriate for young children, and even on these rides your child needs to be fairly stalwart.

GETTING ORIENTED AT ISLANDS OF ADVENTURE

BOTH UNIVERSAL THEME PARKS are accessed via the Universal CityWalk entertainment complex. Crossing CityWalk from the parking garages, you can bear right to Universal Studios Florida or left to Universal's Islands of Adventure.

Bob: Roller coasters at Islands of Adventure are the real deal—not for the timid or for little ones.

Islands of Adventure is arranged much like Epcot's World Showcase is—in a large circle surrounding a lake. Unlike Epcot, however, the Islands of Adventure areas evidence the sort of thematic continuity pioneered by Disneyland and the Magic Kingdom. Each "land," or island in this case, is self-contained and visually consistent in its theme, though you can see parts of the other islands across the lake.

You first encounter the Moroccan-style Port of Entry, where you'll find Guest Services, lockers, stroller and wheelchair rentals, ATM banking, lost and found, and shopping. From the Port of Entry, moving clockwise around the lake, you can access Marvel Super Hero Island, Toon Lagoon, Jurassic Park, The Wizarding World of Harry Potter, the Lost Continent, and Seuss Landing.

ISLANDS *of* ADVENTURE ATTRACTIONS

MARVEL SUPER HERO ISLAND

THIS ISLAND, WITH ITS FUTURISTIC AND RETRO-FUTURE design and comic-book signage, offers shopping and attractions based on Marvel Comics characters.

The Amazing Adventures of Spider-Man
(Universal Express) ★ ★ ★ ★ ★

APPEAL BY AGE	PRESCHOOL ★ ★ ★	GRADE SCHOOL ★ ★ ★ ★ ★	TEENS ★ ★ ★ ★ ★
YOUNG ADULTS ★ ★ ★ ★ ★		OVER 30 ★ ★ ★ ★ ★	SENIORS ★ ★ ★ ★

What it is Indoor adventure simulator ride based on *Spider-Man*. **Scope and scale** Super-headliner. **Fright potential** Intense; kids tall enough to ride usually take it in stride. **Bottleneck rating** 9. **When to go** The first 40 minutes the park is open. **Special comment** Must be 40" tall to ride. **Authors' rating** One of the best attractions anywhere; ★ ★ ★ ★ ★. **Duration of ride** 4½ minutes. **Average wait in line per 100 people ahead of you** 4 minutes. **Loading speed** Fast.

Continued on page 396

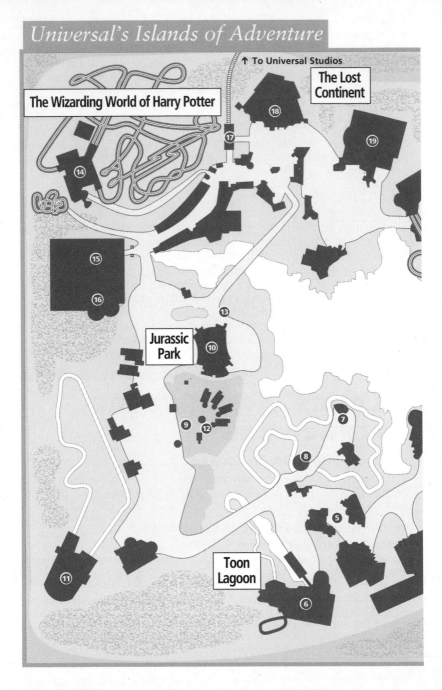

Universal's Islands of Adventure

↑ To Universal Studios

The Lost Continent

The Wizarding World of Harry Potter

Jurassic Park

Toon Lagoon

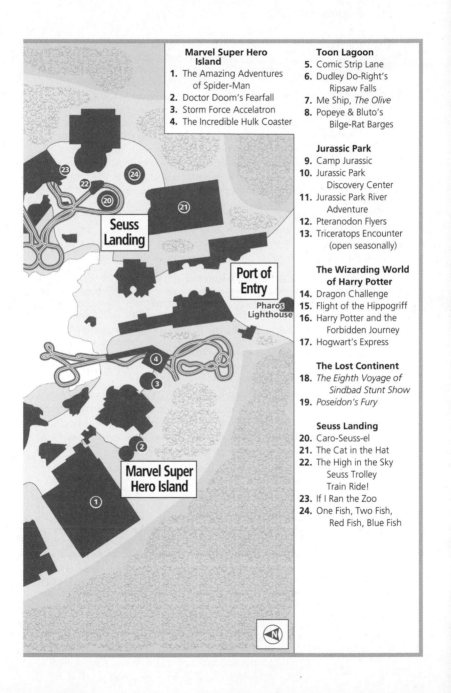

Marvel Super Hero Island
1. The Amazing Adventures of Spider-Man
2. Doctor Doom's Fearfall
3. Storm Force Accelatron
4. The Incredible Hulk Coaster

Toon Lagoon
5. Comic Strip Lane
6. Dudley Do-Right's Ripsaw Falls
7. Me Ship, *The Olive*
8. Popeye & Bluto's Bilge-Rat Barges

Jurassic Park
9. Camp Jurassic
10. Jurassic Park Discovery Center
11. Jurassic Park River Adventure
12. Pteranodon Flyers
13. Triceratops Encounter (open seasonally)

The Wizarding World of Harry Potter
14. Dragon Challenge
15. Flight of the Hippogriff
16. Harry Potter and the Forbidden Journey
17. Hogwart's Express

The Lost Continent
18. *The Eighth Voyage of Sindbad Stunt Show*
19. *Poseidon's Fury*

Seuss Landing
20. Caro-Seuss-el
21. The Cat in the Hat
22. The High in the Sky Seuss Trolley Train Ride!
23. If I Ran the Zoo
24. One Fish, Two Fish, Red Fish, Blue Fish

Seuss Landing

Port of Entry

Pharos Lighthouse

Marvel Super Hero Island

Continued from page 393

Covering 1½ acres and combining moving ride vehicles, 3-D film, and live action, Spider-Man is frenetic, fluid, and astounding. The visuals are rich, and the ride is wild but not jerky. Spider-Man is technologically on a par with Disney's Hollywood Studios' Tower of Terror, which is to say that it will leave you in awe. Ride as early in the morning as possible or in the hour before closing. Already considered by many to be the best theme-park attraction on the planet, Spider-Man reopened in March 2012 with a newly upgraded version of the popular attraction. The ride's new 4K digital high-definition animation, new musical score, and new 3-D Spider-Vision glasses are just the beginning. Included in the changes to the ride are lifelike animation; an upgraded ride vehicle audio system featuring 16 channels of sound; enhancements to lighting, sets, graphics, props, and scenic detail; and a cameo from legendary comic-book icon and *Spider-Man* cocreator Stan Lee. This ride is an absolute must. Soar above buildings without ever leaving the ground! Kudos to Universal; this is the ultimate deception. Ride several times to take in all the details.

Doctor Doom's Fearfall *(Universal Express)* ★★★

APPEAL BY AGE PRESCHOOL — GRADE SCHOOL ★★★ TEENS ★★★★
YOUNG ADULTS ★★★★ OVER 30 ★★★ SENIORS —

What it is Lunch liberator. **Scope and scale** Headliner. **Fright potential** Frightening for all ages. **Bottleneck rating** 10. **When to go** The first 40 minutes the park is open. **Special comment** Must be 52" tall to ride. **Authors' rating** More bark than bite; ★★★. **Duration of ride** 40 seconds. **Average wait in line per 100 people ahead of you** 18 minutes. **Loading speed** Slow.

Here you are strapped into a seat with your feet dangling, blasted 200 feet up in the air, and then allowed to partially free-fall back down. We've seen glaciers that move faster than the line to Doctor Doom. If you want to ride without investing half a day, be one of the first in the park to ride.

> This attraction is best experienced with your mother right next to you. Hold her hand for personal comfort (it makes you look good too) and brace for her expression of absolute terror.

Ian

The Incredible Hulk Coaster *(Universal Express)* ★★★★½

APPEAL BY AGE PRESCHOOL ★ GRADE SCHOOL ★★★★★ TEENS ★★★★★
YOUNG ADULTS ★★★★ OVER 30 ★★★★ SENIORS ★★★

What it is Roller coaster. **Scope and scale** Super-headliner. **Fright potential** Frightening for all ages. **Bottleneck rating** 10. **When to go** The first 40 minutes the park is open. **Special comments** Must be 54" tall to ride. **Authors' rating** A coaster-lover's coaster; ★★★★½. **Duration of ride** 2¼ minutes. **Average wait in line per 100 people ahead of you** 9 minutes. **Loading speed** Moderate.

The Hulk is a great roller coaster, one of the best in Florida, providing a ride comparable to Montu (Busch Gardens) with the added thrill of an accelerated launch (instead of the more typical uphill crank). Plus, like Montu, this coaster has a smooth ride. The Hulk gives Dragon Challenge a run as the park's most popular coaster. Ride first thing in the morning.

> You-know-who made me ride it, and for the duration of the ride I lost my very polite European ways.
>
> Unfortunately, Liliane lost her very polite European ways at about 140 decibels. My ears hurt for days.

Liliane

Storm Force Accelatron *(Universal Express)* ★ ★ ★

APPEAL BY AGE	PRESCHOOL ★★★★	GRADE SCHOOL ★★★	TEENS ★★★
YOUNG ADULTS ★★★	OVER 30 ★★★		SENIORS ★★★

What it is Spinning ride. **Scope and scale** Minor attraction. **Fright potential** Nauseating but not frightening. **Bottleneck rating** 9. **When to go** The first hour the park is open. **Authors' rating** Teacups in the dark; ★★★. **Duration of ride** 1½ minutes. **Average wait in line per 100 people ahead of you** 21 minutes. **Loading speed** Slow.

Dark   Queasy

Storm Force is a spiffed-up version of Disney's nausea-inducing Mad Tea Party. Ride early or late to avoid long lines. Skip it if you're prone to motion sickness.

TOON LAGOON

TOON LAGOON IS CARTOON ART translated into real buildings and settings. Whimsical and gaily colored, with rounded and exaggerated lines, Toon Lagoon was Universal's answer to Mickey's Toontown Fair in the Magic Kingdom. The main difference was that (as you will see) you have about a 60% chance of drowning at Universal's version.

Comic Strip Lane

What it is Walk-through exhibit and shopping and dining venue. **Scope and scale** Diversion. **Fright potential** Not frightening in any respect. **Bottleneck rating** 0. **When to go** Anytime.

This is the main street of Toon Lagoon. Here you can visit the domains of Beetle Bailey, Hagar the Horrible, Krazy Kat, the Family Circus, and Blondie and Dagwood, among others of whom your kids have never heard. Shops and eateries tie into the cartoon strip theme. This is a great place for photo ops with cartoon characters.

Dudley Do-Right's Ripsaw Falls *(Universal Express)* ★★★½

APPEAL BY AGE	PRESCHOOL ★★★	GRADE SCHOOL ★★★★	TEENS ★★★★
YOUNG ADULTS ★★★	OVER 30 ★★★★		SENIORS ★★★

What it is Flume ride. **Scope and scale** Major attraction. **Fright potential** The big drop frightens guests of all ages. **Bottleneck rating** 8. **When to go** Before 11 a.m. **Special comments** Must be 44" tall to ride. **Authors' rating** A minimalist Splash Mountain; ★★★½. **Duration of ride** 5 minutes. **Average wait in line per 100 people ahead of you** 9 minutes. **Loading speed** Moderate.

Wet   Scary

Inspired by the *Rocky and Bullwinkle* cartoons, this ride features Canadian Mountie Dudley Do-Right as he attempts to save Nell from evil Snidely Whiplash. Story line aside, it's a flume ride, with the inevitable big drop at the end. Universal claims that this is the first flume ride to "send riders plummeting 15 feet below the surface of the water."

Small children will be intimidated by the big drop. Try Popeye & Bluto's Bilge-Rat Barges first.

Liliane

Right, Liliane. Popeye & Bluto's Bilge-Rat Barges is perfect for small children . . . as long as they have wet suits and life jackets.

In reality, though, you're just plummeting into a tunnel. This ride will get you wet, but on average not as wet as you might expect (it looks worse than it is). If you want to stay dry, however, arrive prepared with a poncho or at least a big garbage bag with holes cut out for your head and arms. While younger children are often intimidated by the big drop, those who ride generally enjoy themselves. Ride first thing in the morning after experiencing the Marvel Super Hero rides.

Me Ship, *The Olive* ★★★

APPEAL BY AGE	PRESCHOOL ★★★★		GRADE SCHOOL ★★★★
TEENS ½	YOUNG ADULTS ½	OVER 30 ½	SENIORS —

What it is Interactive playground. Scope and scale Minor attraction. Fright potential Not frightening in any respect. Bottleneck rating 4. When to go Anytime. Authors' rating Colorful and appealing for kids; ★★★.

The Olive is Popeye's three-story boat come to life as an interactive playground. Younger children can scramble around in Swee'Pea's Playpen, while older sibs shoot water cannons at riders trying to survive the adjacent Bilge-Rat raft ride. If you're into the big rides, save this for later in the day.

Popeye & Bluto's Bilge-Rat Barges
(Universal Express) ★★★★

APPEAL BY AGE	PRESCHOOL ★★★	GRADE SCHOOL ★★★★★	TEENS ★★★★
YOUNG ADULTS ★★★★		OVER 30 ★★★★	SENIORS ★★★

What it is White-water raft ride. Scope and scale Major attraction. Fright potential Ride is wild and wet but not frightening. Bottleneck rating 8. When to go Before 10:30 a.m. Special comment Must be 42" tall to ride. Authors' rating Bring your own soap; ★★★★. Duration of ride 4½ minutes. Average wait in line per 100 people ahead of you 7 minutes. Loading speed Moderate.

Rough   Wet

This white-water raft ride for the whole family is engineered to ensure that everyone gets drenched; the ride even provides water cannons for highly intelligent non-participants ashore to fire at those aboard. The rapids are rougher and more interesting, and the ride longer, than the Animal Kingdom's Kali River Rapids. If you didn't drown on Dudley Do-Right, here's a second chance.

Liliane

Remember you will get wet. It is OK on a hot summer day, unless it's first thing in the morning. Now is the time to use the raingear or plastic bags to protect yourselves. Most important, keep your footwear dry.

JURASSIC PARK

JURASSIC PARK (for anyone who's been asleep for 20 years) is a Steven Spielberg film franchise about a fictitious theme park with real dinosaurs. Jurassic Park at Universal's Islands of Adventure is a real theme park (or at least a section of one) with fictitious dinosaurs.

Camp Jurassic ★★★

APPEAL BY AGE	PRESCHOOL ★★★		GRADE SCHOOL ★★★
TEENS —	YOUNG ADULTS —	OVER 30 —	SENIORS —

What it is Interactive play area. **Scope and scale** Minor attraction. **Fright potential** Not frightening in any respect. **Bottleneck rating** 3. **When to go** Anytime. **Authors' rating** Creative playground; confusing layout; ★★★.

Camp Jurassic is a great place for children to run and explore. Sort of a Jurassic version of Tom Sawyer Island, kids can explore lava pits, caves, mines, and a rain forest.

Very small children should not be left to explore this place alone, as they will get lost inside the playground and might get very scared. Kids over age 8 are guaranteed an adventure and lots of fun. I loved the playground and regret that, due to my height, I was not allowed on the pteranodon whatchamacallit.

Ian

Jurassic Park Discovery Center ★★★

APPEAL BY AGE	PRESCHOOL ★★★	GRADE SCHOOL ★★★★	TEENS ★★★
YOUNG ADULTS ★★★		OVER 30 ★★★	SENIORS ★★★

What it is Interactive natural history exhibit. **Scope and scale** Minor attraction. **Fright potential** Not frightening in any respect. **Bottleneck rating** 3. **When to go** Anytime. **Authors' rating** ★★★.

The Discovery Center is an interactive, educational exhibit that mixes fiction from the movie *Jurassic Park,* such as using fossil DNA to bring dinosaurs to life, with various skeletal remains and other paleontological displays. Cycle back after experiencing all the rides or on a second day. Most folks can digest this exhibit in 10–15 minutes.

Don't skip the Discovery Center. On a hot summer day, it is a great place to cool off. The best exhibit of all is the one where an animatronic raptor hatches from an egg. Young children will delight in the hatching and are afforded an opportunity to name the baby dino.

Liliane

Jurassic Park River Adventure *(Universal Express)* ★★★★

APPEAL BY AGE	PRESCHOOL ★★★	GRADE SCHOOL ★★★★★	TEENS ★★★★★
YOUNG ADULTS ★★★★		OVER 30 ★★★★	SENIORS ★★★★

What it is Indoor-outdoor adventure river-raft ride based on the *Jurassic Park* movies. **Scope and scale** Super-headliner. **Fright potential** Visuals and big drop frighten guests of all ages. **Bottleneck rating** 9. **When to go** Before 11 a.m. **Special comment** Must be 42" tall to ride. **Authors' rating** Better than its Hollywood cousin; ★★★★. **Duration of ride** 6½ minutes. **Average wait in line per 100 people ahead of you** 5 minutes. **Loading speed** Fast.

Wet

Scary

Guests board boats for a water tour of Jurassic Park. Everything is tranquil as the tour begins, and then, as word is received that some of the carnivores have escaped their enclosure, the tour boat is accidentally diverted into Jurassic Park's maintenance facilities. Here, the boat and its riders are menaced by an assortment of hungry meat-eaters. At the climactic moment, the boat and its passengers escape by plummeting over an 85-foot drop. Young children must endure a double whammy on this ride. First, they are stalked by giant, salivating (sometimes spitting) reptiles, and then they're sent catapulting over the falls. Unless your children are fairly stalwart, wait a year or two before you spring the River Adventure on them.

Pteranodon Flyers ½

APPEAL BY AGE	PRESCHOOL ★★★	GRADE SCHOOL ★★★	TEENS ★
YOUNG ADULTS ★★		OVER 30 ★	SENIORS ★★

What it is Slow as Christmas. **Scope and scale** Minor attraction. **Fright potential** Not frightening in any respect. **Bottleneck rating** 10. **When to go** When there's no line. **Special comment** Adults and older children must be accompanied by a child 36"–52" tall. **Authors' rating** All sizzle, no steak; ½. **Duration of ride** 1¼ minutes. **Average wait in line per 100 people ahead of you** 28 minutes. **Loading speed** Slower than a hog in quicksand.

This ride swings you along a track that passes over a small part of Jurassic Park. We recommend that you skip this one. Why? Because the Jurassic period will probably end before you reach the front of the line! And your reward for all that waiting? A 1-minute-and-15-second ride.

Triceratops Encounter *(open seasonally)* ★★★½

APPEAL BY AGE	PRESCHOOL ★★★	GRADE SCHOOL ★★★★	TEENS ★★★
YOUNG ADULTS ★★★½		OVER 30 ★	SENIORS ★★

What it is Prehistoric petting zoo. **Scope and scale** Minor attraction. **When to go** After experiencing all the rides. **Fright potential** Huge but not scary. **Bottleneck rating** 7. **Special comments** Expect long waits in line. **Authors' rating** Clever and different; ★★★½. **Duration of experience** 5 minutes. **Average wait in line per 100 people ahead of you** 30 minutes.

Guests are ushered in groups into a "feed and control" station, where they can view and pet a 24-foot-long animatronic triceratops. While the trainer lectures about the creature's behaviors, habits, and lifestyle, the dinosaur breathes, blinks, chews, and flinches at the touch of the guests. Though not a major attraction, Triceratops Encounter is well executed. Make it your first show/exhibit after experiencing the rides.

THE WIZARDING WORLD OF HARRY POTTER

IN WHAT MAY PROVE TO BE THE COMPETITIVE COUP of all time between archrivals Disney and Universal, the latter inked a deal with Warner Brothers Entertainment to create a fully immersive Harry Potter–themed environment based on the best-selling children's books by J. K. Rowling and the companion blockbuster movies from Warner Brothers. The project was blessed by Rowling, who is known for tenaciously protecting the integrity of her work. In the case of the films, she demanded that Warner Brothers be true, almost to an unprecedented degree, to the books on which the films were based.

The 20-acre Wizarding World draws its inspiration from all the *Harry Potter* movies and books, creating an amalgamation of landmarks, sights, creatures, and themes that are faithful to the films. The

Wizarding World is situated in the northwest corner of the park between The Lost Continent and Jurassic Park. Let's begin our exploration at Wizarding World's main entrance on the Lost Continent side of the theme area.

Passing beneath a stone archway, you enter the village of **Hogsmeade**. The **Hogwarts Express** locomotive belches steam on your right (until it's relocated to the Studios with the opening of Diagon Alley; see page 383), and the village, depicted in winter, stretches before you, following the contours of a gently curving street. While decidedly different and visually rich, the winter thing seems like a stretch in the dog days of August. On your left opposite the train

 B o b : The Wizarding World will suck up guests like a vacuum on steroids. This means, among other things, that crowds will be considerably lighter in other sections of Islands of Adventure, especially in the morning.

station is **Zonko's,** a joke and novelty shop specializing in such necessities as shrunken heads, extendable ears, and screaming yo-yos. If your sweet tooth is on a rampage, the shop also sells sweets such as Fever Fudge, Nosebleed Nougat, and our personal favorite, Puking Pastilles. Connected to Zonko's through an interior passage is **Honey-Dukes**. For those whose appetite has recovered from disgorging their Puking Pastilles, HoneyDukes—specializing in Acid Pops, Exploding Bonbons, and Fizzing Whizbees—offers another opportunity to expand your midriff.

Across the street from HoneyDukes next to the train station is the entrance to the Dragon Challenge dueling roller coasters. Next door to HoneyDukes and set back from the main street is the **Three Broomsticks,** a rustic tavern serving English staples such as fish-and-chips, shepherd's pie, Cornish pastry, and turkey legs. A children's menu includes standards such as mac and cheese and the obligatory chicken fingers. The Three Broomsticks is also a good, albeit expensive, venue for ice cream and dessert treats. Adjacent to the restaurant is the **Hog's Head** pub with a nice selection of beer, as well as The Wizarding World's signature nonalcoholic beverage, Butterbeer. Except for some meager snacks from vendor carts, no other hot food or sandwiches are available in The Wizarding World. The Three Broomsticks doesn't participate in any of Universal's meal plans.

The only restrooms in The Wizarding World are in the middle of Hogsmeade, where they're labeled PUBLIC CONVENIENCES. Remember where these are located, especially if you're planning to ride Forbidden Journey or Dragon Challenge and are prone to motion sickness. Roughly across the street from the Hog's Head pub, you'll find benches in the shade at the **Owlery,** where animatronic owls (complete with owl poop) ruffle and hoot from the rafters.

Next to the Owlery is the **Owl Post,** a functioning post office where any postcards you mail will be delivered with a Hogsmeade postmark. The Owl Post also sells stationery, toy owls, and the like. To access the Owl Post, enter through an interior door following the wand-choosing demonstration at **Ollivanders** (see below) or through **Dervish and Banges,** a magical supplies and equipment shop, which is interconnected with the Owl Post. The Owl Post front door is used exclusively as an exit. Because it's so difficult to get into the Owl Post, Universal sometimes stations a team member outside to stamp your postcards with The Wizarding World postmark.

Next to the Owl Post is the previously mentioned Ollivanders magic wand shop. Here, following a script from the *Potter* books, you can buy a wand. You can pick it out yourself, or in an interactive experience, a wand will choose you. This is one of the most truly imaginative elements of The Wizarding World. The store is musty and stacked to the ceiling with boxes of wands. A wand keeper sizes you up and presents a wand, inviting you to try it out. Naturally your attempted spells produce unintended, unwanted, and very amusing consequences. The experience is delightful, but the tiny shop can accommodate only about 24 guests at a time. Usually only one person in each group goes through the process of being chosen by a wand, and then the whole group is dispatched to the Owl Post and Dervish and Banges to actually make purchases. Wands run $32 and up. If Ollivanders is a priority, experience it first thing in the morning or after 7:30 p.m. Average wait time during summer and other busy periods is 45–85 minutes 9:30 a.m.–7:30 p.m. If you're just looking to buy a wand without the interactive experience, there's usually a cart set up between Filch's Emporium and the Flight of the Hippogriff exit, with little to no wait.

Liliane: Once you enter The Wizarding World of Harry Potter, be ready to get stuck in a time warp. The attractions are out of this world, and the details are enough to make every Harry Potter fan wish the day would never end.

At the far end of the village is the massive **Hogwarts Castle,** set atop a rock face and towering over Hogsmeade and the entire Wizarding World. Follow the path through the gates of Hogwarts to the Harry Potter and the Forbidden Journey attraction. To the right of the castle and at the base of the cliff are the Forbidden Forest, Hagrid's Hut, and the Flying Hippogriff children's roller coaster. Located in the village near the gate to Hogwarts Castle is **Filch's Emporium of Confiscated Goods.** The shop offers all manner of Potter-themed gifts and apparel, including Quidditch clothing, magical creature toys, film-based chess sets, and of course, Death Eater masks (breath mints extra). Because the shops are so jammed, Universal sells some merchandise, including wands, through street vendors. Wizarding World items are also for sale in Port of Entry shops.

ACCESSING WIZARDING WORLD

WIZARDING WORLD crowd management has been a work in progress for Universal. Trying to herd tens of thousands of guests, all wanting to alight in the same few acres of the park, has been a monumental challenge. A variety of measures have been tried, abandoned, modified, and run up the flagpole yet again, all with mixed success. Now, with a few years of Wizarding World operation under its belt, Universal has settled on a flexible system with three basic crowd-control options predicated on the expected level of attendance for any given day. No matter what the crowd level, however, if you're staying in one of Universal's three on-site hotels and have early-entry privileges for The Wizarding World, use them, arriving as early in the early-entry period as possible.

Crowd Control Option One is for off-season and slow days when the park is not crowded. On these days you can enter and depart The Wizarding World as you please. The waits for the rides will still be over an hour at times, but gaining entry to The Wizarding World is not an issue. Sometimes Option One will be in force in the morning, transitioning to Option Two as crowds build through the course of the day.

Crowd Control Option Two is for days when attendance is high and the park is nearly full to capacity, for example, during spring break, high summer season, or the days before or after a large holiday. It is at this level that barricades are placed at both entrances to The Wizarding World. You can go to either entrance and obtain a pass to come back into the Harry Potter area at a designated time. The pass is free and similar to Disney's Fastpass. This option allows you to enjoy other areas of the park while waiting for your scheduled time in The Wizarding World. At the specified time, return to either Wizarding World entrance and present the pass to the barricade crew.

Once admitted to the Harry Potter theme area, you will still have to wait for each ride, store, and concessions, as well as for the one restaurant in the area. It's common when Option Two is in effect for the entrance barricades to be removed during the last hour or two the park is open, thus allowing you to come and go as you please.

Crowd Control Option Three is for when the park is at full capacity, usually during holidays such as Easter, Christmas, Thanksgiving, and New Year's Eve. On these days the barricades around Wizarding World are in place all day, and the demand to get into the area is much higher.

Be forewarned that on Option Three days, return passes are fully distributed by noon or earlier. This means that if you are not in line to enter Islands of Adventure before the park opens, there is a chance that you might not be able to enter The Wizarding World at all. We strongly counsel you to arrive an hour before opening on these busiest of days and, once admitted, immediately obtain a return pass. Automatic machines resembling Disney Fastpass machines are located in Jurassic Park just past the Jurassic Park River Adventure and in Lost Continent close to the entrance to the *Sindbad* show. At both locations there is no need to use a park entrance ticket (as with Disney's Fastpass) to obtain a return pass. The machines use touch screens, and you can get one ticket for your whole party. The touch screen asks two questions, starting with how many are in your party. It then allows you to select one of two return times. After answering the questions, a ticket is printed.

On Option Two and Option Three days, do not exit The Wizarding World until you have done and seen everything of interest. This applies to both day guests and hotel guests. Do not defer anything in the area for later in the day or depend on being able to get back in. Schedule food breaks before or after your visit. If you leave Wizarding World, the only way back in (for hotel guests or day guests) is to obtain another pass (providing they haven't all been distributed), unless the entrance barriers have been removed, thus allowing free access to The Wizarding World.

Dragon Challenge *(Universal Express)* ★ ★ ★ ★ ½

APPEAL BY AGE	PRESCHOOL —	GRADE SCHOOL ★ ★ ★ ★	TEENS ★ ★ ★ ★
YOUNG ADULTS ★ ★ ★ ★		OVER 30 ★ ★ ★ ★	SENIORS ★ ★

What it is Roller coaster. **Scope and scale** Headliner. **Fright potential** Frightening to guests of all ages. **Bottleneck rating** 4. **When to go** After Harry Potter and the Forbidden Journey. **Special comment** Must be 54" tall to ride. **Authors' rating** As good as the Hulk coaster; ★ ★ ★ ★ ½. **Duration of ride** 2½ minutes. **Average wait in line per 100 people ahead of you** 9 minutes. **Loading speed** Moderate.

Lose Things   Rough   Queasy

This high-tech coaster launches two trains, the Chinese Fireball and the Hungarian Horntail, on tracks that are closely intertwined. Each track is configured differently so that you get a different experience on each. Previously the two trains barreled at each other in what appeared to be an imminent collision, closing at one point to only a foot or so apart. In 2012, however, there were two incidents where loose objects from one train hit and injured riders on the other train. Following a thorough investigation (and a lawsuit), Universal permanently altered the launch so the trains were dispatched sequentially instead of simultaneously, resulting in more of a chase than a race, and eliminating the danger of loose stuff whopping riders in the chops. If you're speculating on the nature of the objects involved, consider riders trying to take pictures with their cell phones—what could possibly go wrong? Dragon Challenge is the highest coaster in the park and also claims the longest drop at 115 feet, not to mention five inversions.

Dragon Challenge, formerly Dueling Dragons, was renamed and incorporated into the new Wizarding World of Harry Potter in 2010. The story line is that you are preparing to compete in the Tri-Wizard Tournament (from *Harry Potter and the Goblet of Fire*). As you wind through the long, long queue, you pass through tournament tents and dark passages. You'll see the Goblet of Fire on display and hear the distant roar of the crowd in the supposed stadium above you.

We prefer the front row on either train, but coaster loonies hype the front row of Chinese Fireball and the last row of Hungarian Horntail.

By now everybody knows that yours truly hates roller coasters, but the decorations along the queuing line were well worth 60 seconds of near-death experience. Next time I'll grab that Goblet of Fire!

Liliane

Flight of the Hippogriff *(Universal Express)* ★ ★ ½

APPEAL BY AGE	PRESCHOOL ★ ★ ★ ★		GRADE SCHOOL ★ ★ ★ ★
TEENS ★ ★	YOUNG ADULTS ★ ★	OVER 30 ★	SENIORS ★

What it is Children's roller coaster. **Scope and scale** Minor attraction. **Fright potential** Frightens a small percentage of preschool riders. **Bottleneck rating** 5. **When to**

go First 90 minutes the park is open. **Special comment** Must be 36" tall to ride. **Authors' rating** A good beginner coaster; ★★½. **Duration of ride** 1 minute. **Average wait in line per 100 people ahead of you** 14 minutes. **Loading speed** Slow.

Previously called the Flying Unicorn, the coaster underwent a name and theme change when it was incorporated into The Wizarding World. Located below and to the right of Hogwarts Castle next to Hagrid's Hut, the Hippogriff is short and sweet but not worth much of a wait. Fortunately, waits usually don't exceed 20 minutes, even in the non-Express line. Have your children ride soon after the park opens, while older sibs enjoy Dragon Challenge. Even if you don't ride, it's worth a stroll down to see Hogwarts Castle from the cliff bottom and to check out Hagrid's Hut situated above the path for the regular line.

Harry Potter and the Forbidden Journey ★★★★½

APPEAL BY AGE	PRESCHOOL −	GRADE SCHOOL ★★★★★	TEENS ★★★★★
YOUNG ADULTS ★★★★★		OVER 30 ★★★★★	SENIORS ★★★★★

What it is Motion simulator dark ride. **Scope and scale** Super-headliner. **Fright potential** Intense special effects and wild ride. **Bottleneck rating** Off the chart. **When to go** Immediately after park opening or after 8 p.m. The ride has a Universal Express line, but for the time being, it is not being used. **Special comments** Expect *long* waits in line; must be 48" tall to ride. The seats are designed for certain body types. Sample seats are at the beginning of the queue, and just before the boarding area is a bench with four fully functional seats. To ride, the overhead restraint has to click three times. If you don't pass muster, you'll be escorted to a place where you can wait for the rest of your party. **Authors' rating** ★★★★½. **Duration of ride** 4⅓ minutes. **Average wait in line per 100 people ahead of you** 4 minutes. **Loading speed** Moderate.

This attraction is the big banana of The Wizarding World and provides the only opportunity to actually come in contact with the *Harry Potter* characters. Half of the attraction is a series of preshows that sets the stage for the main event, a dark ride. To understand the story line and get the most out of the attraction, it's critical to see and hear the entire presentation in each of the queue's preshow rooms. You can get on the ride in only 10–20 minutes using the single-riders line, but everyone should go through the main queue at least once. If you see a complete iteration of each of the preshows in the queue and then experience the 4⅓-minute ride, you'll invest 25–35 minutes even if you don't have to wait.

From Hogsmeade you reach the attraction through the imposing Winged Boar gate and progress along a winding path. Entering the castle on a lower level, you walk through a sort of dungeon with various icons and prop replicas from the *Potter* flicks, including the Mirror of Erised from *Harry Potter and the Sorcerer's Stone* (*Harry Potter and the Philosopher's Stone* outside the United States). Later you emerge outside and into the Hogwarts' greenhouses, which comprise the larger part of the Forbidden Journey's queuing area. The greenhouses are not air-conditioned, but fans move the (hot) air around. Also, blessedly, drinking fountains are in the greenhouse, but there are no restrooms—take care of that before getting in line for the attraction.

Once through horticulture purgatory, you reenter the castle, moving along its halls and passageways. One chamber you'll probably remember from the films is a multistory gallery of portraits, many of whose subjects come alive when they take a notion. The four founders of Hogwarts—Rowena Ravenclaw, Helga Hufflepuff holding her famous cup, Godric Gryffindor nearby, and the tall, moving portrait of Salazar Slytherin straight ahead—argue about Quidditch and Dumbledore's controversial decision to host an open house for muggles (garden-variety humans who are neither wizards nor witches) at Hogwarts. Don't rush through the gallery—the effects are very cool and the conversation among the portraits is essential to understanding the rest of the attraction.

After navigating some more passages, you reach Dumbledore's office, where Dumbledore appears on a balcony and welcomes you to Hogwarts. The headmaster's appearance is your introduction to Musion Eyeliner technology, a high-definition video projection system that produces breathtakingly realistic, three-dimensional, moving, life-size holograms. After his welcoming remarks, Dumbledore dispatches you to the Defence Against the Dark Arts classroom to hear a presentation on the history of Hogwarts.

As you await the lecturer, Harry, Ron Weasley, and Hermione Granger pop out from under an invisibility cloak. They suggest that you ditch the lecture in favor of joining them for a proper tour of Hogwarts, including a Quidditch match. After some repartee between the characters and a couple of special effects surprises, it's off to the Hogwarts Official Attraction Safety Briefing and Boarding Instructions Chamber—OK, we made up the name of the room, but that's what goes on there. The briefing and instructions are presented by talking portraits including an etiquette teacher. Later on, even the famed Sorting Hat gets into the act. All this leads to the Room of Requirement with hundreds of candles floating overhead. This is where you board the ride.

After all the high-tech stuff in your queuing odyssey, you will naturally expect to be wowed by your ride vehicle. Surely it's a Nimbus 3000 turbo-broom, a Phoenix, a Hippogriff, or at least the Weasleys' flying car. But no, what you will ride in the most technologically advanced theme-park attraction in America is, ta-da . . . a bench!?! Yes, you heard right, a bench. Not that there's anything wrong with a bench. We're just saying that maybe the well ran a little dry in the imagination department.

But as benches go, it's a doozy, mounted to a Kuka robotic arm that can be programmed to replicate all the sensations of flying, including broad swoops, steep dives, sharp turns, sudden stops, and fast acceleration. The ride vehicle moves you through a series of alternating sets and domes where scenes are projected all around you. The movement of the Kuka arm is synchronized to create the motion that corresponds to what is happening in the set or film. When everything works correctly, it's mind-blowing. You'll soar over Hogwarts Castle, get tossed into a Quidditch match, spar with the Whomping Willow, narrowly evade an attacking dragon, and fight off Dementors.

Many riders experience various degrees of motion sickness on Forbidden Journey. The best defense against motion sickness is not to ride on an empty stomach. If you have a child who doesn't meet the minimum-height requirement of 48 inches, a child-swapping option is provided at the loading area. Be advised that the seats on each bench are compartmentalized, so your child will not be able to see you or hold your hand.

Upon entering Forbidden Journey's outside queue, you have two choices, left line or right line. They are unmarked, but the right line is for those who have bags or loose items (and therefore require a locker). Our wait-time research has shown that, in some cases, not having a bag (and not needing a locker) can save you as much as 30 minutes of standing in line! The locker area is small, crowded, and confusing. Given this, it may make more sense to risk paying the $3 and stashing your things at the lockers beside Dragon Challenge.

The single-rider line is equally unmarked and relatively few guests use it. Typically, on most attractions, the wait in the single-rider line is one-third the wait of the standby line. At Forbidden Journey it can be as much as one-tenth! Because the ride experience is individual (you can't see the other riders, including members of your party), the single-rider line is a great option. To access the single-rider line, enter the left line (no bags) and stay to the left all the way into Hogwarts Castle. After passing the locker area, take the first left into the unmarked single-rider line. If you use the single-rider line, however, you will miss much of the interior of the castle. A good way to experience the castle *and* cut your waiting time is to tell the greeter at the castle entrance that you want to take the **Castle Only Tour.** This self-guided tour allows guests who don't want to experience the ride to view the many features of the castle via an alternative queuing lane. The beauty of the Castle Only Tour is that you can pause as long as you desire in each of the various chambers and take in the pre-shows at your leisure without being herded along. At the end, if you want to ride, ask to be guided to the single-rider line. Using this strategy you'll maximize your enjoyment of the castle while minimizing your wait for the ride. Note that the Castle Only Tour is often unavailable on peak attendance days and might be deep-sixed for good if Forbidden Journey someday becomes a Universal Express attraction.

Hogwarts Express *(opens 2014)*

What it is Transportation attraction. **Scope and scale** Super-headliner. **Fright potential** Potter villains and spirit creatures menace the train. **Bottleneck rating** 10+. **When to go** Immediately after park opening. **Special comment** Two-park ticket required to enter Universal Studios. **Duration of ride** 4 minutes. **Probable wait in line per 100 people ahead of you** 7 minutes. **Loading speed** Moderate.

The Hogwarts Express provides transportation to Diagon Alley at Universal Studios with some Potterish adventures along the way. For a full discussion of this attraction, see page 386.

THE LOST CONTINENT

THIS AREA IS AN EXOTIC MIX of Silk Road bazaar and ancient ruins, with Greco-Moroccan accents. (And you thought your decorator was nuts.) This is the land of mythical gods, fabled beasts, and expensive souvenirs.

The Eighth Voyage of Sindbad *(Universal Express)* ★ ★

APPEAL BY AGE	PRESCHOOL ★ ★ ★		GRADE SCHOOL ★ ★ ★ ★	TEENS ★ ★ ★
YOUNG ADULTS ★ ★ ★		OVER 30 ★ ★ ★		SENIORS ★ ★ ★

What it is Theater stunt show. **Scope and scale** Major attraction. **Fright potential** Special effects startle preschoolers. **Bottleneck rating 4. When to go** Anytime as per the daily entertainment schedule. **Authors' rating** Not inspiring; ★★. **Duration of show** 17 minutes. **Probable waiting time** 15 minutes.

A story about Sindbad the Sailor is the glue that (loosely) binds this stunt show featuring water explosions, 10-foot-tall circles of flame, and various other daunting eruptions and perturbations. It's billed as a stunt show, but the production is so vacuous and redundant that it's hard to get into the action. See *Sindbad* after you've experienced the rides and the better-rated shows. The theater seats 1,700.

I place seeing *Sindbad* in the same category as colonoscopies —once every 10 years is enough.

Not to be missed is the Mystic Fountain at the entrance to the theater. The fountain may not grant you wishes, but it will talk to you. But watch out: it's a fountain with attitude. Keep your umbrella handy.

Liliane

Poseidon's Fury (Universal Express) ★★★★

APPEAL BY AGE	PRESCHOOL ★★	GRADE SCHOOL ★★★★	TEENS ★★★★
YOUNG ADULTS ★★★★		OVER 30 ★★★★	SENIORS ★★★★

What it is High-tech theater attraction. **Scope and scale** Headliner. **Fright potential** Intense visuals and special effects frighten some preschoolers. **Bottleneck rating** 7. **When to go** After experiencing all the rides. **Special comment** Audience stands throughout. **Authors' rating** ★★★★. **Duration of show** 17 minutes, including pre-show. **Probable waiting time** 25 minutes.

The Greek god Poseidon tussles with an evil wizard-ish guy using fire, water, lasers, smoke machines, and angry lemurs. (*Note:* Lemurs are not actually used—just seeing if you're paying attention.) The plot unravels in installments as you pass from room to room and finally into the main theater. There's some great technology at work here. *Poseidon* is by far and away the best of the Islands of Adventure theater attractions. Frequent explosions and noise may frighten younger children, so exercise caution with preschoolers. We recommend catching *Poseidon* after experiencing your fill of the rides.

SEUSS LANDING

A 10-ACRE THEMED AREA BASED ON Dr. Seuss's famous children's books. As at the old Mickey's Toontown in the Magic Kingdom, all of the buildings and attractions replicate a whimsical, brightly colored cartoon style with exaggerated features and rounded lines. There are four rides at Seuss Landing (described below) and an interactive play area, **If I Ran the Zoo,** populated by Seuss creatures.

If you have only young children in your party, Seuss Landing is the place to spend lots of happy time. A great stop in Seuss Landing is Dr. Seuss's All the Books You Can Read bookstore. Last but not least, if your kids cannot get enough of Dr. Seuss, check out **seussville.com.**

Liliane

Caro-Seuss-El *(Universal Express)* ★★★½

APPEAL BY AGE   **PRESCHOOL** ★★★★   **GRADE SCHOOL** ★★★★
TEENS —   **YOUNG ADULTS** —   **OVER 30** —   **SENIORS** —

What it is Merry-go-round. **Scope and scale** Minor attraction. **Fright potential** Not frightening in any respect. **Bottleneck rating** 8. **When to go** Before 11 a.m. **Authors' rating** Wonderfully unique; ★★★½. **Duration of ride** 2 minutes. **Average wait in line per 100 people ahead of you** 9 minutes. **Loading speed** Slow.

Totally outrageous, the Caro-Seuss-El is a full-scale, 56-mount merry-go-round made up exclusively of Dr. Seuss characters. If you are touring with young children, try to get them on early in the morning.

The Cat in the Hat *(Universal Express)* ★★★½

APPEAL BY AGE   **PRESCHOOL** ★★★★   **GRADE SCHOOL** ★★★★   **TEENS** ★★★
YOUNG ADULTS ★★★★   **OVER 30** ★★★★   **SENIORS** ★★★★

What it is Indoor adventure ride. **Scope and scale** Major attraction. **Fright potential** Not frightening in any respect. **Bottleneck rating** 8. **When to go** Before 11:30 a.m. **Authors' rating** Seuss would be proud; ★★★½. **Duration of ride** 3½ minutes. **Average wait in line per 100 people ahead of you** 5 minutes. **Loading speed** Moderate.

A must for preschoolers, guests ride on "couches" through 18 different sets inhabited by animatronic Seuss characters, including The Cat in the Hat, Thing 1, Thing 2, and the beleaguered goldfish who tries to maintain order in the midst of bedlam. Well done overall, with nothing that should frighten younger children. This is fun for all ages. Try to ride early.

The High in the Sky Seuss Trolley Train Ride!
(Universal Express) ★★★½

APPEAL BY AGE   **PRESCHOOL** ★★★★   **GRADE SCHOOL** ★★★½   **TEENS** ★
YOUNG ADULTS ★★½   **OVER 30** ★★½   **SENIORS** ★★★

What it is Elevated train. **Scope and scale** Major attraction. **Fright potential** Not frightening in any respect. **Bottleneck rating** 8. **When to go** Before 11:30 a.m. **Authors' rating** ★★★½. **Special comments** Relaxed tour of Seuss Landing; must be 34" tall to ride. **Duration of ride** 3½ minutes. **Average wait in line per 100 people ahead of you** 11 minutes. **Average wait in line per 100 people ahead of you** 9 minutes. **Loading speed** Molasses.

Trains putter along elevated tracks, while a voice reads one of four Dr. Seuss stories over the train's speakers. As each train makes its way through Seuss Landing, it passes a series of animatronic characters in scenes that are part of the story being told. The trains are small, fitting about 20 people, and the loading speed is glacial. Save the train ride for the end of the day or ride first thing in the morning.

If I Ran the Zoo *(Universal Express)* ★★★

APPEAL BY AGE   **PRESCHOOL** ★★★★★   **GRADE SCHOOL** ★★★   **TEENS** —
YOUNG ADULTS —   **OVER 30** —   **SENIORS** —

What it is Interactive playground. **Scope and scale** Minor attraction. **Fright potential** Not frightening in any respect. **Bottleneck rating** 2. **When to go** Anytime. **Authors' rating** Whimsical and funny; great for preschoolers; ★★★.

FAVORITE EATS AT UNIVERSAL'S ISLANDS OF ADVENTURE		
LAND	SERVICE LOCATION	FOOD ITEM		
PORT OF ENTRY		
Croissant Moon Bakery	Croissants & panini		
TOON LAGOON		
Ale to the Chief	Nathan's hot dogs		
Blondie's: Home of the Dagwood	Sandwiches		
JURASSIC PARK		
Pizza Predattoria	Pizza		
WIZARDING WORLD		
Three Broomsticks	Mad Eye Meatloaf		
LOST CONTINENT		
Fire Eater's Grill	Gyro		
Mythos Restaurant	Risotto & pizza		
SEUSS LANDING		
Circus McGurkus Cafe Stoo-pendous	Fried chicken; mashed potatoes with gravy		
Green Eggs and Ham Cafe	Green eggs & ham sandwich platter (Green herbs, not food coloring, are the reason for the green eggs.)		

A playground with 19 different interactive elements, this area is great silly-dilly fun for little tykes. How silly? The sign at the entrance of this crazy zoo should give you a clue: "Keep track of adults. They get lost all the time." And yes, you should know by now that there is no way the kids will stay dry.

One Fish, Two Fish, Red Fish, Blue Fish
(Universal Express) ★ ★ ★ ½

APPEAL BY AGE	PRESCHOOL ★ ★ ★ ★	GRADE SCHOOL ★ ★ ★ ★	TEENS ★ ★ ★
YOUNG ADULTS ★ ★ ★		OVER 30 ★ ★ ★	SENIORS ★ ★ ★

What it is Wet version of Dumbo the Flying Elephant. **Scope and scale** Minor attraction. **Fright potential** Not frightening in any respect. **Bottleneck rating** 8. **When to go** Before 10 a.m. **Authors' rating** Who says you can't teach an old ride new tricks? ★ ★ ★ ½. **Duration of ride** 2 minutes. **Average wait in line per 100 people ahead of you** 9 minutes. **Loading speed** Slow.

Imagine Dumbo with Seuss-style fish instead of elephants, and you have half the story. Guests steer their fish up or down 15 feet in the air while traveling in circles trying to avoid streams of water projected from "squirt posts."

I followed Dr. Seuss's advice: If you never did, you should. These things are fun. These things are good. And all wet there I stood! My favorite ride in Seuss Landing!

Liliane

ISLANDS *of* ADVENTURE TOURING PLAN

ISLANDS OF ADVENTURE ONE-DAY TOURING PLAN FOR FAMILIES

WE PRESENT ONE ISLANDS OF ADVENTURE TOURING PLAN geared toward the whole family. Because there are so many attractions with the potential to frighten young children, be prepared to skip a few things and to practice switching off (works generally the same way as at Walt Disney World; see page 245). For the most part, attractions designed especially for young children, such as playgrounds, can be enjoyed anytime. Work them into the plan at your convenience.

Be aware that in this park, there are an inordinate number of attractions that will get you wet. If you want to experience them, come armed with ponchos, large plastic garbage bags, or some other protective covering. Failure to follow this prescription will make for a squishy, sodden day.

This plan is for families of all sizes and ages and includes thrill rides that may induce motion sickness or get you wet. If the plan calls for you to experience an attraction that does not interest you, simply bypass that attraction and proceed to the next step. Be aware that the plan calls for some backtracking. The plan can be found in clip-out form with a map on page 476.

UNIVERSAL CITYWALK

AT CITYWALK you will find a number of great restaurants, clubs, shops, outdoor entertainment, a concert hall (Hard Rock Live), and the Universal Cineplex 20 movie theater. CityWalk has a number of combination restaurants and clubs. Open to families with kids until 9 p.m., many of the venues offer live entertainment.

For mom's and dad's night out, great entertainment is available at Rising Star, a karaoke bar where a live band backs the singers; reggae at Bob Marley—A Tribute to Freedom; Pat O'Brien's dueling-piano club; Jimmy Buffett's Margaritaville; the Latin Quarter for Nuevo Latino music; the Red Coconut Club, an upscale lounge with cocktails and dancing; and The Groove, a club with high-tech lighting and visual effects. If you want to go clubbing, $12 plus tax admits you to all of the clubs. For details, call Universal CityWalk information at ☎ 407-224-2691.

How To Make it Work

CityWalk is open daily, 11 a.m.–2 a.m., and parking is available in the same garages that serve the theme park at the rate of $15 a day for cars and $20 for RVs, trailers, and other large rigs. Regular parking drops to $5 6 p.m.–10 p.m. and is free after 10 p.m. If you park before 3 p.m., you can receive an $8 cinema parking rebate with movie ticket purchase; after 3 p.m., receive a $5 rebate with movie ticket purchase. If you stay at one of the Universal resorts, it's a short walk, but water taxi and bus transportation are also available to transport you to CityWalk. For added fun, try one of the pedicabs that will take you from CityWalk to your resort for a modest tip. Call ☎ 407-224-FOOD for dinner reservations. Visit **universalorlando.com** and select "At CityWalk" under "Events" for special events.

▌▌ SEAWORLD

MANY DOZENS OF READERS have written to extol the virtues of SeaWorld. The following are representative. An English family writes:

Bob : Discount coupons for SeaWorld admission are available in the free visitor magazines found in most (but not Disney) hotel lobbies.

The best-organized park [is] SeaWorld. The computer printout we got on arrival had a very useful show schedule, told us which areas were temporarily closed due to construction, and had a readily understandable map. Best of all, there was almost no queuing. Overall, we rated this day so highly that it is the park we would most like to visit again.

A woman in Alberta, Canada, gives her opinion:

We chose SeaWorld as our fifth day at the "World." What a pleasant surprise! It was every bit as good (and in some ways better) than WDW itself. Well worth the admission, an excellent entertainment value, educational, well run, and better value for the dollar in food services. Perhaps expand your coverage to give them their due!

Bob : If you don't purchase your admission in advance, take advantage of the automatic admission machines located to the right of the main entrance. The machines are a pain in the rear, asking for your name, age, home zip code, and billing zip code, but if you have a credit card, the machines are a lot faster than standing in line at the ticket windows.

OK, here's what you need to know (for additional information, call ☎ 407-351-3600, 888-800-5447, or visit **seaworld.com**). SeaWorld is a world-class marine-life theme park near the intersection of I-4 and the Beachline Expressway. It's about 10 miles east of Walt Disney World. Opening daily at 9 a.m. and closing between 6 and 11 p.m., depending on the season, SeaWorld charges about $89 admission for adults and $81 for children ages 3–9 including tax at the gate. If you purchase online at **seaworldparks.com,** the same tickets will cost you about $79 and $71 respectively. Several multipark tickets are available as well, including the six-park combination Orlando Flex Plus Tickets that include admission to SeaWorld, Aquatica,

SEAWORLD   413

STAR RATINGS FOR SEAWORLD ATTRACTIONS	
★★★★★	**Manta** (roller coaster)
★★★★½	**Antarctica: Empire of the Penguin**
★★★★½	***One Ocean*** (high-tech Shamu and killer whale show)
★★★★	**Kraken** (roller coaster)
★★★½	***Clyde and Seamore Take Pirate Island*** (sea lion, walrus, and otter show)
★★★½	**Shamu's Happy Harbor** (children's play area)
★★★½	**Shark Encounter**
★★★½	**Wild Arctic** (simulation ride and Arctic-wildlife viewing)
★★★	***A'Lure: The Call of the Ocean*** (Cirque du Soleil–type presentation)
★★★	***Blue Horizons*** (whale, dolphin, and bird show)
★★★	**Pacific Point Preserve** (sea lions and seals)
★★★	***Pets Ahoy!*** (show with performing birds, cats, dogs, and a pig)
★★★	***TurtleTrek*** (IMAX-style 3-D film about sea turtles)
★★½	**Journey to Atlantis** (combination roller coaster–flume ride)
★★½	**Stingray Lagoon**
★★	**Alligator Habitat**
★★	**Skytower** (400-foot-tall observation tower)

Universal Studios, Islands of Adventure, Wet 'n Wild, and Busch Gardens. Parking is $15 per car, $20 per RV or camper.

Figure 8–9 hours or more to see everything, 6 or so if you stick to the big deals. Discovery Cove is directly across the Central Florida Parkway from SeaWorld. Parking at Discovery Cove is free.

 Bob: Be forewarned that you can't take pre-packaged sandwiches or drinks into SeaWorld or its swimming park, Aquatica.

SeaWorld is about the size of the Magic Kingdom and requires about the same amount of walking. In terms of size, quality, and creativity, it's unequivocally on par with Disney's major theme parks. Unlike Walt Disney World, SeaWorld primarily features stadium shows or walk-through exhibits. This means that you will spend about 80% less time waiting in line during 8 hours at SeaWorld than you would for the same-length visit at a Disney park.

But, you'll notice immediately as you check the performance times that the shows are scheduled so that it's almost impossible to see them back to back. A Cherry Hill, New Jersey, visitor confirms this rather major problem, complaining:

The shows were timed so we could not catch all the major ones in a 7-hour visit.

FAVORITE EATS AT SEAWORLD		
LAND	SERVICE LOCATION	FOOD ITEM		
KEY WEST AT SEAWORLD		
Captain Pete's Island Eats	Hot dogs & fresh funnel cakes		
THE WATERFRONT		
Voyager's Smokehouse	Barbecue ribs & chicken		
SHARK ENCOUNTER		
Sharks Underwater Grill	Floor-to-ceiling glass allows guests to dine and observe some 50 sharks and other fish. (table service only)		
WILD ARCTIC		
Mango Joe's	Fajita sandwiches		
FRONT GATE PLAZA		
Sweet Sailin' Candy Shop	Candies & hand-dipped chocolate turtles		

Much of the year, you can get a seat for the stadium shows by showing up 10 or so minutes in advance. When the park is crowded, however, you need to be at the stadiums at least 20 minutes in advance (30 minutes in advance for a good seat). All of the stadiums have splash zones, specified areas where you're likely to be drenched with ice-cold saltwater by whales, dolphins, and sea lions. Finally, Sea-World has three of the best coasters—Journey to Atlantis, Manta, and Kraken—in Florida. If you're a coaster lover, be on hand before park opening and ride all three rides as soon as the park opens.

DISCOVERY COVE

THIS INTIMATE PARK is a welcome departure from the hustle and bustle of other Orlando parks; its slower pace could be the overstimulated family's ticket back to mental health.

Liliane: With a focus on personal guest service and one-on-one animal encounters, Discovery Cove admits only 1,200 guests per day.

The main draw at Discovery Cove is the chance to swim with an Atlantic bottlenose dolphin, from among the 45 here. The 30-minute experience is open to visitors age 6 and up who are comfortable in the water. Discovery Cove is located across the street from SeaWorld.

Other exhibits at Discovery Cove include the Grand Reef, the Explorer's Aviary, and the Freshwater Oasis. Snorkel or swim in the Grand Reef, which houses thousands of exotic fish, as well as an underwater shipwreck and hidden grottoes. In the Aviary, you can touch and feed gorgeous tropical birds. The park is threaded by a "tropical river" in which you can float or swim and is dotted with beaches that serve as pathways to the attractions.

Discovery Cove is open 9 a.m.–5:30 p.m. daily. Admission is limited, so purchase tickets well in advance; call ☎ 877-4-DISCOVERY or visit **discoverycove.com.** Prices vary seasonally $229–$359 per person, plus tax (no children's discount). Prices for Florida residents start at $219. Admission includes the dolphin swim, self-parking, Continental breakfast, lunch, drinks, snacks, and use of beach umbrellas, lounge chairs, towels, lockers, and swim and snorkel gear. Discovery Cove admission also includes unlimited admission to SeaWorld and the Aquatica water park for 14 days surrounding your visit to Discovery Cove. If you're not interested in the dolphin swim, you can visit Discovery Cove for the day for $169–$219 per person, plus tax, depending on the season. For only $20 more you can add unlimited admission to Busch Gardens in Tampa Bay for 14 consecutive days. The passes are valid before or after your Discovery Cove visit. For an additional $59 ($49 for Florida residents), experience the SeaVenture underwater walking tour at the Grand Reef. Equipped with a special helmet, guests get to see and touch a variety of sea creatures underneath the water. The experience, including orientation and the underwater tour, lasts about an hour long, 20 minutes of which are underwater, for groups of up to six people per excursion.

 Liliane: The price is high, but the prize is right. Swimming with a dolphin across the bay was one of the most amazing things I have ever done in my life.

PART TWELVE

THE BEST
of the REST

The WATER THEME PARKS

WALT DISNEY WORLD HAS TWO SWIMMING THEME PARKS. Typhoon Lagoon is the most diverse Disney splash pad, while Blizzard Beach takes the prize for the most slides and most bizarre theme (a ski resort in meltdown). Blizzard Beach has the best slides, but Typhoon Lagoon has a surf pool where you can bodysurf. Both parks have excellent and elaborate themed areas for toddlers and preschoolers.

Bob: During summer and holiday periods, Typhoon Lagoon and Blizzard Beach fill to capacity on weekdays and close their gates before 11 a.m.

Disney water parks allow one cooler per family or group, but no glass and no alcoholic beverages. Both parks charge the following rental prices: towels are $2; lockers are $13 small, $15 large (plus $5 refundable deposit); life jackets are available at no cost. Strollers are welcome but are not available for rent. Admission costs for each park are $52 per day for adults and $44 per day for children (ages 3–9).

The best way to avoid standing in lines is to visit the water parks when they're less crowded. We recommend going on a Saturday or Sunday, when most visitors are traveling, or on a Monday. Like the four major Disney parks, the swimming parks participate in the Extra Magic Hours program. Each day, Disney resort guests can enter either of the water parks 1 hour before the park is open to the public. On select days during the summer and some spring holiday periods, evening Extra Magic Hours are offered at Typhoon Lagoon only on two to five designated evenings a month; on these days, Typhoon Lagoon stays open until 10 p.m., 3 hours beyond the normal closing time. For our money, Typhoon Lagoon is the best possible place to be on a hot Florida summer evening. As a postscript, Disney is cutting costs left and right. Don't be surprised if Extra Magic Hours go the way of the dodo.

Bob: If you have a car, drive instead of taking a Disney bus.

Just like at the major theme parks, the key to a successful visit to the water parks is to arrive early. If you are going to Blizzard Beach or Typhoon Lagoon, get up early, have breakfast, and arrive at the park 30 minutes before opening. Wear your bathing suit under shorts and a T-shirt so you don't need to use lockers or dressing rooms. Wear shoes. The paths are relatively easy on bare feet, but there's a lot of ground to cover. If you or your children have tender feet, wear protective footwear that can be worn in and out of the water as you move around the park. Shops in the parks sell sandals and waterproof shoes.

 Liliane: Wallets and purses get in the way, so lock them in your car's trunk or leave them at your hotel.

You will need a towel, sunblock, and money. Carry enough money for the day and your Disney resort ID (if you have one) in a plastic bag or Tupperware container. Though nowhere is completely safe, we felt comfortable hiding our plastic money bags in our cooler. Nobody disturbed our stuff, and our cash was easy to reach. However, if you're carrying a wad or worry about money anyway, rent a locker. Another great device is a waterproof card case with a lanyard to hold park tickets, a credit card, some cash, and your hotel key. You can buy them at the water parks for about $10; more sophisticated versions are available at any good outdoors or sport shop.

 Liliane: Lost children stations at the water parks are so out of the way that neither you nor your child will find them without help from a Disney cast member. Explain to your children how to recognize a Disney cast member (by their distinctive name tags) and how to ask for help.

Personal swim gear (fins, masks, rafts, and so on) is not allowed. Everything you need is either provided or available to rent. If you forget your towel, you can rent one (cheap!). If you forgot your swimsuit or lotion, they're available for sale. So are disposable, waterproof cameras, which are especially fun to have at Typhoon Lagoon Shark Reef.

Establish your base for the day. Many beautiful sunning and lounging spots are scattered throughout both swimming parks. Arrive early, and you can have your pick. The breeze is best along the beaches of the lagoon at Blizzard Beach and the surf pool at Typhoon Lagoon. At Typhoon Lagoon, if children younger than age 6 are in your party, choose an area to the left of Mount Mayday near the children's swimming area.

Though Typhoon Lagoon and Blizzard Beach are huge parks with many slides, armies of guests overwhelm them almost daily. If your main reason for going is the slides and you hate long lines, try to be among the first guests to enter the park. Go directly to the slides and ride as many times as you can before the park fills. When lines for the slides become intolerable, head for

 Liliane: While I do not feel any better on a water roller coaster than I do on the dry thing, I love the water parks. My all-time favorite water ride is Teamboat Springs, the 1,200-foot whitewater raft flume at Blizzard Beach.

the surf or wave pool or the tube-floating streams. The lazy rivers at both parks are perfect for relaxation. Float through caves, beneath waterfalls, past gardens, and under bridges. Life is beautiful and the water is soothing. Did you know that in the winter months Disney actually heats all the water park pools?

Ian: Grab an inner tube and go on Cross Country Creek or Castaway Creek. It's best when you go with a group like your family. Sometimes I hop off the tube and find an underwater jet on the side of the bank. If you go underwater, the jet will shoot you out really fast. It's a blast! Don't worry; the water isn't deep. A good trick to play on someone in your family is to push their inner tube under a cave waterfall. The water is ice cold. It's fun to watch them freak out.

Both water parks are large and require almost as much walking as the major theme parks. Add to this wave surfing, swimming, and climbing to reach the slides, and you'll definitely be pooped by day's end. Consider a low-key activity for the evening.

It's as easy to lose a child or become separated from your party at one of the water parks as it is at a major theme park. On arrival, pick a very specific place to meet in the event you are separated. If you split up on purpose, establish times for checking in.

Children under age 10 must be accompanied by an adult. The water parks are great fun for the whole family, but if you have very young children or if you are not a thrill-seeking water puppy, the pool of your hotel might serve just as well. The water parks, however, were made to order for teens. Note that during the winter months, Disney closes Blizzard Beach and Typhoon Lagoon for refurbishing,

Captain Nemo surfaces at Blizzard Beach by mistake.

Blizzard Beach

ATTRACTION | HEIGHT REQUIREMENT | WHAT TO EXPECT

CHAIR LIFT UP MT. GUSHMORE | 32 inches | Great ride even if you go up only for the view. When the park is packed, use the single-riders line.

CROSS COUNTRY CREEK | None | Lazy river circling the park; grab a tube.

DOWNHILL DOUBLE DIPPER | 48 inches | Side-by-side tube-racing slides. At 25 mph, the tube races through water curtains and free falls. It's a lot of fun but rough.

MELT-AWAY BAY | None | Wave pool with gentle, bobbing waves. The pool is great for younger swimmers.

RUNOFF RAPIDS | None | Three corkscrew tube slides to choose from. The center slide is for solo raft rides; the other two slides offer one-, two-, or three-person tubes. The dark, enclosed tube makes the ride feel as if you've been flushed down a toilet.

SKI PATROL TRAINING CAMP | 60 inches for T-Bar | A place for preteens to train for the big rides.

SLUSH GUSHER | 48 inches | A 90-foot double-humped slide. Ladies, cling to those tops—all others hang on to live.

SNOW STORMERS | None | Three mat-slide flumes; down you go on your belly.

SUMMIT PLUMMET | 48 inches | A 120-foot free fall at 60 mph. This ride is very intense. Make sure that your child knows what to expect. Being over 48 inches tall does not guarantee an enjoyable experience. If you think you'd enjoy washing out of a 12th-floor window during a heavy rain, then this slide is for you.

TEAMBOAT SPRINGS | None | 1,200-foot white-water group raft flume. Wonderful ride for the whole family.

TIKE'S PEAK | 48 inches and under only | Kid-size version of Blizzard Beach. This is the place for little ones.

TOBOGGAN RACERS | None | Eight-lane race course. You go down the flume on a mat. The ride is less intense than Snow Stormers.

alternating maintenance in such a way that one water park will be open at all times. If it is very wintry, Disney will close both parks.

Blizzard Beach and Typhoon Lagoon now offer premium spaces for rental. Premium spaces can accommodate up to six people and cost $300 plus tax for the full day. There are four premium spaces in each water park, and they include the personalized services of an attendant, private lockers, all-day drink mugs, cooler with bottled water, lounge furniture, tables, and rental towels. Advance reservations are available by calling ☎ 407-WDW-PLAY.

You can also rent a premium beach chair space at both parks. The deal includes two lounge chairs, umbrella, cocktail table, and two towels. Limit is up to four people; if you have more than four people in your party, a second reservation is

Ian: The Slush Gusher at Blizzard Beach is really cool. It's really steep and wavy on the way down. You have to cross your arms and legs because water will rush up your swimsuit. Stay as still as possible, and you will go really fast. A speed sign at the bottom shows how fast you came down. Be careful, because if you try to open your eyes, water goes in, and sometimes water goes up your nose.

Typhoon Lagoon

ATTRACTION | HEIGHT REQUIREMENT | WHAT TO EXPECT

CASTAWAY CREEK |. None | Half-mile lazy river in a tropical setting. Wonderful!

CRUSH 'N' GUSHER | 48 inches | Water roller coaster where you can choose from among three slides: Banana Blaster, Coconut Crusher, and Pineapple Plunger, ranging 410–420 feet long. This thriller leaves you wondering what exactly happened—if you make it down in one piece, that is. It's not for the faint of heart. If your kids are new to water-park rides, this is not the place to break them in, even if they're tall enough to ride.

GANG PLANK FALLS | None | White-water raft flume in a multiperson tube.

HUMUNGA KOWABUNGA | 48 inches | Speed slides that hit 30 mph. A five-story drop in the dark rattles the most courageous rider. Ladies should ride this in a one-piece swimsuit.

KEELHAUL FALLS | None | Fast white-water ride in a single-person tube.

KETCHAKIDDEE CREEK | 48 inches and under only | Toddlers and preschoolers love this area reserved only for them. Say "splish splash" and have lots of fun.

MAYDAY FALLS | None | The name says it all. Wild single-person tube ride. Hang on!

SHARK REEF | None; kids under age 10 must be accompanied by an adult | After you're equipped with fins, a mask, a snorkel, and a life vest, you get a brief lesson in snorkeling. Then off you go to the other side of the saltwater pool, where you swim with small colorful fish, rays, and very small leopard and hammerhead sharks. If you don't want to swim with the fish, visit the underwater viewing chamber. Surface Air Snorkeling—a SCUBA-like pursuit involving a "pony" tank, a small regulator, and a buoyancy vest—is also offered. Participants must be at least 5 years old. To sign up and get more information, visit the kiosk near the entrance to Shark Reef.

STORM SLIDES | None | Three body-slides down and thru Mount Mayday.

SURF POOL | None | World's largest inland surf facility with waves up to 6 feet high. Adult supervision required. Monday–Friday, in the early morning before the park opens (hours vary), surfing lessons are offered (surfboard provided). Cost is $150 for 2½ hours; minimum age is 8; class size is 12. Call ☎ 407-WDW-SURF. The price does not include park admission.

needed. Reserve in advance by calling ☎ 407-WDW-PLAY. Cancellations must be made no later than 9 a.m. the day prior to the reservation to avoid a penalty. These rentals are also available on a same-day basis if any locations are left (check at Shade Shack for Blizzard Beach and at High and Dry Rentals for Typhoon Lagoon.) Cost is $40 plus tax and must be paid at time of reservation.

BEFORE YOU GO

1. Call ☎ 407-939-6244 before you go to find out the official park opening time.

2. Purchase admission tickets online before you arrive.

3. Decide if you want to picnic or not, and then plan or pack accordingly. Pets are not allowed at the water parks.

FAVORITE EATS AT THE WATER PARKS

LAND | SERVICE LOCATION | FOOD ITEM

BLIZZARD BEACH

Avalunch | Hot dogs & cheesecake
Cooling Hut | Popcorn, nachos, & Itzakadoozie
Lottawatta Lodge | Pizza, burgers, salads, & kids' meals
Warming Hut | Hot dogs & chicken wraps

TYPHOON LAGOON

Happy Landings | Ice cream, cookies, & waffle cones. *Garbage pail:* Ice cream, fudge, nuts, and sprinkles in pail with shovel.
Leaning Palms | Pizza & kids' meals inside sand pail with shovel
Lowtide Lou's (seasonal) | Chicken wraps & tuna sandwiches
Typhoon Tilly's | Fish, barbecue pork, & kids' meals inside sand pail with shovel

Refillable mugs: If you or the kids enjoy soda, your best bet is to get a refillable mug, available at both water parks. For the price of the mug ($10), you are entitled to free refills throughout the day (only on the day of purchase). Select locations.

A WORD FROM THE WEATHERMAN

THUNDERSTORMS ARE COMMON in Florida. On summer afternoons such storms often occur daily, forcing the water parks to close temporarily while the threatening weather passes. If the storm is severe and prolonged, it can cause a great deal of inconvenience. The park may actually close for the day, launching a legion through the turnstiles to compete for space on the Disney resort buses. If you depend on Disney buses, leave the park earlier, rather than later, when you see a storm moving in. Most important though, instruct your children to immediately return to home base at the sight of lightning or when they hear the first rumble of thunder.

We recommend that you monitor the local weather forecast the day before you go, checking again in the morning before leaving for the water park. Scattered thunderstorms are to be expected and usually cause no more than temporary inconvenience, but moving storm fronts are to be avoided.

We get a lot of questions about the water parks during cold-weather months. Orlando area temperatures can vary from the high 30s to the low 80s during December, January, and February. When it's warm though, these months can serve up a dandy water park experience as this Batavia, Ohio, woman attests:

I will say that going to Blizzard Beach in December was the best decision ever! We went on a Monday in December. There was no one there! They told us at the entrance that if the park didn't reach 100—yes, I said 100—people by noon, they would be closing. Well, I guess they got to 101 people because it stayed open and was totally empty. There was no wait for anything all day! In June we waited in line for an hour for Summit Plummet. In December it took us only the amount of time to walk up the stairs. We had the enormous wave pool to ourselves. We did everything in the entire park and had lunch in less than 3 hours. It was perfect. The weather was slightly chilly at 71° and overcast with very light rain, but the water is heated, so we were fine.

SAFETY FIRST

TOO MUCH FUN IN THE SUN isn't a good thing if you get sunburned or become dehydrated. Drink lots of fluids, use sunscreen, and bring a T-shirt and a hat for extra protection. Read all signs and follow the rules. Lifeguards are on duty throughout the parks. At Typhoon Lagoon, a first-aid station is located behind Leaning Palms. The Blizzard Beach first-aid station is between Lottawatta Lodge and Beach Haus.

WET 'N WILD

WET 'N WILD (ON INTERNATIONAL DRIVE IN ORLANDO, one block east of I-4 at Exit 75A; ☎ 800-992-WILD or 407-351-1800; **wetnwildorlando.com**) is a non-Disney water-park option. If you are looking for a colorful atmosphere, Wet 'n Wild will not deliver; however, the park is packed with incredible slides, flumes, and activities for all ages. Water puppies will get their fill, and kids can go wild.

Tickets with tax at the main gate are $55 for adults and $50 for kids ages 3–9, plus tax. Always call or check online for special deals and discounts (especially for AAA members, Florida residents, and members of the military). An annual pass is $82 if purchased online, and an annual pass for weekdays runs $58 (both are plus tax and include parking). The park also offers half-price admission in the afternoon. Parking fees are $12 for cars and vans and $16 for RVs. Lockers can be rented for $6–$11 plus tax depending on size, and towel rental is $4; both require a refundable deposit of $3. Life vests are provided for free. Pets are not allowed inside the park, and there is no kennel.

Mears Transportation operates a shuttle to Wet 'n Wild that stops three times a day at Disney hotels. It's the same shuttle that commutes between Walt Disney World and Universal Orlando. Cost is $19 for guests age 3 and older. If you are staying on International Drive, you can take the International Drive trolley (visit **iridetrolley.com** for schedules and fees).

Liliane: What I like best about Wet 'n Wild is that the park is open 9:30 a.m.–9 p.m. daily throughout the summer. This is a huge advantage over the Disney water parks that generally close 6–7 p.m.

As with all thrill slides, lines can become unbearably long, so arrive early. Also keep in mind that most slides are geared more toward older children. All the slides outside the Blastaway Beach have a 48-inch height requirement, except for multipassenger slides, for which the minimum height is 36 inches if an adult accompanies the short rider. The only exceptions to this policy are the rides at Wake Zone, with a height requirement of 51 inches (The Wild One) and 56 inches (Knee Ski and Wake Skating).

Wet 'n Wild

ATTRACTION | HEIGHT REQUIREMENT | WHAT TO EXPECT

THE BLACK HOLE | 48 inches if riding alone; 36 inches if riding with an adult | Two-person tube; 1,000 gallons of water per minute; all this in the dark. Do we need to say more? While not the wildest ride in town, it sure is dark in there.

THE BLAST | 48 inches if riding alone; 36 inches if riding with an adult | Two-person tube ride inside a waterworks where all the pipes are broken. You cannot get any wetter.

THE BOMB BAY | 48 inches | You stand on a pair of doors that open, dropping you down a 76-foot slide. You're gonna need a lot of nerve to stand on those doors and wait for the drop.

BRAIN WASH | 48 inches | Extreme six-story tube ride with a 53-foot vertical drop into a 65-foot funnel; tube holds two or four riders.

BUBBA TUB | 48 inches if riding alone; 36 inches if riding with an adult | Long straight track with three hummocks to impede momentum.

DER STUKA | 48 inches | Speed flume descending from a six-story tower.

DISCO H2O | 48 inches if riding alone; 36 inches if riding with an adult | Four persons in a raft are ushered down a tube into a 1970s-era nightclub complete with lights, music, and a disco ball.

THE FLYER | 48 inches if riding alone; 36 inches if riding with an adult | A calmer toboggan-style ride more suitable for families with smaller children.

MACH 5 | 48 inches | Mat slide. For a really fast ride, grab a newer mat.

THE STORM | 48 inches | Half slide, half toilet bowl. This ride is exhilarating and disorienting; when the lifeguard begins hollering, just stumble toward his voice and give him a thumbs-up.

THE SURGE | 48 inches if riding alone; 36 inches if riding with an adult | Four-person raft ride sends you flying down 600 feet of banked turns. Wild!

Other Wet n' Wild attractions include **Blastaway Beach** with a kid-size version of the adult menu. The area is located to the left of the main gate; look for the oversize sand castle capped off with a big blue bucket. The bucket actually fills with water and tips over, soaking the people in front of the castle. Replacing the former children's area in 2012, Blastaway Beach is the largest water park children's playground in Florida. The giant sand castle alone spans two pools (upper and lower), covering more than 15,000 square feet with more than 85,000 gallons of water powering more than 100 soakers, jets, waterfalls, water cannons, 17 slides, and the aforementioned bucket.

The 17,000-square-foot wave pool at **Surf Lagoon** is perfect for body bobbing. If you prefer to ride the waves with tubes, you can rent those at the main rental stand. Another great way to relax is the **Lazy River.** Be forewarned though: The circuit is short and the current fast. If you lose your tube, swim down the river or wait patiently until an empty one passes within reach.

Wake Zone, situated on a lake roughly the same size as the rest of the park, offers wakeboarding, kneeboarding, and tubing. The lines can be long, especially since the attraction only runs from noon until sunset and is open on weekends only mid-March–June, daily during the summer, and weekends only September–mid-October. Be sure to call before going to Wet 'n Wild to see if the area is open on the day of your visit.

When you get hungry, the main food pavilions are the centrally located **Bubba's BBQ, Manny's Pizza,** and **Surf Grill,** together offering such staples as burgers, pizza, and barbecue-pork sandwiches, as well as more-nutritious (and nontraditional) items such as veggie burgers and tabbouleh. Wait times are long, and prices are high but not outrageous. Guests may bring a picnic, but alcohol and glass containers are not allowed (although beer can be purchased inside the park).

You can take in all the attractions at Wet 'n Wild in 1 day, especially in the summer when the park is open until 9 p.m. It is a huge park, and a whole day playing in the water under the hot Florida sun will poop you out. Try to get back to the hotel for a midday nap, and don't plan on dragging already tired kids to a restaurant for a sit-down dinner.

BEFORE YOU GO

1. Call ☎ 800-992-WILD or 407-351-1800, or visit **wetnwildorlando.com,** the day before you go to find out the official park opening time.

2. Purchase admission tickets online before you arrive.

3. Visit the website to determine what attractions are appropriate for the kids in your party.

▮▮ AQUATICA *by* SEAWORLD

AQUATICA, ORLANDO'S FIRST NEW SWIMMING PARK to open in more than a decade, is located across International Drive from the back side of SeaWorld. From Kissimmee, Walt Disney World, and Lake Buena Vista, take I-4 East, exit onto the Central Florida Parkway, and then bear left on International Drive. From Universal Studios, take I-4 West to FL 528 and from there exit onto International Drive. Admission costs about the same as at the Disney water parks and at Wet 'n Wild: $55 for adults and $50 for kids, including tax. If you don't want to wait in a queue to purchase tickets, buy them in advance at **aquaticabyseaworld.com** or use the credit-card ticket machines to the left of Aquatica's main entrance. You can save $10 per ticket if you purchase your tickets online. Also available online: one day at Aquatica and unlimited visits to Banana Beach Restaurant for $55 ($50 for kids ages 3–9). The same combo will cost you $70 ($65 for kids) if purchased at the gate. If you plan on visiting SeaWorld AND Aquatica, consider the combo ticket, priced at $99 for adults and $91 for kids ages 3–9; the combo ticket allows for one visit to each park within one year and constitutes a saving of $30.

Aquatica is comparable in size to other water theme parks in the area. Attractively landscaped with palms, ferns, and tropical flowers,

Aquatica by SeaWorld

ATTRACTION | HEIGHT REQUIREMENT* | WHAT TO EXPECT

CUTBACK COVE AND BIG SURF SHORES | None | One cove serves up bodysurfing waves, while the other puts out gently bobbing floating waves. A spacious beach arrayed around the coves is the park's primary sunning venue. Shady spots, courtesy of beach umbrellas, ring the perimeter of the area for sun-sensitive guests.

DOLPHIN PLUNGE | 48 inches; must be able to maintain proper riding position unassisted | Corkscrewing romp through a totally arced tube until you blast through the clear tube at the end. The viewing of the dolphins is nearly impossible because you're flushed through the clear tube so fast and with so much water splashing in your face, the ride is over before you've seen anything.

HOOROO RUN | 42 inches | A six-story open-air run down a steep, straight, undulating slide.

KATA'S KOOKABURRA COVE | 48 inches and under only | Wading pool and slides for the preschool crowd.

LOGGERHEAD LANE | must be in a single or double tube | Take a tube and enjoy this lazy river, which at one point passes through the Fish Grotto, a tank populated by hundreds of exotic tropical fish.

OMAKA ROCKA | 48 inches | A wide diameter, enclosed, one-person tube ride. The name is derived from the wave action inside the tube, which washes you alternately up one side of the tube and then the other.

ROA'S RAPIDS | 51 inches and under required to wear a life vest | Floating stream with a very swift current but without any rapids. There is only one place to get in and out.

TASSIE'S TWISTERS | must be able to maintain proper riding position while holding on to both handles unassisted | An enclosed slide tube spits you into an open bowl, where you careen around the bowl's edge much in the manner of the ball in a roulette wheel.

TAUMATA RACER | 42 inches; must be able to maintain proper riding position unassisted | A high-speed mat ride down a steep hill.

WALHALLA WAVE | 42 inches; must be able to maintain proper riding position unassisted | Circular raft that can accommodate up to four people and splashes down a six-story enclosed twisting tube.

WALKABOUT WATERS | 36–42 inches for slides into main pool and over 42 inches tall for larger slides | 15,000-square-foot children's adventure area. If your children are under the age of 10, this alone may be worth the admission price. It's impossible not to get wet and impossible not to have fun!

WHANAU WAY | must be able to maintain the proper riding position while holding on to both handles unassisted | Tubes carry one or two passengers down one of four slides with a few twists and one corkscrew.

*Guests under 48 inches are required to wear a life vest.

it's far less themed than Disney's Typhoon Lagoon and Blizzard Beach but much greener and more aesthetically appealing than Wet 'n Wild. You can take in all the attractions in 1 day, but as with all water parks, remember that an entire day of action in the Florida sun will wear out the most active kids and most grown-ups too.

As at other water parks, there are lockers, towels, wheelchairs, and strollers to rent, gift shops to browse, and places to eat. The three restaurants at Aquatica are **WaterStone Grill,** offering specialty sandwiches, fried fish, wraps, and salads; **Banana Beach Restaurant,** an all-you-can-eat venue dishing up burgers, hot dogs, and chicken; and **Mango Market,** a diminutive eatery serving pizza and chicken tenders. WaterStone Grill and Mango Market serve beer.

BEFORE YOU GO

1. Call ☎ 888-800-5447 or 407-351-3600, or visit **aquaticabyseaworld .com** the day before you go to find out the official park opening time.

2. Purchase admission tickets online before you arrive.

3. Visit the website to determine what attractions are appropriate for the kids in your party.

DOWNTOWN DISNEY
(a.k.a. Disney Springs)

DOWNTOWN DISNEY COMPRISES THE Disney Village Marketplace, Pleasure Island (soon to be The Landing), Disney's West Side, and coming in 2016, Town Center. When complete, the entire shopping, dining, and entertainment complex will be called Disney Springs. You can roam, shop, and dine without paying any sort of entrance fee.

If you have a car, use it. There is bus transportation from all the Disney resorts to Downtown Disney, and some resorts offer boat transportation. The problem is that buses make stops at a number of locations at Downtown Disney, so you might sit on the bus for 20 minutes or more before you finally disembark for your destination. The boats are better than the buses but take about four times as long as driving your car. The boat route, however, is very pretty and a good choice if you're not in a hurry. Shops open as early as 9:30 a.m., but there is really no reason to arrive at the crack of dawn—for once.

MARKETPLACE HIGHLIGHTS

ALTHOUGH THE MARKETPLACE offers interactive fountains, a couple of playgrounds, a lakeside amphitheater, and watercraft rentals, it's primarily a shopping and dining venue. The centerpiece of shopping is the 50,000-square-foot **World of Disney,** the largest store in the world selling Disney-trademark merchandise. Kids will particularly enjoy the **LEGO Imagination Center.** You'll know you're there when you see the 30-foot sea serpent made out of more than a million LEGO blocks that lives in the lake right in front of the store. Outside the store is a play area filled with LEGO blocks for children to enjoy.

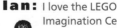 **Ian:** I love the LEGO Imagination Center at Downtown Disney. You can make your own LEGO cars and drop them down a slope.

Once Upon a Toy is a joy. The biggest draws at this 16,000-square-foot store are classic toys with a Disney twist.

Here you can find Mr. Potato Head with Mickey Ears or a sorcerer's hat and the classic game Clue set in The Haunted Mansion.

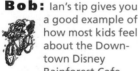

Liliane: Get only the hairstyle and makeup at Bibbidi Bobbidi and take your own pictures.

Bibbidi Bobbidi Boutique transforms your little girl into a princess, albeit for a price. A Fairy Godmother-in-training (the shop owner) and her helpers offer salon services for princesses age 3 and up. Hairstyle and makeup cost $55, adding a manicure will cost you $60, and the royal makeover (including your choice of a princess costume with accessories and a photo shoot with imaging package) starts at $220. Hairstyling for young Prince Charming is also available; the Knight Package costs $16. Prices include tax.

THE WEST SIDE HIGHLIGHTS

THE BEST THING at Downtown Disney and probably in all of Walt Disney World is **Cirque du Soleil's** *La Nouba*. Mesmerizing, thrilling, superb, and beautiful hardly do the show justice, but it is all of those and more. Tickets range $65–$154 for adults and $53–$125 for kids ages 3–9 (tax included). Florida residents are eligible for a 20% discount. If you are not familiar with Cirque du Soleil, visit the website at **cirquedusoleil.com.** You can book online or call ☎ 407-939-7600.

Pop Gallery is the place to go for high-end paintings and sculpture, while **D-Street** offers an eclectic assortment of urban-chic (read bizarre) apparel. New to the West Side is **Splitsville,** an upscale bowling, billiards, and dining venue covering 45,000 square feet on two levels. Or try **Characters in Flight,** where you ascend 400 feet over Downtown Disney in a tethered balloon (the characters are painted on the balloon—don't expect to float around up there with Br'er Fox). The weather-dependent ride is 8–10 minutes and runs $18 for adults (age 10 and up) and $12 for children (ages 3–9). Operating 8:30 a.m.–midnight, the balloon ride is wheelchair accessible.

Ian: The Rainforest Cafe is like having dinner in a tree house. Tree branches are everywhere. Birds are chirping, monkeys, orangutans, and gorillas are all around too. Don't worry; they're not real. Every once in a while thunder and lightning appear and a rainstorm happens. The ribs are very good. You have to get the chocolate volcano for dessert. It's incredible!

Bob: Ian's tip gives you a good example of how most kids feel about the Downtown Disney Rainforest Cafe. Getting a table during normal dinner hours, however, is only slightly less difficult than eloping with Daisy Duck. If the kids are all over you to go, try the saner, more manageable Rainforest Cafe at the Animal Kingdom. You'll be done and out the door in less time than it takes to get seated at the Downtown Disney location.

Harley Davidson offers motorcycle apparel, including leather vests. Catch all the latest box office hits at the **AMC Downtown Disney** state-of-the-art, 24-movie theater complex, all under one roof and offering flicks in an Art Deco setting. For information on showtimes and tickets, log on to **amctheatres.com** and select AMC Downtown Disney 24.

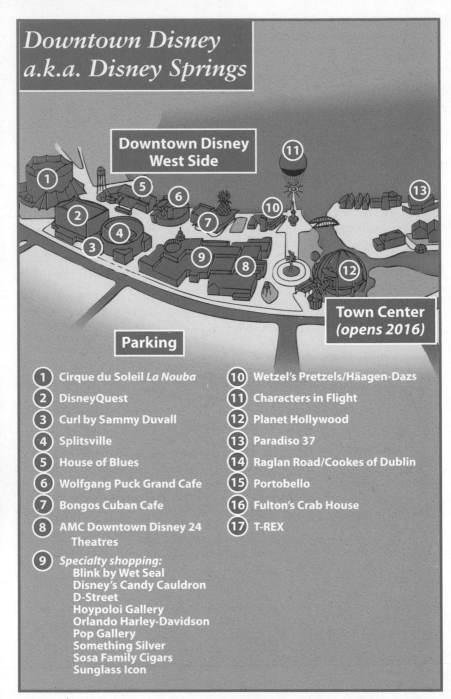

Downtown Disney a.k.a. Disney Springs

Downtown Disney West Side

Town Center (opens 2016)

Parking

1. Cirque du Soleil *La Nouba*
2. DisneyQuest
3. Curl by Sammy Duvall
4. Splitsville
5. House of Blues
6. Wolfgang Puck Grand Cafe
7. Bongos Cuban Cafe
8. AMC Downtown Disney 24 Theatres
9. *Specialty shopping:*
   Blink by Wet Seal
   Disney's Candy Cauldron
   D-Street
   Hoypoloi Gallery
   Orlando Harley-Davidson
   Pop Gallery
   Something Silver
   Sosa Family Cigars
   Sunglass Icon
10. Wetzel's Pretzels/Häagen-Dazs
11. Characters in Flight
12. Planet Hollywood
13. Paradiso 37
14. Raglan Road/Cookes of Dublin
15. Portobello
16. Fulton's Crab House
17. T-REX

Village Lake

Downtown Disney Marketplace

The Landing
(opens 2016)

Parking

(18) **Babycakes NYC/Bodie's All American/Pollo Campero**

(19) **LEGO Imagination Center**

(20) **World of Disney/Bibbidi Bobbidi Boutique**

(21) *Specialty shopping:*
   Arribas Brothers
   Basin
   Ghirardelli Soda Fountain
      & Chocolate Shop
   Rawlings Making the Game
   Ridemakerz
   Team Mickey Athletic Club
   Tren-D

(22) **Once Upon a Toy**

(23) **Disney's Pin Traders**

(24) **Earl of Sandwich/Mickey's Pantry/The Spice & Tea Exchange**

(25) **Wolfgang Puck Express Cafe**

(26) *Specialty shopping:*
   The Art of Disney
   Disney's Design-a-Tee
   Disney's Wonderful World
      of Memories

(27) *Specialty shopping:*
   Goofy's Candy Co.
   littlemissmatched
   Marketplace Fun Finds

(28) **Rainforest Cafe**

(29) **Waterside Stage**

(30) **Cap'n Jack's Marina**

(31) **Disney's Days of Christmas**

Restaurants include the **House of Blues,** which serves Cajun specialties; **Planet Hollywood,** offering movie memorabilia and basic American fare; **Bongos Cuban Cafe,** serving Cuban favorites; and **Wolfgang Puck Cafe,** featuring California cuisine.

DISNEYQUEST If your children are age 11 or older, DisneyQuest on Disney's West Side is an option you might want to consider. Disney-Quest is Disney's pioneering prototype of a theme park in a box, or more literally, in a modest five-story building.

DisneyQuest contains all the elements of the larger Disney theme parks. An entrance area facilitates your transition into the park environment and leads to the gateways of four distinct themed lands, referred to here as zones. As at other Disney parks, everything is included in the price of your admission.

 Bob: Weekdays before 4 p.m. are least crowded at DisneyQuest.

It takes about 2–3 hours to experience DisneyQuest once you get in. Disney limits the number of guests admitted to ensure that queues are manageable and that guests have a positive experience.

DisneyQuest is aimed at a youthful audience, say 8–35 years of age, though younger and older patrons will enjoy much of what it offers. The feel is dynamic, bustling, and noisy. Those who haunt the electronic games arcades at shopping malls will feel most at home at DisneyQuest.

From the turnstile, you enter the Departure Lobby and a "Cyberlator"—a sort of "transitional attraction" (read: elevator) hosted by the genie from *Aladdin*—that delivers you to an entrance plaza called Ventureport. From here you can enter the four zones: Explore Zone, Score Zone, Create Zone, and Replay Zone. As in the larger parks, each zone is distinctively themed. Some zones cover more than one floor, so looking around, you can see things going on both above and below you. In addition, Disney-Quest offers two restaurants and the inevitable gift shop.

Each zone offers several attractions, most based on technologies such as simulators that work well in confined spaces. The Explore Zone is representative. You enter through a re-creation of the tiger's-head cave from *Aladdin.* The headline attraction in Explore Zone is the Virtual Jungle Cruise, where you paddle a six-person raft. The raft is a motion simulator perched on top of blue air bags that replicate the motion of water. Responding to the film of the river projected before you, you can choose several routes through the rapids. The motion simulator responds to sensors on your

 Ian: You've got to try Cyberspace Mountain at DisneyQuest! Ride the roller coaster you design on a computer. You can choose to ride in space, the jungle, or inside a volcano. You sit in a simulator and feel like an astronaut flying through space. And don't miss the Virtual Jungle Cruise. It's totally wild! I worked up a sweat on this one. Feels like you're in a real video game. Everybody is yelling and screaming as you try to paddle in the right direction. Watch out for dinosaurs and waterfalls. You will get wet, really, but not too much.

paddle. As if navigating the river isn't enough, man-eating dinosaurs and a cataclysmic comet are tossed in for good measure.

Some DisneyQuest attractions tap your imagination. In the Create Zone, for example, you can use a computer to design your own roller coaster, including 360-degree loops, and then take a virtual reality ride on your creation in a motion simulator. Sid's Make-a-Toy, also in the Create Zone, lets you design a toy and receive the parts to actually construct it at home. Other creative attractions include virtual beauty salon makeovers and painting on an electronic canvas.

Like all things Disney, admission to DisneyQuest is not cheap. But especially for teens and technology junkies, it's an eye-opening experience and a fun time.

A one-day admission is $48 for adults and $42 for kids ages 3–9 (prices include tax). Children under age 10 must be accompanied by a responsible person 16 years and older. Kids under the age of 3 are admitted free of charge, but strollers are not permitted inside DisneyQuest. You can leave and re-enter anytime you want on the day of your visit: Just make sure your wrist gets stamped upon arrival. Annual passes are available.

 Liliane: Yawn, yawn, yawn. This place needs a serious redo. Quite frankly, forget about the redo; the space could be put to better use. And parents with kids under age 3, don't even think about it.

Believe it or not, there are height restrictions at DisneyQuest, and here is the countdown: **Cyberspace Mountain:** 51 inches; **Pirates of the Caribbean—Battle for Buccaneer Gold:** 35 inches; and **Buzz Lightyear's Astro Blasters:** 51 inches.

No need to leave DisneyQuest when hunger strikes. Wonderland Cafe and FoodQuest serve the usual fare, and once you are ready to leave, the exit is through the obligatory gift shop.

PLEASURE ISLAND (A.K.A. THE LANDING)

AFTER A 20-YEAR RUN, Disney shut down the Pleasure Island nighttime entertainment complex. In March 2013 Disney announced the multiyear transformation of Downtown Disney into Disney Springs. Upon completion in 2016 guests will be able to enjoy more than 150 shops, restaurants, and other venues, including a waterfront promenade. Disney Springs will be completed in phases, opening little by little over the next three years. The part of the former Pleasure Island situated near the lagoon will become The Landing, while the part adjacent to the parking lot will be extended and become Town Center. A multistory parking garage will add 6,000 spaces and hopefully remedy some parking and traffic woes. Now the focus is on family-friendly shops and restaurants, including **Raglan Road,** an Irish pub and restaurant featuring live Celtic music; **Sosa Family Cigar Co.,** a posh smoke shop; **Curl by Sammy Duval,** a surf shop; and several outdoor food-and-beverage locations. **Paradiso 37** features the cuisines of the Americas (that would be North, Central, and South) served both indoors and out.

FAVORITE EATS AT DOWNTOWN DISNEY

LAND | SERVICE LOCATION | FOOD ITEM

MARKETPLACE

- **Earl of Sandwich** | Sandwich paradise
- **Ghirardelli Soda Fountain & Chocolate Shop** | Ice cream & chocolate treats
- **T-Rex*** | Burgers & kids' menu in Jurassic setting with T-Rex dinosaurs
- **Wolfgang Puck Express** | Soups, salads, & pizza

WESTSIDE

- **FoodQuest** | Pizza, pasta, & salads
- **Forty-Thirst Street** | Mini-doughnuts & coffee
- **House of Blues*** | Cajun food & kids' menu. For shows in the music hall next door, check out **hob.com**.
- **Planet Hollywood*** | Burgers. Great for teens who will love checking out the Hollywood memorabilia.
- **Wetzel's Pretzels** | Pretzels with a twist

PLEASURE ISLAND

- **Raglan Road*** | Irish food & live music

* table service only

HOW TO MAKE IT WORK

IT REALLY DOES NOT MATTER if you make Downtown Disney your destination for the day or if you decide to go on the spur of the moment. Fun can be had by all anytime. Family restrooms (with a changing and nursing area) are located in the Marketplace near Once Upon a Toy and the Art of Disney.

SHOPPING There are five ATMs at Downtown Disney. All major credit cards are accepted, and if you are a Disney resort guest, you can have your shopping purchases delivered to your hotel (this only works if you are not checking out the next day). Pickup is usually at the primary gift shop of your resort (no room delivery), but even so, it sure beats lugging stuff around.

BEFORE YOU GO

1. Determine in advance what all members in your party want to do. Pick up a map at Guest Relations and enjoy the area.

2. Downtown Disney is a great place to give your teenagers some space. Agree on a time and place to reunite and turn them loose. While teens enjoy Disney-Quest or the latest flick at the AMC movie theater, mom and dad can have a peaceful dinner at the Portobello Yacht Club or Wolfgang Puck Cafe.

3. Pets are not allowed at Downtown Disney. Best Friends Pet Care (**bestfriendspetcare.com**) is located near Port Orleans Resort.

OUTDOOR RECREATION

UNLESS YOU'RE A GAMBLER OR A NUDIST, you'll probably find your favorite activity offered at Walt Disney World. You can fish, canoe, hike, bike, boat, play tennis and golf, ride horses, work out, take cooking lessons, and even drive a real race car or watch the Atlanta Braves's spring training.

Your kids will go nuts for the **Wilderness Lodge Resort,** and so will you. While you're there, have a family-style meal at the kid-friendly Whispering Canyon restaurant and rent bikes for a ride on the paved paths of adjacent Fort Wilderness Campground. The outing will be a great change of pace. The only downside is that your kids might not want to go back to their own hotel.

More fun is available at **The ESPN Wide World of Sports,** a 220-acre competition and training complex. During late winter and early spring, the venue is the spring training home of the Atlanta Braves. Disney guests are welcome at the sports complex as paying spectators, but none of the facilities are available for guests to use. Prices vary; to book tickets and to learn what events (including Major League Baseball exhibition games) are scheduled during your visit, call ☎ 407-939-GAME or visit **disneyworldsports.com.**

Located 40–60 minutes south of Walt Disney World is the **Disney Wilderness Preserve,** a wetlands-restoration area operated by the Nature Conservancy in partnership with Disney. There are hiking trails, an interpretive center, and guided outings on weekends. Trails wind through grassy savannas, beneath ancient cypress trees, and along the banks of pristine Lake Russell. The preserve is open Monday–Friday, 9 a.m.–5 p.m.; closed on Thanksgiving and December 25. Admission is free, though donations are appreciated. Reservations are highly recommended. If you're interested, call the preserve directly at ☎ 407-935-0002 or visit **tinyurl.com/disneywildernesspreserve.**

GOLF

IF GOLF IS YOUR THING, call ☎ 407-938-GOLF (4653) for information, tee times, and greens fees at Palm Golf Course (★★★★), Magnolia Golf Course (★★★½), Lake Buena Vista Golf Course (★★★), or Oak Trail Golf Course (★★½).

- **ARNOLD PALMER COURSE** *(formerly the Legacy)* ★★★★ ☎ 407-396-3199
- **ARNOLD PALMER'S BAY HILL CLUB & LODGE** ★★★★ ☎ 407-876-2429 **bayhill.com**
- **CHAMPIONSGATE INTERNATIONAL COURSE** ★★★★ ☎ 407-787-4653 **championsgategolf.com**
- **CHAMPIONSGATE NATIONAL COURSE** ★★★½ ☎ 407-787-4653 **championsgategolf.com**
- **CROOKED CAT** ★★★★ ☎ 407-656-2626
- **FALCON'S FIRE GOLF CLUB** ★★★★ ☎ 407-239-5445 **falconsfire.com**
- **GRAND CYPRESS GOLF CLUB** ★★★★½ ☎ 407-239-4700 **grandcypress.com**
- **PANTHER LAKE** ★★★★½ ☎ 407-656-2626
- **TOM WATSON COURSE** *(formerly the Independence)* ★★★★ ☎ 407-396-3199

There is, of course, golf beyond Mickey's Kingdom. The greater Orlando area has enough high-quality courses to rival better-known golfing meccas, such as Scottsdale and Palm Springs. But unlike these destinations with their endless private country clubs, Orlando is unique because almost all its courses are open for some sort of public play. We compiled a list of off-Disney golf courses for dad's or mom's special day off (see the chart on the previous page).

The 900-page *Unofficial Guide to Walt Disney World*, by Bob Sehlinger and Len Testa, contains an entire chapter on Orlando-area golf, with in-depth profiles of all the best golf courses.

MINIATURE GOLF

CONSIDER MINIATURE GOLF FOR THE WHOLE FAMILY at **Fantasia Gardens Miniature Golf,** located across the street from the Walt Disney World Swan or at **Winter Summerland** right next to Blizzard Beach. Fantasia Gardens Miniature Golf is a beautifully landscaped garden with fountains, animated statues, topiaries, and flower beds. At Winter Summerland the Christmas holiday theme is prevalent, with ornaments hanging from palm trees. At Castle Hole watch out for a snowman that sprays water on unsuspecting guests when their golf balls pass beneath him.

Fantasia Gardens is quite demanding and not nearly as whimsical as Winter Summerland. Adults and older teens will enjoy the challenge of Fantasia Gardens, but if your group includes children younger than 12, head to Winter Summerland. Another Winter Summerland plus is that it can be reached easily via Disney transportation. To access Fantasia Gardens you must take a bus to the Walt Disney World Swan Resort and walk to the course from there. Admission with tax to both courses is $13 for adults and $12 for children ages 3–9. Opening hours are 10 a.m.–11 p.m. For more information call ☎ 407-WDW-PLAY (939-7529).

THEME PARK TRIVIA QUIZ ANSWERS

MAGIC KINGDOM
1. (C)   **2.** (C)   **3.** (D)   **4.** (D)   **5.** (C)   **6.** (D)   **7.** (A)   **8.** (C)   **9.** (B)   **10.** (A)

EPCOT
1. (D)   **2.** (B)   **3.** (B)   **4.** (D)   **5.** (D)   **6.** (C)   **7.** (A)   **8.** (C)   **9.** (A)   **10.** (B)
11. (C)   **12.** (B)

DISNEY'S ANIMAL KINGDOM
1. (C)   **2.** (A)   **3.** (D)   **4.** (B)   **5.** (D)   **6.** (B)   **7.** (B)   **8.** (D)   **9.** (C)   **10.** (D)

DISNEY'S HOLLYWOOD STUDIOS
1. (A)   **2.** (A)   **3.** (C)   **4.** (A)   **5.** (B)   **6.** (A)   **7.** (C)   **8.** (B)   **9.** (C)   **10.** (B)
11. (A)

INDEX

The Magic Kingdom

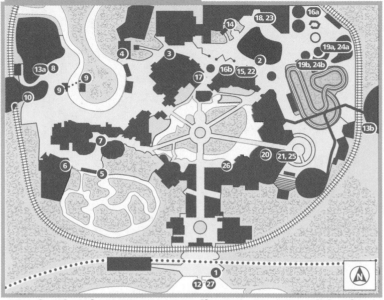

Magic Kingdom Happy Family One-Day Touring Plan

1. If you're a Disney resort guest, arrive 30 minutes before opening. Otherwise, arrive 50 minutes before opening. Obtain park maps and the *Times Guide*. Stroller rentals are under the train station on Main Street.

2. **FAMILY:** Ride the Seven Dwarfs Mine Train in Fantasyland (opens 2014).

3. **FAMILY:** Ride Peter Pan's Flight.

4. **FAMILY:** See The Haunted Mansion.

5. **FAMILY:** Take the Jungle Cruise.

6. **FAMILY:** Ride Pirates of the Caribbean.

7. **PARENTS:** Experience The Magic Carpets of Aladdin.

8. **TEENS:** Obtain Fastpasses for Big Thunder Mountain in Frontierland.

9. **PARENTS:** Take the raft to Tom Sawyer Island. Allow at least 30 minutes to run around the island. Try the barrel bridges and tour Fort Langhorn.

10. **TEENS:** Ride Splash Mountain.

11. **FAMILY:** Eat lunch.

12. **PARENTS:** Take a midday break of 3–4 hours back at your hotel.

13. **TEENS:** Ride a) Big Thunder using the Fastpasses obtained earlier. Explore the rest of the park. If you can, get Fastpasses for b) Space Mountain, and ride during the time shown on them. If Fastpasses aren't available, Space Mountain's wait times usually drop at 3 p.m. during the parade.

14. **PARENTS:** Return to the Magic Kingdom

and reunite your group at *Enchanted Tales with Belle* in Fantasyland. See the show.

15. **FAMILY:** Have one member of your group obtain Fastpasses for The Many Adventures of Winnie the Pooh.

16. **PARENTS:** Get character autographs at a) Pete's Silly Sideshow or b) Princess Fairytale Hall (opens late 2013) in Fantasyland.

17. **FAMILY:** See *Mickey's PhilharMagic.*

18. **FAMILY:** Have one member of your group obtain Fastpasses for Under the Sea: Journey of the Little Mermaid.

19. **PARENTS:** Obtain Fastpasses for a) The Barnstormer and b) Dumbo.

20. **FAMILY:** See *Monsters, Inc. Laugh Floor.*

21. **FAMILY:** Obtain Fastpasses for Buzz Lightyear's Space Ranger Spin.

22. **FAMILY:** Ride Winnie the Pooh using the Fastpasses obtained earlier.

23. **FAMILY:** Ride Under the Sea using the Fastpasses obtained earlier.

24. **PARENTS:** Ride a) The Barnstormer and b) Dumbo using the Fastpasses obtained earlier.

25. **FAMILY:** Ride Buzz Lightyear using the Fastpasses obtained earlier.

26. **FAMILY:** See the evening parade and fireworks from Main Street. A good viewing spot is between The Plaza and Tomorrowland Terrace.

27. Depart the Magic Kingdom.

You can customize this touring plan and get real-time updates while you're in the park! See **touringplans.com** for details. Start time for Fastpass+: Pooh, 6:35 p.m.; Under the Sea, 7:05 p.m.; Barnstormer, 7:35 p.m.; Dumbo, 7:40 p.m.; Buzz, 8 p.m. Priority order is Under the Sea, Pooh, Buzz, Barnstormer, and Dumbo if Fastpass+ choices are limited.

The Magic Kingdom

Magic Kingdom One-Day Touring Plan for Grandparents with Small Children

1. If you're a Disney resort guest, arrive 30 minutes before opening. Otherwise, arrive 50 minutes before opening. Obtain park maps and the *Times Guide* when you pass through the turnstiles. Stroller rentals are under the train station on Main Street.
2. Ride the Seven Dwarfs Mine Train in Fantasyland (opens 2014).
3. Obtain Fastpasses for Dumbo.
4. Ride the Tomorrowland Speedway.
5. Ride Buzz Lightyear's Space Ranger Spin.
6. Return to Fantasyland; ride Mad Tea Party.
7. Ride Dumbo using the Fastpasses obtained earlier.
8. Take the Walt Disney World Railroad from Fantasyland to Frontierland. Walk to Adventureland and obtain Fastpasses for Jungle Cruise.
9. Ride Pirates of the Caribbean.
10. Take a spin on The Magic Carpets of Aladdin.
11. Take the Jungle Cruise using the Fastpasses obtained earlier.
12. Explore the Swiss Family Treehouse.
13. Eat lunch outside the park and return to your hotel for a midday break.
14. Return to the park and take the raft to Tom Sawyer Island. Allow 30–45 minutes

to explore. (Take the railroad from Main Street to Frontierland to reduce walking.)
15. See *Country Bear Jamboree*.
16. Obtain Fastpasses for Peter Pan's Flight in Fantasyland.
17. See *Mickey's PhilharMagic*.
18. Meet characters at a) Pete's Silly Sideshow or b) Princess Fairytale Hall (opens late 2013) in Fantasyland.
19. Eat dinner.
20. Obtain Fastpasses for Under the Sea: Journey of the Little Mermaid.
21. Ride It's a Small World.
22. Ride Peter Pan using the Fastpasses obtained earlier.
23. Obtain Fastpasses for The Many Adventures of Winnie the Pooh.
24. See *Enchanted Tales with Belle*.
25. Ride Under the Sea using the Fastpasses obtained earlier.
26. Ride Winnie the Pooh using the Fastpasses obtained earlier.
27. See *Monsters, Inc. Laugh Floor*.
28. See the evening parade and fireworks from Main Street. A good viewing spot is between the Plaza and Tomorrowland Terrace.
29. Depart the Magic Kingdom.

You can customize this touring plan and get real-time updates while you're in the park! See **touringplans.com** for details. Start time for Fastpass+: Dumbo, 10:05 a.m.; Peter Pan, 7:40 p.m.; Under the Sea, 7:25 p.m.; Pooh, 8:35 p.m. Priority order is Under the Sea, Peter Pan, Pooh, and Dumbo if Fastpass+ choices are limited.

The Magic Kingdom

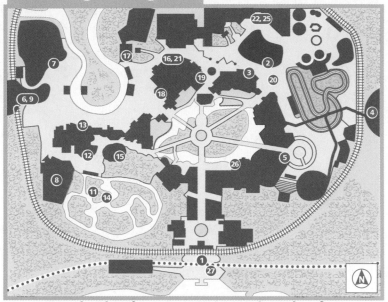

Magic Kingdom One-Day Touring Plan for Tweens and Their Parents

1. If you're a Disney resort guest, arrive 30 minutes before opening. Otherwise, arrive 50 minutes before opening. Obtain park maps and the *Times Guide* when you pass through the turnstiles. Stroller rentals are under the train station on Main Street.
2. Ride the Seven Dwarfs Mine Train in Fantasyland (opens 2014).
3. Try The Many Adventures of Winnie the Pooh on the way to Tomorrowland.
4. Ride Space Mountain.
5. Ride Buzz Lightyear's Space Ranger Spin.
6. Obtain Fastpasses for Splash Mountain in Frontierland.
7. Ride Big Thunder Mountain Railroad.
8. Experience Pirates of the Caribbean in Adventureland.
9. Ride Splash Mountain using the Fastpasses obtained earlier.
10. Eat lunch.
11. Obtain Fastpasses for the Jungle Cruise in Adventureland.
12. See *Walt Disney's Enchanted Tiki Room.*
13. See *Country Bear Jamboree.*
14. Take the Jungle Cruise using the Fastpasses obtained earlier.
15. Explore the Swiss Family Treehouse.
16. Obtain Fastpasses for Peter Pan's Flight.
17. See The Haunted Mansion in Liberty Square.
18. See *The Hall of Presidents.*
19. See *Mickey's PhilharMagic* in Fantasyland.
20. Take a spin on the Mad Tea Party.
21. Ride Peter Pan using the Fastpasses obtained earlier.
22. Obtain Fastpasses for Under the Sea: Journey of the Little Mermaid.
23. Eat dinner.
24. Explore the park, revisit favorite attractions, or shop.
25. Ride Under the Sea using the Fastpasses obtained earlier.
26. See the evening parade and fireworks from Main Street. A good viewing spot is between the Plaza and Tomorrowland Terrace.
27. Depart the Magic Kingdom.

You can customize this touring plan and get real-time updates while you're in the park! See **touringplans.com** for details. Start time for Fastpass+: Splash, 11:15 a.m.; Jungle Cruise, 1:20 p.m.; Peter Pan, 4:20 p.m.; Under the Sea, 6:10 p.m. Priority order is Peter Pan, Under the Sea, Splash, and Jungle Cruise if Fastpass+ choices are limited.

The Magic Kingdom

Magic Kingdom Two-Day Touring Plan for Parents with Small Children: Day One

1. If you're a Disney resort guest, arrive 30 minutes before opening. Otherwise, arrive 50 minutes before opening. Obtain park maps and the *Times Guide* when you pass through the turnstiles. Stroller rentals are under the train station on Main Street.
2. Ride the Seven Dwarfs Mine Train in Fantasyland (opens 2014).
3. Ride Peter Pan's Flight.
4. Ride It's a Small World.
5. Obtain Fastpasses for Splash Mountain in Frontierland.
6. See *Country Bear Jamboree.*
7. Take the raft to Tom Sawyer Island in Frontierland. Allow 30–45 minutes to explore the island.
8. Return to the mainland; ride Splash Mountain using the Fastpasses obtained earlier.
9. Eat lunch and return to your hotel for a midday break of 3–4 hours.
10. Return to the park and experience *The Hall of Presidents* and the *Liberty Belle*

Riverboat (order doesn't matter).
11. Obtain Fastpasses for The Many Adventures of Winnie the Pooh in Fantasyland.
12. Meet Disney characters at a) Pete's Silly Sideshow or b) Princess Fairytale Hall (opens late 2013) in Fantasyland.
13. Take a spin on the Prince Charming Regal Carrousel.
14. Eat dinner.
15. Ride Pooh using the Fastpasses obtained earlier.
16. Obtain Fastpasses for Under the Sea: Journey of the Little Mermaid.
17. See *Mickey's PhilharMagic.*
18. Try the Mad Tea Party.
19. Ride Under the Sea using the Fastpasses obtained earlier.
20. See the evening parade and fireworks. A good viewing spot is between the Plaza and Tomorrowland Terrace restaurants.
21. Depart the Magic Kingdom.

You can customize this touring plan and get real-time updates while you're in the park! See **touringplans.com** for details. Start time for Fastpass+: Splash, 11 a.m.; Pooh, 5:50 p.m.; Under the Sea, 7:15 p.m. Priority order is Under the Sea, Splash, and Jungle Cruise if Fastpass+ choices are limited.

The Magic Kingdom

Magic Kingdom Two-Day Touring Plan for Parents with Small Children: Day Two

1. If you're a Disney resort guest, arrive 30 minutes before opening. Otherwise, arrive 50 minutes before opening. Obtain park maps and the *Times Guide* when you pass through the turnstiles. Stroller rentals are under the train station on Main Street.
2. Ride the Astro Orbiter in Tomorrowland.
3. Ride the Tomorrowland Speedway.
4. Obtain Fastpasses for Dumbo in Fantasyland.
5. Ride The Barnstormer.
6. See *Enchanted Tales with Belle.*
7. Ride Dumbo using the Fastpasses obtained earlier.
8. Head to Adventureland; ride The Magic Carpets of Aladdin.
9. Obtain Fastpasses for the Jungle Cruise.
10. Ride Pirates of the Caribbean.
11. Eat lunch.
12. See *Walt Disney's Enchanted Tiki Room.*
13. Take the Jungle Cruise using the Fast-passes obtained earlier.
14. Explore the Swiss Family Treehouse.
15. Back in Tomorrowland, get Fastpasses for Buzz Lightyear's Space Ranger Spin.
16. See *Monsters, Inc. Laugh Floor.*
17. Ride the Tomorrowland Transit Authority PeopleMover.
18. Ride Buzz Lightyear using the Fastpasses obtained earlier.
19. Revisit favorite attractions, play interactive games, explore the rest of the park, or shop.
20. Depart the Magic Kingdom.

You can customize this touring plan and get real-time updates while you're in the park! See **touringplans.com** for details. Start time for Fastpass+: Dumbo, 10:10 a.m.; Jungle Cruise, 12:30 p.m.; Buzz, 2:30 p.m. Priority order is Buzz, Jungle Cruise, and Dumbo if Fastpass+ choices are limited.

The Magic Kingdom

Magic Kingdom Two-Day Sleepyhead Touring Plan for Parents with Small Children: Day One

1. Arrive around 11 a.m. Obtain park maps and the *Times Guide* when you pass through the turnstiles. Stroller rentals are under the train station on Main Street.
2. Obtain Fastpasses for the Seven Dwarfs Mine Train (opens 2014) in Fantasyland.
3. See *Mickey's PhilharMagic.*
4. Take the raft to Tom Sawyer Island in Frontierland. Allow 30–45 minutes to explore the island.
5. Eat a quick lunch.
6. Ride the Seven Dwarfs Mine Train using the Fastpasses obtained earlier.
7. Obtain Fastpasses for Splash Mountain in Frontierland.
8. Experience *The Hall of Presidents* and the *Liberty Belle* Riverboat in Liberty Square (order doesn't matter).
9. See the afternoon parade from Liberty Square.
10. Ride It's a Small World in Fantasyland.
11. Obtain Fastpasses for Peter Pan's Flight.
12. See *Country Bear Jamboree* in Frontierland.
13. Ride Splash Mountain using the Fastpasses obtained earlier.
14. Obtain Fastpasses for Dumbo in Fantasyland. You can take the railroad from Frontierland to Fantasyland to reduce walking.
15. Obtain Fastpasses for Under the Sea: Journey of the Little Mermaid.
16. Ride Peter Pan's Flight using the Fastpasses obtained earlier.
17. Experience Prince Charming's Regal Carrousel.
18. Ride Dumbo using the Fastpasses obtained earlier.
19. Obtain Fastpasses for The Many Adventures of Winnie the Pooh.
20. Ride Under the Sea using the Fastpasses obtained earlier.
21. Take a spin on the Mad Tea Party.
22. See Winnie the Pooh using the Fastpasses obtained earlier.
23. Revisit favorite attractions, play interactive games, explore the park, or shop.
24. Depart the Magic Kingdom.

You can customize this touring plan and get real-time updates while you're in the park! See **touringplans.com** for details. Start time for Fastpass+: Seven Dwarfs, 1:30 p.m.; Splash, 3:35 p.m.; Peter Pan, 6:50 p.m.; Dumbo, 7:15 p.m.; Under the Sea, 7:25 p.m., Pooh, 8:35 p.m. Priority order is Seven Dwarfs, Peter Pan, Splash, Under the Sea, Pooh, and Dumbo if Fastpass+ choices are limited.

The Magic Kingdom

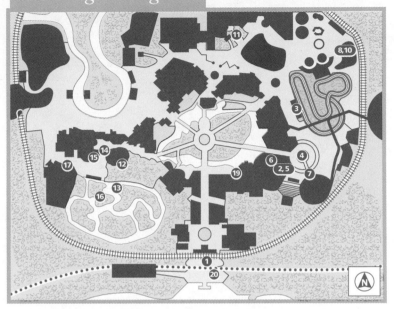

Magic Kingdom Two-Day Sleepyhead Touring Plan for Parents with Small Children: Day Two

1. Arrive around 11 a.m. Obtain park maps and the *Times Guide* when you pass through the turnstiles. Stroller rentals are under the train station on Main Street.
2. Obtain Fastpasses for Buzz Lightyear's Space Ranger Spin in Tomorrowland.
3. Ride the Tomorrowland Speedway.
4. Take a spin on the Astro Orbiter.
5. Ride Buzz Lightyear using the Fastpasses obtained earlier.
6. See *Monsters, Inc. Laugh Floor.*
7. Ride the Tomorrowland Transit Authority PeopleMover.
8. Obtain Fastpasses for The Barnstormer in Fantasyland.
9. Eat a quick, late lunch.
10. Ride The Barnstormer using the Fastpasses obtained earlier.
11. See *Enchanted Tales with Belle.*
12. In Adventureland, explore the Swiss Family Treehouse.
13. Obtain Fastpasses for the Jungle Cruise.
14. Ride The Magic Carpets of Aladdin.
15. See *Walt Disney's Enchanted Tiki Room.*
16. Take the Jungle Cruise using the Fastpasses obtained earlier.
17. Ride Pirates of the Caribbean.
18. See any missed attractions, play interactive games, shop, or explore the park.
19. See the evening parade and fireworks. A good viewing location for the fireworks is between the Plaza and Tomorrowland Terrace restaurants.
20. Depart the Magic Kingdom.

You can customize this touring plan and get real-time updates while you're in the park! See **touringplans.com** for details. Start time for Fastpass+: Buzz, 12:25 p.m.; Barnstormer, 1:10 p.m.; Jungle Cruise, 4:10 p.m. Priority order is Buzz, Jungle Cruise, and Barnstormer if Fastpass+ choices are limited.

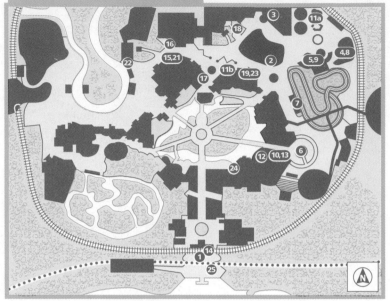

The Magic Kingdom

Parent's Magic Kingdom Plan: One Afternoon and One Full Day (Full Day)

1. If you're a Disney resort guest, arrive 30 minutes before opening. Otherwise, arrive 50 minutes before opening. Obtain park maps and the *Times Guide* when you pass through the turnstiles. Stroller rentals are under the train station on Main Street.
2. Ride the Seven Dwarfs Mine Train (opens 2014) in Fantasyland.
3. Ride Under the Sea: Journey of the Little Mermaid.
4. Obtain Fastpasses for The Barnstormer.
5. Obtain Fastpasses for Dumbo.
6. Ride the Astro Orbiter in Tomorrowland.
7. Take a spin on the Tomorrowland Speedway.
8. Return to Fantasyland and ride The Barnstormer using the Fastpasses obtained earlier.
9. Ride Dumbo using the Fastpasses obtained earlier.
10. Send one member of your party to obtain Fastpasses for Buzz Lightyear's Space Ranger Spin in Tomorrowland.
11. Meet characters at a) Pete's Silly Sideshow or b) Princess Fairytale Hall (opens late

2013) in Fantasyland.
12. Return to Tomorrowland and see *Monsters, Inc. Laugh Floor.*
13. Ride Buzz Lightyear using the Fastpasses obtained earlier.
14. Leave the park for lunch and a midday break.
15. Return to the park and obtain Fastpasses for Peter Pan's Flight in Fantasyland.
16. Ride It's a Small World.
17. See *Mickey's PhilharMagic.*
18. See *Enchanted Tales with Belle.*
19. Obtain Fastpasses for The Many Adventures of Winnie the Pooh.
20. Eat dinner.
21. Ride Peter Pan using the Fastpasses obtained earlier
22. See The Haunted Mansion in Liberty Square.
23. Ride Winnie the Pooh using the Fastpasses obtained earlier.
24. See the evening parade and fireworks. A good viewing spot is between the Plaza and Tomorrowland Terrace restaurants.
25. Depart the Magic Kingdom.

You can customize this touring plan and get real-time updates while you're in the park! See **touringplans.com** for details. Start time for Fastpass+: Barnstormer, 10:15 a.m.; Dumbo, 10:25 a.m.; Buzz, 11:10 a.m.; Peter Pan, 6:20 p.m.; Pooh, 6:20 p.m. Priority order is Peter Pan, Pooh, Buzz, Barnstormer, and Dumbo if Fastpass+ choices are limited.

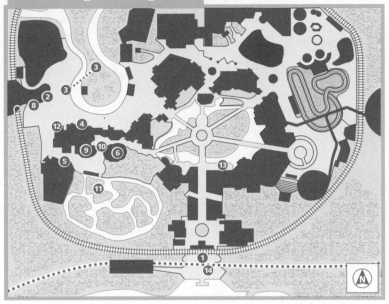

The Magic Kingdom

Parent's Magic Kingdom Plan: One Afternoon and One Full Day (Afternoon)

1. Arrive at the Magic Kingdom entrance around 4 p.m. Obtain park maps and a copy of the daily entertainment schedule when you pass through the turnstiles. Stroller rentals are under the train station on Main Street.
2. Obtain Fastpasses for Splash Mountain in Frontierland.
3. Take the raft to Tom Sawyer Island. Allow 30–45 minutes to run around the island. Be sure to try the barrel bridges and tour Fort Langhorn.
4. See *Country Bear Jamboree*.
5. Ride Pirates of the Caribbean in Adventureland.

6. Climb the Swiss Family Treehouse.
7. Eat dinner.
8. Ride Splash Mountain using the Fastpasses obtained earlier.
9. See *The Enchanted Tiki Room*.
10. Ride the Magic Carpets of Aladdin.
11. Take the Jungle Cruise.
12. See the evening parade from Frontierland. A good viewing spot is in front of the doors to the Frontierland candy shop.
13. See the evening fireworks from Main Street. A good viewing location for the fireworks is between the Plaza and Tomorrowland Terrace restaurants.
14. Depart the Magic Kingdom.

You can customize this touring plan and get real-time updates while you're in the park! See **touringplans.com** for details.

Epcot

Epcot One-Day Touring Plan for Parents with Small Children

1. Arrive at the entrance to Epcot 30 minutes prior to opening. Pick up a park map and daily entertainment schedule when entering the park. Stroller rentals are just inside the main entrance and to the left.

2. If your children are tall enough, ride Soarin' at the Land Pavilion in Future World West. Otherwise, continue to the next step.

3. Exit the Land Pavilion and walk straight toward the middle of Future World. In Future World Plaza, get character autographs at the Epcot Character Spot. Return to the Land Pavilion and take the Living with the Land boat ride.

4. See *The Circle of Life*, also in the Land Pavilion.

5. Ride Journey into Imagination with Figment, in the Imagination Pavilion in Future World West.

6. Eat lunch and return to your hotel for a midday break of 3–4 hours.

7. Return to Epcot and ride Spaceship Earth.

8. Ride The Seas with Nemo and Friends in Future World West.

9. See *Turtle Talk with Crush*.

10. If time permits, see *Captain EO* in the Imagination Pavilion.

11. Eat dinner.

12. Begin a counterclockwise tour of World Showcase with the *O Canada!* film.

13. See *The American Adventure*.

14. Play the Agent P World Showcase Adventure at the Norway Pavilion.

15. Ride Maelstrom, also in Norway.

16. Take the Gran Fiesta Tour Starring the Three Caballeros.

17. See *IllumiNations*. Excellent viewing locations can be found along the walkway around World Showcase lagoon.

18. Depart Epcot.

You can customize this touring plan and get real-time updates while you're in the park! See **touringplans.com** for details.

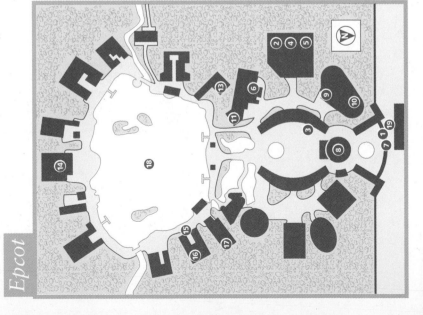

Epcot

Epcot One-Day Sleepyhead Touring Plan for Parents with Small Children

1. Arrive at the entrance around 11 a.m. Pick up a park map and daily entertainment schedule when entering the park. Stroller rentals are just inside the main entrance and to the left.
2. Obtain Fastpasses for Soarin' in the Land Pavilion in Future World West.
3. See The Seas with Nemo and Friends.
4. Experience *Turtle Talk with Crush*.
5. Return to the Land Pavilion and see *The Circle of Life* film.
6. Eat lunch. The Land's Sunshine Seasons food court is the best counter-service option in Future World.
7. Take the Living with the Land boat ride.
8. Ride Journey Into Imagination with Figment at the Imagination Pavilion.
9. See the *Captain EO* 3-D film, also at the Imagination Pavilion.
10. Ride Soarin' using the Fastpasses obtained earlier.
11. Ride Spaceship Earth.
12. Get character autographs at the Epcot

13. Character Spot in Future World Plaza. If time permits, see *Ellen's Energy Adventure* in Future World East.
14. Begin a clockwise tour of World Showcase at Mexico, with the Gran Fiesta Tour boat ride.
15. Eat dinner.
16. Sign up for Agent P's World Showcase Adventure in Norway.
17. Take the Maelstrom boat ride at Norway.
18. Continue touring World Showcase.
19. See the *O Canada!* film in Canada.
20. See *IllumiNations*. Excellent viewing locations can be found along the walkway around World Showcase lagoon.
21. Depart Epcot.

You can customize this touring plan and get real-time updates while you're in the park! See **touringplans.com** for details. Start time for Fastpass+: Soarin', 1:35 p.m.

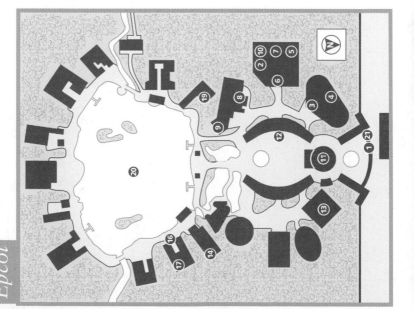

Epcot

Epcot One-Day Touring Plan for Tweens and Their Parents

Note: This touring plan omits the Germany and United Kingdom Pavilions in favor of Agent P's World Showcase Adventure game.

1. Arrive at the entrance to Epcot 30 minutes prior to opening. Pick up a park map and daily entertainment schedule when entering the park. Stroller rentals are just inside the main entrance and to the left.

2. As soon as the park opens, send one member of your group to get Fastpasses for Soarin' at the Land Pavilion in Future World West.

3. Ride Test Track in Future World East.

4. Ride Mission: Space.

5. Ride Sum of All Thrills in Innoventions East.

6. Return to the Land and ride Soarin' using the Fastpasses obtained earlier.

7. Take the Living with the Land boat ride.

8. Eat lunch.

9. See *Captain EO* at the Imagination Pavilion.

10. Experience The Seas with Nemo and Friends.

11. Ride Spaceship Earth near the park entrance.

12. If time permits, see *Ellen's Energy Adventure* in Future World East.

13. Begin a clockwise tour of World Showcase at the Mexico Pavilion.

14. Take the Gran Fiesta Tour boat ride.

15. At Norway, sign up for Agent P's World Showcase Adventure and tour the pavilion.

16. Take the Maelstrom boat ride at Norway.

17. Tour the China Pavilion and see the *Reflections of China* film.

18. Tour the Italy Pavilion.

19. Eat dinner.

20. See *The American Adventure.*

21. Tour the Japan, Morocco, and France Pavilions.

22. See the film *Impressions de France.*

23. Tour the Canada Pavilion and see the film *O Canada!* if time permits.

24. See *IllumiNations.* Excellent viewing locations can be found along the walkway near Canada and the United Kingdom.

25. Depart Epcot.

You can customize this touring plan and get real-time updates while you're in the park! See **touringplans.com** for details. Start time for Fastpass+: Soarin', 10:05 a.m.

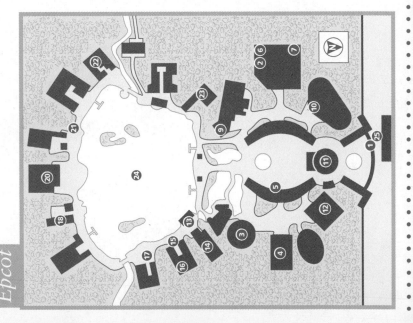

Epcot

Parent's Epcot Touring Plan: One Afternoon and One Full Day (Full Day)

1. Arrive at the entrance to Epcot 30 minutes prior to opening. Pick up a park map and daily entertainment schedule when entering the park.

2. As soon as the park opens, obtain Fastpasses for Soarin' at the Land Pavilion in Future World West.

3. In Future World East, ride Test Track.

4. Ride Mission: Space. Do not use Fastpass.

5. In Innoventions East, ride Sum of All Thrills.

6. Ride Living with the Land in the Land Pavilion.

7. Now might be a good time to pick up a second Fastpass for Soarin', if available.

8. Ride Journey into Imagination with Figment at the Imagination Pavilion.

9. See *Captain EO* at the Imagination Pavilion.

10. Ride Soarin' using the Fastpasses obtained earlier.

11. Eat lunch. Sunshine Seasons has the best food in Future World. The Garden Grill in the Land Pavilion is the closest sit-down

restaurant. Or try the counter-service restaurant at Mexico in World Showcase.

12. Experience the Gran Fiesta Tour boat ride at Mexico. This begins a clockwise tour of World Showcase.

13. Sign up for Agent P's World Showcase Adventure at Norway. There's enough time in this plan to play several games around World Showcase.

14. Ride Maelstrom and tour the stave church in Norway.

15. See *Reflections of China*.

16. Tour Germany.

17. Visit Italy.

18. See *The American Adventure*.

19. Explore Japan.

20. Visit the Morocco Pavilion.

21. Depart Epcot.

You can customize this touring plan and get real-time updates while you're in the park! See **touringplans.com** for details. Start time for Fastpass+: Soarin', 10:05 a.m.

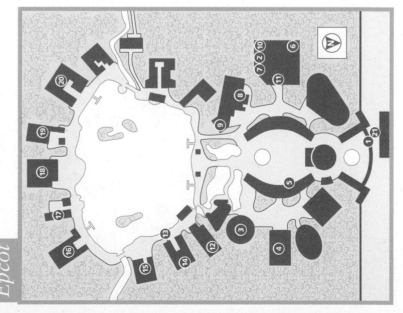

Parent's Epcot Touring Plan: One Afternoon and One Full Day (Afternoon)

1. Arrive at Epcot at 1 p.m. Pick up a park map and daily entertainment schedule when entering the park. Make dining reservations by calling 407-WDW-DINE if you have not already done so.
2. Ride Spaceship Earth.
3. Tour the remaining attractions in Future World East.
4. See the Universe of Energy.
5. See The Seas with Nemo and Friends in Future World West. If you have young children, also see *Turtle Talk with Crush* at the Seas Pavilion.
6. See *The Circle of Life* at the Land Pavilion in Future World West.
7. If you have not already done so, sign up for Agent P's World Showcase Adventure on the walk from the middle of Future World to World Showcase.

8. See *O Canada!* at the Canada Pavilion in World Showcase.
9. Visit the United Kingdom Pavilion.
10. In France, see *Impressions de France*.
11. Eat dinner. Good nearby restaurants include Le Cellier at Canada, Restaurant Marrakesh at Morocco, and Teppan Edo at Japan. Reservations are recommended.
12. See *IllumiNations*. Good viewing spots can be found along the waterway between France and Canada.
13. Depart Epcot.

You can customize this touring plan and get real-time updates while you're in the park! See **touringplans.com** for details.

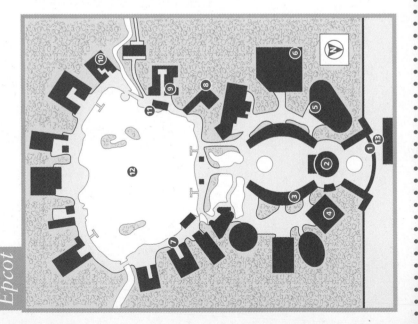

Epcot

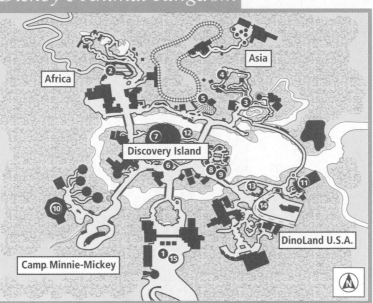

Animal Kingdom One-Day Touring Plan for Parents with Small Children

1. Arrive 25 minutes prior to opening (40 minutes mid-June–mid-August and during holidays). Pick up a park map and entertainment schedule. Stroller rentals are just past the entrance, to the right.
2. As soon as the park opens, experience the Kilimanjaro Safaris in Africa.
3. Ride Kali River Rapids in Asia. You will get wet. Use ponchos or plastic bags to keep dry.
4. Walk the Maharajah Jungle Trek.
5. See *Flights of Wonder.* Check the daily entertainment schedule for showtimes.
6. See *It's Tough To Be a Bug* on Discovery Island.
7. See the exhibits at the Tree of Life and walk the Discovery Island trails.

8. Eat lunch. Good nearby locations include Flame Tree Barbecue and Pizzafari.
9. Meet Mickey and Minnie at the Adventurers Outpost, across from Flame Tree Barbecue.
10. See *Festival of the Lion King* (currently in Camp Minnie-Mickey, relocating to Africa late 2013 or early 2014).
11. Check the next performance time of *Finding Nemo—The Musical.*
12. Find a good viewing spot on Discovery Island for the afternoon parade.
13. If time permits, let the kids play at The Boneyard in DinoLand U.S.A.
14. If time permits, try TriceraTop Spin.
15. Depart the Animal Kingdom.

You can customize this touring plan and get real-time updates while you're in the park! See **touringplans.com** for details.

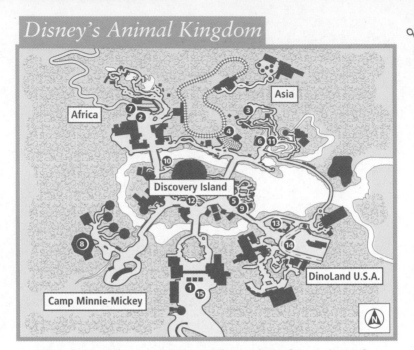

Disney's Animal Kingdom

Asia

Africa

Discovery Island

Camp Minnie-Mickey

DinoLand U.S.A.

Animal Kingdom One-Day Sleepyhead Touring Plan for Parents with Small Children

1. Arrive around 11 a.m. Pick up a park map and entertainment schedule. Stroller rentals are just past the entrance, to the right.
2. Send one member of your party to obtain Fastpasses for Kilimanjaro Safaris in Africa.
3. Take the Maharajah Jungle Trek in Asia.
4. See the next showing of *Flights of Wonder* in Asia.
5. Eat lunch. A good nearby location is Flame Tree Barbecue on Discovery Island.
6. Send one member of your group for Kali River Rapids Fastpasses in Asia.
7. Take the Kilimanjaro Safaris using the Fastpasses obtained earlier.
8. See *Festival of the Lion King* (currently in

Camp Minnie-Mickey, relocating to Africa late 2013 or early 2014).
9. Meet Mickey and Minnie at the Adventurers Outpost, across from Flame Tree Barbecue.
10. Find a good spot on Discovery Island for Mickey's Jammin' Jungle Parade.
11. Ride Kali River Rapids using the Fastpasses obtained earlier.
12. See *It's Tough to Be a Bug* on Discovery Island.
13. If time permits, visit The Boneyard playground in DinoLand U.S.A.
14. If time permits, ride TriceraTop Spin.
15. Depart the Animal Kingdom.

You can customize this touring plan and get real-time updates while you're in the park! See **touringplans.com** for details. Start time for Fastpass+: Safaris, noon; Kali, 4 p.m.

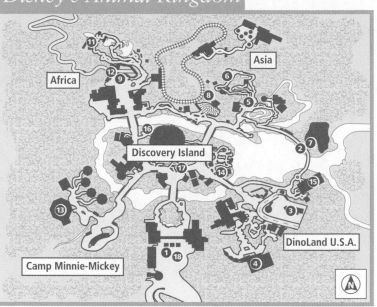

Disney's Animal Kingdom

Animal Kingdom One-Day Touring Plan for Tweens and Their Parents

1. Arrive 25 minutes prior to opening (40 minutes mid-June–mid-August and during holidays). Pick up a park map and entertainment schedule. Stroller rentals are just past the entrance, to the right.
2. As soon as the park opens, send one member of you group to get Fastpasses for Expedition Everest in Asia.
3. Ride Primeval Whirl in DinoLand U.S.A.
4. Ride Dinosaur.
5. Take a ride on Kali River Rapids in Asia. You will get soaked. If you'd like to save getting wet until later in the day, obtain Fastpasses or ride at the end of the tour.
6. Take the Maharajah Jungle Trek in Asia.
7. Ride Expedition Everest using the Fastpasses obtained earlier.
8. See the *Flights of Wonder* show in Asia.
9. Send one member of your group to get

Fastpasses for Kilimanjaro Safaris.
10. Eat lunch.
11. Walk the Pangani Forest Exploration Trail in Africa.
12. Ride the Kilimanjaro Safaris using the Fastpasses obtained earlier.
13. See *Festival of the Lion King* (currently in Camp Minnie-Mickey, relocating to Africa late 2013 or early 2014).
14. Meet Mickey and Minnie at the Adventurers Outpost, across from Flame Tree Barbecue.
15. See *Finding Nemo—The Musical*.
16. Find a good spot on Discovery Island for Mickey's Jammin' Jungle Parade.
17. See *It's Tough to Be a Bug* on Discovery Island.
18. Depart the Animal Kingdom.

You can customize this touring plan and get real-time updates while you're in the park! See **touringplans.com** for details. Start times for Fastpass+: Everest, 10:10 a.m.; Safaris, 12:30 p.m.

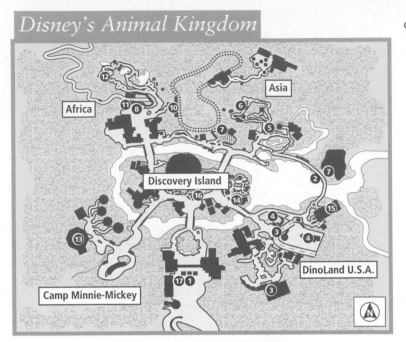

Animal Kingdom One-Day
Happy Family Touring Plan

1. Arrive 25 minutes prior to opening (40 minutes mid-June–mid-August and during holidays). Pick up a park map and entertainment schedule. Stroller rentals are just past the entrance, to the right.

2. **TEENS:** As soon as the park opens, send one member of you group to get Fastpasses for Expedition Everest in Asia. The fastest way to Everest is through Asia, not DinoLand.
   PARENTS: Don't feel the need to rush to an attraction. Explore The Oasis on Discovery Island, pointing out any unusual animals. Hungry? Find the Royal Anandapu Tea Company between Kali River Rapids and Expedition Everest in Asia.

3. **TEENS:** Ride Dinosaur in DinoLand U.S.A.
   PARENTS: Ride TriceraTop Spin.

4. **TEENS:** Ride Primeval Whirl in DinoLand U.S.A.
   PARENTS: Check out The Boneyard playground in DinoLand U.S.A.

5. **FAMILY:** Take a ride on Kali River Rapids in Asia. You will get soaked. If you'd like to save getting wet until later in the day, obtain Fastpasses or ride at the end of the tour.

6. **FAMILY:** Take the Maharajah Jungle Trek in Asia.

7. **TEENS:** Ride Expedition Everest using the Fastpasses obtained earlier.
   PARENTS: See the *Flights of Wonder* show in Asia.

8. **FAMILY:** Send one member of your group to get Fastpasses for Kilimanjaro Safaris.

9. **FAMILY:** Eat lunch.

10. **FAMILY:** Take the Wildlife Express train to Rafiki's Planet Watch/Conservation Station. See the exhibits. Note the writing on the bathroom walls. Take the train back to Africa when you're done.

11. **FAMILY:** Ride the Kilimanjaro Safaris using the Fastpasses obtained earlier.

12. **FAMILY:** Walk the Pangani Forest Exploration Trail in Africa.

13. **PARENTS:** See *Festival of the Lion King* (currently in Camp Minnie-Mickey, relocating to Africa late 2013 or early 2014).
    TEENS: Free time. Revisit favorite attractions or explore the rest of the park.

14. **PARENTS:** Meet Mickey and Minnie at the Adventurers Outpost, across from Flame Tree Barbecue.

15. **FAMILY:** See *Finding Nemo—The Musical.*

16. **FAMILY:** See *It's Tough to Be a Bug* on Discovery Island.

17. Depart the Animal Kingdom.

You can customize this touring plan and get real-time updates while you're in the park! See **touringplans.com** for details. Start times for Fastpass+: Everest, 10:10 a.m.; Safaris, 12:30 p.m.

Disney's Hollywood Studios

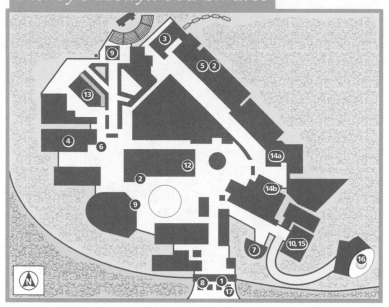

Disney's Hollywood Studios One-Day Touring Plan for Parents with Small Children

1. Arrive 30 minutes prior to opening (40 minutes during summer, holidays, and special events). Grab a park map and daily entertainment schedule when you enter the park. Rent strollers as needed at the gas station on the right side of the park entrance, just past the turnstiles.
2. As soon as the park opens, send one adult to get Fastpasses for Toy Story Mania! If any of your kids are *Star Wars* fans, have another adult sign them up for the *Jedi Training Academy*, near Star Tours on Echo Lake. *Jedi Training* typically fills up by noon.
3. Take the Studios Backlot Tour.
4. Ride Star Tours: The Adventures Continue.
5. Ride Toy Story Mania! using the Fastpasses obtained earlier.
6. See the *Jedi Training Academy*. Check the daily entertainment schedule for showtimes.
7. See *Beauty and the Beast—Live on Stage*. Check the daily entertainment schedule for showtimes.
8. Eat lunch and return to your hotel for a

midday break of 3–4 hours.
9. See the *Lights! Motors! Action! Extreme Stunt Show* or the *Indiana Jones Epic Stunt Spectacular!* Check the daily entertainment schedule for showtimes.
10. If your kids are tall enough and willing, get Fastpasses for The Twilight Zone Tower of Terror.
11. Eat dinner.
12. See *The American Idol Experience*. Check the daily entertainment schedule for showtimes.
13. See *Muppet-Vision 3-D*.
14. Catch a performance of a) *Voyage of the Little Mermaid* or b) *Disney Junior—Live on Stage!* Check the daily entertainment schedule for showtimes.
15. Ride the Tower of Terror using the Fastpasses obtained earlier.
16. See *Fantasmic!* Plan on arriving 60 minutes early to get good seats, or 30 minutes early for standing room only.
17. Depart the Studios.

You can customize this touring plan and get real-time updates while you're in the park! See **touringplans.com** for details. Start times for Fastpass+: Toy Story, 10:45 a.m.; Tower of Terror, 7:45 p.m.

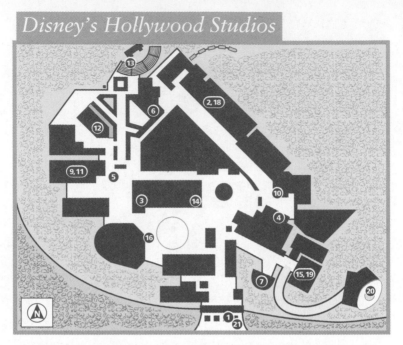

Disney's Hollywood Studios

Disney's Hollywood Studios One-Day Sleepyhead Touring Plan for Parents with Small Children

1. Arrive at the entrance to Disney's Hollywood Studios around 11 a.m. Grab a park map and daily entertainment schedule when you enter the park. Rent strollers as needed at the gas station on the right side of the park entrance, just past the turnstiles.

2. Obtain Fastpasses for Toy Story Mania! at Pixar Place.

3. If any of your kids are *Star Wars* fans, have another adult sign them for the *Jedi Training Academy,* near Star Tours on Echo Lake. *Jedi Training* typically fills up by noon.

4. See *Disney Junior—Live on Stage!* Check the daily entertainment schedule for showtimes.

5. See the *Jedi Training Academy.* Check the daily entertainment schedule for showtimes.

6. Let the kids play on the Honey, I Shrunk the Kids Movie Set Adventure.

7. See *Beauty and the Beast—Live on Stage.* Check the daily entertainment schedule for showtimes.

8. Eat lunch.

9. Obtain Fastpasses for Star Tours: The Adventures Continue.

10. See *Voyage of the Little Mermaid.*

11. Ride Star Tours: The Adventures Continue using the Fastpasses obtained earlier.

12. See *Muppet-Vision 3-D.*

13. See the *Lights! Motors! Action! Extreme Stunt Show.* Check the daily entertainment schedule for showtimes.

14. See *The American Idol Experience.* Check the daily entertainment schedule for showtimes.

15. Get Fastpasses for The Twilight Zone Tower of Terror.

16. If time permits, see the *Indiana Jones Epic Stunt Spectacular!* Check the daily entertainment schedule for showtimes.

17. Eat dinner.

18. Ride Toy Story Mania! using the Fastpasses obtained earlier.

19. Ride the Tower of Terror using the Fastpasses obtained earlier. (You may have free time before they're valid.)

20. See *Fantasmic!* Plan on arriving 60 minutes early to get good seats, or 30 minutes early for standing room only.

21. Depart the Studios.

You can customize this touring plan and get real-time updates while you're in the park! See **touringplans.com** for details. Start times for Fastpass+: Toy Story, 5:15 p.m.; Star Tours, 1:20 p.m.; Tower of Terror: 7 p.m.

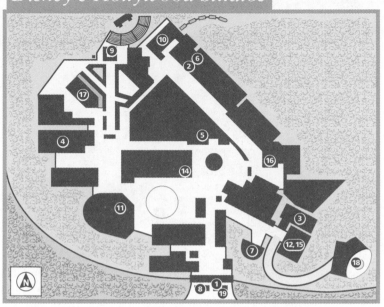

Disney's Hollywood Studios

Disney's Hollywood Studios One-Day Touring Plan for Tweens and Their Parents

1. Arrive at the entrance to Disney's Hollywood Studios 30 minutes prior to opening (40 minutes during summer, holidays, and special events). Grab a park map and daily entertainment schedule when you enter the park. Rent strollers as needed at the gas station on the right side of the park entrance, just past the turnstiles.
2. As soon as the park opens, send one adult to get Fastpasses for Toy Story Mania!
3. Ride the Rock 'n Roller Coaster.
4. Ride Star Tours: The Adventures Continue.
5. See The Great Movie Ride.
6. Ride Toy Story Mania! using the Fastpasses obtained earlier.
7. See Beauty and the Beast—Live on Stage. Check the daily entertainment schedule for showtimes.
8. Eat lunch and return to your hotel for a midday break of 3–4 hours.
9. See the Lights! Motors! Action! Extreme Stunt Show. Check the daily entertainment schedule for showtimes.
10. Take the Studios Backlot Tour.
11. See the Indiana Jones Epic Stunt Spectacular! Check the daily entertainment schedule for showtimes.
12. Obtain Fastpasses for The Twilight Zone Tower of Terror.
13. Eat dinner.
14. See The American Idol Experience. Check the daily entertainment schedule for showtimes.
15. Ride The Twilight Zone Tower of Terror using the Fastpasses obtained earlier.
16. See Voyage of the Little Mermaid.
17. If time permits, see Muppet-Vision 3-D.
18. See Fantasmic! Plan on arriving 60 minutes early to get good seats, or 30 minutes early for standing room only.
19. Depart the Studios.

You can customize this touring plan and get real-time updates while you're in the park! See **touringplans.com** for details. Start times for Fastpass+: Toy Story, 10:45 a.m.; Tower of Terror, 7:45 p.m.

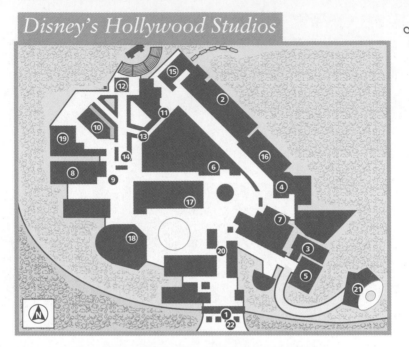

Disney's Hollywood Studios

Disney's Hollywood Studios One-Day Happy Family Touring Plan

1. Arrive at the entrance to Disney's Holly-wood Studios 30 minutes prior to opening (40 minutes during summer, holidays, and special events). Grab a park map and daily entertainment schedule when you enter the park. Rent strollers as needed at the gas station on the right side of the park entrance, just past the turnstiles.
2. **FAMILY:** As soon as the park opens, ride Toy Story Mania! at Pixar Place. If any kids are interested in signing up for the *Jedi Training Academy,* do so near Star Tours, after riding Toy Story Mania!
3. **TEENS:** Ride Rock 'n Roller Coaster. Consider using the single-rider line or Fastpass if the wait exceeds 25 minutes.
4. **PARENTS:** See *Voyage of the Little Mermaid* in the Animation Courtyard.
5. **TEENS:** Ride The Twilight Zone Tower of Terror.
6. **FAMILY:** Ride The Great Movie Ride.
7. **PARENTS:** See *Disney Junior—Live on Stage.* Check the daily entertainment schedule for showtimes.
8. **TEENS:** Ride Star Tours: The Adventures Continue.
9. **PARENTS:** See *Jedi Training Academy.*

10. **FAMILY:** See *Muppet-Vision 3-D.*
11. **FAMILY:** Eat lunch.
12. **TEENS:** See the *Lights! Motors! Action! Extreme Stunt Show.*
13. **PARENTS:** Explore the Honey, I Shrunk the Kids Movie Set Adventure.
14. **FAMILY:** See the Streets of America if you didn't get enough on the way to *Muppet-Vision 3-D.*
15. **FAMILY:** Take the Studios Backlot Tour.
16. **FAMILY:** See *Walt Disney: One Man's Dream* near Toy Story Mania!
17. **FAMILY:** See *The American Idol Experience.* Check the daily entertainment schedule for showtimes.
18. **FAMILY:** See *Beauty and the Beast* or the *Indiana Jones Epic Stunt Spectacular!*
19. **FAMILY:** Eat dinner. Good sit-down choices include Mama Melrose's and The Hollywood Brown Derby.
20. **FAMILY:** Tour Hollywood and Sunset Boulevards.
21. **FAMILY:** See *Fantasmic!* Plan on arriving 60 minutes early to get good seats, or 30 minutes early for standing room only.
22. Depart the Studios.

You can customize this touring plan and get real-time updates while you're in the park! See **touringplans.com** for details. Start times for Fastpass+: Toy Story, 10:45 a.m.

Universal Studios Florida

Universal Studios Florida One-Day Touring Plan

1. Call ☎ 407-363-8000 the day before your visit for the official opening time.
2. Arrive 50 minutes before opening and pick up a map and entertainment schedule.
3. Line up at the turnstile. Ask if any rides or shows are closed, and adjust touring plan.
4. As soon as the park opens, ride Despicable Me in Production Central.
5. Ride Transformers: The Ride—3-D.
6. Take The Simpsons Ride in Springfield U.S.A.
7. Ride Kang and Kodos' Twirl 'n' Hurl.
8. See E.T. Adventure in Woody Woodpecker's KidZone.
9. Play at the Curious George Goes to Town interactive playground and Fievel's Playland.
10. Tour the Street Scenes and eat lunch.
11. Work in the following shows according to their schedules: *A Day in the Park with Barney, Animal Actors on Location, Universal's Horror Make-Up Show,* or *Beetlejuice's Graveyard Revue.*
12. Tour The Wizarding World of Harry Potter–Diagon Alley, and eat dinner.
13. Experience *Shrek 4-D* in Production Central.
14. See *Universal's Cinematic Spectacular—100 Years of Movie Memories.*
15. Depart Universal Studios Florida.

Universal's Islands of Adventure

Universal's Islands of Adventures
One-Day Touring Plan

1. Call ☎ 407-363-8000 the day before your visit for the official opening time.
2. Arrive 50 minutes before opening and pick up a map and entertainment schedule.
3. Line up at the turnstile. Ask if any rides or shows are closed, and adjust touring plan.
4. As soon as the park opens, ride The Amazing Adventures of Spider-Man in Marvel Super Hero Island.
5. Ride Storm Force Accelatron.
6. Ride The High in the Sky Seuss Trolley Train Ride! in Seuss Landing.
7. Ride Caro-Seuss-el.
8. Ride The Cat in the Hat.
9. Ride One Fish, Two Fish, Red Fish, Blue Fish.
10. See *Poseidon's Fury* in The Lost Continent.
11. Ride Pteranodon Flyers in Jurassic Park, if the wait is 10 minutes or less.
12. Tour Camp Jurassic.
13. Eat lunch and work in the next show of *The Eighth Voyage of Sindbad Stunt Show*.
14. See The Mystic Fountain.
15. Ride Flight of the Hippogriff in The Wizarding World of Harry Potter–Hogsmeade.
16. Tour Me Ship, *The Olive* in Toon Lagoon.
17. If your kids are tall enough, try Dudley Do-Right's Ripsaw Falls and Popeye & Bluto's Bilge-Rat Barges.
18. Repeat any favorite attractions, shop, or tour the rest of the park.
19. Depart Universal's Islands of Adventure.

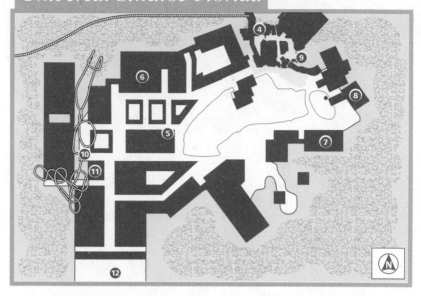

Universal Studios Florida

The Best of Universal Orlando in a Day

1. Call ☎ 407-363-8000 the day before your visit for the official opening times.
2. Arrive at Islands of Adventure 60 minutes before opening, and pick up a map and entertainment schedule. *(See map on next page.)*
3. Line up at the turnstile. Ask if any rides or shows are closed, and adjust touring plan. *(See map on next page.)*
4. As soon as the park opens, walk quickly to The Wizarding World of Harry Potter and take the Hogwarts Express train to Diagon Alley. *(See map on next page.)*
5. Once off the train, see Transformers: The Ride 3-D in Production Central.
6. See Revenge of the Mummy.
7. Ride The Simpsons Ride.
8. See Men in Black Alien Attack.
9. In Diagon Alley, ride the Gringotts Wizarding Bank coaster, eat a quick lunch, and tour Diagon Alley.
10. Ride Hollywood Rip Ride Rockit.
11. See Despicable Me: Minion Mayhem.
12. Exit Universal Studios Florida and walk to Universal's Islands of Adventure.

This plan continues on the next page.

Universal's Islands of Adventure

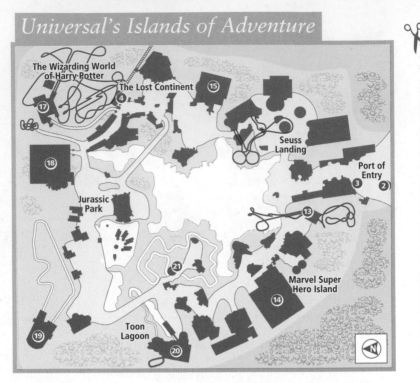

The Best of Universal Orlando in a Day *(cont'd.)*

13. Ride The Incredible Hulk Coaster on Marvel Super Hero Island.
14. See The Amazing Adventures of Spider-Man.
15. Experience *Poseidon's Fury* in The Lost Continent.
16. Eat a quick dinner.
17. Ride Dragon Challenge in Wizarding World.
18. Ride Harry Potter and the Forbidden Journey.
19. Take the Jurassic Park River Adventure.
20. Ride Dudley Do-Right's Ripsaw Falls.
21. Ride Popeye & Bluto's Bilge-Rat Barges.
22. Repeat any missed attractions or revisit favorites as time permits.